THE RISE OF FREE TRADE

CRITICAL CONCEPTS IN THE HISTORY OF ECONOMICS

There are critical ideas in economics which refuse to go away. Debates about such issues as whether economies flourish most under systems of free trade or state intervention, about the determinants of value or the stability of money recur in every era. In many cases earlier generations of economists have made significant and insightful contributions which could illuminate current problems but which are not widely available.

Critical Concepts in the History of Economics aims to remedy this by making available important but rare contributions to economic analysis. Focusing on the questions which have dominated economic thinking for more than three centuries, the series provides major works of reference which make available rich sources of material to a new generation of scholars. Each set comprises four volumes of original texts, which have been carefully retypeset and augmented with an extensive introduction.

THE RISE OF FREE TRADE
Edited by Cheryl Schonhardt-Bailey
Volume I: Protectionism and its Critics, 1815–1837
Volume II: Assault on the Corn Laws, 1838–1846
Volume III: Freer Trade and its Critics, 1847–1906
Volume IV: Free Trade Reappraised: The New Secondary Literature

Already published:
MERCANTILISM
Edited by Lars Magnusson

Forthcoming:
QUANTITY THEORY OF MONEY

THE RISE OF FREE TRADE

Volume III
Freer Trade and its Critics, 1847–1906

Edited and with an Introduction by
Cheryl Schonhardt-Bailey

London and New York

First published 1997
by Routledge
11 New Fetter Lane, London EC4P 4EE

Simultaneously published in the USA and Canada
by Routledge
29 West 35th Street, New York, NY 10001

Typeset in Garamond by
J&L Composition Ltd, Filey, North Yorkshire

Printed and bound in Great Britain by
TJ Press (Padstow) Ltd, Padstow, Cornwall

British Library Cataloguing in Publication Data

A catalogue record for this book is available from the British Library

Library of Congress Cataloging in Publication Data

The rise of free trade/edited by Cheryl Schonhardt-Bailey.
p.   cm.
Includes bibliographical references and index.
1. Free trade–Great Britain–History–19th century–Sources.
2. Great Britain–Commerce–History–19th century–Sources.
I. Schonhardt-Bailey, Cheryl, 1961–
HF2045.R57   1966
382'.71'0941–dc20

96–22601
CIP

ISBN 0–415–14031–5 (Set)
0–415–15628–9 (Vol. I)
0–415–15629–7 (Vol. II)
0–415–15630–0 (Vol. III)
0–415–15631–9 (Vol. IV)

For Andrew
With love and gratitude

CONTENTS

CONTENTS

AKNOWLEDGEMENTS

The editor and publishers acknowledge with thanks permission to use the following copyright documents in volume III.

1 Sir Edward Sullivan, *Protection to Native Industry* London: Edward Stanford, 1870), pp. vi; 1; 2–3; 13; 15; 17–19; 25–36; 38–40; 42–3; 46–50; 52–3; 57–63; 66; 68–70; 76–82; 84–6; 89–91; 94–7; 100; 103; 106–8; 115–18; 121–2; 124–8; 132–4; 136–40; 142–3; 148–9.

2 Henry Fawcett, MP, *Free Trade and Protection. An Inquiry into the Causes which have Retarded the General Adoption of Free Trade Since its Introduction into England* (London: Macmillan & Co., 1879), pp. 3; 4–6; 11–12; 17; 28–9; 45–8; 50–1; 61–7; 69–75; 122–3; 125–8; 130–7; 148–51; 156–60; 162–9.

3 Sir T.H. Farrer, Bart., *Free Trade versus Fair Trade* (London: Cassell & Co., Ltd., 1886), pp. 99–150; 159–76; 220–4.

4 G. Armitage-Smith, *The Free-trade Movement And its Results* (London: Blackie & Son, Ltd., 1898), pp. 130–53; 158–64.

5 'Ritortus', 'The Imperialism of British Trade,' *The Contemporary Review*, 76, (July–December 1899), pp. 132; 137–52; 282–303.

6 C.F. Bastable, *The Theory of International Trade With Some of its Applications to Economic Policy* (London: Macmillan and Co., Ltd., 1903), pp. 22–48; 110–27.

7 Percy Ashley, 'Letter to Mr. Balfour,' (4 July 1903), British Museum Additional MSS 49780.

8 Alfred Marshall, 'Memorandum on Fiscal Policy and International Trade,' (a Memorandum to Arthur Balfour) (31 August 1903), PRO, Cab. T168/54, pp. 1–12; 14–44.

9 'The Assistant Editor', 'Special Supplement: The Economics of Empire,' *National Review*, 42 (September 1903), pp. 1–13; 16–28; 60–76; 78–83; 91–2; 94–7; 100–1; 103–6.

10 A.C. Pigou, 'Mr. Chamberlain's Proposals,' *Edinburgh Review* 200(310) (July–October 1904), pp. 449–69; 474–5.

11 J.L. Garvin, 'The Principles of Constructive Economics as Applied to the Maintenance of Empire,' in Committee of the Compatriots' Club (ed.), *Compatriots' Club Lectures, First Series* (London: Macmillan and Co., Ltd., 1905), pp. 1–12; 20–47; 52–6; 59–61; 63–5; 71–5; 77–81.

12 A.C. Pigou, 'Protection and the Working Classes,' *Edinburgh Review* 203(415) (January–April, 1906), pp. 1–10; 11–13; 20–25; 27–32.

13 John M. Robertson, *Trade and Tariffs* (London: Adam and Charles Black, [1904]1908), pp. 215–26; 239–45; 247–53.

14 E.W. Hamilton, 'Preferential Treatment, Notes on Some Points Concerned With,' Confidential Cabinet Paper (6 June 1903), British Museum Additional MSS. 49780.

15 Author Unknown, 'Most-Favoured-Nation Treaties v. Retaliation,' Confidential Cabinet Paper (29 August 1903), PRO, Cab. 37/66/56, pp. 1–7.

16 Charles Thompson Ritchie (Chancellor of the Exchequer), 'Preferential Tariffs,' Confidential Cabinet Paper (9 September 1903), PRO, Cab. 37/66/58, pp. 1–9.

17 The Rt. Hon. Joseph Chamberlain, MP, 'Letter from the Rt. Hon. J. Chamberlain, MP to Arthur Balfour' (9 September 1903), in Arthur J. Balfour (ed.), *Fiscal Reform Speeches Delivered by the Right Hon. Arthur James Balfour, M.P. From June 1880 to December 1905 Together with a Reprint from The Pamphlet 'Economic Notes on Insular Free Trade' and Letters from and to the Right Hon. J. Chamberlain, M.P. (September 1903), With a Preface.* (London: Longmans, Green and Co., 1906), pp. 66–8.

18 Arthur J. Balfour, 'Letter to Joseph Chamberlain,' (16 September 1903), in Arthur J. Balfour (ed.), *Fiscal Reform Speeches Delivered by the Right Hon. Arthur James Balfour, M.P. From June 1880 to December 1905 Together with a Reprint from The Pamphlet 'Economic Notes on Insular Free Trade' and Letters from and to the Right Hon. J. Chamberlain, M.P. (September 1903), With a Preface* (London: Longmans, Green and Co., 1906), pp. 69–70.

19 Arthur J. Balfour, *Economic Notes on Insular Free Trade*, 5th impression (London: Longmans, Green and Co., 1903), pp. 3–32.

20 Harold Cox (Secretary of the Cobden Club), *Mr. Balfour's Pamphlet: A Reply*, 3rd impression (London: Fisher Unwin, 1903), pp. 2–16; 18–32.

21 Arthur J. Balfour, Speech Delivered at Sheffield on the Occasion of the Annual Conference of the National Union of Conservative and Constitutional Associations (1 October 1903) (reprinted, with revisions, by permission of *The Times* from *The Times* of 2 October 1903), in Arthur J. Balfour (ed.), *Fiscal Reform Speeches Delivered by the Right Hon. Arthur James Balfour, M.P. From June 1880 to December 1905 Together with a Reprint from The Pamphlet 'Economic Notes on Insular Free Trade' and Letters from and to the Right Hon. J. Chamberlain, M.P. (September 1903), With a Preface* (London: Longmans, Green and Co., 1906), pp. 97–110.

22 Joseph Chamberlain, Two Speeches (6 and 7 October, 1903), reprinted, with an introduction by the Right Hon. Austen Chamberlain, MP, in Charles W. Boyd (ed.), *Mr. Chamberlain's Speeches*, vol. II (London: Constable and Company, Ltd., 1914), pp. 140–82.

23 John Morley, *Parliamentary Debates*, 4th series (8 February 1904, House of Commons) (London: Wyman and Sons, Ltd.), cols 623–44.

24 Gerald Balfour, *Parliamentary Debates*, 4th series (8 February 1904, House of Commons) (London: Wyman and Sons, Ltd.), cols 656–64.

25 Lord Balfour of Burleigh, *Parliamentary Debates*, 4th series (18 February 1904, House of Lords) (London: Wyman and Sons, Ltd.), cols 149–51; 153–62.

26 Duke of Devonshire, *Parliamentary Debates*, 4th series (19 February 1904, House of Lords) (London: Wyman and Sons, Ltd.), cols 348–50; 354–64.

27 Author Unknown, 'Free Trade and the Position of Parties' (Commentary on *Hansard's Parliamentary Debates*), *Edinburgh Review*, 199(408) (January–April 1904), pp. 547–55.

The articles in these volumes were made available to me by, and with the assistance of, The Goldsmiths' Library (University of London), the Public Record Office (Kew), the British Museum and the British Library of Political and Economic Science (London School of Economics). The documents in Vol. II were previously published in the Thoemmes Press volume, *Free Trade, The Repeal of the Corn Laws* (Routledge/Thoemmes Press, 1996). My ever patient, ever diligent and ever cheerful research assistant Jojo Iwasaki persevered in obtaining obscure sources for these volumes. I am tremendously indebted to her for her help. The LSE Government Department Staff Research Fund provided partial funding for this project for which I am grateful. Craig Schonhardt lent his artistic talents to designing the covers to these four volumes. In a roundabout way, Doug Irwin created the impetus for this project by alerting me in 1993 to the upcoming 150th anniversary of the repeal of the Corn Laws. David Lake very graciously provided a one-day turnaround in commenting on my lengthy introduction. Doug Irwin, Bob Pahre and Anthony Howe also provided helpful suggestions on the Introduction. Finally, my love and heartfelt gratitude goes to my husband, Andrew Bailey, who came to my rescue on various occasions during this project. Trained as a British economic historian, Andrew's advice and guidance has lent a depth to these volumes that I alone could not have achieved. That these volumes are dedicated to him is little compensation for his intellectual contribution and unfailing support.

I

THE POLITICAL ECONOMY DEBATE

A

FREE TRADE VERSUS FAIR TRADE

1 PROTECTION TO NATIVE INDUSTRY*
Sir Edward Sullivan

Preface

. . . It is assumed that Protection to native industry means Protection to corn: but this is not so; on the contrary, the object of those who advocate Protection to native industry is to wipe off entirely and absolutely every remaining tax on food, on raw materials of any and every description, and to substitute for it a tax on Foreign manufactured goods . . .

Chapter I: Growth of Trade

. . . About the same time that gold and steam revolutionized the commerce of the world, an enthusiastic band of political economists propounded a new commercial faith called Free Trade, that was to inaugurate a new era for mankind, to obliterate all national jealousies, to extend the brotherhood of nations, and to impart such blessings to the human race as it had never hitherto entered into the commercial heart to conceive.

The principles of the new faith were roughly as follows: consumers being in all cases more numerous than producers, their interests should be consulted first: all the world should buy in the cheapest, sell in the dearest market: all distinctions of home and foreign markets should be abolished: all duties and tariffs, and restrictions of any kind should be done away – the whole world was to be the market in which each nation was to meet on perfectly equal terms, and to contribute what best it could: A was to give to B what it could produce cheaper and better than B, B was to return the compliment, and so on through the whole alphabet of nations – all nations, and every body of workers were to be left entirely to their own merits to compete in the world's markets, without favour or restriction. It was a

* Sir Edward Sullivan, *Protection to Native Industry* (London: Edward Stanford, 1870), pp. vi; 1; 2–3; 13; 15; 17–19; 28–36; 38–40; 42–3; 46–50; 52–3; 57–63; 66; 68–70; 76–82; 84–6; 89–91; 94–7; 100; 103; 106–8; 115–18; 121–2; 124–8; 132–4; 136–40; 142–3; 148–9.

grand ideal conception of universal fraternity: the world was to become one unselfish family; its members working together for the general good, that is the good of the consumer.

No one can doubt the conception was a grand one, that if practicable it would have advanced incalculably the prosperity of the human family. Whether it is practical is quite a different thing.

It is no use following out to their fullest extent the theories of free trade: theories they still are, and such probably they will remain till long after our time – it might, however, easily be proved that under the most favourable and universal conditions its blessings would not be quite equally distributed. Some nations, either from natural causes, or accidental conditions, from superior intelligence, thriftiness, capital, advantages of situation and markets would then, as they do now, get more than their fair share of the world's business; whilst others from the reverse of the above causes, might be left entirely out in the cold, and find themselves minus the trade they still enjoy; or it might easily be shewn that, in a community where the producers constitute a very considerable minority, that is in a manufacturing country, it might be convenient, and even necessary for the general good of the community, that the interests of the former should be considered, though distinct and even antagonistic to those of the consumer. Free trade means the perfectly free exchange of goods, raw and manufactured, in every part of the world, or it means nothing at all: it means that all nations and languages, all consumers and producers all over the world must agree to be guided by the same laws, and buy and sell without restriction . . .

Chapter II: Free Trade and Free Ports

There is no doubt there are many articles of manufacture foreigners will produce cheaper than we can, but it is not wise or reasonable that we, as a nation, should therefore give up producing them. It is necessary for a community as crowded as ours that every industry should exist amongst us to give employment to our redundant population.

With a vast over-crowded population confined to our geographical limits by the "melancholy ocean," and unable to expand, a number of small industries are absolutely necessary to the existence of our workpeople, and every industry however small becomes of vital importance. We cannot part with one of our industries or any portion of one of them, without loss to some portion of the community. The country wants new industries, more of them, more work of any and every description instead of less. We cannot afford to lose one means of employment, to allow our workpeople to be thrown out of one single industry, to have their means of support taken from them in the smallest item in favour of the workpeople of other nations whom superior advantages, more economical and thrifty habits, a

4

fostering home support and artificial legislation enable to undersell them. Every class of our workpeople, however small the industry in which they are engaged, form a part of our community; they are members of the body politic, and it is necessary to our national well being, that all our members should be healthy, and as few unemployed as possible; every one should have work and earn wages, and moreover, where the possibility of doing so exists, it is the duty of the Government to see that it is done. It is only in the case of absolute necessity that the interests of one class should be sacrificed to the convenience or even advantage of any other . . .

If we allow any trade to be taken from the country we have to support those employed in it in some other way; it is far better for British consumers to pay a little more for the work of foreign operatives, than it is to be taxed to support their own at home, in idleness and want, in the poor-houses and prisons of the country . . .

There are very few articles of English manufacture that cannot be produced cheaper in some other country. I say cheaper, not better. The English workman can and does produce the very best work, but not the cheapest. It is now a question of the cheapest work. For England, therefore, with a redundant population, no expansive capabilities, every outlet for labour over-crowded, with dear food, dear clothing, dear house-rent, a double rate of wages, an extravagant, thriftless race of workers, to challenge the rest of the world to cheap production, is simply swagger. It is simply inviting competition in a race in which all the world knows we must be beat.

In reply to this we are told that our manufacturing industries, far from being ruined, are prosperous. It is true they are not yet ruined, but many are more depressed than they have ever before been. Very many of them are sick – very sick; far more so than those unacquainted with them have any idea of, and a few years more of such depression will see many of them *in extremis*. There are many who argue that our manufacturers would at once give up manufacturing if it did not pay; and no doubt it is a very natural assumption, that if a manufacturer continues his business it is a proof he is making money by it; but it is very often the case that he continues to manufacture only because he cannot afford to stop. They little know how many manufacturers continue to struggle on in business merely because they do not know how to get out of it. A man with twenty, thirty, fifty, or a hundred thousand pounds sunk in works and machinery cannot give up business without ruin. The causes that diminish the demand for his produce diminsh also the value of his plant; his capital and interest are imperilled at the same time and by the same cause. It is not to be expected, it is not in the nature of Englishmen, that he should at once throw up the sponge, and declare himself beat; he will continue to tread the mill though he gets nothing for it; he will struggle on for years, losing steadily perhaps, but yet hopeful of a change. Millions of manufacturing capital are in that condition in England at present. Capitalists continue to employ their capital in manufacturing industries because it is already invested in them; but in many cases it is earning no profit, and in others diminishing year by year.

It takes some time to scatter the wealth of England. The growth of half a century of industrial success is not kicked over in a day. Moreover, it is only now, only within the last three years, that the foreign producers have acquired the skill and capital and machinery that enables them really to press us out of our own markets. The shadow has been coming over us for many years, but it is only just now we are beginning to feel the substance; their progress corresponds with our decline . . .

There are four fiscal conditions that appear consonant with common sense: The first is universal Free trade, which means the removal of all trade restrictions, and the remission of all duties whatever, the perfectly free exchange of all goods and commodities all over the world. The second is Reciprocal or limited Free trade: the exchange of commoditites on an agreed and equable scale. The third, is imposing a Customs duty on all foreign manufactures for the purposes of income or of protection to native industry. The fourth is to establish Free Ports, neither to ask nor to receive any general or equable exchange of commercial facilities; but to say to the world, we will receive all you choose to send us, raw material or manufactured, without any duty or restriction whatever, notwithstanding you continue to impose heavy and prohibitory duties on our manufactured goods.

This latter policy may be of advantage to a community where a manufacturing class scarcely exists; or to a country where the manufacturing or producing class is proportionately very small as compared with the consuming class; or to some imaginary community that possesses cheaper labour, cheaper raw material, more capital, enterprise, skill, &c. than all the rest of the world besides!

It has been the making of Hamburgh, where the producing class scarcely exists: it would be of vast advantage to America, where the producing class as compared with the consuming class is proportionately very small; it has been attended with tremendous loss in England, where the producing as compared to the consuming class is proportionately larger than in any other country in the world. Say what you will, it was one of the most reckless commercial experiments ever tried, for a manufacturing nation suddenly to throw open her ports and court foreign competition without in any shape or kind securing any return.

In America the manufacturing industries are very small; the natural resources are immense; the expansive capacities of the country are illimitable; even now scarcely a tenth of it is fully populated. Millions upon millions of fertile acres are at the disposition of its inhabitants: and even if the free importation of foreign manufactures did, in some degree, depress the manufacturing population, they are so small a minority as compared to the community, and they have such facilities for turning their energies into other channels that the national prosperity or wealth would not in any degree suffer: land is the raw produce of America, and manufacturing farms and cities must for many years be their best trade . . .

In any consideration of this question it is most important to draw a distinct line between Free Trade in its true and extended signification, and simply declaring our own ports free: it is often sought to assume they are identical, whereas in reality nothing can be more different. It cannot be too forcibly stated, or too often repeated, that the only effect of what is called our Free Trade legislation has been to make England a vast free port, a Hamburgh on a grand scale; she is the emporium for the manufactures of the whole world; it is of importance to lay some stress on this distinction, because the prosperity of Hamburgh, resulting from her being a free port, is often advanced as an argument for our adopting a like policy. Now, from the fact that in Hamburgh there are no producers to talk of, whilst in England there is a larger proportion, as compared to the consumers, than in any other country in the world, it is evident that any argument drawn from the success of this commercial policy in Hamburgh falls to the ground when applied to England, where the conditions and requirements of the country are not only quite different, but actually reversed.

The question of the day is not whether Free Trade is a good thing – we cannot get it on any terms do what we may; but whether it is for the advantage of all classes of the community, or even for the majority, that England should be a free port; that she should admit the manufactures of the whole world without restriction, and without limit, or whether there is not evidence that this policy will cause ruin to a very numerous portion of the community, without very much benefiting the other. The effect of throwing open our ports to foreign competition has been to make England a vast emporium of foreign goods: the surplus stocks of all countries and all industries are sent here on the chance of a market; they must be sold when they come here; if at a fair price, so much the better, if not at a loss. So much the better for the consumer it will be said; but reverse the medal, and how will this affect the producer?

At present we have neither Free Trade, or Reciprocity, or Protection. We have declared England a vast free port; we admit all foreign goods, duty free, without restriction of any kind; but the ports of the world are as tightly closed to us as ever: we have the words Free Trade constantly ringing in our ears, and paraded on every occasion, but it is only a sounding word, it has no meaning when examined by our experience; we have never tried Free Trade; we have never seen it in operation; we may picture to ourselves what it is, but we can no more really judge of it from what we have seen, than a man can judge of a horse by looking at a cow. Free Trade is a misnomer as applied to our commercial policy. You cannot designate a small part of anything by the name that is given to the whole, and you might as well call a horse's tail a horse as to designate by the grand name of Free Trade the fag end of commercial equality that now exists.

We have no more Free Trade now than we had fifty years ago; but we have Free Ports, which is quite another thing.

Chapter III: Corn

The abolition of the Corn Laws affected directly the agricultural and indirectly the manufacturing interest.

The abolition of the duties on manufactured goods affected directly the manufacturing and indirectly the agricultural interest.

Now, after twenty years' experience, it is very amusing to look back and see how, in both cases, the results have exactly disproved the anticipations and theories of the parties most interested. The abolition of the Corn Laws, and of all Customs duties on foreign manufactures, were both carried by the manufacturing class in the teeth of the protracted opposition of the agricultural interest. The latter fancied they saw in this policy nothing short of ruin; whilst the former congratulated themselves on having secured cheap food and an extended market for their produce.

These anticipations have been exactly reversed; whilst the agricultural class are more healthy and prosperous than they have ever been before, the manufacturers and operatives are calling out that they are ruined.

It was the belief of the agricultural interest generally that free trade in corn would ruin both landlord and tenant, throw the land out of cultivation, and force the labouring population to emigrate. It has, on the contrary, proved to be a blessing to all concerned. It has been a decided legislative, commercial and social success, from whatever point you regard it: so great a success that no one in his senses wishes to alter it. It has kept the price of food at a very constant level; it has supplied us with what we could not possibly supply ourselves; it has removed one of the most dangerous and irritating of imposts; it has satisfied every one. The landed interest that was directly threatened, and fairly enough expected immediate ruin, is now by far the most prosperous interest in the country; and I doubt whether in any part of the three kingdoms any considerable number of landlords or tenants could now be rallied to the cry of Protection to Corn.

The abolition of duties on manufactured goods that more directly affected the interests of the manufacturers and operative class was carried by them with acclamation: far from anticipating ruin, they saw before them a golden future that was to add immeasurably to their wealth and happiness. They have been woefully disappointed; and there is scarcely a manufacturing interest in the country at this present moment that would not hail with enthusiasm a return to Protection to native industries . . .

It would almost appear that the abolition of all import duties on food in general, and corn in particular, is necessary to the prosperity, even to the existence of the community. I believe it is as necessary to our prosperity that we should have Free Trade in corn, as that we should have protection to native industry.

So great and evident have been the success and blessings of removing all duties on corn and meat, that the effort of every one should be directed to removing all remaining duties on other articles of food, that next to bread and meat are the greatest blessings to mankind.

Is it not absurd, and stupid, and irritating to the working classes to admit duty free all they produce, to tax all they consume; to admit duty free, clocks, watches, silk, paper, gloves, glass, ribbons, hats, boots, shoes, millinery, the finer kind of cotton goods, and linen, and scores of other industries, and to continue a heavy tax on cocoa, coffee, sugar, tea and tobacco? . . .

The present state of affairs hits them doubly hard, they suffer both ways; the value of their wages isdiminished by the amount of the Customs duty charged on the necessary articles of food they consume; and the amount of their wages is reduced by the free admission of foreign articles of manufacturing to compete with those they produce.

If we are to have Customs duties at all, whether is it most reasonable, to tax wine, silks, and all other luxuries of the rich; or tea, sugar, coffee, cocoa, and tobacco, the actual necessaries of the poor?

The consumption of the articles of foreign manufacture admitted free is confined *entirely* to the rich, the consumption of the necessaries that are still taxed is confined very much to the poor . . .

The landed interest is the most prosperous interest in the country at this present moment, and every landlord and tenant is aware of it; and the Tory party would indeed be stupid if they now attempted to revive the cry of protection to corn: I do not believe there are a dozen fanatics in the country who desire it.

Except in theory, Protection to corn and Protection to native industry have nothing whatever to do with each other, and those who maintain that the logical corollary of returning to Protection to native industries is to return to Protection to corn, are the most illogical of reasoners . . .

Chapter IV: Special Interests

My belief is that the special interests of the manufacturing and operative classes, more especially of those engaged in the production of articles of luxury of all kinds and in the innumerable small industries of the country have suffered from the result of making England a Free Port. They have suffered by loss of demand, by work which would have come to them going elsewhere, and they have the prospect, almost the certainty, that if things progress in the present groove, they will suffer still more; but we are told there should be no special interests; that no class of the community can have special interests without injuring some other class; that what is good for one must be good for all, or, if this is not the case, it ought to be. Theoretically, it is so, and I have always observed that a man who wishes to be thought more enlightened than his neighbour, and able to see further into a brick wall, generally prefers theory to practice or experience. But the upper and middle class have special interests too; they have a special interest in buying clarets and silks, and gloves and fans and boots, and velvets and millinery, and a score of articles of luxury and comfort, cheaper than they could buy them if England were not a Free Port: they have their special interests, which are to buy as cheap as they can, below cost price if possible, and this is evidently opposed to the special interests of the operative class; but the truth is, the whole community is made up of special interests; each class has its special interests, and these interests are often antagonistic to the special interests of other classes in the community: the special interests of some classes are however more urgent than those of others; for instance, the fever patient has a special interest in quinine, the gourmet has a special interest in truffles; but these special interests cannot be considered of equal importance; the gourmet can live without truffles, but the fever patient may die without quinine.

It is the same with our own industries. The upper and middle-class consumers have a special interest in getting their luxuries cheap, as cheap as they possibly can, irrespective of the interest of the producer. The producers have a special interest in having a remunerative market for their produce; but you cannot compare the magnitude of those two interests. It is a matter of convenience and luxury to the former, of actual existence to the latter.

The object of good government should be to adjust all the special interests of the several and antagonistic classes of the community, not favouring any one too much, and avoiding any policy that can be construed by any class as an injury to their interests.

When any special interest claims the exceptional consideration of the State, it becomes a question whether the demand for consideration is urgent, and whether it can be granted without injury or injustice to any other class in the community. The manufacturing industries of the country are now demanding the exceptional consideration of the State. Is their necessity urgent, and can assistance be granted without injuring any other class in the community? The manufacturing class ask to have their industries, their means of existence, preserved to them. The rich and consuming class ask to have their luxuries cheapened. Now, certainly bread and cheese are of more importance to a poor man than turtle and venison to a rich one! . . .

Those unacquainted with manufacturing industries can have no idea of the strength and number of the temptations that already exist to induce the English manufacturer to remove his capital and enterprise to Prussia, Austria, France or Belgium. Some have already done so, and if the present condition of affairs continues many more will do so;[1] it will become a necessity of their existence; they will then have two markets to manipulate – the English where they are admitted duty free; and their own foreign markets where they are protected.

At present emigration is confined to the operative class; but there is another emigration that is threatened that will be far more ruinous in its effects, viz., an emigration of capital and manufacturers; what can the British operative do if his employer and his capital disappear together? . . .

Chapter V: Producer and Consumer

In every community the numbers of the consumers very much exceed that of the producers; in some the proportion is greater than in others; their interests are everywhere and in all cases the same; it is to get the best possible article at the lowest possible price: they have no direct interest in any operative community whatever; no reason to buy from the English if the French, or Belgian, or German can supply the same article as good and as cheap. It is one of the canons of Free trade that the good of the many should be preferred to the good of the few; that the consumers being more numerous than the producers, their interest should be considered first: this is true up to a certain point, but no further; it is like many other matters, a question of comparison; if it were a question whether some particular legislation would benefit the consumers to a considerable extent, and injure the producers to a trifling extent, there would be no doubt about its being a wise and politic act; or it might be absolutely necessary for the good of the community that the interests of the producer should be sacrificed for the benefit of the consumer; but when it comes to a question whether it is wise or just that the special interests of the consumer should be advanced at the expense of the special interests of the producer, it immediately becomes a question of degree: what is the relative interest in the community as represented by the consumer and the producer? Of course the consumers are more numerous in this country than the producers; it is the universal condition of society; but still there is no community existing, or that ever has existed, in which the relative proportions so nearly approximate. It becomes a question, then, to what extent it is just to make the producer suffer for the *convenience*, for it does not amount to more, of the consumer? . . .

But there is another view of the question. Producers are also very large consumers; and any legislation that injures the former, very much affects the latter also. I should say almost the largest and most steady consumers of England are the producers, the manufacturers, the operatives, and the small tradesmen and householders, and the vast population that crowds the manufacturing districts. All of them are excellent consumers when their industries are prosperous, but they cannot consumer when they are out of

11

work, and have no money in their pockets to spend. These classes are not only very considerable consumers, but they are especially consumers of home products and manufactures. All their money is spent on homemade articles, none of it in foreign luxuries; their earnings are spent on essentially English articles of manufacture – English boots and shoes, English clocks and watches, English cotton and linen, ribbons, blankets, flannel, stockings, fustian, hats and bonnets, &c., &c.; probably they never expend a shilling on any article of foreign manufacture. The number and capacity of this class, as consumers, is directly affected by their condition as producers, and the same act of legislation that lessens their power or inducement to produce, lessens their power and inducement to consume.

The very reverse is the case with the upper and middle class consumers; their money is chiefly expended on foreign manufactured goods, not British. The wealthy class, noblemen, bankers, merchants, manufacturers, who increase their expenditure, spend their surplus wealth on wine, pictures, clocks, silks, satin, and articles of foreign luxury chiefly, they spend hardly anything on British manufactures; to speak roughly nearly every manufacturing industry in England might shut up, cease to exist, and the rich and middle class consumers, those with fixed incomes in fact, would still be supplied with everything they require from abroad with very little additional cost.

The result of making England a vast Free Port, and increasing the consumption of foreign articles of manufacture at the expense of our own, has been to weaken very much the tie that should connect the two great divisions of our community, the rich consumer and the poor producer.

A very large proportion of our consumers are entirely independent of our producers; they consume comparatively nothing that is English, and hardly know what we produce. To a very considerable extent the consumers of England are independent of the producers . . .

England is taxed higher per head than any other European country: and every article we manufacture bears some proportion of this taxation. The rates that a manufacturer has to pay on his works is a standing charge on his expenses of manufacturing: it must be added to the cost of his goods, and must of course make them more expensive . . .

The manufacturers of other countries less lightly taxed have a decided and evident advantage over ours: when we admit their manufactured goods duty free, we admit goods less highly taxed for public necessities, on an equality with our more highly taxed goods: but the result of the necessities of our taxation, which throw an additional cost on our manufactures, should not be visisted on the manufacturer or the operative. The Government or the Public have at any time, a perfect right to say to the producer, your goods and work are too dear, and therefore we must admit the foreigner to compete with you; but the English producer, on the other hand, may with perfect truth reply, admit the foreigner, if you please; but at any rate put him on an equality with us, and charge him with a duty equal to the rate of taxation you compel us to pay for the public good.

To the extent that the rate of taxation and other standing charges in England, which the manufacturer cannot escape, and which increase the cost of his work, exceed those of other countries, to that extent our producers ought to be protected. I think common sense should decide this . . .

Chapter VI: Unfair Competition

For all manufacturing purposes England is now only a department of Europe: all nations are allowed to import their goods duty free, and she is therefore compelled to sell her own at any price foreigners may choose to take for theirs. She is no more independent of the rest of Europe as respects the price she can obtain for her goods than Lancashire is of Yorkshire, or London of Manchester. She ought therefore to be placed on an exact equality with other nations against whom she is to compete; any special advantages other nations may possess over her, or any special disadvantage she may be suffering under, as respects them, places her in an unfair position.

I have several times used the expression "unfair" competition of the foreigner, and it is a term strictly deserved in many of their trades. Those who are unaccustomed to business do not realize the dangerous power the present state of our commercial policy gives to the foreign producers to harass, even to destroy, several of our native industries.

It is one of the first axioms of manufacturing industry that the more you can extend your production with the same plant, the cheaper will be the cost of the article you produce; this is owing to wear and tear of machinery and buildings, cost of management, and other standing charges being spread over a greater surface of products; all manufacturers therefore try to extend their production as much as possible, and they will sell their increased make at cost price, or even at a small loss, if their larger quantity enables them to reduce the average cost of the whole quantity they produce.

The position of the foreign manufacturer with his own market closely protected, and the English market entirely free, gives him an opportunity of carrying out this principle to the danger and disadvantage of the British manufacturer that he takes good care to push to the utmost . . . when their home demand is good they naturally sell more in their own dear market than in our cheap one, and we see less of their goods; but the moment their own demand slackens, their surplus goods are turned into our market to be sold at any price they will fetch. The English producer does not share in any degree whatever in improving trade on the Continent; he is not admitted to it; but the foreign producer partakes equally with our own in any rise in the English markets; moreover, the power they possess at any moment to swamp our markets acts very injuriously on the British manufacturer; no calculation will enable him to foretell prices and so regulate the amount of his production, when at any moment, without any warning, all his calculations may be upset by increased foreign importation; this very much interferes with steady production; the amount of the importation of foreign manufactured goods is regulated by two causes: a rise of price in our market, a fall in price in theirs; and it is unfair and injurious to the British manufacturer to be placed so completely at the mercy of the foreigner . . . Foreign manufacturers understand and practise trade combination far more extensively and successfully than we do. Already many of their largest industries are combined, and act together with great discipline and unanimity. It is very easy to see how this danger might become most imminent. America, for instance, notwithstanding her enormous customs duties, consumes immense quantities of European manufactures, but as she regularly increases these duties, and will continue to do so, the natural conclusion is that she will soon begin to supply herself, and the consumption of European articles of manufacture will fall off. The foreign manufacturers, who have calculated on this consumption, and extended their operations to meet it, will therefore begin to stock; or they must sell somewhere else: they will not, however, break through their good remunerative prices at home: they will not compete with each other in their home market, but they will pour all their surplus goods into our markets to compete with our industries . . .

Take glass for instance, one-third of all the glass consumed in England comes from France, Belgium, and Prussia, whilst not one foot or ounce of English glass is admitted into those countries. This is not because foreign glass is better, or the facilities for producing it greater in those countries than in England; on the contrary, many kinds of English glass are better than foreign glass, and England possesses as great facilities for the production of cheap glass as any continental country. How is it then that the foreigners monopolize one-third of the total glass consumed in this country? They do not this by fair upright competition, but by the very means I have just been explaining. The English can produce their glass as cheap, or very nearly so, as the French, Belgians, or Prussians; but these nations having a closed market at home, where all competition is excluded, and where they make a very large profit on the larger portion of their make, are enabled to sell the remainder in England at a price fifteen or twenty per cent. lower than they are getting in their own country; but the two prices taken together will still yield a good average on their whole production.

The English glass manufacturers are able and willing to sell at the same average prices as the foreigner, but they have no chance of doing so; they are excluded from the dearer market abroad, and confined entirely to the cheaper market at home.

Now of course this way of cheapening production is hailed with glee by enthusiastic Free traders, as tending to the advantage of the consumer: buy at the lowest price is their motto, below cost if possible, and never mind how it is done; but this is neither wise nor honest. It is not wise to allow any portion of our producing community to be unfairly depressed, and it is not honest to encourage a state of affairs that is manifestly fraudulent.

When foreign glass is sold at a depreciated rate in the English market, it not only replaces British glass for home consumption, but also for exportation. Exporters to foreign countries naturally buy the cheapest articles they can; if foreign glass is cheaper than British, they buy it in preference. They, of course, do not care that it is unfairly depreciated, and is unfairly competing with British glass . . .

Chapter VII: Labour

Owing to custom, education, habit of life, climate, national peculiarities, cheaper lodgings and food, and other causes, the Belgian, French, German, and Swiss operatives can work and do well, educate their children, and live altogether respectably and contented, at wages varying from 30 to 50 per cent. below those required by the English operative.

This applies to nearly all our industries, more especially to those requiring long hours, patience, and industry, rather than to those requiring great physical exertion.

For instance, the proportionate difference in wages between Continental Europe and ourselves is more observable in watchmaking, spinning, weaving, paper-making, cabinet-making, millinery, lace, gloves, boots, shoes, &c. &c., in the fabrication of luxuries of all kinds, than in iron working, mining, engineering, and other laborious trades and occupations . . .

Twenty years ago the English had better and cheaper fuel, better and cheaper machinery, far larger capital, superior practical and technical education and experience than the rest of Europe put together; and these advantages more than balanced their higher wages. In spite of high wages, the English manufacturer and operative then had a monopoly of many industries that have since spread rapidly among the manufacturing communities of Europe. Many articles that they then produced cheaper and better than the rest of the world can now be produced as well and as cheaply by other nations.

Increased confidence, the spread of mechanical knowledge, the magical effect of an additional circulation of gold, the effect of steam navigation in equalizing the rates of transit, and the price of commodities, has removed many of the advantages England then possessed. The manufacturers and operatives of France, Belgium, Germany, and Switzerland, can now get their raw material at the same price as we do, and can deliver their manufactured article in our markets as cheaply as we can. They have now as much capital, as cheap fuel (or nearly so) a good deal of it English, as much technical and mechanical knowledge, as cheap and as good machinery (most of it also actually English or copied from it) as we possess in this country – all these things, therefore, being equal, they have still an advantage of from 30 to 50 per cent. in wages; and it is this difference that enables them in almost every article to undersell us in our own markets . . .

All other conditions being equal, the Foreign operative must either raise his wages from 30 to 50 per cent., or the English operative must lower his to the same extent, before they can be said to be equally weighted in the international race. But it is of no use the English operative waiting for the Foreign operative to raise his wages if at the same time he raises his tariff also! This has been the practice in America; operatives' wages have been steadily rising, but co-equally have risen the Customs duties on the goods they produce . . .

Chapter VIII: Cotton

A good farmer will depend for his rent on a number of crops; he will not limit his produce to one, and lay his whole farm down in grass or in corn, for grass or corn might fail, and where would he be then? This is true wisdom, and this is what a good Government ought to do for a nation; we have to pay our national rent – and to do so we ought to have a number of crops, great and small, to depend upon . . .

Of late years we have adopted the very opposite policy, we have trusted too much to one crop and neglected the prosperity of others; a great deal too much importance has been attached to the cotton interest in England. The chief, if not the sole reason for throwing open our ports to the world, was to extend our cotton trade. Cotton was our great staple, and it was argued, that if we admitted foreign manufactures duty free, other nations would in return receive our cotton. It was believed the cotton interest would be immensely extended, and to secure this result, it appeared of comparatively little importance that a number of smaller interests should suffer or fail altogether . . .

The French Treaty was negotiated solely and entirely in the cotton interest, but for cotton we should never have heard of it; it was believed we had a monopoly of cotton, that foreigners must buy of us, and that if we could get the duty reduced to 15 per cent. *ad valorem*, we should immensely increase our trade. These expectations have proved illusory.

For many years the French, Prussians, Belgians, Swiss, Austrians and Americans, have each had the germ of a large cotton industry; capital, confidence, cheap transit and *protection* are now rapidly developing them; they require less of our cotton every year, they will soon require none at all;

they can manufacture cotton as good and as cheap as we can, and in some qualities can even supply us at a less price than we can ourselves.

We were assured we had a monopoly of the French cotton supply; and that nothing could affect it. But, as it turns out, there is hardly an article of which the French do not send us more than we send them; in grey and bleached calicoes they take from us £760,000, and send us £880,000. In prints they take from us £24,800 and send us £120,000; in dyed goods they take £6,400 and sends us over £40,000 . . .

If we were to keep a debtor and creditor account, taking even the whole of the stuffs exported as going into consumption in France, the account would stand thus: – Exports from France to England 61½ million francs; exports from England to France, 32½ millions; excess in favour of France, nearly 29 millions of francs in worsted goods alone. In a comparison of the whole manufactured articles imported and exported by France from and to England there is a balance in favour of France of £23,233,593.

The stimulus given to French manufacturing industries by having the English ports opened to them is very well illustrated by the growth of the woollen trade at Roubaix. The number of spindles has increased from 1,300,000 in 1862, to 1,750,000 in 1867; and the exports of woollen yarns has increased 250 per cent.! It is pleasant to hear that "some of the largest establishments at Roubaix state, with just pride, that they are almost exclusively working for the English market;" and yet we are told the woollen trade is prosperous!

It is quite true that some years ago England had a monopoly of the cotton trade, and France and other nations, were obliged to buy of us, because there was no cotton in the market; but the gradual loss of this monopoly became inevitable with the change of the commercial conditions that had given it to us; it is as certain as anything in this world, that wherever labour, machinery, fuel, and capital, are cheap and plenty, and a demand for cotton goods exists, there cotton factories will start up to supply it; it is the simplest of all industries, the best understood, the most profitable both for capital and labour.[2] As foreign factories increase foreign fabrics will gradually supply the place of English fabrics; formerly English cotton goods could stand the heavy *ad valorem* duty, because there was no competition; now there is, it is increasing and will continue to increase every year, and must inevitably deprive us of a good deal of our trade.

In the early stages of the cotton industry it is of great importance to get the material in the best and fittest possible state for manufacturing; it is more convenient in many cases, and gives employment to more hands, and is more profitable to manufacture cotton goods from cotton yarn, than to produce it from the raw article. In many parts of Austria and Switzerland, it is still difficult to get raw cotton, and there cotton yarn is entirely employed; wherever cotton yarn is bought, we know cotton industries are springing up; every nation that takes less of our cotton goods and more of our yarn is on the high road to self-supply: as they profit by every cwt. of yarn they convert into piece goods, so we lose by every cwt. we sell as yarn instead of in its fully manufactured form. The labour employed in converting yarn into piece goods, is about five times as great as that employed in converting raw cotton into yarn; to that extent therefore the interest of the operative class lies directly in completing the manufacture of cotton, rather than in selling it in the shape of yarn; this applies also to the earlier stages of other industries, silk and woollen.

In 1868 France took nearly 30 per cent. less of our cotton, linen and woollen manufactures than she did in 1866, and about 70 per cent. more cotton, linen, and woollen yarn; and the same unmistakeable evidence of increasing manufacturing industry is plainly visible in all our cotton dealings with foreign nations.

If we examine the returns we find a far larger proportion of the raw cotton that comes into this country at present is re-exported than formerly; in 1854 one-ninth of the cotton exported into this country was re-exported; in 1868 one-fifth or nearly double the proportion was re-exported.

Our exports of raw cotton and cotton yarn to France have increased from eleven and-a-half millions in 1854, to twenty-four and-a-half millions in 1868; whilst our exports of manufactured cotton to France have fallen off 30 per cent. since 1866 . . .

The cotton trade of continental Europe with France and China must receive an immense stimulus from the opening of the Suez Canal. Trieste and Marseilles will be brought close to the eastern markets and must necessarily get a very large proportion of their trade. Hitherto her maritime superiority has given England great advantages over less skilful nations; this superiority is over, and slighter ships and timid mariners will now be enabled to reach the golden East with a very small taste of the dangers and diffficulties of the ocean route.

In addition to the rapidly increasing cotton industries of Europe, America is largely extending her cotton mills both in the North and South,[3] and India will soon commence to manufacture on a large scale.

In spite of high wages, high protective duties will foster the cotton manufacture in America; and although it is not likely that we shall yet feel their competition in European markets, it is almost certain she will soon supply her own requirements. In India we may possibly have a very much more formidable rival: the natives of India are especially adapted to the sort of work required in the manufacture of cotton: they grow the raw material on the spot, and any quantity of skilled labour can be procured at from 12s to 14s a month. When cotton mills are started in India on a large scale, and with the requisite amount of capital, I see scarcely any limit to the economical manufacture of cotton goods.

Nothing connected with the cotton question appears to me so childish and ridiculous as the Manchester wail about the scarcity of cotton; they decline to face the difficulty fairly, and to acknowledge that our mills are standing because our monopoly is gone; because other countries buy and manufacture cotton that used formerly to come as a matter of course to us. There is as much cotton grown and as much converted into piece goods as ever, only it is not we who are doing all the buying and selling. They will persist in attributing the depressed stated of the industry to the price of the raw cotton. Only give us cheap cotton, they say, only compel the Ryots of India to grow more cotton, and of a better quality, and to sell it cheaper, and pack it cleaner, and our prosperity will immediately return. They appear to think that the two or three hundred millions inhabiting India have no other mission or object in life but to grow raw cotton for the Lancashire mills, and to consume Lancashire piece goods! . . .

Moreover the distance from India to Europe must always limit the trade in raw cotton, except when stimulated by exorbitant prices. The cotton manufacturer desires that the native of India should send his cotton from India to Lancashire to be made into shirts, which he is to buy back again at a profit, and wear out as soon as possible. But when you consider the cost of collecting the raw cotton together in India, transporting it to the coast, shipping it to England, unshipping at Liverpool, rail to the different factories, packing and unpacking, return charges to Liverpool, reshipment to India, unshipping at Bombay or Calcutta, with all the expenses of spreading it over the country, does it not appear reasonable and natural that it should eventually be manufactured on the spot; especially as the population is docile and industrious, handy beyond all other nations in the pliancy and quickness of manipulation, and economical to a degree that we in this country cannot conceive.

I take it to be beyond any question whatever that, taking a broad view of the question, it is impossible that cotton can for many more years continue to be brought all the way from India to Europe to be manufactured and retransported.

Probably our manufacture of cotton has been less affected by our commercial legislation than any other of our industries. Neither Free trade or Protection, can very much increase, or diminish the share that will come to England, it is regulated by much grander causes. So long as our maritime superiority, a more universal command of raw material, larger capital, superior machinery and fuel, &c. gives us an advantage over other nations, equal or greater than they possess over us in the matter of cheap labour, so long shall we go on manufacturing at a large rate: as these advantages diminish, so will our production. Other nations, as they begin to get more plentiful supplies of the raw material, increased capital, better machinery, &c., will produce more and more manufactured cotton: it is not likely our home trade will very soon be taken from us, but we shall every year be more and more dependent on it: our home demand has now fallen away 30 per cent. in three years, not from foreign importations, but because so many other trades are depressed and half ruined by foreign competition, that our operatives, the largest class of the consumers of cotton, cannot afford to buy it.

Chapter IX: [The] French Treaty

. . . The objects and intentions and anticipations of Mr. Cobden, and those who supported his policy in negociating the French treaty were perfectly honest: he believed it was another step towards Free trade: he found that all his prophecies and anticipations of universal reciprocity had failed, and he naturally grasped at this idea of negociating a commercial treaty with France, as promising some small opening for the realization of his hopes.

Individually, I never could understand the policy or the sense of the Commercial treaty: it always appeared to me absurd to go through the form of negociating a treaty when we had it in our power to do all we have done in the matter just as easily without it; there could be no earthly object in placing ourselves under an obligation to the French for no reason at all.

If it had been a case of reciprocity, of removing corresponding duties on certain articles of manufacture on both sides: there would have been some reason in it, but this was not the case at all; we removed the Customs' duties absolutely, entirely from forty-three articles, most of them articles of French industry; they, on the contrary, did not remove the duties from one single article of English industry. Now, there was no necessity for having a treaty to enable us to do this: we could have done it just as well without one. When you know it is a case of heads you win, tails I lose, surely it is hardly worth the trouble of tossing! . . . Of course, for decency sake, they were obliged to go through the form of an exchange: and this they did in their own way: they did not abolish the duty on any single article of English manufacture; they contented themselves with reducing the duties on a certain number. In some cases they lowered the 50 or 60 per cent. *ad valorem* Customs' duty to 30 or 15 per cent.: in some cases they actually substituted for total prohibition a 30 per cent. *ad valorem* duty.

They followed a very intelligible and I believe a very sound principle: they admitted at low rates all raw materials required for manufactures: coal, iron, cotton, wool, &c. with the machinery necessary to turn them into manufactured products, and continued to impose *ad valorem* duties that were actually prohibitory on all our manufactured goods: they did not in one single case lower their Customs' duties to a point that would allow any article of English manufacture to be sold in their markets at a profit, that was not already in that position; there have always been a few articles we produce, and they do not, or not so cheap and so good as we do, and these they must buy from us under any conditions, to prohibit them would be absurd: these continue, but they have not been added to in one single case.

Now, if it was only a question of the English treaty, French manufacturers would be quite safe, and we should hear no sound of grumbling: the advantages are all on their side: they have taken care to fix a rate of duty that excludes English manufactured goods from their market; but unfortunately the favoured nation clause admits into France, Belgian, Prussian, Austrian and Swiss articles of manufacture at the same *ad valorem* duty that is imposed on British goods of the same kind; the duty that is sufficient to exclude in the latter case is not sufficient in the former: and consequently many French industries find themselves galled by foreign manufactured produce admitted under the wing of the English treaty, but having nothing to do with English industries.

The French were merely throwing dirt in our eyes when they reduced their *ad valorem* duties from 50 or 30 to 15 per cent. on articles that would be equally as well prohibited by an *ad valorem* duty of 5 per cent.: or in changing total prohibition for a 30 per cent. *ad valorem* duty on articles that could not be sold at a profit, even if admitted without any duty at all: yet this is actually what was done! . . .

Every single one of the thirty-three or thirty-four articles admitted duty free from France by the treaty are articles of luxury or convenience, whose use is entirely confined to the wealthier and more luxurious classes in the community, not a single one is directly or indirectly, or in any degree whatever of any service or advantage to the working classes; not one single article admitted duty free is either consumed by the working classes, or cheapens his labour, or adds to his comfort, or directly or indirectly benefits him in the remotest way; but on the other hand all of them are articles he produces . . .

The effect of this suicidal policy is not so immediately evident, because the industries that have suffered most are, with the exception of silk, small industries, employing limited communities, working at their own homes or in small shops, and without any influential capitalist to represent their distress. No immense body of men, like the cotton workers, are thrown out of work at once: if there had been, the treaty would not have lasted a year, or we should have had a revolution; but numerous smaller bodies have been thrown out of work; a number of small industries are partially or entirely ruined, and it is this that causes the distress and misery that now overflows the manufacturing districts . . . But although the Government of France took good care not to allow free entry to a single manufactured article that could in any degree injure any of her existing industries, she took every pains to introduce as easily as possible every article that could stimulate or create new ones: she wanted raw material and machinery, and every facility was eagerly seized for introducing them.

Either the most extraordinary ignorance exists amongst our Free trade professors respecting the relative effect of making England a Free port on the manufacturing industries of France and England, or there is an amount of wilful misrepresentation that does them little credit. In 1865 the total

21

exports from England to France amounted to $25\frac{1}{2}$ millions sterling; the exports from France to England amounted to 53 millions, of which over 40 millions were French products and manufactures.

The relative value of this international trade is shown more by its nature than by its amount, it was nearly as follows: 72 *per cent.* of our exports to France were raw materials, ($\frac{7}{8}$ths of which were Foreign and Colonial produce, merely passing through the country, and $\frac{1}{8}$th coal and iron.) 16 *per cent.* were half raw materials, chiefly yarns of different descriptions, on which most of the labour remained to be done in France. 12 *per cent.* only were fully manufactured articles, a very large proportion of which consisted in the machinery of all kinds required to manufacture the raw and half raw matereials we supplied them with.

Our manufactured goods paid duties from $27\frac{1}{2}$ per cent. on glass and potteries, to 20 per cent. on cutlery, 13 per cent. on cotton, to $7\frac{1}{2}$ on metal work.

Of our imports from France, 16 *per cent.* were raw materials, all home produce consisting chiefly of brandy, wines, oil, corn, &c., true produce of the soil, annual and inexhaustible, and on which a vast amount of labour had been employed.

31 *per cent.* were half raw materials, and $52\frac{1}{2}$ *per cent.* were fully manufactured articles on which all the labour was employed in France, and all of which were admitted duty free in England.

It is thus a fact that 88 per cent. of the articles exported from England to France in 1865, consisted of Foreign and Colonial raw produce, on which no labour had been expended in this country, and of half raw materials on which comparatively little had been employed, and of the coal and iron necessary to manufacture them, whilst of the remaining 12 per cent. a very considerable portion consisted of spinning and weaving, and other machinery necessary to extend the manufacturing industries of the country.

This was in 1865. Take a later date. In the debate in the French Chambers, January 18, 1870, Monsieur Johnstone said: – "Our exports to England are four times as large as our importations from that country: we have exported goods to the value of 400 millions of francs more than we have imported." . . .

Almost every one of the French manufactured articles that we admit duty free are, as a rule, sold at a higher price in France than in England: the French manufacturer will lower his price almost below cost to beat the English producer in the British market, but he yet manages to secure a fair average price on his whole make by selling at a much higher price in his own market where he is protected; and is thus enabled most unfairly and most unjustly to filch their market from the British workers.

Now this is a disadvantage that is so manifestly unjust that one would suppose our statesmen would in the simple exercise of their duty towards their own countrymen seek to remedy it. But no; the theory of Free Trade is right, even though the practice is fatal . . .

The gentleness and tenderness with which the French Government treated their home industries, and the care with which they sought to guard them from any sudden dangers or loss from foreign competition, was in direct opposition to our treatment of our own industries whose prosperity or existence was threated by our commercial legislation. In those cases in France where a fall in the *ad valorem* duty from 30 to 15 per cent. was decided on, four years were allowed manufacturers and operatives to prepare for the contest, to improve their make, &c. &c. Not so with us; no time or preparation was allowed to our operatives or manufacturers; on the contrary, the possibility of any change was persistently denied till the mine was completed and exploded under our feet. No warning was given to the silk manufacturer to prepare for unrestricted foreign competition, but suddenly, as a thief in the night, the Bill was introduced that has almost annihilated an industry yielding some seven or eight millions sterling.

When the ruin of the silk trade consequent on the French treaty appeared to be inevitable the operatives and manufacturers were told they must improve their machinery, their designs, their quality, and manufacture cheaper and better than they had hitherto done; but to ruin a trade first, to throw it into bankruptcy and then to tell it to go ahead is absurd: that is not the way to stimulate its efforts and its energy, to bring new capital and enterprise into it; on the contrary, the very causes that make fresh capital and energy necessary make it impossible to get them. Energy, enterprise, capital steadily leave an industry that is declining or threatened with disaster.

Those who negociated the French treaty might have known, if they had taken the trouble to inquire, that in many points the French were more skilful manufacturers of silk than ourselves, and could beat us in any open market.

Instead of at once throwing our silk trade into a competition that was hopeless they should have given them time and assistance to improve their product up to the standard of those they were to compete with, to tell them to do so afterwards was the most insulting injustice.

They had no right, unless it was absolutely unavoidable, to remove from them without warning the protection that was necessary to their existence, and on which they had counted when investing their capital. The object, no doubt, was to stimulate the cotton industry; but by what new code is it considered just to ruin one industry on the chance of advancing another?

The direct object of all the Free trade legislation we have seen in England, and of the French treaty especially, was to increase the area of our cotton sales. Every other industry, every other interest was considered below notice when compared with cotton; if smaller industries suffered or were ruined, so much the worse for them, cotton at any rate must profit!

The idea was to stimulate the great industry at any cost. The French treaty was the most selfish piece of commercial legislation this country has ever seen, it was originated by cotton men, negociated by cotton men, actuated solely by cotton interests, and with the most supreme indifference for any other manufacturing interest except cotton . . .

Chapter X: Board of Trade Statistics

In the hands of a clever manipulator of figures, the Board of Trade returns may be made to prove anything you like. They are laboriously and conscientiously prepared, and contain a vast amount of useful and varied information; they give us approximately the gross commerce of the country, the principal exports and imports; they tell us where our produce goes, and the nature and value of the produce we receive in return; but they give no insight whatever into the actual condition of our manufacturing industries at home, *our home consumption of home products.*

England's wealth and prosperity does not consist entirely in her foreign commerce; the amount of exports and imports is not alone of itself, conclusive evidence of prosperity. She does not live in imports and exports alone; it is her home consumption far more than her exports and imports that gives occupation to the people and wealth to the country.

Home consumption of home manufactures is the universal test of prosperity, and no information on this subject appears in the Board of Trade returns . . .

For instance, the imports of French silks have increased nine millions in the last ten years, and on the strength of this increased importation it is stated and credited that the community are consuming more silks than they did ten years ago and must consequently be richer, – but this is not so; during the same time the exports of English silks has fallen off a million, and the home consumption of British silks has dwindled to nothing. Very little if any more silk is consumed to-day in England than ten years ago, but French silk is consumed instead of English silk, the work of Foreign hands and looms has replaced the work of our own countrymen; this may be a certain infinitesimal advantage to the consumer, but it is ruin to a considerable body of producers, and if it proves anything at all it is that a large portion of our operative community must have lost their means of livelihood . . .

When we compare the proportion of our manufactured goods exported with the proportion consumed at home, we see at once that without both returns one can get no accurate idea of the condition of our manufacturing industries. Increased exports may mean depression in the home market; and diminished exports may mean increased home consumption. I do not say it is so as a rule; but it is so quite frequently enough to prove the absurdity of relying on any returns of imports and exports as evidence of the true condition of our industries. All is not gold that glitters. At this present moment the increase in some of our exports has resulted entirely from the diminished demand in our home market. In many cases producers have had the choice of selling without a profit at home, of stopping their works, or of exporting to a foreign port on the chance of a profit; naturally they generally try the last first.

The balance of trade is a subject on which Free trade theorists are very strong indeed. They maintain that not only is there no proof of loss when the imports exceed the exports, but actually the very reverse. Now this I believe is untrue. Look at it from any point you like it comes to this, that after we have exchanged all we can in raw and manufactured produce there still remains an enormous balance, say from 70 to 100 millions which we have to pay for in cash.

The fact of our being able to part with from 70 to 100 millions a year for a number of years without shewing signs of exhaustion is a proof of the immense accumulated wealth there was and still is in the country, but it can by no possible sophistry be made to prove that this wealth is increasing.

Whenever the imports exceed the exports, that is to say, whenever a balance remains to be paid for in cash, after all the exchanges have been made, to that extent the country must part with its gold; and, on the contrary, whenever a balance has to be received in cash, after all exchanges have been made, to that extent the country will add to its store of gold. Now a drain of 700 millions sterling in eleven or twelve years is not very much when compared to the funded and realized wealth of England. Still it is a considerable amount, and its effects must be felt both in the country that parts with and in the countries that gain it. This 700 millions has either been withdrawn from the funded and realized wealth of the country, or from industrial enterprises, or it has been diverted from home to foreign articles of consumption; it has gone to create industries and to encourage competition in foreign countries; but it would certainly have been better for our community if it had been expended in creating industries and stimulating competition in our own country.

It is constantly argued that this excess of imports over exports is of no importance, that if it counts at all it is in our favour. That if money goes out something else comes in of equivalent value, in fact the money comes back somehow in return; but I cannot admit the truth of the argument. The money does not come back. We get various articles more or less perishable in exchange for it, but the money, which does not perish, leaves us. I cannot bring myself to doubt that there must be more money in circulation in the community if this balance was retained in the country than if it went permanently abroad. Of course we get value for our money, but it is for the most part in perishable articles, from 50 to 70 per cent. of the value of which consists in the labour of foreign workmen; whilst the money we send to buy these goods does not perish but remains to vivify and to increase trade and industries and find employment in any imaginary degree. It may be argued that this is all right, that our wealth is so boundless and our wants so vast, it is necessary for us to employ additional foreign labour to supply them; but this argument falls to the ground when we find our own operatives out of work and foreigners fully employed supplying us. I do not think it can be doubted that it must be an advantage to a community to export more manufactured goods than they import; it must accumulate wealth in the country and by that means lighten taxation and other burdens . . .

But there are other particulars in our exports and imports that are not satisfactory, and that is the increased exportation of our raw material, coal and iron, and of manufacturing machinery; coal and iron, especially when found united or close together, as in England, constitute the chief natural wealth of the country; they have been the primary cause of our manufacturing supremacy. Even now they are the only weapons that enable us to meet the lower wages of the Continent; to supply these materials to our opponents at the same price and cost that we get them ouselves, is simply to share with them the only advantage we retain, and that alone has enabled us to meet their low cost of labour.

So long as we possessed a considerable advantage in coal and iron to put against their labour, we might compete with them; directly we give them these defeat becomes a certainty. Foreign nations have not been slow in taking advantage of our marvellous generosity in this matter; our exports of coal have considerably more than doubled during the last fifteen years.

Independently of the advantages we give to the foreigner by allowing him to import our coal duty free, there is another reason why this trade should not be looked upon entirely as a subject of congratulation; we call it raw produce, but it cannot be classed with what is generally included under the head of raw produce. Wine and wheat are the produce of the soil and of the seasons, the supply is inexhaustible, renewed and increased year after year; there is no exhaustion about it, it is everlasting. Wine and wheat represent the interest of land, which is the capital; coal and iron are not the interest but the capital itself. The former is permanent and will go on yielding interest for ever; a thousand years hence for all we know the soil of France and America will continue to produce their oil and wine, and wheat in as great, or increasing, profusion as at present; but this is not so with coal and iron: they cannot be renewed through future ages; the supply is limited, exhaustible, diminishing; year by year they must become less; they do not represent the interest of the soil but the soil itself.

In 1868 we exported about five and-a-half millions sterling of coal, and about one and-a-half millions sterling of pig iron; with every ton of this coal and iron we diminished our capital.

It may be argued that the amount of capital represented by these products is so enormous, that it need not strictly be treated as capital,

26

that the quantity exported compared to the whole quantity remaining or consumed, is so small as not to be worth consideration, and there is no doubt some truth in it. I believe we may without danger of exhausting or even perceptibly injuring the national capital during our generation, export coal and iron; but still in doing so, we are diminishing the national capital of succeeding generations of Englishmen; and by enhancing the price of coal at home, and diminishing it abroad, we are parting with two of our special manufacturing advantages, and are assisting foreign industries at the expense of our own . . .

Chapter XI: Reciprocity

A strong effort is being made to discredit the cry for reciprocity or protection to native industries that is spreading amongst the working classes on the ground that it is raised by the "stupid Tories," who take advantage of the present season of depression to try and re-establish the Corn laws.

Now this is not true, the Tories are not the originators or even prime movers of the agitation. It is not a suggestion from above, but a demand from below. It proceeds from the body of the working classes themselves. As yet there has been no prompting, it is entirely genuine.

Of course, very soon the cry will be taken up by one side or the other for political purposes, to strengthen or destroy existing Governments; and if the Tories do not improve the occasion the Radicals will. As yet the working classes have not appealed to either party, politics are not mooted at their meetings; but when they do make this subject the condition of their suuport they will soon find both parties outbidding each other in their behalf.

The vote of the working classes is now of vast importance to each of the political parties. It is sufficient to turn the scale in half the boroughs in the United Kingdom, and the newly enfranchised may be quite sure of humble servants wherever or whenever they can guarantee a majority . . .

Free traders affect to be surprised at this stupid agitation of the working classes, and as I said before attribute it to politcal re-actionists, but every thoughtful man must have felt convinced that whenever the working classes got political power the first use they would make of it would be to protect themselves. Other classes would do the same. It seems almost a law of nature they should do so. The re-establishment of protection to native industry in some shape or another became a certainty when the operative classes gained political power.

We are told the battle of Free trade was fought and won twenty years ago, and that it is ridiculous, an insult to common sense, to argue it over again. No doubt the battle was fought and gained; but it was fought under false colours, and with a totally different class to that which is now clamouring for its modification. The conditions of the problem are totally changed.

27

Then all was theory. Now we have the light of practice and experience to instruct us. The promises of theory have proved vain, illusionary, whilst the lessons of experience have proved hard and startling. The battle was fought twenty years ago with the Tory party, with the landowners. Now it must be fought over again with the working classes.

The working classes supported Free trade twenty years ago because they believed they were battling against the prejudices and special interests of the upper classes, and at the same time advancing their own. Now the whole question is reversed, the upper classes are satisfied; their special interests have been advanced by this legislation. It is the operative class who are now calling out that their special interests have suffered.

The English operatives have found out that they have been cruelly and woefully deceived by their flatterers and advisers. They were assured that if England gave in her adherence to Free trade it would almost immediately become universal. That if only we admitted foreign goods to our markets foreign nations would at once open their markets to our goods.

That though in certain articles the price in our own market would fall, the innumerable fresh markets that would be thrown open to our goods all over the world would far more than counterbalance this trifling loss; that increased demand would more than repay them for any partial fall in price.

They were patted on the head and assured that their superior energy and hardihood and "appetite for hard work," a very favourite term with the flatterers of the working classes, would always enable them to whip the foreigner in any shape and under any condition. They were assured that they were so far ahead of the rest of the manufacturing world, that they need dread no competition; that they were beyond all possibility of danger; that no harm could possibly come to them; that far from running any risk of being driven out of their own market, they would carry the war into the enemies' country and establish a footing in every market of the world . . .

We are told Free trade principles are spreading; why, in Prussia, Austria, Belgium, Switzerland, the idea even of opening their ports and markets, and inviting competition with their own industrial population, has never yet been mooted: whilst in America, the operative's Paradise, the duties on many British manufacturers have been doubled during the last few years;[4] and France, the Promised Land of Free trade, is already trying to withdraw the nominal facilities doled out to us in the Commercial treaty. The only man in France who is at heart, a Free trader, is the Emperor himself.

Is this hopeful for the operative classes in England? Does the direction of public opinion in one single country on this subject afford the slightest hope that any one of them will admit our manufactures duty free? On the contrary. Protection to native industry is more firmly established as a great universal rule of internal polity than any other, and wherever democratic principles extend this principle will intensify.

The operative class are told to wait patiently, in other words to continue without work, till foreign nations have the good sense or the generosity to open their ports to our goods!

Protection to native industry is a question that more directly affects the operative class than any other in the community, who can deny their right to canvass it, and if they think right to call for its repeal?

The working classes have been enfranchised, they have been urged to think and speak for themselves, and it is very probable the first use they will make of this liberty will be to protect themselves and to tear to threads the "peurile [*sic*] doctrines and illusions"[5] of their teachers, and return to the fine old national good sense. Even now, I believe that the most ordinary speaker who would condescend to stump any manufacturing borough or county on the cry of Protection to Native Industry would carry it against Mr. Bright himself. Trade Unions have hitherto had for their object the protection of workmen from each other and from their employers, soon they will seek to protect themselves and their employers against unfair foreign competition.

NOTES

1   There is some little difficulty in reconciling the conflicting statements of those manufacturers who have started factories abroad: for instance, Mr. Mundella, MP for Nottingham, has on two separate occasions elicited cheers by most conflicting statements at the Educational Conference, held at Manchester, Janaury 18, 1868. He said that "his firm employed 700 people in Saxony, and that they could all read and write." (Loud cheers.) A few weeks ago he stated that only 5 per cent. of his work was done in Saxony – 95 per cent. in England. (Loud cheers.) It becomes a simple rule of three sum: if it takes 700 people to do 5 per cent. of his work, how many will it take to do 95 per cent.? Answer – 13,300!

2   In the five Eastern departments there is capital invested in spinning machinery to the amount of eight millions sterling; the trade employs 60,000 workmen, whose wages are calculated as sufficient for the daily support of 150,000 people; their labour is valued at six millions.

3   "American manufacturers are now increasing with great rapidity *under the encouragement* they receive, and this will certainly cause imports to fall off in a few years. Manufactories are being diffused all over the country." – *Vide* President Grant's Address.

4   "American manufacturers are now increasing with great rapidity *under the encouragement* they receive, and this will probably cause imports to fall off in a few years. Manufactures are being diffused all over the country." – *President Grant's Address, Dec.* 1869

5   *Vide* M. Thiers' speech on [the] Commercial Treaty.

2 FREE TRADE AND PROTECTION . . . *

Henry Fawcett

Chapter I: Introductory Remarks

. . . It should, however, be remembered that the adoption of free trade in England was powerfully promoted by circumstances of so purely exceptional a character that they do not now exist in any country where a protectionist tariff either has been, or is proposed to be, introduced. Between England and the countries which now maintain protection there is this fundamental distinction. In England it was agricultural produce that was most carefully protected, whereas in Continental countries, in America, and in the Colonies at the present time, it is home manufacturing indusry that is most zealously shielded against foreign compeititon. In England, therefore, protection made such a first necessary of life as bread, dear; whereas protection in those countries where it now exists increases the price of such commodities as wearing apparel and various articles of household furniture. It at once, therefore, becomes evident that a force of popular indignation could be brought against the maintenance of protection in England which cannot be brought against it in America and Australia. In a period of scarcity and of popular distress such as existed in England in 1843–45 the appeal in favour of free trade became irresistible . . . The ultimate success of the free-trade movement in England was no doubt greatly assisted by the zeal and ability displayed by those who advocated the cause; but without in the slightest degree detracting from the services rendered by the prominent leaders of the agitation, it must be remembered that a speaker or a writer who desires at the present time to convince the American or Australian people of the injurious effects of protection has to employ very different illustrations, has to use very different arguments, and has to make very different appeals from those which thirty years ago exercised such irresistible influence in England . . .

We in England are much too prone to overstate the results of free trade. Scarcely a week elapses without its being said, as if it were a triumphant rejoinder to all that is urged by the American, the Continental, or the Colonial protectionist. "English exports and imports have more than quadrupled since protection was abolished; the income of the country, as shown by the yield of the income-tax, has more than doubled, wages have advanced, and population has increased." But a moment's consideration will show that other causes have been in operation besides free trade to

* Henry Fawcett, MP, *Free Trade and Protection* . . . (London: Macmillan & Co., 1879), pp. 3; 4–6; 11–12; 17; 28–9; 45–8; 50–1; 61–7; 69–75; 122–3; 125–8; 130–7; 148–51; 156–60; 162–9.

promote this wonderful growth of prosperity. Amongst others that might be enumerated it is sufficient here to mention, that about the same time that protection was abolished our railway system was developed, steam was more largely used as a motive power in almost every branch of industry, and the discovery of gold in Australia gave a powerful stimulus to emigration. Again, it should be remembered that the financial reforms which were carried out when free trade was introduced into England produced other very important results besides eradicating protection from our fiscal system. Up to that time the plan had been tenaciously adhered to, of raising revenue from almost every article of foreign produce that was imported. In 1845 import duties were levied upon no less than 1142 separate articles. Of the duties which were thus imposed only those could be considered protective which placed the foreign producer at a disadvantage compared with the home producer. A large number of the articles imported, such as tea, coffee, chicory, sugar, and wine, are not produced in England, and consequently the duties which were imposed upon them could not be protective in their character. When it is remembered that the duties on all these 1142 articles have, with barely a dozen exceptions, been repealed – our customs' revenue being now almost entirely raised from five articles, tea, coffee, tobacco, spirits and wine – it at once becomes evident that the incalculable advantages resulting from the financial reforms which were carried out in England thirty years since cannot be solely attributed to the abolition of protection. A considerable part of the benefit which has resulted is due to the simplification of our fiscal system, which was secured by the repeal of such a large number of duties.

Chapter II: Protection

. . .

Part II – Restraints on Imports

In proceeding to consider the effects which are produced by imposing protective duties on imports, it will be necessary, in the first instance, to point out the very important difference there is between an import duty which is imposed for purposes of revenue, and one which is maintained with the view of protecting some home industry against foreign competition. A country can obtain a very large portion of its revenue, as England does at the present time, from import duties, without there being a trace of protection in its fiscal system. The import duties which are levied in England may be divided into two classes. First, duties are imposed on articles which are not produced in the country itself, such as tea and coffee; secondly, duties are levied on some article, such as malt or spirits; an excise duty exactly equivalent to this import duty being imposed on English-made malt and spirits. When an import duty only corresponds to an excise duty

31

of the same amount, it is evident that the foreign and the home producer are placed in a position of equality, and the import duty cannot be regarded as protective . . .

However careful a country may be to remove all traces of protection from its fiscal system, yet it is impossible to prevent an import duty causing some loss and inconvenience to the countries from which any particular article liable to such a duty is exported. If tea were admitted into England duty free, there would of course be a reduction in its price. The consumption of tea in England would consequently considerably increase; and China, the East Indies, and other countries which supply us with tea, would undoubtedly obtain a somewhat better price for tea owing to this increased demand. Although, therefore, all import duties, even if they are not protective, must be disadvantageous to the countries from which the articles are exported which are subjected to duties, yet there is this fundamental and important distinction between an import duty which is imposed for purposes of revenue, and one which is maintained with the obejct of giving protection to home industry. In the former case, the object those have in view who impose the duty, is to encourage importation; becuase the greater the importation, the larger is the revenue obtained. In the second case, the object being to discourage importation, the smaller the amount of revenue obtained, the more completely will the purpose of the duty have been achieved . . . Hence it may be concluded that the rise in price which is caused by protection, whether it be in agricultural or in manufacturing industry, cannot enable either a higher rate of profit or a higher rate of wages to be permanently secured in the industries which are protected. However greatly the price of any particular commodity is advanced, either by artificially stimulating its export or impeding its import, the capital and labour which are employed in its production only receive a remuneration, the amount of which is determined by the return which is yielded to the capital and labour employed in the general industry of the country. Profits and wages therefore cannot be raised in any particular industry by protection, unless at the same time an influence is brought into operation to increase the general rate of profit and wages in all other industries. It has, however, been shown that protection must exert an influence of an exactly opposite kind. If food is made dearer by protection the remuneration of labour is diminished, the general trade of the country is unfavourably affected, and profits decline. A similar effect will be produced, although its influence may not be so immediately felt, by artificially raising through protection the price of any manufactured article, such as iron. If iron becomes dearer a tax is imposed upon the labourer whenever he has to purchase an article of hardware. Again, dearer iron means more expensive machinery, and, if machinery is more expensive, manufacturing industry is carried on under more unfavourable conditions, and from the diminished returns which are yielded there will be less to distribute both in wages and profits.

There is one class, and one class only, that can derive advantage from a high level of prices being maintained through protection. When the price of any article is increased through protection, the pecuniary value of the land from which this article is procured is proportionally increased. If wheat, by protective duties, is made dearer, the owners of the land on which the wheat is grown can let it at a higher rent; and in the same way those who own coal and iron mines can obtain a higher premium for permission to work these mines if coal and iron are made dearer by the imposition of protective duties on the importation of these minerals.

It may, perhaps, be thought that some doubt is thrown upon the correctness of this conclusion, because since protection was abolished in England, the rent of land, instead of falling, has undoubtedly considerably increased. It cannot, however, be too carefully borne in mind that other influences may simultaneously come into operation which will greatly modify the effects produced by any economic agency such as free trade or protection. Thus, as previously remarked, during the period of the corn laws and the sliding scale pauperism was greatly encouraged by the abuses of the old poor law. The cost of maintaining this pauperism threw such a serious burden on landowners that in many districts the poor rates absorbed nearly the whole net produce of the land, and consequently the increase of rent which was secured through protection was in many instances a very inadequate equivalent for the increasing charge which poor rates were constantly imposing. On the other hand, a short time before the introduction of free trade the administration of the poor law was greatly improved by the reforms introduced by the new poor law. The growth of population and the wonderful development in the trade of the country have so much increased the demand for food and other products, that agricultural prices have, on the average, been maintained in spite of foreign importations; consequently through the operation of these and other favourable circumstances the value of land has increased, and there has been such an important rise in rents that it is probable that no class in the community has been so much benefited by free trade as the landowners, whose ruin it was often confidently predicted would inevitably be brought about by the abolition of protection.

A very competent authority, Mr. James Caird, has shown, in his recently published work on the "Landed Interest", that since 1857 the gross annual value of land in England has risen 21 per cent., in Scotland 26 per cent., and in Ireland 6 per cent.; and he estimates the increase in the capitalized value of the land during this period to be no less than 331,650,000*l.* It is impossible to say what portion of this increase is to be attributed to the operation of free trade. In many instances the land has been rendered more productive by agricultural improvements, and Mr. Caird estimates the

33

amount that has been in this period spent on these improvements to be not less than 60,000,000*l.* After, however, making ample allowance for various circumstances, such as the increase of population and the extension of railways, which have contributed to augment the value of land, it cannot I think be denied that the landowners have been materially enriched by the general increase in national prosperity which has resulted from the development of the commerce of the country since it was freed from the trammels of protection.

At the present time the depression which is affecting so much of the trade of the country is undoubtedly exercising a considerable influence on agriculture. Three bad harvests in succession have brought severe losses upon farmers in many parts of the country; and the difficulties with which they have to contend have been increased by a larger importation of cheap produce from America, while an advance in the wages of agricultural labourers has added to the farmer's expenses. It is evident that of the causes which have brought about the present depression in English agriculture some must be regarded as only temporary in their operation. A cycle of unpropitious seasons has often occurred before, and it may be confidently anticipated that the bad harvests with which the farmers have lately had to contend will be succeeded by good harvests. It ought not, moreover, to be supposed that the farmer receives no compensation for the additional wages which he is now compelled to pay. A labourer cannot do a proper day's work if he is only half-fed, and experience has often proved that the cheapest labour is not always the least costly. So far, however, as the farmer's position is affected by the competition of cheap meat, wheat, and other agricultural produce imported from America, it may no doubt happen that if the continuance of this importation should cause a low level of agricultural prices permanently to prevail, a readjustment of rents may be rendered necessary. It seems, however, probable that with the revival of trade, and with the application of more skill and enterprise in farming, this foreign competiton will become much less formidable than it is at the present time. But even if the continuance of low prices should make farming on its present conditions unremunerative, it is important to remember that the loss will not ultimately fall either upon the farmers or the labourers. Rents will have to be reduced and the owners of land may thus have to surrender some portion of the 300,000,000*l.* which, as we have seen, has been added to the value of their property during the last twenty years. Rents must ultimately be so arranged as to enable farmers on the average of years to obtain the same profits as are secured by other traders. The general condition of the labour market must to a great extent determine the wages which the agricultural labourer will receive, and if an abundance of cheap produce should cause some reduction in rents, it must be remembered that no one will be more benefited than the labourer will be, if he can obtain on easier terms the meat, the bread, the cheese, and all the other articles which supply his daily wants . . .

Chapter III: Free Trade and Reciprocity

. . .

Allusion has already been made to the fact that many who profess thorough adherence to the principles of free trade denounce "one-sided free trade as an absurdity," and assert that if other countries impose restraints on our commerce, we ought in self-defence to impose restraints on their commerce. It will not be necessary to consider the question as one of moral right. It may be admitted that if our manufactured goods are kept out of the American markets by heavy protective duties we should be justified in imposing duties with the view of impeding the importation of American produce. But, however completely our right to carry out such a policy of retaliation may be acknowledged, the important practical question remains for us to consider: what are the consequences which such a policy would produce? The protective tariffs which are maintained by the United States, and other countries, undoubtedly inflict a very serious injury upon our trade; and the simple point to be determined is, whether this injury would be diminished, or whether it would not be most materially aggravated, if we, in order to avenge ourselves, imposed protective duties on their produce. If it were thought expedient to adopt such a policy of retaliation, it might undoubtedly be most reasonably carried out against the United States. The greatest harm which is done to our trade by protection is the loss of free access to the American market, and the tariff of the United States is far more protectionist in its character than the tariff of any other country. This will at once be shown by comparing the import duties imposed on certain English products imported into the United States, France, Germany, Russia, and Austria respectively[1].

It will be seen from the figures opposite that by far the highest import duties, which are levied on English goods, are those which are imposed by the tariff of the United States. Not only are the duties in this tariff exceptionally high, but it embraces a far greater number of articles than the tariff of any other country. By the existing tariff of the United States, import duties are imposed on about 1,5000 articles; and there is scarcely a single English product which is allowed free access to the American ports. By far the greater number of these duties are protective; for it rarely happens in the United States that an Excise duty is imposed on a home product to counterpoise the duty on the same product when imported. The tariff of the United States undoubtedly inflicts a very serious injury on English trade; and it can be a matter of no surprise that the loss we thus have to bear should be the more keenly resented, because England is so good a customer of the United

	UNITED STATES.	FRANCE.	GERMANY.	RUSSIA.	AUSTRIA.
	ad val.	*ad val.*	*ad val.*	*ad val.*	*ad val.*
Iron (Bar) . .	67 to 100%	35%	Free	50%	35%
Copper . . .	30%	Free	Free	Free	Free
Cotton Yarns .	53 to 85%	–	4 to 9%	23%	6 to 9%
Woollen ,, . .	85%	–	$\frac{1}{2}$%	13%	1 to 2%
Jute manufactures	30 to 40%	11 to 26%	5%	10%	4%

States, that of the aggregate amount of her exports, more than three-fifths are purchased by England. In 1877, the value of the exports from the United States was 122,840,000*l.*; and of this entire quantity, 77,820,000*l.*[2] was sent to England. So seriously does the tariff of the United States hinder the importation of English goods into America, that whereas the value of the exports from the United States to England is 77,000,000*l.*, English goods are made so unnecessarily dear in the American markets by protectionist duties, that the value of the goods America annually purchases from us is only of the average value of about 25,000,000*l.* These figures certainly show that, with regard to the injury which is inflicted on our commerce by the maintenance of protectionist tariffs, we have a much stronger ground of complaint against the United States, than we have against any other country. Consequently, in considering whether it would be expedient to impose a duty on some article of American produce, in order to retaliate upon her for the injury which is done to our trade by her protectionist tariff, the strongest case is taken that can be adduced, in support of what is called a policy of reciprocity.

It is frequently said by the advocates of reciprocity, that nothing can be more unjust than to allow various articles of American manufacture to be sent to England to compete on equal terms with our manufactures, when we are forbidden free access to the American market. Whenever trade becomes depressed, great stress is laid upon the injury which we suffer from foreign competiton; and the impression becomes widely spread that this depression is, at least in part, brought about by American goods forcing their way into our markets. But when the statistics of American trade are examined, it is at once made manifest that the injury which is thus done to English trade is so infinitesimal as scarcely to be worthy of consideration. The amount of manufactured goods which is sent from America to England is so extremely small that it could make scarcely any difference if this particular part of the trade betweeen the two countries were to cease altogether. Reference is constantly made to the harm which is done to the cotton trade of Lancashire, and to the hardware trade of Birmingham, Sheffield and other towns, by the importation of cotton goods and of hardware from America. Yet in 1877, a year of great depression, the value of the entire quantity of manufactured iron and steel imported into England from the United States, was only 200,000*l.*, and the value of the manufactured cotton imported from the United States to England in 1876 was 451,876*l.* This importation, small though it is, was exceptionally large. In the previous year, the value of cotton goods imported from the United States to England was only 95,000*l.* And in 1877 it was only 163,000*l.*, or about one-third of what it had been in 1876. The value of the entire quantity of manufactured cotton imported into England in 1876 was 1,810,759*l.*, and in 1877 it fell to 1,764,802*l.* The unreasonableness of supposing that this trifling importation could to any appreciable extent affect the propserity of the English cotton trade, is at once made apparent when it is remembered that the value of the cotton manufactures exported from England in 1877 amounted to no less than 69,227,973*l.*

It therefore appears that no influence of any moment could be produced by levying duties, as the advocates of reciprocity propose, on those articles of American manufacture, imported into England, which come into direct competition with our own manufactures. If we desire to retaliate with effect upon America for the injury which by her tariff she inflicts on our commerce, we must levy duties, not on articles which only constitute a few insignificant items of her trade, but on articles which are exported in such large quantities, that, if the demand for them in England were to decline, the effect would be at once widely felt in America. The commodities which we import in by far the largest quantities from America are products which are either used as food, or which supply the raw material of our most important branches of manufacturing industry.

The following table, the items of which are condensed from the *Statesman's Year Book*, 1879, clearly shows that the produce which we purchase from the United States consists almost entirely of food stuffs, and the raw material of various manufacturing industries: −

Raw Cotton	£23,621,840
Wheat.	15,127,336
Maize.	8,225,437
Bacon and Hams	5,916,077
Beef and Pork .	2,081,121
Cheese .	3,129,829
Tobacco .	1,864,736
Lard	1,415,936
Oil-seed Cake .	1,051,843
Tallow and Stearine	940,008
Butter, Fruit, Hops, various Oils, Wood, Naphtha, Rosin, Skins, Furs, and Caoutchouc	6,253,868
	£69,628,031

As the total value of the exports from the United States to England is 77,825,973*l.*, it appears that at least nine-tenths of these entire exports consist of the articles of food and raw produce enumerated in the above table.

If, therefore, we desire to make the American people suffer some of the same loss and inconvenience which they inflict on our commerce by the protectionist tariff they now maintain, it would be necessary to impose import duties either on raw cotton, wheat, or on some of the articles of food which are imported in such large quantities from America. It would, no doubt, be possible in this way to do a very serious amount of injury to many of the most important commercial interests in America. It is supposed that one-half of the entire labour and capital of America is employed in agriculture. The prosperity of American agriculture would be materially impeded if, by the imposition of heavy duties, American produce was to any considerable extent shut out from the English markets. But the question at once suggest itself: Could we thus punish America without at the same time punishing ourselves? In endeavouring to answer this question it can, I think, be shown that although great harm would be done to America we should inflict a much more serious injury upon our own country.

Suppose, for example, that a duty of ten per cent. was levied on American cotton imported into England. This duty would increase the price of cotton in England, and as a consequence the demand for American cotton would somewhat diminish. England would, in fact, be not so good a customer for American cotton as she was before, and this would be undoubtedly a disadvantage to America. But how trifling is any loss which could be caused to America by this falling off in the demand for her cotton, compared with the widespread mischief which would result to England from the imposition of such a duty. Complaints recur at frequent intervals about the depressed condition of the cotton trade in England. It is often said that the home demand for cotton goods is not so great as it was, and that competition is so active that our manufacturers find it more and more difficult to obtain a profitable market in foreign countries. But if an import duty were imposed on raw cotton everything that is now regarded as unsatisfactory in our cotton trade must inevitably become more unsatisfactory. The duty, by increasing the price of raw cotton, would make cotton goods dear, and this would prejudicially affect the home demand. The consequences however to our foreign trade might be much more serious. If competition with our foreign rivals is now found difficult, what chance would there be of successfully competing with them, if we had to bear the burden of having to pay a higher price for cotton than that at which it could be purchased by foreign manufacturers? The Americans, it is said, are beginning to manufacture cotton goods nearly as cheaply as we can; and they would undoubtedly be able to make them much more cheaply, if we imposed a duty which caused us to pay an unnecessarily high price for raw cotton. The effect of such a duty might be to imperil the prosperity of our own cotton trade; whereas it might at the same time give an important stimulus to the manufacture of cotton in America. With regard therefore to the product which on the average represents in value at least one-third of our entire imports from America, we are precluded from pursuing a policy of retaliation, because any tax which we might impose on cotton would cause America a loss of trifling importance in comparison with the loss which we should inflict on ourselves . . .

It will perhaps however be thought that these objections would not arise if England carried out a policy of retaliation and imposed reciprocal duties against other protectionist countries. It may be argued that whenever an article imported from abroad comes into direct competition with articles of the same kind produced at home, the home trader may be fairly protected against this foreign competition if the countries from which the imports come maintain against us protectionist tariffs. But even if our theoretical right to pursue such a policy is admitted, an insurmountable difficulty presents itself, if it is attempted to be carried out. Whenever there is any decline of industrial activity in this country, complaints are invariably circulated about foreign competition, and the depression of trade is sure to be attributed to the home market being overstocked with foreign goods; it is at the same time said that our merchants find that protective duties exclude them to a large extent from foreign markets. Just at the present time the iron trade is the particular industry which is most depressed, and from the remarks that are frequently made on the subject it appears to be generally assumed that this depression has been to a great extent brought about by iron being sent to our market from Belgium and other countries at a cheaper rate than the English iron-masters can afford to make it. But a comparison of the quantities of iron which England imports and exports, at once shows that foreign competition can have exercised but little influence in creating the present depression. In the year 1877 when the iron trade was most inactive, the entire quantity of iron and steel manufactured and unmanufactured imported into England amounted to only 2,515,034*l.*, whereas the quantity exported was no less than 20,113,915*l.* These figures at once show that the foreign iron-masters cannot sell us iron at a cheaper rate than we can make it ourselves; because if they possessed any such advantages in the production of iron they would drive us out of those foreign markets to which they and we have equal access, and they would gradually appropriate to themselves the larger portion of our export trade. But instead of this taking place the entire value of iron and steel exported from Belgium, the country from whose competition it is said that England has so much to dread, amounted in 1877 to only 1,900,000*l.*, less than one-tenth of the value of iron and steel exported by England during the same year. Hence England has little to fear from Belgium in those foreign markets to which they have equal access. With regard to Belgian iron competing successfully against English iron in our own market, so little reason is there to suppose our trade can be thus injured that the value of the iron exported from Belgium to England in 1877 exceeded by only 210,724*l.* the value of the iron exported from England to Belgium.[3] It therefore appears that the Belgian iron-masters have nearly as much to fear from the competition of England as the English iron-masters have from the competition of Belgium.

Example after example might be repeated similar to the one just described, which would show that the circumstances of England's foreign trade are such, that a policy of retaliation on her part, even if it were desirable, is impracticable. No single case can be brought forward in which English trade suffers to any appreciable extent by foreign products under-selling in our own markets the same articles of English manufacture. Even in those industries, where there are most complaints about foreign competition, not only will it be invariably found that the aggregate quantity which is imported represents a mere fraction of the entire quantity which is produced by the home trade; but it would be erroneous to conclude that this importation, small though it is, displaces goods of an equivalent value from the home market . . . Great stress is laid by the advocates of reciprocity on the injury which was caused to the riband and silk trades of Coventry, Macclesfield, and other places by the abolition of the import duties on foreign silks at the time of the French Commercial Treaty. It is alleged that the French have been enabled so much to undersell us in our own markets, that our silk trade has been almost ruined. It will, however, be found, that although French silks are more largely purchased in this country than formerly, yet any superiority which they are supposed to possess over English made silks does not arise from greater cheapness but depends rather upon the better taste which is often shown by the French, both with regard to colour and to the selection of designs for patterns. It is also believed that the French climate, and the quality of water at Lyons and other French towns, provide more favourable conditions for the dyeing of the silk, and the fixing of the colours, than are to be found in England. In such a case, therefore, if the home manufacturer were protected against foreign competition, protection would be virtually given to him, not to secure him against the cheaper labour of his rivals, but to avert, both from employers and employed, the consequences of not taking the requisite trouble to acquire the skill and other qualities which are possessed by their foreign competitors, or of not being provided with equally great natural advantages. If the English silk manufacturers suffered in consequence of the competiton of cheap French labour, there is no reaosn whatever why the same competition should not make itself felt in the cotton trade and other branches of manufacturing industry; and yet England still holds such undisputed supremacy in the cotton trade, that, whereas the value of the cotton goods which she exported in 1877 was 69,227,973*l.*, the value of the cotton goods exported by France in the same year was only 2,480,000*l.*

But even if it could not be proved as conclusively as I believe it can be, that, so far as our own country is concerned, a policy of reciprocity is impracticable, the most cogent reasons might still be adduced why such a policy should not be adopted. Suppose that the injury which was done to the iron trade by foreign competition were not as imaginary as it has been shown to be, and that Belgian iron and steel were sent in considerable quantities into the English market. If an import duty were imposed with the object of checking this importation, the effect of such a duty would be not only to raise the price of the iron imported, but the price of all the iron produced in England would be advanced by an amount equivalent to the duty. At the present time, the aggregate quantity of iron imported into England is not one-fortieth of the quantity produced in England. But for the sake of argument let it be assumed that the quantity of iron imported is much larger than it is; that after an import duty has been imposed, England imports one-tenth of all the iron which she annually uses. Under these circumstances it is evident that the duty would have the effect of taking from the general body of the English people, in the form of the increased price which they would be compelled to pay for iron, an amount ten times as large as that which the duty yields to the State. Suppose that the home consumption of English made iron and steel is 3,000,000 tons a year. If, therefore, the price of iron were raised one pound a ton by the imposition of an import duty of this amount, the English people would be taxed to the extent of more than 3,000,000*l.*, and the proceeds of this tax would not be devoted to the purposes of the State, but ultimately would be appropriated by those who were the owners of iron mines. The rise in the price of iron, thus artificially created, might in the first instance confer an advantage upon those who were concerned in the manufacture of iron, whether as employers or employed; but, as already explained, competition would force down profits and wages to their normal rate, and the benefit would ultimately accrue to the owners of the mines.

The effect of thus raising the price of iron, in order to benefit a special limited class, would be widely felt throughout the entire nation. Every one who used an article which was wholly or partly made of iron, would find the price he had to pay for it artificially and unnecessarily increased. The consequence of this rise of price to the general community would be precisely the same as if a tax were imposed on every article in which iron was used, on ships, machinery, railway metal, ploughs, harrows, spades, and on a countless number of articles in domestic use. It will be subsequently shown that if one special trade were thus subsidised at the public expense, others would promptly come forward to press their claims for similar consideration. It would soon appear that no valid reason could be assigned why the protection given to one industry should be denied to others; and the system, once commenced, would be rapidly and inevitably extended.

As a policy of reciprocity seems to derive its chief support from those who propose it as a remedy for industrial depression, it will be desirable, before leaving the subject, to show how materially this depression would be increased by the adoption of such a policy. Reverting to the example which has just been considered, it is obvious that if an import duty were placed on iron, and its price were thus raised, every industry in which iron was used would be carried on under more unfavourable conditions. The shipping trade, for instance, has shared in the general depression as much as any other industry in the country. But, depressed as it has been, it would become still more depressed if everyone who wished either to build or purchase a ship found that the iron of which it was constructed was taxed, in order to make it dearer. A mischief of a serious and a permanent kind might result to the trade, for if by the exclusion of foreign iron, English iron were kept at an abnormally high price, it might become advantageous for English shipowners to build their ships, not on the Tyne or the Clyde, but in some foreign port where cheap foreign iron could be used. Again, every manufacturer who purchases machinery, would in consequence of iron being dearer, have to pay a higher pirce for his machinery, and consequently the cost of producing his goods would be increased; he would thus be placed at a disadvantage with his foreign competitors. It therefore appears that whenever an attempt is made to protect one industry against foreign competition, an additional burden is thrown upon other industries, which places them at a disadvantage with their foreign competitors. . . .

Chapter V: Commercial Depression

The very serious depression which has affected the trade of so many countries during the past three or four years has given a new interest and vitality to a discussion as to the relative advantages of protection and free trade. This commercial depression seems to be producing exactly the opposite effects on public opinion in the United States and England. In the former it is undoubtedly to a considerable extent undermining the confidence which many before felt in the efficacy of protection to secure prosperity; while in England, where scarcely any one until lately ventured to utter a dubious word with regard to the benefits conferred by free trade, an inclination is now being shown in many quarters again to lapse into some of the fallacies of protection.

Allusion has already been made to the fact that in many English chambers of commerce, resolutions have been recently passed in favour of reciprocity. What is termed "one-sided free trade" has been strongly condemned by some of those who were, until recently, the stoutest defenders of the principles of unrestricted commerce. The opinion certainly seems to be spreading, that a country commits an act of foolish self-sacrifice, if she persists in opening her markets freely to the products of other countries, when her own products are excluded from foreign markets by protectionist tariffs. This change in public opinion, far from exciting any surprise, may be regarded as the natural result of the manner in which the advocates of free trade and protection respectively have in former years pleaded their cause. Before the present commerical depression, the trade of England had, for a quarter of a century, uninterruptedly advanced with unprecedented rapidity. In the days when we were enjoying this prosperity it used to be perpetually referred to, as affording a conclusive proof of the extraordinary advantages conferred upon a country by free trade. The many other circumstances which have assisted in producing this prosperity were very generally ignored; the statistics of increasing exports and imports were triumphantly appealed to with confidence that nothing more was required for the vindication of free trade, and for the refutation of the doctrines of protection.

Such a mode of considering the subject, naturally accustomed people to the idea that the commercial progress of England was wholly due to free trade; consequently many of those who, in prosperous times, were foremost in expressing their approbation of free trade, are now the first to blame it for the depression which has fallen upon the commerce of the country. Exactly the reverse of what has occurred in England is happening in the United States. Until quite recently the United States enjoyed a prosperity scarcely inferior to that of England. Although, as I have endeavoured to show, she enjoyed this prosperity, not in consequence, but in spite of protection, it was not unnatural that as long as this prosperity continued, the people of the United States were induced to believe that it was the result of protection . . .

It will not be difficult to show that nothing connected with the present commercial depression should cause the English people in the slightest degree to waver in their attachment to the principles of free trade. If commercial depression had alone fallen on those countries which maintain a free trade policy, or if the severity of this depression could be shown to be in any way proportionate to the extent to which the commerce of the country was unrestricted, there might be then some justification for the demands which are now in certain quarters made, that we should relinquish our present commercial policy in favour of some form of protection, such for instance as the imposition of reciprocal duties. But however severe may be the depression from which England and other free trade countries are suffering at the present time, the depression has certainly been much greater in the United States and in other countries where protective duties are maintained . . . In 1877 the aggregate exports and imports of the United States were 219,500,000*l.*, whereas in the same year the exports and imports of Great Britain were no less than 646,700,000*l.* Throughout the present period of commercial depression there has been a considerable falling off in the amount of produce imported into the United States. Her

43

imports between 1874 and 1877 have fallen from 113,000,000*l.* to 90,000,000*l.*, representing a reduction of about 20 per cent. During the same period the imports into England, instead of diminishing, have slightly increased in value, and consequently the capacity of the English people to pay for foreign produce has not been materially affected by the present decline in industrial prosperity. There has no doubt been a falling off in the export trade of England, but this decline is by no means so serious as at first sight it might be supposed to be. Between 1860 and 1870 there was an extraordinary increase in the export trade of England. During this period the exports advanced from 164,500,000*l.* to 244,000,000*l.*, and at the present time, when the depression of trade is most severe, the exports from England are 8,000,000*l.* a year more than they were in 1870. It therefore appears that the steady progress of English trade has not been arrested. All that has happened is that her trade has not been maintained at the abnormally high point to which, during two or three years after 1871, it was to a great extent artificially forced, by a speculative demand so unsound that it could not be permanently continued . . .

Some hesitation might be felt with regard to the soundness of the principles of free trade, if it could be shown that in a time like the present, industrial depression fell least heavily upon those countries whose tariffs were most protectionist. What is happening, however, is exactly the reverse of this; for at the present time, no country maintains such high protective duties as the United States; and in no country has depression been so severely felt, especially in those very industries which have been most carefully protected against foreign competition. The temporary falling off in the export trade of England is due to a general decline in the foreign demand, and has not been in the slightest degree produced by our being driven out of neutral markets by the competition of protectionist countries . . .

In the meantime, however, it may be desirable to direct attention to the fear which has lately been expressed, that the maintenance of our import trade at its present high point, now that there is a certain diminution in exports, is a subject for grave misgiving, and shows that the seeds of future mischief are being sown which are certainly hereafter to bring disaster upon our national industry. These fears have their origin in the large excess which there is at the present time in the value of the goods which are imported by England, compared with the value of goods exported. Taking the figures of the latest year (1877), for which they are given in the *Statistical Abstract*, issued by the Board of Trade, it will be seen that this excess amounts to no less a sum than 142,000,000*l.* Recalling the language, and possibly also reviving some of the fallacies of the mercantile system, it is apparently by some supposed that the balance of trade, being, as it is termed, so unfavourable to England, is an indication that at the present time the nation is living beyond its means; that the English people are annually spending more than they earn, and that, in order to make good the deficit, we are gradually using up our savings and devoting capital to income. The maintenance of our imports at a time of industrial depression, instead of being regarded with satisfaction, should rather, it is argued, be considered as a measure of the prodigality with which the people are living, and with which the nation is exhausting its resources. Those by whom these opinions are entertained seem to find additional cause for alarm in the fact that in no other country is there any considerable excess of imports as compared with exports, while in some countries the exports considerably exceed the imports in value. Thus, in the United States, this excess of exports over imports is 16,600,000*l.* In India it is about 13,500,000*l.* I think, however, it can be shown that the maintenance of the present large import trade of England, far from indicating that there is anything unsound in her national economy, may be fairly regarded as one of the most satisfactory features in her present condition.

In the first place, it is to be remarked, that in preparing a statistical table of exports and imports, the value at which any article which is imported is estimated includes the cost of carriage, and the profits of the merchant who imports it: whereas, in estimating the value of exports, both the cost of carriage and the profits of the exporting merchant are excluded. Thus, if a quarter of wheat is bought at New York at 40*s.*, and the cost of shipping this wheat from New York to Liverpool is 4*s.*, and the profit of the importing merchant is 2*s.*, its value when imported is reckoned at 46*s.* In order, however, to show the different manner in which the value of exports is estimated, let it be assumed that a merchant buys a thousand pounds worth of machinery for shipment to Australia; the value of this machinery in forming a table of exports would be stated at 1,000*l.* But in estimating the amount which Australia has to transmit to England for this machinery, account has to be taken not only of the freight, but also of the exporting merchant's profits. Suppose that the freight is 100*l.*, and that the profit is 150*l.*, Australia will pay 1,250*l.*, and England will receive an amount exceeding by 25 per cent. the amount stated to be the value of the machinery exported. As by far the greater part of the foreign trade of England is carried on in her own ships, and by her own merchants, it follows that England receives for her exports an amount considerably larger than is represented by the value of these exports, because, in addition to their value as given in at the port from which they are shipped, there is to be added the cost of carrying them to the various countries to which they are exported, and the profits of the merchants who export them. On the other hand, from the amount which England has to pay for her imports, there is to be deducted the cost of bringing them from the countries from which they are imported. Thus, for the quarter of wheat which is imported into Liverpool from New York, and which is entered as worth 46*s.*, England has to pay America only 40*s.*; the remaining 6*s.* is received by the English shipowner and the importing merchant. England therefore has to pay to foreign countries, for the goods she imports from them, an amount very considerably less than is represented as the declared value of these imports. On the other hand, she receives from foreign countries, for the goods she exports, an amount which is much greater than that which is represented as the declared value of these exports. It would therefore follow that even if the amount which she has thus to pay for her imports were exactly equal to the amount which she receives for her exports, there would in the Board of Trade returns still appear to be a considerable excess in the value of the imports when compared with the value of the exports. Far, however, from the existence of such an excess being an indication that England was living beyond her means, and was being drained of her resources, it would simply show that our foreign trade was chiefly carried on by our own merchants and by our own shipowners, and that they were enjoying the profits resulting from this trade . . .

There is also another circumstance which causes the aggregate of England's imports to be considerably in excess of her exports. No other country has so large an amount of capital embarked in various foreign investments. Although it is impossible to form an exact estimate of the amount of English capital which is invested, not only in foreign loans, but also in various industrial undertakings, such as foreign mines, railways, banks, shipping companies, etc., yet it cannot be doubted that the interest which has to be annually remitted to England on the capital thus embarked represents a very considerable portion of the amount by which her imports exceed her exports. It has been calculated by competent authorities that the balance annually due to England as interest on capital invested in India and in America alone, is about 30,000,000l.,[4] and this debt has to be liquidated by these countries sending to England either goods or bullion. Hence the amount of the exports sent to England from America and India must not only be sufficient to pay for the goods imported from England, but must also be sufficient to pay the interest on the large sums of English capital invested in America and India. Those countries, therefore, which are largely in debt to foreign nations, must export more than they import; and in those countries which possess surplus capital and lend it abroad, the imports will exceed the exports. Consequently, the comparisons unfavourable to England which are often made by American protectionists between the industrial position of their own country and that of England, because of the large excess of English imports over exports, have so little foundation, that this excess may be regarded as affording evidence of the great extent to which they and other countries have been assisted by English capital . . .

American protectionists have lately been expressing great satisfaction because the exports from their country exceed in value the imports; they apparently consider that in this respect the industrial condition of their country compares most favourably with that of free trade England. In the opinion of the French protectionists there seems to be no weapon with which the renewal of the Commercial Treaty with England can be so effectually assailed, as to point out that under the operation of that treaty the trade of France has been so entirely changed, that whereas her exports were formerly in excess of her imports, and she was thus enriched by foreign commerce, now her imports exceed her exports, and she is consequently being drained of her resources. It can, however, be readily shown, after the explanation which has been given of the circumstances which cause the imports of a country to exceed her exports, that the present position of the foreign commerce of the United States and France, far from affording any justification for a protectionist policy, may be regarded as greatly strengthening the case in favour of free trade. If the goods which America sends to England exceed in value those which she receives from England, it is evident that America is in debt to England; and that this indebtedness is due to the fact that she has borrowed capital from England, and that, in carrying on her foreign trade, she is largely employing English ships and English merchants . . .

The statistics of the English exports and imports of bullion and specie during the last few years show in a very striking manner that a great excess of imports over exports may be entirely due to the circumstances before explained. Instead of there being any drain of money from England to adjust a so-called unfavourable balance of trade, the amount of bullion and specie which has been imported into England during the ten years from 1867 to 1876 has exceeded by no less than 53,800,000*l.* the amount which has been exported; although during this period the aggregate value of her imports exceeded by no less than 804,000,000*l.* the value of her exports. It therefore appears that so large an excess of imports over exports, as that which characterises the foreign trade of England, need not necessarily be accompanied by any drain of bullion or of specie; for during the period when this excess of imports has been most marked, England has on the average of years been adding about 5,000,000*l.* to her stock of bullion and specie, and this is supposed to be the amount which is annually required for fresh coinage and for various manufacturing purposes[5] . . .

In view of the disappointment which is sometimes expressed, that after England has adopted free trade for thirty years, severe depression should have fallen on some branches of her industry, it becomes important to show that although the effects of this depression are more severely felt in protectionist than in free-trade countries, yet if the commerce of every country were as entirely freed from protective restrictions, as is the commerce of England, periods of depressed trade would inevitably occur. The depression from which various branches of industry are suffering at the present time, may be regarded as the natural outcome of the prosperity which these same industries were enjoying a few years since. It is not more certain that night will follow day, or that winter will follow summer, than that a time of exceptional prosperity in trade will be succeeded by a period of corresponding depression. The extremely high profits which were realised by coal-owners and iron-masters five years since, have undoubtedly produced the low rate of profit which is returned to capital invested in these industries at the present time. Whenever any particular trade becomes exceptionally remunerative, people eagerly strive to share the advantages which that trade offers; a largely increased amount of capital is pressed into it; new mines are opened, or new works or manufactories are built, and the means of production are greatly extended. If the demand which originally created the exceptional activity is not permanently maintained, those engaged in the trade are in the position of possessing appliances for a great increase in the supply, at a time when there is either a diminution of the demand, or when there is no increase corresponding to the larger supply. The inevitable consequence is a rapid fall in prices, and a diminution in profits and wages, such as that which has taken place in all those industries which were most prosperous a few years since . . .

When profits are exceptionally low, there is just the same inducement to contract a business as there is to extend it when profits are exceptionally high. In the present state of the coal trade, few new mines will be opened to take the place of those which are gradually being exhausted; the supply will thus become restricted, there will be a tendency for prices to rise, and a sudden increase in the demand may again produce a rise in prices as marked as that which occurred five years since, and thus exceptional prosperity and exceptional depression succeed each other in regular cycles. As an example, it may be mentioned that within the last fifty years there have been in the English cotton trade five periods of great prosperity, succeeded in each instance by periods of corresponding depression. The large returns which are yielded both to capital and labour in periods of prosperity should be regarded as exceptional. The employers and the employed in any trade should never fail to remember that the equalising force of competition is ever present to prevent an abnormally high rate of profits and wages being permanently secured by those engaged in any particular branch of industry. Consequently a portion of the remuneration which is secured both by capital and labour in a time of exceptional activity, should be regarded as a reserve, to compensate the employers and the employed for the reduction in profits and wages which will inevitably ensue . . .

Chapter VI: Commercial Treaties

The opposition which is at the present time offered to the negotiation of commercial treaties, has undoubtedly caused great surprise and disappointment to the advocates of free trade. When the commercial treaty, between France and England, was negotiated, it was confidently anticipated that through the agency of such treaties a very powerful stimulus woud be given to the progress of free trade. Although the Anglo-French Treaty has benefited the trade of the two countries to a far greater extent than was expected, yet the opposition to the treaty has so much increased in France that its renewal now appears to be extremely doubtful. A similar hostility to commercial treaties is shown in other countries; and it cannot be denied that the negotiation of these treaties will now meet with much more formidable difficulties than had to be encountered a few years since. It therefore becomes important to inquire how this change of opinion has been produced, and whether it is due to causes which should in the slightest degree make England waver from the policy of complete free trade which she has adopted.

In a period of industrial depression any circumstance which is prominently connected with the commerce of a country, is sure to be singled out as one of the chief causes by which this depression has been produced. In the United States bad trade is making many, who one placed implicit faith in protection, doubt its efficacy; and in England, where in prosperous times there was an unanimous approval of free trade, the opinion is now not unfrequently expressed that we have carried out a policy of commercial freedom almost too thoroughly and too precipitately. France has not escaped the industrial depression which at the present time exists in other countries; and wherever a trade, which has been affected by the treaty, happens to be suffering from this depression, those who are engaged in it fasten on the treaty for special denunciation. The opposition therefore which is now shown to the renewal and negotation of commercial treaties, is no doubt partly due to the prevailing industrial depression. It is also to be borne in mind that a commercial change, however great may be the advantage which it confers upon the community as a whole, can rarely be introduced without causing some loss to certain special classes. The benefit which is diffused over the rest of the nation is little spoken of. The million may gain by finding some article of general consumption cheapened. They accept the boon without either recognising, or taking the trouble to ascertain, the source from which it comes. The many who are benefited are silent; the few who are injured are ceaseless and clamorous in their complaints.

Between 1858, just before the negotiation of the Anglo–French Treaty, and 1877, the imports from France to England have increased from 13,271,000*l.* to 42,360,000*l.* and the exports from England to France from 9,242,000*l.* to 22,960,000*l.* This great increase in the trade between the two countries shows that the French and the English obtain from each other, respectively, a larger quantity of commodities which could not be obtained at all unless they were imported, or which can be imported at a cheaper rate than they can be produced at home. In thus opening the French market more freely to the English, and the English market more freely to the French, it may no doubt have happened that the demand for some particular article may have been reduced in consequence of the home demand for it being diminished. Thus in 1858 the amount of silk manufactures, and silk imported from France into England was only 2,300,000*l.*; it was 9,800,000*l.* in 1875. Although it appears from these figures that the English purchase a greater quantity of French silk than they did before, it does not necessarily follow that less silk is in the aggregate manufactured in England. The home and foreign demand for an article may both be so much increased that a larger importation may be accompanied by a considerable augmentation in the home production. Thus the value of woollen cloth and yarn imported into France just before the Treaty in 1859 was 100,000*l.*; the value exported in the same year was 7,000,000*l.* Thus the value of these goods exported exceeded that imported by 6,9000,000*l.* After the Treaty had been in operation for sixteen years, the value of the woollen cloth and yarns imported into France, had increased to no less an amount than 3,7000,000*l.* But in the same time, the value of these goods exported from France had increased to 14,000,000*l.* It therefore appears that although the French woollen manufacturers complain more than any other class of traders of the injury that has been inflicted upon them by the increased importation into France of woollen goods from England, yet at the very time when this increased importation has been taking place the French woollen manufacture has been developed to a remarkable extent; for the figures just quoted show that during the time the Treaty has been in operation, an increase of the import of woollen goods of 3,600,000*l.* has been accompanied by an increase in the export of no less than 7,000,000*l.* The amount, therefore, by which the export of woollen goods has increased, exceeded by nearly 100 per cent., the amount by which the imports have increased. Such facts as these are persistently ignored by the French protectionists who oppose the renewal of the Treaty. They constantly refer to the additional quantity of manufactured articles imported from England, as if each bale of woollen or cotton goods sent from England to France necessarily caused a corresponding decrease in the quantity of these goods manufactured in France. The depression in the woollen trade in France cannot be produced by foreign importation, when there has been so great an increase in her export of woollen manufactures. This depression has undoubtedly been brought about by causes analogous to those which have produced depression in England and other countries; it simply represents one of those vicissitudes or reactions to which every trade is liable.

The opposition which is being offered in France to the renewal of the Commercial Treaty with England, has been assisted by another circumstance to which it is desirable to direct attention, because it affords an instructive example of the influence which economic fallacies, which are generally supposed to have been long since exploded, can still exercise on public opinion. There is no single point on which greater stress is laid, by various chambers of commerce in France, that have been most prominent in opposing the Treaty, than the change which has lately taken place in the relative amount of French exports and imports. For some years previous to 1876 the exports from France exceeded her imports. The average annual amount of this excess was about 9,000,000*l*. In 1876 the balance was turned in the opposite direction; for, in that year, the value of the produce imported into France exceeded the value of that exported by 16,000,000*l*. This change in the condition of her trade seems to have created great alarm; the fear is widely expressed that France is being drained of her resources, and the Commercial Treaty is consequently the more strongly denounced because it is considered to have been instrumental in producing this "unfavourable balance of trade." No trustworthy conclusions with regard to the industrial posititon of a country can be drawn from her trade statistics of a single year. This excess of French imports over exports may be due to accidental and temporary circumstances; but if it should continue to be a permanent feature of the trade of France in the same way as it is of that of England, it would follow, as was shown in the last chapter, that there had been a marked improvement in the condition of France: that whereas formerly she was so much in debt to foreign countries that each year she had to send a considerable amount of produce abroad in order to liquidate this indebtedness, these countries have become so much indebted to her, her wealth has in fact so much increased, that, besides receiving payment for the goods she exports, there is annually due to her a surplus amounting to many millions.

When it is thus seen that the renewal of the Treaty is opposed on so many different grounds, it may not improbably happen that an attempt to negotiate another treaty between France and England will fail. If this should be the case there are many of our own countrymen who will no doubt think that England should depart from the policy which she has been pursuing, that she should take some steps to defend her own interests, and that she should no longer continue, as is so often said, "to give everything to foreigners and get back nothing from them in return." . . .

Such a proposal has already met with considerable support from several English chambers of commerce; and it has been suggested that if the treaty is not renewed, the English Government should be asked to impose duties on silks and other articles of French manufacture. It therefore becomes important to consider what would be the result of carrying out the policy thus indicated.

The value of the manufactured silk annually imported into England from France is about 6,000,000*l*.; and this importation would no doubt be considerably reduced if an import duty of 10 per cent. were imposed. Let it be assumed that this duty is a general one, and is levied on all manufactured silk from whatever country imported. The only effect of attempting to confine such a duty to French silks would be that the purpose of the duty would be almost entirely defeated. Nothing would be more easy than for the French manufacturer to send his silks, in the first place, to another country, prior to their exportation to England, and thus secure their entrance into the English market duty free. If the duty were imposed on all foreign silks, the price of these would be increased in the English market by somewhat more than the amount of the duty. The foreign manufacturer would thus be placed at a disadvantage in the English market, compared with the home manufacturer; and the English people would purchase a larger quantity of English silks and a less quantity of foreign silks. The price of silks in the English market, whether of foreign or of home manufacture, would be increased. The advance in the price of the former must be sufficient to compensate the foreign manufacturer for the duty which he now has to pay. The rise in the price of English silk could not permanently be of any advantage to silk manufacturers or their operatives, because, as has been so frequently shown, the competition of capital and labour, seeking remunerative employment, prevents the continuance of an abnoramlly high rate of profit and wages in any special industry. An increased amount of capital and a greater proportion of the labour of the country would be employed in the silk trade; but after the trade had settled down to its regular condition, a larger return could not be yielded to this capital and labour than is yielded in other industries. With regard to the interests of the consumer, as distinguished from those of the producer, it is evident that every one who had to purchase silk, would have to pay a higher price for it. This extra price would, however, only represent a part of the loss to the general consumer. French silks are not always purchased in England on account of their greater cheapness; they are often preferred because they are considered to be superior in colour, and are more attractive in other respects. Without desiring to express any opinion as to whether this preference is well-founded, it is obvious that if a protective duty were imposed, those who wished to buy French silks would be fined, because they preferred them to silks of English manufacture. It therefore follows, as is the case with all taxation imposed with the object of protecting home industry, that the amount which the taxation yields to the revenue of the State, very inadequately represents the loss and inconvenience which are caused to the general community.

A more serious objection, however, against imposing a duty on some article of French manufacture, with the view of punishing the French for refusing to renew the Commercial Treaty, arises from the fact that if such a policy were once commenced it is impossible to foresee the extent to which it might not be developed. It may, for instance, be said that silk is a luxury; and that there could be no very great hardship if those who purchased such a luxury had to pay a somewhat higher price for it. If we could impose a duty on French silk, and then stand still, little harm might possibly result. But every trade in England which is injured, or which supposes itself injured, by foreign competiton, would immediately set up a claim for legislative protection. The very first bale of cotton goods that might be sent from America to England, after the silk manufacturer had obtained protection, would inevitably unite the whole cotton interest in Lancashire to demand that their trade should enjoy a similar security against foreign competition. Parliament would be petitioned, deputations would wait upon the Government, and an amount of political influence would be brought into activity which there would be no chance of successfully resisting. It is almost impossible for a country to depart, however slightly, from the principle of free trade, without rendering a further departure inevitable. From each step that is taken in the paths of protection, increasing momentum is acquired, which will hurry a country on still farther in a policy of commercial restriction.

As it appears therefore to be impracticable for a country to resort to retaliatory import duties, unless it is prepared to sanction an indefinite extension of protection, it may be desirable to consider whether greater success would attend the imposition, as has been often proposed, of an export duty on some article for which there is a demand in those countries to whose markets free access for English goods is denied. There are many, for instance, who consider that it would be highly advantageous for England to impose an export duty on coal. It is supposed that through such a duty we might obtain a considerable revenue from foreign countries; and it is also thought that the possible increase of the duty might be kept as a weapon in reserve, which might be used to threaten foreign countries, if they subjected our commerce to increased restrictions. It is thus said that nothing would probably exert a more powerful influence in preventing the French increasing their duties on English goods, than if they could be told that from the very moment they increased these duties we should compel them to pay a higher price for every ton of English coal they purchased. It can, however, be easily shown that it is rarely, if ever, possible to impose an export duty without producing consequences, and incurring risks, which, at the time the duty is imposed, are not foreseen. As an example it may be mentioned that when the Anglo-French Treaty was discussed in the English Parliament, a considerable amount of support was given to a proposal to levy an export duty on coal. It was then very generally thought that England possessed such advantages in the production of coal, that the imposition of a moderate export duty would scarcely affect the foreign demand for English coal. In thus compelling foreigners to contribute to our revenue, whilst no injury was done to any branch of our own trade, it was argued that we should be partly compensating ourselves for the loss inflicted upon us by the commercial restrictions of other countries. From events which are now happening, it appears that if such an export duty had been sanctioned, foreign countries would gradually have ceased to purchase coal from us, and would have obtained it from other sources. Thus, a certain quantity of

American coal is at the present time being sent to Europe; and it is confidently anticipated by the people of the United States that they will be able in future greatly to extend this trade. It may, therefore, with certainty be concluded that if the export of coal from England had been burdened with a duty, we should soon have entirely lost the foreign market for our coal. In a period of depressed trade like the present, the main- tenance of such a duty would be impossible. There has been a great diminution in the profits of the proprietors of coal-mines; their workmen are suffering great distress in consequence of the reduction of wages to which they are obliged to submit; and it would be felt that there could be no justification whatever for adding to the difficulties which have thus to be encountered, by continuing to maintain a duty which, though it might yield nothing to the state, would have the effect of destroying the foreign demand for English coal.

Equally serious objections apply to every proposal which has been made for the imposition of a retaliatory export duty. Thus it has been suggested by some economists of authority, that with the object of benefiting our manufacturers, it would be desirable to impose an export duty on English machinery. Various foreign countries, it is said, which restrict the importa- tion of our goods by protective duties, employ English machinery, to a large extent, to manufacture articles which compete with the products of our own industry; and in this way we supply the weapons of our own dis- comfiture. But if such a duty had been sanctioned it would, like an export duty on coal, have led to consequences which at the time of its proposal were not anticipated. Although at one time the machinery which foreign countries imported was chiefly obtained from England, yet there was nothing to warrant the conclusion that these countries must always neces- sarily look to England for the mechanical appliances which their own industry did not supply. We possess neither a monopoly of inventive skill, nor a monopoly of the iron, copper, and other materials from which machinery is constructed. The American people are at least as inventive as ourselves, and with their inexhaustible mineral resources, there is no reason why machinery of American manufacture should not be as cheap and as good as machinery made in England. It would therefore be impos- sible to impose an export duty on English machinery without greatly diminishing the foreign demand for it, and we should thus inflict a very serious injury on an important branch of English trade with no other result than compelling the French, the German, and the American manufacturers either to purchase their machinery from their own countrymen, or instead of buying it from England, to import it from some other country. This falling-off in the foreign demand may, however, be regarded as representing only a part of the harm which might be done by such a duty. With the gradual diminution of the foreign demand for English machinery, an important stimulus to enterprise and invention would cease to operate.

Nothing is so likely to secure constant watchfulness to introduce every possible improvement into machinery, as the knowledge that in foreign markets we shall have to contend with the keen and active competition of other countries. It might also happen that if there were any discouragement to mechanical invention in England, foreign machinery might be more largely employed in our own industry, and thus a double disadvantage would result: for there would be a decline not only in the foreign, but also in the home demand for English machinery.

As therefore it appears to be impossible for England, without inflicting upon herself very serious injury, to impose either import or export duties with the object of bringing pressure to bear on those countries which refuse to arrange commercial treaties with her, the question will no doubt be asked: "Can nothing be done?" It is, for instance, often said that it cannot be right for England to pursue a policy of passive indifference, and to continue to adhere strictly to the principles of free trade, when on all sides her proposals for commercial treaties are rejected, and when her access to foreign markets is being barred by more onerous restrictions. To the inquiry: "What ought under these circumstances to be done?" – it seems that we are irresistibly led to the conclusion, that, however much we may be prompted by a natural feeling of annoyance and disappointment to adopt retaliatory measures, we cannot by any possibility enter upon such a course of retaliation, without greatly aggravating instead of mitigating the mischief which is done to our trade by the protectionist tariffs of other countries. It has been shown that whether it be by the imposition of protective duties on the goods which we import from these countries, or by the levying of an export duty on the products which they purchase from us, England cannot carry out a policy of retaliation without very seriously imperilling her own industrial interests. Nothing would give more encouragement to foreign protectionists than the slightest departure on our part from the principles of free trade. Such a departure would be welcomed as an omen that we had at last found it necessary to secure our industry against the evils of foreign competition. If, however, we are firmly resolved not to be drawn by any provocations, great though they may be, from a policy of commercial freedom, events will again and again occur which we may confidently anticipate will gradually bring conviction even to the staunchest supporters of protection, that the policy we thus maintain is not less just to others than beneficial to ourselves. Circumstances connected with the present industrial depression are undoubtedly giving a powerful assistance to the cause of free trade. So long as prosperous times continued, wealth was so rapidly accumulated in the United States, that the American people could hardly be expected to take much heed when they were told that if protection were abolished their country would become even still richer. Now, however, when this prosperity has temporarily passed away, and wide-spread distress prevails, every cause that may have heightened this industrial depression is inquired into with anxious solicitude, and the wisdom of maintaining restricted tariffs is now doubted by many who, until recently, were their most unhesitating supporters. Two or three years ago, protection seemed to occupy a far more unassailable position in the United States than in any other country. The comparative ease with which a period of industrial depression has been tided over in England, contrasted with the serious consequences which it has brought upon the United States, has caused so important a section of the American people to look with favour upon free trade, that it seems not improbable that the principles of unrestricted commerce will gain ground most rapidly in the country where protection has hitherto held its strongest position . . .

NOTES

1 See Parlimentary Return, No. 291, 26th June, 1877, "Import Duties on British Goods (Foreign Countries)." The Return was issued by the Board of Trade, and was prepared under the direction of Mr. R. Giffen.
2 Statistical Abstract, 1878.
3 *Statesman's Year Book*, 1879.
4 See *Economist*, December 15, 1877.
5 See *Statistical Extract*.

3 FREE TRADE VERSUS FAIR TRADE*

Sir T.H. Farrer

Part II: Retaliation

Chapter XVIII: Retaliation on Manufactured Goods Absurd

The second of the two great principles of Fair Traders is Retaliation. They desire to impose retaliatory duties on the goods of foreign countries which do not admit our goods duty free.

These duties are not to apply to our food imports, which have been dealt with already, nor to imports of raw material, but to manufactures only. It is a sufficient practical answer to a proposal of this kind that the weapon is in our hands absolutely inefficacious. Of our imports, ninety per cent. are estimated to be raw materials or food, and ten per cent. only what are called manufactured articles. If we take particular nations, the case is stronger. Our trade with the United States is one-sixth of our whole trade, and their tariff is the most hostile of any; whilst the interest which is affected by their competition is our most suffering interest. But out of their imports into the United Kingdom, which exceeded 100 millions in 1880, about $2\frac{1}{2}$ millions only were manufactures; whilst out of our exports to them $24\frac{1}{2}$ millions were manufactures. Will they not laugh at us? or, if not disposed to laugh, will they not treat us as they have treated the Canadians, and place still further obstacles on our imports?

To France we exported in 1880 upwards of 12 millions' worth of manufactured and half-manufactured goods; $2\frac{1}{2}$ millions' worth of raw material; and one million's worth of food. From France we imported 23 millions' worth of manufactured and half-manufactured goods, 3 millions' worth of raw materials, and nearly $15\frac{1}{2}$ millions' worth of food. Here there is more to retaliate upon than in the case of the United States, but the proportion of manufactures which we sent to France is greater than the proportion which she sends to us. We send her little but manufactures, whilst she supplies us largely with food. To Germany we exported in 1880 nearly 14

* Sir T.H. Farrer, Bart., *Free Trade versus Fair Trade* (London: Cassell & Co., Ltd., 1886), pp. 99–150; 159–76; 220–4.

millions' worth of manufactured and half-manufactured goods, less than 2 millions' worth of raw materials, and less than $1\frac{1}{2}$ million's worth of food. From Germany we imported in 1880 a little over $4\frac{1}{2}$ millions' worth of manufactured goods, $3\frac{1}{2}$ millions' worth of raw materials, and $16\frac{1}{4}$ millions' worth of food. If we are to play a game at who can do most to stop each other's manufactures, it is clear that Germany will have the best of the match. What is true of these countries is true of others. We are *par excellence* the manufacturing country, and for us to play the game of who can best destroy manufacturing industry is simple suicide.

Chapter XIX: Proposal to Tax Manufactures and Leave "Raw Material" Free – Difficulty of the Distinction

Is the received Policy of distinguishing between Raw Materials and Manufactures well founded?

But when we are told that raw material must be admitted free, and that manufactures are to be taxed, I should like to ask what distinction can be drawn between these two classes of goods which would justify a different tretament? When I look down the list of so-called raw materials, I see nothing which is not both the produce of some previous labour and the means or material of some further labour; and when I look down the list of so-called manufactured articles, I find the same thing. I am unable to draw any line between the two, or to find any principle by which to distinguish them.

If the quantity of labour employed in producing the article is to be the test, the labour employed to produce so-called raw materials may, and often does, far exceed the labour necessary to turn that raw material into a manufactured article. There may be more labour in getting coal, or in growing wool, than in spinning or weaving. If we are to be guided by the operation of the article as a means or a stimulus towards further production, I am unable to see how the raw produce of the soil operates for this purpose more directly or more effectually than the article into which it is subsequently converted by human labour. I do not see why the alkali out of which glass or chemicals are made is not as efficient a means of production as the salt out of which the alkali is made. Let us take any list in which an attempt has been made to distinguish between raw products and manufactures. We get into difficulties at once. The alkali, for instance, to which I have referred, heads one list of manufactured articles, but it is chiefly useful as a material to be employed in subsequent manufactures. "Apparel and haberdashery," which come next,

Raw Materials and Manufactures impossible to distinguish.

are, no doubt, manufactures as complete as it is possible to conceive; but even here the boots of the navvy, the shirt and apron of the operative, the blouse of the French labourer, the jersey of the sailor, or even the neat cloth coat and shirt of the clerk or manager, are as much the means and essential conditions of further production as the stone, the iron, or the wool which these persons are employed in manipulating or disposing of. Horses come first in one list of "raw produce;" but a farm horse is at once the final product of skill in breeding for generations, and is a direct instrument in further production. "Clocks" come first in another list of manufactured articles and there is certainly no more finished article of human ingenuity than a clock; but is not a clock the *sine quâ non* of every place where productive labour is at work? Is it not the great economist of time, which is the principal of all factors in production? I might go through the list in the same way, pointing out how each article of large or general use is, on the one hand, the result of previous labour, and the means for further labour. Nay, the same thing is true of food also. Food is the means of keeping the human machine going, without which there can be no productive labour; it is the most obvious, if not the most important, of raw materials; it is to the man and woman what the coals are to the steam-engine. We admit this when we class food and raw materials together as articles which are not to be taxed, or which are to be taxed more sparingly and cautiously than other things. But, like other raw materials, food is not really more necessary to further production than other articles of general human use. The house in which the artisan lives, the clothes which he wears, the tools which he uses, are no less means and instruments in making the articles which he produces which he produces for sale than the food which forms his blood and muscles, the coal which drives his steam-engine, or the material of fibre, of wood, or of metal which he is converting into use. We may go farther, and say that the so-called luxuries, the tea, sugar, and tobacco, which make life tolerable to himself and his children, are also instruments by which his powers of production are increased. Nay, we may assert, with the most exact truth, that the wine which refreshes the brain of the man of science, the statesman, or the physician, is in the highest degree conducive to the production of wealth. All active and useful human life is on cycle of unintermitted and contemporaneous production and consumption – of production, in order to procure articles of

Raw Materials and Manufactures impossible to distinguish.

consumption; of consumption, in order the more effectually to produce. There may, of course, be useless and even mischievous consumption of excessive or pernicious luxuries but these are, economically speaking, a trifle in the vast mass of human consumption; and there may also be foolish and ill-directed production. But, generally speaking, all human consumption is a direct means of production; and this makes me doubt whether there is any real sense in the commonly-received doctrine that it is better, on economical grounds, to tax articles of consumption – that is, articles which are in a fit state to be at once eaten, worn, or otherwise used by man – than articles which he has to do something more to before he can use them. But this is, I am glad to say, a controversy on which I need not enter; from the Fair Traders, or from some of them, I am too glad to accept the admission that raw material is not to be subject to a retaliatory duty; and only mention the point now because, if we admit that manufactures are to be taxed, we may find it difficult to stop there.

I have said, "or from some of them," because the Fair Traders are not consistent with themselves. Mr. Farrer Ecroyd, for instance, in a letter published by their League, considers the free admission of raw materials necessary, and he is a man who does not juggle with words. But in a later manifesto of the Fair Trade League, published in 1884, consisting of letters by Mr. Sampson Lloyd and notes in illustration of them, I find that the writers are impressed with the above arguments concerning the difficulty of distinguishing raw material from manfactures. What is the conclusion they draw? Not, as one might expect, the natural conclusion, that we cannot exclude manufactures whilst admitting "raw materials;" but that "raw materials" must be defined afresh, by excluding from the term "raw materials" articles used in manufacture *which can be produced at home.* "Raw material" thus acquires, in the language of these writers, a meaning which will puzzle economists; and the Fair Trader, whilst professing in terms to give our manufacturer the free import of materials, refuses to allow him to use, under that designation, any foreign article used in manufacture which is produced abroad and which can also be produced at home! This, of course, is Protection pure and simple, and helps to show what really needs no proof – that Fair Trade is but a shuffling name for Protection.

Mr. Sampson Lloyd's letters.

New definition of raw material as an article which cannot be produced at home!

Chapter XX: Other Proposals for Retaliation

The Retaliation of the Fair Trade League is, as we have seen, ridiculous from its impotency; but this does not show that all Retaliation would be inefficient, or, if efficient, undesirable. Proposals for Retaliation, if once adopted, will not stop where the Fair Traders leave them, and there are arguments in favour of the principle of Retaliation which require a more complete answer than is to be found in the impracticability of a given plan. I do not know that these arguments have ever been more fairly, clearly, and vigorously stated than by Lord Salisbury, in his speech at Newcastle, on the 12th October, 1881. He said: –

> "I now only wish to say a word with respect to a matter which, perhaps, through being exciting, occupies some considerable portion of public attention at the present moment. It has been said that we of the Conservative active party are anxious to return to the state of things existing before 1840 in respect to fiscal matters, and sundry terrible consequences have been deduced from the assertion. I, for one, do not possess the desire, nor do I think that such a return would be for the public welfare; but it does not do for the Government to ignore the commercial difficulties under which the country labours by the simple device of accusing their opponents of a desire to return to the state of things to which I have referred. Whenever the evil of the present state of things is pointed out to them, they, instead of replying, call us lunatics, or beat the great tom-tom of Free Trade in order to drown our voices. It is undoubtedly the fact, and I do not think that any one can traverse the statement, that in one respect the apostles of Free Trade thirty-five years ago made a gigantic miscalculation, when they said that if the country adopted their principles the rest of the nations of the world would follow their example. (Cheers.) It was repeatedly held out, both by Mr. Cobden and Sir Robert Peel, and undoubtedly it influenced many minds at the time. I am very far from stating that as their only reason. I do not mean to say that their policy would have been different if they had had a different belief; but they had the belief, and took every opportunity of communicating it to others, that our example would be followed by other nations of the world. That, I take it, is an undoubted fact in history.

Arguments in favour of Retaliation.

Lord Salisbury at Newcastle in 1881.

Arguments for Retaliation. Lord Salisbury.

61

Well, that has not been the case. The third of a century
has passed by, and all the nations by which we are
surrounded have not only not become more Free Trade,
but on the whole have become more Protectionist.
America, I believe, is more Protectionist; the Protectionist feeling is rising in France. Both of them, mind you, are
complete democracies, so there is no pretence for saying
that this particular form of opinion has been imposed by
the ruling classes. They are countries where it is undoubtedly the sentiment of the people, and nothing else,
which governs the conduct of the Government: and in
both these countries the feeling of Protection has increased, and is increasing. In Russia, on the other hand, a
despotism of the closest type, still you have the same
phenomenon. A feeling of Protection is increasing, and
the measures of Protection are multiplying. In a kingdom
like Germany, with certain constitutional liberties, but
ruled undoubtedly by the acutest brain that this century
has seen in Europe, you still see this remarkable phenomenon – that the tendency towards Protection is
increasing. In our own colonies, where, if anywhere, we
ought to have some influence, there too, unfortunately,
the Protectionist feeling is strong, and our own productions are shut out from the markets of our own children.
Now, that is a fact which I say it is idle to ignore. It is
childish to imagine that our example now, after so many

Arguments
for Re-
taliation.
Lord
Salisbury.

years, will alone have any effect upon these nations. They
have their own experience; they have their own philosophers to teach them. Many of them are, and certainly
believe themselves to be, as far advanced in intellectual
culture as ourselves. What is there to induce them to
defer to our judgment, and to follow our example in this
respect? If we intend to act upon them, we must find
other motives; and I think we have a right to ask, without
pledging ourselves to any opinion until the facts are
known, that there should be a thorough investigation
into the question whether we are now pursuing the right
course for the purpose of inducing those other Governments in some degree to lower the terrible wall of tariffs
which is shutting out the productions of our industry
from the markets of the world. There is no reason that
we should pledge ourselves to any particular course until
the facts are known. But if you make a suggestion of this
kind, you are immediately told, 'This is Reciprocity and

Retaliation, and behind it lurks the shadow of Protection.' Reciprocity and Retaliation! But what are these commercial treaties, if they do not involve the principle of Reciprocity? Sir Charles Dilke will very soon meet the French Minister of Commerce, and they will be talking over the respective products of their respective tariffs, and practically Sir Charles Dilke will say to the French Minister of Commerce, 'If you will give me this relaxation of duty upon cotton, I will give you this relaxation of duty upon wine.' But what is this but Reciprocity? And when Sir Charles Dilke finds that the French Minister of Commerce is difficult to deal with, he will say, 'Well, but if you do not give us this duty, if you do not give us this relaxation upon cotton, I will not give you a relaxation of duty upon wine.' What is that but Retaliation?

"Therefore I say, ever since you adopted the principle of commercial treaties, ever since that memorable date, 1860, the principle of what they are pleased in their own language to term 'Reciprocity and Retaliation' is conceded.

"It is merely a question of policy arising upon the state of facts in each particular case, whether you have the means of any alteration of your tariff which you can with due consideration for your own interests adopt, whether you can so do it in the case of the tariff of your neighbour; and it seems to me that that is a sensible course of conduct to adopt. There is no doubt that by abandoning duties which are useful to you for revenue purposes you confer a great benefit upon foreign countries. Why should you not ask for a price in exchange for that benefit? Why should you not obtain for your own industries a benefit corresponding to that which you are conferring upon them?

"I do not know, until inquiry has been made and opportunities gained of ascertaining whether it presses either upon the food of our people, or the raw material of our industry, both of which must be held sacred – I do not know what opportunities we may have of exercising this salutary influence upon foreign Powers; but in spite of any formula, in spite of any cry of Free Trade, if I saw that by raising a duty upon luxuries, or by threatening to raise it, I could exercise a pressure upon foreign Powers, and induce them to lower their tariffs, I should pitch

Arguments for Retaliation. Lord Salisbury.

63

orthodoxy and formulas to the winds and exercise the pressure."

This argument derives its strength from Commercial Treaties

Now, if I wished to find a strong argument against all tariff bargains, I should point to this speech of Lord Salisbury's. He may exaggerate the sanguine views entertained by Sir R. Peel and Mr. Cobden of the prospects of universal Free Trade; he may also exaggerate the present tendencies of other countries to Protection; and the Retaliation he suggests – viz., upon that inappreciable part of our imports which consists of luxuries – is, unless he means to include amongst luxuries the tea, sugar, and tobacco which are the comforts of our working people – as impotent as that of the Fair Traders.

But, unlike many of the Fair Traders, he states his case fairly, and he puts in very clear terms the impression which our commercial treaties have made, and are making, on many minds besides his own – an impression from which it is very difficult to escape, especially for a diplomatist. Our minister at a foreign court will tell you, "Don't trouble me with your arguments; tell me with what force you will back them." If the Foreign Secretary is to make a bargain, he must have something to bargain with.

"X." in the Pall Mall Gazette.

Lord Salisbury may, however, be thought by some Free Traders to be a poor economist, and a diplomatist of a very suspicious type; but he has support where one would least expect it. I have seen arguments not very different in character in a perfectly unsuspicious quarter. In the *Pall Mall Gazette* of the 8th and 12th August, 1881, were some letters signed X., by an ardent advocate of commercial treaties, in which, after pointing out, first, that such a treaty as Cobden's, which only reduced duties and gave no preferences, differs *toto cælo* from such treaties as the Methuen Treaty, which gave

Arguments for Retaliation.

a distinct preference and stipulated for the maintenance of differential duties; and, secondly, that exports are as important a factor in trade as imports – two facts which no sound Free Trader would for a moment deny – the writer proceeded to draw the conclusion that it is the business of the Government of this, and of every other country, to do as much for its exports as for its imports, and, after dismissing the notion of differential duties of a Protective character, suggested a differential duty on wines as a legitimate means of compelling France to admit our exports. A large part of his letters consists in the exposure of the fallacy which he supposes the school of Ricardo to commit when they say, "Take care of the imports and the exports will take care of themselves." He points out with perfect truth that a limitation on our exports is as much a limitation on our trade as a limitation on our imports, and he implies that however free our ports may be to foreign imports, it will do us little or no good if the hostile tariffs of foreign countries continue to limit our exports.

A notion similar in substance, but much more recklessly expressed, finds its utterance in the constant misrepresentations we have lately heard of the views and objects of the authors of our present policy. We are told that what Mr. Ricardo, Mr. Cobden, Sir Robert Peel, and others had in view, as the principal object and result of their Free Trade policy, was the abolition of foreign restrictions on our exports; that they believed themselves, and prophesied to the people, that if we in England would take off our duties, foreign nations would certainly take off theirs; that in this they deceived and were deceived; that foreign nations have not followed our example; and that these short-sighted politicians, were they now with us, would at once admit their mistake and revise their policy.

We have been told, for instance, by Lord Salisbury in his speech at Dumfries in 1885, that Mr. Bright having raised a formidable agitation against the Corn Laws, Sir Robert Peel, rightly or wrongly, was of the opinion that it was necessary for the interest of the country that that agitation should be closed, and that on this account, without waiting for any negotiations with foreign Powers, he introduced the system of Free Trade which Mr. Gladstone has carried further; and we are told by Lord Penzance, in the *Nineteeth Century* of March, 1886, that the whole fabric of free imports was rested by its framers on the conviction that foreign countries would abandon Protection. Now, what were the real facts? The first step taken by Sir Robert Peel was his first reform of the Tariff in 1842, and in his cautious fashion he based it rather upon financial necessities than upon Free Trade principles. In doing this he had postponed certain further reductions of duties, on account, amongst other reasons, of commercial negotiations then in progress. Thereupon Mr. Ricardo, in two successive years, 1843 and 1844,[1] brought forward a motion urging the immediate remission of our own duties without waiting to see what other nations would do. In the very interesting debates upon these motions, some members, amongst others Mr. Disraeli, defended the principle of Reciprocity. Sir R. Peel and Mr. Gladstone clearly agreed with Mr.

More reckless Advocates of Retaliation.

Misrepresentation of the Origin of the Policy of fighting hostile Tariffs by Free Imports.

Arguments for Retaliation. Debates of 1843 and 1844.

Ricardo in the principle he advocated – a principle on which they subsequently acted – but objected to its immediate application, and to the abstract form in which his motion was couched. Mr. Ricardo himself, Lord Grey (then Lord Howick), Mr. Ewart, Mr. C. Villiers, and Mr. Cobden, supported the motion on the ground, which was admitted on all hands to be true, viz., that for 25 years we had been struggling by means of our own duties to obtain reciprocal reductions from other nations, and had failed entirely, a fact which is constantly and conveniently ignored by the present advocates of Reciprocity. They said, further, that if the great object of this country were to obtain reductions in foreign tariffs, the best way to effect it would be to reduce our own, to show foreign nations that we believed in our own principles, and to convince them by our own consequent prosperity that our policy was the true one. In their anticipations of the wisdom of foreign nations, and in their under-estimate of the strength of protected interests, they were perhaps too sanguine. But this was not the only ground, or indeed the real ground, on which they supported the motion. That ground was the principle, true then as now, that whether foreign nations maintain their own duties or not, it is for our interest to abolish ours, and that if we would but do this in our own interest our own trade must prosper, let foreign nations do what they will. As regards Sir Robert Peel, he has himself stated his reasons for adopting a Free Trade policy in one of the finest speeches he ever made.[2] Mr. Disraeli had asserted that – "We can only encounter the hostile tariffs of foreign countries by countervailing duties;" and Sir Robert Peel's speech was an emphatic refutation of this doctrine, and an uncompromising defence of the opposite principle – viz., that you can best fight hostile tariffs by free imports – a principle upon which his great tariff reforms were really founded. The immediate suspension of the Corn Laws was due, he said, to the temporary scarcity of food; but the ultimate repeal of that, as well as of other Protection laws, he founded on principles of Free Trade – a principle which he asserted as positively, and defended as powerfully, as Mr. Bright, Mr. Cobden, or Mr. Ricardo. These great economists were right. Their policy was adopted, and our trade did prosper. No one of these distinguished men doubted, as "X." seems to suppose, that foreign Protective tariffs are a great impediment to our trade, or that it is most desirable that they should be reduced or repealed. What they said was – "A

Our interest is to abolish our own Protective duties, whether other nations reduce theirs or not.

Arguments for Retaliation. Origin of our present policy.

foreign tariff is one impediment; over that you have no power. Your own high tariff is another and a separate impediment, with an additional and cumulative effect; over this you have power. Remove the impediment over which you have power, and do not wait for the removal of the further impediment over which you have no power. You will gain much if you do not gain all. Half a loaf is better than no bread." But the consideration of this fundamental question deserves a new chapter.

Chapter XXI: Hostile Tariffs Must be Met by Free Imports: Statement of the Principle.

The fallacy by which "X." and Lord Salisbury and many others are misled consists in thinking of a high tariff as a complete barrier, a solid wall, a watertight sluice which allows of no passage. If this were the case, it would be quite true that one high tariff is just as great an impediment to trade as two, and that there is no use in removing one unless you can remove both. If every foreign country were to build an impervious wall round itself, so that no trade could enter, it would not signify how much or how little of a wall there may be round England; no trade could pass either one way or the other. But even in the pre-Huskisson days of absolute legal prohibition, the wall was broken through by the smuggler; and, in the present day, no nation practises absolute prohibition even on paper. The metaphor of a barrier-wall misleads, as metaphors constantly do. If we are to have a metaphor, Lord Palmerston's metaphor of two turnpikes, one at each end of the bridge, each of which offers some obstacle to the traffic, is a much better one. At the present time every nation, however Protective in its tendencies, does what it thinks best calculated to promote its own exports, and therefore cannot destroy, but only check its imports, which are the necessary concomitants of exports. No existing tariff is such as to keep out foreign goods altogether; each tariff has its weakest point, its lower and less Protective duties. Moreover, as a matter of fact, all nations are not Protectionist. In many tariffs Protection is a secondary or partial object; and in other countries importation is altogether free. There are, therefore, abundant means of export; there are even abundant channels, often direct, often circuitous and indirect, by which, so long as a Protectionist country exports at all, the exports of a free country can reach, and in the nature of things must reach it.

Fallacies in the arguments of Lord Salisbury and others.

Principle of Free Imports.

Protective Tariffs impediments, not barriers.

67

Trade will go on, and does go on, in spite of hostile tariffs, although the number of transactions is, in consequence of such tariffs, less than it otherwise might be; and each trade transaction is, from its very nature, profitable to both parties engaged in it.

Position of a Free Trade country in the midst of Protectionist countries.

Let us, however, consider a little more carefully what the position of a nation is which opens its ports whilst other nations are shutting theirs; what our position would be, on the hypothesis (which is untrue) that, whilst we retain a Free Trade tariff, all other nations put heavy duties on our goods. I think it can be proved that, though we shall not have as much trade absolutely as we should have if other nations were free like ourselves, we shall be better off relatively; the trade and the production of the world will be less, but we shall have a larger share of it.

Effect of Protective Duties as between two Countries only.

The point, though elementary, is so important that it is worth while to consider it attentively. Let us first take the simplest case, that of barter between two merchants living in two different countries, and let us think what would be the effect on their dealings of a tax, imposed in either country on the importation of the commodities in which they deal. Suppose that A, a Frenchman, makes 100 yards of silk in France; and B, an Englishman, makes 100 yards of cloth in England. They exchange these one for the other. Suppose

Principle of Free Imports.

that the French Government puts on the English cloth a duty equal to the value of the cloth; suppose, further, that the cloth is a necessity to the Frenchman, and that it is only to be got from England. The effect of the French duty upon the Frenchman will be, that he will have to pay twice as much for the same quantity of cloth as before; in other words, he will have to pay 200 yards of silk for his 100 yards of cloth. Then suppose that the English Government puts on the French silk a duty equal to the value of the silk, and suppose, as before, that the silk is a necessity to the Englishman, and can only be got from France. The effect on the Englishman will be that he will have to pay 200 yards of cloth for his 100 yards of silk. The effect of the two duties combined will be that the Frenchman will have to give 200 yards of silk for 100 yards of cloth, and the Englishman will have to give 200 yards of cloth for 100 yards of silk – the extra 100 yards of silk and 100 yards of cloth going into the pockets of the respective governments.

Of course, the real thing will be entirely different; the goods will not be either necessaries or monopolies; and the effect of the duties will be to transfer the industries, and, in so doing, to reduce both consumption and production. The effect of the French duty on the Frenchman will be to make the Frenchman buy less English cloth, to make him pay more for it, to make him buy inferior cloth from a French maker, and to make him sell his silk to the French cloth-maker for less than the Englishman would give for it. Its effect on the Englishman will be to deprive him of the best market for a part of his cloth, to make him buy less French silk, and to make him buy something with the rest of his cloth which is of less value to him than the French silk.

The further consequence of the English duty on silk to the Englishman will be to make him buy less French silk, to make him pay more for it, to make him buy inferior English silk instead, and to make him sell his cloth to the English silk manufacturer at a less price than the Frenchman would give for it. Its effect on the Frenchman will be to deprive him of his best market for a part of his silk, to make him buy less English cloth, and to make him buy French cloth instead at a higher price.

The effect of one duty, supposing the duties still to be equal, will be as great as that of the other; they will act cumulatively in transferring English and French industries from what they do best to what they can do less well; the French industry from silk-making to cloth-making, the English industry from cloth-making to silk-making.

Principle of
Free Imports.

The aggregate production of the two parties will be diminished equally by both duties; and if one duty is taken off, the mischief to both parties will be just one-half what it would be whilst both duties are continued.

Let us now take the case of two nations who exchange goods with one another; and let us, after the manner of Bastiat, call one of them Libera and the other Vincta.

Libera determines to put no duties on the goods of Vincta – Vincta puts a duty of 20 per cent. *ad valorem* on the goods of Libera. The result will be damaging alike to Libera and Vincta; Libera will be able to sell less to Vincta, and to buy less from Vincta in return; Vincta will be able to buy less from Libera, and will be able to sell less to Libera in return. Now, suppose that Libera, irritated by Vincta's conduct, determines to retaliate, and to impose in her turn a tax of 20 per cent. on the goods of Vincta. What will be the result? Precisely the same as before, only that it will be double and cumulative. Vincta will be able to sell still less to Libera, and to buy still less from Libera in return; Libera will be able to buy less from Vincta, and to sell still less to Vincta in return. Both duties have had an equal effect in diminishing the buying and selling on both sides. But their action has been cumulative; the duties imposed by Libera have doubled the loss to each originally caused by the duties imposed by Vincta. Libera has done herself no good, but has done equal mischief to herself and her rival by retaliation. It will even, in this case, clearly be her interest to cease following the example of Vincta, to revert to her original policy, and become Libera again; and it will not be the less her interest to do so because she is at the same time doing good to Vincta.

Effect of Protective Duties as between three or more Countries. Abstract illustration.

Principle of Free Imports. Abstract illustration.

But now let us consider the case of three countries, which we will call Libera and Vincta No. 1 and Vincta No. 2. Suppose that they have a triangular trade with one another and that these three trades (that of Libera with Vincta 1, that of Libera with Vincta 2, and that of Vincta 1 with Vincta 2) are each equal in amount, and that each of them is represented by 6. Then 18 will represent the aggregate trade of all three, and each will possess an equal share of it, which will be represented by 6. Now suppose that Vincta 1 and Vincta 2 each put equally heavy duties on their respective imports, Libera remaining free as before. The trade between Libera and each of the others will be subject to one set of duties, but the trade of Vincta 1 and Vincta 2 with each other will be subject to two sets of duties. The aggregate exchange, and with the exchange the production of all three countries, will be diminished, but not in equal proportions. The trade between Vincta No. 1 and Vincta No. 2 will be diminished in a larger proportion than the trade of each with Libera. If we suppose that each set of duties has the effect of diminishing the trade on which it is charged by an amount represented by 1, the whole diminution will be equal to 4, and the aggregate trade of the three countries will now be represented by 14 intead of 18. Of this diminution, 1 will fall on the trade between Libera and Vincta No. 1, which will now be 5 instead of 6; 1 on the trade between Libera and Vincta No. 2, which will also be 5; and two on the trade between Vincta No. 1 and Vincta No. 2, which will now be 4. Each country will, of course, have half the trade between itself and each of its neighbours, and the whole trade will now be divided as follows: – Libera will have 5 instead of 6; Vincta No. 1 and Vincta No. 2 will each have $4\frac{1}{2}$ instead of 6. The following diagram will make this clear: –

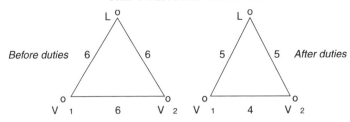

In the same way it may be shown that if of three countries trading with one another under three tariffs equally Protective, one does away with Protection, the production and trade of all will be increased, but the largest share of the increased trade will fall to the one which opens its ports. When she opens her ports she must do good to her neighbours as well as to herself, though not so much good – a thing which it is important to remember in examining the consequences of adopting a Free Trade policy. Its adoption by one country is followed by an increase of the trade of other countries as well as of her own, though her own trade reaps the greatest benefit.

Principle of Free Imports.

I am not very fond of illustrations of this kind. They are apt to appear to be mathematical demonstrations, when they are really only rude and abstract illustrations of one of the many elements which go to make up the infinitely complex and delicate conditions of human business. But taken merely as an illustration, I believe the above formula represents a general truth. Perhaps a more homely illustration will make the matter clearer. Suppose a large village or small town with three general shops in which everything is sold, from lollipops to hardware. Two of the shops are rented from the squire, who also owns nearly all the land in the parish. He says to the tenants of these two shops – "I want to do good to my estate and those who live on it, and therefore I shall require you, in buying for your stock-in-trade such articles as the estate produces, to buy your articles from your neighbours in preference to buying them from strangers. The parish produces corn, wood, vegetables, fruit. There is a local pottery, a local flour mill, a local forge for tools and hardware. All your stock of these things you shall buy from the producers in the parish; or, if you buy them from strangers, you shall pay me a percentage on your purchases, to be used for the good of the estates." The third shop, happening to be on a bit of land not belonging to the squire, is not subject to his patriarchal theories, and buys all its stock of goods, whether

Concrete illustration

71

of a kind produced in the parish or not, wherever it can buy them cheapest and best. I think we can tell which of these three shops will sell the best articles, will sell them at the lowest prices, and will have the largest and most profitable custom. The case runs on all fours with those countries of which two compel their producing classes to buy their goods at home, and of which the third leaves them free to buy where and how they best can.

Principle of
Free Imports.

To carry our homely illustration a little farther, let us suppose that our squire, alarmed at the success of the independent shop, and the decay of the two which belong to him, says to the rest of the tenants on his estate, "I have compelled my shops, for your sakes, to buy their stock of you. It is not fair, it is not tolerable under such circumstances, that you should take your custom to that odious free shop, or to the neighbouring town. You shall buy as well as sell at the shops belonging to the estate, and we will all support one another against these horrid strangers." I think our squire would soon find, in his flitting tenants and diminished rents, ample reason for regretting that he had meddled with their buying and selling.

The Nation
which re-
mains free
will get the
largest share
of the Trade.

So far, then, as artificial restrictions are concerned – and it is only with these we are now dealing – the country which keeps its own ports open whilst the ports of other countries are shut will not do as much trade as if the ports of all were open, but of the reduced trade which is left by the restrictions it will do a larger share. If England keeps her ports open whilst the United States, France, Germany, Italy, and other countries shut theirs, the aggregate trade of all of them, and even the actual amount of England's share, will be less than if all of them were open; but her share of what is left will be greater than that of the others, and it will be proportionately greater than it was when the ports were open. It is to her open markets rather than to those of the closed countries that each foreign country will prefer to export, and return trade is apt to follow in the same channel. To her will come raw materials, half-manufactured goods, food, clothing, everything which aids production directly or indirectly. No market is likely to be so closed against her but that she will be able to get something into it, and in doing so she will, by her command of the materials and instruments of production, be better able to compete than her rivals, who have made the materials and instruments of production dear. To all open neutral markets – and they are many – she will have full access. In all neutral markets, open or closed by duties, she will have an advantage. Her open market will attract imports; her command of all that is needed for production will give comparative cheapness to her exports. She will lose absolutely some of the direct trade with her Protectionist rivals which she might have had if it were not for their duties, but they will lose that trade also, and she will have advantages in competing with them in other markets which they will not have . . .

Chapter XXXI: Relation of the Prosperity of Other Nations to Our Own

Before attempting to prove anything by facts and figures, let us be on our guard against a mistake, by which our Protectionist friends are constantly leading us into pitfalls. It is a very important and a very dangerous mistake, for it involves the very principle which lies at the bottom of the Free Trade controversy. To read Protectionist literature, one would imagine that no nation could thrive except at the expense of another; that trade, at any rate between nations, is a sort of betting or gambling game, where the gain of one is the loss of another. If the list of French exports grows as ours grows, still more if it increases by a percentage faster than our own, we are in danger. If the American export account appears to exceed our own, we are lost, and so on. Unless our sale list keeps far ahead of and grows faster than that of all other nations, we are losing our position, and dwindling among the races of mankind. But the truth is that trade is reciprocal: our trade cannot grow without making the trade of other nations grow too. Every act of trade is a sale by one man and a purchase by another, and every such sale and purchase involves a second purchase by the first man and sale by the last. Every act of trade is an act of barter – or, rather, one-half of an act of barter. Except in the case of transfers of goods made to pay existing debts, every sale by an Englishman to a Frenchman involves a sale direct or indirect by a Frenchman to an Englishman. Every English export to France involves a French import from England, a French export on account of England and an English import on account of France. And the whole transaction is a gain to both traders and to both countries. An increase in the English export list, arising from the removal of our own restrictions, necessitates an equal and corresponding increase in the French export list; and the

Our Trade can only grow by making the Trade of other Nations grow too.

73

increase in the French exports, which follows the removal of our restrictions, is the proof and consequence of an increase in English trade. We cannot do good to ourselves without doing good to our neighbour. Nay, if we are doing much the larger trade of the two, it may very well happen that by removing some artificial restrictions which we have placed on our trade with him, we may arrive at the result of increasing our neighbour's trade by a percentage on his trade greater than the percentage by which we increase our own – a catastrophe which excites the liveliest alarm in the minds of those who think the infant of two years lives faster than the youth of twenty, because in one year the infant has doubled his age, whilst the youth has added only one-twentieth to his.

Folly of supposing our wealth to consist in the poverty of others.

It would be seen to be the height of absurdity if a manufacturer, a merchant, a farmer were to look on the prosperity of his customers as signs of his own decay. Conceive the village baker saying to the shoemaker, "You are making too much by my custom; you have enlarged your shop, you are taking an apprentice; you eat more of my bread, it is true, but I cannot bear to see you so rich. I shall do without shoes, and go barefoot, in order that your balance may be less at the end of the year." And yet this is the spirit in which we often look at foreign statistics. The very growth in them which we envy is often the necessary result of the increase of our own trade, which again is the result of our own free policy. When we reduced our tariff between 1840 and 1860, we increased our own exports and imports; but we increased those of America and Germany and France at the same time.

Consequently, in comparing national statistics, the question is not whether we increase faster than or as fast as other nations, though this question may often be answered in the affirmative, but does our Free system enable us to do trade with other nations which we should not do without it, and does it enable us to do trade from which they cut themselves off by a system of Protection?

Competition.

In saying that trade is necessarily a mutual benefit, I do not forget Competition, or the partial and local suffering which it occasionally causes. Competition becomes wider, if not more severe, as communication extends. But competition is one form of a higher law, of which in this case we can see the beneficent results, and which neither men nor nations can disregard with impunity. Free Trade cheerfully obeys this law; *it has regard to sellers who want to sell what other people want to buy, and to buyers who want to buy what other people want to sell.*

Protection discourages such buyers and sellers, and encourages instead of them, and at their expense, *the sellers who want to sell what nobody wants to buy.* If in the race of competition we were entirely thrown out; if, whilst other nations were prospering, our forges were extinguished, our looms idle, our pauperism on the increase, and our consumption seriously diminishing, it would be time, not to reverse our policy, but to reconsider our position. But whilst the very opposite of this is the case, it is the height of folly to look with jealousy on the growing wealth of other nations who can sell what we want to buy, and buy what we want to sell . . .

Chapter XXXV: German Trade in Recent Years.

The excellent reports recently made by our Ministers and Consuls upon the trade of Germany give us much valuable information and enable us to supplement the statistics.[3] The case is full of interest and also full of warnings. It contains a warning to those Free Traders who have been unwise enough to attribute our commercial prosperity to Free Trade alone, and who have been content to rest the case against Protection on this argument. It is an undoubted fact that German manufactures, both for home consumption and for export, have largely increased during the last five or six years; and that this increase has been coincident with the adoption of a Protectionist policy. It contains a warning to our own manufacturers, whether capitalists or labourers, that if they wish to compete successfully with Germans, not only in German but in neutral markets, they must not fall behind the Germans in technical education, in thrift, in industry, in pushing powers, and in readiness to learn and meet the wants of customers. It contains a warning to inquirers on this subject that in considering whether depression exists, they must go beyond the word depression and find out what it means, and that they must not mistake growing exports for successful trade. On this point I have dealt more fully below. Lastly, it contains a further warning to inquirers that in reading and drawing conclusions from the published statistics of trade between the two countries, or from the official reports, valuable as both are, great caution must be exercised. For instance, statistics of export from this country to Hamburg comprise goods not meant for Hamburg or Germany, as there are no means of distinguishing goods intended for consumption in Germany from goods in transit; and statistics

Official Reports full of interest and warning.

75

of trade to or from Germany may appear under the head of Belgian or Dutch exports or imports – as much of the trade of Germany goes through Belgium or Holland. And if statistics need accurate interpretation, official reports must not always be taken for gospel. Thus, for instance, Mr. Mulvany, our Consul at Düsseldorf, to whose practical knowledge Mr. Scott, the Consul-General, bears ample testimony,[4] is of opinion that the welfare of the working classes in Germany has improved immensely, owing to the wise policy of the German Government in giving up Free Trade; that land-owners and farmers have suffered by the low price of foreign imports; that it is fortunate for Germany that American bacon has been all but prohibited, and that the value of land will soon be quite re-established by moderate Protective tariffs. Such an opinion from a British Consul would seem to deserve attention. But when we find that Mr. Mulvany is the son of an Irishman who has set up successful iron-works in Germany, and who has been a strong promoter of the import duties by which these iron-works are protected from English competition,[5] we cease to attach so much value to his report. Nor is it only in matters of opinion that caution is necessary. For instance, Mr. Strachey, Her Majesty's Chargé d'Affaires at Dresden, whose valuable report on the effect of the German tariff[6] would be even more useful than it is if attention were less distracted from its substance by the ambitious brilliancy of its style, rejects with scorn the suggestion that the German Government favours German exporters by charging them lower freights than are charged on imported goods.[7] But, on the other hand, we find in the synopsis of answers from the Consuls,[8] statements as the following, positive statements that "Reduced rates are given for through freight of certain goods to certain ports on the North Sea"; "Differential freights have been established favouring exports of coal, salt, spirits, &c."; "Low freights are given on State railways to German coal, &c. &c." – statements, I may add, which are amply confirmed by reports from other sources.

History of German Trade.

The history of German trade during the last twenty years may be shortly stated as follows:[9] – Before 1866, Germany was a patchwork of different States, and exported agricultural produce. Between 1866, the year of the Austrian war, and 1869, her manufacturing industry was largely developed, and her agricultural imports came to exceed her exports. After the French war in 1870, German unity was confirmed and extended; the national spirit was further awakened; the indus-

76

tries of Alsace and Lorraine were added to the commercial resources of the Empire; internal barriers were removed; coinage, weights, and measures were reformed; the railway system was revised and consolidated; a new commercial code was passed; two hundred millions sterling was passed into the country by France in payment of the indemnity; and German trade received an unprecedented stimulus. The consequence was an immense development not only of sound enterprise but of wild speculation, followed, in 1874–8, by the inevitable collapse. During this period Free Trade was in the ascendant, and it is probably a misfortune that in 1877, just as the collapse was becoming acute, such duties as remained were further reduced. During this period of Free Trade the iron manufacture and exports rose rapidly, while imports of iron fell off.[10] The collapse in prices led to a cry for Protection. In 1878 an Imperial Commission was appointed to consider the subject, and the Protectionist tariff of 1879 was the consequence. It is right to add that this tariff was not entirely due to the demand for Protection. The German Government was in need of revenue, and, owing to the peculiar constitution of the Empire, it was difficult to raise it except by indirect taxation. After the adoption of this tariff came the temporary revival of 1879–1880, which was felt in Germany as well as elsewhere, followed in later years by a period of large business but low prices. The tendency to Protection is still in the ascendant and seems to be growing in strength. Though there is a strong party in favour of Free Trade, the Protectionists have the upper hand. Article after article has been protected; the tariff of 1885 is much higher than that of 1879, and it includes a heavy tax on foreign corn. Protection has followed its usual course. Each step has made a further step unavoidable, until at last the food of the people, the prime necessary of industrial life, and formerly an article of export, is made dearer and scarcer by a heavy import duty.

If we ask what has been the state of trade and manufacture during these years, and what it is now, we receive answers which show a large increase of business. The statistics of German trade can, as above stated, only be given since 1872, and changes in them, which were made in 1879, render the comparison of previous with subsequent years less satisfactory than it would otherwise be. Such as they are, the figures are given in the table, No. XX. in the Appendix.

Taking a period of three years from 1872, and quinquennial periods subsequently, the figures are: –

Statistics of German Trade.

Annual Average.	Population in millions	Imports, special		Exports, special.	
		Amount in thousand £	Per head	Amount in thousand £	Per head
			£ s. d.		£ s. d.
1872–4	41	177,048	4 6 3	116,258	2 16 7
1875–9	42	183,946	4 6 1	134,679	3 3 0
1880–4	45	154,377	3 8 3	155,400	3 8 8

And for the last five years: –

Years	Imports, Special.		Exports, Special.	
1880	£141,035		£144,770	
1881	148,150		148,850	
1882	156,475		159,525	
1883	163,185		163,610	
1884	163,040		160,247	

Since 1872 our own imports have increased faster than those of Germany, but her exports have increased faster and more than ours. During the last five years both her imports and exports have held their own better than ours, and better than those of France. The imports of Germany were larger from 1872 to 1879 than they have since been: her exports steadily increased from 1872 to 1883. From 1872 to 1879 her imports largely exceeded her exports; from 1880 onwards her exports and imports have been nearly equal. The excess of imports in the earlier years is probably due to the payment of the French indemnity. The absence of any such excess in more recent years is very remarkable when considered in connection with the further facts to which I shall have to call attention.

During the period embraced in these returns we find that there has been an immense development of manufacturing industry, which is still progressing. The general export figures are given above. The production of pig iron in Germany increased from two and a quarter millions of tons in 1873 to upwards of three millions and a half in 1884, whilst in the United Kingdom it increased in the same time from upwards of six millions and a half to seven millions and a half.[11] The returns for Great Britain in 1884, as compared with 1883, show a decrease of production of iron, whilst those for Germany show an increase.[12] The net imports of raw cotton[13] into Germany increased from upwards of $2\frac{1}{4}$ million cwt. in 1877 to upwards of three million cwt. in 1884. The net imports of raw jute increased from 236,000 cwt. in 1877 to 668,000 cwt. in 1884. Meanwhile the exports of woven goods increased, whilst the imports diminished. The same thing is true of many, if not most, other articles. As regards British trade with Germany the aggregate has increased, but its proportion to the whole trade of Germany has decreased.[14] British manufactured articles have been displaced in Germany by German products, more especially in iron, in textiles, in chemicals,[15] and in cheap glass and pottery.[16] German goods are rivalling English goods in neutral markets, and are being sold in our own. They are being imported to England, and some are re-exported as English goods. The Germans rival us successfully in cheapness, though not generally in excellence. Nor are we alone. French imports into Germany have suffered more by German competition than our own.

As regards the recent period of depression, it appears that since 1882 large concerns have been increasing their business, whilst smaller concerns are still unable to make way against difficulties. When the question is asked whether there is depresion at present, it must be answered by another, viz., what is meant by depression? If by depression is meant diminution in the volume of business, it cannot be said to exist, except perhaps in particular trades and in particular places At Königsberg, Memel, and Breslau the loss of the grain trade has caused loss of business. Sugar, iron, chemicals, and shipping are all suffering everywhere from glut and over-production, and it would seem that business in these articles is contracting. But, speaking generally, the mass of articles produced, consumed, and exported is large; employment is brisk, and wages are comparatively high.[17]

Depression in Germany

These statements show that German powers of production have made immense advances within the last twenty years, and that in the last five or six years they have not been more crippled or restricted than our own. If we were to treat a policy of Free Trade on the one hand, or Protection on the other, as the sole cause of commercial prosperity, these statements would afford a strong argument against Free Trade. But the policy of legislative interference with trade is only one of many factors. We have, for instance, in these reports, a number of other considerations insisted upon, which are quite sufficient to account for the development

Advance in German Trade and its causes.

of German trade. I can only mention them shortly, referring to the reports for greater detail. They are: –

1st. The energy thrown into business by the accomplishment of national unity and the development of the national spirit. This has been the motive-power of every other change.

2nd. The unification and improvement of laws, of weights and measures, of coinage.

3rd. The excellence and cheapness of internal carriage by land and water. The purchase of German railways by the State, facilitated by the French indemnity, has enabled the Government to reform and lower railway rates.

4th. The absence of strikes and agitation among workmen.

5th. The rate of wages, which, though much higher than it was, is still lower than the English rate.

6th. The prevalence of thrift and industry amongst employers and employed.

7th. The excellence of the technical education given in the public schools.

Last, but by no means least, the pains and skill evinced by German traders in pushing their wares and in adapting their goods to the wants of their customers. Their agents are ubiquitous, and their efforts in search of custom as incessant as they are ingenious and varied.

On this point Mr. Scott's remarks are well worth the attention of English manufacturers. He is speaking of the German market, but what he says is equally true of other markets. Our representatives in all parts of the world are unanimous on this point. He says: "It seems to be a subject of very general complaint that English producers are imperfectly acquainted with the requirements of the German market, and unwilling to alter their standard of supply to meet them; they are said to be entirely dependent on the middleman for this very requisite information; and the English dealer, on his side, is believed not to have as yet realised the fact that the day has gone by when the German consumer was content to take the supply which the English dealer thought the best for him; that the German market has now got a standard of its own, and one not to be despised, which native producers are quite able to attain to. If, therefore, British producers think the German market worth supplying, they should make greater efforts to ascertain the exact nature of the German demand more directly and promptly than they do at present, and be prepared with a suitable supply of goods."[18]

In short, the German manufacturer seems to neglect no means of pushing the sale of his own goods and ousting his rivals. It is by the legitimate means of thrift, skill and industry that his real successes are won. But he does not neglect less legitimate methods. Thus we are told that he copies his rivals' designs, and that he appropriates his trade marks. He exports pig iron marked "English Foundry No. 3," and so-called "Low Moor Plates."[19] He makes German cutlery and sends it to England to be re-exported to America with English trade marks.[20] He makes surgical instruments, sends them to England, and re-imports them with English names.[21] He makes "genuine" Leicester articles in Germany, and exports them to England with English labels.[22] The inferior German writing paper is made with English water-marks.[23] German potters copy our best makers, bring out scamped fac-similes at half our price, and export largely, competing with us by this means both in our own and in the American markets.[24] German candles are inferior to English, but they are labelled "candles" or "fine candles," and are made up in English pounds.[25] Birmingham, it is true, follows suit in imitating Berlin, but is, in Germany, promptly repressed by German law.[26]

Such practices make it sound strange to hear that a habit is growing in Germany of treating competition "not as a legitimate and indeed essential wheel of the great industrial machine, but as a malignant force of modern depravity which is the peculiar resort of capitalists, Jews, and English manufacturers." It is odd enough to hear such terms as "an infamous breach of honesty," "piracy," and the like, applied to successful trade competition by a foolish Socialist professor, but to hear them applied to the importation of Nottingham thread by a German thread-maker is indeeed amusing![27]

With all these factors at work, the Protective tariff of Germany is but a small thing in comparison with other factors, more especially if it is remembered that, bad as it is and much as it is growing, it is very far indeed from being prohibitory. Indeed, there is in the want of indirect revenue felt by the German Government a guarantee that Protection will never be carried to the extent of prohibition.

What has Protection done for it?

As regards the actual effect of the German Protective tariff, it is extremely difficult to disentangle different causes and effects, so as to trace its operation with any degree of certainty. But there are certain features in the accounts we have of German trade which point to the conclusion that

81

Protection has in Germany, as elsewhere, been both useless and mischievous.

In the first place, it seems clear, as a matter of history, that whilst the moderate Protection given by the tariff has fostered some forms of industry into a quicker development than they would have attained without it, it has not been the sole or a chief, or indeed an important, factor in developing German manufacture generally. From Mr. Strachey's very interesting report it appears that during the years prior to 1879, in which the Empire was progressing towards Free Trade in iron, and during the years in which Free Trade was an accomplished fact,[28] the iron industry of Germany, perhaps the most important of all, was rising rapidly in importance; that the iron exports were increasing, and that they were entering into serious competition with the produce of England and of Belgium, whilst at the same time the imports were decreasing. The crisis which followed this growth, and which was the origin of the Protective tariff, was common to the whole world. As Mr. Strachey tells us, the iron duties were repealed when the great cosmic crisis which followed the German struggle with France was in its acutest phase, and they were re-imposed just as the bottom was reached. Thus the adoption of the tariff of 1879 was coincident with the beginning of recovery, and it is impossible to distinguish between the effects derived from Protection and the development due to the natural vitality of the iron trade.

Again, as to textiles, Mr. Strachey tells us that in 1878, just before the date of the Protective tariff, it was proved, before an Imperial Committee, that in most of the leading staples native German industry commanded the home markets; that Germany had as good as no import of the articles which constitute the bulk of the cotton manufacture, and that there was a large and growing export.[29] So with knitted fabrics, the success of Chemnitz over Nottingham is not due to the tariff.[30] As regards woollen goods, we find that in the period which preceded 1879 the German weavers were to a great extent masters of the home market in woollens and worsteds.[31] As regards linens again, English manufactures, before the tariff of 1879, scarcely entered Germany, and there was a large export of German linen.[32] In these cases the new tariff merely accelerated the process which was already going on. Upon jute manufacture it had a greater effect.[33] The great success of Germany in mixed silk goods is due to their skill and not to the tariff;[34] whilst their victory over Lyons, so far as it is due to legislation, is owing, not to the German Protective duty on German silks, but to the high Protective duty which France has imposed on foreign cotton yarns. So far as the German tariff is concerned, it checks its own silk manufacture by a similar duty, but one of lower amount. Chemicals, again, in which Germany has been especially successful, receive little Protection and some hindrance from the tariff.[35] Her large manufactures of leather, wood, paper, pottery, and glass owe little or nothing to it.[36]

In short, it is clear that German manufacturing industry generally was making great progress under a system of Free Trade; and that the utmost that can be claimed for Protection is to have given additional stimulus to some branches of it. Cotton spinning appears to be an interest which has benefited more than most by Protection,[37] and we shall see presently what the effect of this benefit is on other industries. Under these circumstances it is, to say the least, extremely doubtful whether even in each protected industry growth and progress would not have been as great without Protection as it has been with it.

But this is only a small part of the question. No one doubts that a single special interest may be fosterd by a protective duty. The real questions are, What is the effect of such a Protective duty on other interests? Whether any single interest can be protected without involving Protection for others? And what is the final effect of Protection on the production and consumption of the country? Fortunately, we are not without means of giving an answer, however imperfect, to these questions.

If it has fostered some industries, it has impeded others.

In the first place, it is clear that the duties by which Germany protects particular manufactures do interfere with other manufactures, and are complained of, perhaps more loudly than the facts warrant. Thus, makers of machines and of all sorts of goods made with iron and steel complain of the duties on those metals, and find or seek compensation in Protective duties on the articles they make.[38] The duties on cotton yarn have stimulated cotton spinning, but take from the weavers as much as they give to the spinners,[39] and the export commodities of Germany are at a great disadvantage in the markets of the world with the cottons of countries in which yarns are untaxed. The taxation of cotton yarns also injures the weavers of mixed goods, whether of woollen or silk.[40] The taxation of woollen yarns injures the weavers of wool.[41] The taxation of linen yarns injures the weavers of linen.[42] The makers of clothing complain of the duties on linen, woollen stuffs, &c.[43] Alizarine-makers need soda, and soda is taxed.[44] Strontium is of value for the most depressed of manufactures, that of sugar, but, at the beck of two or three Westphalian miners, strontium is taxed.[45] The makers of soap, perfumery, candles, and varnish require oils; but German oil-makers must be protected.[46] The makers of essences and liqueurs complain of taxes on seeds.[47] Leather-dressers complain of taxes on articles used in tanning.[48] German timber is protected, and the vast number of trades which use wood cry out.[49] Paper suffers from the tax on chemicals.[50]

Whatever the actual effect of all these Protective taxes may be in restricting and repressing manufacture – and in many cases it must be considerable – the complaints made by the manufacturers are unanswerable in point of principle, and they are met, not by removing the duty on the material, but by giving the finished manufacture the protection of a higher duty. Germany is like France and Canada, a practical illustration of the universal truth that Protection takes from one at least what it gives to another, and that if a nation begins by protecting one interest it must go on protecting others until the charmed circle is complete.

It has made things dear in Germany.

If this is the effect of German Protection on the materials used in manufacture, what is its effect on the German consumer? There is ample evidence in these reports that the prices of many, if not of most, manufactured articles are higher in Germany than in countries which have no Protective tariff. This, we are told, is the case with steel rails;[51] with cotton goods, which to persons accustomed to London prices seem enormously dear;[52] with woollen goods;[53] with linen;[54] with chemicals;[55] with articles made of leather;[56] with pottery;[57] and, as we know so well, with sugar. In short, the German consumer suffers as the consumers in other Protectionist countries do from Protective duties. Life is made dearer and less pleasant to him. For readers in this country it is needless to labour this point. Free Traders or Protectionists, we have all of us, I hope, except a few Fair Traders, got beyond the astounding doctrine that Protection raises prices to the seller without raising them to the buyer – a doctrine with which German Protectionists seem still to console themselves.

About German consumers, then, there can be no doubt. But how about German producers? Are they not doing well?

If we find that prices in Germany, if not high, are yet in many cases higher than they are in England; and if at the same time the volume of business in Germany is large and constantly growing larger, we seem to have the elements of great prosperity for produceers. Do the reports bear this out? Quite the contrary. If there is one feature in these reports on which all the reporters are unanimous and which applies universally to all branches of trade, it is that business, though large, is unremunerative; that profits are nothing or next to nothing; that there is a general glut of manufactured articles; and that the only hope for manufacturers is in some new market, some fresh demand which shall raise prices and make it worth while to go on producing. If this is what is meant by depression – and it is really what is meant by it in this country – there can be no doubt that it exists in Germany to as great an extent as it does in England. It is almost superfluous to quote authorities. But I may quote one or two extracts from recent newspapers. In the *Times* of 21st July, 1886, occurs the following statement: – "An additional proof is afforded of the critical position into which the German iron industry has fallen, by the announcement that the large rolled iron concern of F. Remy, of Dortmund, has suspended payment . . . The fact that in a recent contract for steel rails at Altona the lowest German tender was underbidden by one from England has caused absolute alarm. Hitherto, owners of German works have been able to recompense themselves for low-priced foreign contracts by keeping up prices at home." And again in the *Ironmonger* of 14th August, 1886, I find the following: – "More than thirty German Chambers of Commerce have expressed in their annual trade reviews for 1885 their conviction of the necessity of reverting to a more liberal foreign commercial policy. The Chambers of Carlsruhe, Darmstadt, Munster, Leipzig, Hanau, and many others, complain of the injurious consequences of the Protective system. It is also regarded as significant that the organ of Prince Bismarck reproduces prominently a portion of the Leipzig report, in which the Government, whilst congratulated on its opposition to the bimetallists, is urged to reverse its present commercial policy." The consular reports all tell the same story. In the three great articles, iron, sugar, and chemicals, the depression is very great[58] – greater, probably, than in England or elsewhere. As regards trade generally Mr. Scott says that "the returns tell us that the return on capital is everywhere steadily decreasing. Prices of products in nearly

It has raised prices, but not profits, which are in many cases next to nothing.

85

all the chief branches of industry have been steadily falling, and the profits of producers and middlemen are being reduced in many instances to a minimum . . ." The report of the general Handelstag of Germany has summed up the description of 1883 in five words: "*From maximum exertions minimum profits.*" "General over-production – or, rather, the general belief in the existence of over-production – is spoken of as the one great cause." Mr. Mulvany, who has, we have seen, such a firm belief in the recuperative effects of Protection, says, nevertheless:[59] "The depression of trade, or, perhaps more correctly speaking, of prices, is notorious." "The greater portion of capital invested in industry yields little or no interest, only a small portion a fair rate, and none a high rate." "A continuance of depression may become dangerous to master and man." From Königsberg[60] the report is that depression has reached its lowest point, and that it is caused by increased competition, very slow sale, and very small profits, often disappearing in loss. From Saxony we learn that[61] "the depression is almost universal and there are scarcely any branches of production which it has not reached." From Würtemberg: "The volume of transactions shows progress. The profits earned seem to decrease in a corresponding ratio."[62] We have, then, increased production; increased exports; prices higher at home than abroad; and, at the same time, aggregate profits decreasing so much that in many cases they approach or even reach zero.

Goods are sold cheap abroad and dear at home!

To this remarkable state of things we have to add one other fact, which seems to me to be very significant. The German manufacturer is selling cheap abroad, and keeps his head above water by selling dear at home. Of this there can, I think, be no doubt. Mr. Scott says:[63] "The producer, in order to keep a grasp of foreign markets and to keep his business going, is throwing it into foreign countries at unremunerative prices, in many cases lower than those at which he places it at home . . . As he has in many branches at present the practical command of the home market to the almost entire exclusion of foreign competition, he is able to go on increasing his production for the present in spite of diminished profits, but it would require more than ordinary temerity to make a forecast of his future." Mr. Mulvany tells us that the German manufacturers are "steadily pushing their products into the markets of the world – it is true, in many cases without any profit – indeed, on large quantities, exported at a dead loss."[64] Again, according to Mr. Strachey the existence of a double scale of prices, one for home buyers, another for foreigners, is a common, if not a general fact. The following are instances:– As regards iron (the production of which appears to be about 2.8 million tons, and the home consumption about 1.8 million, leaving 1 million for exports)[65] we are told that the magnates of Essen and Bochum formed a coalition which secured the sale of their goods in Germany at prices far above English, while in foreign markets they were flinging their rails away;[66] and, again, that the Protective duty has enabled the German rail-makers to combine to fix home prices which are, or have been, fully 25 per cent. above their terms for foreign markets.[67] And, again, that the Chamber of Bochum reported that in 1882 the foreign trade was hardly profitable, and that German producers habitually accept for goods sent abroad prices lower than they will take from home dealers.[68] Again, with respect to some important chemicals, in which there has been great over-production, Mr. Strachey says that the German makers keep up their prices in the home market to an artificial height by a trade convention, and, in the usual manner, throw their remaining supplies abroad at the lowest prices.[69] Again, in the manufactures of articles of leather, in which also there is a glut, export prices are systematically lower than those taken from the home purchaser.[70] In pottery the consignments for foreign markets are made 15 or 20 per cent. lower than the dealings in Germany. And finally we know – as shown below in Chapter XLVIII. – that the German Government pays its sugar producers a bounty of at least a million a year, which operates as an inducement to them to sell sugar to Englishmen at half the price which, thanks to the duty, they are enabled to charge to their German brethren.

This is surely a very remarkable state of things. It is quite intelligible that a trader should sell some goods at no profit in order to obtain custom in other and more profitable goods; it is quite intelligible that a manufacturer should here and there, and by way of exception, sell surplus stock without profit – or even at a loss. But that the mass of traders of any nation should habitually sell goods to foreigners at a low price, and should recoup themselves by selling them to their own countrymen at a comparatively high price, is a practice which, so far as I know, is unprecedented. And that any Government should enable and encourage them to pursue this practice by protecting them in the monopoly of the home market, and should think that by so doing they were increasing the wealth and productive powers of the country, would be incredible of any men out of Bedlam, if it did not seem to be the policy of the present rulers of Germany. To induce manufacturers to sell dear at home and cheap abroad; to make your country-men pay for dear goods, and to give them away to the foreigner, is a policy of which our own Protectionists and Fair Traders, however great their absurdities, would be heart-ily ashamed.

Agriculture extremely depressed.

Of agriculture nothing has been said hitherto, but it is, after all, the greatest interest in Germany. Of the whole population 42 per cent. are still dependent on agriculture, and 45 per cent. on all other industries put together.[71] Formerly it played a much larger proportional part. In 1865 a large surplus of grain was sent abroad. The same process has since gone on in Germany which has gone on in other European countries: manufacture has increased disproportionately to agriculture; labour has flocked to the towns; and corn has come from remote quarters of the earth. Germany has become an indus-trial nation, and one-fourth of her home consumption of grain is now supplied from abroad. This process was pro-ceeding very rapidly under the peculiar circumstances men-tioned above, before Germany adopted the policy of protecting manufactures. That policy, whatever its impor-tance as compared with other factors in the process, must have accelerated it. It must have helped to attract labour from the country to the towns, and have made it dearer and scarcer to the agriculturist; it must have increased the cost to the farmer and the peasant of all manufactured articles. In the meantime the competition of foreign corn lowered agricul-tural prices. The necessary result is very great depression in the agricultural interest. The Prussian Minister of Agriculture reports that within recent years the prices of nearly all agri-cultural products have fallen 25 or even 30 per cent., while the cost of production has increased in the same time 75 per cent.[72] Nor has the depression in cereals been made up for by increase in cattle. Within fifteen years sheep have declined from 28,000,000 to 19,000,000, though pigs have increased, doubtless fostered by the exclusion of American bacon.

Now, if the German Government had no protected man-ufactures this agricultural depression must have been borne, as it is in England, and the German artisan would have had the full benefit of the new sources of food supply which have for us and for Europe, postponed the Malthusian difficulty. But the protection given by German laws to other industries made the claim of agriculture irresistible; and the vicious circle of Protection has been completed in Germany, as in other Protectionist countries, by a tax laid on the food of the people. In 1879 a duty was laid on grain of about 2*s*. 6*d*. a quarter. In 1885 these duties were increased, and apparently on the average doubled,[73] so that, the clothes and tools of the people having been made dearer to them for the sake of the manufacturer, their food is now made dearer to them for the sake of the farmer and landowner. Nor is this a trifling matter. If, as is stated to be the case, Germany produces 50 millions of quarters of cereals, and imports nine millions, a tax of 5*s*. a quarter on the imported grain would impose on the people an extra charge, not of £2,250,000, which would be the actual amount of the tax on this imported grain, but of £14,750,000, by which sum the price of the whole 59,000,000 quarters consumed would be raised.

Tax on corn.

Having thus put together such of the leading features in the German trade as the statistics and reports furnish, let us see what the lesson can be drawn from them on the subject of Protection, premising that in so large, complicated, and uncertain a matter conclusions must be doubtful.

Conclusions concerning German Trade.

Under the influence of circumstances, some of which she shared with other European nations, whilst others were peculiar to herself, Germany with a Free Trade *régime* was becoming, and had indeed become, a successful manufacturing country. In a moment of commercial reaction and collapse she adopted a Protectionist policy. This policy has grown and extended its limits as it has done elsewhere – and, though less intense than in some countries, it now embraces all, or almost all, products of labour, including the food of the people. Under this policy certain industries have been exceptionally and unnaturally fostered, and this has helped to produce a glut, which makes those industries unprofitable. In other cases of the kind, as in the United States, relief by exportation is impracticable, because Protection has raised the cost of production. But Germany has met this difficulty in a very remarkable way. Whilst selling dear at home she makes it a practice to sell cheap abroad, and thus maintains her exports. We have found in her statistics of trade the feature, very uncommon in the case of a prosperous trading nation, that her imports hardly keep pace with her exports, and do not exceed them. This feature in her statistics might be explained by the fact that she was investing largely abroad, and sending goods abroad to pay for them, as we did in 1872. But it may also be explained by the fact that foreign nations are paying her little for what she sends to them, or, in other words, that the foreign trade, for which she is making such great efforts, is not profitable to her. This latter explanation seems to be the more likely, since it is consistent with the universal complaint that trade, though large, is unprofitable, and with the practice of her traders, who, as we have seen above, make their profits out of their own countrymen and sell for export at unremunerative prices. This, of course, they could not do without the help of Protective duties. If this is the true account of the maintenance of the volume of German exports during the recent period of depression, we may be annoyed that such a nation as Germany should add to the general depression by fostering unnaturally cheap exports at the expense of her own people – just as we are annoyed at her disturbing the sugar trade by her system of bounties – but we need not be alarmed. Such a course cannot last. Nor can it make Germany richer or more powerful, for purposes of competition or otherwise. And in the meantime we get cheap goods at her expense . . .

Chapter XLV: General Remarks on the Present Commercial Depression

One general
feature of the
present
depression is
over-
production
or glut.

It is quite clear that the present depression is universal, and that in Protectionist countries it is as intense, probably much more intense, than it is in our own. Nor, except perhaps in the United States, are there any signs of future recovery which do not exist in this country. It would, as I have said, be impossible and out of place here adequately to consider the various symptoms of the disease as it exists in different countries; still more to discuss the numerous remedies which have been suggested. But there are one or two observations, bearing on the subject of this book, which may be made with advantage.

There is one feature common to the disease in all places and in all countries – viz., a glut of manufactured goods; more iron, more steel, more ships, more sugar, more cotton, woollen, linen, jute, and silk fabrics than can be used or disposed of at a profit. The volume of trade has not decreased, or has decreased by very little; but prices are unremunerative and profits very low. Supply has overtaken and more than overtaken demand. From all nations comes the same story: from Free Trade nations such as England,

Belgium, and Switzerland; from semi-Protectionist nations such as France and Germany; from Protectionist nations such as Russia and the United States. In the case of corn there can scarcely be said to be a general glut, though certain markets may be overstocked for a time; and even non-European countries which formerly supplied it suffer by the development of new sources of supply. Now, there are many causes of glut and over-production over which Governments and laws have little or no control, and in which demand and supply reign supreme. But there are also causes of glut which are due to human action, and these have been largely at work in the present commercial crisis. It is precisely those things which Governments are trying to foster by Protective duties and prohibitions in which the glut is most conspicuous. Metals and metal wares, textiles, sugars, these are the things which are produced in such abundance that they find no sales or find no profitable sale; and these are the things which, if made abroad, the United States and Russia, France and Germany, Canada and the Australian Colonies (always excepting New South Wales) are excluding from their markets. At first sight this appears a paradox. Can exclusion and restriction promote extravagant production? That it causes dearness and scarcity is obvious to every one except a thorough-going Protectionist, but that it should also cause over-production and unremunerative prices is what might not at first sight seem probable. And yet this is what economists have taught, and, as the event proves, have taught truly.

The first and immediate effect of Protection in a country is to raise prices to the consumer. Whilst this lasts importation goes on; the duty actually received on imported articles goes into the public exchequer; whilst the increase of price of home-made articles goes into the pocket of the native producers. The profit thus made gives an unnatural stimulus to production. Capital is improperly and unhealthily attracted to the protected trade; and the home competition becomes at last so severe as to reduce the price of the home-trade article almost to the level of the foreign article. Protection ceases to raise the price, though it keeps out the foreign article. Then comes a plethora of home-trade goods; the trade ceases to be profitable; manufactories are shut up, and workmen are turned off, or have to take very low wages. Exportation may take place for the moment, but it cannot last or be profitable, because Protection has so raised the cost of

Effect of Protection in increasing glut.

91

manufactures as to make it impossible to compete with foreign manufacturers in neutral markets.

This is exactly what we are told has happened in the United States, in Russia, in France, in Germany, in Canada, and in other Protectionist nations. Protection has caused a glut; glut has caused reduction of profits; and loss of profits has caused reduction of work and employment. Germany and Russia, and possibly other nations, have managed to meet this glut by the original experiment of selling dear at home and cheap abroad – of giving directly or indirectly a bounty on exportation. Such a practice is suicidal; it gives unnaturally cheap goods to other nations at their expense; it must consequently injure them and it cannot last. But whilst it continues it disturbs legitimate business, and in so doing injuriously affects the trade of the world.

This causes general loss and suffering.

So long as seasons and climates vary, so long as men are subject to hopes and fears, commerce and industry will be subject to some of those ebbs and flows which cause so much uncertainty and so much human suffering. To what is inevitable we must submit. But it is sad to think that these ebbs and flows are aggravated by the folly of Governments which, by intercepting the gifts of Providence in one direction, and by applying an unnatural stimulus in another, check natural production, and stimulate unhealthy industries into unnatural activity, to be followed by equally unnatural and unnecessary prostration.

This one cause of depression is human and preventable.

So great is this mischief that if it were possible by a league amongst all nations to prevent any one of them from interfering with supply and demand, such an object might almost justify temporary Retaliation. But any such scheme is Utopian, and to attempt it by means of Retaliation would be like seeking for universal peace by general war. There is nothing for us in the meantime but to accept the cheap goods other nations insist on sending to us, and to wait till they learn that they are injuring themselves.

Attempt to imitate England by non-natural means.

It seems probable that it is the great prosperity of England in the earlier part of this century which has misled the world. England led the way in manufactures, and especially in iron and in textiles. Other nations said to themselves: England's prosperity is due to manufactures, and to manufactures of a particular kind. If we can but make the same things as she does we shall be as prosperous as she is. We will compel our people to do this, at whatever hazard to things which we can make better than England. England shall not have manufacture all to herself. And thus because England happened to have peculiar facilities for doing particular things to the great advantage of herself and of the world, other nations which have not the same facilities for doing those particular things, but greater facilities for doing other things, have set themselves to do what they ought not to do, and have not done what they ought to do. And in this they think that they are imitating England's example!

It must not be supposed that because I have thus emphasised that one cause of depression with which this book is specially concerned, I attribute the depression solely to this cause, or overlook its general character, and the numerous causes which have contributed to it.

The depression is general throughout the trading world; it is a depression of values rather than of volumes; of prices and of profits rather than of wages. Production and consumption are on the whole as large or nearly as large as they have ever been, and a much larger number of persons subsist in greater comfort than has ever been the case before. At the same time the reduction in prices and profits has at last reached wages and employment; speculation and enterprise are deadened; and it is as yet uncertain whether and how far production may be affected. To dogmatise on such points would be absurd. Nor does it seem to me possible to state positively and definitely what are the causes of the depression, and what importance is to be attached to each of them. It is obvious that they are not simple but many, and of different kinds, and that whilst some are temporary, others are of a more permanent character. Bearing this in mind, we may, perhaps, summarise the different causes which have been suggested as follows:–

General character and numerous causes of depression.

Some causes temporary, some more permanent.

Among the more temporary causes may be mentioned –

Temporary causes.

1. A reaction from the inflation of 1871 and the following years.

2. The comparative cessation of work in constructing the American and other railway systems, and the reaction from the abnormal demand for labour and materials which was created by that construction.

3. The reaction from the abnormal demand for shipping which prevailed down to 1884.

4. The collapse in the prices of coal and iron, caused by these reactions.

5. A succession of bad harvests in England and Continental Europe.

6. Changes in rapidity of communication and in the mode of doing business; by which stocks are economised, and the merchant and middleman dispensed with.

Among the more permanent causes, which seem to have made the present depression chronic, may be mentioned –

1. The natural fall in the rate of interest and profits, caused, as economists tell us, by saving and investment progressing faster than population and demand.

2. The appropriation to labour of so large a share of the proceeds of industry that the margin left for profit on capital, and for reward of skill and energy, is insufficient to encourage saving, investment, and enterprise. This must be regarded at present merely as a speculative suggestion.

3. The appreciation of gold, and the consequent fall in prices, which operates on the mind and imagination, if not on the pocket, and thus chills enterprise and speculation.

4. The competition of the agriculture of other quarters of the globe with that of Europe.

5. The natural competition of all civilized and progressive countries in manufacture.

6. The unnatural stimulus given to this competition by Protective systems and by Bounties, causing in the first instance a withdrawal of capital and labour from those objects to which they might be most profitably applied; and causing in the second instance glut, over production, and suffering to the protected interests themselves.

Of these causes most cannot be prevented or interfered with by human agency; some of them are distinctly beneficial to mankind; and some bring with them their own cure.

None of them point in the sligthest degree to the principle of freedom of exchange as a cause of depression or distress; whilst the last which I have mentioned, viz., the system of Protection and Bounties, is a violation of that principle. I have placed it among the chronic causes of depression, but trust that I may be wrong in so doing, and that Protectionist nations may recover their senses and, by recurring to a more natural system, show that this particular form of commercial disease is temporary, as well as unnecessary and self-created . . .

NOTES

1 See Hansard, vols. 68 of 1843, and 73 of 1844.
2 Hansard, 1849, vol. 106, p. 1429.
3 See Part II. of Second Report of Committee on Depression of Trade, c. 4715, i., pp. 157 to 199; also Mr. Strachey's Report on the effect of the German Tariff, c. 4530 (1885), pp. 1 to 75.
4 App. Part II. to Second Report of Committee on Depression of Trade, pp. 170, 171.
5 Ditto, p. 171.
6 Parl. Paper, c. 4530 (1885), p. 1.
7 Appendix to Part II. of Second Report on "Depression of Trade," Mr. Scott's Report, p. 194.
8 Ditto, p. 187.
9 Ditto, p. 158. See also Mr. Strachey's Report, Parl. Paper, c. 4530 (1885).
10 Strachey, c. 4530 (1885), p. 4.
11 Strachey, c. 4530, p. 8.
12 Ditto, p. 7.
13 Ditto, p. 47.
14 Scott, c. 4715, i., p. 160.
15 Ditto, p. 160.
16 Strachey, c. 4530, pp. 63–65.
17 Scott, c. 4715, i., p. 159.
18 Scott, c. 4715, i., p. 161.
19 Strachey, c. 4530, p. 16.
20 Scott, c. 4715, i., p. 161.
21 Strachey, c. 4530, p. 13.
22 Ditto, p. 23.
23 Ditto, p. 62.
24 Ditto, pp. 63–64.
25 Ditto, p. 53.
26 Ditto, p. 58.
27 Ditto, pp. 23, 24.
28 Strachey, c. 4530, p. 4.
29 Ditto, p. 21.
30 Ditto, p. 23.
31 Ditto, p. 31.
32 Strachey, c. 4530, p. 32.
33 Ditto, p. 36.
34 Ditto, pp. 40, 43.
35 Ditto, p. 48.
36 Ditto, p. 66.
37 Ditto, p. 26.
38 Strachey, c. 4530, p. 17.
39 Ditto, pp. 22–26.
40 Ditto, pp. 29, 43.
41 Ditto, p. 31.
42 Ditto, p. 33.
43 Ditto, pp. 30, 32.
44 Ditto, p. 48.
45 Ditto, p. 51.
46 Ditto, pp. 52, 53, 54,

47 Ditto, p. 54.
48 Ditto, p. 57.
49 Ditto, p. 60.
50 Ditto, p. 62.
51 Strachey, c. 4530, p. 14.
52 Ditto, pp. 21, 26.
53 Ditto, p. 32.
54 Ditto, p. 33.
55 Ditto, p. 51.
56 Ditto, p. 57.
57 Ditto, p. 63.
58 Scott, c. 4715, i., p. 159.
59 Ditto, pp. 169, 170, 171.
60 Ditto, pp. 182, 185.
61 Ditto, p. 193.
62 Scott, c. 4715, i., p. 195.
63 Ditto, p. 160.
64 Ditto, p. 170.
65 Scott, c. 4715, i., p. 159.
66 Strachey, c. 4530, p. 7.
67 Strachey, c. 4530, p. 14.
68 Ditto, p. 18.
69 Strachey, c. 4530, p. 51.
70 Ditto, p. 57.
71 Scott, c. 4715, i., p. 1.
72 Scott, c. 4715, i., p. 157.
73 Strachey, c. 4530, p. 66.

4 THE FREE-TRADE MOVEMENT AND ITS RESULTS*

G. Armitage-Smith

Chapter VII: Fifty Years of Free-Trade

The essence of the Protectionist contention is that articles excluded by tariffs will be produced *at home*, and thus home industries will be encouraged. The weakness of this contention, so far as it fails to recognize the advantage obtained from the exchange of products in foreign trading, is examined in the previous chapter. We shall deal withonly one question here. Did the protective system, during the thirty years of its application to agriculture, feed the people of this country? The labourer who exclaimed, I be protected and I be starving! summed up the results of the Corn-laws on this point. The history of the thirty years from 1815 to 1845 is a continuous record of distress; periods of scarcity and privation, fluctuating prices alternately starving labourers and ruining farmers, bread riots and disturbances, in manufactures uncertainty and loss. At length a famine in Ireland, following closely upon manufacturing depression and starvation in Great Britain, terminated the system devised to secure an abundant home-supply of food at steady and profitable prices. No principle could have received a fuller trial, and none could have failed more completely. With a population less than half the present population of Great Britain, the condition of the people was such that multitudes daily employed in the occupation of rearing cattle and growing corn, rarely tasted any meat except bacon, and many could not earn sufficient bread to maintain their own families in health and energy.

The test of a principle is in its *total effects*, not in any partial or peculiar advantage to individuals; every monopoly benefits the holder, but it does this at the expense of others; and if we inquire into the results of the Corn-laws, we find they were a cause of great misery, want, and suffering to a large proportion of the community, and of loss and injury to many others.[1] The abolition of the restrictions gave immediate relief, an era of prosperity began, and fifty years of free-trading show no such instances of suffering and distress as those which preceded it. On the contrary, the progress of the nation in comfort and material well-being has been continuous and marvellous. Fluctuations have accompanied the advance; the Crimean War, the American Civil War, and other misfortunes have imposed checks, but the outcome of the change is that Great Britain is the best-fed country on the globe, although it is the country which produces the smallest proportion of its own food. Common observation reveals the fact that the lot of

---

* G. Armitage-Smith, *The Free-trade Movement And its Results* (London: Blackie & Son, Ltd., 1898), pp. 130–53; 158–64.

the working-man has entirely changed, and that his economic condition in the present day would be an enviable one to those circumstanced as were the labouring classes of the early forties. Statistics of wages and prices show that, with easier work and shorter hours, a labourer gets now about 65 per cent, factory operatives 75 per cent, and a skilled mechanic 90 per cent more of necessaries than he did fifty years ago. Sir R. Giffen has stated that nearly the whole of the economic advantage of the last fifty years has gone to the working-classes, that is, their position has not only changed absolutely as regards the comforts of life, but relatively as regards other classes in their share of the general prosperity.[2]

This wonderful transformation is of course not to be assigned exclusively to the Free-trade movement; the marvellous progress of science, the conquest of man over the forces of nature, and their subjection to his purposes, are features of the century which need no detailed enumeration to remind us of their vast import. But the reform of 1846 and the subsequent fiscal changes were factors of the deepest importance in the scientific development and industrial progress of this country; and the Free-trade movement may be credited with rendering possible the freest application of scientific discovery and invention, so as to lead the nation to a standard of life hitherto inconceivable.

As a self-supporting country Great Britain must have continued to devote the chief part of her labour and capital to obtaining food from her soil; and we have seen what was the average of comfort when that was attempted. Her population must have remained smaller, and her resources in other industrial direcitons could not have been utilized. Under Free-trade she was enabled to give full play to her mechanical and manufacturing genius and reap the full advantage of her mineral wealth, relying upon an abundant supply of cheap food in exchange for her other products. The abolition of hindrances to trade gave to the nation fresh possibilities, and called into activity the energy and skill by which they could be realized. The scientific discoveries and wonderful inventions which have enriched Great Britain through her various industries, and have even made agriculture a mechanical industry to some extent, could never have found an opening in this country; the vast industries of coal, iron, machinery, of cotton and wool, &c., could never have been developed under a system which compelled the country to produce its own food, and excluded the agricultural products which are now purchased by means of these industries. Free-trade was therefore a necessity prior to the full and profitable expansion of those industries which have enriched Great Britain during the last fifty years. The industrial revolution, with its mechanical inventions, factory-system, and the steam-engine, began its operation more than fifty years earlier, but the masses were, notwithstanding, poor and half-starved until the advent of Free-trade.

The Free-trade movement really involved at root much more than the revoking of the Corn-laws and the reform of our fiscal system, though these were the actual matters about which it was definitely fought out and decided. It meant the adoption of the idea of enlarged opportunity for enlightened individual action, and for true freedom of contract, both as regards trade and labour, on the largest and fullest scale possible. Adam Smith had advocated natural liberty in this sense; he contended for the removal of all restrictions which operated injuriously, he urged the justice of workmen's combinations and the necessity for education as a means of conferring higher freedom and opportunity, as well as the removal of protective tariffs and bounties on food. Errors sometimes arise in regard to Free-trade among its most ardent devotees owing to a too narrow interpretation of its doctrine. Having for its aim the promotion of the wealth of nations, in principle it would apply to any measure, which, by removing obstacles to trade in any direction, makes for that end. Commercial treaties (in the absence of fuller measures) are consistent with the spirit of Free-trade, which is one of peace and good-will, displacing jealousy and warfare by means of friendly business relations. Arrangements between nations, involving give and take of many kinds, recognize mutual interests; in various ways the world is being educated to appreciate the advantages of improved intercourse and enlarged markets. International communication (through telegraph, post, travel, newspapers, and financial relations) all point to the advantages of diminished friction. It is difficult to believe that artificial obstacles to the full enjoyment of nature's products can be permanently maintained. So long as the pressure is not felt acutely the burden may be tolerated, but there are many evidences that sections of other nations smart under a consciousness of the injury inflicted upon them by tariffs on foreign merchandise.

Great Britain, with her growing population, found the pressure of tariffs upon food intolerable in a time of scarcity, and the lesson of the economic advantage of free exchange was brought home to her by the most impressive kind of teaching that could be conceived. No other country has had the principle enforced in the same manner, and those who in protective countries fully realize its worth are confronted with the difficulty of dealing with interests which would suffer loss if the tariff-fed manufactures of those countries were suddenly placed in competition with the products of other countries. But the trend of events is towards universal trading. The boundaries of race and nation are being effaced in the operations of exchange, and gradually the economic area will expand to comprise the whole productive world. Science cannot continue to bring nations nearer together, bestowing fresh gifts of wealth and power upon all, without at length the fact dawning upon them that to resist nature's generosity, by imposing artificial limits upon the acceptance of her lavish productiveness, is much the same as to refuse to enjoy the use of steam-power, or to deny themselves the fruitful discoveries of electricity.

Statistics of wealth, commerce, rates of wages, savings, consumption of food, &c., of shipping, revenue, and of the expansion of the great staple trades, give indubitable evidence of the vast advance in comfort of the nation since the abolition of the protective *régime*. In considering these figures we must remember that though young countries, like the United States and Australia, rich in natural gifts, and fed with streams of emigrants from Great Britain, have advanced rapidly during the past fifty years, their progress starts from a comparatively recent date, while that of Great Britain is the growth of a more mature and relatively populous country. To compare their progress in some respects with that of Great Britain would be to compare the growth of the child with that of the man. Taking note of like circumstances, no country has made the same relative progress as Great Britain during the past fifty years.

In 1840 the population of the United Kingdom was $26\frac{1}{2}$ millions, it is now nearly 40 millions, living at a vastly higher level of comfort. The population had grown rapidly from 1800 to 1840 under the stimulus of the new factory industries and under the influence of the Poor-laws, which practically gave a bounty on births, but the standard of living had not advanced; with the removal of restrictions of trade, improvement began, and it has proceeded at an accelerated rate. Meanwhile the nation has supplied the Colonies and the United States with some millions of its able-bodied offspring as emigrants, and has further provided hundreds of millions of capital from its savings to enable them to develop the newer regions in which they have settled. Although the population of Great Britain increased 50 per cent. (from $12\frac{1}{2}$ millions to $18\frac{3}{4}$ millions) between 1811 and 1841 the export trade made no progress: it declined from 1815 to 1836, and had barely recovered by 1844.[3] In 1845 our total foreign trade (imports and exports) only amounted to £160,000,000, or less than £5, 15*s.* per head of the population, and the exports were greater in value than the imports. The effect of the repeal of the Corn-laws was an immediate increase in our foreign trade; the exports for the twenty-five years following 1845 were nearly three times those of the preceding twenty-five years, though some of this increase much be attributed to the effects of the gold discoveries. By 1854 this commerce amounted to £268,000,000, and the imports exceeded the exports by £32,000,000. In 1896 the total foreign trade had grown to £738,00,000, being £18, 10*s.* per head of the population, and the imports were in excess of the exports by £130,000,000. This large surplus, which has been annually increasing for more than forty years, is practically all profit to Great Britain, arising from interest on foreign investments, profits on trading, earnings of British vessels, &c.

The increase in money values of our foreign trade does not fully represent, however, its real magnitude; the general fall in prices during the last quarter of a century should be taken into account, in which case the business would need to be estimated at probably some 50 per cent.

more. A better idea, perhaps, of the magnitude of our foreign trade is gained from the statement that it is more than the total foreign trade of Germany and the United States together, and that while it amounts to £18 per head of the British nation, the foreign trade of Germany is only £7 per head of its population, and that of the United States is £4, 10s. It must be remembered that in this immense trade 70 per cent. of the exports are manufactures, and an equal proportion of the imports consists of agricultural produce (food and raw materials), and that the industrial interchange has been stimulated by the removal of impediments to free exchange. Great Britain possesses about 30 per cent. of the commerce of the world in manufactures, while France and Germany jointly control about an equal amount.

Consequent upon this enormous growth of business with distant parts, and under the same stimulus of free enterprise, another vast source of wealth has grown up in our ship-building and carrying trade. Great Britain owns more than half the tonnage of the mercantile shipping on the globe, and does more than half the conveyance of goods by sea. During the last fifty years her carrying power has grown fourteen-fold, her sailing tonnage (2,189,000 tons) is only slightly greater than that of 1840, but her steam tonnage has been developed from an insignificant amount to more than 10,213,000 tons, about 55 per cent. of the steam tonnage of the world. Her ships employ a quarter of a million of seamen, ship-building has become one of her most thriving and highly-paid industries, and during the last fifteen years has annually added to her mercantile sea power some 600,000 tons. It will be seen that this great expansion has taken place *since* the repeal of the Navigation Acts in 1849, and it is under the system of free competition that the United Kingdom has become the general carrier of the world, and that her commercial navy has grown in so remarkable a degree. Meanwhile under protective tariffs the United States shipping has declined, until only 23 per cent. of her foreign trade is carried in her own vessels. Out of a total tonnage on the globe of 25,907,451 tons the United Kingdom and her Colonies possess 13,482,876 tons, the United States comes next with 2,326,838 tons, Germany has 2,029,912 tons, and France with bounties on both ship-building and freights possesses only 1,162,382 tons.

Railway development and home trade have run parallel with that of iron ship-building and foreign commerce. Railways were in their infancy when Queen Victoria ascended the throne. In 1845 only 2400 miles had been laid in the United Kingdom, fifty years later this had increased to 21,174 miles. The enormous traffic is one further proof of the prosperity of the nation; in 1896 the passengers conveyed numbered 981,603,296, the goods amounted to 356,468,009 tons. The British railways, created by voluntary enterprise, represent wealth valued at more than £1,000,000,000. No doubt the railways, roads, canals, may be said to be concerned with the internal development of the country; they have been necessitated, however, by the manufacturing expansion which received so strong an impulse from the new conditions of trade. Internal transport is a needful accessory to commercial development, with its elaborate specialization and localization of industry, and the extent of the machinery of transport is an indication of the degree to which this differentiation has been carried.

If we next glance at the textile trades (cotton, wool, flax, silk, hemp and jute), we find our factories employing more than one million operatives, and manufacturing one-fourth of the raw materials produced in the world. Thus we provide about one-fourth of the clothing of civilized races from materials which, with the exception of wool and flax, are entirely imported from other countries. In the interval since 1846 these various industires have increased not only in extent and value, but in efficiency and output per man. During the last fifty years the total value of the manufactured products of all the textile trades has grown from some £90,000,000 to about £190,000,000 per annum. Between 1854 and 1895 the import of raw wool increased from 104.9 to 771 million lbs. The cotton trade alone daily pays in wages £100,000 and turns out 14,000 miles of cotton cloth. At present we consume at home a little more than half the cotton goods manufactured and export the remainder. With some vicissitudes due to various causes, such as the American Civil War (which checked the supply of cotton), to the construction of mills in India, to the natural development of the cotton industry in other countries, and to the fluctuations arising from the dictates of fashion in dress materials, &c., this large section of our staple employments has gone on increasing its consumption and advancing in value and importance. Wages have risen, the standard of living of the artisans employed has considerably improved, and there have been no such periods of depression as that of 1842, when half the spinners of Stockport failed, and thousands of operatives were standing in the streets. The cotton famine of 1862–1863 has been the sole serious interruption, and this was due to a definite cause, beyond the reach of economic foresight.

The great expansion of the manufactures of Great Britain has been accompanied by a proportionate development of her industries in coal and iron, as in turn the prosperity of the manufactures are dependent upon these natural resources. It is by means of their joint results that payment is made for the enormous amount of foodstuffs which annually enters the kingdom. In 1840 the output of coal was about 30 million tons; in 1896 about 195 million tons were raised, this output being valued at £57,231,000. The whole mineral wealth produced was worth £76,601,000 and 838,000 men were employed in its extraction. More than 40 million tons of coal are now exported yearly. The production of iron has increased between 1835 and 1896 from $\frac{3}{4}$ million tons to $8\frac{1}{2}$ million tons. Great Britain exports annually about 4 million tons of iron and steel goods. The annual value of iron and steel manufactures is £115,000,000, and the increase in value continues in spite of the enormous reduction in cost which has been caused by recent inventions and new processes. Machinery, cutlery, tools, steel rails, engines, and apparatus of various kinds form a considerable part of our exports, as well as of the provision for the demands of home industries, and employ skilled artisans at several times the amount they could possibly earn in agriculture if Great Britain were a self-supporting country. The only extensive industry which has not advanced during the Victorian era is agriculture . . .

There are many other proofs of the national prosperity and progress during the fifty years, that can easily be made visible by the use of statistics, a few of which may be indicated. It is computed by official statisticians that the capitalized wealth of the United Kingdom has increased since 1840 from about £4,000,000,000 to £11,806,000,000; that is, from £155 to £295 per head of the population, and many facts tend to show that the wealth is widely diffused. The value of house property alone has increased nearly fourfold; and since the character of its housing is a very real test of the comfort of a people, it is of interest to observe that the proportion of houses rented at sums above £20 has increased from 7 to 20 per cent of the whole in the same period. The income-tax, reimposed by Sir Robert Peel in 1843 as a means of remitting taxes on commodities, was then assessed on property and incomes valued at £250,000,000, and each penny then yielded £800,000 of taxation. In 1895 it was assessed on £700,000,000, and each penny produced £2,200,000.

Increase of business calls for an enlargement of the special machinery for effecting exchanges and payments. The expansion of banking thus forms an excellent index of the growth of commerce; the deposits and capital of the banks of the United Kingdom have advanced between 1840 and 1895 from £132,000,000 to £1,111,000,000; that is, from £5 per head to £28 per head of the population. In the same period the accounts settled by the Bankers' Clearing House have advanced from £950,000,000 to more than £7,000,000,000. With this great development of general banking there has been a corresponding addition to Savings-bank deposits; these increased between 1841 and 1897 from £24,500,000 to £176,000,000. In 1861 Post-office Savings-banks were devised to carry thrift to the doors of all classes and there are now some eight million depositors in Savings-banks of all kinds in the United Kingdom. Meanwhile other openings for investments have been brought within the range of the working-classes, not only in building clubs, co-operative, trade, and friendly societies (the deposits in which, together with the Savings-banks deposits, amount to more than £280,000,000), but the system of joint-stock enterprise with limited liability, which has proved a most potent instrument for converting labourers into capitalists, has enabled large numbers of workmen to become owners of shares in municipal stock, gas and water companies, railway companies, and various industrial enterprises.

In the budget speech of 1897 the chancellor of the exchequer stated that during the Queen's reign the National Debt had been reduced by £175,000,000, while the revenue had risen from £52,000,000 to £112,000,000; meanwhile taxation had been so reduced and its incidence rearranged, that, while a labourer earning 13s. 2d. a week paid 43s. 3d. a year in taxes in 1841, he would now pay only 12s. 3½d. a year.

Perhaps in no way can the advance in the material condition of the masses be indicated with more assurance than by their consumption of necessaries. As the rich may be assumed to have had always a sufficiency of necessaries, a reduction in prices would affect only their consumption of luxuries, and not of necessaries; any increase in the average consumption of ordinary commodities therefore has arisen from a larger consumption by those classes who formerly had an inadequate supply; the addition, though spread over the whole population by an average, is really in the lower grade of incomes. Between 1840 and 1895 the average consumption of wheat, corn, and flour in the United Kingdom has grown from 290 to 360 lbs. per head, of meat from 75 to 110 lbs. (and meat in 1840 was to the labouring classes mainly bacon), of sugar the consumption rose from 15 to 88 lbs., of tea from 1¼ lbs to 5¾ lbs., of tobacco from .86 lbs. to 1.7 lbs. If Ireland, which only consumes 40 lbs. per head of meat, be omitted, the consumption of meat by Great Britain becomes 120 lbs. per head, which is far in excess of that of any other European country: Germany consuming 75 lbs., France 70 lbs., and Belgium 56 lbs. per head. The consumption of imported butter, bacon, cheese, and eggs has been multiplied tenfold in the fifty years. If diet, as asserted by the medical authorities, be a chief determining factor in the endurance and efficiency of labour, there can be no doubt as to the advantage possessed by British workmen of to-day over those of the protective era, and also over the labourers of most other European countries at the present time.

It was on January 1st, 1840, that the penny post was introduced, taxes on advertisements were abolished in 1853, and on newspapers in 1855, the duty on paper was removed in 1861, the Education Act for England was passed in 1870. It is difficult to realize the full benefits of these measures, all of a character removing restrictions upon knowledge and communication, and all steps in the development of individual freedom. There was no daily paper published outside London in 1841, now the daily issue of papers in the United Kingdom is about seven millions. The average number of letters per head of population in the United Kingdom was in 1839 only three, and in 1895 it had risen to fifty-three, for England alone it was eighty per person. The mass of cheap literature, which now appeals to a reading public, speaks both for education and for leisure. A free press, untaxed papers and advertisements, free education, and means of extending those opportunities for gaining knowledge, which have formed so considerable an element in the progress of the nation, have removed some of the most effectual barriers between different classes, and have tended to promote a feeling of the common claims of humanity.

Among other significant changes, which have followed upon the improvement in material condition, is the steady diminution in crime, convictions having latterly fallen to about one-third of the number in 1840, although the population has increased fifty per cent.; pauperism has also been reduced one-half. Better food, improved dwellings and sanitation, and reduction in the severity of labour under modern conditions have told favourably upon health and the duration of life; the death-rate has fallen materially, sickness is diminished, and human life has been prolonged. Very real evidences of the substantial improvement in the condition of the masses are to be found in the abbreviation of the hours of labour (for British labourers work fewer hours than those of any other country), in the increase of holidays and excursions, and the dress and manners of the people. We read, for example, in a recent Oldham newspaper: "Holiday club subscriptions for seaside, &c., amounted this year to £150,000. Nearly every factory and public-house has its club, and the average takings are £750 a year". The contrast with the descriptions of the same district in 1842 is very significant. The multiplication of free public libraries and newsrooms, of which there are now more than 200 in the country, is a further addition to the comfort and well-being of the industrial classes.

Hospitals and dispensaries for the free treatment of disease have increased, and subscriptions for their support, received from all classes, indicate not only the growth of sympathy and social sentiment, but the existence of a surplus upon which the benevolent feelings can operate. The Metropolitan Hospital Sunday Fund alone has raised for this purpose some £900,000 in twenty-five years. In Burdett's *Hospitals and Charities* for 1897 we read that the working-men of Wigan contributed £58.24 per 1000 of the population to their hospital, Wolverhampton £41.73, Birmingham and Sunderland each £30.1. These are suggestive facts indicative alike of material progress, regard for health, and the increase of that consideration and sympathy with suffering which mark an advance in refined feeling.

The amount expended by the working-classes upon athletics is a proof of a different kind, but a forcible one, that they have both energy, time, and money to spare. A starving people has neither the spirit nor the means for sport. During the first half of this century our working-classes had little to spend on amusements. The healthful pleasures of football, cricket, cycling, and boating are no monopoly of the rich in this country; and indeed the very extensive industries called into existence by cycling alone are sufficient to demonstrate that a very large proportion of the community is able to secure, not only necessaries, but some share in the luxuries of life and in its amusements. Again, theatres and concert-rooms multiply at a very rapid rate, especially those which cater for the working-classes. We learn from statistics that while, during the last fifteen years, teachers have increased 15

105

per cent., shopkeepers 27, bank-clerks 30, commercial clerks 34 per cent, the class of public entertainers has been augmented 50 per cent.

Thus in every field of observation there is most convincing evidence of the great and general advance in material prosperity, which has been made since the policy of restriction on commerce was abandoned. That the problem of poverty yet remains, and that there is a residuum of helpless, shiftless poor in our large towns, and that many classes are yet ignorant and struggling for a wretched susistence, hidden away in back streets and alleys, – these, and facts like these, only prove that there are weighty social questions still unsolved, and that moral and economic reforms have to penetrate to a much lower level. Vicious propensities and ignorance are not eradicated by fiscal legislation. Free-trade is not an idol, nor is its adoption a charm to cure social diseases; there is neither fetish-worship nor miracle-working in the recognition of a sound economic principle. The whole doctrine is summed up in the liberty and opportunity for men to employ their labour and expend their earnings to the best advantage without let or hindrance. But liberty of purchasing will not make the ignorant skilled nor the idle industrious; it will not prevent the waste which arises from drunkennness or gambling, nor save a man and his family from the consequences of vice or imprudence. These evils demand other remedies; many efforts are being made to combat them and to reduce these dark spots on the social horizon. The progress of the last fifty years lends hope that the comforts and advantages which have been extended to so large a proportion of the community will, in time, penetrate to these lower strata also; meanwhile, to no class is cheap food a greater boon than to the struggling workers on the verge of bare subsistence.

Chapter VIII: Why Free-Trade is not Adopted in Other Countries

One of the most frequent objections brought against the Free-trade policy of Great Britain is that other countries have not adopted it. It is said, "We stand alone, and it is presumptuous to think that we are wiser than all other nations", "The verdict of the world is against us". Much attention has been drawn to the sanguine but unfortunate prediction of Cobden that if England led the way other European nations, convinced by her example, would follow within five years.[5] But fifty years have now passed, and not only have the European nations failed to follow the example of Great Britain, but some have increased their tariffs, while the United States have advanced still further on the lines of Protection, and even most of our Colonies have rejected the policy of the mother-country in its favour. This constitutes apparently a weighty expression of opinion against the Free-trade doctrine, and calls for some examination.

In the first place, however, Cobden did not rest the argument for this policy upon its adoption by others. His prediction was no more than an

106

expression of his own firm conviction that the merits of a doctrine, so clearly grasped by his own mind, would be brought home with equal force to others when its actual operation in Great Britain afforded visible evidence of its advantages. But he did not make sufficient allowance for difference of circumstances or for interested opposition. Adam Smith had been more awake to these difficulties when he wrote; John Bright also had no expectation of the sudden conversion of Europe; and Peel distinctly stated that his action rested on the conviction, slowly and surely attained, of the necessity of Free-trade for Great Britain, and not upon any anticipation of its becoming the policy of other countries. Scientific doctrines are not settled by votes, and new principles have ever to fight their way to general acceptance; and when their application in practice proves adverse to the interests of particular classes there can be less hope of their speedy adoption. Moreover, as the circumstances of all countries are different, special reasons can be advanced to show why Protection has taken root so firmly in many countries. Yet it is not strictly true that Great Britain has no followers. In Europe several of the vigorous and flourishing smaller countries – Switzerland, Holland, Belgium, Denmark, and Norway – are all but Free-trading, and New South Wales has always been a staunch supporter of the policy of the mother-country.

Nor must we forget the nature of the trade of other countries. Great Britain is unable to provide herself with sufficient food; raw materials and food-stuffs together account for nearly 75 per cent. of her imports while manufactured goods are about 75 per cent. of her total exports. This is the case with no other country. It is true that France and Germany both import some corn,[6] but their chief imports, and almost the entire imports of most other protective countries, consist of manufactures, materials for manufactures, and luxuries, on which the pressure of duties is less severely felt than would be the case if they were levied upon the immediate necessaries of life. While, then, different circumstances have fostered the protective principle in Europe, the United States, and the Colonies, in all of them the facility for collecting revenue by the customary method of duties on imports gave it an easy footing; and in all it has been maintained by the sentiment of supporting home industry, and the fallacy that more employment is found for labour in the country by excluding foreign competition.

The circumstances that have favoured the growth of Protection in the United States are its vast extent and large resources, great variety of climate, fertile soil and abundance of minerals. While rightly endowed by nature with a multiplicity of products, it has been supplied by Europe with vigorous labourers, and with abundant capital. Each such adult immigrant to the States from Great Britain, endowed with average strength and skill, has been estimated as equivalent to a gift of £200 in his personal capital. A unique concurrence of favouring conditions in the United States has made for wealth, in spite of the impediments raised by legislation, and has enabled the nation to maintain a high standard of living, and to bear its burden of taxation. It must further be remembered that the states comprising the Union, trade freely with one another, and this freedom extends over 51 states and territories differing so widely as New York and Texas, Florida, and California. The United States covers an area of 3,500,000 square miles, and includes almost every variety of climate and every kind of product. Were it severed from the rest of the world, its people might live in comparative affluence, and miss very few of the comforts and luxuries found elsewhere. It is not remarkable that they should be able to uphold a system of Protection in these circumstances. In no sense, however, can that system be said to be the product of healthy conditions. In its origin it was a reaction against the oppressive "colonial policy" and "sole-market theory" of Great Britain, which helped to provoke the War of Independence; partly in retaliation and partly for revenue purposes the American colonists began to tax our exports. In 1789 President Hamilton advanced the plausible principle that "infant industries" should be protected as a temporary expedient in order to enable them to become firmly established, and that when they no longer required this safeguard, the duty would be abolished. With this object duties of $8\frac{1}{2}$ per cent. were adopted for seven years. The war between Great Britain and France led to complications with the United States, which then increased its tariff as an act of hostility. Reduced in 1815, it was again raised in 1816, and from that time its fluctuations have been frequent. Between 1847 and 1860 reduced tariffs were followed by a period of great prosperity. Then came the Civil War, and the need for revenue led to greatly increased import-duties, which rose to 47 per cent. Some relaxation followed the war, but from that time the tariff has been the sport of financiers and political parties. With every increase of duty fresh vested interests have been created, and tariff-fed industries call for yet further aid. What has happened to the "infant industries" of a hundred years ago? Without the help of duties, ranging from 40 to 100 per cent they are still unable to compete with Great Britain, and the tariff is perpetually under manipulation. A "national policy" was advanced by Mr. M'Kinley in 1890, by which duties were still further augmented; the avowed aim of this policy was "to encourage home industries", "to keep money in the country", and "to exclude goods made by *pauper labour*". With all its natural gifts and extensive territory, the United States has, in consequence of its inflated prices, become a most expensive country to live in; yet American workmen apparently fail to see that high prices do not necessarily mean high real-wages. The bounty of nature is counteracted by measures which end in the creation of monopolies and millionaires, while labour troubles are frequent, and the contrasts of wealth and poverty, sufficiently glaring in Old-world cities, are enormously magnified in the New.

Tariffs have become recognized instruments for creating vested interests, politics are rendered corrupt, and the newspapers complain that politicians combine in log-rolling and in reciprocal voting with the object of securing an increased share in the plunder of the community. If the principle of stimulating infant industries into striving and energetic adult industries ever had an opportunity for fair trial it has surely been in the United States, with all its magnificent natural resources; and yet the duties, adopted for a brief seven years a century ago, are still in existence, while the rate is enormously increased and the period of operation is unlimited.

It might be expected that the cotton manufacture would become a successful industry where the raw material is a natural product and so many other causes are favourable, yet the whole export of manufactured cotton by the United States is less than £3,000,000 while that of Great Britain, which fetches the raw material 3000 miles, is £60,000,000. In the States the cotton manufacture has been a protected industry since 1816, when a duty of 25 per cent. was imposed; yet, after eighty years of fostering, this industry is protected by a tariff ranging from 30 to 60 per cent. *ad valorem*. The iron industry is an even more telling example against "the infant industry theory". It was protected in its early development by a duty fixed at 20 per cent. in 1816; yet, in order to avoid the competition of English iron goods, the duty has been augmented by the Dingley tariff to 60 per cent. *ad valorem*, under the plea of the "national policy", which is adopted now that the "infant industry" theory is no longer tenable. If the iron industry can compete successfully with British goods, legislation imposing a duty of 60 per cent. to exclude the latter is surely superfluous.

The effect of the tariff of 1890 upon woollen goods was to render them nearly three times the price of the same article in Great Britain. Mr. M'Kinley sustained his protective doctrine with the remarkable dictum that "cheap goods were a badge of poverty", and he found a strong supporter in Mr. Jay Gould, the millionaire, who supplied the additional argument that "high prices would teach working men thrift". Nor is the doctrine entirely extinct in the United States, that commerce between nations is war. Only a few years ago Senator Evarts declared in the United States that "trade between nations stands for war in a sense never to be overlooked and never to be misunderstood". President M'Kinley's message on the occasion of his accession to office takes somewhat different ground, and seeks to combine the conflicting aims of securing high prices, increasing employment by high tariffs, and "checking deficiencies in revenue by protective legislation which is always the firmest prop of the Treasury"; and yet these ends are to be secured "by extending the reciprocity law of 1890 under which a stimulus was given to our foreign trade". This combination of aims will no doubt recommend the policy to different groups of Protectionists, but it displays an amount of confusion and contradiction which is almost hopelessly bewildering.

The tariff will no doubt succeed in creating high prices by the exclusion of foreign manufctures, but it strikes a blow at American farming so far as the latter depends upon foreign consumption for markets. In 1895, out of a total of £158,000,000 of exports from the United States, agricultural produce amounted to £110,000,000. If the United States renders payment for its exports difficult or impossible in foreign goods, the British corn-importing trade will naturally move towards freer markets. Argentina affords just such a market, and she is becoming a rival to the United States for British manufactures. No measure could be more favourable to the extension of commercial relations with our Colonies also than that the United States, by pursuing a policy of isolation, should make it less easy to dispose of her wheat in Great Britain; and if at such a stage, the Colonies, following the example of Canada, reduce their tariffs to the mother-country, her trade will naturally flow to their shores, while the tide of emigration, both of labour and capital, will tend to set strongly in the same direction.

The duties on linen and sewing-thread supply another illustration of the waste and expense caused by the protective system in America. A duty of 35 per cent. on linen has long existed, but the new tariff raises this duty by various additions ranging from 50 to more than 100 per cent. The duty on sewing-thread is also increased from 40 to 67 per cent. On the linen duties the *New York Journal of Commerce* thus comments:– "There is practically no linen industry in this country, and there probably never will be. The conditions of our climate do not favour the growing of flax, even in parts of the country which seem best suited for it; and the industrial habits of our people do not favour the attention to the mass of tedious and toilsome details that go to the preparation of this fibre for the loom." The loss incurred by forcing an industry in such circumstances is obvious.

The moral of the tariff system in the United States is, that the benefit to be derived from imposing a temporary protective duty is a delusion, – the weakly infants do not grow up to independence, but are always requiring additional nourishment. As in opium-taking, the doses have to be increased to maintain the unhealthy system. The tendency of the new tariff is towards prohibition, but the President's message also contemplated an extension of markets for American produce, although the fundamental fact in trading is that a nation cannot sell without buying. It is of the manufactures of Great Britain that the United States is most jealous. The tariff is not levied so much against the labour of inferior races as against the highly-productive labour of Great Britain. Through blindness to the fact that the object of trading, as of all work, is to satisfy wants, the tariffs of the United States are being pushed more and more towards a point where much of the labour of the country will be employed at an economic loss. Waste cannot increase wealth, and misdirection is a species of waste, since it causes capital and labour to be employed with a loss of efficiency.

New and unexpected difficulties are arising out of tariffs in America; both South and West are calling for Protection to *their* infant industries against the East. So long as they were agricultural and mining only, they adhered to the "national policy"; but some of the San Francisco papers now urge that the plea for protection against foreign products holds good equally against those from other parts of their own country. Consumers in California are advised to give the preference to the products of their own States, and to reject those of the Eastern States. Thus the fallacious principles so long upheld in international relations are beginning to be applied at home between state and state. This is consistent but serious, and should it be maintained it promises to put an end either to protection against foreign countries, or to the free-trading between the States. The latter alternative would raise very weighty problems. The latest alterations in the United States tariff endeavour to give some of the privileges of monopoly to the wool-growers of the West; but no protective duty can help the grain and meat farmers, who are taxed heavily on every article of their consumption. So also a duty has been demanded on imported long-staple cotton by the cotton-growers of the South, and both West and South are urged to fight for protection for their young manufacturing industries. The Western farmer has hitherto been too weak to resist Protection, which has always told against him. Will the Western manufacturer be sufficiently strong to carry it to its logical conclusion of protecting every state and district from every other, and if so, how will it affect the Federation?

In the Australian self-governing Colonies Protection grew out of the system under which duties were levied upon imported goods for revenue purposes. These duties were, after a time, extended to foster infant industries, on the representation that *temporary* and *moderate* duties would soon accomplish the firm establishment of manufactures, and give a desirable diversity of employment. The duties have more recently been advocated as a means of producing higher wages. The Colony of Victoria has taken the lead in the protective movement. It deliberately adopted Protection in 1865, and duties of 10 per cent. were then levied upon clothing, furniture, boots, and woollen goods. As in other cases, the duties, once commenced, were afterwards increased to sustain the vested interests created, and the period of operation was extended. But after thirty years of Protection, Victorian industries, with duties of 30 per cent, are as far from independence as at the beginning.

J.S. Mill's unfortunate, though somewhat guarded, admission, that temporary Protection might be adopted in a young colony to start new industries, is often quoted in justification of such attempts. Mill, however, contemplated only a very brief period of support to enable an industry, in the success of which there were strong grounds for belief, to be started on a scale sufficiently great to overcome initial difficulties, and to prevent it from being crushed at the outset by the rivalry of old-established competitors. This policy might be theoretically sound, on the assumption that governments are omniscient, and can foresee what industries will soon be thus established so as to stand alone. In practice, however, this state of things is not realized. Governments are not endowed with this prescience, nor are political parties proof against the representations and demands of their supporters. The experience of a century of the "young industry" policy in the United States, and of more than thirty years in Australia, bears out what might have been anticipated – that such aid cannot be restricted to industries sure to succeed, and proves that the academic exception to free-trading had no practical application. Cobden in this matter showed more insight into the facts of politics than the philosopher. Sir Louis Mallet reports a conversation with him only a few days before his death, in which Cobden said with peculiar earnestness: "I believe that the harm which Mill has done to the world by the passage in his book on *Political Economy* in which he favours the principle of Protection in young communities has outweighed all the good which may have been caused by his other writings".[7] Without endorsing this remark as regards the impossible estimate of the value of Mill's writings, it must be admitted that the theoretical conditions contemplated in Mill's defence of Protection for young colonies do not seem really to exist; since in practice it is impossible either to predict what industries will become self-supporting, or to resist the claims which are made for the application of the principle of temporary succour to other fresh industries, or the plaintive appeal for further aid to save from ruin those already established by the aid of tariffs . . .

In all times there have been natural movements and changes in industry, although the forces which created them operated slowly in more primitive conditions. The family system of spinning and weaving in homes gave place to more complex production in factories. Village manufactures ceased and passed to towns; thus agricultural labourers lost their various other employments which had been subsidiary, but had now become specialized. Industries have frequently changed their localities. Norwich, Suffolk, and the valleys of Somerset and Gloucester have ceased to be the great centres of the woollen industry, which moved to the coal-fields of the North with the invention of machinery and the steam-engine. Similarly the iron industry left the forests of Sussex for the coal-fields of Yorkshire, Lanark, and other counties. Coventry, once the leading centre of the silk industry, turned to watch-making; and when the American machine-made watch destroyed the trade, with ready adaptation it took up the bicycle industry, and is now much more prosperous than at any previous period. Under a protective system the silk industry might have remained its staple trade, and we might still be having distress among protected weavers instead of a prosperous and increasing population of mechanics. Paper-making and printing have found suitable settlements at certain rural towns in Buckinghamshire and Kent, within easy distance of the metropolis. Great Britain about 1770 was exporting corn to the Colonies and to Russia; a century later she is dependent upon them for part of her own supply; in the interval their agriculture and her manufactures have been developed. India has long

112

been one of the most considerable markets for Lancashire cotton goods. She is now setting up cotton mills, and is creating a demand for English machinery and the products of Yorkshire ironworks . . .

These examples are sufficient to show that it is a natural law that industries tend to move to, and flourish in, the localities best adapted to their requirements; and that owing to discoveries, the spread of science, and the rise of new conditions, this locus is not permanent, but is ever changing to take advantage of more favourable circumstances. By artificial obstructions, such as protective tariffs, we may attempt to direct and retain industries, but only at a considerable loss, and waste of natural productiveness. Progress is a product of the combination of the two universal laws of unity and variety – of persistence and change. Free commerce avails itself of both; restraints on commerce tend to destroy some of the advantages to be derived from change, and so far retard national progress.

Although, for reasons adduced, Free-trade has not been adopted by other countries or by most of the Colonies, yet there is strong indirect evidence for the soundness of the principle of commercial freedom in the *internal* fiscal arrangements of large states and federations of states. In all cases of the extension of the boundaries of a country, or the inclusion of a new member, fiscal federation is adopted. The United States place no restrictions on the trade between the several states, and every new territory admitted to the Union is placed on the same footing; the same principle is adopted in the Dominion of Canada, and in Russia and Germany. But if Protection has any economic advantage, its virtue would not cease with the political inclusion of a territory in a country; the local industries should require the same defence as formerly. It is found, however, that the larger the country the greater is the gain from the removal of these restraints. The reason is plain, the field of commercial intercourse is greater, and there is a nearer approximation to complete free-trading. If a country is of vast extent and its climate and products very varied, and if it possesses minerals as well as abundance of land, such a country is most favourably situated for industrial independence, for it has within itself resources of all kinds, and it will suffer less than others from attempts at being self-sufficing. On the other hand, the smaller the country and the more specialized its products, the greater is the advantage which it gains from contact with others. Relations of mutual interchange with countries differing economically from themselves become essential to small and populous countries, and such in an eminent degree is the case of Great Britain.

Under a natural system of trade, industries adapt themselves to wants; under Protection they are apt to be either abnormally stimulated and to over-produce, as is the case with the sugar industry in France; or the privilege tends to develop them into strong monopolies, often sufficiently powerful to completely control an industry. In all protective countries the interests of some classes thus become an obstacle to the adoption of

113

Free-trade, a difficulty seen very clearly by Adam Smith. In free-trading Great Britain few syndicates have succeeded in maintaining high prices,[8] foreign competition, sooner or later, comes in and defeats attempts at artificial monopoly rates. The United States, the country in which Protection has had its strongest hold, have become the home of trusts and corners. There are some twenty of such gigantic trusts, many of them erected upon the exclusion of foreign competition, which control the most extensive industries and fix prices at monopoly rates. The sugar trust has already been mentioned; a glass trust flourishes under the shelter of a duty of 120 per cent. on foreign window-glass, while another trust in mother-of-pearl buttons is protected by 1400 per cent tariff against foreign competition. The iron, copper, nickel, and tin industries are all monopolies in the United States, and have become mines of wealth to their proprietors. The latest of these is the tin monopoly, which was created by the M'Kinley tariff, not only to the great injury of the British tin industry, but also of some other America trades. Minerals could be worked at a reasonable profit in the States, but the effect of the monopoly created by a tariff is, that under the plea of developing the home industry and national resources, syndicates are formed which secure duties almost prohibitive, and enable the owners to obtain exorbitant prices and profits.

A further serious evil attaches to the tariff system as regards the internal trade of a country. Tariffs are at best a clumsy machinery for regulating trade, but their frequent alterations make them most potent instruments for disturbing trade and creating depressions and crises. It is now understood in the industrial and commercial world that steadiness is a desideratum of healthy business, and that violent fluctuations, however created, lead only to uncertainty and injury in the long run. The latest tariff bill in America illustrates the action of such interference with trade. From the time it was proposed it created disturbance and dislocation; speculations based on its probable results disordered the markets, some imports were vastly increased in anticipation of its prohibitive effects, while other industries held back to await its promulgation. The bill was frequently altered to meet the demands of the representatives of different trades.[9] During the whole period it was under consideration the utmost uncertainty prevailed, business hesitated, industry languished, and trade was stagnant. Many interests were involved, and none could forecast the issue. And this gratuitous injury to trade is a consequence of a system which professedly organizes trade for the benefit of the community.

While, then, various reasons can be adduced for the maintenance of the protective system in other countries, it is plain that the strongest impediment to its abolition is self-interest – a principle which finds abundant illustration everywhere, but which, in the case of protected industries, is enlisted very widely in a cause economically injurious to the community as a whole. By a mistaken policy many industries have been started in those

114

countries, which can only flourish through the exclusion of competition afforded by the tariffs; those interested fight therefore for the maintenance of the tariffs, and their influence is great in the Legislature. The principle, being admitted, gains wider application, monopolies are built upon it, and interests are created embracing powerful secions of the community, hence its abolition is difficult; strong defences are sought and plausible arguments created on its behalf. In Great Britain the repeal of the Corn-laws was opposed by only one large interest, and its resistance was weakened by the allies of famine and misery which came at a critical moment to join its opponents. It was a question of food and sustenance in Great Britain which drove home the economic argument; the like conditions do not exist in any other country . . .

NOTES

1   Various causes of distress operated during the first forty years of the century – bad harvests, the war, with its burden of taxation and debt, the Poor-law, which, until 1834, fostered an idle and inefficient population – the rapid changes in manufactures also dislocated industry. The Protective system accentuated all the evils arising from these various causes, created scarcity of food, and prevented the means of profitable employment.
2   "Hence, while capital has increased, the income from capital has not increased in proportion. The increase of earnings goes exclusively, or almost exclusively, to the 'working-classes' " . . . "What has happened to the working-classes in the last fifty years is not so much what may be called an improvement as a revolution of the most remarkable description." – ("On the Progress of the Working Classes" – *Financial Essays*, vol. ii.) See also *Labour in the Longest Reign*, pp. 9–16, by Sidney Webb, for similar testimony as regards men in organized trades.
3   See Porter's *Progress of the Nation*, pp. 361–362.

DECLARED VALUE OF EXPORTS OF THE UNITED KINGDOM

1815, ...	£51,632,971
1821, ...	38,870,851
1831, ...	47,020,658
1844, ...	58,584,292

4   Statistics from *Lloyd's Register of British and Foreign Shipping*, 1897–8, quoted in *Whitaker*, p. 728.
5   Speech in the House of Commons, Jan. 15th, 1846: "I believe that if you abolish the Corn-laws honestly, and adopt Free-trade in its simplicity, there will not be a tariff in Europe that will not be changed in less than five years to follow your example."
6   France imported 99 million bushels of grain in 1894, 43 millions in 1895, and 35 millions in 1896.

7   Quoted in a letter of Sir Louis Mallet, given in the Appendix to Mr. Gowing's admirable *Life of Richard Cobden* (Cassell & Co.).

8   This is true at all events of necessaries and articles of general consumption; no doubt the prices of some articles (diamonds, iodine, quicksilver, &c.) with a very limited supply are controlled by monopolies.

9   An interesting side-light is thrown upon the working of the protective system by the indignation and protests against the Dingley Tariff in the United States coming from Americans visiting Europe. This latest fiscal device has not only intensified the ordinary effects of Protection, but represents the American Government as agent of a "New York Tradesmen's League", composed mainly of tailors and milliners. The Act prohibits Americans from bringing home more than $100 worth of personal effects, all excess being charged at about 60 per cent. duty. The measure inflicts annoyance and inconvenience upon some 60,000 or 70,000 American citizens who visit Europe in the year, and is calculated to yield some £50,000 excess duty, while it entails increased expense in customs-officials, and has created a system of spies on board ship and detectives in the Custom-house in the interest of the so-called "Merchants' Board of Trade". – See *The Times*, 19th October, 1897.

B

TARIFF REFORM AND THE EMPIRE

5 THE IMPERIALISM OF BRITISH TRADE*

Ritortus

I The Rise and Decline of British Industrial Supremacy

On the whole it must be upheld, as the characteristic of the entire period of the growth of England's commercial greatness since the time of Elizabeth, that it was the English trader who was the standard bearer of the expansive power of England. It was he who, according to Hume, "tried his fortune in towns and states abroad with cloth and manufactures," and not with the aid of powder and shot and Colonial Ministers. We have also Mill's support in this view: "Industry rather than war," he wrote, "was the natural source of power and importance to Great Britain." No claims were pegged out then for posterity; trade was not expected to follow the flag but the flag followed trade.

It is the glory of the English race that the pluck of the individual laid the foundations of the Empire. It is a spurious, effeminate, and utterly un-English doctrine, clashing with the teachings of three centuries, which would now insist that our flag, borne by some Colonial Minister, went first and that the English trader meekly followed. Such a doctrine may be good enough for Continental nations, but must be rejected by any Englishman worthy of the name. We ought never to forget this truth, and we ought never to allow our modern supine *café chantant* Jingoes to osbcure this vital fact in our history.

In one respect, however, the British Government was manly enough to stand by the British manufacturer and trader during that period. It gave him the necessary protection when alone he was unable to fight those elementary powers which determine international values. Against the previously acquired superiority of Continental manufactures which were earlier in the field than he, he was protected by the prohibition of their importation. Thus he was enabled to carry on his industrial struggle and to overcome, to

* "Ritortus", 'The Imperialism of British Trade', *Contemporary Review*, 76 (July–December 1899), pp. 132; 137–52; 282–303.

the advantage and glory of England, the odds that were against him. Against the superiority of the Dutch in the carrying trade at that period, due to the lower rate of profits in Holland, as Mill pointed out, England enacted her navigation laws. She thereby caused men and capital to rush into this industry and tore the monopoly of the carrying trade from the Dutch. When England conquered India she secured the then rising manufactures of Manchester against a deadly rivalry by excluding Indian cottons from English markets. In fact, though the laws of international exchange had in those days not yet been recovered, England often acted unconsciously on them from that common sense which is the inheritance and just pride of the Britisher.

By acting thus England vigorously upheld the interests of her producing classes, instead of sacrificing them to false theories and sentiment as she has done during the last fifty years.

At the time when England – on the foundations thus laid and secured – was approaching the perfection of her commercial and industrial development, the principles of our national science of economics and the theory of foreign trade were discovered and set forth by thinkers such as Ricardo, Torrens, and others. We were taught how, by means of foreign trade and by the superiority of our manufactures, we could purchase goods from abroad with less labour and with greater advantage than if we had to produce them ourselves. We were shown that according to general principles the advantages of foreign trade were best secured by perfect and reciprocal Free Trade, and that, under the law of Free Trade, profits would rise and capital accumulate quickest. Nothing can be more true, more logical, than the principles of foreign trade bequeathed to us by the great economic writers.

But it must not be forgotten that this theory of foreign trade was based on the unconditional assumption of the existence and continuance of that mutual course of trade in which foreign commodities were purchased with home commodities, and in which the equilibrium of trade was undisturbed by payments not originating in commerce. This disturbance was a new development which grew out of our commercial manufacturing supremacy, and was to lead us to a new supremacy. The former was bound to give way to the latter. The moving force in this new phase is no longer the superior efficiency of our labour, but the superiority of our capital, the fruit of the labour and industry of former generations. Theretofore we had, as we have seen, acquired only a species of property and a "vested interest" in the industrial products of all the regions of the earth; henceforward our capital went forth to acquire for us a real property in the soils and industrial undertakings themselves of those regions. Our capital served us, as Lord Castlereagh said, in the stead of cannon and guns to conqueur the world.

But no one seems to have understood the economic nature of this new development and its effect on foreign trade. Though the investments of capital abroad created payments outside of regular trade transactions and

118

interfered with them to the point of almost putting an end to them, the fundamental difference between true commerce – that is, between exchange of commodities on the one side, and payments without any return and not originating in commerce on the other side – is not grasped. On the contrary, our Ministers and economists of to-day continue to talk of trade and interests of trade when they mean nothing but concessions, investments, and interests of capital, and constantly mistake the concession-hunter, especially when backed by banks and syndicates, for the trader. But for this short-sightedness many of the evil effects of this change which overtook trade might have been averted while its beneficial effects were fostered. A wiser policy, adapting the true laws of international exchange to the new condition of things, might have turned our capitalistic conquest of the world to its full advantage.

The decline of England's mere industrial supremacy was long since foreseen, as a remote contingency, by our great economists. General economic principles pointed to it. Malthus taught us a century ago that it was unreasonable to expect that any one country, merely by the force of skill and capital, should remain in possession of markets, uninterrupted by foreign competition. It is, according to him, an accidental and temporary and not a natural and permanent division of labour which constitutes one State the manufacturer and carrier of others.

In one place Malthus seems to point directly to the case of England:

"If a country," he says, "owing to temporary advantages of this kind, should have its commerce and manufactures so greatly preponderate as to make it necessary to support a large portion of its people on foreign corn, it is certain that the progressive improvement of foreign countries in manufactures and commerce might, after a time, subject us to a period of poverty and of retrograde movements in property and population.

"As long as agricultural nations continue to apply their increasing capital principally to the land, this increase of capital will be of the greatest possible advantage to the manufacturing and commercial nation. It is indeed the main cause and great regulator of its progress in wealth and population.

"But if in the natural progress of these agricultural nations they turn their attention to manufactures and commerce, their further increase of capital and skill will be the signal of decay and destruction to the manufactures and commerce of that commercial nation which they have before supported."

In the following passage Malthus warns us that it is from America this danger may come.

119

"According to general principles," he says, "it will finally answer to most landed nations both to manufacture for themselves, and to conduct their own commerce. That raw cotton should be shipped in America, carried some thousands of miles to another country, there to be manufactured and shipped again for the American market, is a state of things that cannot be permanent. A purely commercial State must always be undersold and driven out of the market by those who possess the advantage of land."

We were, therefore, well forewarned. On general principles, a rising competition was to be expected. It soon sprang up, and we ought to have been well on our guard.

With the restoration of peace after the Napoleonic wars the industry of the Continent revived. Torrens [see (vol. I: 15)] bears testimony to the fact that the difference between the efficacy of British and of foreign labour became less and less; that the goods produced in England by a single pair of hands no longer exchanged for the goods produced in other countries by ten or twenty pair of hands; and that as the produce of British industry exchanged for the produce of a less quantity of foreign productions, including the precious metals, prices and profits and wages of necessity declined. The industrial processes heretofore the monopoly of England were to an ever-increasing extent transferred into other countries, and our customers became our rivals.

This development was accelerated by ill-judged legislation and by that short-sighted commercial policy to which, I regret to say, we still adhere. Instead of seeking the benefits of free international exchange through true and universal freedom of trade, with due appreciation of the change in trade referred to above, and thereby trying to ensure, if not a further development, at least the maintenance of that industrial superiority which we held, we alone abandoned Protection and gave gratuitous concessions to industries abroad without having first secured reciprocal Free Trade. We admitted duty free the agricultural produce and manufactures of the whole world, which we had helped to develop by our capital, while the world, for the most part, refused to admit our home manufactures.

Foremost amongst those who waged a tariff war against us was the United States of America, the nation which was the richest in land, and therefore the most dangerous competitor. It was fundamentally wrong to have ever based any hopes on the possibility that America would always take our manufactures in exchange for her corn.

Torrens gives a careful survey of the actual state of our commercial relations with the United States in his time, and condemns the policy of one-sided Free Trade which we then adopted. It will be interesting to read, in the light of the present day, his comparative estimate of the industrial position of the two countries made fifty years ago:

"The difference between the rates of profits and of wages in England and the United States is a practical solution of the question which we proposed for consideration – namely, Whether the financial policy adhered to by the United States, or the opposite policy adopted by England, is most in accordance with the true teaching of economical sicence. Under the financial policy adopted by the United States, the producing classes obtain a greater proportion of the benefits resulting from foreigntrade than that which is due to the efficacy of their industry.

"Under the opposite policy adopted by England the producing classes obtain a less proportion of the advantages resulting from foreign trade than that which is due to the efficacy of their industry.

"In the United States the rewards of industry are more than commensurate with its efficacy; the attraction of higher profits and higher wages turns upon their shores, from all the other quarters of the globe, a never-ebbing tide of capital and labour; their progress is the most rapid that the world ever saw.

"The United Kingdom presents a different picture. Here the rewards of industry are not commensurate with its efficacy. The tide of capital and labour recedes from the British shores."

This is the way one of the greatest English economists and expounders of Free Trade looked upon the development of the mutual relations between England and America a few years after the adoption of one-sided Free Trade by the former. America, backed by her tremendous resources in land and encouraged by the Free Trade policy of England, had even then entered upon a serious industrial struggle with us. Torrens saw that the future boded ill to England. That which Torrens overlooked, and that which was always overlooked by the writers of his time, was the all-important fact that the capital which in a never-ebbing tide was turned upon American shores, and which receded from British shores, remained British after all and secured to the British capitalist the higher profits in America.

The dangers to the English manufacturer foreboded by Torrens have, however, become real. It is true there were fools who raised the cry of "Made in Germany," but very justly did the *Times* remark some time ago, in a very interesting article on "American Foreign Trade," that throughout the controversy over the "Made in Germany bogey" the more level-headed experts in this country never doubted that we had in America a far more powerful commercial rival than we had in Germany, and that these experts were already being justified by the event. The shipments of manufactures from the United States have indeed increased at a phenomenal rate, and will in the last fiscal year, for the first time in the commercial history of the United States, be of greater value than the imports of manufactured goods.

Cobden's fears[1] are at last realised, and for once a prediction of his has been fulfilled: it is now the sentiment of the people of England generally, and perhaps also the inward conviction of our Government – notwithstanding its touting of the American alliance – that our chief and most dangerous rival in manufactures is the United States. A remarkable article – "The Menace to England's Commercial Supremacy" – appeared in the April number of the American *Forum*. The writer asserts that the decay of English manufactures is as inevitable as that of English agriculture. His reason for this assertion is that English capital has helped to develop the industries of the world, and that the very position of England as a great creditor nation will largely contribute to the undoing of her own industries. "It is indisputable," the writer adds, "that the British have reason to regard with apprehension, if not with a stronger sentiment, the outcome of their efforts to obtain profit at our expense."

This foreigner seems to me to gauge the situation justly. It is high time we should do the same and face it.

II The New Departure

The rising rivalry of our competitors in manufactures, together with our one-sided Free Trade policy, would not only have prevented us from progressing any further in manufactures and wealth, but would surely have landed us in a most undesirable position, if the expanding and conquering power of our capital had not come to our rescue. We ought never to lose sight of this momentous fact. We must try to understand its full bearing. It was the decisive turning-point in the economic development of the country. On the true estimate of its importance, therefore, will depend the right appreciation of our interests and likewise the aim of our future policy.

Our tremendous industrial fabric could not be shaken to its foundation all at once. We may still for a long time to come hold our own fairly well against all competitors, but we have lost the monopoly of manufacturing. Our chief power no longer consists in the supremacy of our industry. It is shifting gradually, and leaning more and more on capital . . .

England could not remain the workshop of the world; she is fast becoming its creditor, its mortgagee, its landlord. The Limited Liability Companies Act of 1862 is more or less the starting-point of this our latest development. It gave our capital the great power of combining and the courage for starting on its conquering career abroad.

It is true that our capital had emigrated before 1862, but the amount which had left England previous to that date was comparatively small. The effect of its emigration on the trade and industry of England passed more or less unnoticed. It was only since the beginning of the sixties that this movement increased to a degree unknown before, and that its effect began to be strongly felt. An article in the *Edinburgh Review* in 1865, entitled "Seven per Cent.," bears witness to the radical change then taking place. The article is quoted by Mill in his "Principles," and by its masterly style and treatment of the question undoubtedly betrays Mill as its author. It takes up the subject of the almost unprecedented rise in the money rate which had taken place since 1864, and frightened the business world. It ascribes this rise to the comparatively vast and sudden expansion of the joint stock system, to the new Limited Liability Companies Act, and to the growing availability and diffusion of English capital for foreign purposes.

The article, it must be observed, does not consider these causes to be only temporary, but looks on them as "fundamental and permanent changes in the relation of the aggregate of English capital and foreign demand." The writer, therefore, justly recognises in the supply of this foreign demand a distinctly new departure from the old ways of international exchange and foreign trade. He remarks that at first the new companies mainly supplied English industry and benefited our manufacturing districts and our producing classes. Soon, however, the companies found the rates of money higher abroad than at home, and lent their capital to foreigners for the benefit of their shareholders. Nevertheless, the writer is disposed to believe that although England has suffered under this new competition for loanable capital, yet no country will in the end reap greater advantages from it than England herself, who of all countries has the greatest capital at her command.

Such a judgment expressed so many years ago shows the extraordinary perspicacity of the author. Even then he had fully grasped the new condition of things which was to carry England over the dead point to which her industrial power alone would have brought her. Our tremendous capital garnered in the days of our industrial superiority could not possibly have found occupation at home without lowering the rates of profit. For that reason we should soon have dropped to that stationary state into which nations fall when profits decrease and accumulation of capital stops, while foreign competition with our manufactures would have crippled us. Malthus, therefore, declared it indispensable for England to find for her increasing capital "a larger arena abroad."

Ricardo, in his famous "Essay on the Profits of Stock,"[2] expresses himself in a similar way. In a letter addressed to Malthus on this same subject, he writes: "Accumulation of capital has a tendency to lower profits. If with every accumulation of capital we could tack a piece of fresh fertile land to our island, profits would never fall." That is just what our capital has done for us. It has been adding one piece of land after the other to our islands, until our capitalists may triumphantly say, "The world, the world is ours."

Mill believed the perpetual overflow of British capital "into colonies or foreign countries" to have been for many years the principal means by which the decline of profits in England had been arrested. He himself counselled the sending of English capital abroad, in order to produce food for the increasing population of England, the ordinary operations of international exchange, and the capital of the nations from which we buy it, not being sufficient to procure it. In one of his most interesting chapters Mill wrote as follows:

"The expansion of capital would soon reach its outward boundary, if the boundary itself did not continually open and leave more space.

"The mere continuance of the present annual increase of capital, if no circumstance occurred to counteract its effect, would suffice in a small number of years to reduce the rate of net profit to one per cent."

Happily for us all, we cannot in our times arrest the free flow of capital from one country to another. By the elementary laws of nature it will go from countries where profits are decreasing, into countries where they are larger, as surely as water flows from the mountains to the ocean. The superabundant capital of Great Britain, therefore, finding no longer profitable employment in the agriculture, manufactures, and trade of her own territory, began, by necessity, to overflow her boundaries, to take possession – first of the carrying trade on the seas, and then of the soils, the industries, and the commerce of the countries beyond the seas. It laid its hands on everything it could develop and make profitable. It thereby kept up profits and increased England's wealth.

Mill expresses this very happily when he writes: "England no longer depends on the fertility of her own soil to keep up her rate of profit, but on the soil of the whole world." It is important that this be understood to the letter. It is truly the whole world, and not only that part of it which is mapped out as our Colonial possessions, which is fast becoming England's domain and empire.

Mill saw this clearly. He is very careful to say always "Colonies *or* foreign countries" when speaking of this new process of acquisition. Nevertheless, this point is often forgotten or lost sight of by our modern Imperialists, who talk so grandiloquently of the extension of our Empire, and yet narrow its limits to the red lines on the world's map. Unconsciously, however, they feel the truth of this when they speak of our Imperial interests in China, in Turkey, in Africa, or elsewhere. Our Imperial interests actually pervade the whole world. The whole world, therefore, it cannot be too often repeated, forms the true basis of our Empire. We are no longer a small and isolated industrial nation which exports and imports, and with its commodities commands and buys the produce of other nations; we are fast becoming an Imperial nation, which by its capital and investments commands the productive forces themselves of other nations. We develop or help to develop them; we draw them into our orbit and bind up their interests inseparably with our own. It is thus that the British Empire takes form and substance.

It will be worth our while to pause here for a moment in order to consider the nature of our capitalistic conquests and to illustrate our arguments by referring to notable instances.

Let us first take the colonies, because just now much is made of our trade with them by our Imperialists and by our Colonial Minister.

Let these gentlemen remember that the colonies, from beginning to end, have all been established and built up by the capital of the mother country. If they cannot remember this, we should advise them to look it up in Ricardo, to whom Mr. Chamberlain has often referred of late in support of his new conception of Free Trade. Let them also look at the innumerable land, mortgage, mining, railway, &c., companies which, comfortably seated in the City of London, divide up amongst themselves the soil and properties of the colonies. Let them open, for instance, Mulhall's "Dictionary of Statistics," and ponder over the remark on page 589: "As regards the amount of wealth per inhabitant, the United Kingdom stands second only to Australia, and when we consider that most of Australia is mortgaged to British capitalists, we may say that in reality the United Kingdom has most wealth per head."

As Australian wealth is mortgaged to British capitalists, so also is Australian trade. In fact, there is no longer free trade between us and Australia, by which commodities are freely bartered for commodities with our kith and kin – the picture of which fills Mr. Chamberlain's imagination. On the contrary, the exports to Australia represent to a large extent capital for new investments, while the imports from Australia represent to a large extent payment to the mortgagees or absentee landlords in England.

The same may be said of almost any other British colony. Canada, at this moment the spoiled darling of England, is the latest example of our capitalistic acquisitions. The preferential treatment accorded as a free gift to Great Britain will naturally serve to facilitate and increase British investments in Canada. If this were the intention which originated the preferential treatment, it was no doubt a clever and effectual move, as Canada needed British capital for her development.

Glad, indeed, may the colonies be if English investors send out their investments – as they happily do for the most part – in the shape of commodities. In such cases there is "value received"; but there is no "value received" if no actual capital be transmitted to a country, and if, nevertheless, it be saddled with debts running up to millions of pounds by mere share transactions on the London Stock Exchange. Such is the special privilege of the pitiable countries on which modern Imperialism is allowed to experimentalise and to peg out claims for posterity, a process which in these cases comes dangerously near "sweating" those countries for the benefit of existent Stock Exchange interests. Africa may soon have to tell a tale on this subject.

Where is the difference between colonies and foreign countries with regard to capitalistic occupation? we may now ask. In foreign countries, as in the colonies, we see the same companies – land, mortgage, mining, railway, &c.. We cannot even say that we have invested a greater amount of capital in the colonies in order to develop their resources than we have done in foreign countries. On the contrary, the amount of capital we have placed in the United States is infinitely greater than that of the capital we have outstanding in all our colonies put together.

We have helped to build up the United States on a grander scale than any of our colonies, and, from a merely economic point of view, we may look upon this country as upon our largest and greatest colony. So much, indeed, are we dependent on the profits we draw from the United States that the condition of affairs in that country reacts more powerfully on the state of affairs in England than does the business condition of any other country in the world.

It could be clearly seen in the months preceding the election of President McKinley how much more important for us was the protection of our capital invested in the States than the preservation of our mere trade interests. Though McKinley was known to be a most advanced Protectionist, yet the City of London took his side strongly against Bryan. The City did not object to Mr. McKinley's high tariff, for it protected the innumerable industrial establishments owned by British capitalists in the United States; but it saw the danger to its interests in the silver agitation of Bryan. Not that this agitation would have affected very seriously the real trade and exchange of commodities between the countries, for this it could not do; but that it would have affected very seriously the payments in gold which the City looked for from America. The night of the election will not soon be forgotten in Lombard Street. City men trembled in their shoes, and sat up throughout the night in their offices watching the incoming telegrams on the results of the polls. Confidence was only restored when McKinley's victory was declared, and profits, interest, and power of English capital in the United States again secured. The head of a firm of Customs lawyers wrote to the Republican State Committee at that time as follows: "Several of our correspondents in Yorkshire write that, in the event of McKinley being elected, ten or twelve manufacturers, employing 7000 or 8000 hands, will remove their plant and business to the United States." . . .

After all we have said it will be clear that we must approach the question of the disparity of exports and imports from quite another side than that from which it has hitherto been treated. Without the guidance of these economic principles, which we have shown to be the laws of our development, it is only natural that this question should be looked upon as bewildering, if not alarming. Our imports increase by leaps and bounds;

our exports – which we have considered hitherto as the means wherewith to buy our imports – languish.

The excess of our imports has of late grown beyond all expectation . . .

If since the middle of the century we have sent out our capital to produce abroad; if we have farmed with it the soil of foreign countries; if by means of it we have dotted the whole globe with our industrial establishments – then we must of necessity import an increasing share of the produce of our capital abroad without exporting for it in return. Our imports from abroad were bound to increase; our exports from home were bound to suffer. It was a radical change which upset the equilibrium of international exchange, and rendered the theory of trade from country to country inapplicable to the revolutionised state of commerce.

It is due only to our deplorable deficiency in economic knowledge and our want of economic thought that this new state of affairs has been so little realised. Economic writers, it is true, avow that England is the greatest creditor country in the world, and that other countries have to pay interest to her. They do not see, however, that England is no longer a mere creditor who draws interest, but is also a landlord and proprietor who draws rents and profits. They admit, also, that the payment of interest in international trade is made by commodities, but they draw no conclusions from these admissions as to the nature of the changes which such payments must of necessity produce in the prices and the exchanges of the paying and the receiving countries. They cling to the idea that trade is still nothing but an exchange of commodities for commodities from one country to another, and that imports are still bought and paid for by exports. They do not understand how we can receive imports without paying the long bills which they make out to be due by us for imported food and manufactures. We still hear it incessantly repeated that we pay the foreigner such and such sums for wheat, so much for butter, meat and so forth – whereas we do not pay the foreigner at all. It is, on the contrary, the foreigner who pays us with his commodities. We receive them as our due or our own; we make no return to him, nor do we give any equivalent. Our great authorities, to whom we owe so much gratitude for our enlightenment in matters economic, have not failed to shed light also on this subject.

Mill, having developed the theory of international trade in all its ramifications, expressly points out how the very international payments with which we deal here necessarily disturb the equilibrium between imports and exports: "The remittances being made in commodities and being exports for which there is to be no return, it is no longer requisite," he says, "that the imports and exports pay for each other; on the contrary, there must be an annual excess of exports over imports (or imports over exports) equal to the value of the remittance."

And yet, notwithstanding this clear statement, men have been puzzled by the recent disparity of imports and exports! Even in the paper of Sir Robert

Giffen on the excess of imports, alluded to above, we miss a just appreciation of this point and a clear distinction between the two opposite kinds of imports – namely, between imports which are bought and paid for and imports which are made in payment of obligations without any return. Although he ought to know that the United States and all other indebted countries must send their wheat or other produce to us without being credited for it, yet Sir Robert Giffen writes as though these countries could draw on England in order to pay with the drafts their purchases elsewhere. As a matter of fact, the drafts from these countries against their produce are sent with the goods to England in order to pay, with their proceeds, creditors in England . . .

Therefore many of the dreaded commodities "made in Germany" and exported from thence may have been "made in English factories in Germany" and exported by orders from England. Many bushels of wheat exported from the United States were, from the very start, English property, or at least mortgaged to English capital. Many steel rails or cottons sent from America to Japan, India, or China, nay, even to England, may have been made in American mills owned or financed by Britishers. Who knows whether the firm which made the Atbara Bridge did not belong to British capital? All exports and imports of this kind, usually ascribed to the countries whence they come and whither they go, and swelling the exports and imports of these countries, represent in reality British trade. They are made on British account, for and by British capital. The profits which they yield, and which are ultimately remitted to British investors, are the share that British enterprise and British capital have in the trade of the respective countries. The fact is, the trade of the world, as well as its soil, if we do not foolishly disturb it, or meddle with it from unwarrantable jealousy, is becoming more and more one, and becoming more and more British, in whatever country it is going on and under whatever flag it sails.

If we wish to have a clear understanding of the phenomenon of our swelling imports we must put aside all preconceived notions of trade and mutual exchange, and must look upon the incoming tide of commodities as upon our income derived from our extensive and multifarious properties abroad. We receive this income in all kinds of commodities and, as we must say once more, we pay nothing for them in return. It is simply ridiculous to complain that by this importation we are getting poorer. On the contrary, by it we are every year getting richer. This is best shown by the statistics of the increase of our national wealth since the time when this importation began. The general wealth of the United Kingdom was estimated by Porter in 1840 at £4,000,000,000 sterling. According to Mulhall it rose in 1882 to £8,720,000,000 sterling; in 1888 to £9,400,000,000; and in 1895 to £11,806,000,000 sterling. This shows a very big increase up to 1895. The increase must have been still greater within the last three years in consequence of the general improvement in commerce and trade which set in after 1895. The increased imports in these years, no doubt, were the evidence of our increased profits.

It would be of the greatest interest to know exactly what are the sources for which our income is drawn, and particularly what part of it comes from abroad. Unfortunately on this very point the income-tax returns are not satisfactory. They give all sorts of unimportant distinctions, but they fail to give an accurate account of the chief divisions of wealth which we derive from little England and from our Empire abroad.

Mulhall, in his "National Progress during the Queen's Reign," complacently writes:

> "The loss of agricultural capital since 1880 has averaged thirty millions; but the increase of wealth in all other pursuits has been so steady and uniform, that the bulk of the nation has regarded such loss with philosophic equanimity. From a purely economic point of view, a continuance of the present system is most desirable."

The annual Budget speeches of our excellent Chancellor of the Exchequer show the same complacency. Notwithstanding the agricultural decline, notwithstanding the depression in others of our most important home industries, the Chancellor of the Exchequer surprises us every year by an ever-increasing surplus of revenue, which makes us appear to be rolling in wealth. It is evident, as Mill remarked, that England, in the acquisition of her riches, is no longer dependent upon her own resources, but, for half a century past has drawn her wealth from a far wider field . . .

III The Burning Question and the Answer

The burning question of to-day is – whether the capitalistic era which is now slowly superseding the industrial era of England is not fraught with dangers. We ought to ask ourselves very seriously whether, in the acquisition of wealth and in the establishment of manufactures abroad, we are not moving too fast for our well-being at home. We are in duty bound to watch that our capitalistic expansion does not react too forcibly on the social fabric of England, and injure the vital interests of the nation.

For once I agreed with Mr. Chamberlain when he said in his Wolverhampton speech:

> "The centre and the heart of this Empire, the hub of the wheel, from which radiate all its colonies and dependencies, is to be found in these three small islands . . . but these three islands, upon which all depend, with the enormous possibilities of good, could not themselves enjoy any measure of prosperity, could barely enjoy the confidence even of existence, but for that gigantic trade upon which everything depends

129

... Therefore the first duty of the Government is to maintain and defend this trade, the foundations of which were laid by our ancestors."

It is only regrettable that Mr. Chamberlain does not carry this idea further, but "in his manner" confounds national trade, capitalistic expansion, and Imperial interests, and therefore cannot see how the one may be seriously injured by the unchecked growth of the others.

We can scarcely hope for any help from him, however much he may talk of the first duty of the Government to maintain and defend the trade in these three small islands. Whatever he offers – to-day an International Zollverein, to-morrow an Imperial expansion by conquest, or, in the *Economist's* graphic phraseology, a "grabbing for posterity" at all costs – will neither improve our national trade, which to-day he calls gigantic, and which to-morrow may be, to his great mind, only of parochial importance, nor advance our true Imperial interests. If we must get rid of the Manchester school we must certainly not replace it by a Birmingham school.

Mr. Chamberlain's proposals for maintaining and defending our trade are really, to use his own words, not worth being touched, "not even with tongs." They are in conflict with the most fundamental laws of trade, of which he evidently does not know much. However fools may fight about the question whether trade follows the flag or the flag follows trade, trade will after all follow its own laws. These laws, if allowed full play, and if not meddled with by Colonial Ministers, will all work in our favour. They have, however, been almost continuously ignored for the last fifty years, and we cannot hope for our salvation save from their rehabilitation.

We have seen in what manner and to what degree our capital investments abroad enriched us when our profits at home threatened to decrease. The large excess of imports over exports, far from making us poorer, was only the means by which we received the incomes from our extensive properties beyond the seas. There can be no doubt that the tremendous stream of wealth which set in from our outer domain towards our shores, in the shape of commodities, must have given an impetus to certain new branches of enterprise at home. It has engendered in certain sections of the community a feeling of ease and well-being which has deceived even thoughtful observers into the belief that all is well in this best of all worlds. But there can be no doubt that this stream of wealth has choked many of our national enterprises and injured many of the most vital interests of our islands. We cannot, therefore, share this convenient optimism. On the contrary, we fear that the advantages arising from our inflowing wealth from all parts of the world, beneficial though they may be to certain classes of our population, are overrated, and that the grave disadvantages to our producing classes in general, and to the community at large, are overlooked. There are ugly signs of a decline, if not decay, in some of our most important industries. Our agriculture, which we proudly call our greatest industry, is smitten by chronic disease. Other industries, on which we thought our national greatness rested, seem almost on the eve of meeting the same fate. It is no secret that Manchester itself is feeling the pinch. Only the other day Mr. Albert Simpson, in the *Manchester Guardian*, called our attention to the serious depreciation of cotton mills, and to the fact that no new capital is entering the trade, whilst employment is gradually decreasing.

Our iron industry has lost its leading position, and is far surpassed by that of the United States. We must not allow ourselves to be deceived by the boom which for the time being has given us a lift and galvanised our home industries into a semblance of life. The relatively low prices which continued to rule until quite recently ought to have given us warning that this life was far from being real. It was chiefly brought about by demands caused by armaments for war, and by the new rush of capital into all sorts of remunerative or speculative investments after long famishing years of low interest. We are afraid it will not be very long before we are in the slump again, and resume our downward course; for the competition with ourselves which we have created abroad must soon begin to tell again, and to show its peculiar economic effects. The newly born American pseudo-imperialism which has helped to boom business in the United States cannot last, and we may be sure that its collapse when it comes will be quite on an imperial scale. We shall then realise anew how much our profits are dependent upon the business in the United States; and it may be safely predicted that this time it will be our manufactures, more even than our agriculture, which will have to suffer from the forced sales of the products of the new huge manufacturing combinations in America.

In the decline of our home industries the future of our labouring classes is sure to be involved. The industrial labourer will soon share the lot of the agricultural labourer, who, for want of employment in our rural districts, has lost his livelihood at home, and is forced to seek it abroad by following in the wake of our capital. The cheap prices of food and the exceptionally high nominal wages which at present prevail may delude the labouring classes as to their real positions, but they cannot and will not last for ever. We cannot but consider both as more or less transitory.

It is commonly thought, and seems at first very natural to suppose, that, for the present, all limitations of production of food is at an indefinite distance, and that ages must elapse before any practical necessity arises for taking the possible limits of production into serious consideration.

This John Stuart Mill declares to be not only an error, but "the most serious error to be found in the whole field of political economy. The question," he adds, "is more important and fundamental than any other; it involves the whole subject of the causes of poverty in a rich and industrious community."

With the rapidly increasing population of the world we are probably much nearer to a restriction in the production of food than the present generation, which takes no thought for the morrow, cares to admit. The cheap prices of food now ruling are the effect of our capital having taken into cultivation, within the last thirty years, immense tracts of fertile lands beyond the seas and temporarily outrun population. The high rate of wages which our labourers at present enjoy is caused, not only by the world-wide demand for labour which has sprung up from the rapid expansion of modern capital over the whole globe, but chiefly by the possibility given to labour of flowing into and freely acquiring those fresh and fertile lands which were suddenly opened to it. This naturally served as a powerful regulator of wages, and contributed much to keeping them up for the time being. But, as Ricardo puts it: "Whilst the land yields abundantly wages may temporarily rise, and the producers may consume more than their accustomed proportion; the stimulus which will thus be given to population will speedily reduce the labourers to their usual consumption. When poor lands are taken into cultivation or when more capital and labour are expended on the old land, with a less return of produce, this effect must be permanent."

It is impossible that the countries beyond the seas which send us our food on exceptionally low terms will continue to do so for all time to come. They cannot eternally supply as cheaply as they do now an ever increasing demand. Within measurable distance their superior soils will be taken up and cultivation extended to inferior soils.

Prices of food will then rise and profits will fall; for the law of Ricardo that profits of stock are determined by the yield of inferior soils taken into cultivation will prove as true to-day as it was in his time. With an increasing population wages will fall also. Things will then begin to look serious . . .

Statesmen worthy of the name ought to consider seriously this "most important and fundamental question" of John Stuart Mill. The gain which the moneyed classes draw from their investments abroad, and the temporary golden rain which through them falls at present on that part of the community which is in their pay or ministers to their luxuries, cannot possibly last for ever, and cannot compensate us for the misfortunate which will overtake us if we allow our great national industries to be sacrificed.

We are not possessed of that philosophic equanimity with which Mr. Mulhall, in the passage quoted above, views the decline of British agriculture and declares the continuance of the present economic system to be most desirable. We are rather of Ricardo's opinion that it is always regrettable for a nation to be deprived of important and beneficial branches of trade. We cannot but see in the paralysis of our agriculture and in the decline of our other great industries a national calamity, and we feel assured that we have been landed in this our present predicament, notwithstanding all our riches, by the utter neglect of all sound laws of trade. The sooner we revert to these laws the better it will be for us.

The movement which we have outlined, of our flowing capital seeking investment and expanding abroad, was in itself a very natural one, and was, if kept within natural bounds, beneficial to our economic development. Up to the present it has prevented, as we have shown, the profits of our capital from falling, and has acquired for us immense new potentialities. With these potentialities we ought to have at least been able to maintain our home industries, if not in their former monopoly or supremacy, yet in a prosperous and flourishing condition; with our capitalistic expansion we ought at least to have defended the "mighty trade, the foundations of which were laid by our ancestors," and to have kept sound the centre and the heart of the Empire built upon these foundations. We ought to have given to this Empire that solid economic structure which would have secured to ourselves and to the world at large those "enormous possibilities of good" a vision of which flashed through the mind of Mr. Chamberlain. This we could have done if we had been true to the teachings of our great ancestors, and if we had not, by an unjust, an unscientific, and a short-sighted policy, dangerously precipitated the movement of capitalistic expansion then in the course of development.

It was the perverse fate of England that she, the very country which gave to the world the science of national economy, should have become unfaithful to the principles of this science, and should have followed the voice of a charmer who juggled away these principles and substituted for them, by legerdemain as it were, a mere sham.

Torrens gives the following expression to this thought, in regretting that Sir Robert Peel should have been misled by Cobden:

> "Sir Robert Peel, suddenly awakening from the long delusions of his early life, and eager for guidance through paths he had failed to explore, turned to the voice of the charmer no adder's ear. Not possessing the mastery of scientific principles which would have enabled him to perceive the limitations to which they are liable in practice, he embraced the Cobden creed with the headlong zeal of a recent convert. *Regardless of the necessary laws which govern the terms of international exchange, he substituted direct taxation for import duties, while foreign countries continued to enforce their tariffs; and thus destroyed the equality without which no real freedom of commerce can exist."* . . .

Cobden called himself "a practical man," and did not trouble himself much about scientific principles. From the teachings of our great econo-mists, which he neither understood nor cared to understand, this only had he gleaned – that, in order to enable him to reduce wages and raise profits, he needed cheap food for the Manchester labourers. This was the true inwardness of his principles. In his parliamentary speeches he protested, with an adroit display of philanthropy, against this imputation. He pre-tended that the rate of wages had no more connection with the price of food than the moon's changes. But, in his "Russia by a Manchester

133

Manufacturer," he allowed the truth to leak out. In this pamphlet he confessed that there was, indeed, a very close connection between cheap food and cheap wages, and that he wanted the former in order to enforce the latter.

In order to procure cheap raw material, this later saint of Free Trade and arch-enemy of bounties and monopoly became director of a monopolistic concern, the Algerian Cotton, Land, and Irrigation Company, and had enormous privileges and extravagant bounties on exportation of cotton granted it by the French Government. To secure for the cotton mills of Manchester immunity from poor-rates, he, though always posing as the friend of the labourer, was ready – as the *Times* of January 15, 1863, pointed out – to withdraw, without a pang of conscience, from the operatives the very funds upon which they must have depended in a crisis. In short, Cobden tried his best to increase the profits of his industry at the expense of the labourers, by all kinds of quackery, tricks, and jugglery; but he failed. The inexorable laws of international exchange were against him. The only result of his machinations was to expose English manufactures, through one-sided Free Trade, to the then rising competition from abroad, and to lay the axe to their roots. With an utter disregard for economic truths, Cobden told the landlords that only badly tilled farms would go out of cultivation. The derelict fields of England are a sad comment on this prophecy!

Torrens, the great Free Trader who opposed Cobden's school as the school of imperfect Free Trade, dismissed all further discussion with an adversary so unworthy of his steel in the following remarkable and amusing letter – well worth preserving:

"The inevitable consequence of the adoption of your scheme of one-sidism would be a decline in the rate of manufacturing profits.

"It is somewhat curious to mark the points regarding which we agree, as well as those respecting which we differ. We are agreed upon the fact that the adoption of your principle of one-sidism would cause a fall of rents; but in dealing with this fact we march in opposite directions. I, borrowing my theory of rent from Malthus and Ricardo, urge the farmer and the farmer's labourer to resist one-sidism, because, if this theory be correct, *the fall of rent occasioned by one-sidism would throw inferior soils out of cultivation, and diminish the demand for agricultural labour.*

"You, deriving you theory of rent from some process of transcendental logic, not yet presented to the public, urge the farmer and the farmer's labourer to support one-sidism, because, if your occult theory be correct, the fall of rent which one-sidism would occasion, instead of throwing out the poorer soils, would give an increased employment on the land.

"Again, we agree in desiring that monopoly should be abolished, while we disagree as to the means by which the abolition can be effected.

"I contend that monopoly cannot be abolished by removing restrictions on one side, and leaving one party with an advantage over the other.

"You see in me an advocate of monopoly. *I see in you monopoly personified.*

"You have discovered a new theory of rent, and you protect your discovery as effectually as if you had drawn round it Bishop Berkeley's wall of brass. This seems to me somewhat inconsistent in a free trader.

"Why do you not bring your discovery into the open market? Though a little learning may be a dangerous thing, yet, as half a loaf is better than no bread, we should like to obtain a few grains of your bonded knowledge, though subject to some restrictions, and however limited the supply.

"Once more, we appear to be entirely agreed as respects the estimation in which each holds the arguments of the other. You pronounce my reasoning absurd; and I venture to suspect that your logic is occasionally defective. Our controversy is thus conducted upon a principle of perfect reciprocity, and, as reciprocity is all that I contend for, I subscribe myself yours very truly,

"R. TORRENS"

By the adoption of Cobden's one-sided Free Trade and the remission of import duties in England whilst other countries insisted on retaining their tariffs, the international demand for the goods of the several countries was of necessity altered.

The demand for foreign produce in Free Trade England naturally increased; the demand for British goods in protective countries naturally decreased. For this reason the value of British goods was lowered in foreign markets. They had to be offered at cheaper prices, and, the demand for them from abroad falling off, to bear the burden of foreign tariffs. This, as Torrens had predicted, naturally lowered profits in England, and in order to make good the loss English manufacturers were compelled to cut down wages, or to resist an increase of wages which other wise might have taken place. The state of things, therefore, which obtained during and after the revolutionary wars, when the extraordinary demand for British goods had given to England her enormous industrial supremacy, was now reversed. At that time the value of all foreign products fell in relation to the produce of English labour. Now, after the adoption of Free Trade, the value of English products fell in relation to the produce of foreign labour.

In the case of the United States of America, Torrens describes this process in the following manner:

"Because America imposes heavy duties upon the products of British industry, while England imposes no countervailing duties on the great staples of American industry, it will be apparent upon a due consideration of the subject, that the whole of the American duty falls upon the British producers, in the form of a deduction from their profits, or from their wages, or both."

Such a disturbance of international demand by import duties, with its effect on international values, is constantly ignored by our modern free-traders. They repeat *ad nauseam* the old threadbare truisms that imports must always be paid for by exports, and that if we take care of the imports the exports will take care of themselves.

They refuse to understand that truisms like these, even supposing that commerce should continue to be nothing but a mere exchange of commodities for commodities, and that the equilibrium of this exchange should not be disturbed by payments not originating in such commerce, have no bearing whatsoever on the paramount question, which is, *whether the prosperity of a country will be promoted* by admitting foreign produce free of duty, whilst foreign countries refuse to relax their tariffs. Even on the above supposition, the real question at issue is not whether the increased amount of our exports would be proportionate to the increased amount of our imports, but whether the requisite amount of exports could be effected without such a reduction in the value of British goods as would cause a decline both in British profits and British wages. This question must be answered in the negative. A country which rashly abolishes its tariffs will and must always be the loser if other countries do not follow suit. In order to save it from such an experience, it is maintained unanimously by all economists that Free Trade could confer an advantage on countries only if it were reciprocal, and that the adoption of one-sided Free Trade was nothing but the offer of a bounty to protective countries upon the retention of their tariffs. In the very name of Free Trade, therefore, it was insisted upon by all our classic writers that equalising, countervailing, or retaliatory duties should be imposed in order to maintain or enforce the principle of reciprocity. Torrens, in his letters to the Marquis of Chandos, insisted on our forcing Russia to abolish her tariffs against us by retaining or re-imposing duties on her products. Pennington demanded that the unfavourable effects of hostile tariffs on the trade of England should be counteracted by retaliatory duties; and Mill declared that the only mode in which a country could save itself from being a loser by the duties imposed by other countries on its commodities was to impose corresponding duties on theirs.

If we did not act on this advice, we cannot wonder that Peel's and Cobden's prophecy of an early abolition of tariffs by foreign countries was not realised, but that, on the contrary, foreign countries were too far-sigthed to abandon the conspicuous advantages which our Free Trade had created for them. We continue, therefore, to suffer from the inequality of foreign demand for our commodities, and the constant tendency to lower the value of our goods in foreign lands and of our profits in England. We do our best, as we shall soon see, to artificially drive our capital into more favoured lands.

For some time after the adoption of Free Trade, the evil effects of the new policy were not revealed in their magnitude, except to some few astute observers. The tremendous momentum of the unique force of English industries was too great to have admitted of a sudden collapse. The almost uninterrupted series of wars which raged from 1854 to 1871, even to 1877, counterbalanced the effect of the Free Trade folly. It not only checked the industrial development and competition in the respective countries, but also increased enormously the demand for the produce of British labour. The experience of the Napoleonic wars was almost repeated, and the supremacy of British industry temporarily restored. The outflow itself of our capital to foreign lands acted in the beginning as a stimulus to our home industries, for before our competitors were in the field this outflow was effected almost solely by means of English commodities needed for the new enterprises abroad. The hurtful consequences of the sinister Free Trade policy were thus kept so much in abeyance that the Free Trade school could and did audaciously claim this exceptional and temporary trade prosperity as the result of their one-sided fetish.

Six years, however, after the adoption of the Free Trade policy, Torrens gave the following description of its influence on the state of affairs in the United Kingdom:

"As regards Ireland, agriculture declined rapidly since the repeal of the Corn Laws, and as regards Great Britain, the blindest devotee to the policy of Sir Robert Peel will scarcely venture to exemplify its success by reference to the recent statistics of British agriculture. The statistics will dissipate the popular illusion that the policy of Peel has accelerated the prosperity of the country. The industrial condition of the country, as revealed by these figures, demands grave consideration. We have an extension of foreign commerce, accompanied by a diminution of commercial wealth; this may be accounted for by the following three facts: The incomes of the classes depending on the land have been diminished. The terms of international exchange have been so altered to our disadvantage that the value of British goods in foreign markets has fallen in a greater proportion than that in which the quantities exported to foreign markets have been increased. The general fall in the rate of profits throughout all the departments of industry has caused the amount of British capital annually invested in foreign securities and foreign speculations to exceed the amount annually accumulated; the reduction of the rate of interest driving capital abroad."

137

That which was clear to the genius of Torrens in 1852, when he wrote the above lines, became painfully felt by the nation a quarter of a century later. Torrens anticipated the precipitating influence which the Free Trade policy would necessarily have on the emigration of British capital. It no longer remained a natural and spontaneous emigration of superfluous capital; on the contrary, capital was actually driven out, and forced out, by the artificial lowering of its profits at home and the raising of them behind the Customs barriers of foreign nations. It paid the capital better to establish factories behind those barriers, and under their protection, than to fight them in an unequal battle by a reduction of prices.

Torrens on general principles looked askance at the emigration of our capital; especially he regretted its being artificially forced. And yet, as we have already seen, he did not take into account that special effect which later on, in the natural course of things, the payments of profits, dividends, and interests on this capital were to produce on our home industries. No one of our great classic writers before Mill had made this particular question the subject of his inquiry, for the simple reason that the question itself had not arisen in his time. Mill was the first to throw light on it, but his teachings have passed unheeded.

The capital which left our shores did not emigrate in the sense in which our great economists had alone considered its emigration, that is to say, in the sense that it was lost to England. It never was naturalised, so to speak, in the foreign countries, but it remained English, and made the respective countries tributary to England.

Thus, apart from the inequalities forced on us by our one-sided Free Trade policy, a new cause of disturbance was created for our commerce, which revolutionised the latter and hopelessly upset the very idea of an equilibrium of trade.

The tributes were paid in commodities. The "dumping of foreign stuff" on English shores, the glutting of English markets with foreign goods which had to be sold for account of English creditors, began.

The sales could only be effected by offering the goods at lower prices. With continually rising imports of this kind the slaughter of prices became chronic. We must see in these sales the true, the real cause of that terrible fall in prices which for more than thirty years has puzzled the public mind, disorganised our home production, and impoverished our debtors. Our own industries had to bear the brunt of this new state of things; they were forced out of their own markets by the tributes of the foreigner. Free Trade no longer existed; it was replaced in an ever increasing degree by what must be more correctly termed a pawn trade.

It is another proof of our absolute thoughtlessness, not to say ignorance, in matters economic, that the true nature of this change and its effect on commerce and on prices has never been recognised in its true significance. All the nonsense that has been written by monometallists and bimetallists about the fall of prices in the last thirty years might have been spared us if we had taken the trouble to read, mark, and inwardly digest the following masterly passage, in which Mill gave us, a generation ago, the perfect description and the complete theory of the payment of tributes:

"If before the (tributary) country became liable to the annual payments foreign commerce was in its natural state of equilibrium, it will now be necessary, for the purpose of effecting the remittance, that foreign countries should be induced to take a greater quantity of exports than before, which can only be done by offering those exports on cheaper terms, or, in other words, by paying dearer for foreign commodities. The international values will so adjust themselves that either by greater exports or smaller imports, or both, the requisite excess on the side of exports will be brought about. The result is that the country which makes regular payments to foreign countries, besides losing what it pays, loses also something more, by the less advantageous terms on which it is forced to exchange its productions for foreign commodities."

Or, in other words,

"the paying country will give a higher price for all that it buys from the receiving country, while the latter, besides receiving the tribute, *obtains the exportable produce of the tributary country at a lower price.*"

Here we have it stated in a most lucid manner and by the highest authority, that through the payments of tributes the natural equilibrium of trade is overthrown, and that this is effected by the lowering of prices. One has only to compare this classic statement of Mill's with Sir Robert Giffen's explanation in his paper formerly alluded to – of the inequality of exports and imports – in order to form a sad perception of the collapse of economic thought in the present day.

Sir Robert Giffen is justly looked upon as one of our chief modern economic lights. His views may therefore be taken as fairly representative of modern economic opinion; but beyond stating the fact that the purchasing power of our foreign customers was diminished through the increased difficulty of paying their debts to us, owing to the fall of prices, and that we gained at their expense, Sir Robert Giffen gave us very little enlightenment on the nature and the effects of international debt-paying. By expressly saying "whatever the cause of the lower prices may be," he betrayed that he had no glimmer even of any connection between such debt-paying and the lowering of prices, although he ought to have known from Mill that the latter were the agency through which the former was effected, and that debtor countries, by paying tribute, "lose not only the tribute itself, but something more." The very fact, therefore, of paying tribute and debt to us made our foreign customers poorer. Our gain at their expense was doubtful: we may have acquired wealth, but we have lost the markets for our exports and we see our industries ruined! . . .

Under our present economic system our industries not only lose their foreign markets by foreign restrictions, but also by the diminution of the purchasing power of foreign customers. At the same time, English industries find themselves constantly undersold in English markets by forced sales of foreign commodities on account of English creditors. Last, but not least, industries find the general cost of production in England increased by the rise of the level of general prices in England – that is to say, of prices of all things not imported from abroad. The prices of these things are necessarily raised by the influx of the tributes, while the prices of imported articles fall.

All home industries, therefore, which are in competition with commodities imported from tributary countries, are sure to be driven to the wall, and are doomed to certain extinction. They must ultimately be ousted; for no industry in the long run can stand falling prices of its products and rising cost of its production, with weakened markets.

British agriculture had to succumb the first to the inroad of foreign produce, for it was first with agricultural produce that foreign countries began to pay their debts. Other industries, if not already attacked, will in due time share the same fate, for foreign countries will, by-and-by, find it cheaper to pay with manufactures . . .

We therefore must give to the burning question, asked in the beginning of this chapter, the answer that we are moving too fast in our new capitalistic departures. Our artificially fostered and almost forced expansion makes us look out too eagerly for high profits and quick expansion abroad. A sham Imperialism turns our heads. We lose sight of the manner in which it reacts on our truly national interests centred in these islands. The chief duty of a true national policy should be to defend their industry and their trade. Until now we see them sacrificed to the Moloch of false Imperialism.

We are the last to object to a sound Imperial policy and expansion. No one can take a greater pride in the progress of our economic development and in the rise of our Imperial position than we do. We will not be deterred from working to that end by any necessary sacrifices . . .

Things develop fast in our times; one half-century more may see that by far the greater part of our wealth is lying abroad. We have seen how the fruits which we reap from this wealth and which we import into England react – according to the laws of trade and values – on our industries at home and, consequently, on the social fabric of England. If this reaction is painful now, how much more so will it be later on, when a much larger stream of wealth will pour into our islands from abroad! English capital and English labour will be driven out in an ever increasing degree, and England will become more and more the pleasure-ground of the new Imperialist, the foreign investor. This, at least, will be the direction in which we shall be moving – indeed, in which we are already moving. There are noticeable signs of such a movement; so plain, indeed, are they, that he who runs may read. Some may approve of this development, and look upon it as a most desirable and natural end. They believe in wealth at all costs. We do not agree with them; we think that we have overdone somewhat the keeping of our cows in Australia, Canada, or Argentina, cultivating our wheat-fields in Manitoba or in India, spinning our cotton in China and Mexico, or making our machinery in Germany and the United States. We believe that in what we are pleased to call "developing foreign countries" we have neglected the development of our own land, England, and allowed her to fall back . . .

Before the Cobden school invented the paramount rights of the consumer, in order to catch votes at elections, economic science guarded first of all the rights and interests of the producer. It is with the interests of the producer that the interests of every country are bound up, and there is no doubt that it is the home producer who has the strongest claim on our assistance. "In order to encourage the home trade," writes Torrens, "it is the first duty devolving on a Government to secure to every member of the community a perfect empire over the produce of his industry. The way to render men industrious is to convince them that their earnings are their own, and that they labour for themselves." Mill puts the case of the producer even stronger still:

"What a country wants to make it richer," he writes, "is never consumption, but production. The legislator, therefore, needs not give himself any concern about consumption. He has to look solely to two points – that no obstacle shall exist to prevent those who have the means of producing from employing those means as they find most for their interest; and that those who have not at present the means of producing, to the extent of their desire to consume, shall have every facility afforded to their acquiring the means, that, becoming producers, they may be enabled to consume. These general principles are now well understood by almost all who profess to have studied the subject, and are disputed by few except those who ostentatiously proclaim their contempt for such studies."

Ricardo declares "that the end of all commerce is to increase production, and that by production you increase the general happiness."

We are sorry to say that the "general principles" expounded in the above quotations, notwithstanding Mill's assertion to the contrary, we are still far from being understood. And yet it seems to us that in the carrying out of these principles lies the very first and chief condition of that self-reliance and independence which is the pride of Englishmen and the only basis of British trade.

Give to an Englishman the perfect empire over his produce, secure to him the full scope for his energies, and he will soon acquire the means

141

which enable him to consume, without caring for the treacherous cheapness which Cobdenites dangle before his eyes.

"The cheapness of an article," as Mill expressly remarks, "is not measured solely by the money price, but by that price compared with the money income of the consumer." If, therefore, you secure to the producer a greater money income through his energies, even a higher price of the article will be cheap to him. . . .

It is in accordance with the doctrines of Free Trade – which requires first of all that labour and production should not be artificially handicapped in relation to the labour and production of other countries – that the natural equilibrium between the different branches of industry should be maintained. This latter principle, established first by Torrens, then accepted in his "Treatise on the Protection of Agriculture" by Ricardo, and afterwards by all later economists of any significance, requires that in all cases of artificial interference with production a countervailing duty should be established in order to restore the natural equilibrium. Ricardo, the founder of the theory of foreign commerce, the great champion of Free Trade, was for this very reason of the opinion that "the importation of corn should not be for all times allowed without the payment of any duty whatever." . . .

By the imposition of reciprocal and countervailing duties the financial expansion might be retarded. Capitalists would be slower to invest abroad, for the levying of countervailing duties would be equivalent to a reduction in their profits and dividends drawn from abroad; Stock Exchange values probably would suffer; the concession-hunter would be discouraged; but then, ours most surely is not to be an Empire which shall sweat foreign nations, fatten the foreign investor, enrich the stock-jobber and company-promoter, and choke the home producer. We will not be Empire-floaters, but Empire-builders. We will keep sound the centre and heart of this Empire. Mr. Chamberlain has left the Cobden Club. That does him honour. Better late than never. After that we might have expected something from him. In his speech on the West Indian grants he came somewhat near the truth. "The main object of Free Trade," he said, "is to secure the natural course of production and exchange; that each nation is to produce what it is best fitted to supply and to exchange its produce without artificial preferences." But by an unfortunate quotation from Hume – that Free Trade could only properly exist where the nations were in like circumstances and where they were at liberty to apply the same means to the same end with equal facility – he spoiled his case. Under such conditions there would obviously be no trade at all. His knowledge of the principles of trade is evidently limited.

If Mr. Chamberlain, appealing to these principles, asserts that countervailing duties would be justified against the sugar bounties of France and Germany, in favour of the West Indian colonies, because of their artificially interfering with the course of production, we should like to ask him why he does not stand up frankly, first of all, for the introduction of countervailing duties in favour of the home producer?

To ask countervailing duties against continental bounties for the benefit of London capitalists who have their sugar plantations in the West Indies, in Mauritius, in Queensland, in Argentina, or in Brazil – plantations fostered and protected by all kinds of Government privileges and bounties – while English producers and labourers are left without any protection against the much more devastating powers of foreign tributes, is simply idiotic. The British home producer who, by means of cheap sugar, has succeeded in building up paying industries of jam and biscuit making, is again to be sacrificed to the interests of capital invested abroad. This clearly shows that Lombard Street and St. Swithin's Lane, and no longer the English producer and labourer, are the determining factor in our politics. We cannot, however, and must not accept this state of things as final. From our old political parties we can expect very little. They continue to run in their old grooves, though circumstances, as we have shown, have radically changed. The rising power of capital is fast dissolving the old parties as it threatens to dissolve our very Constitution. We seem to *ruere in servitium* of this new capitalistic Imperialism, and to allow it, as we did in the case of the typical Empire-builder in South Africa, to override the authority of Parliament and to set aside the demands of justice. Both our old historical parties have broken down before this new power. Those few leaders of Liberalism who still fight against it, by upholding Cobdenism as an unshakable dogma, yield up all effective weapons for mastering it. It seems as if a new party were required to undertake the arduous task of combating the domination of capital, and of reinstating the English producer in his former rights and his old independence. As we have said before, this is a very big and urgent question, and one of the very highest statesmanship.

It is hardly worth our while to point out the hollowness of all schemes which aimed at constituting an Imperial Zollverein and creating Free Trade within the boundaries of our colonial possessions. The very reference to its prototype, the German Custom Union, reveals a hopeless deficiency in economic reasoning. The German Zollverein was a Custom union between States financially independent of each other, and forming one comparatively small territory. Between these States Free Trade was possible; within their territory only the laws regulating internal commerce, and not those regulating international trade, were brought into play.

Between England and her possessions real Free Trade is impossible. The possessions are built up by and dependent on English capital. The trade between them, far from being free, is more or less mortgaged or pawned to it. The trade, therefore, is fettered by the necessity of paying profits and interest to English capital. We have seen in what manner and in what degree international values had to adjust themselvse to the requirements of such payments. Values had to be lowered disastrously in the colonies, while their exports to England disastrously lowered the prices of the same kind of goods in England. Hereby all payments became more onerous. Gold exports came in sight and threatened to overturn the credit system. Not only for revenue purposes, but still more in order to retrench obligations abroad, the majority of the colonies had to take refuge in Custom duties.

For these reasons the Zollverein idea was no sooner advanced than it was dropped. The colonies could not possibly accept it on account of their indebtedness.

The first principle to be followed in our treatment of the colonies must be this – that we leave to them their full independence to arrange their economic policy according to their own interests. It is their business to make their economic dependence on our capital as tolerable to themselves as possible. We must avoid even the appearance of meddling with their affairs for our advantage. Only thus can we secure their invaluable political coherence. No one appreciates this coherence more highly than we do; but we see it endangered by all nonsensical plans of drawing the colonies, as a whole, economically closer to us.

A true national policy, on the other hand, must be to take care of ourselves. Good policy, like charity, begins at home. We must defend "that gigantic trade centred in our islands of which our ancestors laid the foundations." We must defend it against all odds to which, as we have seen, it is exposed. Our first duty will be to defend it against the inroads of one-sided Free Trade and of one-sided pawn trade, by restoring perfect Free Trade, reciprocity, and equality by means of reciprocal and countervailing duties. That done, we shall be at liberty to arrange our commercial inter-course with each foreign country or with each colony according to the peculiar circumstances of the case. We might hereby create a great elastic commercial system working in harmony with the interests of all countries concerned. We might hereby ensure to our World-Empire the conditions of a sound and healthy growth.

With the security thus accorded to our home producers in agriculture and manufactures we shall have a *locus standi* for approaching those necessary internal reforms which in the pursuit of sham Imperialism have been too long neglected. If we procure security of rent and capital to landlord and farmer, we can undertake the necessary reform of the Holdings Act. If we procure security of profits and wages to manufacturers and labourers, we can take up social reforms in favour of the labourer. Last, not least, we can take in hand the much needed reforms of taxation; reduce direct taxation which presses hardly on our own industries, and restore indirect taxation which will benefit them. Nothing, under the circumstances, can be more just than such a taxation. By the enormously increased imports which we receive without return the international demand is affected in such a manner that it would throw on the British capitalist the burden of import duties levied on the goods sent in payment of his income from abroad. It is therefore he whom this taxation would chiefly affect, in the shape of a reduction from his rent or profits – drawn from abroad. Nothing can be more just; for not only does the capitalist cause increased expenditure to our Exchequer for the protection accorded to his interests abroad – as we now see by the deficit we have to meet – but he has also escaped until now all taxation and contributions to the Imperial Exchequer from his investments in foreign countries. In fact, he almost enjoys immunity from taxation, while he lays increased taxation on the home producer who is already ground down by the influx of the investor's profits. Our representatives abroad have to work every year more and more to secure to the foreign investor his concessions; he therefore is a very fit subject from whom to obtain a just contribution to the public revenue. Our Empire abroad has never yet been duly taxed. The burden and heat of the day has fallen solely on the home producer.

There is, then, a wide field of action and beneficial reform before us. Both require statesmanship of the highest order. We have arrived at a period of our national and Imperial development when we need again the guidance of great minds such as those which laid the foundation of our development in the period uder review . . .

NOTES

1 See (vol. III: 23).
2 See (vol. I: 3).

---

6 THE THEORY OF INTERNATIONAL TRADE . . . *

C.F. Bastable

Chapter II: The Theory of International Values

The general account of the character of, and the advantages which result from, international exchange given in the preceding chapter, suggests a further investigation of great importance, but one which will necessarily be of a somewhat complicated kind. It may concisely be stated in the following

* C.F. Bastable, *The Theory of International Trade* . . . (London: Macmillan and Co., Ltd., 1903), pp. 22–48; 110–27.

shape:– What are the conditions which determine the divisions of the gain resulting from foreign trade among the different parties to the exchange? Or, In what way will the values of commodities which are the subject of foreign trade be affected by the conditions under which that trade is carried on? In working out this problem, it will be most convenient to follow somewhat closely the course adopted by J.S. Mill, not only since his treatment is the most thorough, but also because students have generally gained their first notion of the subject from his pages.[1]

Let it, then, be assumed that there are but *two* nations, countries, or "trading bodies" in existence, and that these nations trade in but, indeed we may say can produce only, two commodities. Let the countries in question be styled A and B, the commodities x and y. Let it further be granted that a unit of productive power in A can produce $10x$ or $20y$; and that a unit of productive power in B can produce $10x$ or $15y$. It follows, from the law of comparative cost, that it will be the interest of A to confine itself to the production of y, and of B to devote its resources to the production of x. The question which has now to be answered is: What are the terms on which the exchange of x and y take place? And in the answer to that question lies the solution of the problem of international *values*, as distinguished from that of international *trade*.

Before, however, entering on this inquiry, it will be best to dwell for a little on some assumptions made in, and one some special features of, our supposed case. (1) It is assumed that the commodities x and y are both capable of being proportionally increased up to any assignable limit by a proprotionally increased amount of productive power, from which it follows that their value is determined by, or at least moves parallel with, their cost of production, so that in A $10x$ will exchange for $20y$, and in B for $15y$. The existence of different costs of production for different amounts of commodities produced, of a set of non-competing industrial groups, and of all those retarding agencies which have been loosely summed up under the name of "custom," are for the moment ignored. Nor is such a method of procedure illegitimate. The expediency, and even the necessity, of employing provisional hypotheses in economic observation, has been recognised by Leslie as well as by Cairnes, by Dr. Ingram as well as by Mr. Sidgwick. In Germany it is conceded by Schmoller.[2] The real error lies, not in the use of hypotheses, but in forgetfulness of the fact that they are unreal, or, at all events, incomplete. (2) The term "productive power" may be noticed. It is used to escape the awkwardness, if it be not something more, of estimating the exertions of a country in units of labour or of capital – a mode of procedure which leaves it open to the critic to speak of the omitted element as if it were an essential condition.[3] There can be little difficulty in conceiving a given amount of labour working with an average amount of capital, and thus producing a definite amount of a commodity. (3) There is a further caution which will save the student from some confusion as he proceeds; it is that the "units" spoken of need not necessarily, or even usually, be the same in both countries; for instance, the unit in A may be one day's labour and £5 capital; in B it may be ten days' labour and £30 capital. The apparent equality of productive power in the case of the commodity x – 10 in each country – is adopted to secure, as it were, a common denominator, and to enable the division of gain to be more easily understood. (4) Finally, we must add that all impediments to exchange, arising from cost of transport and from customs duties, or any other cause, are for the present neglected.

Having cleared the way by the foregoing remarks, let us now follow out the working of our hypothetical case. When each country produced for itself, the total production was $20x + 35y$. When each country applies itself to the product in which it has the greater comparative advantage (or less disadvantage) the total production becomes $20x + 40y$, that is, a gain of $5y$. It is the conditions which determine the division of this amount of $5y$ between A and B that must now be looked for. The analogy bewteen international and individual exchanges . . . seems at first to suggest that the problem is a hopeless one, for if A and B were individuals, it is plain that the ratio of exchange might lie anywhere between $10x$ to $15y$ and $20y$. In fact, we come to what Jevons has called the "failure of the equations of exchange";[4] and such is substantially the conclusion at which J.S. Mill arrived on closer reflection.[5]

There are, however, several modifying circumstances in international, as opposed to individual, exchange which assist us in indicating generally the conditions that we are in search of. Why, it may be asked, should the terms of an exchange between separate individuals be so hard to predict? Simply because it is hard to get the needed information. "The result of the bargain," in a case of the kind, "will greatly depend upon the comparative amount of knowledge of each other's positions and needs which either bargainer may possess or manage to obtain, in the course of the transaction. Thus the power of reading another man's thoughts is of high importance in business, and the art of bargaining mainly consists in the buyer ascertaining the lowest price at which the seller is willing to part with his object, without disclosing, if possible, the highest price which he, the seller [buyer?], is willing to give. The disposition and force of character of the parties, their comparative persistency, their adroitness and experience in business, or, it may be, feelings of justice or of kindliness, will also influence the decision."[6] In such a case even the main influencing force – the comparative urgency of demand – is unknown to an outsider. In international exchange, on the other hand, there is the steadying effect produced by the existence of a large number of persons on each side. It may be impossible to estimate the amount of x which A (an individual) would give for y; but if A be a body of persons, its demand will come under the law of averages, and can, with the aid of statistics, be determined within tolerably narrow limits. Returning to our particular case, let us assume that the trade

147

between A and B is opened at the ratio – suppose of $10x$ for $16y$. At that rate we find that 1000 times $10x$ is demanded by A, and that 1000 times $16y$ is demanded by B, and that thus there is no unsatisfied demand on either side; it follows that the trade is in equilibrium, and that $10x$ to $16y$ will be the ratio of exchange. A will gain $4y$ and B will gain $1y$, by the opening of the trade. The result may, however, be different; for A may require a larger amount of x at the ratio $10x$ to $16y$, say 1100 times $10x$, while B only requires 1000 times $16y$ at the assumed ratio. It will therefore be necessary for A to offer a greater amount of y in exchange for x, say $10x$ for $17y$. Now, it is apparent that at this new ratio A cannot require more than it would at the lower rate, and, in all probability, will require a less amount, which we shall suppose to be 1050 times $10x$. On the other hand, B cannot require less of y at the new ratio than at the older and more unfavourable one, and, indeed, will be likely to require more, which increased amount we shall assume to be 1050 times $17y$. Here, again, we have a state of equilibrium, the demand on either side being satisfied. It is possible that several ratios may satisfy the condition to which, as we have just seen, international exchange conforms; but, owing to the fact that large groups of persons are the source of demand on each side, it is probable that the equation of demand once satisfied will not lightly be departed from, so that, to some extent, it will not only be a position of equilibrium, but also one of stability, though, in some cases, a departure from it would perhaps lead to a new state of equilibrium at a different ratio.

The foregoing inquiry leads directly to J.S. Mill's conclusion in his first and soundest exposition of his theory. The ratio of exchange, in the case of commodities, which are the subject of international trade, depends on the comparative intensity of demand on each side, always, of course, operating within the limits set by comparative cost. As Mill has pointed out, it is conceivable that all the gain by exchange would go to one country; for, suppose that A only requires a limited amount of x, which will not be increased by a reduction in its value, while B requires a large amount of y, it is possible, and, under such conditions, even likely, that the terms of exchange will be $10x$ for $15y$, since B, in order to satisfy its demand for y, will offer increasingly favourable terms, even up to the limit set by its power of producing y for itself.

This "first elementary principle of international values,"[7] important as it is, stands in need of large developments and additions before it can be applied to actual cases. Up to the present we have paid no attention to the industrial constitution of the countries or nations whose supposed bartering we have been using as a guide in our inquiry. The proposition just developed may be further explained by looking at the results of different systems of organisation. If we make the unlikely supposition that A and B are both "socialistic" States, the exchange will then be in form exactly the same as that between individuals. The ratio of exchange must be arranged by treaty, and will be a high act of State,[8] so that any attempt to determine it would be practically impossible. When the usual state of individualistic industry is to be found, we have seen that reciprocal demand may be regarded as a fairly steady condition for determining the ratio of exchange; but it appears that it is possible to alter the ratio by means of the combination of dealers on each side. It is, as we shall see, also possible to affect the ratio of exchange by the imposition of charges on the act of exchange, or on the transfer of the commodities from country to country;[9] still the fundamental condition is what Mill has called "the equation of reciprocal demand," and all other operating forces work through it.[10] It is therefore requisite to see the extent to which the results attained by our purely hypothetical case are affected in the complex conditions of international trade. We may first give up the conception of the commodities x and y as being always produced at a fixed cost, and regard them as subject to the laws of diminishing or increasing return; the consequence which will necessarily follow is, that the limits set by cost of production which, up to the present, we have regarded as fixed become movable. Increased demand for a commodity subject to the law of diminishing return, will remove the limits set by comparative cost, and may also allow of the commodity being partly produced in both countries; thus, in the case already considered, some units of productive power in B may produce $25y$, others $20y$; but the unit on the margin will, *ex hypothesi*, produce but $15y$. Now, when international exchange commences at, say $10x$ to $17y$, all units in B which produce less than that amount are withdrawn from the production of y, and directed to that of x; but those which produce $17y$, or any greater amount, remain employed as before. The law of diminishing return may also affect A. Some units there may produce $40y$, some $30y$; but those at the margin will, *ex hypothesi*, produce but $20y$. The extended production which results from increased demand will probably lower the margin of cultivation, or, to speak more generally, of production; but when the margin comes down to $17y$, there will be no further gain by international exchange to A, so long as $17y$ is given for $10x$. The law of increasing return operates in the opposite direction; thus, if the increased demand for y, which arises from the growth of international exchange, causes it to be produced in A with greater ease, so that each unit will produce, say, $25y$, then it is clear that, in order to dispose of the additional supply, y must be offered at lower terms; and it may also be inferred that if y be subject to the law of diminishing return in B, as we have supposed, some more units of B's productive power will be withdrawn from the production of y and devoted to that of x. It is of course not likely that the same commodity will be subject to such contrasted conditions in two different countries. It is, however, possible that the recent development of agriculture in the United States and Canada has taken place under the law of increasing return, and that its effect on British farming is more noticeable, since the latter comes under the law of diminishing return. The same considerations may, too, explain the predominance of a manufacturing country, when once attained, since its productive power is steadily increasing, and thus extending the field of international exchange to the dismay of the native producers of manufactures in other countries; but whatever be the limits of their operation, it is demonstrable that the operation of the law of diminishing return tends to limit the area of international exchange, while that of the law of increasing return is calculated to extend it.

Another of our assumptions has been that there is perfectly free competition, which implies complete mobility of labour and capital within each of the countries or nations A and B; though, in considering the general features of the subject, we have seen that both these factors of production are, in a greater or less degree, impeded by the existence of customary conditions, as well as by the ignorance of producers, which is a necessary result of the great and increasing complexity of industrial organisation.

It now becomes necessary to consider the effect which the admission of this new element produces on the rates of international exchange. It is evident that hindrances to free competition may take one of two forms; for the whole body which produces x in either of the countries A and B may be rigidly marked off from that which produces y, or, again, each of those commodities may be produced by a number of groups which are not in effective competition with one another. In the former case, the element of cost of production is absent as a regulator; and, in truth, the producers of x and those of y are two completely distinct trading bodies, or in the economic use of the term "nations"; so that we have reached the complex case of three or more trading bodies which we shall investigate later on. In the second form of arrested competition it is probable that some of these groups will be in effective competition with the producers of the other commodity, be it x or y; and to that extent, the changes in the distribution of productive power will be just as in the case of perfectly free competition. Where competition is arrested, the group will be to that extent a distinct nation, and will have to be treated as such. The limits which custom, and, in less degree, cost of transport, set to effective competition, are, in general, not of so rigid a character as has just been represented. The production in an industry which is carried on under customary conditions, or with exceptional advantages of any kind, whether resulting from situation or trading, will not indeed alter under any slight change in the terms of supply brought about by the opening or development of foreign trade; but a large and sweeping variation will tend to break down the barriers of even the best-established custom, and to neutralise the effect of special aptitudes or facilities.

One peculiar feature of changes in the relations of non-competing groups, which is brought about by foreign trade, ought to be emphasised. We have seen that the advantage of foreign trade is due to the superior productiveness of industry, in consequence of its more efficient operation, by being applied to those industries only in which it possesses a relative advantage; and for this object, an actual change in the distribution and employment of productive force is needed. Where, however, there is no effective competition, no change can take place, and what really happens is a readjustment of the terms of exchange, so that what is gained by one group is lost by another, and, in appearance, there is no advantage to the country as a whole. On closer examination it will be discovered that a real advantage is gained, but that it consists, not in a more effective employment of productive power, but in the breaking down of a monopoly. For let it be assumed that the conditions of exchange in B are such as to establish the terms of $10x$ for $15y$, and further, that this ratio is the result of supply and demand, unaffected, or only partially affected, by cost of production; now, if by foreign trade the terms of exchange would be so altered as to give $10x$ for $17y$, but that the producers of y, being a non-competing group, are unable or unwilling to transfer their efforts to the production of x, and, instead, are ready to give $17y$ for $10x$, so that there is no necessity for carrying on foreign trade, is it not evident that the producers of y have hitherto been in possession of, at least, a qualified monopoly, by means of which they have been able to exact from the producers of x peculiarly favourable terms, and that by the opening of foreign trade this monopoly has been abolished, or to some extent diminished? The same considerations apply to the case of personal or local aptitudes, the gains of which always tend to be reduced by the opening up of other sources of supply. The importance, in a practical sense, of this fact will be best seen in relation to the protectionist controversy.

Up to the present we have retained the main elements of our original hypothesis, viz. two "nations," two commodities, and absence of all impediments to exchange. In order to approach, in some degree, the complexity of actual trade, let us insert each of the omitted elements, but in reverse order. Retaining the idea of two countries and two commodities, we first add the element of cost resulting from impediments to exchange, whatever be their character. To the legitimacy of this procedure, as adopted by Mill, objection has been made by Mr. Sidgwick;[11] but by the manner in which the general problem has been stated in the preceding chapter, this difficulty has been removed. Cost of transfer is not a necessary element in exchanges between individuals, or even between adjacent groups, and in many cases it is a very slight one.[12]

The effect of impediments will, of course, be to lessen the gain by foreign trade. In our hypothetical case we saw that $5y$ was the gain obtained by the opening of international exchange; but if we assume that the ratio of exchange is $10x$ to $17y$, and that the cost of transfer of each of these amounts is $1y$, the gain will be reduced to $3y$, and the ratio of exchange will not, in general, be the same in both countries, since the cost of transfer, or some of it, will have to be added to the commodity in the importing country. It follows that the alteration of value will produce a readjustment of the terms of international exchange; but it is impossible to say in what way the loss, arising from the sum of impediments, will be divided between the two countries. We have seen that in one unlikely case the whole gain of exchange might accrue to one country [p. 148], and under similar circumstances the whole cost of transfer might be placed on one of the parties; thus, if in A the demand for x was so intense as not to be reduced by its higher value, while in B the demand for y was so weak as to decrease more than proportionally to its rise in value, then the whole cost would fall on A, and the value of y would be the same in both countries, though, as, in such a case, B would, if there were no cost of carriage, have obtained the whole gain from foreign trade, the impediments would in reality be a deduction from its gains. It may, at any rate, be said with confidence, that the effect of impediments on foreign trade is, in general, to inflict a loss on both parties, but that we do not possess sufficient data to enable us to divide the amount of loss, any more than that of the total gain from foreign trade.

Impediments to transfer are – as Mill remarks – one, but not, as he seems to assert,[13] the only reason for the production of the same commodity in different, or, to keep to our case, in both countries. Let us assume, what is not unlikely, that the cost of placing $10x$ in A, and $17y$ in B, will come to $6y$, then the total gain – $5y$ – will be swallowed up, and be replaced by a loss of $1y$; so that the exchange would cease. The existence of impediments to transfer is, in fact, a tendency operating in somewhat the same way as the law of diminishing return, the effect of both being to limit the field of international exchange.

Another step towards reality may now be taken. Let us assume that A and B produce not x and y only, but also a third commodity z, and that one unit of productive power in A will produce $100z$, while one in B will only produce $90z$. Previous to the introduction of z, the terms of exchange have been, suppose, $10x = 16y$. B is now able to offer to A not x only, but also z, and it will be A's interest to take some of the commodity z at $17y = 90z$, as there would be a gain of $5z$ by the transaction, since in A $1y = 5z$ $\therefore$ $17y = 85z$. The exact terms of exchange will depend on the amount of x and z required by A compared with that of y by B; but whatever it may be, there is no doubt but that B's position, as a trader, will be improved. In like manner, a commodity w may be added, whose conditions of production are such that a unit of productive power in A produces $50w$, in B $40w$; here, if the ratios of exchange be, as would follow from the last case, $10x = 17y = 90z$, it will be A's interest to offer $45w$ for $10x$, since it thus gains $5w$; it is, too, for B's advantage to accept these terms, as it will also gain a similar amount.

The actual rates finally established will, in the more complex as in the simpler case, depend on the play of reciprocal demand; but it cannot be overlooked that the introduction of several commodities on each side will produce a steadying effect, in addition to that exerted by the presence of a large number of dealers and consumers. The terms of exchange will be set by the comparative demand of each nation for all the products of the other, which are the subject of foreign trade; and it is further implied in the very fact of exchange that "the exports of each country must exactly pay for the imports" (the cost of carriage being omitted). The extreme limits within which the terms of exchange can vary, will be set by the difference in the comparative cost of production of those commodities in respect to which the difference is widest; but as any tendency to move close to either of those points will be accompanied by a diminution in the number of articles entering into the trade and in the sum of exchanges, with a subsequent reduction of the total amount of gain, it will, in general, be likely that the terms of exchange will be near to the middle point (which, in our particular instance, would be $10x$ to $17\frac{1}{2}y$), or, more accurately, to a position determined by an average obtained from the comparative costs of all the commodities exchanged between A and B.

One special case has not yet been discussed, and as it has supplied critics with a specious objection, it ought to be noticed here. Suppose that the country B, instead of being able to produce y at the amount of 15 per unit of productive power, is absolutely incapable of so doing, or can gain from its own resources only a very small amount, say $1y$ for each unit. How, it has been asked, are the terms of exchange to be settled? And further, is not the possibility of such a case an evidence of the erroneousness of the theory?[14] The answer to this very plausible objection is to be found in the express statement of an element which is implicitly contained in Mill's theory, viz. the limit set to exchange by the comparative utility of the commodities x and y to the consumers in B. So long as the comparative costs of production were closer than the comparative utilities, there was no necessity for dwelling on this latter condition; that is to say, that so long as B could, from its own resources, obtain $15y$ for $10x$, there was no need to refer to the limit of utility, which, for an average amount, we shall assume to be $8y$ for $10x$. When, however, this power of producing at home the commodity required is withdrawn, the limit set by utility comes into operation, and it would furnish the really ultimate and complete limiting condition in cases of absolute monopoly on both sides.[15] It must, too, be added that utility varies with the quantity demanded, and that value is determined by the final or marginal utility, or the advantage to the consumer of the last increment obtained, so that in no respect does Cournot's criticism hold good.

The last step in turning our originally abstract and unreal hypothesis into an interpretation and illustration of international trade has now to be taken. Let us add to the two countries A and B a third country C, which is capable of producing the three commodities x, y and z, but in which the ratios of exchange, resulting from the comparative effects of the productive agents, are $10x$, $14y$, and $80z$. From inspection it is plain that the most economical arrangement will be the production of y by A, of z by B, and of x by C; for the total production, when each country produces for itself, will be $30x + 49y + 270z$, whereas, when each country takes up the production of that commodity in which it possesses a relative advantage, the total becomes $30x + 60y + 270z$, thus giving a gain of $11y$. It is also a consequence of the comparative conditions of production that C is able to supply x on better terms than A and B, who has previoulsy done so. Whether such will be the actual result, however, depends on the comparative intensity of the combined demand of A and B for x, as compared with the demand of C for y and z – a proposition which will also apply to the cases of A and B with regard to their respective products. The existence of two independent sources of supply for each of the commodities will, in addition, prevent the division of gain in any case being very much in favour of one of the parties. If, for instance, A and C were isolated from the rest of the world, $10x$ might conceivably exchange for almost $20y$; but the competition of B, who will find it expedient to withdraw from the production of z, in which it could, at the most, get $18y$ for $90z$, produced by the same sacrifice as it would cost to produce $10x$, will prevent such a result; so that the probable outcome would be the modification of any terms of exchange by which the advantages of the trade were very unequally divided.

A further consequence of great importance, and one which even popular doctrines on the subject fully recognise, is the effect on the parties already trading of the introduction of a new country. Up to the present it has appeared that a country always gains by foreign trade: the sum of its wealth is increased, or, in any case, better distributed. The effect of an extra trading body coming into the field may be to remove some of these advantages. It is possible that the competition of C may not permit of B's obtaining such favourable terms in the exchange of its products x and z. Nay more, it is evident that C would, under the assumed conditions, force B to abandon the production of x, and to confine its efforts to the production of z, in regard to which it did not, so long as its foreign dealings were confined to A, possess the greatest comparative advantage. In fact, B would be undersold by C. It is, however, possible that the increased demand for the commodity z, which would be the natural consequence of the introduction of C, would, to some extent, compensate for the loss inflicted on B. Whether this would be the case or not, it remains certain that the total production would be increased, and thus that the other countries (and A in particular) would gain more than B had lost., When more than two nations are introduced, it is also evident that the exports and imports passing between any two of the nations need not be equal. In an extreme case it is conceivable that, with three countries, each might only receive commodities from one, and only send them to the other; thus A might send y to C, who sent x to B, imports and exports will only be found over the whole trade of any country. The sum of its imports must equal that of its exports. That is, of course, assuming there are no other relations between it and other countries.

Having introduced each of the elements which, in the original hypothesis, were removed for facility of reasoning, let us suppose that a number of "nations," A, B, C, D, etc., trade with one another in respect to a number of commodities, x, y, z, u, etc.: what will be the consequence? The analogy between international exchange and that between independent individuals has already been dwelt on.[16] In each case there is room for somewhat wide variations where but two parties are concerned.[17] When a number of individuals within any nation are engaged in trade, a market, using that term in its wider meaning, grows up, and the terms of exchange become more definite, so that we may say that commodities, when freely produced, tend to exchange in the ratios of their respective costs of production; but the influence of cost of production does not prevent some individuals from receiving large rewards for what are to them slight exertions, and which may even be a source of pleasure.[18] The gains which persons thus obtain by their special taste for an employment which is usually regarded as onerous, are of the nature of rent, and deserve more attention than economists have been willing to bestow on them. In international trade similar phenomena are to be met with; but they have scarcely been noticed at all. The competition of different countries tends to establish a definite rate of exchange, and any aberrations from the terms thus settled are rectified by the play of reciprocal demand. The best evidence of the truth of this proposition is furnished by the exceptions which are found to exist. They all occur in the case of commodities produced in a single country, and even then are not always to be met with.

To rightly understand the nature of international trade, it is, above all things, necessary to constantly bear in mind its great complexity. The existence of numerous nations, in the economic sense, each the producer, actually or potentially, of many commodities – the fact that the cost of each of these commodities will vary according to the amount produced, some-times increasing, sometimes diminishing, as the production is extended – the operation of customary conditions within each nation giving rise to groups possessing what are virtually qualified monopolies – the limiting effects of the various impediments to transport, as also the operation of local advantages within each nation, have all to receive full recognition in the theory of international trade, and have to be realised when seeking to interpret any special phenomenon. It is obvious that without the use of special hypotheses, it would be impossible to work out any theory on so intricate a subject.[19]

Some further considerations bearing on the theory of international values may most suitably be considered here. (1) It may have occurred to the reader, that all through the preceding discussion the powers of production of the supposed countries, A and B, have been regarded as being approximately equal in amount; and the objection naturally arises, Would this theory apply to the case of trade between a small country and a large one: to take a concrete instance, beteen the Isle of Man and England? On examination it appears that there is no failure of the elementary principle, which regards comparative intensity of demand as fixing value. The small country A, let us assume, will, by its demand for x, but slightly affect the total demand in the large country B, and there will not be any serious alteration in its value, since the amount of y which A brings into the market is, *ex hypothesi*, small in proportion to the total amount of y. It therefore follows that the production of both x and y will continue to be carried on in B, while A will give its entire efforts to the production of y, and will therefore obtain almost the entire gain of the trade. With different costs of production of y in B, it is probable that B will receive some advantage, since the production of the most costly part of y will be abandoned by it. It is hardly necessary to add that the competition of other nations would have a tendency to deprive A of this special advantage; but nevertheless the probability is, that a small country gains by opening up trade with a large one – a point of some practical importance.[20]

(2) The way in which the gain of each nation has been computed also stands in need of further elucidation. For convenience we assumed that each nation had two units of productive power, which were not necessarily of the same amount in each country, and we considered the distribution of the gain resulting from the readjustment of the industrial forces, so far as these selected units were concerned. In the actual working of foreign trade, it is the whole productive power of a country which undergoes alteration, and it is as the result of this readjustment that gain is obtained. It is therefore plain that the definite figure $5y$, which we adopted in the earliest form of our hypothesis, is entirely illustrative, and that any quantitative estimate of the gain arising from international trade is not to be looked for. By altering the figures used for illustration, various divisions of the gain from trade may be arrived at; but then the differing results are obtained from altered *data*.[21] From the side of international value, the general conclusion must be, that the advantage of foreign trade consists – first, in lowering the value of imported goods, as compared with those produced at home, or in limiting the gains of special groups of producers, to the advantage of the society in general; and, second, in permitting the productive power of a country to be employed in those commodities for which it is specially fitted. In the ordinary illustrations this twofold benefit is lumped up in the gain on the process of exchange; but a not uncommon instance will bring the two elements into light. Suppose an improvement in the production of the commodity x to take place in B, so that $12x$ will be

produced by a unit of labour, this, of itself, would tend to lower the value of x, as measured in terms of y; but since it is the readjustment of industry resulting from foreign trade that has made it possible for x to be more cheaply produced, it follows that the gain of B will be obtained by that extra efficiency, while it is probable that some of the advantage will be retained in exchanging x for y, so that a double element of gain will be present. The nature of the commodities exchanged, and the extensibility of the demand for them, are in this latter case the determining conditions. The operation of the laws of increasing or diminishing return, as the case may be, also affects the question; if the commodities which a country imports are not subject to the latter law in the country from which they are obtained, but would be if produced at home, the country will gain considerably by the existence of a trade which prevents one set of the articles which it con-sumes from being produced at a constantly increasing cost. Should it happen that the law of increasing return is applicable to the production of the country's exports, it gains by the continuous augmentation of its industrial efficiency. The present position of England in respect to its foreign trade is somewhat of this kind; so that we might say, *a priori*, that her gains from commercial intercourse would be peculiarly large; and the evidence of statistics seems to verify this deduction.

(3) The effects of impediments to exchange on the course of trade is also deserving of some further notice. Among these impediments may be placed – (*a*) actual cost of carriage, such as shipping freights and railway charges; (*b*) brokers' and agents' commissions; and (*c*) import and export duties, whatever be their aim. With respect to the first of these deductions from the total gain, the important fact specially emphasised by Sidgwick, that transport is a double operation, is fundamental. The import has to be brought in, and the payment for it sent back; and, as the aim of men, regarded as traders, is to reduce all the expense incurred to obtain a given object, it follows that every effort will be made to diminish this cost of transfer. Another interesting point is the costliness of the very agents of transport. Ships and trains – to take the two most prominent agents – are not moved without difficulty, and therefore it is desirable to find profitable employment for them both on their outward and return journeys. The course of trade is often determined by the possibility of finding a return cargo; and instances may even be found of the creation of an industry for this purpose.[22]

No better illustration of the actual working of the abstract principles which have been considered in the present chapter, can be found than the way in which the cost of the double journey is divided in the case of the English coal exports, so thoroughly investigated by Jevons.[23] Those places which have no return cargo to furnish are compelled to pay the total cost of the two voyages; their exports in payment being, as we shall see, adjusted by means of the foreign exchanges. The effect of commissions

157

is, of course, the same as that of freights; but it must be remembered, that the rate of profit expected by a trader is that to be obtained in the country where he resides, and, owing to the generally hazardous character of foreign trading, will naturally be even higher, so that it is probable that a country with a low rate of interest will be at an advantage in engaging in the carrying trade.

German writers, and Mangoldt in particular, have laid stress on the distinction between "active" and "passive" nations, *i.e.* between those that carry on foreign commerce themselves, and those that simply admit traders from other countries. Such a distinction belongs rather to the historical development of commerce than to the abstract theory. It is of course plain that the traders of the "active" country have at first an opportunity for special gain, since they will avail themselves of any advantages that the conditions of a passive country afford . . . In time, however, this "opportunity" gain disappears and is replaced by the usual interest on enterprises of the same class, and the equally normal profits of the undertaker or *entrepreneur* . . .

Chapter VII: Taxation for Revenue in its Effects on Foreign Trade

When treating of the various conditions affecting international values, we found it necessary to consider the results which followed from impediments to exchange, without making any distinction as to their origin; and such a method of procedure was evidently legitimate, since the effect on value was produced by the mere existence of the impediment, not at all by its special features. There is, however, one kind of hindrance which, on account of its practical importance, needs a separate investigation, viz. that caused by duties levied on imports and exports. For the present we will only inquire into the operation of revenue duties as distinguished from those which seek to "protect" native industry. The aim of the persons imposing the former is – or ought to be – to obtain a maximum return, and therefore the greater, *cæteris paribus*, the amount of goods passed from country to country, the greater will be their satisfaction. "Protective" duties, on the other hand, are only completely successful when all foreign goods are excluded, and therefore attain their end most effectually when they bring in no revenue whatsoever. We are, however, here dealing with facts, not with desires or intentions, and consequently, when a duty, ostensibly levied for protection, does bring in some return, we shall regard it as being, to that extent, a revenue duty. There is, of course, no protection where an equivalent tax is imposed on the home product, even though no revenue is obtained on the importation of the article; since it is certain that the removal of the tax would not cause any change, as the native producers would retain the same relative advantage. The reason for a special treatment of the particular class of impediments under consideration lies in the fact that, while all other hindrances require efforts to overcome them, and are thus a dead loss, taxes may increase the State's revenue, and help it to meet the expenses incurred in the discharge of its functions. Still they are a deduction from the gain of exchange, and their influence and true effects can only be known by regarding them from that point of view.

Taxes may be levied either on exports or on imports;[24] and it will be found most convenient to commence by examining the operation of the former class of imposts. Suppose, then, that – all other things remaining the same – a country imposes an export duty on one of its staple products, the natural result will be a rise of price, owing to the enhancement of its expenses of production for foreign markets; the foreign demand for the commodity in question will in all probability be reduced, and the change in demand will almost necessarily entail an alteration in the conditions affecting the equation of indebtedness, but in what direction it is beyond the power of abstract reasoning to point out without more precise facts to work on. Two conditions of particular weight in determining the final results are – (1) the position of the exporting country as a producer; and (2) the nature of the demand for the commodity in the importing countries. Should the exporting nation possess a monopoly of the production of the taxed article, it is evidently possible that the tax may at least partially fall on foreigners; but if other countries produce the commodity, it is almost certain that exportation will cease, and that a loss will be inflicted on native producers, while no revenue will be obtained. It is, therefore, only in instances where a virtual monopoly exists that export duties have ever been even suggested. The extent and the intensity of the foreign demand will also affect the productiveness of the tax, as well as its incidence. Where an increase of price largely reduces the quantity sought for, it is possible that the amount exported may be less in value than before the imposition of the duty, and thus the equation of indebtedness may be altered to the disadvantage of the exporting nation. These facts lead directly to the proposition usually adopted by writers who have entered on this topic, viz. that an export duty is only expedient, on economic grounds, where the country imposing it has a monopoly of the article taxed, for which article, moreover, the foreign demand is intense.[25] It is supposed that in such a case the duty would fall on the foreign countries which consume the taxed commodity. The export duty on opium in India, and also that levied on wool in mediæval England, have been regarded as illustrating this proposition, and for similar reasons an export duty on cotton has been advocated in the United States. The *data* set forth above do not warrant the conclusion so confidently drawn, since they will be found on investigation to be incomplete. It is not the demand for any single commodity which determines the equation of demand – omitting, for simplicity, the still more involved relations arising from the forms of indebtedness in general – but the comparative demand for all the exports and for all the imports [pp. 152–3, 154–5]; from which it follows that even if the demand of the taxed commodity be undiminished, yet that for other exports of the taxing country may be reduced; and, since the purchasing power of the importing countries will necessarily be lessened by the increased expenditure on the taxed article, such a consequence is very likely. As all international trade is connected through the operation of the foreign exchanges, the loss to the taxing country may perhaps be experienced in its trade with countries which do not import the taxed commodity, but whose relations with it are affected by the alterations in the general terms of exchange produced through the operation of the duty. For the purpose of illustration, we may take the possible effects of the export duty on Indian opium. Even granting that the Chinese demand for that drug remains unaffected by the tax, it yet may happen that the demand of China for English manufactures will be reduced thereby, and that in turn the terms on which India receives silver from England will be altered. The consequence of this change might indeed be such as to favour India, and thus present an additional inducement for the imposition of the duty; but it would be impossible to decide which would be the final result.

Some further considerations bearing on this very difficult subject should not be overlooked in any attempt to estimate the influence of export duties. One of these is the operation of the law of diminishing return. Where that law governs production, an export duty will, to some extent, fall on rent, since if it slightly reduces the amount exported, the production of the most costly portion will be abandoned, the price, apart from the tax, will fall, and to that extent the owners of the more productive agents still employed in turning out the taxed commodity will suffer. As demand is frequently fluctuating, and the raw material in nearly all industries is more or less subject to the law whose effect we are considering, it is impossible to show that this result is not always to be found in the case of export duties.

Again, taxes on exports may be defended as, under certain conditions, being equivalent to a national association to raise their price. Thus, reverting to our Indian example, it might be argued that under free competition the price of opium would be fixed by cost of production at the lowest profitable amount,[26] but that the duty will raise the price, and thus have the same effect as a combination of dealers or a trade union in the market for commodities or for labour. We have already [p. 149] recognised the existence of this possible case; but to estimate its probability, the whole state of international indebtedness has to be examined, and especially the conditions of reciprocal demand as regards other commodities.

It should be remarked that export duties on exhaustible articles which are aids to production – as in the cases of English coal and Peruvian guano – have to be mainly judged on non-economic grounds; but the reasons which justify such measures will prescribe duties on home consumption as well.[27] From the financial point of view, all duties on exports which are not highly productive are objectionable, since they fail in the first object of taxation. Export duties have not in general been popular, as they conflicted with the views of the mercantile theorists, who aimed at increasing exports, and who consequently preferred to give premiums on exportation, instead of loading it with duties. It was only in the case of raw materials that such taxes were tolerated, and then only with the object of preserving them for the use of the native manufacturers of finished products.[28]

Import duties next claim our attention. They, too, are impediments to trade, and, in general, tend to reduce its advantage. Like export duties, they operate on the terms of exchange, through the necessary readjustment in the equation of reciprocal demand. As when dealing with taxes on exports, let us suppose that – no other change taking place – a country imposes a duty on a particular commodity which is imported, and which, to simplify the inquiry, we will assume is not produced in the taxing country. The price will at first be raised by the amount of the duty, and probably the demand will be diminished. This diminution will lead to a further alteration, since, the demand being reduced, the importing country will have a balance in its favour which will have to be liquidated by a flow of bullion towards it; and the terms of exchange will be altered to suit the new state of things; but, as with export duties, the actual result cannot be predicted. Here, again, there are conditions of primary importance for forming a correct judgment on the probabilities of the case – (1) If the demand of the taxing country for the commodity be weak, it is possible that the alteration may be to its advantage; and (2) if there be no other country which requires the taxed product, it is evident that its position is made still stronger; for the weakness of demand will lower the value of the imported article, and the absence of any other market will render it advantageous for the producers to sell at any terms above those set by the limits of comparative cost. In truth, these conditions are analogous to those which we met when dealing with export duties.[29] There the most favourable instance for the duty was monopoly of production, combined with intensity of demand. Here it consists in weakness of demand, with monopoly of consumption, if the phrase be permitted.[30] Instances of this latter kind are, however, of rare occurrence; there are very few articles which are only used in one country, and the demand for which at the same time falls rapidly on a slight elevation of price. It would, therefore, appear that it is extremely difficult to tax foreigners by the instrumentality of duties on imports.[31] It, however, not infrequently happens that some particular class of producers may find their best market in a particular country. An import tax imposed by that country on their product, if it seriously reduces demand, may fall on them. Possible instances are supplied by the alleged effect of the duties under the U.S. tariff of 1890 on the prices of tin-plates, Sumatran tobacco, and Canadian farm produce. An import duty in England on Irish cattle would, it is likely, fall in part on Irish producers. It must be added that it is very difficult to discover the real operation of such taxes. Price movements are due to many different causes, which are not easily disentangled, and the precise weight to be assigned to each is hardly ever capable of determination.[32] Import duties have, however, been generally preferred to taxes on exports; but their aim has been either to afford "protection" to native producers, or the more reasonable and legitimate one of obtaining revenue from the consumers of the imported articles.

Though it is not easy to discover a case in which import duties, imposed by one country only, would fall on the foreign countries that export the taxed commodity, yet a modified form, which closely resembles it, is far from being uncommon. Suppose that a number of countries all impose similar duties on articles which are the staple products of certain other nations: here the taxing countries may constitute the principal market for the product; their demand may be reduced by the tax, and, if so, some, and even perhaps most, of the loss from the impeded exchange would be borne by the producing countries. Thus, let us assume that all the various nations of Europe were to levy the same amount of import duty on tea, which is the product of a different group of nations – economically speaking – viz. China, India, Japan, Ceylon, and Java: there is nothing absurd or unreasonable in supposing that a reduction in the quantity demanded would, at first, be the result; leading to an offer of all Eastern products on more advantageous terms. In this particular case the conditions would favour such a change, since an elevation in price of an article not absolutely necessary, but still generally consumed, quickly reduces the demand. A similiar extension of the propositions relating to export duties is also justified. A tax on the export of wine in all wine-producing countries might fall, for the most part, on the countries which imported it; but here the condition of intensity of demand would probably be absent, and, if so, the rent of vineyards would have to bear an indefinite amount of the duty. In general it must be said that, as the conditions of supply and demand, in domestic trade, can be affected by skilled combinations, so the same forces in foreign trade can be made to yield like results by the use of analogous means. Export duties are, as we have said, similar in effect to combinations of producers, as import duties to those of consumers. Nor does the resemblance cease here. The two sets of influences are alike in their weakness as in their strength. The outside dealer who does not join in the combination is yet able to profit by its result; and, in like manner, the producing nation which does not impose export duties gets the advantage of the increased demand which is directed towards its part of the produce. Thus, suppose that France, Spain, Italy, and Germany imposed an export duty on wine, but that Portugal did not, then manifestly the latter country would profit by the duty, while getting also the advantage of increased demand. So likewise if, while all other European

162

nations levied duties on imported tea, England admitted it free of tax, she would profit by the reduction of demand, and thus get her own supply at a cheaper rate than if there were no duty – in fact, she would gain the same advantage as the taxing countries by the operation of the duty, while her inhabitants would not suffer from the inconvenience of restricting their demand, which would be the consequence of the higher price in the other countries. The above conclusion is, of course, drawn without prejudice to cases in which the tax may be the best mode of raising revenue from the native consumers. It only applies when the duty is not imposed on purely fiscal grounds, but rather as a mode of manipulating the equation of reciprocal demand.

The considerations just adduced appear to have an important bearing on a question which has been much discussed of late years, viz. the effect of foreign tariffs on British trade. The advocates of high tariffs in the United States and other countries have contended that the duties imposed on imports from England have been paid by the English producers, and have not raised prices. A similar idea is, to some extent, to be found prevailing in England. In seeking to deal with this matter, we must first lay aside the case of protective duties, which have been reserved for further examination, and confine our attention to duties which bring in revenue. The existence of high duties in most foreign countries may, it is clear, reduce the demand for English products, and thus affect the terms of exchange to that country's disadvantage. The loss, however, would fall on the nation as a whole, not on the special class of producers for export, unless they possessed a monopoly, when the duty would, indeed, be a deduction from the monopolists' gains, which can hardly be regarded as those of producers proper. That such has been the actual result is not established by anything like the amount of evidence required. The fact (if fact it be) that the difference in prices between English and American iron is not as great as the amount of the import duty does not prove it, since, if it were generally true, no iron would be imported, and the duty would not be one of revenue. The occasional import of iron at a low price is equally unsatisfactory, since there is no way of judging of the special circumstances – as, *e.g.*, bankruptcy of a particular firm – which may have made such a step desirable. Nor is it necessary to prove a diffference in price between English and American iron (the duty excluded); for, if the iron industry be carried on under normal conditions, it is not possible that English producers will sell their product cheaper in foreign countries than at home, as, by lowering the price of the home product slightly, the demand would be so increased as to carry off the stock now sent abroad, and the action of competition would almost necessarily have this effect, since, were it otherwise, iron must be above its cost value in England, or below it in America; but in the former case a monopoly value would exist; in the latter, English exporters would be trading at a loss. It follows, therefore, that, regarding

163

the trade as a continuous one, the prices of imported iron in America must exceed those in England by an amount equal to the sum of the impediments to transfer, *i.e.* cost of carriage and duty. The real adjustment of the incidence of revenue duties will be through the scale of prices prevailing in the countries concerned; and it is quite possible that the heavy taxes on English manufactures, especially in the colonies, where they operate chiefly as revenue duties, may have some such effect; but nothing beyond this admission is warranted by evidence, nor is it easy to see in what way the actual existence of such a condition of things could be established or refuted.

The foregoing remarks suggest another aspect of the question of tariffs – What is the position of a single country without such duties when trading with a number of countries, all of which have them in full force against the productions of all other nations? We have seen that a country without duties may gain the advantages of the export or import duties imposed by other countries, and at the same time be free from their disadvantages. The nation of our supposition is in a somewhat similar situation. Her trade is, indeed, affected by the duties of other countries; but, then, so also is the trade of each of those countries, while she has an advantage when competing with any of the duty-levying nations for the consumption of the products of a third country. The terms of exchange are altered by the operation of the duties, and, in addition to this advantage, she gets the commodities she needs by as much less as the amount of the duty in other nations. In the export trade she has the benefit of her cheaper imports, so far as they are auxiliary to production, which, in a highly-developed system of industry, must be generally an important factor; and she further possesses the advantage given by the influence of freights [p. 157], by reason of which, other things being equal, her exports will be preferred to those of the countries which levy high duties. When the advantages and disadvantages of such a position are compared, it is highly probable that the former will be found to exceed the latter; but, for a more precise determination, the size and number of the various taxing countries should be taken into account; for the smaller the number of taxing nations, the less opportunity there will be for obtaining the advantages just pointed out. The conclusions thus arrived at, by deduction from the elementary conditions governing international values, are, in some degree, verified by the position of England as regards her foreign trade, more especially in respect to competition with other countries in neutral markets. It should, however, be carefully noted that all such statements must be taken subject to the qualifications necessarily involved. They are drawn from the examination of a few leading features of foreign trade applied under conditions which have been much simplified, and are thus far removed from reality – a characteristic which makes them quite unfit for that sweeping application to practice which has been the greatest weakness of the older English economic school. But, this caution notwithstanding, these more refined considerations present a double advantage, for (1) they indicate the proper direction of statistical inquiry, and thus enable those conversant with the facts of trade to supply the suitable clothing which will render them, when corrected, capable of interpreting the phenomena of international exchange,[33] and (2) they discharge a useful negative function in refuting the doctrines of so-called practical men, which are in reality made up of unsound deductions from defective premises. The most thorough investigation of the general forces which are at work in determining the course of foreign trade, shows the great complexity of the phenomena to be dealt with, as well as the improbability of any conscious intervention being likely to alter the course of exchange in the interests of a particular country.

Bounties, either on exportation or importation, are, from the scientific point of view, "negative taxes" – to use Cournot's phrase.[34] They artificially reduce the value of the commodities to which they are applied, just as ordinary duties raise it; and, therefore, they tend to increase the amount of foreign trade, and so far produce a gain which will be divided among the trading countries, according to the conditions of demand existing at the time: but in addition they involve an outlay on the part of the nation which pays them greater than the gain obtained, since the necessity of the bounty proves that the industry supported by it is less profitable than that to which, without interference, the productive power of the country would have been directed. It is probable that most of the advantage will go to the nations which import the subsidised product; and it is certain that the expense of the bounty will fall wholly on the country bestowing it. If the commodity be subject to the law of diminishing return, the lowering of the margin of production may raise the cost of the most expensive part, when the bounty will partly go towards rent, and partly be lost in the extra cost of production. The well-known instances of the bounties on beet-root sugar illustrate instructively the operation of both these cases, since the raw material is subject to the law governing all extractive industry, while the manufacture product conforms to the ordinary rule. It is possible that in an industry where the amount of produce rapidly increases with concentration and application of labour and capital on a large scale, the gain thus obtained would equal, or perhaps exceed, the loss incurred by the artificial redistribution of production; but even here the loss to the State's revenue would not be compensated, and there is little chance of the development, under a bounty system, being superior to that which would result from complete freedom. From the scientific point of view, it is, however, right to indicate the possibility of such a case, though its realisation is hardly within the region of practice.

One particular class of taxes presents such peculiarities that it is best treated apart, viz. that of charges levied on the money-material. What, *e.g.*, would be the effect of an export duty on Australian gold? In this case the law of demand is perfectly regular, and the raising of the value of bullion ought apparently to be met by a reduction in the quantity needed for exportation. As, however, there are other gold-producing countries, and as gold does not apparently change in price, the result would be that the tax would fall on the producers, and therefore, if the industry were regularly organised, necessarily on the owners of the mines. Assuming effective competition, it follows that the production of gold would be diminished, and its value would rise, thus benefiting all gold-producing countries, and in some degree the whole world, since the gold employed as money is, of course, a dead loss, *i.e.* so far as its functions could be discharged by a smaller amount. What holds true of export duties partly applies to taxes on the importation of the precious metals, which, in general, take the form of seigniorage. So far as internal trade is concerned, they enable the country to manage with a smaller stock of bullion, while they allow of its preserving the due scale of prices; but they hinder the working of foreign trade, and check the speedy adjustment of the exchanges. Should all countries establish a similar amount of seigniorage on their coins, it seems clear that it would in reality be a tax on the production of the precious metals, that is, so far as their production is carried on in the ordinary way, otherwise it would be equivalent to a general rise of nominal prices. It, perhaps, ought to be added that the absence of all mint charges is in fact a bounty on the importation of bullion, as Dudley North clearly saw.[35]

Before quitting the subject of taxes for revenue, which are calculated to affect the course of foreign trade, it may be advisable to look at such duties, taken as a whole. Thus regarded, they appear as a deduction from the gains by international exchange, against which their yield in revenue to the States imposing them should be set off; but in this calculation of advantages and disadvantages, all the elements involved must be considered. Every duty on the transfer of commodities is more or less a "privative" tax. It hinders some persons purchasing the article, and diminishes their enjoyment, without any corresponding advantage to the revenue. All import and export duties – the case of taxes on money excepted – have this effect. They therefore cause greater loss than gain; as each duty, in some degree, reduces the field of exchange, and the resulting utility. That such is the outcome of these taxes, in their extreme form, Mill fully recognised; for even when suggesting retaliatory import duties, he adds: "Only it" (the nation imposing them) "must take care that these duties be not so high as to exceed all that remains of the advantage of the trade, and put an end to importation altogether."[36] It is one of the many strange things in his economic writings, that he should suppose that the movement from complete freedom to total cessation of exchange took place *per saltum*. It is evident that each addition to the duties on either side would remove some of the advantage of exchange, and that every reduction would somewhat increase it. Duties on commodities may be necessary to the financier; but his object should be

– entirely disregarding the fiscal policy of other nations – to obtain the maximum of revenue. A purely revenue duty aiming at "retaliation" – if such be not even a contradiction in terms – is manifestly uneconomical, and thus offends against the fourth of Adam Smith's famous maxims, all of which should be substantially obeyed in a sound financial system.

NOTES

1 Professor Nicholson, in his important *Principles of Political Economy* (vol. ii. pp. 268 *sq.*), has followed Cournot by handling the problems of foreign trade in terms of money without any preliminary discussion from the point of view adopted in the text. His treatment is interesting and suggestive, but, on the whole, the older method appears to be preferable. For a fuller notice see Appendix C.

2 Cp. Leslie, *Essays*, p. 158; Cairnes, *Logical Method*, pp. 77–84; Ingram, *History of Political Economy*, pp. 187, 242; Sidgwick, *Principles*, Introduction, chap. iii.; Schmoller, *Jahrbuch* (1888), p. 256.

3 Thus Cournot, *Théorie des Richesses*, p. 344, objects to the undue exaltation of capital by the English school, though, curiously enough, it is labour that Ricardo and J.S. Mill mainly consider in their theories of international value.

4 *Theory of Political Economy*, p. 134.

5 Cp. "Ten yards of cloth cannot exchange for more than twenty yards of linen, nor for less than fifteen, but they may exchange for any intermediate number." – *Principles*, iii. 18, § 2, with iii. 18, § 6, and iii. 18 § 8.

6 Jevons, *Theory*, pp. 134–135. Cp. Bagehot, *Economic Studies*, pp. 136–145.

7 J.S. Mill, *Principles*, iii. 18, § 2.

8 For a good argument against socialism, based on the difficulty of conducting international trade under that *régime*, see Leroy-Beaulieu, *Le Collectivisme*, pp. 393–399.

9 See Chap.. VII.

10 The attempt made by Mill to amend his theory by introducing the addiitonal element of the amount of capital set free from the produciton of exports is, as he even seems to admit, a failure; for, in the case of two countries and two commodities, the amount of freed capital, or, as I should prefer to say, "productive power," is evidently determined by reciprocal demand, so that nothing is gained by the laborious and confusing discussion in secs. 6, 7, 8 of chap. xviii. Professor Edgeworth's authority may be quoted in support of this criticism. See his "International Values" in *Economic Journal*, vol. iv. p 609.

11 *Principles*, p. 206.

12 It is not at all clear that Mr. Sidgwick's criticism would hold as against Mill. Even granting that cost of carriage is a necessary element, may it not still be legitimate to make provisional abstraction of it, in order to facilitate reasoning?

13 "Cost of carriage has one effect more. But for it, every commodity would (if trade be supposed free) be either regularly imported or regularly exported. A country would make nothing for itself which it did not also make for other countries." – *Principles*, iii, 18, § 3.

14 See Cournot, *Théorie des Richesses*, pp. 344–345, for this objection. Like all the doctrines of that acute thinker, it deserves examination.

15 This operation of utility is fully recognised by Mill. "The utility of a thing, in

the estimation of a purchaser, is the extreme limit of its exchange value: higher the value cannot ascend." – *Principles*, iii. 2, § 1. In criticising the statement in the text, Professor Edgeworth [pp. 623–624) seems to have overlooked the particular passage in Cournot to which it is intended as a reply. Cournot urges that in the case of an article not producible in A, the advantage obtained would be *infinite* – "an exaggerated deduction which warrants us to distrust the theory." This contention seems satisfactorily encountered by reference to the limit set by the utility of the article to consumers, which may be small, and is never infinite.

16 See p. 13.

17 In a tribe of savages, "if any exchanges took place between individuals within the community, they would obviously be governed, not by cost of production, but, like the exchange between Esau and Jacob, by the urgency of the respective needs of the parties." – Leslie, *Essays*, p. 181.

18 "The laborious effort fitted to produce a given result does not represent the same sacrifice for different people: it is one thing for the strong, another for the weak; one for the trained workman, another for the raw beginner." – Cairnes, *Leading Principles*, p. 95.

   Cp. Sidgwick, *Principles*, p. 58: – "In fact, when we consider the higher kinds of skilled labour, it must be evident that the labourer often gets more enjoyment out of his work than he does out of anything else in life."

19 Cournot, *Théorie des Richesses*, pp. 349–350, objects to the hypothetical procedure as adopted by Mill, and prefers to deal with the complex problem; but his results are not encouraging.

20 The consideration noticed in the above paragraph has been developed in an interesting way by Professor Nicholson, *Principles of Political Economy*, vol. ii. pp. 302 *sq.*

21 Cournot, *Théorie des Richesses*, p. 345, objects to Mill's theory, on the ground that taking y instead of x as the common "denominator" or measure (see p. 24), the percentage of gain obtained by each party would be different. Thus, if instead of taking $10x$ or $15y$ in A, we suppose that a unit in A produces $13\frac{1}{3}x$ or $20y$, then on the hypothesis that the ratio of exchange after international trade is opened is $10x : 18y$, Cournot argues that the percentages of gain to A and B will be $16\frac{2}{3}$ and $11\frac{1}{9}$ respectively, while if the original figures were retained the percentages would be 20 and 10, and adds that "mathematical questions do not admit of such ambiguities." His contention is regarded by Professor Edgeworth as "hitting an inaccuracy on a very plausible interpretation of Mill; on any interpretation an inelegancy" (*Economic Journal*, vol. iv. p. 624, cp. p. 609). It is, however, certain that the difficulty is entirely imaginary. As pointed out in the text, the particular figures are merely illustrative. The varying percentages which Cournot obtains are due to the illegitimate changes which he makes in the units employed. In the original illustration he estimates the percentage by taking the produce of the less efficient unit in A (15) and that of the more efficient unit in B (20); in the second and altered one he take the produce of the more efficient unit in A ($13\frac{1}{3}$) and that of the less efficient unit in B (10). As a necessary result different percentages are obtained. A more natural method would be to calculate the amount of gain by taking the total result of the two productive units in each country, reducing the two commodities to a common measure, by which process precisely the same percentages would be obtained in either case.

22 The Glasgow potteries mentioned by Hearn (*Plutology*, p. 310] are a case in point.

23 *Coal Question*, chap. xiii.

24 Transit duties are probably earlier than either import or export duties, but they have now little importance. They no doubt may bring in revenue to the State at the expense of foreigners, but they tend to reduce and divert traffic, and accordingly lower the gains of transport agencies in the country employing them. The duty levied on opium passing from the native estates to China through British India is the best known example of such a charge. Cp. *Wealth of Nations*, p. 379.

25 See Thorold Rogers, *Six Centuries of Work and Wages*, p. 79. The four conditions there specified are all included under the two mentioned in the text.

26 For this doctrine, cp. Sidgwick, *Principles*, p. 183.

27 See Jevons, *Coal Question*, pp. 354–364. For the export duty on English coal, imposed in 1901, see *Economic Journal*, vol. xi, p. 225.

28 See *Wealth of Nations*, book iv. chap. viii; cp. Bastable, *Public Finance*, p. 513.

29 This resemblance has been elsewhere described by saying "that there is a kind of symmetry in the action of both classes, so that import duties are really export ones reversed." Professor Edgeworth, in his examination of international value from the mathematical economist's standpoint, denied the existence of this symmetry, and declared that "the want of symmetry between the effects of . . . taxes on exports and imports is the conclusion which can be most peculiarly and exclusively attributed to the mathematical method" (*Economic Journal*, vol. iv. p.. 435). Further consideration, however, led him to the conclusion "that the symmetry predicated" above "does in general exist."

30 "Buyers' monopoly" is Sidgwick's phrase, *Principles*, p. 340.

31 The different conclusion arrived at by Mill, *Principles*, v. 4, § 6, may be explained by his confining his attention to the case of two countries, by which course the element of monopoly, both in supply and demand, is implicitly introduced.

32 The controversies as to the real effect of M'Kinley tariff illustrate the statement in the text. See Edgeworth, *Economic Journal*, vol iv. pp. 45, 46, and Mr. Shearman's criticism, *ibid.* vol. iv. pp. 524–527. Cp. Professor Nicholson's remark (*Scottish Geographical Magazine*, Sept. 1891), "The incidence of import and export duties, especially when the direct effects are considered, is the most complicated and difficult problem in economics."

33 The studies of Sir R. Giffen (*Reports on Foreign Trade*) and Professor Flax ("The Commercial Supremacy of Great Britain," in *Economic Journal*, vol. iv. pp. 457 *sq.* 595 *sq.*; vol. ix, pp. 173 *sq.*, and "British Trade and German Competition," *Economic Journal*, vol. vii, pp. 34 *sq.*) may be referred to as admirable examples of statistical method. On the other hand, Mr. Williams's *Made in Germany* may be noticed as affording a warning of the dangers that beset the incautious.

34 *Théorie des Richesses*, p. 374.

35 *Discourses on Trade* (1691).

36 *Essays on some Unsettled Questions*, p. 29.

7 LETTER TO MR. BALFOUR*

Percy Ashley

Private

> The Settlement,
> Tavistock Place,
> W.C.
> 4th July, 1903

Dear Mr. Balfour

Herewith I send you the completing part of the summary of Wagner. It is, I am afraid, rather tabular and statistical, but his main line of argument is fairly clear. Combining this with the account of his views contained in the memo. on the German tariff controversy, one might I think, summarise his argument in something like the following way: –

(I) The great development in the British Export industry came in the fifties and sixties; it was due partly to natural advantages, but still more to the fact that Great Britain was the first largely-industrialised state, and was undisturbed by such troubles as harassed continental Europe and the United States during that period.

(II) Since then, in spite of the increase of markets of one kind or another (in China, the Colonies, etc.) British exports have not increased at all considerably, except because of (a) coal, (b) machinery. The general statistics tend to show that our export of British produce is as a whole almost stationary; or at least has not increased in proportion to the increase of population.

(III) This is due to the industrialisation of other nations – a process rendered possible in regard to those branches of production in which we once stood almost alone (textiles, steel and iron), by their Protective Systems, which have enabled foreign producers (a) to keep our goods out of their home markets; (b) by means of the profits which they can thus make at home, to compete with us in other markets; (c) to harass our manufactures even in the British markets.

(IV) This is, however, the inevitable fate of any country which devotes itself entirely to industry – it is already threatening Germany. The problem is: What is a nation to do when it finds itself coming to this predicament?

(V) Such a nation must prepare itself for an economic re-adjustment: it must aim at securing the home market to its own manufacturers. (This is Carnegie's doctrine, that if you secure the home market the export business will take care of itself.) And it must seek to render as easy as possible the transfer of surplus labour and capital from one industry, which would have too much of both under the new conditions, to another which had too

---

* Percy Ashley, "Letter to Mr. Balfour" (4 July 1903), British Museum Additional MSS, 49780.

little; it should prevent an *abrupt* transition. To accomplish these two purposes a moderate protective tariff is the most effective instrument.

(VI) The ultimate aim should be self-sufficiency; and clearly the larger the area which you possess, and the more varied its resources, the greater the chance of attaining the desired end.

Such I gather to be Wagner's general doctrine, and I confess that there seems to be a good deal to be said for it. But there are some fairly obvious comments. (I) It is true that our rate of increase of exported produce has slackened, but it is very doubtful if we could reasonably have expected that we should do more than hold our own, in the fierce rivalry. (II) Much of the competition is purely artificial; it is only rendered possible by the tariff policies and the action of the trusts; and both in Germany and the United States there is growing opposition. (III) If the transfer of industries is economically desirable, it will invevitably take place: the difficulty about trying to ease the transition by moderate protective duties is that once these are imposed vested interests in them are created, and the original purpose becomes lost from sight. (That seems to me to apply equally to Brentano's idea of fighting "dumping down" by means of tariffs.) (IV) Self-sufficiency is no doubt an ideal, but to attain it requires (a) a large area; (b) a central directing force; (c) a common purpose shared by all the inhabitants of that area. We have the first in the British Empire; we may possibly get the second; unless the Colonies abandon their attempts to become industrial, I see no prospect of the third. (V) Such a policy would entail a rapid increase in population in Australia, Canada, and New Zealand, and the Cape – the home population remaining much as it is. But as there is no sign of this rapid increase, there would have to be a redistribution of the white population of the Empire.

I have been considering, as far as I can, some of the other points which you put to me; and particularly the problem of what is going to happen when practically all foreign countries have tried to close themselves against our manufacturers by tariffs, and we are consequently unable to export manufactured goods largely. Of course at the present time our exports of manufactured goods (British, Foreign and Colonial Produce) only pay for less that 3/5 of our imports; but in regard to the general problem just stated there seem to me several considerations which must be taken into account.

First of all, it is obviously impossible for any large number of countries to become self-sufficing unless their wants remain extremely limited, and their standard of life low. The small countries of the Balkan peninsula, Spain and Portugal, Norway and Sweden (to mention only European examples) can never be self-sufficing; and of the large countries many have not the resources and climatic conditions necessary for many branches of production.

171

Secondly, it is evident that when a protective and a non-protective country are fighting to secure admission into the markets of a third country, the non-protective country has a distinct advantage – for its producers get food, raw materials, and semi-manufactured materials cheaper than the manufacturers in a protective country; and have their cost of production by so much reduced.

Thirdly, it is quite evident that some industries must go. We cannot, I think, hope to hold the cotton trade, except for special kinds of goods whose production is favoured by the dampness of the British climate; we cannot expect to command (in fact, we have already ceased to command) the iron and steel trade. But, if scientific and industrial ability remains to the country, new industries will develop. The fact that in 1872 the textile and iron and steel *and coal* trades accounted for 83% of our total exports of British Products, but in 1898 for only 69% (and in 1900 for 74%) may mean that those particular industries are stationary or declining somewhat; but, *since our total exports have increased rather than declined,* it means also that we have a more varied supply of commodities to export, i.e., that a greater variety of industries is arising in this country.

Fourthly, our manufacturers have carried the war into the enemy's country by going within the tariff walls. So Coats have set up works in Germany and are supplying the foreign markets from there; and British capital and British management are setting up works of many kinds in many places. The manufacturers possibly could not have obtained sufficient labour for such extensions in this country; and even if they have not extended operations, but only changed the place, whilst the British workers in that industry may have suffered, (that is unhappily an inevitable result of all industrial development) – yet the industry is British and is promoting the wealth of this country.

Fifthly, our demand for imports is growing and clearly we are paying for them somehow. It is by our exports, by our services in transport and middleman operations; and they represent the profits flowing to this country from (a) British industries established abroad, (b) other British investments abroad. I see no evidence that these other investments abroad are declining as a whole; admittedly they are in the United States, but against this they are certainly increasing elsewhere, and especially in British Possessions. As for the talk about "living on our capital" I see no evidence whatever. If it were so, surely the wealth of the country would be declining – you can't both spread your capital and have it; yet, taking such indices as we have, the capital of the nation is not declining. The income tax returns (which represent return on capital to a large extent) are steadily rising; the deposits in the Join Stock Banks, and the Savings Banks are rising persistently.

Admittedly, it *may* happen that we become more and more a creditor country – a *banking* country rather than an *industrial* country – and this might have a serious effect on some classes of the population. But though we are becoming more banking and less industrial (relatively though not absolutely) I cannot see that any such suffering to the working class (beyond that amount which inevitably accompanied all economic change, and against which economic history shows conclusively that no legislation can guard) – I cannot see that any serious suffering is likely to befall the workers.

This is so long a letter that I will not trespass further upon your time. But I should like to add this – that as a strong Imperialist I should welcome anything which might make, or tend to make, Imperial Union closer and more real. I should welcome any economic legislation which would promote that; my only fear is that the price which this country might have to pay would be a great deal too heavy.

If there are other enquiries which I might make, or other points which you would like to consider, perhaps you will let me know.

Yours very truly

[signed]

Percy Ashley.

---

8 MEMORANDUM ON FISCAL POLICY AND INTERNATIONAL TRADE*

Alfred Marshall

Prefatory Note

This memorandum is written from the point of view of a student of economics rather than an advocate of any particular policy. I have not held back my own conclusions on the question to which my attention was directed. But I have endeavoured to select for prominence those considerations, which seem at once important and in some danger of being overlooked, whether they tell for or against my conclusions.

The problem of the incidence of import duties is extremely complex, and two methods of simplifying it have had great attractions. One method is to treat it as an abstract problem: two countries about which nothing is known

* Alfred Marshall, "Memorandum on Fiscal Policy and International Trade" (a Memorandum to Arthur Balfour) (31 August 1903), PRO *Cab. T168/54*; pp. 1–12; 14–44.

are supposed to trade with one another; and abstract reasoning shows that almost every distribution of the incidence is possible in some conceivable case or other. This is well as a foundation.

But the application to real conditions has not yet been adequately worked out. Thus propositions which are true under certain conceivable, but unreal, conditions are liable to be quoted in such a way as to suggest that they apply to this real world in which we live.

The second method is to fall back upon the observation of price movements. This method ignores the fact that import duties affect the relative purchasing power of money in different countries, and thus expand or contract the measuring rod by which their own effects are estimated. It is therefore generally avoided by students. And, indeed, when applied to the broader problems of fiscal policy it is not only unscientific in principle, but also misleading in practice.

When, however, it is applied to the case of one or two relatively small import duties, it points to results which are very nearly true. For the purchasing power of money is not materially affected by this small disturbance: and the effects of the tax on the price to the consumer measure accurately enough its direct effects on his material well-being.

In these cases our course is fairly clear, provided we can isolate the effects of the tax from those of other disturbances which occur at the same time. That is not an easy task, but it is often practicable.

The problem is too large and difficult to be handled in a Memorandum. But it is passing from the student's closet to the market-place; and it seemed to me therefore right to attempt to present its chief outlines in a short compass; and I have done so in the first part of this Memorandum. I can but hope for a lenient judgment on its grave imperfections.

Heads (C), (D), and (E) deal with existing conditions in a broad way. It is possible to omit the severer discussions under heads (A) and (B).

Part II is concerned with the indirect effects of various systems of import duties, which are often much more important than the direct effects. In some of them the economic element predominates, and in others the ethical and the political. It is impossible to discuss fiscal policy without reference to all, and many of my opinions, therefore, are given with exceptional diffidence. But I have endeavoured to keep distinct, though not separate, those suggestions which fall mainly within the province of the economist from those which do not . . .

Part I – The Direct Effects of Import Duties

(A) The Problem Cannot be Completely Solved by a Simple Study of Price Movements

1. The first issue to which my attention has been called is the incidence of import duties. It is my opinion that, in nearly all important cases, they are

borne almost exclusively by the consumer. But there is no absolute rule in the matter. Taxes can be conceived on a large scale, and have actually existed on a small scale, in which a perceptible part of the burden of an import duty is borne by foreigners. And, of course, in this as in all other cases, a part of the pressure of every new tax, of whatever kind, is apt to rest temporarily on producers, merchants, shippers, and others, until they are able to shift it to its permanent resting-place on the shoulders of consumers.

2. The problem is difficult, and it will be well to start by guarding against an attempt to deal with it by a simple study of price movements. That is an unsafe basis to build upon, for it seems to show that there is a strong *primâ facie* case, derived from international price comparisons, for the conclusion that the main burden of an import tax falls on the consumer. But, unfortunately, these comparisons are apt to prove too much. They appear to show that the consumer must bear the whole burden of every such tax, together with the profits on it of each stratum of traders through whose hands it passes. But the *primâ facie* case thus made out is not valid.

3. The *primâ facie* case is this:– As a general rule the exporters are indifferent as to the market to which they send their goods; and select that which will yield them the best price after paying all the costs. If, therefore, the cost of delivering any commodity in a certain market is increased by the levying of an import tax of 1*l.* upon it, exporters will avoid that market until, by making the commodity scarce in that market, and rather more abundant than before in other markets, they have raised its price (duty paid) in that market by 1*l.* relatively to its price in other markets in which there has been no new tax. The ultimate consumer may, therefore, be expected to have to pay this 1*l.* together with profits on the extra capital required for moving the commodity by all the dealers through whose hands it passes on its way to him. And price statistics show that he has to do so.

4. Hence in this *primâ facie* case for the conclusion that the whole burden of every import tax is borne by the consumer, there is a weak point. Both the general argument and that based on a comparison of observed prices neglect the fact that the purchasing power of money in any country may be affected by its tariff policy. For taxes on certain imports into a country raise their value in that country relatively to things which are not taxed: and one of these is gold. Therefore the purchasing power of gold is generally low in a country which levies many high import duties; and when we know that a certain fiscal policy has raised the price of any given commodity to a consumer by, say, a quarter, we have not got an answer to the question how great the burden on him really is.

5. The answer to this question can be found only by going back to the great truths which Committees of the House of Commons at the beginning of the last century investigated, and which was stated forcibly by Ricardo. It is that gold is a mere commodity in international trade; and that the levels

of international prices do not govern the course of international trade, but are governed by it. Reasoning on this basis is troublesome; but there is no other method by which the problem in hand can be adequately grasped. All attempts to evade its difficulty and take refuge in an apparently simple study of price movements are delusive.

(B) The Main Issue

6. Suppose two countries, A and B, to trade with one another, and only with one another; and to levy no taxes on imports. The price of A's goods in B will differ from their prices at home only by costs of transport, and *vice versâ*. But now A puts a tax of 50 per cent. on all imports, except of course gold. The prices of A's goods will remain higher in B than at home merely by the cost of carriage. But the prices of B's goods in A are now bound to rise 50 per cent. relatively to their level in B, for unless and until that happens it will answer to send gold instead of goods from B to A. This rise in price of B's goods in A's markets takes place whatever be the urgency of B's demand for A's goods. But it is mainly on the urgency of that demand that the incidence of the tax depends; and the observed price movement *taken by itself*, proves nothing conclusively.

7. The burden of the tax will be thrown mainly on B if B's demand for A's goods is so urgent (so inelastic to use a technical term) that when, in consequence of the tax, merchants begin to lessen the supply of A's goods, each of these goods can be disposed of for a much greater quantity of the labour and general commodities of B than before. For then, while every day's labour, and every home commodity in A will exchange for about as much of other home produced commodities or services as before, each of them will exchange for much more than before of B's goods *in bond*. It might conceivably exchange for just double as much as before of B's goods *in bond*; and therefore for just as much as before *duty paid*, and in this case, the whole burden of the tax would be thrown upon B.

Here the solution of this particular problem ends, so far as essentials go. But its secondary consequences in terms of price movements should be added. Since A's goods can be disposed of in B's markets on such favourable terms, gold will be sent from B to buy them. Therefore, gold will become very plentiful in A; prices generally will rise there, and a rise in money wages will follow in due course. Therefore, though B's goods in A sell for twice the price they do at home, yet their prices will not represent much more effort than before; it may not represent any more effort at all. In B, on the other hand, gold will have become relatively scarce, and will command more of B's goods and services than before. Therefore, although A's goods sell in B for only their price at home, together with cost of carriage, yet their real cost to B will be very much increased. The consumers in A will be nearly as well off as before, and their Government will have got the taxes mainly at the expense of B.

8. But A will have to bear the burden of her own taxes in case B is in no urgent need for her goods. For then, when the merchants slacken their deliveries of A's goods in B, the market will be unresponsive. Each bale of A's goods will bring back about as much of B's as before. A day's labour in A, or a bale of A's goods will command about as much as before of B's goods in bond, and their taxes will be paid in the main by those who consume them in A. In this case there will not probably be any considerable movement of gold, and the *primâ facie* suggestions of price statistics will correspond pretty closely to the actual facts. [A's Government might possibly spend a great part of the taxes on imported goods, and if the private consumers in A were in urgent need of their old supplies of B's goods, they might have to force the trade, and to accept less and less of foreign goods in return for each bale of their own. This would, of course, lead to an exploitation of gold from B, and might ultimately force B to bear even more than the whole burden of the taxes.]

9. The two countries A and B, being taken to be shut off from all trade except with one another, it is *primâ facie* reasonable to suppose that B's demands for A's goods are somewhat urgent; and that, therefore, the burden of the taxes will fall in a considerable measure on her. But in the real world B always has access to other markets, and therefore she will not consent to pay any of A's taxes unless A has something like a monopoly as regards nearly all her exports; or else, from geographical or other causes, B is very much at A's mercy. That is to say, the ordinary conditions of trade, as it actually exists, bear a much closer resemblance to the case discussed in the last section than they do to those of the section before that, in which a great part of the burden of A's taxes was shifted on to foreigners.

(C) A Broad Treatment of Some Representative Cases

10. The effect of an import duty is felt in the first instance at the frontier. If the commodity is bulky, it may very well be imported in spite of a heavy duty, and yet be sold in other parts of the country at a low price. To take a strong instance, timber is sometimes almost without value on the Pacific slope, while in other parts of the United States its price responds to taxes on importations from Canada. But in countries no part of which is far removed from a frontier suitable for importation, such as the United Kingdom and Belgium, the full effect of an import duty is felt by nearly all consumers, even of commodities as bulky as wheat.

11. Again, it is not denied that exceptional geographical causes may put a country very much at the mercy of a stronger country which lies between it and the main movement of the world. Possibly Germany, and even Austria-Hungary, may be able to throw a small part of their importations on

countries lying to the east of them. And yet Germany cannot throw on England any share of the burden of her own import duties, even though there are a few chemical and other German products, which England cannot easily forego. England can always take these as her first choice, and for the rest of her trade Germany must force her way with goods which England has no special reason for obtaining from her rather than from other sources. And what is true of Germany with regard to England is true of England with regard to the whole Western world. There may be some small markets in which her connections by steam-ship or otherwise give her an advantage tending towards a mitigated monopoly. But in the aggregate they count for little. There is thus no considerable exception to the rule that England has now to pay the burden of her own import duties.

12. There has, indeed, never been a country, the whole of whose exports were in such urgent demand abroad, that she could compel foreigners to pay the whole of any taxes which she imposed on her imports. But England's exports approached to it twice: once they consisted chiefly of wool, which was indispensable to Flemish weavers. And again, in the first half of the nineteenth century, they consisted chiefly of manufactures made by steam machinery, which was not in general use anywhere else; together with tropical products, which she had special facilities for obtaining. It is possible that the rest of the world would have given twice as much of their own goods as it did for many of them, rather than go without them. As it was, England did no doubt throw a considerable part of the burden of her taxes (import and export) on the foreign consumer: though it may be true that by making her taxes (or prohibitions of import) heavy just where they ought to have been lightest, she so checked that growth of the vitality of the masses of her people which ought to have resulted from her new command over the forces of nature, as to hasten the day in which she would cease to hold the unchallenged leadership in industry.

13. But any powers which she may have had of throwing a considerable part of the part of the burden of her import duties on foreign consumers of her products have been destroyed by two inevitable causes. Her arts and resources of production have become the common property of all countries of the Western world, and in some important cases have been developed by others faster than by herself: and the growth of her population has made her demand for many of her imports more urgent than is the demand of any other country for any of her exports. In this respect she is, however, not in a weaker position than Holland and Belgium, and not in a very much weaker position than Germany.

14. I assume that we are concerned with the settled trade relations and not with exceptional or temporary incidents. Almost every trader has opportunities of springing hard bargains upon particular customers, who have made their plans on the expectation that he would deal with them in a regular manner. Such undignified action brings its own nemesis. But prac-

tices which would be thought bad business as between individuals, have been suggested in the present controversy as appropriate for international trade policy; and it may be well, therefore, to state clearly that I do not deny that small gains may be snapped by sudden import duties.

15. For instance, if a country is the chief purchaser of an important speciality for which a second has exceptional advantages, then an import tax on it would be borne in the main by the producer for some considerable time. This might occur in the case of a tax levied by England on Greek currants, or on some classes of heavy wines. There is no important commodity the supply of which is in this position. But as we shall see presently the relations between those countries which are large exporters of wheat and those which are large importers of its have several minor peculiarities.

16. Similarly if manufacturers in any country have adopted expensive plant to the needs of a particular foreign market, they may pay nearly the whole of an unexpected tax levied on their goods there; for it is better to work with but low returns on their investment than to let their plant lie idle. Conversely, if a tax in the importation of certain goods is suddenly removed those producers whose plant is specially adapted to those goods may be able to add nearly the whole amount of the tax to their price and reap very high profits until new plant is ready to meet the increased demand resulting from the cessation of the tax.

17. Of course a room may become colder as the newly-ligthed fire in it obtains strength; and again, darkness may set in earlier on a day when the sun sets at 5.30 than on another day when it sets at 5.15. But no one could gain credit by pretending that such facts prove that the fire did not make the room warmer than it would otherwise have been, or that the setting in of darkness is not mainly controlled by the hours of sunset. And yet cases in which the effect of remission of an import duty has been overridden by bad harvests, or a great temporary rise in freights, or other causes, have been gravely adduced as affording grounds for the belief that "low prices [of wheat] of recent years . . . are only remotely connected, if at all, with our policy of free importation" (letters by "An Economist" to the "Times" of the 25th June, 1903). I propose later on to indicate what is in my opinion the true interpretation of the history of English wheat prices since 1820.

(D) Illustrations from Recent German History of the Effects of High Tariffs on the Purchasing Power of Money and Wages

18. Of course a small change in a country's fiscal policy will not materially affect the purchasing power of money in it. Therefore if the imposition of a tax on any minor import raises the price of it to her consumers by the full amount of the tax, relatively to the price at which it is to be had in other countries that have made no such change, then it may be concluded that the

179

full burden of that tax falls on the consumers, until it is shown that the general purchasing power of money in the first country is lower than in the second. The *onus probandi* lies on those who may urge that it is.

19. There are, however, reasons why those who advocate a "protective" policy should be unwilling to lay stress on the undoubted fact that the general purchasing power of money is low in countries with a high protective Tariff. For this fact cuts two ways. On the one hand, it does mitigate that extra burden that a country seems to take on itself by any new import duty which raises the price of a commodity by a given sum of money. But, on the other hand, it calls for a similar deduction from any *primâ facie* statistical evidence that may be offered of the prosperity of the country with the high Tariff. The advocates of the high Tariff gain a little by dwelling on the connection between high Tariffs and high prices, but they lose a great deal.

20. This may be illustrated by the effects of that movement towards high Tariffs which set in nearly twenty-five years ago in Germany. In the preceding, comparatively free trade period, it was reckoned that the purchasing power of money was two-thirds as high again in Germany as in England. (The common way of putting it was: "a thaler equals 5 fr., which equals 5*s*.") I took considerable pains to verify this statement, and found it to be approximately true, even after allowing for the fact that many comforts and minor luxuries had then to be bought either from England, or from world markets which were largely under English influence. Many of these things are now made with good appliances in Germany as in England. Further, German and Alsatian iron ores have been made effective by modern processes applied with consummate technical skilll, and Germany is now abreast of England in the mastery of steel, which is the master of the world. Thirty years ago it used to be said that in active occupations an Englishman could generally do as much in one hour as a German in two; but since then the levelling up has been almost incredible to any one who has not watched it step by step. And now the difference in effective value between the hours' work in the more progressive parts of Germany and the English hours' work is very small. Although by far the greater part of this progress is unquestionably due to education and to improved food, yet it may perhaps be conceded that a small part of it is due to the opportunities which the German protective Tariffs gave to break weak nascent industries against the invasion of the more mature and stronger industries of some other countries, and especially England.

But granting this, it yet remains true that undiscriminating import duties, imposed to gratify powerful interests, and not needed to protect any nascent industry, have (partly, indeed, by strengthening kartelle or trade combinations) so raised prices against the consumer, that the real wages of the German workmen have risen less rapidly than those of the English. Money wages in the more progressive parts of Germany have probably risen rather faster than in England; though, save in the heavy iron industry, the condition of which is temporarily exceptional, they still lag far behind. But the prices of the necessaries of life have risen, while those in England have fallen; so that 6 marks – instead of 3, as was the case thirty years ago – are required, I believe, to purchase as much of them as 5*s.* do in England now. In spite of Germany's best technical advances, in spite of the growing energy of her people, in spite of the development of German iron ores – while those of England are running short, I believe it to be true that the real wages of the German are increasing much less rapidly than those of the Englishman; and that if Germany abandoned protection, which has now no considerable service to render her, the wages of the German would rise a great deal. To hazard a bold guess, I should expect them to rise by about a fifth.

(E) Wheat Prices in England since 1820

21. I now take up the point (see § 17) that, though, of course, the effects of a change in taxation on the price of wheat may be lessened, and even over borne, by fluctuations in harvest, or, again, by changes in freights and other disturbances arising out of a great war, and so on; yet, when this is done, I believe that every movement in the world's market for wheat, and especially in the relative prices of wheat in English and continental ports during the nineteenth century, will be found to be such as could have been anticipated from the doctrine that a tax on such a commodity as imported wheat raises the prices of that wheat by at least the full amount of tax . . .

25. It is, indeed, an almost universal rule that a tax on the importation of a commodity lessens its consumption more or less; and the consequent diminution of demand tends to induce foreign producers to offer it on terms which are lower, though not always perceptibly lower. Wheat has conformed to this rule throughout all history, so far as is known, until about forty years ago. But now nearly the whole of the English people can afford to buy as much bread as they want, and yet have enough left to buy some more expensive foods, and, as Sir R. Giffin seems to have been the first to observe, a rise in the price of wheat still leaves bread the cheapest food, which they will consent to eat in any quantity; so that, having to curtail their purchases of more expensive foods, they buy, not less bread that they would have done, but more. Consequently, a general tax on the importation of wheat into England now might increase rather than diminish England's total demand for wheat, and, unless it lead to a great increase of supplies from England herself, might raise and not lower the net price which foreigners obtained for their wheat.

But in spite of Germany's recent great advance in wealth, a rise in the prices of wheat and rye compels many people to substitute potatoes and other cheap foods for part of their consumption of bread; and therefore an increased tax on imported grain, harvests being normal, is sure to diminish importation.

26. But so large a part of the best wheat land in the United States is already taken up, that these farmers are relatively, if not absolutely, diminishing in numbers. The growth of wheat as a sole crop is going out, and the supply is becoming increasingly sensitive to changes in the price which can be obtained for it . . . From 1820 to 1840 the average price of wheat in England was about double that in the specially wheat-producing districts of Germany, and quite half as much again as in the industrial districts of Westphalia and the Rhine Provinces; while now the price in Germany is about a third as much again as in England. In France, with an almost stationary population, protection has compelled the people to pay about as high a price for their wheat now as they did early in the century. These facts prove, not indeed that the present cheapness of wheat in England could have been produced by England's present fiscal policy alone, but that they could not have been produced without that policy.

29. If a tax were imposed in England only on foreign and not on Colonial wheat it would, under existing circumstances, diminish the English demand for foreign wheat, and thus probably cause it to be offered on slightly lower terms: i.e., the price here would probably not rise by the full amount of the tax. But as this higher price would have to be paid on the whole of the wheat consumed here, the revenue would not gain nearly as much on the aggregate as the consumer lost. We thus pass from the direct incidence of taxes of imports to the more general results of various international trade policies.

Part II – England's Fiscal Policy Considered With Reference to the Economic Changes of the Last Sixty Years

(F) England's Fiscal Policy Assumes the Relative Maturity of her Industries

30. The second question on which my opinion is invited is, "How far, and in what directions, the circumstances which formerly made Free Trade the best policy for this country have been altered?"

31. The principles on which our present fiscal system was based sixty years ago seem to me to be not ultimate, but derivative. They were obtained by applying certain truths, which are as universal as the truths of geometry or mechanics, to certain conditions which were transitional. If these principles are converted into dogmas, the same error is made as if the rules laid down for building a bridge, when the only materials available consisted of pine logs, were regarded as sacred dogmas governing for ever the construction of bridges for purposes, and under conditons of which the original builders had never dreamed, and when the materials to be used were steel or granite. The art of engineering involves an organized study

and judgment of the proportions of diverse considerations, tending in opposite directions. No one can be certain of getting the right proportions even for the problem which he knows best. Not by applying without question the judgments as to proportion, which were made by the great men who founded our present system, but by forming our own judgment on weighing the facts of our own generation as they did of theirs, can we show ourselves worthy to be their followers.

32. Looking back, it is easy for us to see that they made a grave error of judgment as to the proportions of one leading problem of their own age, though not of their own country. They misjudged both the needs and the potentialities of backward countries, and especially of new countries. They assumed that every country which has latent resources and faculties for an advanced industry will attract that industry to it from other countries as easily and surely as one county of England would under like circumstances attract it from other counties. But this is not true now, and it was even less true then . . .

35. List and Cary, the great German and American founders of modern protective policy, insisted on two fundamental propositions: one was that Free Trade was adapted to the industrial stage which England had reached, and the other that State intervention was required on behalf of pioneer industries in less advanced countries. Had English Free Traders appreciated fairly the force of the second of these positions, their powerful arguments that Protection was an almost unmixed injury to England would perhaps have been accepted by the whole civilized world. As it was, this, their one great error, put many of the most far-seeing and public-spirited statesmen and economists in other countries into an attitude of hostility to their position as a whole. It has caused, and it is causing to-day, able men to deny, directly or indirectly, economic truths as certain as those of geometry; because English predictions, based on misapplications of them, suggested by this one great error, have proved both misleading and mischievous.

(G) The Bases of England's Fiscal Policy Sixty Years Ago

36. It has been noted that at the very time at which English economists were preparing the way for uncompromising Free Trade, England's exports consisted to so large an extent of things of which she had some partial monopoly that she might hope then – as she cannot hope now – to throw on foreigners some perceptible share of the burden of her import duties. Accordingly, they did not condemn all import duties, but only those which were levied in an inconvenient way, such as duties on raw material; or were unjust, such as those which pressed heavily on the poor; or, lastly, were *differential*. By differential taxes are, of course, meant taxes levied exclusively or with special weight on commodities which are produced in certain places or by certain methods, or are imported by certain routes or in certain ships,

while other commodities, capable of serving more or less well the same needs, are treated differentially, and escape the tax in whole or in part.

37. They objected to a differential tax that it set consumers and traders on evasions, either by substituting for the taxed commodity some other which was less serviceable, but not taxed, or by obtaining the commodity in part from some other and more costly source of supply. In so far as either of these substitutions was made, the consumer was prejudiced, and the revenue gained nothing. In so far as the tax is not evaded, the revenue gained all that the consumer lost – subject only to deductions for cost of collection, &c. They found that in a few exceptional cases, such as tea, coffee, tobacco, &c., there was very little evasion, and therefore little waste. But they found by a study of detail, and not by any general or *a priori* reasoning, that in the case of all commodities for which the English climate was suitable, or for which inferior substitutes could be obtained, the evasions caused by a tax were very great, and the waste was so great as to exceed many times the very small part of the burden of the tax which could be thrown upon foreigners. They therefore advocated the abolition of all such taxes as contrary to the principles of economy in taxation.

38. A chief corner-stone of our present fiscal policy was the great universal truth that the importation of goods which can be produced at home does not displace labour, but only change the direction of employment. Of course, any violent change is, to some extent, an evil; but there is a strong *primâ facie* possibility that if the business men of a country, when left to follow their own judgment, decide that it would be more costly to make certain goods at home than to import them in exchange for other home-produced goods for which there is a foreign demand, their judgment is right. But, unfortunately, when those in the industries with which the imported goods compete set themselves to persuade the public and Government that a protective import duty should be levied, their private interests are at a great strategic advantage in competing with those of the public. For it is possible to point out the particular places in which additional employment would be given by the tax. It is easy to find out the particular employers and workmen whose profits and wages would be raised by it; to invite the employers to subscribe to a "campaign fund" on its behalf; and to urge both employers and employed to exert all the political influence, direct and indirect, which they possess, in putting pressure on the Legislature in their favour. Good strategy prompts that as much as possible of the argument and appeal in the special interests of any one industry should come, not from those who have a direct stake in that particular industry, but from others who have a "log-rolling" understanding with them. Then, as now, unscrupulous politicians would boast that by going from one constituency to another and holding before each a protective duty which would give a visible bounty to a considerable portion

of the constituency, they could work up an eager cry for a protective policy, which would drown any arguments based on the general interest.

Those who cared more for the well-being of the masses of the people than for class interests or for political power found themselves in a difficult position. For, though they knew that such taxes must lessen employment and lower real wages in the aggregate, and that those industries which gained by the taxes would gain at the expense of a greater aggregate loss to other industries, yet they could not always point out the particular industries which would suffer most; while the far more numerous workers who have nothing to gain by such taxes had seldom any organization and were not vocal. Thus the benefits of such taxes, because easily seen, and by persons who could easily make themselves heard, were apt to count at the polling booth, and even in the counsels of statesmen of upright intentions, for more than the evils; for those evils, though greater in the aggregate, were less easily seen, and did not directly appeal to vocal classes.

39. Fortunately for the success of Free Trade, many of the existing protective duties were ill-chosen; they pressed on raw materials, and thus limited employment in a conspicuous way; and the evils of one of them – that which fell upon the food of the people – were palpable enough. But this accidental gain somewhat diverted attention from the general argument by which economists proved that protective taxes lessened rather than increased the aggregate employment, wages, and profits. It is, therefore, even more important now than it was then to lay stress on that argument.

40. The argument starts from the fact that employment in making a thing is not provided by the mere desire to have it, but by that desire combined with the appliances for making it, and the means of supporting those at work. The older economists expressed themselves badly, and laid too great stress upon the *capital stocks* of machinery, raw material, food, &c.; whereas more recent economists lay greater stress on that *inflow* of new supplies of food, raw material, machinery, &c., which constitutes the national income or dividend. This change of emphasis is very important in some connections, but not in regard to the particular point now in hand. Then, as now, the basis of economic doctrine was that the source of all wages and profits (as well as rents) was in the aggregate efficiency of national production; things obtained from foreigners in exchange for recent exports, or as interest on exports loaned in earlier years, being counted in place of the said exports. The economists then argued:

Firstly, whatever increases this total efficiency of production increases that aggregate supply of goods (of past and recent make) which affords employment and income (wages, profits, and rent) to the various classes of the nation.

Secondly, if goods which can be produced at home are yet imported freely from abroad, that shows that they can be got generally at less cost by

185

making other things with which to buy them from abroad than by the direct method of making them at home.

[There may be exceptional cases in which goods are sold with but little attention to cost of production; and there may be other cases when a home industry is temporarily disorganized, and it is reasonable for the public to incur some sacrifice for its relief. Again, certain classes of the community may have no direct interest in particular taxes, as for instances, taxes on very fine lace or on very coarse tobacco. But such cases, because exceptional and on a small scale, have little relevance to this broad issue.]

Thirdly, therefore, a tax which puts obstacles in the way of the importation of things which consumers prefer to buy from abroad does not enlarge employment or raise wages, and is not in the interest of "producers." It is sure to be in the interest of some producers (if among producers are counted landlords and other owners of natural sources of production). But it is sure also to injure other producers more than it benefits the favoured groups; because it lessens the aggregate flow of desirable things available as a basis of employment and for distribution among the various classes of the nation.

This fundamental truth is, of course, not inconsistent with the counsel that, as the prudent husbandman puts seed-corn into the earth, so a nation shoud be ready to sacrifice something of present income in order to develop industries which are immature, and even exposed to the competition of others which are strong. But this counsel had no application to England, because her industries were relatively mature.

41. The next great fallacy which the founders of our present system had to combat was that, though Free Trade might be for the advantage of all nations if adopted by all nations, it was a mistake to open English ports freely unless and until foreigners would reciprocate this generosity. To that two replies were made.

The first was that foreigners would certainly adopt England's policy as soon as they saw how successful it was. The events of the next few years gave some support to this hope. But it was based on a misconception of the position. It ignored the fact that protection to immature industries is a very great national good; and that, though this may be bought at too great a cost, it would have been foolish for nations with immature industries to adopt England's system pure and simple.

Their second answer was sufficient by itself and was complete without a flaw. It was that if, in spite of taxes levied by other nations on her goods, she could get them in exchange for her own at less cost than she could make goods like them for herself, it was in her interest to do so. Of course, here again there might be exceptional cases. It might be possible to retaliate by taxes the chief burden of which would be borne by foreign consumers of English goods; but, as has already been noted, it was decided not to try for such small gains.

186

42. A suggestion of more practical importance was that the remission of taxes on goods coming from any country should be made conditional on the lowering of taxes levied by that country on English goods. This course was adopted in some cases. But it was not in harmony with the large and bold comity, and of England's leadership in the comity as well as in industry, which were the glory of the great and noble, if somewhat too sanguine, men who threw England's ports open as wide and as quickly as they could.

43. This decision of theirs has not the strength of a scientific demonstration. It does not rank with their refutation of the fallacies that differential taxes on the importation of goods which can be produced at home are essentially wasteful, and tend as a rule to lessen employment and depress real wages. On the contrary, it is based on a judgment of relative quantities; and such judgments are at best fallible, even for the time and place in which they are held.

But, further, relative quantities change rapidly even in an age of apparent stagnation; while the last sixty, and especially the last twenty, years have been full of subversive changes. Each age must judge such matters for itself, and none has as yet been called on to judge for itself so independently as that which is now opening out.

(H) Transition to Present Conditions

44. To any one who approaches with an open mind the fiscal problem adopted by England sixty years ago, there appears a strong presumption that the more perfectly it was adapted to the conditions of that time the more certainly would it fail to meet exactly the widely different conditions of the present time. Even if all the chief forces in operation now had been working then, the great changes in their relative proportions must, it might reasonably be supposed, have called for great changes in the policy designed to meet them.

I for one was so much impressed by those arguments of Carey and his followers which had found scarcely any echo in English literature that I went to the United States in 1875 to study the problems of national industry and international trade from the American point of view, and was quite prepared to learn, not indeed that the American system was applicable to England, but that it might contain ideas capable of adaptation to English conditions.

I came back convinced that a protective policy in fact was a very different thing from a protective policy as painted by sanguine economists, such as Carey and his followers, who assumed that all other people would be as upright as they knew themselves to be and as clear-sighted as they believed themselves to be. I found that, however simple the plan on which a protective policy started, it was drawn on irresistibly to become intricate

187

and to lend its chief aid to those industries which were already strong enough to do without it. In becoming intricate it became corrupt, and tended to corrupt general politics. On the whole, I thought that this moral harm far outweighed any small net benefit which it might be capable of conferring on American industry in the stage in which it was then.

Subsequent observation of the course of politics in America and elsewhere has strengthened this conviction. It seems to me that the policy adopted in England sixty years ago remains the best, and may probably remain the best, in spite of increasingly rapid economic change, because it is *not* a device, but the absence of any device. A device contrived to deal with any set of conditions must become obsolete when they change. The simplicity and naturalness of Free Trade – that is the absence of any device – may continue to outweigh the series of different small gains which could be obtained by any manipulation of tariffs, however scientific and astute.

45. Among the changes which may be urged as affording a *primâ facie* case for reconsidering the fiscal policy adopted by England sixty years ago are:–

(i) The increase in the strength and purity of Government in its administrative machinery, and the broadening of the functions which it is expected to perform, and does perform, with general approval.

(ii) The growing strength of Protectionist countries which partially exclude English manufactures, and England's relatively slow progress in some branches of industry and trade.

(iii) The growth of powerful industrial organizations or combinations, fostered by tariffs and other Government favours, whose power to manipulate trade gives cause for anxiety.

(iv) The new relations between England and other English-speaking countries, resulting partly from the development of electrical and steam communication, and opening up new possibilities of a commercial federation either of the British Empire or of Anglo-Saxondom.

I propose to offer a few remarks under each of these heads.

(I) The Enlarged Resources and Increased Efficiency of Government

46. It is commonly charged against the English economists and statesmen of sixty years ago that they had an undue distrust of Government. They certainly did distrust Government as they knew it; but it is not certain that they were very wrong in doing so. Government then was, indeed, less corrupt and incapable than it had been when it evoked the wrath of Adam Smith, and made him deny, not as is commonly supposed, that there were many important things which Government might undertake to do, but that it was at all likely to perform efficiently many important duties. Even after the Reform Bill Government remained largely under the dominion of the more selfish members of the well-to-do classes, and it discharged very

imperfectly those urgent duties which none but the Government could perform at all. There was, therefore, little to be gained by urging it to take up tasks in which private enterprise and philanthropy could make some headway.

47. Since then the shorthand reporter, the electric, telegraph, and the improved printing press have combined with the general movement towards higher ethical standards in the task of cleansing Parliament and in strengthening Governmental departments. And in England this tendency has been further strengthened by the influence of Free Trade in diminishing the money value of political power – an influence which, in my opinion, would have been partially reversed if success had attended the Fair Trade movement of twenty years ago, or should attend the similar present movement for fiscal reform.

48. The experience of other countries seems to show that even now there is danger to a Parliament which listens to the representations of interested classes when framing its fiscal policy. Perhaps the case of Germany is the strongest, because German public officials have been always recognized as inferior to none in honesty of purpose, and there are probably few persons in the world who have a higher standard of honour in private life than the "Agrarian" members of the Reichstag. But yet the undignified selfishness which they and certain powerful manufacturers have shown both in legislation and in controlling the votes of their dependents has probably done more than anything else to increase the probability that a German working-man, who takes life seriously and has a strong feeling of duty, will be an ardent Socialist.

49. England's dangers are not the same, but they are not very different. She excels all other countries in the solid strength of her Trade Unions; and perhaps her greatest danger is that they be tempted to use that strength for the promotion of the interests of their class, or of particular groups of them, at the expense of wider interests. There is no more urgent duty incumbent on those who care for the higher as well as the material wellbeing of the country than to resist this temptation, and the worst method of preparing for this task is to bring back again into English politics the notion that there is plenty of money to be got by influencing votes in Parliament, both directly and through control of the public press.

50. Further, though Government is in some respects better placed for grappling with such difficulties than it was, yet, on the other hand, the amount of constructive work which the modern age is requiring from it is probably growing much faster than its power of getting through its work. This is partly because human life is much larger and more complex than it was, partly because our growing knowledge and wealth and standard of public duty makes us ever less willing to acquiesce in grave social ills, and even in minor discomforts, which cannot be adequately handled save by the authority and force of Government, and partly because the increased

intellligence and probity of Government officials generally make us willing to take the risks of Government for intervention in many matters in which Adam Smith and his immediate followers would have justly asserted that such a remedy would probably be worse than the evil. Connected with these undertakings there must necessarily be openings for certain classes of employees, and also of builders, manufacturers, traders, &c., to reap money gains through Imperial or municipal politics. We must proceed with, and even enlarge, many of these undertakings. But that is an additional reason in favour of the simple policy of Free Trade, in preference to an intricate system of duties which would occupy much of the best time and strength of Parliament and Government, and which might tend to lower the tone of public morality.

(J) The Advance of the United States, Germany, and Other Countries

51. Old countries cannot in any case expect to grow as rapidly as those which are only just beginning to develop some of the best of their resources. Still less can they hope to do so if some of their own best mineral and other resources are running short. By far the larger part of whatever relative retrogression England may be showing as compared with those two powerful countries the United States and Germany, which are progressing most rapidly, is directly traceable to a recent development of their great resources and the partial exhaustion of England's iron mines.

52. The United States present a unique combination of agricultural and mineral riches worked in a temperate climate by a mixture of races of great energy and alertness. The material resources of national prosperity are a good climate and large areas yielding generous returns to labour in the production of the staple foods and textile materials, together with coal or water power and iron ore. In all these respects, excepting climate and coal, the United States is incomparably better supplied than England is; and in the earlier stages of nearly every great branch of production, labour of a given efficiency will go much further – in some cases more than twice as far. The best English ideas have nearly always been accessible to Americans. When early in the century England took great pains to prevent the exportation of her best machinery, the manufacturers of Europe set themselves to smuggle the machines or drawings of them out of England piecemeal and under various disguises. But the prouder Americans inquired exactly what was the operation which the machine took over from the human hand, and then devised one for themselves; and it sometimes turned out better than the English one. Foreign trade, therefore, was not necessary to the United States. Her domestic trade is larger than that of the whole civilized world was 200 years ago. Protection could not possibly do her much harm. And it is probable that the help given by her to a few industries which really

190

needed help about compensated for the economic loss (but not for the moral injury) caused by the protective policy in other directions.

53. As to Germany it has already been suggested that the protective policy to which she has latterly given herself has, on the whole, hindered rather than helped the use which she has made of the high industrial energies of a population very much greater than that of the United Kingdom. If we take coal and iron together, and remember that the very rich beds of inferior iron ore in Luxemburg, Lorraine, &c., have been rendered available for making steel by recent inventions, her mineral resources are about equal to those of this country; and, of course, her agricultural resources are much larger. Her position for foreign commerce is in some respects better than that of England. For the ocean routes from her ports are not very much longer than those from English, and she has almost exclusive access to large areas of Eastern Europe which are ready to use Western goods, but are not yet ready to make such goods themselves. In fact, the greater part of the increase in Germany's foreign trade during recent years, of which much has been written, is with these countries, and is due to advantages which scarcely any fiscal policy could destroy.

54. Germany, like the United States, owes much of her strength to the large population within her own borders, among whom there is absolute Free Trade. One of the chief causes which retarded her rise was the fact that Prussia, the largest and most vigorous German State, was not a compact unit, but a number of disjointed fragments divided from one another by artificial frontiers. The Zollverein, following an earlier Swiss, and a still earlier French, precedent, was the most important movement towards Free Trade that the world has ever seen, except the contemporary reform of the British fiscal system. It abolished in every direction artificial hindrances to the "simple" and "natural" tendency of each man to deal with those persons who are best able to meet his wants in return for his meetings theirs. It stopped the laborious passing of goods in bond from one Prussian island to another; it put an end to vexatious inquiries and diminished the labour of custom-house officers. In short, its influence was largely in the opposite direction to that which would be exerted by the commercial federation of the British Empire; though in many respects similar to that which would be exerted by a commercial federation of Anglo-Saxondom, as I shall argue later.

(K) The Burden Which Foreign Tariffs Inflict on England

55. As the United States, Germany, and other countries have advanced in industrial efficiency, their growing wealth has enabled them to consume very largely increased quantities of all those goods which England is specially expert in producing, and also to produce many goods which are serviceable to her either for direct consumption or for use in her industries.

Their progress has necessarily worsened her position relating to theirs. But it has positively improved her position in many directions, and very probably it might have on the balance improved her position positively it if had not been for two causes. One of these is conspicuous: it lies in the high import duties which most of them levy on her goods. The other – which in the long run will probably be more important – is less conspicuous: it is that the most recent developments of manufacturing methods and appliances have tended to lower the relative value of those industrial faculties to which England owed her leadership. Let us look at these two causes.

56. In discussing the incidence of a tax on imports in Part I, the keynote of our main argument was that the country B whose goods were taxed would seek other markets for them until they had risen in value in the taxing country A sufficiently to throw nearly the whole burden of the tax on the consumer. The part which would be borne by the producers in B might indeed be temporarily very great if they had made their arrangements specially for sale in A's markets, and in some other exceptional cases. But as a rule, in the actual world, B would quickly find some other markets for her goods, nearly as good as A's had been before the tax, and would have a further resource in directing new applications of her capital and labour to other branches of production for home or foreign markets, and possibly even in diverting some capital and labour, which were already in the taxed industry, to others. Thus, it was argued in section 3 that if A put a tax of 1*l.* on one of B's commodities, "exporters will avoid A until, by making the commodity scarce there, and rather more abundant in other markets, they have raised its price, duty paid, in A by 1*l.*, relatively to its price in other markets in which there had been no new tax." There was then a presumption that (save in the exceptional case in which nearly all A's exports have a monopoly value) A's consumers will bear nearly the whole of the tax imposed on B's goods, a burden which could be measured (after allowance for changes in the international distribution of gold, and, therefore, in general prices) by the change in price of B's goods, duty paid, in A's ports, as compared with their price in others where no new tax had been levied. That is to say, it was assumed that A's tax on B's goods could not exert a very great influence on the value of B's goods in the ports of other countries. But now that we are dealing with broad changes in systems of taxation, and not with isolated movements of taxes, attention is demanded for considerations which were before relatively unimportant.

57. If A puts a tax on one of B's goods, B can send it to C, D, E, &c., in rather larger quantities, without appreciably glutting their market, or she can send other goods to A or to C, D, E, &c. But if A, C, D, E, &c., all put a heavy tax on one of B's goods, B must either very much diminish her export of it or bear a large part of the burden of the tax. And if A, C, D, E, &c., all put heavy taxes on all B's exports, then B is almost sure to bear a large part of the burden. She might, indeed, turn much of her capital and

labour chiefly to producing things for her own consumption, but she is almost sure to be in urgent need of some imports, and in order to obtain them she must export. If several of her goods are in urgent demand abroad, she may be able to get most of what she wants to import by exporting rather reduced quantities of these goods, and only of these goods. Their scarcity will give them high purchasing power abroad, and she will then not pay a very great part of the foreign import duties, though she will, of course, be hampered and inconvenienced in many ways. If, however, she has no exports which approach to a monopoly value abroad, she must turn her attention more and more to providing for home consumption, and must be content to allow a considerable part of the burden of foreign duties on her exports to enter into the real cost to her of whatever *net* imports she requires.

The word "*net*" is here important. The foreign raw material which enters into her exports (*e.g.,* American cotton, which England re-exports as calico) does not count as an import for this purpose. Nor, again, do those which she draws in the payment of interest, &c., on capital which she has already exported: such imports are not affected by the taxes levied abroad on her exports.

58. England is undoubtedly in a much worse position than she would be if the commodities for which she has a special aptitude were not generally liable to heavy taxes abroad. The taxes which press upon her most are those levied by the United States, by her own Colonies, and by other new countries which have a surplus of agricultural and mineral products, such as she needs. The taxes on her imports levied by such a country as Germany are of relatively small importance to her. It is to the advantage of both that they should exchange textiles or metal goods whenever the merchants see their way to a profitable exchange. But if England made things for home consumption with the capital and labour with which she makes her exports to Germany, and Germany acted in like manner, neither of them would be seriously injured. To put an artificial obstacle in the way of the trade would be a gratuitous folly, but its total economic effects would be small after the immediate effect of the disturbance had passed away.

On the whole, the general rise in import duties levied on manufactures is a serious evil to England. And, unfortunately, the power which England has of putting pressure on other countries to lower their tariffs is lessened by the second of the two great changes which have impaired the strength of her position. I proceed to consider that.

(L) Changes Affecting England's Industrial Leadership

59. The progress of the arts and resources of manufacture has benefited England more than almost any other country in one important but indirect way. It has so reduced the cost of carriage by land and sea that raw materials

and food can come to her, even from the centres of great continents, at a less cost than, sixty years ago, they could from the near neighbourhood of the sea-shores and great rivers of the Continent. But the 300,000 miles of railways which have been built during the last sixty years in America, Asia, Africa and Australia are rendering greater service to Englishmen than to any other people except those in whose lands the several railways are placed.

But in almost every other respect the progress of the arts and resources of manufacture has benefited England less than any other country. For, even sixty years ago, the excess of the cost of the manufactures needed for her own consumption over that of the raw material by which they were made was very small. If it could have been reduced to nothing she would have gained by the change very much less than she has gained by the lowering of the cost of imported food and raw material for her own use.

On the other hand, countries which used to be dependent on imported manufactures have gained all round: they have gained by lowered cost of transport, and they have gained by the lowered cost of manufacture of commodities for direct use; and that almost equally, whether these goods are manufactured by themselves or imported. For competition compels England, Germany, and other Western countries to give to consumers almost at once the full benefit of any economy in manufacturing processes which they have obtained.

60. In so far as the increasing economy of transport and manufacture enables Western goods to be made even of imported material and disposed of in backward countries where before they could not compete with hand-made products, the exporting country gets a great share of the benefit. But people's most urgent needs for some classes of manufacture are now satisfied by manufactures which, with modern processes, absorb very little labour, and therefore sell under competition for very little. For instance, further economies in the manufacture of pins might diminish rather than increase the total value of the export of pins, and the number of people to whom that industry gives employment.

Therefore, England's gains from the further progress of manufacture, except in so far as it led to yet further cheapening of long-distance transport, might be less than those of most other countries, even if that progress made a proportionately increasing demand for those industrial faculties by which England obtained her leadership; but it does not.

61. The very perfection of the textile and other machinery by which England won her industrial leadership has enabled it to be worked fairly well by backward races. She is thus at a steadily increasing relative disadvantage in trading not merely with people like Japanese, who can assimilate every part of the work of an advanced factory, but also with places where are abundant supplies of low-grade labour, organized by a relatively small number of skilled industrialists of a higher race; as is largely done in

America, and as certainly will be done on an ever-increasing scale in other continents.

62. Consequently, England will not be able to hold her own against other nations by the mere sedulous practice of familiar processes. These are being reduced to such mechanical routine by her own, and still more by American, ingenuity that an Englishman's labour in them will not continue long to count for very much more than that of an equally energetic man of a more backward race. Of course, the Englishman has access to relatively larger and cheaper stores of capital than any one else. But his advantage in this respect has diminished, is diminishing, and must continue to diminish, and it is not to be reckoned on as an important element in the future. England's place among the nations in the future must depend on the extent to which she retains industrial leadership. She cannot be *the* leader, but she may be *a* leader.

63. The economic significance of industrial leadership generally is most clearly illustrated just now by the leadership which France, or rather Paris, has in many commodities which are on the border line between art and luxury. New Parisian goods are sold at high prices in London and Berlin for a short time, and then good imitations of them are made in large quantities and sold at relatively low prices. But by that time Paris, which had earned high wages and profits by making them to sell at scarcity prices, is already at work on other things which will soon be imitated in a like way. Sixty years ago England had this leadership in most branches of industry. The finished commodities and, still more, the implements of production which her manufacturers were giving their chief attention to in any one year were those which would be occupying the attention of the more progressive of Western nations two or three years later, and of the rest from five to twenty years later. It was inevitable that she should cede much of that leadership to the great land which attracts alert minds of all nations to sharpen their inventive and resourceful faculties by impact on one another. It was inevitable that she should yield a little of it to that land of great industrial traditions which yoked science in the service of man with unrivalled energy. It was not inevitable that she should lose so much of it as she has done.

64. The greatness and rapidity of her loss is partly due to that very prosperity which followed the adoption of Free Trade. She had the full benefit of railways, and no other country at that time had. Her coal and iron, better placed relatively to one another than elsewhere, had not begun to run short, and she could afford to use largely Bessemer's exacting but efficient process. Other Western nations partially followed her movement towards Free Trade, and in distant lands there was a rapidly increasing demand for manufactures which she alone was able to supply in large quantities. This combination of advantages was sufficient to encourage the belief that Englishmen could expect to obtain a much larger real income and to live much more luxuriously than anybody else, at all events

in an old country; and that if he chose to shorten his hours of work and take things easily, he could afford to do it.

65. But two additional causes of self-complacency were added. The American Civil War and the successive wars in which Germany was engaged, partially diverted the attention of these countries from industry, checked the growth of their productive resources and made them eager to buy material of war, including railway plant and the more serviceable textile materials at almost any cost. And lastly, the influx of gold enriched everybody who could borrow money with which to buy materials, could apply moderate intelligence in handling them, and could then sell them at a raised level of prices and discharge his debt with money of less purchasing power than that which he had borrowed.

66. This combination of causes made the sons of manufacturers largely content to follow mechanically the lead given by their fathers. They worked shorter hours, and they exerted themselves less to obtain new practical ideas than their fathers had done. And a part of England's leadership was destroyed rapidly. In the 'nineties it became clear that in the future Englishmen must take business as seriously as their grandfathers had done, and as their American and German rivals were doing; that their training for business must be methodical, like that of their new rivals, rather than merely practical on lines that had sufficed for the simpler world of two generations ago; and that the time had passed at which they could afford merely to teach foreigners and not learn from them in return.

67. This notion of leadership is different from, almost antagonistic to, measurement of a country's leadership by the volume of her foreign trade, without reference to its quality. Such measurement is very misleading.

Of course, the statistics of foreign trade are specially definite and accessible; and since the fluctuations of business confidence and activity are reflected in foreign trade among other things, the habit has grown up of using export statistics as a *primâ facie* indication of the time and extent of such fluctuations. For instance, vital statisticians have frequently pointed to the parallel movements of export and marriage-rate statistics. Even for this purpose export statistics are not very trustworthy; while for broader purposes they are quite untrustworthy.

Other things being equal, an increase in the efficiency of those industries in which a country is already leading will increase her foreign trade more than in proportion. But an increase in the efficiency of those in which she is behind will diminish her foreign trade.

England has recently been behind France in motor-car building, and behind Germany and America in some branches of electrical engineering. A great relative advance on her part in those industries would enable her to make for herself things which she had previously imported, and would thus diminish her foreign trade. On the other hand, even a small advance in her power of spinning very high counts of cotton yarn would increase her

196

foreign trade considerably; because that is a thing for which other nations have an elastic demand, and are almost wholly dependent on England.

68. England's export trade, though still very much larger in proportion to population than that of Germany and America, is not increasing as fast as theirs. But this fact is not wholly due to causes which indicate relative weakness.

The chief cause of it is that the improvements in manufacture and in transport, aided by Free Trade, enable England to supply her own requirements as regards food, clothing, &c., at the cost of a continually diminishing percentage of her whole exports. Her people spend a constantly diminishing percentage of their income on material commodities; they spend even more and more on house-room and its attendant expenses, on education and on amusement, holiday travel, &c. Present censuses show a progressive increase in the percentage of Englishmen who earn their living by providing for these growing requirements. That is to say, the number of Englishmen who devote themselves to producing things which might be exported in return for foreign products; and therefore England's foreign trade, measured in money, increases but slowly. Of course, if her foreign trade be measured by the quantity of things exported and imported, it is increasing very fast; but still it is not increasing as fast as that of Germany and America. How far is this really an evil?

69. American conditions are very dissimilar to ours. But let any one compare in detail German and English trade statistics, and point out the desirable foreign commodities with which England is ill supplied. The earnings of England's capital invested in foreign countries and in ships on the ocean enable her to bring home 8*l.* to 9*l.* per head worth of foreign commodities for her own consumption, in addition to those which she brings with her nominal exports. Her people think that these, taken together, are enough; and prefer expensive summer holidays to increasing still further above the German level their consumption of oranges or silk. Who shall say that they are wrong? It is useless to point out things which we might export and do not: unless it can be shown that the extra things which we should be able to import by so doing are more desirable than the things and services which we are providing for ourselves, and which we should need to give up in order to make those things for export.

70. The real test of relative progress which foreign trade offers lies in the skill with which each nation applies her industry to producing great results with small manual effort; or, in other words, in making commodities cheap relatively to effort, and effort dear relatively to commodities. In view of her failing stores of iron ore, England rightly exports an ever-increasing proportion of machinery and implements which are of small bulk relatively to their value, and that is an indication of the qualities of leadership; but her imports of electrical plant and aniline dyes show that her hold on leadership is insecure, and can be retained only by renouncing the easy self-compla-

cency engendered by the abnormal prosperity in the third quarter of the last century.

71. The position, then, is this: On the one had, England is not in a strong position for reprisals against hostile tariffs, because there are few of her exports which other countries need so urgently as to be willing to take them from her at a largely increased cost; and because none of her rivals would permanently suffer serious injury through the partial exclusion of any products of hers with which England can afford to dispense.

And, on the other hand, it is not merely expedient – it is absolutely essential – for England's hopes of retaining a high place in the world, that she should neglect no opportunity of increasing the alertness of her industrial population in general, and her manufacturers in particular; and for this purpose there is no device to be compared in efficiency with that of keeping her markets open to the new products of other nations, and especially to those of American inventive genius and of German sedulous thought and scientific training.

And, therefore, though it be true that the import duties of Western nations inflict greater loss on England than they did sixty years ago, it seems that she stands to gain little and to lose much by any attempt to coerce them into lowering their tariffs.

72. Especially does it seem contrary to England's interests to levy import duties with the object of giving English diplomatists something to bargain with when discussing foreign tariffs. English business would be disturbed by the opinion that such a duty was probable; and again by its actual imposition, and again by the probability that it would be removed, and again by its actual removal. It would disturb business in every way; and it would set particular classes of business men on influencing Government, as it has done in other countries where diplomats are intrusted with a power of this kind. In fact, it would be easy to impose protective duties and hard to remove them; and the plan would lead to a number of protective taxes based on no scientific system, and conducive neither to the material nor the moral prosperity of the country.

73. But England already grants to every nation with which she deals better terms than that nation gets from any other. It is not unreasonable that she should demand in return the "most-favoured-nation" treatment, and that she should regard any refusal to grant it as an act of deliberate commercial hostility, which would justify her in considering whether or not it was worth while to make reprisals. It is, of course, true that the existence of this clause sometimes deters an astute German or other diplomatist from pressing for specially low duties on goods in the production of which England happens to have some advantage over his own country, and that the most-favoured-nation treatment is not the ideally best for England in all details. But it gives England nearly all that she could obtain by interminable tariff wars, and at no cost. It might, therefore, be well that every foreign

nation should know that so unfriendly and unjust an act as the refusal or most-favoured-nation treatment to England might be met by a small tax levied on all the chief commodities, not of urgent necessity to England, imported from her. Being small and evenly distributed, it would not bring into existence an artificial home industry dependent on the tax, and claiming that to remove the tax would break an implied promise of continued support. It would therefore not be likely to lead to Protection.

(M) Trusts and Cartels

74. It is, however, urged that special treatment is required of the products of powerful single firms or combinations of firms which, protected by a high tariff, sell at a high price at home, and find additional employment for their workers by producing goods to be sold below cost price abroad. It is further alleged that they can sell such goods more easily in Free-trade England than elsewhere. The economics of combination is a vast subject; but I will venture to submit a few fragmentary remarks on the subject.

75. Speaking generally, American trusts in the proper sense of the word have ceased to exist. What are called "trusts" are single Corporations so vast as to obtain a dominant control approaching to monopoly in some large branch of industry. They aim at constructive economies, and do not always exert themselves much to keep competition out of the trade; they boast that their large scale of buying, producing, and selling enables them to make a profit at prices which leave no margin for smaller producers. Especially in their early days, some of them appear to have acted cruelly and unscrupulously; but, as a rule, they now avoid action, which is palpably against the public weal, and it is rather the fear of what they may do in the future, when they are more firmly in the saddle, than of what they are doing just now, which is causing so much of the best American thought to be given to the duties of the State with regard to them. The best opinion seems to be that as a Joint-stock Company has less right to privacy than an individual business man, so a Corporation of semi-monopolistic scope may be fairly compelled to make returns to the Government for publication of a kind which it would not be well to demand from an ordinary private Company. If those returns tend to show that it is making a bad use of its power, and, in particular, is selling below cost price with the set purpose of ruining rivals, it may be required to level up its prices, or to level them down at its option, to the same amount for the same thing (cost of carriage being allowed for) all over the States. Secondly, it is urged that if a trust sells more cheaply abroad than at home, it thereby proves that it has no right to be defended by a protective duty; and though there are several important trusts which are independent of the tariff, yet the growing power of trusts generally is causing many able and influential persons who have defended the policy of Protection to turn towards Free Trade.

76. The discussion of the combination policy in Germany, though immensely in advance of that in this country, lags behind that of the United States; but in the main tends in the same direction. The cartels are, however, very different from the trusts. They are federations more or less strongly knit together and not amalgamated. Each firm retains much autonomy, except in the matter of selling, and, in some cases of buying. Their constructive economies are not, as a rule, to be compared to those of the American Trusts, but they effect some important economies in the advertising and distribution of their products, and they are ruthless in restricting their supplies to the home consumer in order to compel him to pay an artificially high price for them. They are an almost unmixed curse to Germany. It is probable that if Protection were introduced into England, monopolistic power would be sought by the German rather than by the American route; and in that case Protection would, in my opinion, do in this one way alone far more harm than it could do good, even according to the most sanguine of the estimates which have been put forward by the best informed of its advocates.

It should be noted that the strongest cartels are, as might be expected, in trades which make half-finished goods. They often sell their products to English and other manufacturers at prices which enable the finished product made of them to undersell the German product in foreign markets. This is only one of many instances of the intricacy and friction which their system introduces, and is tending to form a strong public opinion against it.

77. The statement that a trust or cartel can more easily sell surplus goods in England than in any other market in which it habitually sells seems only in part true. It may be conceded that if the tax remains fixed in amount, then a given fall in the price of the goods in bond will make a less proportionate fall in their price duty paid than it would in their price where there was no duty, and, therefore, might not stimulate sales so much. But this is a relatively small point, and there seems to be no other difference between the two cases.

78. It is not to be denied that the cartels and the trusts are annoying to English manufacturers. But it is hard to devise a remedy that will not be worse than the disease. It is not possible to prohibit all selling below the full normal price; it is not easy to say when such a lowering of the price is reprehensible, still less when it is an offence. English manufacturers, especially in the iron industry, were for more than half a century by far the chief ill-doers in this direction, and the memory of their ill-deeds rankles sorely in American minds. Even now the accusations levied against some combinations of English shipping companies, not without indirect Government subsidies, are exceptionally bitter. And it might be hard to take formal action against foreigners who were selling cheaply in English markets without laying ourselves open to very sharp retorts, and even retaliations.

79. My own conclusion is that our first duty is to study the problem of combination. Meanwhile we should take no hurried action. Least of all should we "protect" in order to exclude a few parcels of goods sold cheaply, to the great annoyance of one group of English traders and the benefit of another group. At most we should consider whether it might be worth while in any specially flagrant cases to charge particular specified cargoes with a tax corresponding to the "unfair" lowering of the price at which they were sold here. This would be troublesome; but the mischief could be kept within a small compass.

(N) Increased Opportunities for Imperial or Anglo-Saxon Federation

[Section N is listed in the original Contents page (not shown) as comprising subsections 80–84, but the original numeration begins at Subsection 81.]

81. Looking at the details of the imports and exports of our Colonies, taking account of the geographical relations between Canada and the United States, and allowing for the fact that the technical problems which the agriculturalists and even, to some extent, the manufacturers of all our Colonies have to face are those of the United States rather than of England, I can see no likelihood that they will be willing to give a permanent effective preference to English goods over those of the United States, unless in return for an indirect subsidy so vast as to drain the resources of the United Kingdom. And, of course, they will not allow British manufacturers to retard the growth of their own.

82. All the shifting schemes which have been vaguely adumbrated for a bargain between the Colonies and England seem to me to ignore the rules of arithmetic. In *each* part of the transaction the gains which either side is invited to expect are greater than the loss which the other is to incur; and yet, as the scheme includes differential duties which are essentially wasteful, the aggregate material gain must be less than the aggregate material loss. The schemes might be hopeful if they started with the firm suggestion: Imperial unity is an ideal worth much material loss; let us consider how best to share this loss among us. As it is, the schemes seem to me to likely to breed disappointment and friction between England and her Colonies.

83. It is, indeed, suggested that, if England subsidize Canada to make railways and grow wheat, the world's stock of wheat will be so much increased that its price will fall. But for that purpose the subsidy must be on a vast scale. We should bear all the cost, and Germany and other wheat-importing countries would share the benefit. Canadian wheat cannot reach us easily without the active friendship of the United States: in time of war it could not reach us at all against the will of the United States; and yet emphatic stress has been laid on estimates – very much exaggerated, so far

as I can form an opinion – as to the share of the wheat-exporting trade which Canada might be expected to take away from the United States.

84. Geographical and economic considerations seem to me to favour attempts to promote intimate commercial arrangements throughout Anglo-Saxondom on the way towards its closer political union, but to put a veto on the approach to the political union of the Empire viâ the commercial. For the Empire alone steps towards closer political union should, in my opinion precede those towards commercial union.

ALFRED MARSHALL

---

9 SPECIAL SUPPLEMENT: THE ECONOMICS OF EMPIRE*

The Assistant Editor

I

At the close of the Napoleonic campaigns, England found herself in the most remarkable position that a country has ever occupied. A speck upon the circumference of the planet, she possessed the effective empire of the world; an island, she was the absolute dictatrix of the sea; an industrial and commercial nation, she had secured in the long war the complete monopoly for practical purposes of manufacture and shipping. Her accumulated wealth and productive energy were equal to those of the whole Continent combined. In spite of the vast expenses of the twenty years' conflict in which she had swept the sea with her fleets and subsidised the allied military power of whole nations, not only were her means unexhausted, national capital had never increased so fast. Her resources were greater at the end of the struggle, for all its colossal cost, than they had been at the beginning. She held direct dominion over a fourth of the land and all the ocean.

But also, and this is the fact most important for our present purpose, she held even over the rest an indirect dominion. Before the age of railways the water was the world's highway in a more exclusive sense than it is now, and

---

* "The Assistant Editor", "Special Supplement: The Economics of Empire", *National Review*, 42 (September 1903), pp. 1–13; 16–28; 60–76; 78–83; 91–2; 94–7; 100–1; 103–6.

the commercial communications of mankind were in our hands. We were in touch with all nations, and nations not actually contiguous could only come in touch with each other through us. Colonial and tropical merchandise, raw cotton, Eastern silk, coffee, tea, sugar, and spices had to be received through British vessels or dispensed with. But the island was the centre of machine manufacture as well as the centre of navigation. The growth of the cotton trade in the fifty years before Waterloo has been justly described as the most wonderful industrial development that has yet been witnessed. Not only was there nothing outside these islands equal to Lancashire, there was nothing resembling Lancashire. The woollen trade was still greater than it had been when Defoe wrote in exultation, "Take our English woollen manufacture, and go where you will you find it." The linen trade was well nigh as extensive as it is to-day. In silk we held our own. In metals, in hardware and cutlery, boots and shoes, earthenware, china, glass, and the rest, we were as unrivalled as in textiles. For all purposes of manufacture we were the workshop of the world. For purposes of distribution, in respect of the things we did not produce, we were the warehouse of the world. We were the carriers of the world. We were the bankers of the world. Unless other nations bought our wares they could not procure such wares at all, and the extent of our sales was only limited by the means of our customers and the mediæval measures by which the fiscal policy of almost every country restricted exchange. In one word, we were as secure even of foreign markets as though they had been our own. The one deep blot upon all this brilliant picture of national prosperity and power was the condition of the people – the pauperisation of agricultural labour and the squalid lot of the overworked and underpaid population which had begun to swarm in manufacturing towns. Of this part of the matter the classical economists then and long afterwards took scant account. If the lot of the poor was wretched, competition had caused it, and competition would cure it. Cheap labour encouraged capital; the encouragement of capital extended employment; and this in its turn would make labour less cheap. If the demand for workers increased faster than the population, the condition of the masses would be improved. If not, the remedy lay in emigration, but not at all in combination among the workers or in legislation by the State.

The weakening of the national and Imperial idea, which may be perceived in these doctrines, resulted from the very completeness of our success up to Waterloo; from the cosmopolitan character of our commerce; and from the absence for many subsequent decades of all serious foreign rivalry upon the sea or in manufacture. With the decay of national feeling throughout the generations that followed the Napoleonic wars there was an increase of human feeling, and a strong tendency to believe in the near approach of universal peace and a universal friendship between peoples, which would find its natural expression in unrestricted trade. Upon the economic side the earlier classical economists, in their attitude towards the masses of our own people, preached the hardest and the coldest creed that could influence a nation. But, in their attitude towards foreign countries, and in their whole conception of international development, they were actuated, on the contrary, by the visionary sentimentalism of Rousseau. This fundamental contradiction of thought explains, as nothing else explains, the whole history of England throughout the nineteenth century. The natural relation of individual men was considered to be one of merciless competition, with which the State should do nothing to interfere. But the natural relation of peoples was considered to be one of harmonious co-operation which the State should do everything to promote, and national prejudice was regarded as the most vicious and artificial of all passions, instead of being, what it essentially is, the vulgar form of the instinct of self-preservation. Yet England, in this scheme of human society, was always to retain the position she actually held as the chief industrial workshop of the world which would generally remain agricultural, supplying this country with all manner of crude products, and taking back in return all manner of finished articles.

The advocacy of this ideal on the part of Englishmen was natural. If it could have been realised, it would have been the permanent guarantee for the retention by this country of an overwhelming proportion of the world's wealth and power. The only difficulty of this theory lay from the beginning, as we shall see, in the total refusal of foreign nations to accept it. America rejected it from the outset. Germany, from the time of the most original and far-sighted of her economic and political writers, Friedrich List, to the time of Bismarck's final breach with Free Trade, rejected it more and more. France, though temporarily affected by the ideas of Cobdenism under the Second Empire, returned, as she was certain to do, to the ideas of Colbert almost immediately upon the recovery of her political freedom after the disasters of 1870. The British school of political economy, always excepting Adam Smith, whom all schools can and do claim as the father of their opposite opinions, under-rated both the power and the value of the national idea, whether at home or abroad. They underestimated both the ambition and the capacity of foreign nations to offer effective rivalry to this country in manufacture. This is, of course, not an indictment against them. It is a matter of historic fact, which must be grasped with the utmost clearness if we are to understand the commercial policy of this country from the beginning of the Great Peace to the repeal of the Corn Laws, and from the adoption of Free Trade to the fiscal controversy of to-day.

With the complete predominance in industrial and mercantile power which has been described, we seemed to be a century in front of the remainder of the world in material development. We were certain under these circumstances of conquering every market to which we might be admitted. This was the reason which made us in favour of the theory of Free Trade. No conceivable theory would have been so well calculated to promote our special interests if we could have realised it. That is why we

204

have never realised it. Real Free Trade would have prolonged our monopoly of manufacture in enabling us to suppress, by our immense competitive superiority, the infant industry of every country in its own market. Hence other countries have been led more and more to exclude us in order to "protect" their industrial growth and to secure their own markets more and more for themselves. The reasons that decided England in favour of Free Trade were, in other words, clearly the reasons which have decided the world at large in favour of Protection, and created the modern economic situation. We believed that our industrial success had been wholly due to an inherent superiority in position, resources, racial character, and commercial aptitude. We thought other nations would dispute it in vain. Other nations believed, on the contrary, that our industrial success was due, above all, to the fact that we had been left in sole possession of the commercial field owing to the political confusion of the Continent, and they believed that our supremacy, with peace in Europe and patience on the part of its peoples, might be seriously disputed and possibly overthrown. In this conception, as we now perceive, foreign countries were right, and the British school of political economy, in the first half of the nineteenth century, was mistaken. In the generation before and after Free Trade we mistook the temporary condition of politics for the permanent conditions of nature. When we adopted Mr. Cobden's policy we thought, as he thought, that the world was tending towards an age of cosmopolitan liberalism and free exchange – towards a universal acceptance, in other words, of English ideas. What was really approaching was the age of Bismarck, militarism, universal tariffs, and destructive competition.

We have free imports. We have no free exports. We define our contention, therefore, at the outset. A country which monopolises all the manufactures must be in favour of unrestricted access to all the markets. So long as it is allowed by other nations to retain this enviable situation it must be inclined to Free Trade. A country, on the contrary, which no longer monopolises any manufacture, and which finds its rivals shutting it out of most of the markets, must desire to make itself secure in some of them. Hence, when it has wholly ceased to enjoy free exports it must reconsider the theory of free imports.

II

Adam Smith was the most practical of writers, and his superiority over all his successors lies in his profound sense of the distinction between the pure science of wealth and the applied science of politics. He never forgets that the power of nations is not only more important than the wealth of nations, but that anything which diminishes the former in the case of any particular country must be detrimental to the latter. The economist in him was subordinate to the Nationalist. He vindicated the soundness of the old

205

Navigation Laws – probably the most severe Protectionist measure in history – upon the principle that "defence is more important than opulence." He was the father of the theory of free exchange, which will probably be adopted by the world in some future and distant generation, though it has not yet been seen in practice. But at the same time Adam Smith was the father of Imperial Federation. In a famous passage he recommended that the American Colonies should be represented at Westminster. If his prescience had been shared by statesmen the separation of the race might never have occurred, and a united North America might actually have been, as he thought, possible, the predominant partner of a British Empire twice as great and powerful as that which now exists. The founder of modern political economy was in no sense an unconditional Free Trader of the modern order. He distinctly sanctions a resort to retaliation in cases where a country aggrieved by foreign restrictions upon its trade has a reasonable prospect of securing equal treatment by resorting to retaliation.

No writer also has explained more clearly than Adam Smith the value of the home market by comparison with the foreign market. Two parties must be benefited by an ordinary transaction in trade. But where the transaction takes place between two citizens of the same country, that country receives both the benefits. In a case of foreign exchange a country receives only one side of the benefit. Another nation receives a benefit which may be equal or superior; and as the second nation may be an enemy to the first the net result of the transaction may mean a relative disadvantage to the first. Thus far Adam Smith is above the quarrels of the day, and both sides may claim him. He may be claimed for Mr. Chamberlain's policy under each of its three aspects – that which implies, in consequence of the German treatment of Canada, the resumption by this country of the power to retaliate; that which seeks to strengthen the home and to extend the colonial market as compensation for the closing of foreign markets; and that which sees in preferential trade the true means towards Imperial Federation. Also, though the author of the "Wealth of Nations" is the father of free exchange as a doctrine – of the Free Trade theory proper – not a sentence can be quoted from his pages showing him to be the father of "free imports" as an actual and unreciprocated policy. Free imports are an inference which successors have drawn from his doctrines, but as we have seen they are nowhere laid down as an express and unconditional article of his doctrines. Upon the contrary, the Navigation Laws, which he defended on political though not on economic grounds, prohibited foreign nations altogether from bringing colonial imports into this country, and were the most complete contradiction to the letter and spirit of Mr. Cobden's policy.

Nevertheless, if free imports are a pure inference from Adam Smith's teaching it is well to see how that inference was drawn. The foundation of his whole system of political economy lies in the principle of the division of employments. In other words he laid down with unsurpassable clearness the unalterable truth that specialisation means efficiency. When many hands made different parts of a pin the article was produced in a quantity and with a speed impossible upon the principle of one person one pin. A man is a better farmer if he is not at the same time a tailor, as a man is a better physician if not at the same time a lawyer. Now the division of employments for purposes of production implies the necessity of exchange and the absurdity of restrictions upon the exchange either of goods for goods or services for services. This is the view that we all accept in our private lives.

It is true that individuals following different employments are necessary to each other. But what is by no means true is that persons following the same employment are equally necessary to each other. The smith is indispensable to the farmer, the farmer to the smith, the tailor to both, the physician to all of them, and the freer they are to give their services to each other the better. Here we have the whole explanation of the theory of free exchange and the whole origin of what is a very different thing, the policy of free imports. Nations were conceived as individuals following different pursuits, each having a special aptitude for producing commodities needed by the rest. In that case Free Trade between different States would be unquestionably as advantageous as the free interchange of goods or services among all parts of one country and all citizens of the same nation. Among nations upon an actual level of industrial development free competition would indeed by the only means of proving to what particular employments they were relatively adapted.

But in constructing a theory of international intercourse upon the analogy of private intercourse, one side of the matter was completely overlooked. There is not only such a thing as division of employments, making co-operation necessary and restriction absurd; there is such a thing also as identity of employments, which involves a completely different relation – the relation not of co-operation but of competition. Here at once the destructive element comes into play, and the theory of free exchange no longer applies. If two persons make two heads of a pin, to recall once again Adam Smith's most familiar illustration, and only one head of a pin is needed, they cannot combine their activities, are no longer beneficial to each other, their interests are no longer identical, but, on the contrary, one can succeed only at the expense of the other. The existence of the farmer is indispensable to that of the village tailor, but the appearance of a second tailor where there was only one before is by no means an unmixed benefit to the first. The whole structure of Cobdenism is founded upon the assumption that *division of employments* with the consequent necessity and advantage of the freest possible exchange, would continue to be a more decisive factor in economic policy than *identity of employments* involving the destruction of interests upon one side by the competitive success of similar interests upon another side.

207

The main question, therefore, in 1903 is not a question of theory, but a question of fact. You cannot in ordinary life assume a man to be a physician who may not be a physician. The point is whether as a matter of fact he is a physician. When free imports were adopted, for instance, we were the only considerable manufacturing country in the world, and our intercourse with the remainder of the world was co-operative, and not to any appreciable extent competitive. America was a large buyer of our goods, and had not yet become an overwhelming producer of corn. Her cotton manufacture, which is now larger than that of Lancashire, was then an industry of entire insignificance. Her iron industry had no effective existence. Now America makes more than twice as much pig-iron as we do, and she makes three times as much steel. She has thrown our land out of cultivation by her agricultural abundance, and at the same time has withdrawn a large part of her former orders from our factories, and will necessarily avail herself of the free-imports system in a time of crisis for the purpose of displacing our iron and steel manufactures in this country by her surplus production. France, in spite of Defoe's exultation, sends us vastly more woollen goods than she purchases, and, in spite of the hopes built upon Cobden's treaty, sells more cotton goods than she buys. Germany, like America, produces more pig-iron than we do, and at no distant date, with her present rate of progress, will make annually twice as much steel.

In 1846, when England was still the chief and almost the sole workshop of the world, and when foreign nations were both our providers of raw materials and food and our customers for finished goods, the actual characteristic of international commerce was a broad division of employments as between an industrial island and an agricultural world. This is why free imports were adopted with confidence in 1846, and were for a long time successful. But again, as a matter of fact, the dominating characteristic of modern commerce now is the identity of employments among the principal industrial nations. Therefore each nation is endeavouring to enlarge its trade at the expense of the others, conceding the narrowest possible market to its neighbours while securing the largest possible market for itself. That is why the whole doctrine of free imports in 1903 is shaken to the base. If division of employments among nations had remained an actual fact, free imports would have remained an indisputable policy; for free exchange would have been in the equal and evident interest of all nations, and Free Trade would have become universal. We have been excluded by hostile tariffs from the markets of competitive countries simply because our most successful and powerful employments were identical with those which the rival industrial nations desired to establish. The co-operative principle of divided employments in international commerce formed the basis of Cobdenism. The competitive principle of identical employments destroys it.

III

At the outset let us do justice to Richard Cobden, and try to understand the point of view of this great but fallacious Englishman – an Englishman as typical in his different way as Cobbett himself, and governed by that fact unawares. When he believed himself to be actuated by cosmopolitan theories he was really impelled by intensely insular ideas. Hence, when he appealed to mankind at large, his most effective opponent, Friedrich List, with just alarm, warned all Germany against him. All Germans of deepest insight knew that their destiny would have to be worked out by war as it had been worked forward by war. They knew that the conflict of interests and ambitions between peoples was only too real. They held that there was no reason for other nations and races to be satisfied because England had got all she wanted in politics, and could desire nothing further but full play for her crushing economic power in all the markets of the world. There was international division of employments only because England well-nigh monopolised all the superior employments. A continued division of employments in that sense would relegate the other peoples permanently to the inferior employments. That was not a position which they could be or were prepared to accept. Cobden was a widely travelled man. But the mark of his mind was that wherever he went he saw nothing that did not strengthen him in his previous opinions. It does not appear that the moving spirit of the Corn Law League had read Friedrich List who, remarkable to say, is not once mentioned in Mr. Morley's biography. If Cobden had read that economist he would have despised List's system of "*national* economy," as the *Edinburgh Review* did, for the reason that it was *national*, though this very fact has determined its ultimate triumph over Cobden's own doctrines. One thing alone he foresaw and clearly predicted – that the manufacturing development of the United States was inevitable and would be formidable. What he unfortunately did not foresee even here was that America, to secure that development of her home production, would attack British exports more and more severely, and would base her whole fiscal policy upon the deliberate repudiation of the Cobdenite theory of exchange. Then with regard to the continental countries, Cobden saw that the actual state of things was division of employments. Owing to his lack of historic sense and of the higher order of imagination, he did not understand that the real ambition of the majority of civilised mankind would be to rise above their lower economic status and to obtain, as nearly as might be, an equality of employments with this country. The sanguine and somewhat facile idealism which helped to make him unsuccessful in business, helped equally to make him a dangerous guide in national policy. But with his unrivalled organising power, his elevated and sincere character, his lucid and persuasive intelligence, he was wonderfully well fitted to play the part of the triumphant agitator against a bad system. The practical bent of his energy was determined by two things. He was a cotton manufacturer – belonging to the greatest and also the most exotic of our trades. That trade depended, as it still does, exclusively upon imported raw material in the first place, and almost exclusively upon export trade in the finished stuffs. But also Richard Cobden, as the son of a ruined yeoman, was helped by his antipathy to landlords and by his knowledge of land. He was a farmer's son, to whose family the Corn Laws had not meant success. We are bound to believe that his political thought and action were coloured by this fact more deeply than Mr. Morley indicates.

As a cotton manufacturer Cobden desired Free Trade – free imports of raw products, free exports of finished products – as a matter of course. The only error lay in overlooking the fact, obvious to us, but not at that time obvious, that other nations would desire to create Lancashires of their own – that foreign nations were certain not to have the same interest in conceding free exports that Cobden had in desiring them. His idealism and his interests worked naturally together against everything that he understood by "monopoly and restriction." But he regarded the Corn Laws, in the expression he frequently used, as "the keystone in the arch of monopoly." Pull that out and the whole of the old fiscal system would collapse. We have seen the theories upon which that result was advocated. We shall now glance at the method by which it was secured.

Free imports are of course a negative. They are not a system, but they are the absence of one. Cobden's aim therefore was purely destructive, and he achieved it because the thing he attacked was bad as it stood. The old tariff had become a stupid and injurious mechanism, and the sliding scale was its most stupid and injurious device. We know now that our mediæval forefathers had originally been shrewder and more practical men than we had long been apt to think. Their conception of commercial policy was not widely different from the late Mr. McKinley's, or from that of the German Emperor, or from that of any modern framer of a national tariff. Their object in imposing fiscal restrictions was not really to restrict trade, but to encouarge home production rather than foreign production. The McKinley Act forced Yorkshire woollen manufacturers to set up factories in America, just as Mr. Chamberlain's policy would force a large number of the American and Continental firms now supplying us with foreign manufactures to create employment here. But Edward III. aimed at and achieved precisely the same object when he founded the greatness of the British woollen industry by inducing the Flemings to settle in this country, and then prohibiting the importation of foreign cloth. The mercantile system in the seventeenth and eigtheenth centuries pursued many very sound aims in practice, even though it framed false theories to account for them. Without the Navigation Laws our control of the world's carrying-trade and our command of the sea could never have been so complete or so secure. We placed every obstacle in the path of our rivals, and forcibly kept down their competition to the utmost of our power. This may have made our wealth absolutely less than a more liberal system might have made it. But being a far greater disadvantage to our rivals than ourselves it helped to make our wealth relatively greater than theirs, and therefore to increase our national power.

None the less at the time of Waterloo the tariff had lost sight of its original purposes and placed its multitude of imposts with blind extravagance and haphazard triviality on raw material, food and foreign manufactures alike. The reaction began with Huskisson in 1823, not with Cobden in 1846. The latter found England already started upon the glissade of fiscal reform, and for him was reserved the work of giving his country the final push . . .

The sliding-scale, with its nominal duties when prices were high and its enormous duties when prices were low, placed a premium upon unscrupulous speculation which resulted in violent fluctuations of the market. Imports were excluded in good seasons by the unremunerativeness of prices, and were not forthcoming in bad seasons because of the uncertainty of the market. With agriculture even more than with respect to the Navigation Laws "defence is more important that opulence," and if Cobden had realised the full moral and economic importance of that fact, English society would have been a much sounder organism than it is to-day, and our industrial power itself would have been placed for all competitive purposes upon a much more solid basis. We shall show this in examining, from a point of view which has never yet received due attention in this country, the creative effect of free imports in England upon commercial development in America. The right reform would have been found upon the one hand in a reasonable fixed duty upon imported wheat, with a rebate upon Colonial wheat according to the wise spirit and practice of our old Colonial system. Upon the other hand, tariff reform, while removing taxes from raw materials in every shape and form, ought not to have gone to the length of conceding absolute and unconditional "free imports" to all products of all nations before we had bargained by treaty with other countries for a reasonable measure of reciprocal treatment in return for the invaluable privilege they were granted in our market. Had this been done there cannot be the slightest question that Cobden's own ideal of free exchange would have been more effectually promoted, and that British exports would have now enjoyed freer access to every great civilised market, while national thought upon the principles of commercial policy and the conditions of competitive success would have been kept alive. But the sliding-scale was the tangible point of attack in the whole framework of our traditional fiscal policy, and Cobden drove the whole weight of popular passion against it like a battering-ram against a cottage wall. His genius as an agitator lay in the clearness with which he concentrated himself upon the effort to "pull out the keystone in the arch of monopoly." It was pulled out, and the whole fabric, with all its abuses and all its safeguards, came down together. Some forlorn fragments of the tradition of centuries, in which we had been neither an unsagacious nor an unsuccessful nation, remained to be knocked away in 1860. With the Repeal of the Corn Laws Cobden's work of largely beneficial but largely hazardous and wholly indiscriminate destruction was done. In all other respects the Imperial, the foreign, and the social policy of Cobdenism and the school of *laisser faire* has been rejected by this country as much as by any other country. The real issue of "national economy" as between a free importing and a Protectionist system had never been, and until now never has been, thoroughly debated. For before the modern rise of foreign competition, full data for comparison between the two systems – not as abstract doctrines but as practical methods applicable to given states of society – did not exist. But the Corn Laws had been triumphantly assailed. In 1846 England became what, after some tentative and temporary imitations, she remains – the only free-importing nation. We did not get free exchange. We are further from the conditions of free exchange in 1903 than we were in 1846. British exports are obstructed on every side as perseveringly as foreign imports are facilitated upon this side. We are the only free-importing nation. We are not a Free Trade nation, because there is no Free Trade . . .

Free exchange would give us full play for our commercial supremacy throughout the world. It was natural that we should desire it. It was inevitable that foreign nations after reflection should decide more and more firmly to refuse it. The extraordinary fact was not that we should have endeavoured to aggrandise our already overwhelming advantage in this manner, but that we should have really held the belief that we were somehow promoting the universal interests of mankind. Our insularity was never so narrow as when we thought we had become cosmopolitan. Free Trade while the conditions of competition were so unequal was inconsistent with the material ambitions and the full economic development of the remainder of the world. This is why free imports have not only led to Free Trade, but, as we shall see further on, have actually been one of the chief factors in creating the universal *régime* of Protection outside these islands.

V

From this point we must enter upon the statistical analysis of British trade if we are to form an intelligent opinion upon either side of the greatest controversy, taken for all in all, that has been opened in British politics since the separation of America. The present issue is distinctly more momentous than the original struggle upon the Corn Laws. It must determine our whole fate as an Imperial Power and as a trading nation. Our commercial supremacy, our maritime supremacy, and with them the security of our dominion, were more complete before Free Trade than they have been under Free Trade. For both sides alike the issue involved in Mr. Chamberlain's enterprise is that of the making or the breaking of the Empire, the consolidation or the decay of our dominion, with the preservation or the loss of our commercial ascendency upon the sea. Isolated free imports involve the refusal of commercial union with the Colonies, as well as of a tariff against foreign manufactures in this country, corresponding to the tariffs against British manufactures in competing countries. The political and economic issues are alike decisive. The defenders of free imports think that preferential trade would be ruin; the advocates of commercial union are convinced that continued "free imports" will be fatal. But Mr. Chamberlain's opponents are under the disadvantage of believing that our commercial supremacy must pass away by natural necessity in consequence of the preponderance of the United States in population and resources, and the preponderance of Germany in population though not in resources. But if our mercantile supremacy must pass away, our mastery of the sea must pass away, the Empire must pass away, and we must ultimately become a subordinate European State.

The opponents of free imports accept none of these conclusions. They believe that our present fiscal position – free imports for all competitors in this market, tariffs in all the markets of our competitors against our goods – means a restraint upon home production as well as upon export which has depressed our industrial and competitive power far below the natural level. They believe that as against Germany our industrial and commercial advantages are decisive, and that for all purposes of ocean traffic the British Empire, which lives by sea-exchange, possesses no less decisive advantages over the immense but self-contained market of the United States.

It remains to develop the arguments of these views and to dissect the arithmetic of the present system. The inquiry divides itself naturally into three periods of thirty years each: (1) from Waterloo to the repeal of the Corn Laws – the period of our monopoly before free imports; (2) from 1846 to 1875 – the period of our monopoly after free imports; (3) from the appearance of foreign competition in the seventies and the consequent disappearance of our monopoly down to the present day, when the whole question of our fiscal policy is reopened.

VI

The First Period – It is frequently imagined that British commerce had been languishing before free imports, but this is to begin with a fundamental error. Our trade was far less stagnant in the thirty years before Cobdenism than it has been in the last thirty years under Cobdenism. This appears to a certain extent from the following tables, showing the values of British exports in the generation after the Great War. There was, to begin with, a reaction from the inflated conditions of commerce during the struggle, but after the first reaction the extent of the progress made may be measured by two tests. Take first the table of real values:

I. PRODUCE AND MANUFACTURES OF UNITED KINGDOM EXPORTED, ACCORDING TO THE REAL VALUE THEREOF.

1815	£49,600,000
1820	35,600,000
1825	38,900,000
1830	38,300,000
1835	47,400,000
1840	51,400,000
1845	60,100,000

But this is in reality far from showing the full extent of the expansion. The great fall in prices during the second quarter of the century conceals in these figures the constant but remarkable increase of the quantities exported that was really taking place. This is shown by the old official or fictitious values. They were entirely conventional, and worthless in themselves, but as they were consistently applied to the same goods year after year by the Mandarins of our old Customs system, sublimely irrespective of the real fluctuations of price, they show how the volume of our exports actually expanded:

II. PRODUCE AND MANUFACTURES OF THE UNITED KINGDOM AT THE OFFICIAL RATES OF VALUATION.

1815	£41,700,000
1820	37,800,000
1825	47,200,000
1830	61,200,000
1835	78,400,000
1840	102,800,000
1845	134,600,000

Thus, in the quarter of a century before Free Trade the increase in the quantity of our exports was about 250 per cent. In the last generation, under free imports, our outward shipments, apart from coal, have increased by less than 40 per cent. in *quantity*.[1] We perceive, therefore, that the effects of the old tariff system in restricting the expansion of commerce have been immeasurably exaggerated, and that the power of free imports alone to promote commerce has also been immeasurably exaggerated. Take iron: the output of pig iron in the United Kingdom increased from 400,000 tons in

1820 to about 1,500,000 tons in 1845 – or nearly fourfold. Take cotton: the piece goods exported rose from 350 million yards in 1820 to 1100 million yards in the year before the repeal of the Corn Laws – a more than fourfold increase. The relative importance of the linen trade was much greater than it is to-day, and wool made slower, but still steady, progress. British hardware and cutlery and every description of British metal manufacture were in demand throughout the world. To sum up the matter, let us quote the *History of the Free Trade Movement,* by one of Mr. Cobden's most convinced and enthusiastic disciples, the late Augustus Mongredien. He is describing what was the real state of the country in 1845, the year before the repeal of the Corn Laws, and this is how he writes:

> The country was flourishing, trade was prosperous, the revenue showed a surplus, railways were being constructed with unexampled rapidity, the working classes were fully and remuneratively employed, the Imperial average of wheat for the week ending June 28 was 47*s.* 11*d.* a quarter, and bread was cheaper than it had been for many years. (P. 133.)

How ludicrous, by comparison with all this, seems Lord Rosebery's melodramatic declaration about the "terror, horror, and famine" of the period before the repeal of the Corn Laws! We were a very great nation, and, by comparison with our neighbours, we were more powerful, more prosperous, and more progressive than we are now.

VII

The Second Period – Yet for the thirty years after the repeal of the Corn Laws Cobdenism seemed to be justified with overwhelming completeness by the event. The adoption of free imports was followed by an unparalleled expansion of commerce, as the fall of Tenterden steeple was followed by the appearance of the Goodwin Sands. There was little more connection between the two fomer phenomena than between the two latter. There was no general decline in the cost of living. The price of wheat did not fall. The price of meat increased. Nor were our manufactures improved owing to any decrease in the general cost of production, for raw materials had been practically free since the tariff reform of 1842.

Expansion of commerce follows expansion of demand. In the thirty years after the repeal of the Corn Laws there was an immense expansion of the world's demand on account of changes which were transforming the conditions of production, transport, and finance throughout the world, but which had no more to do with the alteration recently made in our domestic policy than with the planetary motions. It was Cobden's extraordinary good fortune to secure the adoption of his system exactly upon the eve of a series of political and economic developments, which increased enormously, as we have said, the world's demand for manufactured goods, and at the same time prolonged for another generation our monopoly of the supply. Exports were the index then, as they are now and always must be, of competitive progress. Let us state, in the first instance, and afterwards analyse, the astonishing figures of the British trade returns in years of highest trade from 1846 to 1873:

BRITISH COMMERCE, 1846–1875.

	Exports, Million £.			Imports, Million £.
1846	57.8	...	...	75.9
1847	58.8	...	...	90.9
1848	52.9	...	...	93.5
1849	63.6	...	...	105.9
1853	98.9	...	...	123.1
1857	122.0	...	...	187.8
1860	135.9	...	...	210.5
1866	188.9	...	...	295.3
1872	256.3	...	...	354.7
1873	255.2	...	...	371.3

No familiarity with these figures ever leaves them other than amazing. They represent an uprush of national success without example in the history of commerce, and they may well remain without a parallel in the future. We see the demand for British goods increasing by leaps and bounds. The same demand would, of course, have existed, and would have had to be satisfied from the same source in the same way, if free imports had never been introduced. For the demand was created by three things which had no sort of connection with Cobdenism: (1) the discoveries of gold in California and Australia; (2) the development of railways and steamship communication throughout the world; and (3) the almost universal and continuous wars which followed the close of the Great Peace. The whole world plunged deeply into debt to this country, and our loans went abroad in the concrete form of British goods. The fever of speculation and enterprise was worked up, which reached its height in 1872–73, with the final close, so far as we were concerned, of the conditions which had produced it. We were never again to be the focus of such an economic movement. But Richard Cobden was the least of the persons responsible. The persons responsible were, the anonymous man who picked up the great nugget at South Fork in California; Hargraves, the miner from California, who discovered the first gold in Australia; George Stephenson, the third Napoleon, Prince Bismarck, M. de Lesseps, Ismail Pasha, and Jefferson Davis.

(1) *The Gold Discoveries.* – It will be observed in the above table that for

216

the three years following the repeal of the Corn Laws the value of exports showed no increase. There was no increased trade from free imports alone. But in 1848 the great gold deposits were discovered in California, and before the end of the year adventurers were swarming from all parts of the world. The bay of San Francisco, which had been a beautiful solitude, became crowded with ships and cities. Mining camps sprang up by enchantment in the wilderness. America began to increase her imports by from five to six millions a year. The total imports of the United States were £25,000,000 in 1846. They were £65,000,000 in 1856. We had the lion's share of the increase in goods and freights. But within three years after this movement had commenced it was doubled in force by the Australian goldfind, and a market of first-class importance was instantly created in another wilderness – this time at the Antipodes. Australian imports actually increased tenfold in value between 1851 and 1853; and what had been an almost uninhabited continent became, what it still remains, our third most important customer, India being even then the first, while the United States were second.

(2) *Railway Development.* – In the meantime works another factor of demand. Concurrently with the Californian gold discoveries there was a sudden expansion of the rate of railway construction in America, and the Republic fom 1848 began to add thousands of miles of line to its system. A similar movement was going on throughout the European Continent from Madrid to Moscow, and in South America, in India, in Egypt. British money and British iron played the chief part in creating this development. We did not realise while our exports were bounding in consequence, that the work we were engaged in was the work which would destroy our manufacturing monopoly, transform the industrial conditions of the world, and call foreign competition into being. Our foreign investments went abroad to create in this and other respects the conditions of foreign competition – a very remarkable fact, which a masterly economist of our own time, Professor Adolph Wagner,[2] has made the foundation-stone of his teaching. Throughout the sixties we were exporting bar and railway iron at the average rate of a million tons a year, and the value of our total exports of iron and steel increased with leaping prices from £15,000,000 in 1863, to £38,000,000 in 1873. Nor must we leave out of sight the fact that the same movement was revolutionising the home market. In 1845 and 1846 "no fewer than 347 Acts were carried through Parliament authorising the construction of 7654 miles of railway at an estimated cost of £190,344,087 sterling." In all this huge process "free imports" were the fly on the wheel. We had invented railways, and the world demanded railways from the only country which could supply them.

(3) *The Continental and American Wars.* – The apologists for free imports resist with almost violent indignation the attempt to take 1872 and 1873 as a basis of comparison for the examination of British trade in the

subsequent period. These years, they tell us, were entirely abnormal years, owing to the Franco-German war. But if free imports did not create the prosperity of the early seventies, it is certain that they did not create the prosperity of the country during any part of the period under review. If 1872 and 1873 are to be ruled out as abnormal years, there is not a single year in the previous quarter of a century which can be regarded as a normal year or taken as a basis of comparison. Hence we have the valuable admission of the Cobden Club itself that our commercial expansion in what is called "the golden age of Free Trade" had no more to do with free imports than the principles, let us say, of the Free Food League have to do with free food. In 1848 came "the year of revolutions" and the awakening of the democratic and national movement throughout Europe. The whole political system of the Continent had to be recast before the foundations of industrial success could exist. Once more the appearance of foreign competition had to be postponed for the greater part of one generation, and once more our monopoly was prolonged. Italy and the German Empire were to be created, France dismembered and reorganised, Austria had to be overthrown and reconstructed, Denmark had to be despoiled, and the American Union above all had to be saved. If the climax of 1872 and 1873 was due to the Franco-German war the ascent of our trade to the figures of 1866 was due to the American Civil War, and the consequent cotton boom in India, Egypt, and Brazil – to the development of Prussia, with the triumphs of Schleswig-Holstein and Sadowa. If we go back to 1857 and 1853 the special cause of the upward impetus is found in the great gold-finds, and all through the period railway construction and the increase of steam shipping are assisting all the abnormal influences of war and speculation to force up the trade returns. There was a golden age of demand for British goods. The internal development of colonies and dependencies and foreign nations was increasing their consuming power, and the workshop of the world was still, in the absence of any industrial rival, the only source from which the required supplies could be drawn. But there is not a moment between 1846 and 1873 at which the successive phases in this immense progress of national commerce and wealth need to be accounted for by any reference to free imports.

(4) *Foreign and Colonial Investments.* – Throughout the period of this unprecedented accumulation of wealth, we were lending money to all the world for many purposes besides railways, and were paying the loans in the concrete form of exported goods, chiefly iron.

Finally, before we close our review of the period, let us glance at the true connection between cheap food, national prosperity, and commercial progress. The following table compares the prices of wheat with the value of exports in the years of maximum trade after the repeal of the Corn Laws:

Price of wheat per quarter.		s.	d.	Exports	*Million £*
Average before Repeal, 1841–5	.	54	9	Average 1841–5 54	
Price after Repeal .	1846	. 54	8	. . . .	57.8
	1853	. 53	3	. . . .	98.9
	1860	. 53	3	. . . .	135.9
	1866	. 50	11	. . . .	188.9
	1872	. 57	0	. . . .	256.3

Throughout the period the price of bread rather rose than fell, the price of meat rose remarkably, and the cost of living as a whole increased under free imports. But the nation had higher profits and higher wages, and preferred them though food was dearer than before the repeal of the Corn Laws. In other words, it is successful production that creates prosperity, not cheap consumption. This fact disposes with final effect of the "historic claims" of Cobdenism, and forms a sufficient refutation of the charlatan cries which are now used to alarm the people. Free imports did not reduce the cost of living. Neither will preference raise it. But Mr. Chamberlain brings the nation back to the main point of national economy when he tells it that successful production and competitive progress are the vital conditions of popular welfare, and must be the main objects of commercial policy.

VIII

The Third Period, 1873–1903. – The whole basis of Cobdenism was in reality destroyed by the Treaty of Frankfort. Little as we perceived it at the moment, it was a greater blow to the position of England in the world than to that of France. It opened a new economic epoch; the industrial awakening of the Continent and America was at hand; and with it the end of the manufacturing monopoly we had held for a century. "The hour had struck though we heard not the bell," and our position under free imports was soon to be as though a man should find himself engaged in a struggle against well-armed opponents with nothing to depend upon but his great bodily strength and a total absence of weapons. One of the most singular processes in history has been the extent to which England herself has equipped her rivals for the struggle against her trade. For the last fifty years a large part of her trade has constantly consisted of exports for helping her competitors to dispense with the other part of her exports. For decades we had been providing other countries with the two chief requisites of modern production – capital and railways. In the last thirty years by far the most progressive staples of our exports have been machinery for enabling mankind to dispense with our textiles and coals, which assists their iron and steel manufacture to dispense even with our machinery. In this sense foreign competition is our own Frankenstein's creation. The process was unavoidable. But it creates a situation in which free imports do not assist

219

us, for it has brought to an end the whole theory of international division of employments upon which the Free Trade doctrine rested.

We have pointed out the fundamental contradiction of that doctrine. It assumes the natural state of individuals to be one of competition and the natural state of nations to be one of co-operation. It teaches in each case the profound fallacy of half-truths. Trade Unions in England have proved the power of combination to be as strong as the power of competition when it comes to the contest between capital and labour for the sharing of the profits. The American Trusts, which are permanent in their nature whatever superficial observers may think, and will become more formidable than before when financial disaster compels them to reorganise upon a sound basis, have proved that combination may be a stronger factor than competition in enlarging the mass and reducing the cost of production. Upon the other hand a quite opposite qualification of the Free Trade doctrine of international commerce is true. In that sphere the force of competition continually tends to become more prominent than the factor of co-operation. This may be better understood if stated in yet another way. The free imports doctrine assumes that all imports are equally useful because they must be paid for by exports of one kind of another. But this denies altogether the existence of foreign competition – which is absurd.

There are some things in commerce which nations cannot leave to chance or the blind conflict of their human atoms. If our textile and metal trades were destroyed, for instance, by an immense influx of foreign manufactures, we could pay for what we received by mining an enormous quantity of coal and depleting our mineral deposits at a rate which would exhaust them in twenty years. The Cobdenite doctrine, that imports must be paid for, would be perfectly demonstrated in that process. In the meantime our manufacturing industries would be destroyed – and when the coal was done everything would be done. It is, therefore, theoretically false and practically fatal to assume that all imports are equally useful and all methods of paying for them equally profitable. Yet the whole doctrine of free imports rests upon this falsehood. If international division of employments were complete there could be no such thing as competition. The farmer does not compete with the smith, nor the tailor with either. But, as we have explained, the doctor does compete with the doctor for practice, and the lawyer with the lawyer for briefs. America, Germany, France, Belgium, and now Italy – all these countries alike are manufacturers, as we are – and already in several respects to a greater extent – of iron and steel, machinery, cottons, woollens, linens, hardware, earthenware. More and more the characteristic of the situation as between these nations becomes the identity of their employments. Each aims at rising as high as possible in the scale of employments. They compete with each other; they endeavour to oust each other. If their efforts are made far easier in one country than in any other, the process may go too far. We are exporting more and more coal. Free imports of iron and steel and textiles are more and more attacking our greatest industries. The undoubted, the inevitable tendency of that sort of exchange is to drive us from the higher employments to the lower. Politicians who do not understand that point are unfit to legislate; and professors who show in public manifestoes that they do not understand it are unfit to teach.

The desire of other nations to develop the superior employments which we formerly monopolised, and to preserve them when obtained, is the whole secret of the Protectionist action. There is nothing mysterious in it. It is the simple counterpart of a man's desire to rise in the world and to give in private business no unnecessary assistance to a competitor . . .

But Bismarck, above all, was the destined enemy of the Cobdenite creed. He had attacked and broken its whole conception of international policy. His social legislation repudiated its *laisser faire* conception of domestic policy. And he now gave, for all Continental purposes, the final blow to its fiscal policy . . .

Bismarck was vehemently resisted by the majority (though supported by the ablest) of the professors; by the doctrinaire Radicals; and by the Hanseatic cities, which were as much opposed to him as is Lancashire to Mr. Chamberlain – not foreseeing that they would profit almost more than any other portion of the German Empire from the brilliant result. But supported by the agrarians and the manufactures alike, the Iron Chancellor triumphed, and his triumph made a profound impression on the world. Everywhere, except in England, it was realised that the free imports doctrine had received its death-blow. England might endeavour for some time to persevere in the practice of that policy; but the whole theory upon which it rested had been destroyed by the logic of facts. It was founded upon the co-operative conception of international relations. It was overthrown by the competitive reality of international relations. Where there is no rivalry in trade, free imports of commodities, which a country requires and does not produce, must be desirable and cannot be harmful. When rivalry appears – that is, when true division of employments ceases and identity of employments in vitally important industries begins – the case is altered. It is the obvious interest of a country to concede only the minimum of facility to the necessarily dangerous aims of foreign competition. Free imports give the maximum of facility to foreign competition. This is why every other country has already abandoned them, and this is why they must be discarded here, if our status as a commercial great Power is not to be irrrevocably lost . . .

XIII

Mr. Chamberlain's opponents have determined not to believe in the theory of dumping with regard to iron and steel. But to fully understand that issue, we must consider both sides of it. The increase of foreign imports in this country reduces the competitive power of the trades they attack, and not only lowers the general rate of home production, but reduces exports. It is clear when a country begins to "dump" in this market the products of any given trade, that if we cannot hold our own market against the invader, much less can we continue to export to that country in that trade. The ensuing figures show both sides of the account:

	1891	1902
Imports of foreign iron, steel, and machinery from Germany (with Holland) and Belgium	£2,300,000	£8,100,000
Exports of British iron, steel, and machinery to Germany (with Holland) and Belgium	5,060,000	4,800,000

Eleven years ago it will be seen we still exported to Germany and Belgium nearly twice as much iron, steel, and machinery as we received from those countries. Now the proportions will soon be reversed. These two nations were able to send us twice as much iron and steel last year as we sold to them. Thus British industry is ceasing to be a feeder of foreign enterprise. The Continental iron and steel trades have begun instead to feed certain British trades at the expense of other British trades . . .

When the crash came in Germany and the internal demand collapsed, there was a surplus – and the Westphalian syndicates saved themselves or at least minimised their losses in the only possible way by flinging that surplus upon the British market. The German crisis came in 1900 – the result was seen in the British Trade Returns of 1901. For the purposes of the comparison between the two years it must be remembered that Rhenish iron and steel are shipped through Holland.

THE GERMAN CRISIS AND THE BRITISH DUMPING-GROUND, 1900–1901.

	1900 Tons.	1901 Tons.
Imports from Germany and Holland –		
Pig iron	9,000	24,000
Bar-iron, &c.	2,000	14,000
Iron and steel, unwrought	6,000	90,000
Various manufactures	13,000	18,000
Rails	17,000	19,000
Unenumerated	84,000	117,000
Total weight dumped	51,000	282,000

Machinery being entered only by value, it is more difficult to show what occurred with regard to it, the fall in price for dumping purposes concealing the real increase in the quantities dumped, but the figures are as follows:

	1900	1901
Machinery imported from Holland and Belgium	£577,000	£773,000

In other words, Germany was allowed to save herself at the expense of British manufacturers, who were dragged down with the fall of their rivals, but were made to fall undermost. If a tariff had existed in this market equivalent to the German duty on iron and steel, the Westphalian syndicates would have had to suffer far greater losses; they would have been forced either to sell more cheaply still in this market, or would not have been able to sell at all. They would have had to contract their output by comparison with ours, their competitive power would have suffered a grave injury, and ours would have been improved. This is how dumping works out in practice to the progressive weakening of the national industry. As a result of her crisis Germany would have been third this year in her output of iron and steel had it not been for the facilities for maintaining her output which our fiscal system affords her. But "free imports" existed, and free imports were utilised. The final effect has been to contract British output more than German, and to depress this country still further from its historic position in iron and steel. The process, it will be observed, has three stages: (*a*) there is a German crisis in 1900; (*b*) the Westphalian syndicates fling their surplus upon the British dumping-ground in 1901; (*c*) German output in 1902 shows a recovery accordingly, and British output a relative weakness. These stages appear very clearly in figures that we may draw again from the White Paper:

COMPARATIVE OUTPUT, 1900–1902.

	PIG IRON			STEEL		
	1900.	1901.	1902.	1900.	1901.	1902.
	Tons.	Tons.	Tons.	Tons.	Tons.	Tons.
England	9,000,000	7,900,000	8,500,000	4,900,000	4,900,000	4,800,000
Germany	8,500,000	7,800,000	8,400,000	6,600,000	6,400,000	7,800,000

The ultimate effect upon productive energy we see in 1903, when Germany is exporting a million tons of her annual output to the British Empire, and is enabled by that fact to rank as the second iron and steel power. We are told with curious humour by the resolute apologists of the system which makes these things possible, that the blows inflicted by protected capital upon British capital by ruthless selling below cost price, cannot be continual. True; but they leave as we see permanent effects upon the victim, and permanently reduce his strength and spirit by comparison with his assailant. We can assemble the materials of iron and steel manufacture cheaper in this country than they can be assembled in Germany. We can ship the finished product more cheaply owing to our still unrivalled facilities of access to the sea. The cause of our under-production, and therefore of our competitive weakness, and our disquieting outlook in iron and steel, lies simply and alone in the hopeless strategical disadvantage under which we place ourselves by our present fiscal system. A crisis in the affairs of our rivals, so long as the dumping-ground remains open, must be a greater injury to us in the long run than to them . . .

We already receive nearly a million tons of foreign iron and steel. American competition, when once more directed towards this country by a financial crisis or otherwise, will double or triple that quantity. And identity of employment to that extent on the part of all his foreign competitors must make the position of the British ironmaster untenable. Mr. Chamberlain's opponents cannot argue upon their own principles that the British iron and steel industry will not be destroyed. They must argue upon their principles no less in this case than in the case of agriculture, that it probably will be destroyed. The professors can only tell us in this case, as in the former, that we shall get another trade. What other trade? They certainly cannot tell us . . .

We have now to crystallise our criticism before entering upon reconstructive principles. The industrial problem of England is the problem of home production.

We have instanced the relative position of the three leading manufacturing powers with reference to iron and steel. The same consideration applies to the whole range of national industry. Consider the commercial relation in which these three countries stand to each other. By our imports from America and Germany under the free imports system we strengthen their home market to the extent of over £150,000,000 – estimating the value of the goods they send us in the country of production before shipment. But by the exports we send them under their tariff system our home market is strengthened annually by only £50,000,000 a year. Apart from all questions of freight and commission – distributive and financial profits – it is certain that upon the balance of the transaction we promote the *productive* energy of our rival three times as strongly as they promote ours. They must gain upon us therefore, and they do, and those who secure the advantage in productive power by such a system of exchange will ultimately have it in transport also and in finance . . .

But if the actual relation of the three great markets is such as we have described in point of value of trade, what is the influence of that fact upon competitive conditions? There, we repeat, is the marrow of the matter. The three countries together contain a population of nearly 180,000,000 – the United States, 78,000,000; Germany, 58,000,000; England, 42,000,000. The American trader's position is the best. He makes with equal freedom for the two richest markets – his own, where the tariff gives him a monopoly, and this one, where he is as free to ply his trade against ours in competitive business as in any State in the Union. His field of free sale therefore contains 120,000,000 of people, and he is sure of two-thirds of it. The German merchant has the next best position. His field of free sale contains 100,000,000 of people, and he is sure of the larger half of it. The British trader's field of free sale, this island, contains only 42,000,000 of people – and he is sure of none of it. How can any reasonable mind demand of him that he shall display equal competitive power? It is as impossible for him to do so as for a shop with a small custom to compete against a shop with a large one. The analogy is exact. Let us now work it out in more detail. In the first place, the British manufacturer must play for safety only. He must be forced into under-production and for this reason. If he have a surplus owing to a sudden shrinkage of demand in the home market he cannot save himself by selling it abroad even at cost price, because tariffs ranging from 17 per cent. *ad valorem* in Germany to higher scales of duties elsewhere must be paid by him and not by the consumer. He cannot sell abroad therefore except at a prohibitive rate of loss, and as in times of depression he finds himself undersold on all sides by foreign competitors even in his own market, his whole production must be dead loss. He must therefore avoid over-production at all hazards and does. This is why we are slackening down throughout our whole industrial system, and why we show less enterprise in business than any other nation and less progress. Yet the natural energy of the race was never greater than it is to-day. The "apathetic Englishman" is a myth. He still possesses upon the average more physical vigour than any other race, and when he again feels himself living in an age with real causes to fight for, with great aims to pursue, and with a sense of national driving-power restored to national existence, it will be seen that there is nothing the matter with his mind. But he cannot give his full measure in business. He is in the grip of a theory which he does not really believe in, but which seemed in some mysterious manner to be the unchangeable policy of his country, so that he ceased to have any clear thought whatever upon the subject of fiscal policy and the true principles of commerce. He cannot compete with his rivals in their market, and in his own market he is under disadvantages to which none of them are subject. That is the Englishman's position. It is not conducive to progress. A country compelled to avoid over-production and confined to a policy, relatively, of under-production must fall more and more behind, since another disqualifying factor, as will be seen soon, enters into the problem.

The situation of the American and German manufacturer is that he can afford to play not for safety but for fortune and to pursue in every direction of business a progressive and aggressive policy. The tariff maintains a higher level of profit in every way, but not at the expense of the consumer. For the increase in wages as well as profits goes everywhere with the extended enterprise of capital and the increased demand for labour. Mr. Stephen Jeans, of the British Iron Trade Assocation, has declared that he knew of cases in America where production was from 25 per cent. to 30 per cent. less than the lowest cost of production he had ever heard of in this country although the wages of workmen across the Atlantic were far higher. We may also instance the case of the boot and shoe-factory in Massachusetts where a German inquirer found that all the workers received 15 dollars a week and the cost of labour nevertheless was only 40 cents a pair, while in German boot-factories the men received less than 4 dollars a week, but the cost of their labour was 58 cents on a similar pair of shoes. Both in American and Germany the monopoly of the home market does not mean indolence and inefficiency as all the early theories of Free Trade told us would be the case, but it does mean more energy in the pursuit and inventiveness in the the methods of business than we have seen in this country since we learned to think that "free imports" were in themselves the one blessed and all-sufficient law of national business. The tariff in a word justifies itself by its sheer efficiency as an economic instrument. For what really creates enterprise is the inducement of profit, not, as Cobdenism with its shallow view of human nature thought, the pressure of competition. Where competition prevails under unequal conditions, as in this country, it becomes a discouraging factor. Foreign competition being shut out from the home market industrial capital is in the enviable position of possessing both higher interest and better security. It encourages to the utmost, as our system can never do, progress, invention, enterprise, if you like, speculation; production and if you like over-production. The recurrence of over-production is the sure sign of expansive vigour in a commercial society. It was our own complaint in the days when our profits were highest. The tariff thus stimulates home output to the utmost. But now let us see what happens when the internal vigour so nourished seeks an outlet in a country like ours under free imports and possessing enormous consuming power. The foreign competitor, with the secure profit of his home market behind him, can afford to sell at a very small profit in this country in order to make a trade and he makes a trade by degrees as we have cause to know. But when that trade becomes considerable, we have this situation. The tariff encourages foreign production by high profits and discourages British production by high duties; the free-sale facilities of this country again increase foreign production and depress British production in identical employments. But the governing factor of successful production is quantity of output. You build a factory and have the ordinary fixed charges in connection with it. If you double your output without building a new one, your profit upon the second half of your production must be much greater than upon the first half, at equal prices. You can afford to sell the second half at lower prices than the first and still make the same profit. You can sell the second half at a price actually below the cost of production for the first half and still make a profit. You can always, therefore, hopelessly undermine a rival who only turns out half your output, by selling below his cost of production, while still making a profit for yourself. We may conceive the process as follows:

FIRST-HALF OUTPUT.		SECOND-HALF OUTPUT.	
Cost of production	100	Cost of production	95
Profit, 10 per cent.	10	Profit	15
Price. . . .	110	Price. . . .	110

But now let us see how the second half might be sold at a profit below the cost price of the first:

Cost of production for first-half output	100
Cost of production for second-half output . . .	95
Profit at 5 per cent.	$4\frac{3}{4}$
Price . . . —	$99\frac{3}{4}$

The actual transactions in business life are doubtless a less simple matter than these conventional figures suggest, but they may help to explain the mechanism of underselling to the large numbers of Englishmen who find difficulty in understanding how it can pay the foreigner to sell below the cost of production. To increase output is to cheapen cost. We have shown how the tariff stimulates foreign output. It is also stimulated indirectly by "free imports" here. Our system reduces our productive energy, while the American and the German systems sustain at the maximum the productive energy of those nations. The tariff also facilitates those great capitalist combinations which are indispensable to the efficient organisation of modern business. All of us, like Mr. Roosevelt, while recognising the uses of trusts, object to the abuses, but all of us must see that we too must learn to construct businesses upon a greater scale, and to conduct business in a more daring temper. Nowhere are large combinations more needful than in this country, and nowhere would they be less dangerous. The Trade Unions form a counterpoise here which does not exist elsehwere. Trade Unionism cannot attain among the cosmopolitan millions of the Republic the power and the solidity it possesses among our homogeneous people . . .

We have now worked out the thesis with regard to the effect of free imports upon foreign trade and the home market. They have lost us our supremacy in the one: they jeopardise our existence in the other. Free imports are turning us more and more into a nation of distributors and middlemen. There are whole streets in the City of London almost exclusively occupied by foreign agents or by the agents for foreign firms. These streets represent the Intelligence Department of foreign competition, and no one can accuse this Intelligence Department at least of being undermanned. Its legitimate business is to be in close touch with every part of British life, and to spy out the industrial nakedness of the land. The British manufacturer is better known to his competitors in many respects that he is to himself. The campaign against British business is promoted in this way with as much effect as though it were concerted, and at every moment of our waking lives some British consumer is being ingeniously tempted to injure the interest of some British producer and to promote some foreign interest. As a result, while distributive, commission and agency businesses and profits increase in this country prodigiously, our *productive* power, in which alone a nation can find the permanent guarantee of its prosperity, is checked, enervated and reduced. The fatal feeling spreads through the country that we are on our defence, and have reason to be content so long as we do not lose too rapidly or too much, and while public incidents like Mr. Pierpont Morgan's attempt to corner the Atlantic are avoided. Influenced, more or less consciously, by the whole feeling of Englishmen in his time that there was something predestined and permanent in our manufacturing monopoly, Cobden's ideal of Free Trade was an ideal of commercial conquest. His vision was that the products of our superior employment would reign in all the markets of the world while all nations poured into this country in tribute the products of their inferior employments. This is what Bismarck meant when he called Free Trade the weapon of the strongest, and asserted that England could never have adopted it if she had not first developed through several centuries of ruthless protection and irresistible power. America also, if in some remote day she should have developed her whole industrial forces to a point making her certain of crushing every rival – even America, which has been the protagonist of protection almost from the first moments of her independent history, might then adopt Free Trade . . .

XV

For the maintenance of empire and of our historic place in commerce and upon the seas, and no less for the progress of a crowded nation in a little island, two aims must be clearly and unflinchingly pursued.

The first aim, as we have indicated, must be the security of the home market. From the purely commercial point of view it is many times more valuable than all foreign and colonial markets put together. For a vast self-contained country like the United States the importance of foreign commerce is infinitesimal by comparison with that of internal production and exchange, except indeed for agriculture, which must still export its surplus if it is to make a profit upon its entire cultivation. Germany has mainly created her present wealth by the development of the home market. The interests of the home market have always been the first care of wise legislation. And this for an obvious reason. An international transaction may be at the best of about equal profit to the two countries between which it takes place. But a home transaction of the same kind is twice the immediate gain to the country within which it occurs, for each party to the transaction profits by it, but both profits belong to the same country. This is a principle of which America has never lost sight, and her firm grasp of it gives the clue to her tariff legislation for a century . . .

And the United States has been on the whole firm in her conviction throughout her history that the best fiscal policy in the interests of national wealth is that which makes it as difficult as possible for foreign competition to decrease total wealth by defeating the efforts of any individual citizen. There are some citizens for whom the States can do nothing, but the majority in their various walks of life are average men, neither inspired beings who delight indifficulty, and would be successful anywhere and under any circumstances, nor incompetents for whom it is useless to provide opportunity. For the average man in business at large the Republic has found that the most effective thing to do is to give him the chance in the field of domestic enterprise of making all the dollars there are, either in competition or in combination as he chooses with other American citizens, but reasonably free from foreign attempts to reduce or minimise his profits to the possible disadvantage of the State. Cobden left out the interest of the State altogether, for although he thought that the relations of individuals were governed by competition he also imagined – it was, we repeat, the fundamental contradiction – that the relations of nations were really founded on fraternity. His whole doctrine rested upon a theory of "natural aptitude" fitting every country for some particular industry. If a home trade was beaten by foreign competition that was a proof that the country had no "natural aptitude" for that trade, and would do better to let it go and find another. That was the cardinal fallacy of Cobdenism. We now know that there is no such thing as "natural aptitude" in this absolute sense. *Everything* in manufacture flourishes in America under the inducements provided by the McKinley and Dingley tariffs to national enterprise. But have we a "natural aptitude" for *anything*? Coal and iron are no exclusive possession of ours. Every country provided with coal and iron can compete in every industry we possess. Upon Cobden's theory of "natural aptitude" it would appear that the one industry in which we are inherently fitted to maintain an everlasting superiority is – agriculture! – the yield of English land in bushels of wheat per acre being still unrivalled anywhere in the world. America from the first knew better. She did not want division of employments: she wanted identity of employments. America did not want to exchange with our goods: she wanted to exclude them in order that internal production might be as various and vigorous as possible, that domestic exchange might be as active and reproductive as possible, and that she might create, as she has done, the most powerful home market in the world . . .

XVI

That is the problem of production. There is also a problem of exchange, which for us must be more serious than it ever can be for any other nation. We alone of all the great manufacturing nations have overturned the equipoise between city and country, between agriculture and manufacture, which must always be the ideal of a sound State. We are stating the fact, not condemning the action . . .

For all practical purposes we must regard ourselves as a nation permanently dependent for the food of its people and the crude material of its manufacture upon seaborne supplies. If we were a nation merely, that position in its ultimate sequel, however long delayed, could not be other than fatal. But as we are more than a nation – as we are an empire, which we are learning more and more to regard as a whole – that position must suggest the vital principle of our whole Imperial system. If we had no Colonies, or only in the sense that France or Germany have them, our commercial position would now be hopeless . . .

It remains to discuss from this point of view the fourth proposition with reference to exports: "That in British exports to British possessions, and in them alone, during the last thirty years there has been a great and steady increase both in quantities and values." How completely our commercial supremacy as a whole has been saved by trade under the flag, and how absolutely the future of our maritime power depends upon the economic relations between the Mother Country and her colonies and dominions throughout the world, we shall now see.

The summary up to the present point may be thus given:

(1) The interests of national production demand that the British manufacturer shall have the same advantages in his home market that his competitors enjoy in their home markets. This is the first condition of an adequate improvement upon our part in competitive power.

(2) The interests of our maritime ascendency, since our industry depends on one hand upon imports, demand that we should also secure freer markets for our exports.

(3) The interests of the Mother Country demand the exchange of manufactured goods for food and raw material to a far greater extent than now.

(4) The interests of the Colonies demand the promotion of British manufactures in order that the Mother Country, being by far the greatest consuming centre in the world for imported agricultural produce, may promote in return the development of Colonial cultivation.

(5) The permanence and security of the Empire demand that it should be as self-supporting as possible and should become so not only as completely as possible but as rapidly as possible.

(6) The problem of Imperial power is a problem of Imperial economy,

and the only solution conducive to the effective unity of our political system for purposes of defence – while consistent with the fullest freedom of self-government and the commercial development of all its portions – lies in preferential trade.

In one sentence our whole future as a people, if we wish to keep the place we hold, depends upon the degree of success we shall secure in the attempt to realise this broad conception – a strong home market as the centre of a self-supporting Empire. This is the object of Mr. Chamberlain's policy. His action in raising the issue has been, not wanton, not mistaken, not premature, Sooner or later the issue had to be raised. Facts would have forced it upon us at some future period, when our policy might have been in weaker hands, when the inclination of the Colonies to conclude a commercial union with the Mother Country might have passed away, and when the damage to our industrial and mercantile position under the present system might have been far more difficult to repair. We are fortunate that the question is brought forward by a statesman fit to grapple with it, and at a time when the conditions for a successful change of policy are more favourable than they have been for many years, or may ever be again.

XVII

The Empire depends upon our commerce. Our commerce depends upon the Empire . . .

We being an island, with a population too small for any lasting effort of continental conquest, were compelled by nature to pursue one aim alone and we therefore achieved it – Colonial ascendency. Sea-power cannot in itself be an object. It is the means to an end. It was not the sole condition of our purely insular safety in the days when we could still feed ourselves, and when there was sufficient military force in our population to repel any invader who might succeed in reaching our soil. If we look not at the theoretical fallacies, but at the practical methods of the mercantile system we shall see that it was an old-fashioned form of pure McKinleyism bent upon securing that the process of international exchange should never have the effect of displacing home production by foreign production. The extraordinary tenacity with which this idea was pursued is seen in the fact that the woollen trade in Ireland was suppressed because it threatened to become a seriously competitive manufacture, and the linen trade was established instead, so that the development of one island should not interfere with that of the other. These were the unjust and impolitic exaggerations of the system, but we see how clear and resolute was the aim – the security of home production. By the old Colony laws we took care to monopolise the importation of raw materials and exotic produce from them, and to monopolise the supply of manufactures and other home

231

exports to them. Cromwell's great Navigation Laws, which Adam Smith, though opposed to the rest of the system, thought the wisest of all the commercial regulations we had ever adopted, excluded foreign vessels from the carrying-trade of the Empire, and further reserved for British ships the transport of Colonial produce to foreign countries. The theories upon which all this was done were ridiculed by the classical economists in the days when as we have said the historical sense was in abeyance, and the extent of our triumph had blinded us to the natural insecurity of our Imperial situation. The newer historical school of economists in this country has discovered that the old system secured the creation of the Empire. Its practical effect was tremendous. The expansion of England, as Sir John Seeley has shown, was effected by commercial wars. The cause of our mercantile supremacy did not lie, as modern free importers would have us think, in our trade with foreign countries. It lay in the security of our home production, in our monopoly of Colonial and Indian supplies, and in the completeness with which we had turned both these advantages to account for the purpose of securing the mastery of the seas, the consequent control of the world's communications, and therefore the control of the world's trade . . .

From the point of view of total commerce it will be seen that the British Empire, as a whole, is far more important than Great Britain separately. The aggregate commerce of the United Kingdom is about £850,000,000. The total trade of the Colonies with countries other than Great Britain is according to a recent return about £250,000,000. The total annual commerce of the Empire, regarded as a whole, amounts, therefore, to the stupendous annual sum of about £1,200,000,000. And this is practically all *ocean trade*. That is the point to be grasped. A great proportion of the traffic in the German returns is a purely land traffic, and a considerable part of the imports and exports of the United States pass across the Canadian and the Mexican frontier lines. The ocean-borne commerce of the Empire, as a whole, is by nature, and so long as the Mother Country remains prosperous must continue to be, far greater than that of any other State for generations to come. It is now three times as large as that of the United States, and about seven times as large as that of Germany. In that fact, if we know how to use it, lies our security. The British Empire only needs to understand itself in order to assure its future, and for the British Empire to understand itself simply means that the Mother Country and the Colonies must understand each other . . .

Our real rival in Imperial trade will be the United States unless we give ourselves the benefit of home market principles, and apply to the Empire in a moderate form of imitation the commercial policy of the Republic. In Canada we know how the proportions stand. We are Canada's best customers by far, but in 1902 the Dominion received 60 per cent. of its imports from the United States, and only 24 per cent. from the United Kingdom.

With a large part of the imports from the United States we do not compete, but among other items, including £2,000,000 of American textiles and £5,000,000 of American iron and steel, we should recover some millions of Canadian trade under an increased rebate in our favour. But a withdrawal of the preference clause, such as will presumably take place if Mr. Chamberlain's policy – that is, Canada's policy – should be rejected by the country, would be the death-warrant of our trade with the Dominion. The United States would seize the chance to draw Canada into the reciprocal relations with the Republic that she had been unable to establish with the Mother Country. In that case Canadian citizens would buy from us in the end as American citizens buy – six shillings a head, which would mean the disappearance of the trade now carried on upon the forty-shilling-a-head basis owing to the preference clause and the Imperial connection. Our trade with Canada let us remember is already larger than our trade with any foreign countries except the United States, France and Germany. It is even now a first-class asset of our commerce. Its existence is bound up with Mr. Chamberlain's success . . .

A still more serious danger lies before us in the probable action of the Colonies themselves. We are mistaken if we think that rejecting Mr. Chamberlain's proposals would leave things as they are. It would be seen within a short time to have left them far otherwise with respect to our trade prospects and our Imperial hopes alike. It is in our power to leave things as they are on this side. But as to leaving them as they are upon the Colonial side – that is a matter which will not depend upon us, and will be goverened by the ideas of those who are slaves to none of our economic superstitions. The Colonies, like ourselves, desire the policy that would pay them best. They are mainly agricultural countries, and what they most desire is the development of agriculture. That is what will increase their population and make them great States. Except upon the basis of an extensive and flourishing agriculture no national manufacturing system can be built. But the Colonies, the Dominion and the Commonwealth alike, are now at the parting of the ways. They stand beween the American ideal and the Imperial ideal. They, like the German people since the teaching of Friedrich List, who had lived in America, have been deeply influenced by the American doctrine of the home market. Both in Australia and Canada tenacious manufacturing interests are arising, who put business first in practice precisely as the Cobden Club does in theory. Their object, if they can secure it, is not to have lower tariffs against the Mother Country, but to have higher tariffs against her. They are not yet predominant in either of our greatest Colonies. If preference is adopted they will not become predominant at all in our time. Preference would place in Colonial hands the work of supplying the vast food consumption of the United Kingdom. It would do what Cobden hoped from his policy - it would create larger agricultural populations, but with a definite guarantee that their increased consuming power would mean a larger demand for British goods. Now what is certain is that in Canada and Australia alike the farmers under preference would be in favour of lower tariffs – perhaps in favour of as close an approximation to Free Trade with the Empire as revenue necessities permitted. In any case they would be as naturally in favour of minimum tariffs in favour of the Mother Country as the manufacturing interests would be in favour of maximum tariffs against the Mother Country. But if Mr. Chamberlain's policy were rejected the Colonies would have no reason whatever to pause in a policy of high protection strictly upon the American model. If we had refused preference for their agriculture in our market why should they extend any special consideration to British manufacturers by their tariffs. If we are to be committed to free imports by the refusal of preferential trade, we should see in the Colonies what we have seen in every foreign country . . .

XX

The Empire can never be secure and commerce can never breathe the air of national confidence upon which its progress so largely depends until we feel that we are once again members of a self-supporting system commanding its own means of living. It is the unalterable law that in every sound and safe society agriculture must be internal to the State. For us it cannot be internal to the nation. But all the more is it essential that it should be internal to the Empire. Since we have sacrificed home agriculture we must be dependent upon colonial agriculture, but not upon supplies that the Empire does not control. We must not only maintain a fleet to protect the transit of our supplies once they are upon the seas. We must ensure that under all circumstances so long as our naval power holds they shall reach the sea. That is the political aim indispensable to the recovery of our Imperial security. The second aim is of a more purely economic character. In the scantiness of our agricultural population we suffer under one of the greatest disadvantages that can affect manufacturing industry. Where there is a great agriculture and a great industry side by side the economic balance is perfect. There is complete division of labour and free exchange for mutual support. Cobden never imagined that his system would displace British agriculture to the extent we have seen, but he also imagined that if it did, we should merely change the direction but not the character of our transactions. If American farmers supplied our food they would take our goods just as the home farmers did, and agriculture under the American flag would be the same support to British industry as though it had flourished under our own.

This was not only a mistaken but a disastrous view, and the influence it has exercised upon the industrial position of England has never yet been studied in this country with the attention that the subject deserves. The economic development of America has been carried to its present height by the simultaneous action of two forces – restricted imports and free exports. The system under which we are attempting to work is that of free imports and restricted exports. Grasp clearly that distinction. Reflect upon it a little and you will see that the success of the first system is due to an immense degree to the existence of the second. It is better to have a larger demand for your goods than a smaller demand. Hostile tariffs are, or course, a means of diminishing the demand for your goods and stopping your export wholly or partially. But to deprive a business of customers is the deepest injury you can inflict upon it. We cannot dogmatise upon the merits or demerits of Free Trade because Free Trade has never existed in the world. But we have had free imports. America by her access to this island has practically had free exports. Germany has free exportsfor a fifth part of her trade – the portion she now sends to this country. France in the same way has free imports for a third of her whole trade. Every country which sends goods to this island has, so far, free exports. The country which imagines itself to possess Free Trade is the only country in the world which does not enjoy anything in the shape of free exports . . .

The security of our mercantile predominance can be the only sure and permanent guarantee of our naval supremacy. At present the British consumer pays the American railway rates upon his food-supply as well as the price to the American farmer and freight to British ships. Why should not this vast outlay go every year to the building up of British Colonies and the British Empire now that America has had the benefit of it for a generation. When our American food-import becomes a Colonial food-import, with the line of supply completely British from end to end, our shipping supremacy will be as much a matter of course as the superiority of the United States in its output of iron and steel. Upon this condition the transfer of our agriculture to the wider shires beyond the sea would become the very security for Empire. Our food-supply must be raised upon British soil, and carried from British ports abroad to British ports at home in British ships. Politically, preferential trade is as important for our security as is the existence of the Navy, and more so than the existence of the Army. It would be as much worth paying for if need be, as either of those services, and we can secure it without adding a shilling to taxation, and with no increase of our burthens in any direction without an equivalent decrease in some other direction. Mr. Chamberlain's policy would make the British Empire a natural system resting upon a natural base, when the vast importation of food-supplies and raw material upon which the Mother Country depends for her prosperity, her production, and her life, will be received to a main extent from British possessions. Colonial agriculture, British shipping, and home production would be three links of a chain that nothing could shatter . . .

Whatever degree of preference we might give and receive, nothing can be more certain than these two main points: (1) that Colonial tariffs should be lower upon British goods, higher against foreign than they will be if Mr. Chamberlain's policy is rejected; (2) that if we drew our food-supplies and raw material from the Colonies, we shall send back a far larger volume and value of manufactured goods in exchange for them than we do now. At home a tax upon the foreign-manfuactured and half-manufactured articles, which now supplant home industry, would in part be an aid to revenue when paid by those who cannot afford to lose this market, and in part a premium on home production and home enterprise. It would induce American capital and energy to settle inside the tariff with results as useful as when Edward III. set the precedent by bringing over the Flemings. It would not mean the sacrifice of our foreign trade, for every nation which has strengthened its productive force by adopting the tariff has increased its foreign trade. In our case, we should undoubtedly increase it, for other nations would do with us what they do with each other – they would offer reciprocity in return for lower duties – and so long as our tariff was upon a lower *ad valorem* level than that of other countries, which would be the case, we should be entitled to "most-favoured-nation treatment" precisely as we are now. By bringing special pressure to bear upon the classes of duties especially injurious to British goods, we should make the "most-favoured-nation" clause a reality in many cases where it is now a nullity . . .

THE ASSISTANT EDITOR.

NOTES

1   Values are another question, as will be seen.
2   See (Vol. III: 7f. 222)

10 MR. CHAMBERLAIN'S PROPOSALS*

A.C. Pigou

ART. IX. – Mr. Chamberlain's Proposals.

1. *Speech of the Right Hon. Joseph Chamberlain, MP, at Welbeck, August 4, 1904.*
2. *Report of the Tariff Commission*, Vol. I.: Iron and Steel Trades.
   P.S. King & Son. 1904.

Mr. Chamberlain has opened his second campaign. Throughout his speeches two great themes persistently stand out – the economic condition of England and the political condition of the British Empire. Under each head he has made proposals. On the one hand, he advocates duties upon certain kinds of manufactured imports, no matter from what source they come; on the other hand, duties upon foreign imports of agricultural produce, from which colonial imports shall be exempt. Both proposals alike will, he declares, confer an economic benefit upon the mother country; and, in addition to this, the second will enable us to secure at once valuable concessions from, and a closer union with, our colonial fellow-subjects . . .

I Protection of Manufactures

. . .

Free imports, it is said, may perhaps add to the nation's wealth, but they undermine the fortunes of the working classes.[1] Even, therefore, though Protection should impose an extra charge upon the wealthier part of the community it is still to be desired, according to this view, as a means to benefiting the poor. The injury inflicted upon the working classes has, however, to be demonstrated. The argument implicit in much popular oratory, that, since foreign competition in any industry diminishes employment in that industry, therefore such competition in all industries diminishes it all round, contains the 'fallacy of composition,' and is logically untenable. Nor need we stop at the merely negative conclusion that Mr. Chamberlain's thesis is 'not proven.' The war may fairly be carried into his own country, and he may be invited to explain the relation between that thesis and the recorded facts. If it were true that imports, or – since he prefers to limit the issue – imports of manufactured and partly manufactured goods are detrimental to employment, we should expect the great increase of these which has recently taken place to have been accompanied

* A.C. Pigou, 'Mr. Chamberlain's Proposals', *Edinburgh Review*, 200 (310) (July–October 1904), pp. 449–69; 474–5.

by a growth in the percentage of Trade Unionists out of work. There has been no such growth. During the last forty years our imports of manufactured goods have trebled, and the average level of employment has remained practically unchanged.[2] . . .

A second ill-effect attributed to Free Trade is that it augments the transitions of industry. That it does this in some degree is undoubted, for, under its influence, a nation tends to transfer its resources from less to more productive channels. In these transitions some sacrifice of acquired skill is demanded of the adult workpeople who have to change their trade, and this, wherever it occurs, is a real evil. It must, however, be remembered that transitions great enough to necessitate a movement of adults are very exceptional . . .

A third alleged ill-effect concerns the *quality* of employment. All are agreed that mere opulence is less important than the conditions under which people work. At present, it is said, the trend of our export trade is away from 'staple' and towards 'miscellaneous' industries – jam, pickles, slop clothing, furniture, and so forth. Consequently, the trend of employment is turned in the same direction, with the result that between the last two censuses the numbers employed in tailoring and furniture-making have increased much more rapidly than those engaged in staple industries. But the former group of industries are worked under worse conditions than the latter. Hence it follows that foreign trade is causing more people to work under bad conditions, with deleterious results both to physique and to character. It is therefore desirable that the nature of that trade should be modified, and that, instead of making slops with which to purchase staples, we should make the staples for ourselves.

This argument has been employed by Professor Ashley.[3] We need not inquire how far his view of the condition of labour in the miscellaneous industries is correct. He himself has admitted that a considerable proportion of the tailoring industry is carried on in well-appointed modern factories, and it is unnecessary to remind him of the existence of Port Sunlight. Let it be granted that the facts are substantially as he has described them. It is sufficient to ask whether protection to British staples would be an adequate or a desirable remedy . . .

Furthermore, even supposing that Professor Ashley's remedy would do more good than harm, it does not follow that it ought in practice to be adopted. For there is a way at once simpler and more certain. It is difficult to see why bad conditions in the 'miscellaneous' industries should be attacked in a manner different from that which has been adopted in regard to all the other regulated industries of the country. When the operatives in cotton mills were oppressed and degraded as no workpeople are degraded now, the solution of the difficulty was not found in a tariff upon agricultural imports. It was found in factory legislation, inspection, and sanitary regulations – in protection, in short, not to goods but to men. If the conditions of the miscellaneous industries require a remedy let them be dealt with along these well-tried lines . . .

The next argument which may be urged against the Free Trade position is both older and supported by higher authority. In the *prima facie* case advanced at the beginning of this article it was shown that unimpeded foreign trade enables a nation to obtain what it requires more cheaply than it can do under protection. But this conclusion was only proved as regards *immediate* effects. Nothing that was said could be used in answer to the argument that Free Trade, while adding to wealth immediately, might detract from it ultimately. This was the point upon which Alexander Hamilton and Frederick List seized in answer to the classical school. 'It is true,' wrote List, 'that protective duties at first increase the price of manufactured goods; but it is just as true, and moreover acknowledged by the prevailing economical school, that in the course of time, by the nation being enabled to build up a completely developed manufacturing power of its own, those goods are produced more cheaply at home than the price at which they can be imported from foreign parts.'[4] The argument thus formulated is commonly known as the 'infant industries argument,' and is recognised as formally valid by all modern economists. In the above form it has not, of course, great immediate relevance to the present condition of England; for, in an old country, such as ours, commanding every kind of mechanical skill, it is extremely improbable that any really suitable industry should fail to be started for lack of an initial stimulus. But the infant industries argument is only a special case of a wider generalisation which List also envisaged the perfect clearness. 'The power of producing wealth,' he declared, 'is infinitely more important than wealth itself.'[5] It is in all respects relevant to our case to ask whether protective duties, though for the moment diminishing wealth, might not strengthen productive power. Advocates of tariff reform hold that, if intelligently managed, they would conduce to these results in three respects. First, by making the market for our products *wider*, they would enable manufacturers to increase the scale of their output, and so to secure various economies of production; secondly, by making the market *steadier*, they would add to these economies; and thirdly, by obviating the unfair attacks of foreign monopolists, they would prevent the destruction of industries naturally suited to this country.

A plea for a wider, as distinguished from a steadier, market is based by Mr. Chamberlain's Tariff Commissioners upon the ground that, when works are running full time, their costs are much less in proportion than when they are only partially employed. This fact has long been a matter of common knowledge, and did not need to be demonstrated by the interesting statistics which the Commissioners quote.[6] To establish it is, however, a very different thing from showing that costs will be reduced by a policy which causes *the total British output* of any particular staple good to be increased. There is, in short, an ambiguity in the phrase 'manufacture on a large scale.' It is evident that a mere increase in the already enormous quantity of iron and textile goods made in England could not inaugurate any appreciable economies. In order to this effect the increase would need to be accompanied by a general approximation, on the part of individual firms, towards working up to their full capacity. There can be no doubt that as an immediate consequence of the imposition of import duties this change would take place. But the advantage would not be more than momentary, for, as the protected industry became more profitable, capital would be diverted into it and new works started. When time had been given for things to readjust themselves there is not reason to suppose that the average amount of short time would be less than it is at present, and therefore no reason to anticipate any reduction of costs.[7]

The argument for Protection as a means to steadying the market turns upon its relation to one of the different policies which the Tariff Commissioners confuse under the comprehensive title of dumping. In bad times people do not want to spoil their own market by selling in it cheap. Neither do they want to disorganise their staff by shutting down their works. Consequently, when practicable, it is very convenient for them to *dump their surplus* abroad and spoil the market of somebody else. The policy is facilitated under a protective tariff, because the re-importation of the dumped goods is prevented by the Customs duties. When adopted by foreign firms, it is, of course, directly advantageous to this country, because it enables us to buy what we need at low prices. But, on the other hand, it may involve an indirect disadvantage in the disorganisation and fluctuations brought about in the British industry primarily affected. It is impossible to say generally whether the good or the evil result will be the greater. The answer to that question varies in different cases according to the character of the dumped article and the purpose for which it is employed. Though in many instances the good will certainly predominate, it need not always do so. Circumstances can be conceived in which the exclusion of the article would, if practicable, be advantageous. We have, therefore, to inquire whether this exclusion can and ought to be effected by any form of protective action.

The device which naturally suggests itself is a duty varying inversely with the price at which the importer intends to sell. By this means customs officers could checkmate the intending 'dumper,' for they could levy special rates upon the cargo which he designed to 'dump.' Unfortunately for this plan, however, the dumper himself is the only person who need know what his selling price is going to be. In an imaginary world of 'protectionist men' he would perhaps hand on to the customs officer all essential information. In the real world, however, he will certainly refrain from doing this. If necessary he can make consignments at full prices to an agent at Southampton, instructing him that the goods – which have not, of course, been dumped into England from abroad – are forthwith to be dumped from one part of England to another. No scheme has yet been suggested by which evasions of this kind can be prevented. The plan of imposing discriminating duties upon 'dumped' as distinguished from other imports of the same commodity must, therefore, be regarded as outside the range of practical politics.[8]

A second device is Professor Ashley's scheme for empowering the Executive, without resort to Parliament, to impose temporary high duties on all imports of a particular class at such times as surplus dumping seems likely to do more harm than ordinary imports do good.[9] Under an autocracy, incorruptible and omniscient, this plan might, no doubt, succeed. But political proposals have to be considered in the concrete. No responsible statesman supposes that, in these schemes of taxation, Parliament will consent to waive its present powers. Under such circumstances it is mere academic theorising to suggest that duties can be imposed at one moment and removed at another just as the occasion demands. Professor Ashley's scheme may be advisable in the study, but it will not work in the world.

A third device is the frank imposition of permanent high duties. The disorganising effects of surplus dumping are, it may be said, so serious that, in order to their avoidance, the advantage of imports sent to us in the ordinary way ought to be sacrificed. Apart, however, from the evident costliness of this remedy, it can be shown that the end sought by it would not be obtained. While surplus dumping may increase fluctuations, ordinary imports diminish them. Their expansion checks upward, and their contraction downward, oscillations of price. Take, for example, the case of a strike in the iron trade. Under our present system rising prices draw German iron to England. Even so, the disorganisation of the secondary industries which use iron as a raw material is considerable. But if importation were impeded by the presence of a high tariff their difficulties would be still greater. For every three men who now lose their employment there might then be four or five. In view, therefore, of the fact that the proportion of the imports which are, to those which are not, 'dumped, must always be extremely small, a policy of general exclusion as a remedy against surplus dumping bears a perilous resemblance to one of general starvation in mitigation of the dangers of an occasional debauch. In fact, there seems no ground for departing from the strong opinion expressed by Professor Marshall some twenty years ago: 'Protection has been proposed as a remedy for the inconstancy of industry: I believe that all reasonable arguments and all practical experience prove that it much increases that inconstancy.'[10]

The last device is exemplified in the scale of duties provisionally suggested for the iron and steel industry by Mr. Chamberlain's Tariff Commission.[11] This consists in the permanent imposition of duties ranging up to 10 per cent. It is a conclusion not easy to connect with the remarks about surplus dumping, upon which it in part depends; for, when foreign firms have determined to 'flood' the English market with their

241

surplus at slaughter prices, it is hardly to be expected that a 10 per cent. duty will prevent them from doing so. One of the Commissioners' own witnesses (firm No. 630) tells us that 'American file-makers offer their files to consumers here at 70 per cent. from the Sheffield standard list.' In such circumstances the futility for defensive purposes of anything except really high duties must be patent to everybody. Professor Ashley not only admits but strongly emphasises it. After giving instances of the kind of reduction at which these surpluses are sometimes sold, he writes: 'To meet such prices duties of 50 to 75 per cent. *ad valorem* may be needed, or even prohibition.'[12] His remedy, inexpedient as we hold it to be, is at least intelligibly related to the disease it is designed to cure. Mr. Chamberlain's Commissioners, on the other hand, for their premiss, expatiate upon the deluge, and, for their conclusion, truculently brandish Mrs. Partington's celebrated mop.

A final plea for Protection is that it is sometimes needed to prevent, not the dumping of surplus produce, but destructive dumping. It is conceivable that foreign combinations might deliberately adopt a policy of killing British rivals in order to establish an exclusive control over our market. They might sell in England at low prices – prices so low as to involve a positive loss – until our industries were destroyed, and then, no longer having any competitors to face, might gather in the fruit of their labours by raising prices to a very high level. In the face of a policy of that kind to check the import of their cheap goods, though still involving a direct loss, might nevertheless be sound policy, as tending to save us from monopolistic exactions later. The formal validity of this argument is not disputed. The practical question is: Does this kind of dumping, as a matter of fact, take place, or is there any ground for supposing that it is likely to do so? So far as the facts go there is no evidence that anything of the kind has yet occurred. It is true, no doubt, that Mr. Brailsford and other 'experts' have stated that the Steel Kartell in the last few years has pursued the policy just described. But in the official memorandum prepared for the Board of Trade precisely the opposite opinion is emphatically put forward:

> 'It is, of course, easy to suppose a state of things in which a Kartell or a combination of Kartells might deliberately export at a low price, with the principal or the exclusive aim of injuring and ultimately of entirely ruining and bringing tò a close a particular industry in a foreign country. But it cannot be said that there is any clear evidence of such action on the part of the German combinations, whose export policy up the the present time appears to be mainly the result of supply exceeding demand in the German domestic markets.'[13]

It is not maintained that destructive dumping does not exist at all. On the contrary, it certainly exists in the home market of Protectionist, and sometimes even of Free Trade, countries. There are plenty of cases in which

American Trusts have 'dumped' goods in the markets of native competitors, in order to ruin those competitors and maintain their own monopoly. There have been instances of the same thing even in England. A Birmingham concern, for example, engaged in the manufacture of screws is popularly supposed, at one period, to have succeeded in dumping other English screw-makers out of existence. But destructive dumping into England from abroad does not take place, and for a very simple reason. The only purpose of the policy is to secure the control of the supply, and therewith the power to exact monopoly prices afterwards. In the native market, especially in a protected country, where the competition of foreign imports is hindered by a tariff, there is no reason why that result should not be achieved; but, in the British market, if a German Kartell or an American Trust kills British competitors, what advantage has it? It is still prevented from reaping its reward by the presence of sellers from other foreign countries. It will not, therefore, be worth its while to 'dump' unless it has not merely an American or a German but a world-embracing monopoly . . .

There remains a further indirect advantage which may be claimed for certain forms of protective duties. These may be advocated not upon the ground that they are protective, but that they compel the foreigner to contribute something towards our revenue. The plea is frankly a national one. It is admitted that the world at large would suffer from the diversion of industry into channels where it is relatively inefficient, but it is claimed that in certain cases the direct loss experienced by this country would be less than its indirect gain through the tribute levied upon other nations. Since it is generally agreed among economists that, in some cases, a part of an import duty may be thrown permanently upon the foreigner, this argument cannot be met by any general denial. On the contrary, as Professor Marshall has observed, 'there is no absolute *a priori* proof that these evils' (those involved in the diversion of industry by a differential duty) 'must necessarily outweigh the advantage of shifting a part of the direct burden of a country's taxes on foreigners.'[14] It cannot be denied that special cases might be found in which a duty incidentally protective would confer a net advantage upon us during the first few years of its operation, and sometimes even permanently. Any general attempt to tax the foreigner by means of protective duties is, however, exceedingly unlikely to result in any such net advantage. As Professor Marshall further observes in the course of the letter already quoted,

> 'a study of details shows that, as the world is constituted, an attempt to make other nations contribute to a country's revenue on any considerable scale is foredoomed to failure, and especially that England cannot do it. Again, a study of detail shows that the waste and friction and indirect consumers' loss caused by differential duties on the frontier are

always greater than they appear at first sight, and especially in the case of a densely peopled country which has limited material resources and must trust mainly to a highly efficient organisation of her industry and trade.'

If this view be accepted it follows that, in order to get any net benefit from protective duties levied for revenue purposes, Parliament would need to make a very careful and limited selection of dutiable imports. It can hardly be doubted, therefore, that if, as under the present proposals, a large number of duties are arranged, not with the object of taxing the foreigner, but with the entirely different object of protecting home industries, there must ensue a loss upon the whole. The duties which would be most efficient protectively are not at all likely to be either of the same size or levied upon the same commodities as those which would best serve the purposes of revenue. It is scarcely rational to support Mr. Chamberlain's policy of Protection for its own sake upon the ground that a perfectly wise statesman, whose object was to collect a revenue in the most economical manner, might include in his budget a few differential duties, the protective element in which was secondary and incidental, and which differed from Mr. Chamberlain's no less widely in character than in purpose.

At this point the analytic portion of our disucssion may conclude. The results reached, while neither rigid nor dogmatic, are on all counts adverse to the policy which the Tariff Commission is disposed to recommend. If, however, the argument stopped at bare analysis it would be far from complete. For it is upon the practical side that the case against Protection is strongest. The intellectual difficulty of selecting the right cases for protection and of applying it at the right time is serious. But it is not the only difficulty. In England the supreme financial authority is not a bureaucracy, but a ministry subject to the control of Parliament. In view of the many and great interests which a tariff may affect, it is too much to hope that it would be left entirely unhampered in the contemplation of its intellectual task. The need of conciliating supporters and of avoiding an adverse division might force it on occasions to modify its proposals – not, perhaps, in the direction most conformable to the intellectual ideal. It was said of a certain American tariff that the only kind of manufacture to which it essentially related was the manufacture of a President of the United States. Dangers of that class cannot be ruled out as impossible even in our own country, and the prospect of them has to be reckoned with when the chances are weighed that a really scientific tariff will be framed. Furthermore, even if it be granted that, in its first form, the tariff would be good, can we seriously suppose that either the number or the magnitude of the duties would remain unaltered? When Protection has been granted to one industry it is extremely difficult to refuse it to others. When it has been granted at all it is extremely difficult, in bad times, to reject the plea, which is certain to be made, that the extent of the protection should be augmented. But, if that is difficult, what prospect is there that duties, once imposed, will, when the interests of the State require it, be rigorously reduced or removed? Mr. Chamberlain's supporters continually observe that, despite the example offered to them by England, foreign countries steadfastly continue in the paths of Protection, and this, they hold, is an argument against Free Trade. To their opponents, on the other hand, a different and less encouraging inference suggests itself. When duties are imposed businesses come to be started whose profits depend upon their continuance. Alone, perhaps, no one group of them is strong enough to influence the Legislature. But they are aware of that fact, and, in consequence, combine to resist the introduction of freer trade in one another's commodities. The passage of the recent tariff law through the German Reichstag afforded an excellent object lesson of the working of tariff regulation in practice. In the final result the agrarians contrived to force through Parliament, in the face of Governmental opposition, a set of minimum duties which deliberately sacrifice the general good in the interests of a particular party . . .

II Preferential Tariffs

At the beginning of this article it was observed that the arrangement selected would involve some repetition. The reason for this is that one of the arguments most commonly urged in favour of preferential duties is their partially protective character. They are, in Mr. Chamberlain's view, destined to afford a defence to British agriculture against the onslaughts of foreign competition. They are to bring back into cultivation land which at present is idle, to revive the greatest of our national industries, and to prevent the labourers of the country from being driven into the towns. Like his manufacturing duties they are to achieve their successes without a single accompanying disadvantage. They are to 'extend the production of food, increase the employment of labour,' and at the same time 'to cheapen the ultimate cost to the consumer.'[15] The benefits to the labourer from remissions of duty upon tea and sugar are not a compensation but an 'extra.' It is not till after we have heard that 'my proposals' will 'bring to the labourer more employment and will not raise the cost of living' that they are introduced. Of the new taxes by themselves, considered in complete isolation, it is claimed:

> 'I but open my eyes, and perfection, no more and no less,
> In the kind I imagined full fronts me.'

To opinions of this kind the general argument addressed above to the protection of manufactures is directly applicable. Here as there protective duties must compel us to produce for ourselves goods which could be obtained at less cost by the method of exchange. The price of wheat and the other taxed articles must be raised – not necessarily above what they were before, but above what they would have been without the tax. . . . The broad effect of the duties must, therefore, be to render agricultural produce in general more expensive.

Mr. Chamberlain's supporters may reply that, though this result might follow under merely protective, it will not follow under preferential duties. An obvious answer to such a contention is to inquire how, in that case, it is possible for their policy to benefit the British agriculturist. There is, however, something a little wearisome in the reiteration of this unanswerable dilemma. It is more profitable to face the problem directly. The solution appears to be that conditions are not inconceivable in which preferential duties would so stimulate the developement of railways and other transport facilities in our Colonies that, in the long run, the price of their products would reach a level as low as, or even lower than, that which they would have attained in the ordinary course of things. But this result, though conceivable, is, even in the abstract, highly improbable. It implies that the conditions of agricultural production here and in the Colonies are at present fixed in a region of unstable equilibrium, and that, without preferential duties, the small impetus required to start them moving from thence will not be given. In the concrete the answer is still more conclusive; for there is ample evidence that the desired movement has already begun. The Canadian North-West does not need the touch of a preferential fairy prince to waken her, but is already alive with youthful energy. Hence it is practically certain that the preferential character of the proposed taxes will not prevent them from raising prices above the level which they would otherwise have reached. The economic case against preferential taxes on agricultural imports is the same in principle as that against protective taxes upon manufactured imports. The general argument that productive resources are diverted from more to less economical employments holds good in both instances.

In the case of agricultural duties, however, there is, in addition to this, an important permanent effect upon the *distribution* of wealth. In Mr. Chamberlain's Welbeck speech it is curious to note that the name of an important class in the community – the agricultural landlords – was not once mentioned. The benefits anticipated for farmer and agricultural labourer were expounded in glowing terms, but the very existence of the landlord was ignored. And yet, if Protection is reintroduced, it is to him that nearly the whole advantage thereby conferred upon agriculture is bound, in the long run, to go. No doubt it will not be secured to him immediately. Tenants with long leases will retain part of it for a time. But when leases come to be renewed the landlord has the whip hand, and can raise rents to match the improved prices of agricultural produce. Nor is it in the least relevant to reply that rents are largely influenced by private friendliness and other non-economic considerations. For these influences are operating already just as effectively as they are likely to do under Mr. Chamberlain's proposals. Non-economic and economic factors both play their part. But, when the former remain constant and the latter change, the obvious fact that the former are in existence affords no ground for doubting that the new cause which has been introduced will be followed by its appropriate effect. It is difficult to see how the advocates of agricultural protection can escape from this conclusion. Everybody knows that it is the landlords whom the recent prolonged fall of prices has struck most severely. Their rents have moved in about the same proportion as agricultural prices. Indeed, the parallel between the changes which have occurred in these prices and in incomes assessed to ownership of 'lands' during the last forty years has been very striking. In the following table the price movements as between successive decades are compared with the movements in the value of lands as between the final years of each decade.

TABLE[16]

Value of Lands in the U.K.	Unweighted Index Number of Wheat, Barley, Oats, Prime and Middling Beef and Mutton, Pork and Bacon.
Between 1860 and 1870 rose 10 p.c.	Between 1850–9 and 1870–9 rose 10.5 p.c.
" 1870 " 1880 " 8 "	" 1860–9 " 1870–9 " 11.5 "
" 1880 " 1890 fell 16 "	" 1870–9 " 1880–9 fell 14.8 "
" 1890 " 1900 " 9 "	" 1880–9 " 1890–9 " 1.5 "

Though, however, it is practically certain that the recent fall in prices has hit the landlords hardest, it does not follow that its effects have been confined to them. On the contrary, it may be rejoined that these effects have been largely felt by the agricultural labourer. As between the three years beginning with 1880 and the three beginning with 1900 his wages have only risen 9.7 per cent., while wages in general, apart from agriculture, have risen 18.8 per cent.[17] Under these circumstances it may plausibly be urged that the connexion between his fortune and the landlord's, which has been maintained through the depression, would continue if an agricultural tariff were to convert bad times to good.

The answer to this rejoinder is threefold. In the first place it must be remembered that, though agricultural wages have not increased so fast as industrial wages, they have nevertheless increased considerably. In the second place, an important factor in checking the demand for labourers' services has been one quite independent of foreign trade, the substitution, namely, of mechanical for muscular power in various mechanical operations. Lastly – and this reply is of itself sufficient – such part of the retardation in the wage movement as is really connected with cheap imports is traceable to the *continuous fall*, and not to the *absolute lowness*, of agricultural prices. If these had been merely low, things would have adjusted themselves. In accordance with well-known economic laws there would have occurred a transference of labour from agriculture to other occuaptions, until equilibrium between their respective wage-levels was restored. Since, however, prices were not merely low but falling, supply, though steadily following, failed to come up with demand. Agricultural labour proving, like all labour, unable to adjust itself quickly to changed conditions, remained, until the last year or two, in excess of the farmer's requirements. It suffered on account of changes to which it delayed to respond.

The bearing of this analysis upon our immediate problem is decisive. A fixed duty upon foreign agricultural imports can affect the absolute level of agricultural prices, but, except in the short period of readjustment immediately following its imposition, cannot affect their changes. These could be influenced only by some kind of 'climbing' duty, which Mr. Chamberlain has never ventured to propose. His fixed duties, therefore, cannot confer any permanent benefit upon the agricultural labourer. Precisely similar reasoning applies to the farmer. Hence it follows that the only real beneficiaries of his policy would be the agricultural landlords. A sum of money equal to the increase of prices multiplied by the amount of home-grown agricultural produce would be transferred to them from the pockets of the consumers of that produce. This is the main direct result to be expected from the proposed taxation.

When that result is clearly envisaged the statesman who, in this country, should declare it desirable would need audacity. Under an economy of peasant proprietors such as prevails in France, and to the existence of which Mr. Chamberlain referred with dazzling irrelevance at Welbeck, the case might be different; for it could be claimed with some show of plausibility that the average wealth of these peasant landlords is less than the average wealth of Frenchmen; and, this point established, it could be added that a transference of money from the richer to the poorer is always *pro tanto* an advantage. In Great Britain, however, this argument obviously cuts in the opposite direction. The average agricultural landlord is much wealthier than the average citizen. To put money into his pocket at the expense of the community is to mulct the poor for the endowment of the rich.

The strong condemnation which this conclusion implies has driven certain writers to resort to economic juggling. The performance begins with a truism. It is remarked that an increase in the prosperity of landlords will react upon that of other classes; and from this premiss is evolved the conclusion that an increase in their prosperity ought to be promoted by Protection. Since, however, as has already been shown, whatever extra prosperity is secured to them by this means comes from the public, the indirect reflex benefit *to* the public is scarcely likely to compensate for that expense. If any one asserts that it will, he may be invited to revise a number of opinions which usually meet with acceptance. For it will follow that he has only to give his income away in order to obtain a greater income from the reflex benefits showered upon him by those who receive it. The argument implicitly treats a small quantity of the second order as not merely comparable with, but actually greater than, one of the first order.

There is, however, a more serious reply. Granted that agricultural import duties are bad in their protective aspect, it may still be argued that in their revenue aspect they are good in a more than equivalent degree. In an earlier paragraph something was said upon the general possibility of exacting a contribution to our revenue from the foreigner. In the case of the proposed preferential duties it is, however, necessary to go somewhat further into detail, for Mr. Chamberlain has publicly declared: 'These taxes that I have spoken of will be paid in the main by the foreigner; they will be the foreigners' contribution – and it is a very small one – to our expenditure, but they will bring in a great number of millions a year.'[18] As these hypothetical millions are to be employed in the reduction of duties upon articles of general consumption it is clear that, if they are sufficiently numerous, the public may gain more from them than it loses in its payment to the landlords. The point is, therefore, an important one.

In discussing it we need not dwell too closely upon Mr. Chamberlain's phraseology. To speak of our gain, whatever it may be, as a contribution from the foreigner is not strictly accurate. Paradoxical as the remark may appear, the chief part of the gain would not be directly contributed by any one, but would arise out of a shifting of the margins of agricultural production. This, however, is a minor point. The essential matter is that the so-called contribution is not a *net* gain. There have to be set against it, first, the payment which is made under the new plan to colonial agriculturists, and, secondly, the 'contribution' which is sacrificed upon those commodities – tea, sugar, and so on – the duties upon which are to be reduced. It is only after these items have been subtracted that the net advantage of Mr. Chamberlain's plan from the standpoint of revenue can be found . . .

It must, however, be conceded that the main purpose of Mr. Chamberlain's plan is not economic, and that the economic side of it probably interests him little. His dream is a different and a far more inspiring one: '*Let us unite the Empire, the great aspiration of the wisest and the best of your statesmen.*'[19] It is upon our judgement whether or not his proposals will help forward this result that, in the last resort, they must stand or fall. His case is not finally answered until it has been shown that the commercial ties which he contemplates, so far from proving a cement of empire, are likely to prove a solvent.

In the first place, Mr. Chamberlain has claimed for them the power of advancing *political* unity. He has appealed to history, and has declared that 'commercial union in all previous cases has always preceded closer political federation.'[20] This statement is not, however, in accordance with the facts. That famous advocate of Nationalism, Frederick List, makes a precisely opposite assertion: 'All examples which history can show are those in which the political union has led the way the the commercial union has followed. Not a single instance can be adduced in which the latter has taken the lead and the former has grown up from it.'[21] Mr. Chamberlain's one illustration is the German Zollverein. There, indeed, the seed of commercial union bore political fruit. It needs, however, but little argument to show that between that case and the present there is no analogy. It is not merely that Germany consists of contiguous States and the British Empire of ocean-sundered colonies. The essential point is that the commercial union whose results Mr. Chamberlain applauds was disparate in every respect from that which he seeks to justify by its example. The policy which succeeded was the abolition of all duties between the separate States. The policy which is proposed is the imposition by the separate States of new duties upon foreign imports. No inference from the one to the other can possess the slightest cogency . . .

NOTES

1 Mr. Chamberlain at Liverpool, 'Speeches,' p. 154.
2 Cf. the table compiled by Mr. G.H. Wood, 'Journal of the Royal Statistical Society,' December 1899, and the official Abstract of Labour Statistics, 1903.
3 The Tariff Problem, pp. 106–110.
4 The National System of Political Economy, pp. 144, 145.
5 The National System of Political Economy, p. 133.
6 Report, §§ 55, 56.
7 If, indeed, the wider market secured by Protection led to the growth of combinations on the American pattern economies would not improbably result. It is, however, generally held that the evil effects of these combinations upon distribution are apt to exceed their good effects upon production. Furthermore, the fruit of Protection is at least as likely to be Kartells as to be Trusts, and Kartells are injurious in both respects.
8 Mr. Fielding, in his Budget Bill in the Canadian Parliament, proposed in June last a special duty on dumped goods. 'That duty would be the difference between the price at which the goods were sold in Canada and their fair market value in the country of origin' ('Times,' June 8). It will be interesting to see how the experiment is worked.
9 The Tariff Problem, p. 133.
10 Address to the Co-operative Congress, 1885.
11 Report, §§ 88.
12 The Tariff Problem, p. 133.
13 Cd. 1761, p. 298. It is sometimes argued a priori that destructive dumping must take place, since some foreign goods are sold here more cheaply than in the country of origin. The conclusion does not follow, for, as the Tariff Commissioners rightly observe (Report, § 61), a policy of two prices may be directly profitable to those who pursue it without reference to ulterior results. No

arguments, however, can be framed for Protection against goods imported in pursuance of that policy other than those which are applicable to Protection in general.

14 An export duty on coal, 'Times,' April 22, 1901.
15 Mr. Chamberlain's speech at Welbeck.
16 In this table the figures for Irish lands for 1860 have been estimated from the values of 1862, the earliest year in which they are recorded. The smallness of the fall in lands between 1890 and 1900 as compared with the fall in price is partly explained by the passing of the Agricultural Rating Act.
17 Calculated from tables in Cd. 1761, p. 260.
18 Mr. Chamberlain's speech at Welbeck.
19 Mr. Chamberlain's speech at Welbeck.
20 Mr. Chamberlain's speech to the Agents General, Nov. 18, 1903.
21 The National System of Political Economy, p. 126.

---

11 THE PRINCIPLES OF CONSTRUCTIVE ECONOMICS . . . *

J.L. Garvin

The Doctrine of Development

The strength of the Manchester school lay in the simplicity of its creed. The Imperial school must endeavour to base itself upon an argument equally definite and compact. Statistics up to the present have played an indispensable part in the fiscal controversy, but there is a strict limit to their usefulness: they are trying to the popular head, they make speeches cold, meetings dull, and democracy depressed. Since enthusiasm cannot be generated by arithmetic, no great cause was ever carried by figures. It is essential that the case for Imperial union upon an economic basis should be made as far as possible independent of detail. By the use of undeniable figures we have succeeded in opening a controversy – that is, in creating doubt. But this is negative work, and the effect of our efforts must depend in the long run upon the extent to which we can make our ideas of positive policy intelligible and convincing. If we are not only to create doubt but establish conviction, we must substitute one creed for another, principles for principles, ideals for ideals. "When I got my method by the end," said

* J.L. Garvin, 'The Principles of Constructive Economics . . .', in Committee of the Compatriots' Club (ed.), *Compatriots' Club Lectures, First Series* (London: Macmillan and Co., Ltd., 1905), pp. 1–12; 20–47; 52–6; 59–61; 63–5; 71–5; 77–81.

Bunyan, "still as I pulled it came." The attempt of the present paper is to seek the leading idea from which the fiscal tangle will come straight of itself in the mind of the plain man. That idea seems to be offered by the doctrine of development as applied to modern economics.

The classical economists belonged to the pre-Darwinian age. We differ from them in our whole view of life and of the ends of life – in our whole mental method as well as in our possession of the practical experience of the last sixty years. We now know, for instance, that the security of all the peace interests of nations depends upon the efficiency of their war apparatus. We know that the one thing worse than war is being beaten; that there is no economic injury more penetrating than defeat; that there are no economic factors so potent, so creative, as national strength and the sense of it. We now know that abandoned colonies and dependencies would mean lost markets as well as a broken Empire, and the permanent weakening of national spirit and energy even at home. The doctrine of development starts from the direct denial of *laissez faire*. It holds instead that under modern conditions the economic progress, no less than the political preservation of a State, must largely depend upon the conscious purpose and efficient action of the State itself. Government, in a word, should be the brain of the State, even in the sphere of commerce.

England is not ruined, but for the most part exceedingly prosperous. Our purpose is served, not by denying that fact, but by accepting it and reasoning from it. There are of course serious qualifications to be made. A chart of the world's poverty would show the existence of large depressions in this country, and the lowest soundings of all would be taken in the poverty-deeps of London. There is a steady accumulation of social sediment in all our great cities. It is not our immediate business to dwell upon these things, but rather to admit that the average level of material comfort is higher than in any other country in Europe. For there is no mystery connected with this admission. The octogenarian who had never gone to bed sober for half a century, used to be quoted as an instance of the beneficial effects of alcohol, but we should now take him as proving the vigour of an exceptional constitution. There is no doubt that Great Britain possesses, from the commercial point of view, an altogether exceptional constitution. In her maritime facilities and the character of her internal resources she enjoys, in proportion to her area and population, more natural economic advantages than any other country in existence. We inherit a vast amount of accumulated capital from the comparatively recent days of our monopoly, when we were the industrial centre of the world, and our manufacturing power was equal to that of all other nations combined. Cobdenism discounts our advantages, but has not yet reached the point of neutralising geology, geography, and history! Our gross profits are still greater – they ought to be far greater – than those of any other European people. Trades Unionism enables labour in this country to wrest from capital a maximum percentage of our gross profits.

From this circumstance alone, even if our total earnings were no larger than those of Germany, or were even but slightly lower, the average wages of our working classes would be much higher – the more so as our labour supply is smaller. Foreign competition, recent as it is, has had no time to do more than weaken perceptibly the foundations of our industrial position. It has had no time to break down the mass of the structure. The rivalry of the United States and Germany has been acting with full effect for hardly more than a single decade. Above all, it must be pointed out that we still raise nearly as much coal upon our speck of an island as is raised in the whole of the United States. So long as coal remains the prime motive power of machine-industry, and our position in that respect continues to be anything like as favourable as it is now, our average income per head must be considerably higher than that of any other country in Europe, for reasons with which indiscriminate free imports have nothing to do. We owe to Cobdenism neither our collieries nor our coast-line, nor the historic policy which gave us the mastery of the sea. Yet to the things we do not owe to Cobdenism we unquestionably owe the main fact of our prosperity – the excess of capital and income per head over the average *per capita* wealth of any continental people.

Our natural advantages in many respects are indeed by no means so exclusive as the classical economists thought. But as compared with a country like Germany – which seemed so hopelessly handicapped three decades ago by a poor soil, a bad coast, by traditional penury, by the struggle from the first against an insufficiency of capital, which is even yet by no means made wholly good – we have every natural qualification for exceptional prosperity. To say we have superior prosperity is nothing. So far as we have it, it is evidently owing to our natural resources, to our long monopoly before the rise of foreign competition, to our Imperial position – that is, to our superior advantages of all kinds. The real question is whether we are making the most or the least of these superior advantages. As democracy would put the matter, are we making the best or the worst of ourselves? The present paper sets out from the view that we are no longer making the best of ourselves and are distinctly tending to make the worst. Our fiscal policy acts as a check upon our natural advantages: the policy of other countries acts as a stimulus upon theirs. Under a good system we ought to have made far more progress in the last thirty years than we have achieved. We ought to be still upon the aggressive and not upon the defensive in every neutral market in the world. Our existing prosperity ought to be even greater than it is, and our prospects more secure. The contention to be examined, in a word, is, that indiscriminate free imports in this country are no longer conducive to the highest attainable level of economic progress, that for the island and the Empire alike fiscal *laissez faire* is now a principle of minimum development, and that we must seek in another policy the principle of maximum development.

An altogether new vocabulary would be needed in this country to secure the clearest discussion of the issue involved. To a greater extent than has been generally recognised even yet, we are dealing in names which have no relation to things. Let us begin therefore by reminding ourselves of the actual meaning of some familiar terms: –

(1) *Free Trade* is something which does not exist, which has never existed, which cannot be made to exist, and which, however irreproachable as an ideal, is a conception remaining as purely abstract and remote as that of "the parliament of man, the federation of the world." The theoretical merits of the doctrine are not in any way involved in the present controversy, and there is no occasion to dispute or even to discuss them.

(2) *Free Imports* imply by their mere name the absence of free sale. They cannot be confounded with Free Trade, which implied complete reciprocity in the conditions of exchange. That was the quintessence of its meaning. Further, "free imports" cannot even be called "free imports" without qualification, for the purposes of careful controversy. Our system, if we are to accurately distinguish it from other systems, must always be thought of as "indiscriminate free imports."

(3) *Protection* nowhere means what in this country it is almost universally supposed to mean. It means in modern economics "largely free imports." That is the quintessence of the idea involved in it. It distinguishes fundamentally between imports of raw material and those of manufacture. The latter are taxed, the former are free. The aim is to restrain the taxed import of foreign goods in order to encourage more powerfully the free import of raw material.

(4) *"Free Imports"* v. *"Protection."* There is thus between these terms no such radical antithesis as is commonly supposed. The true distinction is the much narrower and more definite one between "indiscriminate free imports" and "largely free imports." In this sense either of these systems has just as much or as little to do with Free Trade as the other. This country, for instance, possesses practically nothing in the shape of free exchange except in regard to coal. Now, foreign countries called Protectionist actually do possess free exchange – that is, real Free Trade – to a more considerable extent. Germany and France, for instance, have free imports for their raw material and free exports to this market for a very high proportion of their finished manufactures.

(5) *Federal Trade* is the system proposed to be established in order to promote the largest exchange of commodities between the Mother Country on the one hand, and the Daughter Nations and Dependencies on the other, with a view to the greater security of sea power,

as well as to the economic development and political union of the Empire.

Throughout the present paper, therefore, the issue will be regarded as one between indiscriminate free imports and a discriminating system. This implies the abandonment of *laissez faire* and the definite intervention of the State for the purpose of encouraging the more desirable at the expense of the less desirable imports. There is no proposal to reverse Free Trade, for it has never existed. There is no attempt to disparage its principles, for they are remote from the practical issues of the existing generation. If the State is to interfere at all in economic policy, that interference can only take the form of some discrimination between imports and imports. *Laissez faire* was an artichoke of which every leaf but free imports has disappeared. Are we to consider that truth, which did not reside in the root, is likely to reside in the remnant? Or shall the remnant also disappear with the adoption by the State of a definite policy with regard to sea trade and Imperial production? The whole question of Constructive Economics lies there.

Philosophically the term "constructive economics" is one with which it might be possible to pick a slight verbal quarrel. The conflict is more strictly one, to deviate for a moment into jargon, between the passive and the active conceptions of the State, between the static and the dynamic ideas of public policy, between a theory of structure and a theory of energy; or, in one word, between *laissez faire* and *savoir faire*. The issue, as I understand it, is above all one between the doctrine of drift and the doctrine of development. But this being admitted there are great practical uses in the term "constructive economics." All political economy must involve a theory of the State in relation to trade. For more than sixty years the most dogmatic and least exact of the sciences has been dominated in this country by a futile conception of the State. *Laissez faire* assumes that the State has no function, or only a negative one in relation to trade – that commerce only asks of Governments what Diogenes asked of Alexander.

That is the principle of destructive economics which we are organised to combat. The leading principle of constructive economics is that the State, above all others the British state, has a positive and vital function in connection with the commerce upon which dominion depends. We are told by the survivors of the Manchester school that Governments can only hamper the operations of industry – that tariffs, in other words, can only limit production and restrict exchange. It is our business to show, upon the contrary, that the State can still give a powerful and decisive impetus to national industry. A national economic policy can unquestionably promote production. In this country a well-adjusted tariff would stimulate, for instance, manufacturing production.

But you cannot promote manufacturing production in this country, which would then rely to a greater extent than ever upon imported raw material, without at the same time promoting exchange in the largest volume and in the best form. If a national tariff increased our manufacturing power it could not do so without making us larger consumers of raw material from the other parts of the Empire. From our point of view, we can only regard a National Tariff on the one hand, and Federal Trade upon the other, as the inseparable factors of a dual apparatus, or rather as the reciprocating parts of a single mechanism. There we touch the aspect of the case which, as I conceive, especially interests this Club.

For again our theory of the State differs from *laissez faire* in that it avoids like the plague all pretence of laying down universal and eternal principles. We have to discuss the conception of a positive economic policy as applied to the concrete and unique circumstances of the British Empire. But we are all the more bound to place the clearest emphasis upon our leading idea – that of the fundamental unity of the whole question. The historic policy of this country never attempted to distinguish between the respective interests of Trade and Empire. The statesmen of the seventeenth and eighteenth centuries may have taken sometimes an erroneous view of the connection between them. But they had the great merit – Chatham in this respect being always supreme among them – of understanding that the interdependence of trade and Empire was at any rate vital.

Far less can we afford to separate, or can we succeed in separating, those interests now, when the industrial island as a matter of absolute life and death is more than ever dependent upon having access at all times and upon the cheapest terms – of the word cheapest in that connection we are not at all afraid – to the oversea supplies without which our machines would starve as well as our people. For us trade and Empire must sink or stand together. For us the problems of both are urgent. In our belief a home tariff without fiscal federation with the Colonies would be a lever without a fulcrum. We conceive the two things as warp and weft, not to be divided without pulling the texture to pieces. As Mr Balfour said in that remarkable little speech to the overflow meeting at Sheffield, when he repudiated the idea that he was opposed to Preference on principle, it is not within the narrow limits of the four seas that you can develop the wealth, the population, and, in the combination of these two, the power required to keep you in your station among the Empires of the world. Still, as in the old days when the real foundation upon which our greatness yet stands was laid down by the national or positive system, so long and so inadequately known as the mercantile system, ships, colonies, and commerce are the inseparable links of a single chain, and they must slip or hold together. If your ships go, so do your colonies and your commerce; if your commerce goes, so do your ships and your colonies; but also if your colonies should go, so, as we shall see in a moment, must your commerce and your ships.

With respect to each one of these things the condition of your Imperial existence is not success. It is supremacy. For this country there can be no such matter as a second-class position in sea trade with second-class shipping, a second-class navy, and a second-class dominion. We believe it to be in the strictest sense impossible that our supremacy in sea-trade, sea-power, national wealth, and Imperial dominion, can endure permanently or can endure for long without a decisive reversal of the essentially and avowedly anti-Imperial system adopted in 1846, and without a speedy return, with all such wide modifications as the very different needs and circumstances of the time may demand, to the historic and national spirit of commercial policy to which we owe to this day all that is solid still in the foundation and the fabric of the State.

For national policy created sea-power, and sea-power has been not only the instrument of our defence: it has been the great engine of our progress . . .

III The Renewed Need for Development

For a generation we throve mightily, but it was only while the foreign competition, already beaten down under our former system, continued to lie flat. We provided the world with railways and loans. We created their competitive apparatus, and then they one and all adopted or strengthened Protectionist methods of working their competitive apparatus.

The main fact about our situation before 1846 was that our Imperial security and commercial supremacy were absolute in every possible respect. Wages were at least four times as high in this country as they were in Germany. The blots which disgraced our civilisation were chiefly owing to the fact that *laissez faire* meant the neglect of the people before it meant the neglect of the State.

Let us endeavour to tabulate, simply, the indisputable facts about our commercial situation in 1904. They may be stated as follows: –

(1) Our manufactured exports to foreign countries have been stagnant for more than thirty years.

(2) Our manufactured exports to the great protected countries have been slowly but clearly declining for thirty years.

(3) Their manufactured exports to us have increased during the same period in geometrical progression – they have increased, are increasing, and ought to be diminished.

(4) For some time the growth of our colonial trade compensated for the loss in foreign markets. But for two decades that trade also has been showing all the symptoms of arrested development. The recent spurt has been entirely due to the Canadian Preference clause and the South African War – the credit for which cannot be attributed by any stretch of imagination to the principle of indiscriminate free imports.

(5) Excluding South Africa, the truth about our exports of manufactured articles to foreign and colonial markets alike is that as a whole

they have been totally stagnant during the greater part of the present generation.

(6) In spite of the help which we derive from coal the United States is now first in the total value of its exports.

(7) If Germany continues to gain upon us as she did last year, and as she has not ceased to do since Bismark abandoned *laissez faire*, Germany in less than ten years from now will either take second place or dispute with America the first; and we shall be reduced to the third place as an exporting power.

These are the facts about exports. You will agree with me that they could hardly be worse – that the necessity for waking up in earnest could hardly be more urgent. But now take the Cobden's Club's tests. Take imports. Even upon the Cobden Club's own principle of balance the countries which develop the largest exports must in the end have the largest imports. Things are indeed most clearly tending in that direction. The facts about imports are:

(1) In the last twenty years the United Kingdom has increased its total imports for domestic consumption by 30 per cent. Germany, in spite of her Corn Law and protective system, has increased her total imports by close upon 90 per cent. And America, in spite of her M'Kinleyism and her vast internal command of food and raw material, has increased her imports by 40 per cent.

(2) At that rate in a couple of decades more we shall be surpassed, by Germany at least, in imports as well as in exports, and therefore in total value of trade. That is a far more important point than any that has been made with respect to exports. For if Germany is to excel us in the total volume of her trade she must ultimately displace us in shipping.

(3) An unmistakable index of the whole situation is that the imports of our competitors show their demand for the raw materials of manufacture to be expanding faster than our demand.

Again, I think the facts could scarcely be worse even with regard to imports. The most optimistic judgment that the Cobden Club can draw for us from its own tests is that it may be a few decades yet before we fall into the second-class position with respect to total trade and shipping. The third great department of the inquiry touches of course the home market. As to this we shall not possess the same plain data for comparison until Professor Hewins has reported upon the labours of the Tariff Commission. But her again we can make without the slightest fear of contradiction some broad assertions of the most disquieting kind. Stating them as before we say:

(1) That America and Germany in the last twenty years have developed their manufacture without sacrificing their agriculture. Their economic system is absorbing year by year a far greater increase of

population than that for which we are able to find employment under the *laissez faire* system.

(2) Every important British industry has weakened in comparative position during the last twenty years, and is still weakening.

(3) In the manufacturing industry, for which we possess the greatest natural aptitude – I mean the iron trade – we have sunk to the third place. To put it that way does not show the full seriousness of the matter. Again, I will not trouble you with the figures, but what they will show is that, in 1880, we still made nearly as much pig-iron as the rest of the world put together, twice as much as the United States, three times as much as Germany. Now we have been immeasurably distanced by the States. We were finally and far outstripped last year by the Fatherland. Our output, which was larger a couple of decades ago than that of both these countries combined, is now only a quarter of their combined production. They are bound to pour their surplus of iron and steel into our market, just as they poured in their surplus of corn and sugar, and the iron trade is bound to be wrecked just as our agriculture was swamped. This fact alone would mean that the centre of our industrial line is being driven in before our eyes, and that we have reached the critical point in the economic life of England.

We can sum up the whole matter with regard to the home market and national production in this way. America and Germany have increased their manufacturing output beyond comparison more rapidly than we have. Exclusion from their markets has restrained our output. Access to this market has promoted theirs. But – and here we come at once to the foundation principle of constructive economics – the larger the output the lower the cost; the larger the output the larger and cheaper, relatively, the export surplus. The larger and cheaper the surplus the more they will dump if this market remains open, and the cheaper they will dump. Look at it as we like, and we shall see that *laissez faire* promotes the production of our rivals and restricts our own. It claims the name of Free Trade, and produces the characteristic effect it attributes to Protection. Free imports have in reality produced a more far-reaching check upon British trade and industry than the restrictions Cobdenism removed[1] when it swept away the whole of our historic policy, the good and bad together, the parts of it that had become a clog upon our commerce as well as the parts of it which ought to have been retained as a safeguard and a stimulus. In 1846 everything was secure after three centuries of ancestral stupidity; in 1904 everything is jeopardised after sixty years of concentrated wisdom and enlightenment.

We shall find this contrast to be due largely to the fact that before the *laissez faire* era, statesmen never forgot that in political economy the political comes first. *Laissez faire* attempted political economy with the politics left out.

IV The Theory of National Development

The classical economists sincerely believed that they were the people, and that wisdom should die with them. It is important to examine their principles, and to probe the errors of thinking which led their expectations to miscarry. Cobden is justly blamed for his false prophecies because they arose almost entirely from the false principles of that buoyant and vigorous empiric.

Upon the theory of free imports our case ought to be that of Eclipse first and the rest nowhere. The Protectionist nations ought to have taxed themselves to death, under the delusion, as the Americans say, that they were lifting themselves by the straps of their boots. The pernicious thing Protection ought to have neutralised all America's natural resources; a sickly dependence upon the State should have made the American capitalist languid and the German manufacturer incompetent. If Germany has superior technical education, if her whole industry, as we are told, is more intelligently organised than ours, the first result should have been to expose to Germans the evil of their ways and to wean them from perverted ingenuity in fighting against their own interests. German imports ought certainly to have declined when they adopted the tariff and stopped British dumping. Their exports, upon the famous principle of balance, should have declined with the imports. In the home market, Protection ought to have meant limited consumption and reduced production. The healthy pressure of unlimited foreign competition, on the contrary, should have kept the British manufacturer strung up to the highest pitch of superior activity and intelligence. The more our rivals disabled themselves by the so-called restrictive system, the more our trade ought to have bounded. We ought to have swept our competitors long since out of every neutral market in the world.

Such was the prophesied result. The actual picture presents an unsatisfying substitute. We shall most clearly grasp the principles of constructive economics by showing what were and are the fallacies of destructive economics. They can be compressed into a single sentence. The classical economists, like our contemporary Cobdenites, forgot the fundamental distinction between raw material and manufacture; they never made and never attempted to make a thorough analysis of foreign trade in its competitive aspect; they almost ignored the fact – for us gigantic – that foreign trade had a competitive aspect; they advocated the same treatment for competitive and non-competitive imports; they no longer made any real distinction between the things that are partly destructive and the things that are wholly and entirely beneficial; and, far above all, the *laissez faire* school, turning their back upon the whole history of their own country, overlooked the ability of States pursuing a positive policy of economic development to create competitive power where it has not existed. *Created* aptitude in the modern world is as conspicuous a factor as natural aptitude.

Hence the code of orthodox dogma that we are bound to criticise with profanity. Take first the idea of *laissez faire* itself with reference to foreign trade. This idea finds its best expression in a statement attributed to Lord Grenville, which I have taken from a famous protest in 1815 against the Corn Laws, "Public prosperity,'" it says, "is best promoted by leaving uncontrolled the free current of national industry." Fair words! The Cobden Club thinks that something has been done to realise them. But it takes two to make a Free Trade bargain, and other countries have always refused to strike one with us since the competitive era began. In other words, it takes two to remove restrictions upon exchange – that is, upon the "current of national industry" flowing out into the channels of foreign trade. It takes two to set that current free. Free imports into this market have enabled foreign Protection to develop with impunity, with the result of checking the sale of British goods abroad, and sending competitive imports here to check the sale of British goods at home – a double check through foreign legislation upon the output of British goods. Foreign tariffs acting directly upon this market through indiscriminate free imports exert a very powerful influence upon the operations of British capital and industry, which are being gradually forced out of the more natural into less natural channels. There is no *laissez faire* in foreign trade. The system we call *laissez faire* is simply one which leaves foreign restrictions free to act most adversely upon our commerce. The paradox of *laissez faire* is that, by comparison with our protected rivals, our competitive power is knee-haltered.

Thus, free imports are the principle of least development because they limit our market to the utmost, and at the same time expand the markets of our competitors. America and Germany, while keeping a firm grip of their home markets, enjoy in neutral markets the most-favoured-nation clause just as we do, and get more practical benefit out of it, since it is they who in the course of their tariff negotiations actually adjust the most-favoured-nation clause to suit their own trade. They enjoy also the absolute freedom of this vast consuming centre. They have monopoly at home, equality abroad, and an enormous privilege in this market, for which they concede nothing corresponding. Again, let us note that political economy wholly ceases to be a dismal science, and rivals the gay one when the chief Protectionist Powers enjoy most Free Trade, having their imports mainly free and a large proportion of their exports free also.

Let me state here a first positive principle. We cannot claim to force our goods upon foreign nations who desire to manufacture their own just as we do. For this reason the half-way house of retaliation must ultimately be advertised to let. We cannot get Free Trade for Free Trade. That we know.

"Retaliation," therefore, must come to the alternative – tariffs for tariffs. Our first constructive principle is that when foreign nations use their power to contract our market abroad, we must, to begin with, use our power to extend our market at home.

This brings us at once to another of the celebrated sophistries. I quote it from the great petition[2] drawn up by Tooke and presented by the City of London in 1820. It tells us – "The maxim of buying in the cheapest and selling in the dearest market, which regulates every merchant in his individual dealings, is strictly applicable as the best rule for the whole nation." That celebrated form of words has simply no application to the conditions of British business. It is more and more a question to-day of buying in the cheapest market and selling in the biggest, upon the principle of small profits and largest transactions. It is the foreign manufacturer who buys in the cheapest market and sells in the biggest. Have our Cobdenites ever considered the full meaning of the fact that raw material is free under every scientific tariff? Nearly half the imports, roughly speaking, of America, half the imports of Germany, far more than half in the case of France, consist of raw material; those Powers enjoy free imports of all that can develop a trade without hurting any other trade. Thus American manufacturers buy their raw material as cheap as we do. The Germans also buy their raw material as cheap and their labour cheaper. But when it comes to disposing of the finished product and selling it in the widest market they have the conquering pull. America has the whole of her own market and ours – free sale among 120 millions of people. Germany has the whole of her own market and ours – free sale among 100 millions of people. Our only field of free sale is what we share with the other two in this market of 40 millions.

We can no longer afford to give America and Germany points in the game; and to secure equal opportunity for British capital and labour to compete with the protected nations, we must continue to admit raw material as freely as they do, but must restrain the sale of their manufactures in order to increase the sale of our own.

A third principal fallacy, stated by John Stuart Mill, is that either the consumer must bear the tax owing to a rise in prices, or else Protection will not protect. "In the case of manufactured goods," says Mill, "the doctrine of taxing for revenue and protection simultaneously involves a palpable inconsistency . . . The object of the duty as a means of revenue is inconsistent with its affording incidentally any protection. It can only operate its protection in so far as it prevents importation, and to whatever degree it prevents importation it affords no revenue." But this is really a purely verbal dilemma unworthy of so acute a mind, and unworthy, by the way, of Lord Goschen's, who tries to make great play with this point against Mr. Chamberlain's Budget. Where the tariff is well adjusted it is certain that either the foreigner will pay the tax or we shall take the trade. The foreigner can only come in to the same extent at the same price. Part of that price must pass into the Treasury, where none of it went before. The tariff brings a fiscal squeeze to bear upon the profits of every foreign manufacturer who succeeds in forcing competitive goods through it. In these days such a relief of taxation without decrease of revenue is a very important gain indeed to economic life. Two and a half per cent wrung from the sufficiently prosperous pockets of those who now send every year £140,000,000 of wholly and partially manufactured goods into this country, would cover every year the complete cost of three new battleships. One of the principles of constructive economics therefore is that from a purely revenue point of view a moderate tariff levied upon foreign competition is a wise and sound substitute for twopence upon the income-tax.

But when we have cleared away the sophistical superstructure of economic platitude, we touch the fallacy that forms the very groundwork and foundation of the *laissez faire* creed. Dispose of this, and the whole doctrine of free imports collapses. What we are coming to, it is hardly necessary to say, is the theory that imports must be balanced by exports, and that you cannot have imports coming into the country without creating a trade to pay for them. The Cobdenite contention, in a word, is that it does not matter what you import nor how you pay. They refuse to consider the character of the trade. It would be as wise to assure an invalid that so long as he absorbs something into his system powdered glass is as good as boiled chicken. Constructive economics depends as a matter of practice upon drawing a firm and radical distinction between competitive and noncompetitive imports – between those which injure some to benefit others and those which benefit everybody and injure no one – that is to say, we recognise a vital difference between the imports which are partly destructive and those that conduce entirely to the industrial development of the nation. As regards the pure theory of the thing, we know that by exporting a sufficient quantity of our coal in a single year we could import sufficient foreign manufacture to extinguish all British manufacture. Exports and imports would still balance beautifully according to the principle. Consider again the obvious fact that in a long course of trade between two countries, the one may rise from an agricultural to a manufacturing status, and the other country may decline again from manufacture to agriculture, exports and imports balancing all the time; while these two nations nevertheless end by entirely reversing the rôles they began with in the process of exchange.

From this point of view trace out the real idea suggested by this symmetrical doctrine. It is that if exports and imports balance there must be equal benefits conferred upon both sides of the trade. A little thought, however, will expose the really extraordinary error of reasoning here. Suppose you get iron from Germany and ship in exchange coal. The benefit to German manufacture is unmixed. But in this country the iron taken in exchange may close a British iron works, disbanding the labour employed in it, wasting part of the capital that was sunk in it, and perhaps driving the remainder of that capital clean out of the country. Thus, upon our side, the loss in the iron trade may not only wipe out the profit upon the coal shipment, but may leave us with a serious balance to the bad. It is entirely untrue therefore that the law of equality between exports and imports means a law of necessarily equal economic gain to the countries concerned. Protectionist nations take care to get the maximum benefit from every transaction by encouraging the imports that serve the purpose of development sole and simple, and by restraining the imports that may injure or destroy one home industry by the very same act with which they excite a corresponding export upon the part of some other home industry. I do not know if I have yet made this point perfectly clear, but let me try to put it in another way.

Suppose the profit to be equal on the goods of equal value exchanged. The protected countries make their profit upon any one trade with the very least exposure to loss upon any other trade. The Cobdenite country makes its return profit upon any trade with the maximum liability to loss upon some other industry. Germany makes a thousand pounds, say, upon her shipment to us of competitive manufacture. We may make also a thousand pounds upon a balancing export like coal, but may simultaneously lose a thousand pounds through injury to some collateral industry by the German competitive import. There can be no equal benefit so far as the nation as a whole is concerned until we place as effective a check upon foreign competitive imports as they place upon our manufacture, and adjust our fiscal policy as they do to secure that the profit of one trade shall be earned with the minimum liability to loss upon another. In the theory of balance the classical economists only considered the reflex action of imports upon exports. We have to consider the intermediate loss that may be involved by the direct action of the competitive import upon the particular home trade against which it competes.

Cobden had a masterly grasp of the modern Protectionist principle. He owed his success to that fact. He understood that what you exchange for what makes all the difference to your industrial position. His ideal – we cannot too often repeat it – was to exchange cotton for corn – to export manufactured goods and to import food and raw material. The serious fact we have to deal with now is, that we take more manufacture from our protected competitors than we sell to them. If we are to keep the high industrial place we have held we must endeavour like our rivals to increase our exports of manufacture and to check our imports of manufacture.

The natural process of imports and exports should correspond as far as possible with the alimentary processes and the consequent productive exertion of the human economy. The prevailing opinion throughout the civilised world in favour of the so-called Protectionist system, which is really a bad name for a creative or progressive system, will be found to be based upon the conviction and experience that the action, the positive policy, of the State, in this matter, is essential to the fullest development of the nation, and that the unlimited import of foreign manufacture in respect of articles for which the home country is equally adapted, does most effectually diminish or restrain the productive power of home manufacture.

It may be clearly demonstrated that injury to any established industry involves some permanent national loss, and that a manufacturing country can derive no compensation for having its aptitudes for manufacture discouraged in any particular. In face of the steady backing given by foreign tariffs to foreign competition no wise State can maintain an attitude of fiscal *laissez faire* or can abstain from parallel action for the security and progress of home production. Practical policy will place a firm check upon the destructive possibilities of finished imports, and will encourage the developing power of raw imports, to the utmost.

The case therefore lies in five words. "*Protection*" is progress: "Protection" develops. Only so far as the thing is a real method of progress and development are we in favour of it. Where it is resorted to by some countries it becomes indeed the only possible principle of development for other countries. This is all admirably condensed by the famous heretical paragraph in John Stuart Mill's *Political Economy* – the paragraph which John Bright said, quite truly from his point of view, would do more harm than the rest of the two volumes would do good. What Mill begins by admitting is, that Protection is defensible for the industrial development of a new country. But the reasons he goes on to adduce prove it to be equally defensible for the further development of an old country.

He says, "The superiority of one country over another in a branch of production often arises only from having begun it sooner. There may be no inherent advantage on one part or disadvantage on the other, but only a present superiority of acquired skill and experience. A country which has this skill and experience yet to acquire may in other respects be better adapted to the production than those which were earlier in the field; and besides nothing has a greater tendency to promote improvements in any branch of production than its trial under a new set of conditions." That is all most just and true, but now come the really important words: "It cannot be expected that individuals should at their own risk, or rather to their certain loss, introduce a new manufacture." With all the qualifying words in which this statement is wrapped up nothing can change its meaning. The chain of reasoning which we are bound to draw from it runs as follows: –

(1) That Protection develops.
(2) That countries, instead of having natural aptitudes for separate employments, may have identical aptitudes for competitive employments – this being indeed the dominant fact in the industrial world of to-day.
(3) That aptitudes being otherwise equal, Protection must give the decisive advantage to the protected manufacturer.

(4) That under a Free Trade system a country cannot have new industries – one means of development being therefore closed to it.

(5) That some of its capital will probably be sucked away from home investments to the protected areas – since Mill explains clearly that Protection attracts capital by the security it affords – another means of development being lost to the free-importing country.

(6) That you can create competitive power by Protection.

(7) That you can therefore improve competitive power by the same means.

(8) If capital must have equal security as against its competitors to induce it to create an industry, it must have the same security to remain in an industry or to extend one. The security of capital means the efficiency of capital, the encouragement of enterprise, and the progress of industry.

(9) Upon Mill's principle, if you can obtain equality by Protection as against a free-importing country, you can secure superiority by it. If it admittedly raises you from a lower to a higher plane of economic life, the level at which you can be legitimately expected to stop is beyond the competence of any Cobdenite to define.

(10) While there is any latent capacity to develop you ought to go on developing.

(11) Protection upon these principles should act as we know it does. Its defect is not on the side of under-production, but on that of over-production. Its danger is not that it restricts, but that it tends to develop too much.

Well, that is a complaint which we should be glad to see national industry contracting. If occasional periods of over-production were a sign of decay instead of vitality, shipbuilding, exceptionally subject to expansion and contraction as it is, should be our weakest industry, instead of our strongest industry relatively to our competitors. Over-production is a certain sign of great progressive energy.

The future of national industry depends in my conviction upon the more powerful application of national capital to national business. We must increase to the utmost the scope for investment and enterprise throughout the Empire. Although the total population of America and Germany surpasses our own, the whole relative excess of their people, or perhaps more, is still engaged in agriculture. Our purely industrial population is still as numerous as that of either of the United States or Germany. Upon the other hand, our accumulated wealth is probably still greater than that of America, and in any case is far greater than that of Germany.

What we want is to multiply the productive force of our population by the fullest use of our far greater wealth per head – in other words, by the highest co-efficient of machine-power. We need a greater concentration of our own wealth upon our own purposes. We wish to secure, as we have every opportunity to do, a renewed attraction of foreign enterprise and skill. If we want to have again the most vigorous progress and the most up-to-date methods, we must induce capital to embark upon large expenditure. We cannot obtain that result without offering capital in this country some such security as it enjoys elsewhere. We shall never persuade capital to make investments that dumping may destroy. Enterprise cannot be as alert, inventive, sanguine, and self-confident in this country as it is where it is necessarily far more certain of its returns.

An examination of the psychology of Cobdenism would deserve a volume to itself, and would be found a very important branch of the practical question. No one, we may presume, will be found to deny that in every country which admits the raw material of industry free, but discriminates against foreign finished goods, the activity of capital is encouraged — that in other words the creative element in national industry is stimulated — to a greater extent than can be possible under indiscriminate free imports. Cobdenism admits the fact clearly when it declares that capital under the tariff is stimulated at the expense of the consumer. But if capital is stimulated at all its operations must be extended; its effect in developing the productive capacity of a country must be more powerful; it must afford the maximum amount of employment; it must tend to raise wages by the most certain of all methods — that of increasing the demand for labour; and it is not possible that the consumer upon the balance can lose by it, if this chain of reasoning is sound. It will be admitted that the populations of the United States, Germany, France, Italy, Belgium, and so on, never enjoyed since 1846 so high a degree of relative prosperity by comparison with ourselves as they do now.

The psychology of Cobdenism believed that security was enervating, and that the process of subjecting our industry to the unlimited competition of the world would have an especially bracing effect. The facts we have to confront, on the contrary, are, that enterprise in America and Germany is carried on with extraordinary efficiency, and that British manufacturers are accused of lethargy and backwardness. This is not mainly due to any inherent defect of mind, but is mainly due to the lack in this country of equal competitive conditions, of equal inducement to equal enterprise. For the rest it is a perfectly well assured fact that many foreign manufacturers carrying on in the United Kingdom a trade which they do not intend under any circumstances to sacrifice, would be forced by the tariff to found branch establishments in this country, producing here goods that are now made abroad.

The principle of maximum development demands — the truism is almost too elementary to repeat — the maximum efficiency of capital. We can never have the maximum efficiency of capital so long as enterprise is less encouraged in this country than in competitive countries. Upon this point, Mill's admission that you cannot fairly expect new industries to be established under free-importing conditions is sufficient of itself to settle the question.

But the maximum efficiency of capital means the maximum provision of employment, and the maximum rate of wages relatively to the supply of labour. That is where the consumer comes in. In this country the people control their government more directly and certainly than does any other nation whatever. Again, the trades unions, owing partly to their political, partly to their economic power, form the strongest check conceivable under democrative conditions upon the power of combined capital. With us, there can be no increase of profits without a fully proportionate increase in wages. Mr. Winston Churchill, in that favourite speech of his which at judicious intervals he repeats apparently word for word – as regards the peroration certainly word for word – to audiences throughout the country, sums up his case in some such terms as these: "To say that Protection can secure an increase of wealth is a profound economic fallacy – to say that it means a better distribution is a downright lie." If Mr. Churchill would consent to discuss the matter with more attention to modern things and less to traditional names; if he could realise that this controversy is not one between Free Trade and Protection, but between the system of all-free imports and the system of largely-free imports, – the vigour of his vocabulary would be abated and his conception of economic possibility enlarged. That the policy of maximum development as embodied in a scientific tariff can secure an increase of total wealth is a profound economic fact, most brilliantly demonstrated in Germany since 1879. But that increase of national wealth would mean a larger distribution of wealth among the people is what the conditions of this country make certain.

V The Urgency of Imperial Development

The argument widens at this point. To us, the principles of constructive economics are mainly or exclusively important for their bearing upon the unity, the security, and the development of the Empire. Thus far we have considered their application to the United Kingdom only. Even from the purely Imperial point of view this is half our subject. Now, and for some period to come, the maintenance of the Empire must depend to an overwhelming degree upon the power and wealth of the island. I need not urge here the converse truth now to engage us – that the power and wealth of the island must depend at no very remote date upon the maintenance of the Empire. At present we are in every respect the heart of our own dominion. The physiological system of the Empire, as it were, must be considered as a whole by any statesmanship inspired by a spark of imagination or clarified by one scintilla of insight into the factors of international policy and the conditions of our existence as a world-Power. The heart must be a healthy and vigorous organ. Fatty degeneration there would be fatal to all our political hopes as an Imperial people – fatal probably to some of the Colonies – fatal perhaps to the English idea itself.

The chief object of this Club is to urge that the nation cannot limit its view of economic policy by an insular horizon. Did we attempt once more to lead an isolated life we should realise at once the disadvantages of being an island and a small one. There are some disadvantages. We have no hinterland. Nature has fixed our bounds. We cannot incorporate an inch of European territory not at present belonging to the United Kingdom. Railways through Europe and direct shipping services are diminishing our importance to the Continent even as a warehousing centre and place of transhipment. Germany, Russia, Austria-Hungary, and even France have elastic frontiers. The home territory of some or all of these may yet be enlarged by considerable, perhaps remarkable, accessions. The success, for instance, of the pan-German movement which is the natural form of German Imperialism, would at once create a Central European Empire, with a white population larger than that of the United States, stretching certainly from the North Sea to the Adriatic, perhaps from the North Sea to the Bosphorus. This would place a greater European sea-power than any that has yet existed except our own, upon the flank of the route to India and of all our Imperial communications. Such a development of European politics is a practical contingency no less possible than was the partial union of 1870. Again, the ultimate incorporation of the whole or part of Belgium into France is a perfectly thinkable thing.

The island cannot increase its size in that way. Left to itself it would inevitably become a Power of the second class, and afterwards of a lower class. Within the time of those now living, it would be surpassed, as we have seen, by at least one other European State in manufacturing population, in manufacturing production, in the total volume of its trade, in shipping, in naval power. Even the national independence of the island, if not one shred of dominion over sea remained, could not be permanently maintained. Without supreme sea-power, we might defend the shores of Great Britain – not those of Ireland – by military means. But we could not secure our supplies of food and raw material. Any nation displacing us in the sovereignty of the sea could sever the arteries of our economic life at will. Isolated, in a word we should sink to Holland's place. It is not enough to realise that without the Empire we should cease to be Imperial. Without the Empire we could not be independent. If we ever slip from the height to which we have risen we must fall far. We must bring the people to realise that the Imperial matter is the National matter. Our supremacy in sea-power and sea-trade cannot be preserved, as I shall endeavour to show, except by the co-operation of the Colonies and by the development of the Colonies – in other words, by the application of the principles of constructive economics to Imperial policy.

It is important here to obtain a clear view of the attitude to the Cobdenite movement towards the Empire. We all understand that the policy of free imports was more or less connected with anti-Imperial opinions. It was a reaction against the mercantile system of which the old form of colonial reciprocity, with its singular mixture of sense and error, was an integral part. Hence the necessity for all the early free importers to disparage the Colonies. If they were to ensure the triumph of their creed they had to contend not only like Turgot that "Colonies are fruits which cling till they ripen," but that Free Trade would make foreign markets more lucrative than markets under the flag. The enormous difference between Free Trade and free imports lies precisely in the fact that while the one secures the desired access to foreign markets, the other does not. The only markets in which modern nations can make themselves secure are their own. In the seventeenth and eighteenth centuries our ancestors were in the same situation. The colonial part of the mercantile system, like the other parts of that system, sprang out of the requirements of practical policy under the circumstances of their time.

Nothing of this was recognised by the leaders of the Free Trade movement; and to realise the intensity of feeling and conviction with which the *laissez faire* principle was combined with the Little England principle, let us attend to a few of Cobden's sentiments upon the subject of the Empire. His whole belief is summed up in the well-known letter of 1842:

> The Colonial System, with all its dazzling appeals to the passions of the people, can never be got rid of except by the indirect process of Free Trade, which will gradually and imperceptibly loose the bands which unite our Colonies to us.[3]

Cobden himself hated the Empire with the whole vehemence of his heart. The entire Manchester school disliked the Empire and disbelieved in it.

What is really important to note is that such politics were the logical development of such economics. If you thought the existence of the British Empire a political mistake with a certain amount of moral obloquy resting upon it, you were right to support the economic measures through which it might be soonest dissolved. If you thought from the economic point of view that foreign nations were going to throw open their markets more and more widely to British trade, that the connection with the Colonies gave you of itself no special commercial advantage, that separation would promote peace and retrenchment by removing causes of quarrel with foreign nations and enabling the Army and Navy to be reduced – then it necessarily followed that the existence of the British Empire was a political mistake. The ideal of universal Free Trade depended strictly upon the ideal of universal peace. Both were equally persuasive and both are equally remote. Universal peace will only be possible when the lines of the map have been finally adjusted, and no powerful nation owns what any other powerful nation covets. In the same way universal Free Trade will only be possible when every nation has reached full development; when industries no longer tend to shift their centre of gravity from one country to another; when, in short, international commerce has ceased to be in any very important degree competitive, and when a real and permanent division of employment has been actually created. Upon the whole, comparing the ideals of universal peace and universal Cobdenism, the latter aspect of the millennium seems considerably the further of the two. The only way of attaining it was then and is still for some nations to renounce development.

We know, after the experience of half a century from the era of glass exhibitions, that the life of peoples, like that of individuals, is a thing in flux. There is a struggle for existence between nations as between men. Political ambitions overlap. The Powers tend to trench upon each other's margin of subsistence. Positive policy, as we have seen in the last generation, still from time to time creates new States, and old ones are at intervals overthrown. The world's destinies are still decided, as now in the Far East, by war. Modern Japan is entirely the creation, not certainly of *laissez faire*, but of Government action, its political and commercial power developing simultaneously, its economic future being dependent upon its fate in arms. It repeats in this way the history of England under Chatham and that of Germany under Bismarck. Cobden's idealism was a mist of roseate illusion, concealing from him in their stern permanence the stronger lineaments of human nature and human nations.

The Club, on the contrary, takes a creed of Empire as its reason of being. We know that no dominion has ever depended upon liberty so complete wherever liberty may be conceded, or upon power so just where power must be exercised. We believe that the British Empire represents the greatest secular agency for good that has yet existed. That it should continue is, we think, of considerable moment for the better and more interesting futurte of mankind, no less than necessary for the political safety of our self-governing Colonies, and for the interests of these islands in their local character as a great European State. Unlike Cobden and the Manchester school again, we think the British Empire to be not an unnatural but a practicable system, its extremities, while we retain supremacy of the sea, being far more freely and intimately connected by water than are, for instance, the extremities of the Russian Empire by land.

But everything at present is in the experimental stage. As the result of reverses of fortune it is still possible that Canada might cease to be Canadian, that Australia might become a yellow continent, that South Africa might even yet be German-Dutch, that India might pass to who knows what new masters, that England herself might become the Holland of the twentieth century. The British Empire is a thing which may dissolve with strange completeness, or may steadily solidify into all we hope, if we begin even now where we ought to have begun long ago . . .

271

We are not very much afraid of the Empire being disrupted by any spontaneous movement from within; but we have to concern ourselves more closely with the danger of its being disrupted from without, whether by armed attack or economic temptation . . .

Preferential trade is the principle of maximum development for the Colonies – as a tariff encouraging the import of raw material, rather than the import of foreign manufacture, represents the same principle for the nation. The Mother Country's demand for food and raw material ought to act directly on the Colonies' unlimited capacity for supply. This internal process of supply and demand within the Empire itself ought to be, what it might be, the most powerful economic factor in the whole sphere of sea-trade. Only in this way, while securing other incidental objects only less important, can we make the Colonies centres of increase for white population under conditions that will build them up on British lines and keep them under the British flag.

Here, however, comes the difficulty of method. A national tariff, if it were possible to separate the interests of the island from those of the Empire, would doubtless place a duty upon foreign manufacture and leave all other imports free. The preference policy asks democracy for purposes of Imperial development to place a tax upon foreign food. For us these two schemes must stand or fall together. Can the consent of democracy be secured to a proposal so daring? I think it can be secured when democracy is made to understand that as the taxation of foreign manufacture would increase the free import of raw material, providing the maximum of employment and supporting the maximum of population at home, so the taxation of foreign foodstuffs is designed to increase the free import of colonial food-stuffs with a view to providing the maximum of employment in the Colonies and supporting there the maximum population.

Many national economists in Germany, from List downwards, have been opposed to all taxes on food as to taxes on raw material. Such taxes in such opinions are only to be justified by political and not by directly economic reasons. In Germany there is maintained a true Corn Law of a severe description, which restricts all food imports, which unquestionably limits the supply and raises the price, and which can only be plainly defended on grounds of military necessity.

But duties exclusively levied on foreign food imports for the purpose of increasing the free supply of colonial food-imports would have nothing in common with any Corn Laws formerly obtaining in this country or now existing abroad. Their purpose, method, effect, would be radically different. They would represent an economic policy wholly new to the world's experience. Such duties would be calculated to produce greater rather than less abundance, to increase the food supply rather than restrict it. It would be quite as accurate, therefore, to call Federal trade Free Trade as to call it Protection in the old opprobrious sense. The system of preferential trade proposed for the British Empire may be as fully justified on grounds of commercial advantage as on those of political expediency.

Politically every Englishman can grasp the proposition – the vast majority of Englishmen responding to it when thus stated – that the existence of the Empire must depend sooner or later upon the relative number of its free citizens. Hence the importance of keeping under the flag the intending emigrant who counts two upon a division. It is self-evident that preference in this market must increase the number of colonial agriculturists if it increases the profitableness of colonial agriculture. It would deflect into Imperial channels part of the streams of emigration which now flow towards other directions. It is the prevailing opinion of all the Colonies, without exception, that preference would stimulate their growth. There can indeed be no doubt of it . . .

Our demand for the things by which we live must develop supply somewhere. It must develop foreign territory or else the Empire. When such a choice lies in our hands can there be any doubt as to how we ought to exercise it? The existence of isolated free imports in this country has immensely facilitated in different ways the rise of American and German competition. We have gone on nourishing their manufactures while they have gone on repressing ours – a process which evidently tends to inequality.

Again, take the theoretical problem in its concrete aspect. We must either continue to draw the bulk of our imports of food and raw material from the United States, or we must commence to draw them more abundantly from the Colonies. What have we done in the past under conditions of exchange contrary to all that Cobden hoped to secure by his system – or at least by his half a system – that fragment of a creed, that torso of a policy which is all he succeeded in bequeathing to us? We first increased very materially the agricultural wealth and the population of the United States. Then upon that basis America built her present manufacturing power. We gratuitously provided agricultural consumers by the million for the competitive goods of protected manufactures; and that is what we are still doing for the community, which is already far larger, and so far as relates to present earnings richer than we, which hopes to sweep us out of many neutral markets and presses us hard even in Colonial markets.

By spending annually a hundred millions sterling upon the United States, which we might have spent within the Empire we lose in every way. A trade of that character would be conducted within the Empire upon far better terms of exchange. The reason is again plain. Every colonial as a customer is worth to us upon the average from ten to twenty Americans. Even if colonial tariffs should remain at their present level they are a trifle by comparison with the average 70 per cent duty under M'Kinleyism. American manufacture would be strong enough to exclude ours even under a lower tariff. Colonial manufacture under higher tariffs cannot be carried on for many years upon a scale enabling it to exclude British so completely. Again, no single colony equals the United States in potential capacity for every manner of industry. No colony could ever be as economically self-contained as the Republic is, or as independent of us and others. It is certain that the more food and raw material we draw from the colonies instead of from the United States, the greater proportion of manufactures we shall send out in return.

The practical case for preferential trade in a word is this: Whether we shall continue to spend a hundred millions sterling a year in developing American competition, or whether we shall use that vast amount to create Colonial customers and Imperial citizens. Constructive economics must dictate that policy by whatever name called, which means the most energetic effort to develop trade and power under the flag . . .

The permanent security for mercantile supremacy and sea-power lies in preferential trade. British shipping will not be safe a few decades hence unless it is made safe at both ends now. With the development of colonial supplies the bulk of our imports of food and raw material will be of British origin. We shall be certain then, but only then, to have them borne always to our ports in British ships. In every popular movement there must be one main idea to form the focus of all argument. This, in my conviction, should be the main idea of our movement. We conceive a system under which our imports, becoming again in an overwhelming proportion as free as now, shall consist of food and raw materials, the products of British soil, raised by the hands of British subjects, white or native, carried over British railways to British ports, and shipped by British vessels to British people. Under a national tariff, as was contended at the beginning of this paper, we at home should have a higher creative and consuming power than now; we should check the exceedingly dangerous tendency of the Colonies to send more and more of their raw material to foreign markets and to receive foreign finished articles in return; and we should export, in accordance with what ought to be the steady aim of our commercial policy, the maximum percentage of manufactured goods relatively to the volume of our imports.

This is the sole means by which the British Empire can be converted into an organic system with adequate powers of progress and resistance. Preferential trade would place our dominion upon a natural and solid basis, with a clear prospect of permanence. The Sea-State would rest upon a fundamental guarantee – the economic security of sea-power. Again let me emphasise that point. It is the vital one. Under preferential trade the volume of Inter-Imperial exchange, the value and bulk of the Empire's internal commerce, would remain beyond all comparison the strongest factors in the sea-trade of the world. We shall see this if we examine closely the position of our competitors.

Weak policy, as has been shown, would enable the United States to wrest our supremacy from us. Under preferential trade it would be impossible for

274

even the United States to do anything of the kind. And for an obvious reason. The United States, not fiscally, but naturally and on account of the very extent of its territorial resources, is more than any other country what the Germans call a closed system. Its commercial power is mainly a matter of domestic exchange. Producing so much of her food and raw material within herself, America is not at all fitted to rival us in imports. With respect to exports, our relative Imperial position under preferential trade would be stronger still. Our coal shipments alone represent even now the enormous weight of 60,000,000 tons actually – that is to say, a weight of freight greater than is represented by all the exports and imports combined of the United States. But the United States is also tending rapidly to consume more and more of her corn and raw cotton; and as she gradually substitutes shipments of finished goods for cargoes of the bulkier and cruder commodities, the weight of her exports in the future is likely to diminish as its value increases. Canada's commerce, on the other hand, will grow more and more in bulk and weight as well as in value. Detailed figures would establish this proposition if the Club desired, but it is not necessary to encumber the argument with them.

The sea-trade of the Empire, developed by its native as well as its white population, must always employ, if we keep Canada, a vastly larger shipping than the United States will ever need. Germany's trade passes to so large an extent across her land frontiers, that, if we can hold the Empire together, we shall keep down her maritime rivalry with ease. The political possibilities of pan-Germanism with respect to the incorporation of Holland and Austria make it probable, however, that the German Empire will be a more persistent and serious competitor for sea-trade and sea-power than the United States. With a large extension of her European boundaries, her population would be equal or superior to that of the United States, and being more dependent upon sea-borne products that population would need a larger shipping. Under another generation of fiscal *laissez faire*, however, the things of which we might keep a permanent grasp must drift out of our hands. America will become the first maritime and naval power if Canada is incorporated with the States; and Germany, using her military force to extend her frontiers and to complete the racial unification that was not perfectly accomplished in 1870, would assuredly become the second maritime and naval nation. But if we keep Canada by preferential trade, if we use every exertion to develop the population of the white Colonies, if we utilise the immense economic advantages we possess in the tropical territories and the countless native subjects of the Crown, and if we raise the manufacturing and consuming capacity of this island to the point of maximum development by a national tariff stimulating British capital and labour to some degree, as competitive enterprise and employment are stimulated abroad – then the economic foundations of sea-trade, of sea-power, of the Imperial Sea-State, will remain impregnable . . .

Appendix

We shall best recapitulate the argument and throw the cosmopolitan and the national theories of economics into the clearest contrast if we set out here the chief clauses of the London Free Trade Petition of 1820 (admittedly the ablest short statement of the *laissez faire* case ever made), and attempt an answer paragraph by paragraph from the point of view of the modern dynamic or progressive school.

PETITION

To the Honourable the Commons, the petition of the Merchants of the City of London – Sheweth:

1. That foreign commerce is eminently conducive to the wealth and prosperity of a country, by enabling it to import the commodities for the production of which the soil, climate, capital, and industry of other countries are best calcualted, and to export in turn payment for those articles for which its own situation is better adapted.

2. That freedom from re-straint is calculated to give the utmost extension to foreign trade, and the best direction to the capital and industry of the country.

3. That the maxim of buying in the cheapest market and selling in the dearest, which regualtes every merchant in his individual dealings, is strictly applicable as the best rule for the whole nation.

ANSWER

1. The *laissez faire* movement begins here by ignoring the Empire. The advantages claimed for foreign commerce belong more accurately to maritime commerce. Happily for us our maritime commerce need not be *foreign*, and may be to a large or a main extent inter-Imperial. Even under free exchange inter-Imperial trade would be, transaction for transaction, far more conducive than foreign to the wealth and power of the Imperial State, by giving at least equal economic advantages to the island, and securing on the other side the parallel development of British population and territory, instead of foreign population and territory. See also below.

2. There is no freedom from restraint in foreign trade. Measures for the development of the Empire are calcualted to give the utmost extension to our maritime trade by securing the fullest exchange of goods for goods. The best direction will be given to the capital and industry of the country by the interference of the State for the purpose of redressing unequal conditions of competition, and providing the larger scope at home, which is the only possible compensation for restrictions abroad.

3. The protected manufacturer under tariffs leaving raw material free is the person who makes the most complete application of this principle. But the whole formula as applied to modern economic conditions is an antiquated and unreal one. The principle of maximum development is as follows: To utilise the largest possible;

4. That a policy founded on these principles would render the commerce of the world an interchange of mutual advantages, and diffuse an increase of wealth and enjoyments among the inhabitants of each State.

5. That unfortunately a policy the very reverse of this has been and is acted upon by the Government of this and every other country, each trying to exclude the production of other countries with the specious and well-meant design of encouraging its own production, thus inflicting on the bulk of its subjects who are consumers the necessity of submitting to privations in the quantity and quality of commodities; and thus rendering, what ought to be the source of mutual benefit and of harmony among States, a constantly recurring occasion of jealousy and hostility.

demand with respect to what you produce. The State, as in the case of cotton, can be more efficient than *laissez faire* in actually creating larger and cheaper supply, as well as in securing for the nation wider markets. We may revise this famous principle as follows: Buy in the fullest market and sell in the largest.

4. We have not induced the world to accept this view, because it is certainly not true as written. Even free exchange, as Mill recognised in the celebrated heretical paragraph, can obviously confer equal advantage *only upon equally developed nations.* Foreign nations could not have developed their aptitude for manufacture except by protection against the overwhelming advantage we possessed when they began. But their policy of national development has enormously increased the total world-supply of manufactured commodities, and has diffused the maximum increase of wealth and enjoyments among the inhabitants of competitive States. For us a policy founded on the principles of Imperial development will secure the maximum increase of wealth and power for all the inhabitants, whether insular or transoceanic, of the Imperial Sea-State.

5. Answered by Mill, modern history, and previous paragraphs. The tariff only restrains competitive manufacture and encourages to the fullest extent the free import of all the foreign production that is best calculated to nourish home production.

But this section is mainly interesting as introducing to us our friend the consumer. By the present relations between a protected world and a Cobdenite island the injury to us as producers of British manufacture is greater far than the gain to us as consumers of foreign manufacture. It is absurd to say of any State that the bulk of its subjects are "consumers." In every State the really typical and important person is "the producer-consumer." He is immeasurably more numerous and

277

prosperous abroad than in any previous generation. His prosperity is built upon the bases of free raw material, maximum production, and full command of the national market. What the petitioners of 1820 never greater far than the gain to us as consumers of foreign manufacture. It is absurd to say of any State that the bulk of its subjects are "consumers."

In every State the really typical and important person is "the producer-consumer." He is immeasurably more numerous and prosperous abroad than in any previous generation. His prosperity is built upon the bases of free raw material, maximum production, and full command of the national market. What the petitioners of 1820 never sufficiently realised is that free exchange does not necessarily mean the largest exchange; while the largest production means inevitably the largest trade. That is why the policy of development has prevailed, and why foreign commerce and general consuming-power were never so great in the "protected" countries as now.

6. That the prevailing prejudices in favour of the protective or restrictive system may be traced to the erroneous supposition that every importation of foreign commodities occasions a diminution or discouragement of our own productions to the same extent; whereas it may be clearly shown that although the particular description of produce which could not stand against unrestrained foreign competition would be discouraged, yet as no importation could be continued for any length of time without a corresponding exportation, direct or indirect, there would be an encouragement for the purposes of that exportation of some other production to which our situation might be better suited: thus affording at least an equal, and probably a greater, and certainly a more beneficial employment to our own capital and labour.

6. This is the core of the controversy – that since imports must create exports to pay for them under a free import system, all things must be always all right.

The "privailing prejudice" throughout the civilised world in favour of the national or progressive principle is found to be based upon the conviction and experience that an active economic policy on the part of the State is essential to the fullest development of the nation; for it is true that every import must develop a corresponding export. But the vital point is what you exchange for what. It would, of course, be utterly false to say that our manufactured imports stimulate by their increase our manufactured exports. Otherwise these latter would now be immensely greater than they are. Foreign tariffs prevent us from paying for competitive imports by the production of articles to which we are best adapted. We might, theoretically, import enough foreign manufacture to ruin all British manufacture, and might balance the account by exhausting our coal seams. The principle of balance, therefore, gives no security whatever for a country's manufacturing position. The policy which frees all developing imports and taxes all competitive ones gives the fullest security. It means the largest production and the largest exchange.

NOTES

1 As Dr. Cunningham admirably puts it, the conditions of our industry are now "dictated" to us by foreign nations.
2 See Appendix.
3 Morley's *Life*, vol. i. p. 230.

---

12 PROTECTION AND THE WORKING CLASSES*

A.C. Pigou

ART. I – Protection and the Working Classes

1. *British and Foreign Trade and Industry.* [Cd. 1761.] 1903.
2. *British and Foreign Trade and Industry,* (Second Series). [Cd. 2337.] December 1904.
3. *Essays and Addresses on Economic Questions.* By the Right Hon. VISCOUNT GOSCHEN. London: Edward Arnold. 1905.
4. *Handbuch der Volkswirtschaftslehre.* VON ALFRED MARSHALL. Stuttgart und Berlin: J.G. Cotta'sche Buchhandlung Nachfolger. 1905.
5. *Progress of the German Working Classes.* By W.J. ASHLEY. London: Longmans, Green & Co., 1905.

* A.C. Pigou, "Protection and the Working Classes", *Edinburgh Review*, 203 (415) (January–April 1906), pp. 1–32.

279

6. *Speech of the Right Hon. Joseph Chamberlain, MP, at Birmingham,* November 3, 1905.

7. *Speech of the Right Hon. Joseph Chamberlain, MP, at Bristol,* November 21, 1905.

8. *Sir Louis Mallet. A Record of Public Service and Political Ideals.* By Bernard Mallet. London: Nisbet and Co. 1905.

I Introductory.

'I can fancy that an interesting address might be delivered on statistical fallacies, illustrated by copious examples from contemporary politicians and social philosophers. Given a great number of figures partially unknown, given unlimited power and discretion of selection, and given an enthusiast determined to prove his case, and I will not answer for the consequences.'[1]

So wrote Lord Goschen as President of the Statistical Society in 1887; and so his words are printed in the admirable collection of papers that he has recently brought together into a single volume. The warning was just. The 'copious examples' have not been wanting. During the last three years, statistical data have been showered from thousands of platforms upon zealous and untrained audiences by orators as zealous and scarcely more instructed. Nor has the ignorance, misstatement, misrepresentation, so lamentably apparent, been confined to one party in the great fiscal controversy. Popular audiences affect strong speech. Exaggeration was demanded, and the demand has been supplied . . .

On no aspect of the controversy, perhaps, have the misstatements been so numerous as on the relation of Tariff Reform to the fortunes of the labouring classes. Again and again Mr. Chamberlain has dealt with that subject. His gospel never wavers. His 'mathematical certainty' never falters. At Glasgow the torch was lighted. The message flashed through Greenock, Newcastle, Liverpool: 'I call upon the working classes of this country to wake up. I call upon them to demand that they shall be defended against the unfair and unequal competition which, during the last thirty years, has taken thirty millions of wages out of their pockets, in order to put it into the pockets of their competitors.'[2] On the banner of Tariff Reform, in a place of honour beside 'Think Imperially,' is inscribed 'Help for the Working Man.'[3] Tactically it is an excellent device. The *Mail* parades the misery of great hosts whose speedy multiplication not Falstaff's men in buckram rivalled. Exaggeration matters nothing.[4] Overstatement of an evil is forgiven more readily than understatement; and Mr. Chamberlain's statistical nightmares have unfortunately evoked from opponents pæans of prosperity, no less the stuff of dreams. Hence, Tariff Reformers have enlisted on their side the great human force of uninstructed sympathy. In point of rhetoric they could have chosen no better battle-cry . . .

II Arguments from Statistics.

There are two ways in which, if adequate data were available, statistical reasoning could be employed. First, figures indicative of the condition of the working classes at any given period might be collected for a number of Free-Trade countries, and similar statistics for a number of Protectionist countries. If the countries selected were sufficiently numerous, if the fiscal policy pursued in each was not a *result* of the industrial conditions, and if any given policy could be assumed to act in the same sense under all conditions, a comparison of the statistics would be an application of the method of difference, and should show *a posteriori* whether Free trade or Protection was economically the more advantageous. Secondly, statistics indicative of changes in the condition of the working classes might be collected over a series of years for a number of countries, with a view to showing, on the same lines as before, whether prosperity increased more rapidly under Free Trade or under Protection.

It may be said at once that there are no sufficient data for an application of either of these methods. Neither Protectionist nor Free Trade countries are numerous enough to warrant resort to it. In the few of them for which statistics are available, general conditions are so various that the fortunes and progress of the working classes would differ enormously whatever fiscal policy were adopted. Naïvely to attribute differences in the figures to differences in policy is to indulge in ignorant absurdity.

This general conclusion seems so clear that in any ordinary controversy the argument would need to go no further. In the present instance, however, so much stress has been laid by Tariff Reformers upon the case of Germany that their appeal to the circumstances of that country cannot be wholly ignored. This appeal involves a comparison both of existing conditions in the two countries and of recent rates of progress.

The argument by absolute comaprison was worked out in leaflet No. 88 of the Imperial Tariff Committee (President, Mr. Chamberlain). In 1903 the number of emigrants for every 10,000 of the population was in England thirty-five, in Germany six. In 1903 the percentage of unemployed in trade unions was in England 5.3, in Germany 2.3. The amount, per head of population, in savings banks is in England 4*l.* 11*s.*, in Germany 7*l.* 17*s.* The implied inference is that the Protectionist policy of Germany is better for the working man than the Free-Trade policy of England.

Prima facie the reasoning may seem persuasive. Since, however, statistics are susceptible of accidental manipulation, caution suggests that we should trace those figures to their origin. Fortunately that task is an easy one. In 1904 the Board of Trade published an important Blue-book (Cd. 2337), entitled 'British and Foreign Trade and Industry' (Second Series). This Blue-book deals with all the points mentioned in the leaflet, and is cited by the writer as one of the sources from which he drew his information. A comparison of the source with the stream that filters through his hands may prove not uninstructive.

The statistics of emigration quoted in the leaflet have the best show of justification. The following comments are, however relevant. (1) For the 'United Kingdom' of the Blue-book, 'England' has been substituted in the leaflet. (2) The Blue-book shows that our emigration rate in 1903 (35 per 10,000) exceeded that of the previous year by more than ten, and that of any other year subsequent to 1894 by more than fifteen; in the leaflet these facts are suppressed. (3) The Blue-book shows that, of the recent increase in the rate, by far the greater part has been due to emigration to outlying portions of our own Empire, and that in 1903 the destination of nineteen out of every thirty-five emigrants was British; this fact is suppressed. (4) In the Blue-book we read, 'Still less is it an easy task to institute international comparisons, the basis on which the emigration statistics are compiled in different countries being far from uniform.'[5] This also is suppressed.

The second figure in the leaflet refers to savings banks. In this case the deception is more serious. On the first page of the section of the Blue-book headed 'Savings Bank Deposits in the Principal Countries,' the following passage occurs:

'An attempt may be made to compare working-class savings in different countries by a comparison of the statistics of savings banks, co-opera-tive and friendly societies, and other similar institutions. Such compar-isons, however, are usually unsatisfactory for the following reasons, among others:

'1. There are no data enabling a comparison to be made of the total deposits in *all* institutions in which working men deposit their savings.

'2. Even if such data were available, we should not know, for each country, what proportion of the total deposits represents savings of classes other than the working class.

'3. If we confine our comparison to a single class of institution, *e.g.* savings banks, it is vitiated by the fact that the conditions of deposit, *e.g.* maximum limit of deposit, rate of interest, &c. differ in different countries, and the degrees to which savings banks are exposed to the competition of other modes of thrift and other classes of provident institutions also vary very greatly.

'It follows that savings banks are likely to be attractive to working-class savings and to the savings of other classes in different degrees in different countries, so that there will be no uniformity either as regards the extent to which the total deposits in these banks are representative of the whole savings of the working classes, or as regards the proportion of these deposits which are drawn from other than working-class sources.'[6]

The third figure quoted concerns unemployment. Here, again, the leaflet suffers from an accidental slip. The Blue-book section on 'Unemployed Statistics in Foreign Countries' [p. 104) opens with this passage:

'It may be said at once that on unemployed statistics exist 'in any foreign country on a basis which allows a comparison 'to be made of the actual level of employment in that country 'and the United Kingdom respectively at a given time.' The method of the leaflet is illumined by the further fact that in France, also a Protectionist country, the unemployed figure for 1903 was 10.1. This figure, at least as comparable with ours as the German one, is suppressed. Further comment is scarcely required.

So far of the precise figures contained in the leaflet. In addition to these there is the more vague statement: 'The cost of living on the whole is *not higher* in Germany than in England. Butter, pork, eggs, milk, potatoes and other vegetables, beer, spirits and tobacco are all cheaper in Germany.' The following comments may be made. (1) At the beginning of the section in the Blue-book, in which statistics under most of the above heads are cited, we read:

'Comparisons of absolute prices of commodities in different countries are far more difficult than comparisons of rates of change of such prices, inasmuch as we have to be sure that the qualities of the articles compared are approximately the same. In some cases this is impossible; in other cases it would yield a misleading result, seeing that the staple articles most usually consumed in the different countries may not be identical in quality. With these reservations the following figures are given.'[7]

In the leaflet this caution is suppressed. (2) In the Blue-book, comparative figures are given for the important commodities, flour and sugar, indicating that both are decidedly more expensive in Germany than in England. These commodities are not mentioned in the leaflet. (3) Taking all the articles of food, for which the Blue-book gives figures, and weighting them equally, we find that the geometric mean of them all gives prices in England as 6 per cent. higher than prices in Germany; when rice and sugar are omitted, as 17 per cent. higher. On the other hand, it is stated as 'the most probable result from our present imperfect data' that the average level in money of industrial wages in Germany is two-thirds of that in the United Kingdom.[8] If this conclusion, which is not mentioned in the leaflet, is combined with the foregoing price statistics, it appears that the level of *real* industrial wages in this country must exceed the German level by a quarter or a fifth. We do not claim for this result any positive value. It seems, however, to show that the argument from a comparison of *existing conditions* in England and Germany, if it could be permitted as an argument at all, would not work out in the way that Tariff Reformers pretend.

The argument from the comparative *progress* of England and Germany frequently occurs in Mr. Chamberlain's speeches. At Bristol he expressed it thus:

'In Germany, take that as an instance . . . wages have increased in greater proportion than here. Emigration has diminished enormously. It is not diminishing in anything like the same proportion – indeed, it has not practically diminished at all – in England. The savings of the people have multiplied in a much larger degree. The cost of living has diminished there as well as here.'[9]

The statement that the emigration rate has declined more rapidly in Germany is true. Down to 1894 the curves for the two countries moved similarly, and, since that date, the German curve has fallen considerably below the English. In the Board of Trade inquiry[10] various reasons for this change are suggested. We are absolved, however, from going into the matter by the fact that the immediate antecedent of the new movement was a considerable diminution of protection in Germany, brought about by the Caprivi treaties of the early nineties. It can scarcely be argued that an improvement, which began when protection was made less stringent, is primâ facie itself the result of protection.

The statement that the savings of the people have multiplied much faster in Germany is unwarranted. The deposits in savings banks per head of the population did, indeed, increase between 1880 and 1890 by some 86 per cent. in that country as against 30 per cent. in England. Between 1890 and 1900, however, the percentage growth has been practically the same in the two countries.[11] Furthermore, as already observed, it is dangerous to infer from savings banks deposits to savings in general, since large masses of savings are invested in other institutions, of which comparative figures are wanting.

The statement that wages have increased in greater proportion in Germany, coupled with the remark that the cost of living has diminished there as well as here, misrepresents the facts. Both assertions are literally true; but they conceal the conclusion, to which the figures apparently point, that real wages have risen faster here. From the Blue-book [Cd. 1761] it appears that since 1886, the first year for which comparative statistics are available, industrial wages in terms of money have moved as follows, the wages for 1886–90 being represented for each country by 100.

Table I.

Changes in Industrial Wages in terms of money.

—	United Kingdom	Germany
1886–1890 . .	100	100
1891–1895 . .	105.5	105
1896–1900 . .	110.3	113.9

The above table takes account of money wages only. Table II., printed below, takes account of the movement of prices as well as of the wage movement, and thus measures fluctuations in terms, not of money, but of the things that money can buy. It is reached by combining the table just given with Table P, headed 'Changes in average level of retail prices of food to a workman's family in Germany and United Kingdom' in the first fiscal Blue-book.[12]

Table II.

—	United Kingdom	Germany
1886–1890 . .	100	100
1891–1895 . .	109.6	100.8
1896–1900 . .	119.9	113.9

The second Blue-book fails to bring up to date the figures upon which Table I. is based. Consequently, neither table can be carried beyond the year 1900. It should be noted that Table II. corrects for prices of food only, there being no figures for the other items that enter into a workman's weekly budget. So far as any conclusion is warranted by these imperfect data, it is that the statistics of money wages have masked the real relative movement in England and Germany, and that, as a matter of fact, our own workmen have been progressing at a more, and not at a less, rapid rate than their Continental neighbours. As in the case of comparative conditions, so in that of comparative progress, we submit no positive argument. In the present state of knowledge, trustworthy statistical treatment of the problem along either of these lines seems to us wholly impracticable.[13] A wrestling match conducted on ice is futile and proves nothing. It is for our opponent's satisfaction and not for our own that we have accepted his challenge under those conditions.

III The Popular Economic Argument.

We may now turn from the statistical to the economic aspect of the problem. The quotations already given from Mr. Chamberlain's speeches indicate the line of argument on which he relies. The working classes 'lose when those countries are 'allowed to send more manufactures to us,' because, when this occurs, work is taken abroad which might otherwise have been done in England; with the result that industries, capable of employing a great number of men, are contracted, or possibly even destroyed. This reasoning, persuasive enough in itself, is reinforced by instances, taken from the town in which the orator happens to be speaking, of specific local industries that have suffered from the effects of foreign competition. In the face of these things it is not difficult to understand that many admirable and sympathetic men regard free imports as the main cause of unemployment and protection as the infallible cure.

There is, however, a serious logical gap in all this. Nobody denies that foreign competition with any particular British industry tends to contract the scope of that industry, and, hence, the aggregate of wages annually expended in it. That this must happen is, indeed, too obvious for argument. Nor is it less obvious that protection to an industry, everything else remaining the same, would expand that industry and augment its wages-bill. A tariff on imported steel means, *ceteris paribus*, more money spent on steel-making in England. That is a primary 'datum' that nobody can possibly dispute. The Free-Trader's contention is, not that protection of steel will fail to benefit steel-makers, but that it will fail to benefit them so much as it injures the workpeople in other industries. The direct stimulating effect on the favoured trade is, indeed, the more palpable. It is concentrated at one point and is, therefore, plainly visible. The indirect depressing effect, on the other hand, is spread over a great number of industries and is, therefore, concealed . . . The economic considerations popularly advanced are, in fact, as inadequate to that end as the statistical considerations we have already examined.

IV The Correct Method of Approaching the Problem.

So far the discussion has been purely critical. Its purpose has been to clear the ground for more positive reasoning. In this reasoning we shall assume without proof that fundamental analysis of the nature of foreign trade that is common to intelligent disputants on both sides . . . We shall take it for granted that foreign trade consists essentially in the exchange of goods and services on our part against other goods and services on the part of the rest of the world. We shall, in fact, echo the opinion of Professor Ashley, perhaps the best equipped among Mr. Chamberlain's supporters: 'Pro-'perly explained and qualified, the proposition that in the long 'run exports must balance imports is a commonplace too 'evident for discussion.'[14]

Now, it is often supposed by Free-Traders that, by means of this commonplace, they can at once destroy the plea that Protection will benefit the working classes. They argue that, since a tariff must ultimately check imports and exports equally, the workmen in the export industries must lose as much as those in the protected industries gain. This argument is no doubt effective against certain superficial fallacies. But it is itself also superficial. The Free-Trader would do well to recognise this; for, if he refuses, he will find himself in difficulties. He will be compelled, in fact, to support proposals for shifting taxation from non-competitive commodities, such as tea, to imported manufactured goods. That policy would, indeed, diminish manufactured imports, but, since tea imports would at the same time be increased, it would not diminish aggregate imports to the same extent: indeed, it might not diminish them at all. Exports, however, would only contract in correspondence with aggregate imports. Therefore, the net result of the change would be, on the one hand, an increase in the field for labour in the protected industries, on the other hand, either no decrease at all, or, at the worst, a relatively small decrease in the field for it in the export industries. This conclusion is at once obvious and simple. And yet supporters of Tariff Reform have failed to perceive that it is implied in the common Free Trade contention. Their opponents have been proclaiming from the housetops an argument that really helps their side, and the weapon thus put into their hands has been left altogether unused. Truly, the fiscal controversy has proved a tangled skein!

In reality no direct argument either way as to the effect of Protection upon Labour can be drawn from the fact that imports and exports balance. To attempt such an argument is to assume that there is in the country a definite fund for purchasing labour, and that the size of this fund is fixed. It is only on that assumption that labour can be supposed either necessarily *un*-affected when manufactured imports and exports decrease equally, or necessarily *well*-affected when the former decrease most. But the assumption itself is an exploded fallacy. The fund that rewards the services of the various factors of production, labour among the rest, is itself nothing but the aggregated fruits of those services, consisting of them and varying when they do – varying, therefore, when, through foreign trade or any other cause, they are directly or indirectly rendered more productive. The modern and now accepted doctrine is set forth in Professor Marshall's *Principles of Economics*, or in the German version of that great work, whose title heads our article:

'The net aggregate of all the commodities produced is itself the true source from which flow the demand prices for all these commodities, and, therefore, for the agents of production used in making them. Or, to put the same thing in another way, this national dividend is at once the aggregate net product of, and the sole source of payment for, all the agents of production within the country; it is divided up into earnings of labour, interest of capital, and, lastly, the producer's surplus, or rent, of land and of other differential advantages for production. It constitutes the whole of them, and the whole of it is distributed among them.'[5]

From this general principle, it is easy to deduce the correct method of estimating the effect of Protection upon Labour. The first stage is an inquiry into the effect of that policy upon the National Dividend as a whole. For, primâ facie, anything that enlarges that dividend is likely to be advantageous, and anything that diminishes it disadvantageous, to all the agents of production in the country. The ultimate effects, for instance, of an industrial invention will probably be good, and those of an expensive war bad, for all classes. The second stage is an inquiry as to the effect of Protection upon the distribution of the dividend among the various agents. For, this may be altered in such a way that, despite the increase in the whole dividend, the share that goes to certain agents may be, not merely proportionately, but absolutely less than it was before. The third and final stage concerns the effects of Protection on the manner in which Labour receives its share. This may be altered in such a way as to react on character and *morale*. If, for instance, Protection would lessen either the irregularities of employment, or the proportion of people engaged in sweated industries, the consequent improvement in the men might be well worth purchasing even at a cost of some reduction in their earnings . . .

VII. Protection and the Distribution of the Dividend.

. . . Though primâ facie probable, it is not certain, that a reduction of the aggregate dividend would involve an injury to each and every contributory factor of production. It is, on the contrary, possible that a protective system, though diminishing the wealth of the country as a whole, might, nevertheless, improve the fortunes of the labouring classes. Furthermore, it is an essential part of Mr. Chamberlain's strategy to emphasise this possibility. According to him, foreign trade in manufactures is likely to injure the poor in the very act of benefiting the rich. In his speech at Birmingham, he said: 'Year by year the balance of trade gets greater and greater against us. 'Who is it that loses by this? Is it the rich? Not necessarily at all. They may 'continue to make more money than ever – by financial operations, by 'carrying their works abroad, by other devices. The people who lose are the 'working people of this country. . . . The working man, and the working 'man alone, is the sufferer.'[16]

There is, in fact, no necessary harmony between changes in the aggregate dividend and changes in real welfare. Consequently, Mr. Chamberlain's contention is not irrelevant, but demands careful investigation.

In a group among whose members mobility is complete, it is easily shown that the interest of the whole and of the parts is harmonious. Imagine, for example, a community consisting exclusively of workmen, able to pass without friction from any one trade to any other. If the Government of that group puts a duty on imported boots, the immediate result is a gain to the bootmakers and a loss to everybody else. This result, however, cannot continue. For the boom in boots will attract labour into that industry and divert it from other industries, until a common level is again established. There will be a short period of transition, but things will soon settle down, and, when they have done so, no one division of the group can be affected differently from any other. Consequently, if the import duty lessens the dividend of the whole group, it necessarily lessens that of every part.

Now, of course, in real life mobility within the different groups of industrial agents is not complete. Even unskilled labour cannot turn indifferently from one occupation to another. Still less can a skilled sugar-refiner transform himself into an iron-puddler, or a commercial traveller adopt the rôle of littérateur. Within the realm of capital, plant erected for gasworks cannot convert into a motor factory, or the machinery of a cotton mill be turned to the making of guns. Between the various uses of land similar barriers subsist. The conversion of arable into pasture land, or of pasture into building sites, is not a wholly frictionless operation. Within each of these industrial groups mobility does, indeed, exist, but it is hampered by serious impediments.

From the standpoint of the moment these considerations are fundamental. Since, however, protection is never advocated except as a more or less lasting policy, this standpoint is not an appropriate one from which to examine it. For such a purpose we need to take a fairly long view of society, and, when we do this, the impediments to mobility that have been noticed no longer seem to matter. The factors of production present themselves, not as a stock, but as a flow . . . In the long run, therefore, mobility is complete, and the interest of the whole cannot clash with that of any part.

The above argument applies broadly to any group consisting of a single industrial agent. It does not, however, apply to those great nation groups in which a variety of such agents are embraced. For, as between one agent and another, the equilibrating force of mobility is much less conspicuous. When labour is depressed, no 'run' seems long enough to allow it to transfer itself to landowning or capitalism. Is not the better view that the great divisions of the industrial world, land, capital, brain-labour, trained hand-labour, muscular labour, are non-competing, in the sense that, against those who would pass from one to another there is a great gulf fixed?[17]

From the standpoint of a very long period this view is not, indeed, accurate. In nature there are no hard lines, and correct analysis depicts competing character, not as rigidly present or absent, but as more or less present according to the relations of the object, and the length of the period, we are considering. Conclusions based on the assumption of immobility as between groups of industrial agents are thus necessarily imperfect. On the other hand, however, those suggested by the opposite assumption would be more imperfect still; they would be vitiated throughout by the interaction of temporary earnings and permanent efficiency. The truth is that our problem is too complex for exact treatment, and that, in starting from the assumption of immobility, we are merely preferring a less to a greater inaccuracy. Fortunately, whatever error is thereby introduced tells in favour of, and not against the policy that we oppose.

Mobility absent, the interests of the whole and part are no longer necessarily harmonious. The appropriate analysis is as follows. Throughout the whole range of industry the 'law of substitution' prevails. Employers tend to substitute one kind of labour or machine for another until the return from the last sovereign invested in each is the same. Between employers themselves the same law is at work. As a consequence, the national dividend is distributed among the various factors of production in proportion to their marginal efficiencies. So long as the ratio between these remains unaltered, anything that increases the whole dividend necessarily adds to the share of each factor. Protective duties, however, besides affecting the dividend, may also change relative efficiencies. They develope [*sic*] one manufacture, A, at the expense of another, B, and a given factor may play a more important part in the former than in the latter of these. In such a case that factor rises in marginal efficiency relatively to the others, and, consequently, secures a greater proportionate share of the national dividend. The point is easily illustrated. Suppose, for example, that all agricultural imports into Great Britain were subjected to heavy taxation. Much of our industrial energy would thereupon be diverted from manufactures to agriculture. But the function of agricultural land is more important in the latter than in the former industry. Consequently, the marginal efficiency of agricultural land, relatively to that of capital and labour, would be increased, and, hence, the proportion of the national dividend that accrues to agricultural landowners. In corresponding circumstances the same result would emerge in regard to any other factor of production. Nor need the gain achieved be merely proportional. The increase per cent. in the share of the dividend obtained by the favoured factor might exceed the shrinkage per cent. in the dividend itself. In that case, protective duties would involve an absolute, and not merely a relative, gain to that factor.

This is the judgement of pure theory. Since, however, in that sphere, almost anything can be proved *possible*, practice is little helped. What we really need to know is the *probability* of such a result occurring in England at the present time. On that point the following considerations may be submitted. First, we do not know that the part played by Labour in the industrial life fostered by Protection would, as a matter of fact, be any more important relatively to other factors than the part played by it now. So far as the evidence goes, it is just as likely to be less important. Secondly, if it is more important in any degree, Labour's *proportion* of the dividend would,

290

indeed, be augmented; but a *great* increase of importance would be needed to increase its *absolute quantum* – and it is this alone that matters. Thirdly, as between England and the rest of the world, capital is exceedingly mobile. If, therefore, the earnings of Capital here are diminished – and, with the whole dividend reduced and the slice of it taken by Labour augmented, this can scarcely fail to happen – Capital would flow abroad in large quantities.[18] The movement would both react unfavourably on the aggregate dividend and also compel Labour to surrender to Capitalists a larger proportion of what remained. Even, therefore, if Labour were to gain for the moment, it could scarcely retain its advantage. Fourthly – and this is our final point – even though it were true that Protection benefited Labour, it would not follow that it benefited labouring people. For labouring people are not mere embodiments of the factor Labour. They are also themselves Capitalists, whose savings are enormously important. No doubt, as Lord Goschen warns us in his admirable study of the 'Growth of Moderate Incomes,' the available statistics must be used with caution. Part of the investments in savings banks belong to the children of the well-to-do, and there are other qualifications of a similar character. No matter, however, what stress is laid on these points, the general drift of the figures is highly significant. In 1903 the number of depositors in Trustee and Post Office savings banks in the United Kingdom was 11,000,000, the amount of deposits per head 17*l*. 18*s.*, and the aggregate deposits 198,000,000*l*. The number of members of industrial and provident (co-operative) societies was 2,000,000, the amount of share capital per member nearly 13*l*., and the aggregate share capital over 26,500,000*l*. The number of building societies (a frequent form of investment for the poor) was 2,062, and the liabilities 51,000,000*l*.

Industrial companies (the insurance companies of the poor) had on their books (in 1904) 22,500,000 policies, aggregating 221,000,000*l*., and averaging 9*l*. 16*s*. 5*d*. per head. The membership of *ordinary* Friendly Societies was in 1902, the latest year for which statistics are accessible, 5,500,000, and the aggregated capital 36,500,000*l*. The membership of *all classes* of friendly societies was 13,250,000, and the funds 45,000,000*l*.

The membership of all trade unions was (1903) 1,900,000; for the hundred principal unions the income in 1903 was 2,000,000*l*., and the funds in hand at the end of the year 4,500,000*l*.[19]

In the face of such figures it is impossible to treat the working classes as dependent merely on labour. Their stake in capital is also very large. Even, therefore, if it were proved that Protection would benefit labour, it would by no means follow that it would benefit labouring people. For, the dividend as a whole being reduced, capital would probably lose more than labour gained, and the capital of the poor would suffer with the rest. Though solidarity were wanting between factors of production, it would still be prominent between concrete classes. That the factor labour should gain through a policy injurious to the national dividend we have already shown to be improbable; that the class 'labouring people' should so gain is more improbable still.

VIII Protection and the Stability of Industry.

. . . There are . . . three distinct questions. First, how does Protection affect 'employment' in the sense of the aggregate quantum of work that has to be done for given earnings; secondly, how does it affect the average number of men out of a job; thirdly, how does it affect the fluctuations that occur about this latter average?

The first of these questions need not detain us. If, in accordance with previous reasoning, Protection lessens both the National Dividend as a whole, and that slice of it that goes to Labour, the hours of work are apt to be longer and not shorter than they would otherwise have been. The very fact that wages are low necessitates long hours as a means to subsistence earnings. It is a commonplace that hours of labour decline as wages rise, and that they tend to be lowest among the most prosperous sections of the working classes. Protection is likely to increase employment in the sense of exacting more work for the same real wage and lessening the labourer's time of leisure.

The second question is more complex. The average proportion of men out of work depends upon two main causes. In the first place, it cannot be isolated from the general policy pursued by labour in the matter of wages. So far as custom fixes a rigid minimum, forbidding the older or less competent workmen to accept lower rates than their companions, it makes it less easy for them to secure employment. The proportion of men out of work is thus a function of the workpeople's wages policy. So far as it depends upon this, it has nothing to do with the fiscal system in vogue.

In the second place, the average proportion out of work depends in part upon the stability of industry. Much of the enforced idleness that exists is due to the fact that the industrial machine is in a state of motion. Wants change with fashion, means of supplying wants with new inventions and developing transport. Labour and capital strive continually to adapt themselves to this varying process. But they are not mobile or far-sighted enough to adapt themselves completely. Maladjustments occur both in space and time. Supply follows hard on the heels of demand, but lacks the speed to overtake it. Hence, there is necessarily a fringe of men in movement. They are at once a means by which adjustment is sought, and a proof that it is not found. The average number unemployed for this cause varies with what may be called the organisation of mobility, with the development, that is to say, of agencies for moving people, spreading information and cultivating foresight. So far it is clearly independent of fiscal policy. But it depends also, in part, upon the character of the particulars from which the average is derived. In those trades where the variations in these are largest, the average itself is also largest.[20] The variations, however, depend upon the stability of industry, and that in turn partly depends upon fiscal policy. At this point, therefore, for the first time, Protection and the Unemployed come into connection. If Protection makes for stability, it lessens the average number of persons out of work as well as the fluctuations about that average.

Hence, our second and third questions reduce themselves to one. Under both heads, Protection is beneficial if it steadies, injurious if it disturbs, industry. Nor is this all. The National Dividend itself is not, as has been tacitly supposed hitherto, determined independently of the extent to which industry fluctuates. Fluctuations mean the periodic idleness of certain productive resources, and hence, *ceteris paribus*, make the dividend less than it would otherwise be. Consequently, if it could be proved that Protection made for stability, the case against it from the standpoint of Labour would be weakened in three distinct ways.

The Protectionist argument, by which this proof is attempted, turns principally upon certain incidents connected with the modern developement of large-scale industrial organisation. Stated as plausibly as possible – more plausibly, we venture to think, than the Protectionist himself usually contrives to state it – it falls into three divisions, referring respectively to (1) the dumping of surplus produce into England; (2) similar dumping out of England; and (3) the general development of Kartels and Trusts.

In the first place, surplus produce is sometimes dumped into this country by foreign manufacturers who are anxious not to spoil their home market, but have no compunction about disorganising ours. It is not denied that this practice has, *pro tanto*, an influence detrimental to stability in what may be called the 'dumpee' country. If, however, it is argued that such an incident justifies the establishment of a protective tariff, we reply, first, that the incident is comparatively unimportant; secondly, that a tariff such as is proposed would have no tendency to remedy it.

The former point may be illustrated as follows. In 1902 the German crisis led to a large amount of 'dumped' iron and steel coming to this country. The extracts from trade journals, which Mr. Schloss prints as an appendix to his 'Memorandum to the Board of Trade' (in Cd. 1761), do not, however, indicate any great disturbance in England as a consequence. We are again and again told that, in spite of the low prices of the dumped goods, 'local steel-makers still adhere firmly to their quotations.' Furthermore, an inspection of the figures concerning employment in the iron and steel trades, published in the 'Labour Gazette,' does not indicate that 1902 differed appreciably from other years, either in the number of men employed or the number of 'shifts' worked per man per week.

The further point that dumping of the kind contemplated would not be hindered by a general tariff was well argued by the distinguished Professor Dietzel in a recent issue of the 'Economic Journal.' A moderate system of

Protection,' he wrote, 'affords no security that the floods due to over-'production in 'other countries will not wash away the tariff wall.'[21] A country with a surplus tries to spread that surplus over a wide area. Since the normal price in Protectionist tends to exceed that in Free-Trade countries by the amount of the duty, it has no inducement to send more to the latter than to the former group. One may even argue – in this diverging from Professor Dietzel – that, if the duty is *ad valorem*, the danger of surplus dumping is actually greater in Protectionist countries, since, whereas, in a Free-Trade country, the fall in selling price and price received is equal, in a Protectionist country, the duty payable being diminished, the price received falls less than selling price.[22] This point is, no doubt, of little practical interest, since it assumes *ad valorem* duties to be assessed on declared values. The broad conclusion that a general tariff cannot diminish the danger of dumping remains, however, intact.[23]

In the second place, it may be argued that Protection has a steadying effect, in that, by checking re-imports, it facilitates dumping from the protected country when times are bad. *Pro tanto*, this argument is valid. The provision of an effective means for the disposal of surplus acts upon the industries interested in much the same way as the practice of making for stock. On the other hand, however, when an industry steadies itself by dumping surplus abroad, it, at the same time, disturbs the more advanced industries of its own country by providing cheap material for the use of their foreign rivals. Those rivals are thus enabled to undersell native firms both at home and abroad, to cut into their market, and to throw their trade into confusion. In Germany this state of things has already given rise to serious complaints, nor does it appear that any satisfactory way of remedying it has as yet been found.[24] Though, therefore, Protection, by facilitating the dumping process, may, perhaps, promote stability in one or two industries, it is most unlikely to promote it to any appreciable extent in the industrial system of the country as a whole.

In the third place, attention may be directed to the connection that subsists between protective duties and industrial combination. Circumstances are conceivable under which this latter form of organisation would tend to promote stability.[25] If, therefore, these circumstances are realised, it follows that Protection, so far as it involves combination, itself indirectly promotes stability. On the other hand, however, recent experience shows that there is a tendency among combinations of producing firms to frequent disruption from within. So far as this tendency is realised, combination makes strongly against stability. Furthermore, this particular plea for Protection may, perhaps, be put aside *ab initio* upon more general grounds. *Timeo Danaos et dona ferentes*. To purchase a little stability at the cost of a Trust or, still worse, a Kartel system, with its power to mulct the consumer and corrupt the Legislature, is not a bargain that commends itself to those who know the facts.

The three incidents of modern industry on which the Protectionist argument about stability depends have thus been reviewed. In every case it has been found that the alleged steadying influence is at the best extremely small. There must now be noticed on the other side a broad and deep force making for disturbance. Protection narrows the market, and, the narrower the market, as the history of wheat prices in the nineteenth century shows, the greater is the liability to fluctuation. Booms rise higher, depressions sink lower; the hills and the valleys of industry are alike more marked. 'When a period of prosperity occurs in a régime of high Protection' – we quote from Professor Dietzel –

'there will be a violent inflation in the favourably situated industries. The consumers are obliged to buy from them – as in former times the customers from the guild masters. The level of prices, profits, wages, rises enormously, to sink in like degree. When a period of prosperity occurs in a Free Trade region there will be a rise of prices, profits, and wages, but not in nearly so great a degree as in the protected regions. Energy is at once employed throughout the world to work towards the restoration of the disturbed equilibrium between demand and supply, and hence to prevent the waves rising too high. Foreign competition, like oil poured on the sea, moderates the tide of the national industrial system.'[26]

Is it not plain that this broad general tendency altogether outweighs the special incidents on the other side to which reference has been made? Despite recent developments in industrial combination, we can still echo the words that Professor Marshall addressed to the Co-operative Congress in 1885: 'Protection has been proposed as a remedy for the 'inconstancy of industry; I believe that all reasonable argu-'ments and all practical experience prove that it much 'increases that inconstancy.'[27] If this conclusion is accepted, it follows from our previous reasoning that Protection is likely to increase, rather than to diminish, both the average number of men out of work and the fluctuations at once of unemployment and the unemployed.

IX Conclusion.

The positive results of our inquiry may now be summarised in a few sentences. They are not, be it observed, of an abstract or general character, but refer specifically to the conditions existing in this country at the present time. They are: first, a general tariff, such as Mr. Chamberlain proposes, would almost inevitably lessen the aggregate national dividend; secondly, it would not increase the proportion of that dividend that goes to the labouring classes in any way that could save them from absolute loss; thirdly, so far from yielding an incidental compensation to the poor by lessening the numbers out of work or the fluctuations of employment, it would tend to make both these evils worse than they are at present.

These conclusions are precise and definite. If accepted they destroy the plea that protective duties upon manufactured imports would benefit the labouring classes. In urging them against Mr. Chamberlain we are condemning the means that he proposes to employ. With his end, the great object of bettering the condition of the people, we, no less than he, claim to be identified. We welcome the work that he has done in opening men's eyes to the evils of our industrial life, and in rousing their enthusiasm for the cause of social improvement. It matters little that the fire he has kindled seems now a turgid issue of smoke and sparks. The prophet of Protection has given us heat and power. Patriotism, grown sane, will clarify that gift and turn it to true service in the State.

NOTES

1 Goschen, 'Essays and Addresses,' p. 223.
2 Mr. Chamberlain at Birmingham. 'Times,' Nov. 4, 1905.
3 Mr. Chamberlain at Bristol on November 21 announced as his motto: 'More work for the people of this country, and a closer union between the different parts of the Empire.' 'Times,' Nov. 22.
4 This point may be illustrated from the Report of the Joint Committee *re* Unemployed, of the Borough of Finsbury for the winter of 1904–5: 'With regard to the extent of distress, which it has been reported prevailed in Finsbury through lack of employment, it seems clear that statements made by persons who claimed to represent the 'Unemployed' were greatly exaggerated. The leaders of a deputation to the Borough Council stated that they spoke in the name of 700 men who were out of work. Upon being asked to furnish the names and addresses of these men, they were only able, after a lapse of three weeks, to supply a list of 156, and 104 of these had already been dealt with by the Committee' (Report, p. 8).
5 [Cd. 2337] p. 159.
6 [Cd. 2337] p. 174.
7 [Cd. 1761] p. 221.
8 Ibid. p. 290. It is probably right to add to the German wage the compulsory contribution to workmen's insurance on the part of employers. This contribution is, however, too small to affect the argument. It is put by Professor Ashley at 'about 2 per cent. additional wages.' 'Progress of the German Working Classes,' p. 18.
9 'Times,' Nov. 22, 1905.
10 [Cd. 2337] p. 166.
11 [Cd. 2337] p. 195.
12 [Cd. 1761] p. 224.
13 In this view we may claim the energetic support of Professor Ashley. Cf. 'Progress of the German Working Classes' *passim*, especially p. 2: 'It requires but little reflection to understand why it is that a direct comparison, exceedingly difficult and insecure as it must be in the case of any two countries, is

absolutely valueless as applied to Germany and Great Britain.' In the face of this and many similar passages it is interesting to note that the writer of leaflet No. 88 mentions Professor Ashley's book as one of his authorities.

14 'Compatriots' Club Lectures' (First Series), p. 260.
15 'Principles of Economics,' p. 609.
16 Mr. Chamberlain at Birmingham, 'Times,' Nov. 4, 1905.
17 Cf. Edgeworth, 'Economic Journal,' xi. 587.
18 There would probably also be a tendency for some of the remaining capital to seek investment in men rather than in machines, and this, so far, would be good. An argument on those lines, however, if adequate in favour of protective duties, is still more adequate for prohibiting mechanical inventions.
19 Cf. 'Tenth Abstract of Labour Statistics of the United Kingdom, 1902–4.'
20 Cf. the tables in [Cd. 2337] pp. 87–90.
21 Economic Journal, March 1905, p. 2.
22 Cf. 'Professor Dietzel on Dumping and Retaliation,' by A.C. Pigou, Economic Journal, Sept. 1905, pp. 438–9.
23 No doubt, the danger might be lessened either by prohibitive duties or by discriminating tariffs upon particular cargoes. Neither of these devices, however, is included in Mr. Chamberlain's scheme, and the second is wholly impracticable. (Cf. Edinburgh Review, Oct. 1904, pp. 456–8.)
24 Cf. Lotz, 'The Effect of Protection on some German Industries,' Economic Journal, xiv. p. 515 et seq.
25 Cf. A.C. Pigou, 'Professor Dietzel on Dumping,' Economic Journal, Sept. 1905, pp. 440–1.
26 Economic Journal, March 1905, p. 9.
27 Address to the Co-operative Congress 1885.

----

13 TRADE AND TARIFFS*

John M. Robertson

Chapter XVI: The Argument for Retaliation

Unfortunately protectionists are able, now as in the past, to trade upon blind passions; and they are content, after every one of their economic arguments has been answered, to repeat the mere angry cry of retaliation. "Hit back," "don't take it lying down," "treat them as they treat us" – such are the watchwords with which tariffists spread the gospel of Imperial Unity, not reflecting that the very colonies to which they ask us to give a preference "hit" us all the time.

* John M. Robertson, *Trade and Tariffs* (London: Adam and Charles Black [1904] 1908), pp. 215–26; 239–45; 247–53.

It lies on the face of the case that such appeals are made because it is felt that no others will avail. To tell a man that you are proposing to him a highly profitable course of action, as against one which is ruining him, and in the same breath to seek to put him in a rage, is to exhibit a partial consciousness that the first proposition is false. Resentment is not needed to make a business man choose a gainful policy as against a losing one. Mr. Balfour, avowing that the policy of protectionist countries is "doubtless costly to them," is content to appeal rather to fear than to anger – fear of a possible decline of prosperity in the future after half a century of gainful free trade – while admitting that "both the total wealth and the diffused well-being of the country are greater than they have ever been. We are not only rich and prosperous in appearance, but also, I believe, in reality. I can find no evidence that we are 'living on our capital.'"[1] As against alike the appeal to resentment and the appeal to fear, it is the business of rational men to weigh the proposed policy on its merits, economical, political, and even sentimental.

To extract any coherent argument from Mr. Balfour's reasoning is impossible. He admits that even a country with vast natural resources "would no doubt suffer some economic loss" from diminution of exports; and he goes on to say that such a country as our own, "if it found itself confronted with a universal system of augmenting tariffs," would be not only "incomparably worse off" but "worse off than it would have been had it never adopted the free trade policy"; and this because, "while large imports are a vital necessity, the exports required to pay for them are not of a kind which other nations – all, by hypothesis, protectionist – are obliged to take."[2] Now, as Mr. Balfour calls for Protection, he is proposing a course which (save in one contingency) must on his own showing lessen exports, inasmuch as it will in his opinion lessen imports to begin with. The one conceivable cause to the contrary would be a decision of the protectionist countries to lower their tariffs when we put one on. But Mr. Balfour goes on to argue that though it would be *obviously* against the interests of foreign protectionist countries to cut down their own export trade by lessening our buying power, they would not see it! "However sound be the economic doctrine, . . . it is not one which will easily appeal to protectionists. They would not be protectionists if it did."[3] And again: "If argument failed before powerful vested interests were created, it is hardly likely to be effective now."[4] Then from Mr. Balfour's point of view there is little or no hope that the foreigners will lower their tariffs. It is true that all the while an alleged decline in *our* exports is the very reason he gives for turning protectionist himself – the very reason that is urged by his fellow-protectionists for their policy. But it is not our business to find a reconciliation between Mr. Balfour's self-contradictions. What we have here to note is that while he thus avowedly does not expect foreign protectionists to lower their tariffs when we import less from them, because the argument "is not one which easily appeals to them," he finally tells us that this very argument is an inducement "*which they thoroughly understand*,"[5] and that therefore we are to check their exports to us by putting on retaliatory duties!

In the gift of self-contradiction, Mr. Balfour must be admitted to be Mr. Chamberlain's equal, perhaps his superior. Probably no other modern statesman, certainly none with Mr. Balfour's repute for intelligence, ever put forward in justification of a policy such a series of self-stultifications as we have been considering. Having taken note of the confusion, we can but put it aside for what it is, and go on to ask whether they are *any* grounds on which we may expect foreign protectionists to lower their tariffs if we put one on. On the widest survey, there is none. As Mr. Balfour and Mr. Chamberlain both avow, they are proposing "to do to foreign nations what they *always* do to each other." In other words, foreign nations (the protectionist nations, that is) simply go on retaliating, go on raising their tariffs against each other; and we are to join in the process. On this view the case is hopeless. It is true that there are growing movements for free trade in many if not in all protectionist countries. The German Socialists, in particular, are for the most part determined free-traders; and ere long they may carry their point. But in the meantime there is not the least reason to suppose that our resort to a tariff would help them: on the contrary, it would be cited by the German protectionists as a proof that all trading countries now realise the rightness of Protection.

While Mr. Balfour thus actually gives reasons why protectionist countries should not be expected to lower their tariffs in the event of our setting up one against them, he and his followers are alike committed to the pretence that a tariff *is* a means of bringing down other tariffs. They proceed on the simple assumption that it ought to be, in disregard of all experience. "A means of negotiation" is the common expression. Now, a tariff might be such an instrument as between two Governments both of which at heart desired free trade, as Mr. Balfour and Mr. Chamberlain profess to do, but both of which were hampered by their protectionists in the legislature. Huskisson, as we saw, used the retaliatory action of the Prussian Government in 1822 as a pretext for modifying in 1825 the Navigation Act and lessening the duties against Prussia. But Huskisson, we know, was a free-trader; and according to the Anglo-German economic historian Prince Smith,[6] the British Government actually suggested to the Prussian Ministry the retaliatory action which the latter, being also inclined to free trade, was loth to take. Whether or not this is true, it is clear that both Governments *were* disposed towards free trade, and the success of the retaliation in that particular case is the kind of apparent exception which, being explained, leaves the rule intact.

All experience goes to show that, where a strong disposition to protectionism exists, retaliatory duties only in the case of a few articles never have any remedial effect. It was this that happened in 1697–1700, when Flanders retaliated on the English prohibition of Flemish lace by excluding English woollens; and in that case the woollen trade simply overrode the claim of the English lace industry in a fashion which to-day would arouse a storm in any protectionist country. Strong interests do not yield their prey; but in England to-day one protected trade would hardly dare in this fashion to sacrifice others which had been in alliance with them. The historic rule is, obstinacy in evil. Peel, after his tariff reductions of 1842, strove for years – Gladstone being his Minister – to induce the protectionist Governments of his day to come to terms, but had to admit a total failure. It was this failure that convinced him of the futility of tariffs as "instruments of negotiation." He had left on the duties on wine and brandy for that express purpose, and he could gain nothing by them. "Wearied with our long and unavailing efforts to enter into satisfactory commercial treaties with other countries," he declared in 1846, "we have resolved at length to consult our own interests, and not to punish other countries, for the wrong they do us in continuing their high tariffs upon the importation of our products and manufactures, by continuing high duties ourselves." "The best way to fight hostile tariffs is with free imports." He actually established free trade in Britain in the midst of a war of tariffs throughout Europe;[7] and the only countries which at the same time moved in a free trade direction were Holland and the United States, moved not by pressure but by goodwill.

The falsity of the theory of retaliation is further demonstrated by the simple fact of the prevalence of protectionism. Tariffists tell us in one breath that all the world has seen good reason to turn protectionist, and in the next that another tariff will tend to make them turn to free trade. If ninety-nine mutually opposing tariffs have no reciprocally repressive effect, why should a hundredth alter the situation? By which proposition will the tariffist stand? Do the other countries want free trade, or do they not? If they do, why do they fight each other with tariffs, generation after generation? If they do not, how should our tariff coerce them all, any more than they have coerced each other?

As we have seen, tariffs have been generally resorted to in the outset not by way of resentment against and effort to beat down other tariffs, but primarily for revenue purposes; and they have been maintained and heightened by the sinister interests which they generate and strengthen. Even a fresh resort to free trade by hitherto protectionist countries would not induce others to follow which were ruled by protectionists, no matter how loudly the latter might have declared that their tariffs were merely retaliations. The trade interests in the United States have never scrupled to turn their backs on their own pledges when there was any talk of taking off a duty which had been expressly granted as a temporary aid. As Dietzel remarks: "The good example set in 1879 by England, Holland, and Denmark – that is, by a number of countries of the highest importance for our [*i.e.* German] foreign commerce – did not cause our legislative authorities to remain faithful to the 'régime Delbrück': as little likelihood is there that a future adoption of the free trade principle by Russia and the United States would induce it to pursue the same course."[8]

Caprivi, who understood the principles of free trade, did succeed in introducing, from 1891 onwards, a system of low-tariff policy which had been pursued in Germany from 1879 had injured German trade. The reason of his success in conciliating some other continental Powers was that Russia and the United States had greatly raised their tariffs, and the other States were disposed to recoil from a similar policy. He was actually coming down from a high tariff to a lower, not forcing anybody to lower theirs first. In this case a potential free-trader negotiated with States inclined to lower tariffs. In the case of Russia, however, there ensued a tariff war, and only after it had caused vast losses did the two countries come to terms. Even in this case the solution was due to the circumstance that Germany specially needed Russian rye and flax, and that Russia specially needed the German market for those articles.[9]

Apart from cases in which such wasteful tariff wars end in agreements which might have been come to at the outset, there is hardly an instance on record in modern times in which a single retaliation, or the threat of it, has had a salutary effect. In the case of Brazil's threat to tax German manufactures because of a raised German duty on coffee, Germany yielded because the tax on coffee was not protective, and was besides unwelcome to German consumers in general. Certainly the tariff wars are far more numerous than the prompt pacifications. And those wars are in themselves the most emphatic condemnation of protectionism. That which was waged between France and Italy from 1889 to 1898 is estimated to have caused to the two countries a total loss of £120,000,000. In the ten years French imports of Italian goods fell off by $57\frac{1}{2}$ per cent, and Italian imports of French goods by 50 per cent; and though there was a recovery in 1899 it has not since been maintained. Each country has permanently injured its trade with the other. In the years 1893–95, again, France and Switzerland waged a similar war; and here again there there has been a permanent loss, besides the fall of 45 per cent in exports on the French side, and 35 of the Swiss side, while the struggle lasted.[10]

All the while, Britain is on the "most favoured nation" footing with all Powers save Portugal, whose wines she now taxes rather heavily. To sacrifice this immense advantage on the alleged chance of a gain from "retaliation" which has never been seen to accrue in human experience, would be the extremity of national folly, and only individual self-interest could ever propose it. If, finally, the game of retaliation is to be played with even a semblance of thoroughness, the taxation of imported raw materials is inevitable; and this our tariffists still protest their determination not to attempt. Their theory, then, at this as at so many other points, is divided against itself, and the practical dilemma is in itself sufficient to confound them. To retaliate against the United States we should have to tax cotton, which would ruin our cotton industry; and tobacco, the duty upon which Mr. Chamberlain has promised to lighten – it being indeed heavy enough already. To punish Russia we should have to raise the price of kerosene; and to press Italy we should have to burden our importers of raw and thrown silk. The thesis thrown out in passion will not bear an hour's cool scrutiny.

Before leaving this theme it may be well to notice the use made in recent tariffist propaganda of an ill-considered passage in which J.S. Mill, discussing the effect of tariffs, seems to suggest "retaliation," albeit with a totally different meaning from that of the protectionists who make use of some of his words. In one protectionist[11] pamphlet the proposition that we cannot get reductions of tariff from foreign nations "for nothing," is supported by this simple footnote: –

> A country cannot be expected to renounce the power of taxing foreigners, unless foreigners will in return practise towards itself the same forbearance. The only mode in which a country can save itself from being a loser by the revenue duties imposed by other countries on its commodities, is to impose corresponding revenue duties on theirs. – J.S. MILL.

Here the only possible inference for an uninformed reader is that Mill believed import duties fell upon the foreign producers of the taxed articles. Now, Mill held exactly the opposite view. Mr. Vince, like Mr. Chamberlain, selects his quotations (and in this case it can hardly have been by oversight) in entire disregard of the context. After the passage he quotes comes this: –

> Only it must take care that those duties be not so high as to exceed all that remains of the advantage of the trade, and put an end to importation altogether, *causing the article to be either produced at home* or imported from another and a dearer market.

To cause the article to be produced at home is precisely the aim of most protectionists.

Mill's position is to be understood from his previous reasoning. A few paragraphs before that quoted from, he sums up an exposition thus: –

> Those are therefore in the right who maintain that taxes on imports are partly paid by foreigners, *but they are mistaken when they say that it is by the foreign producer.* It is not on the person from whom we buy, but on all those who buy from us, that a portion of *our* custom duties spontaneously falls. *It is the foreign consumer of our exported commodities who is obliged to pay a higher price for them because we maintain revenue duties on foreign goods.*[12]

That is to say, *our* import duties would cause the foreigner to pay more for what he buys from us.

In this opinion Mill was, I think, demonstrably wrong. The truth lies neither in his view nor in that of the protectionists. Mill worked out his argument in terms of pure *a priori* reasoning as to the effect of limitation of import (by raising prices) on reciprocal export. He argues, that is, that if Germany by reason of tariffs imports less from us, she will owe us less, and will consequently send us less, and we shall have to pay more for what she does send us. And *vice versa*. This argument takes no account of Germany's continued *wish to sell to us*, which, as the protectionist so often and so bitterly complains, leads her at times to "dump" upon us below cost price. It further ignores the operation of the exchanges, by reason of which, while German drawers of bills on London would have to pay a higher discount because of our lessened sales to Germany, and so *get less* for their exports, our exporters will get a premium for their bills on Germany, and so, without raising their prices, *get more* for their exports, thus being newly advantaged against the German tariff. But whether Mill was right or wrong,[13] it is mere deception to quote him in a sense flatly opposed to his real meaning. Mr. Vince is all the while arguing that *increase of exports* is the grand desideratum. Mill's argument was that we should take a course which would *further diminish* our exports as well as our imports. It is safe to say that such a counsel, once understood, will never be followed by either tariffists or free-traders.

The argument that "the foreign producer" can be made to pay the tax undergoes yet other manipulations. In the "Speaker's Handbook" of the Tariff Reform League[14] there occurs this oracular citation: –

PROF. SENIOR

A part of the taxes received by the Government of one country is often paid by the inhabitants of another. – *Outlines of Political Economy*, p. 184.

This use of Senior is, if possible, even more misleading than the before-noted use of Mill. The sentence quoted is the first in a paragraph in which Senior argues that when England puts a heavy import duty on tea, "a portion of our duty on tea is, in fact, paid bythe inhabitants of the tea-growing districts of China," inasmuch as, if we did *not* put a duty, the increased demand would cause a rise of price in China which would "have a tendency to raise the rent of land and the wages of labour in the tea-growing districts." In passing, it may be remarked that the effect upon wages would depend upon whether new soil was taken into cultivation, or whether other crops were given up in favour of tea-growing. In the latter case wages might even fall if tea-growing required less labour than the other culture, as sometimes happens where pasture supersedes grain-growing. But taking Senior's proposition to be true, the only "retaliation" it can be made to justify would be one deliberately planned to impoverish foreign landlords and foreign workmen on the score that their Government had impoverished our manufacturers and workmen by lessening the possible demand for their products. On the question whether such retaliation could do us any good, Senior would, of course, reply in the negative, save in so far as he might conceivably believe in the power of retaliation to force the foreign government to reduce his duties. But in the case of its refusal to do so, his whole line of argument commits him to the recognition of the fact that by impoverishing the foreigner we should merely restrict his *power* to buy from us even what he wanted to buy.

This is recognised by Professor Sidgwick, who in turn is exploited by the Tariff Reform League no more ingenuously than they have handled Senior. The "Handbook" cites him thus (italics mine): –

PROF. HENRY SIDGWICK

"Unless foreign products are completely excluded by import duties, such duties will partly have the effect of levying a tribute on foreign producers, the amount *and duration* of which may *in certain cases* be considerable." – *Principles of Political Economy*, p. 493.

Sidgwick's argument is, in brief, that a 5 per cent duty on foreign silks may "after a certain interval" cause half the silks consumed by a nation to be produced by native industry, while the price of the whole may rise only $2\frac{1}{2}$ per cent. Then the imported half will yield the State 5 per cent, while the tax on consumers is only $2\frac{1}{2}$ per cent, "so that *the nation in the aggregate* is at this time losing nothing by protection except the cost of collecting the tax, while a loss equivalent to the whole tax falls on the foreigner." That is to say, what the consumer loses in the extra price which he pays *qua* consumer, he gains *qua* taxpayer. To say nothing of the fact that those who do not buy silk get the gain without bearing any of the counterbalancing loss, this argument overlooks the fact that the rise in price tends (1) to check consumption, and (2) unduly to enrich the silk-manufacturer, until extra capital enters into the trade, when the tendency will be to over-produce for a time, with the result of depressing prices, and so on. But, further, Sidgwick himself admits (3), on the next page, that "the protection given by [nation] A to one branch of her industry may very likely have the secondary effect of inflicting a blow upon another branch." This fatal corollary is of course not quoted by the Tariff Reform League.

Sidgwick's very characteristic handling of the subject of Protection is a warning as to the confusion that may be wrought by what may be termed the non-committal handling of a scientific issue. It is a good instance of the species of academic problem in mechanics in which "the weight of the elephant may be neglected." Beginning in his anxiously detached fashion to discuss the practical issue, he writes (italics mine): –

"I hold . . . that when the matter is considered from the point of view of abstract theory it is easy to show that protection, *under certain not improbable circumstances*, would yield a direct gain to the protecting country; but that from the *difficulty of securing in any actual government sufficient wisdom, strength, and singleness of aim* to introduce protection only so far as it is advantageous to the community and withdraw it inexorably so soon as the public interest requires its withdrawal, it is *practically best* to tax for revenue only."[15]

That is to say, "under certain not improbable circumstances" there would concur other inevitable circumstances which would make the totality of the required circumstances improbable in the highest degree! It is "practically best" to adhere to free trade principles because no government can be found wise and good and strong enough to apply protection with that perfect wisdom, goodness, and strength which alone can enable us to raise the price of silk and the profits of our own silkmakers, and at the same time to lower the profits of the foreign silkmaker, without causing loss to "the nation in the aggregate," whatever may be the extra burden on the consumer of silk. And, all the while, even the most perfect wisdom, goodness, and strength in protecting the silk trade would not preclude injury to other trades! *Solvuntur tabulae!* . . .

Chapter XVIII: The Argument from Unemployment

Our survey of actual experience in protectionist Britain and in the protectionist countries of to-day has shown clearly enough the falsity of the pretence that tariffs mean "work for all." So patently false is it, indeed, that the more intelligent tariffists repudiate it, both in Parliament and outside. None the less, a tariffist journal in London daily flaunts the falsehood: "Tariff Reform means work for all." And since emigration is pointed to as a proof of industrial failure, it follows that a tariff is to find work not only for the present unemployed but for those who are now emigrating. On votes won by such means the bulk of the tariff party seem to rely. It may be well, then, to add to the historic inquiry an examination of the plea on its economic merits, though this means only exposing afresh the central protectionist fallacy in terms of this particular issue.

The Free Trade principle is that freedom involves the maximum yield to labour, by reason of its economic direction on the most advantageous lines – most advantageous, that is, as to economy in production. It is arguable, of course, that it might be "advantageous" for a rich pastoral and agricultural country to bear special taxation in order to develop variety of handicraft among its population. The free trader's answer is that, given the premiss, by far the better course would be to pay directly for the encouragement of the crafts in question, seeing that protection by import duties invariably (1)

305

develops political corruption, and (2) keeps the protected industries in a position of desperate dependence on the tariff, which almost no later exertion can shake off. But we are not here concerned with the problems of "new countries," since such no longer exist. We have to consider our own case.

The question is, seeing that taxes on food or manufactured imports, or both, will tend to raise prices, how can the demand for labour thereby permanently increase? In the United States and in Germany there has gone on, under Protection, an exploitation of their large reserve of natural resources. Apart from coal, what resources have we to exploit to any such extent? The protectionist answer is that many articles now imported will under Protection be made at home, native labour being thus employed where formerly it was not. But the excluded articles must be either (a) goods now sent hither in payment of British services or as interest on British investments, or (b) goods now paid for by exports. In the former case the services or loans in question must, in terms of the argument, go partly unpaid; and the labour formerly employed in distributing and in earning the imported articles now excluded will go unemployed. In the latter case the labour formerly employed in making the goods which used to be exported in payment for the imports will cease. The protectionist replies that it will make the same goods as before in order to pay for the goods now made at home in place of those excluded by import duties. But he here makes the plainly false assumption that the makers of the new goods for home consumption will demand the same goods as were formerly exported to pay for the goods then imported. Obviously they will not. They will demand food and clothing; and the labour thrown out of employment must take to producing these if it is to be employed at all. And how can it? Finally, as the articles now to be made at home will in the terms of the case be dearer than formerly, the demand for them will tend to be less, and thus the whole volume of industry will shrink. How, then, can there be an increased employment for labour? And what of the *export* of our goods, whether to other producing countries or to "neutral markets"? Forgetting his pretence that labour in protectionist countries is well paid, Mr. Chamberlain tells us that we import sweated goods, with which our better-paid labour cannot compete. If, then, our wages and costs rise still further, how can we, save by an increase in efficiency relatively to foreign producers, compete as before in neutral markets?

Now, increase in our exports has been all along insisted on by the tariffists as essential to a healthy condition of our trade. Mr. Chamberlain and Mr. Balfour, however, seem alike unable to make up their minds as to whether increase of exports is the supremely desirable thing, though both speak in that sense. Mr. Chamberlain condemns the buying of tram-rails from abroad, on the score that the making of them, even if more costly, would have employed British labour. But British labour has actually been employed to make the goods which go to pay for the imported rails; and those exported goods figure as exports; whereas, had the rails been made at home, our exports would have been so much less; and Mr. Chamberlain would have continued to argue that, the less our exports, the worse is our industrial condition. What would he finally have?

This insoluble dilemma is the demonstration of the irrationality of the protectionist case. It is a perpetual oscillation between irreconcilable conceptions. The protectionist argues with Mr. Chamberlain that as population increases we must increase our exports, which presumably means further increase of shipping. Then what imports are we to take in payment of the extra exports and the freights? "Raw material," is the reply. But if the term "raw" is to be defined as strictly as possible, how, in the name of reason, can we hope to import mere raw material in payment for an ever-increasing export of manufactures when the manufactures are worth over twice the raw material, quantity for quantity? If, after importing fifty-five millions worth of raw cotton and consuming a large quantity we export a hundred millions' worth of finished cotton goods, are we thereafter to import a hundred millions' worth of raw cotton in order to export something like two hundred millions' worth of cotton manufactures; then import that value in raw cotton, to export four hundred millions' worth of cotton goods, and so on *ad infinitum*? Are we dealing with dreamers or with men of business?

To refuse to be paid at all in partially or wholly manufactured goods is simply to refuse to take full payment for our goods and services, and returns on our foreign investments. To this the argument always comes. On the plea of unemployment we are in effect asked to shut out part of the price paid us for our goods and services, in order that goods to that amount shall be made by native labour. Now, even if we could in that fashion secure for the moment employment for our unemployed – which, we have seen, we certainly cannot – it would be the worst possible way of doing it; for in the process we should be crippling our power to export to either neutral or protected markets, thus making further unemployment inevitable; and we should be enriching inequitably the employers on the pretext of finding wages for their men. An unemployment problem certainly exists; but this is assuredly not the way to deal with it. We should but increase hopelessly the mass of unemployment. And, needless to say, if we contrived to keep up for a year an increase in our exports, we should be emphatically told by our protectionists that whatever unemployment we still had, would be much increased if we should return to free trade! If only the immense increase of exports in the past five years had occurred under Protection, not one protectionist in the country would admit for a moment that the present unemployment was a reason for trying free trade again. They would assert – they would indeed probably believe – that we had to thank Protection for the smallness of the amount of it.

That their specific, on the other hand, would inevitably increase unemployment can be demonstrated upon any line of analysis we may follow. Let us put another concrete case. One of the imports most complained of by protectionists is that of iron in bars or ingots – certainly a manufactured article as compared with raw ore, but equally a raw material for those whose business it is to make iron into tin-plates or into machinery. As is well known, such cheap imports did much to restore to prosperity the tin-plate industry which was so hard hit by the McKinley Tariff. Similarly, our shipbuilders have secured contracts in virtue of their command of "dumped" German steel; and have even beaten German competitors in engineering contracts on the Continent, through being able to buy German steel cheaper than it is sold to Germans. Still further, we have the case of a firm of shipbuilders *and* makers of steel plates, who, when German steel plates were coming in at prices lower than they could themselves afford to sell them at, bought a supply, and were thereby enabled to lay down and sell a ship at a price at which they could not otherwise have built one. Nottingham lace-makers, again, use as the basis of their silk and linen lace a cotton-net (afterwards chemically removed) which is clearly a manufactured article, and which is imported for the purpose.

To tax imported iron, then, or steel, or cotton-net, is to tax the "raw material" of many important industries; and so with a hundred other imports. The tax will raise the price of the higher manufacture, by way of protecting the home manufacture of the lower; and the net effect will be to force some labour from the higher to the lower industry, and to throw more labour absolutely idle. Nothing is more certain than that rise of price normally checks demand, not only for articles which can readily be dispensed with, like lace, but for all products not absolutely indispensable; and lessened demand means lessened employment.[16] Under Protection the tin-plate factories which have thriven on imported German or other iron will be unable to export as they have done to the United States in the teeth of the tariff; and if some extra employment is obtained for the iron forges, it will be heavily overbalanced by the labour thrown idle through the stoppage of the whole of the exports which now go to pay for imported iron. Imports, once more, mean demand, either (*a*) for exports, or (*b*) for home labour which is the price paid for sharing in the goods imported in payment of freights or interest on investments.

This home trade is habitually ignored – sometimes, as we have seen, condemned – by protectionists, though all the while it is an increase of home trade that they profess to desire. The modern expansion of the building trade, which is one of the most satisfactory features of all, is either ignored or mentioned only to lament that the exporting industries do not expand at the same rate, or that, as at present, it is suffering from lack of work. Mr. Chamberlain insists that we shall make our own watches, rails, and bottles, thus exporting less of other products, and so reducing still further that export trade which he usually takes as the real measure of our industrial prosperity, but on the other hand, it is hoped, increasing our home trade. As a matter of fact the home trade would not be increased: the general demand would fall off with the rise in prices; and many constructive enterprises which are undertaken because prices are low would simply be abandoned.

But Mr. Balfour, on the other hand, avowedly sees nothing desirable in the increase of the home trade. He expressly admitted in 1903 that it was gaining ground proportionally to the then lessened rate of expansion in export trade; and he does not deny, further, that while the larger "staple" industries do not expand as formerly, "this is more than made up for by the variety of goods we now manufacture for the foreign consumer." But, he adds, "*from neither circumstance can I derive much satisfaction*. These are precisely the signs which would accompany the struggle of a Free Trade country so to modify its industries as to pierce the barrier of foreign tariffs." Exactly! And was there ever an idler answer?[17] When such "staple" industries as coal-mining, shipbuilding, and machine-making are found to *increase* their export, Mr. Balfour finds that also an evil! Nothing, apparently, will content him but increased export of cheap cottons and woollens.

For such a position there is neither social nor economic justification. Free modification of industry from staple to new forms means the elevation of labour from simpler to more complex activities – an evolution upwards. When done without injury to consumers or to other industries – as happens under Free Trade, but not under Protection – it is a social gain. And while Mr. Balfour thus recognises and disparages such evolution, other propagandists in Mr. Chamberlain's train are telling the workers that Free Trade means the reduction of industry to the lower forms.

Even Professor Ashley thus argues[18] that our industries are tending to decline from skilled to unskilled forms, offering as his proof (1) the increased exports of coal, clay, and spirits, and (2) the decrease in values of exports of cottons and in quantities of exported woollens, while unable to deny (a) the increased *quantities* of cottons (piece goods) exported, and paying no heed to (b) the immensely increased home consumption of woollens and other articles of manufacture, or (c) the continual increase in shipbuilding, and in the numbers of men employed in and through that great industry. At the same time, when he deals with one of the most skilled industries, that of machine-making, he does it only to deplore, with Mr. Balfour, that in that matter we are enabling foreign nations to compete with us in the *use* of machines, as if *that* were not a less skilled form of industry than the making of them! On the other hand, he takes no note of the obvious tendency of Protection to force the home manufacture of such low-grade articles as cotton-net and pig-iron . . .

The more disinterested argument of Professor Ashley yields no better prescription than Mr. Balfour's. His plea for "regulation" of industry would lead logically to Socialism; but instead of a socialistic control in the interests of all he proposes mere protectionism – the subsidising of the few at the cost of the many – without even offering a reasonable proof that Protection will "regulate" the sweated industries of which he desires the restriction.

All the while, those who are proposing to shut out a quantity of our imports in order to have similar goods made at home are proclaiming that they want import duties by way of raising revenue – that is to say, the goods are not to be kept out, but to come in! Thus does the protectionist theory reel and gyrate, flying from pillar to post, doubling, confuting itself, contradicting itself, constant only in confidence of asseveration.

Chapter XIX: The Argument for Revenue

It might have been supposed that any adult who argued the problem long enough to carry on a discussion would see that he cannot propose at once to tax the same goods for revenue and for the purpose of preventing their importation. But that is done daily, hourly, by journalists, propagandists, and statesmen so called, in the name and cause of "tariff reform." As there are certain logical limits which those capable of seeing them cannot pass, we must here assume for the argument's sake that the tariffist is proposing only one of two incompatible courses, and is demanding *not* the exclusion of goods in order to make work, but the admission of them under an import duty.

At the outset we have to pause once more over his secondary – or is it primary? – thesis that the desired revenue is to be taken from "the foreigner," not from ourselves. On this head there is even more than the usual difficulty in extracting a meaning from tariffist contradictions. Mr. Balfour and Mr. Chamberlain alike confound confusion; and different performers among their followers explicitly propound contrary doctrines, while professing unqualified devotion to both.

The proposition that import duties will safeguard the home producer from "unfair competition" must mean, if anything, that they will cause a rise in the prices of the given commodities, the home-made article rising by the amount of the tax, or part of it. If, then, the foreigner is to pay any of the tax, it can only be by way of continuing to undersell or limit the home producer. And if, say, goods which he now sells at 10s. where the home producer wants 11s. are taxed 1s., and he continues to sell them at 10s. (9s. plus the tax), the home producer will be in no way relieved. If, on the other hand, the foreigner simply offers his goods as before, thus enabling the home trader to put up his prices, the foreigner clearly pays no part of the tax. What, then, does the protectionist desire?

The common statement concerning the competition of protectionist countries is, as we saw, that in virtue of their entire command of their own market the foreign producers are able to sell in ours at relatively very low prices. If, then, they could still afford to lower their prices so as to leap our tariff, they will forfeit either the 10 per cent or what part of it may be necessary. In that case we shall receive the amount as public revenue; and if the goods come in sufficient quantity there will be no rise of price, the home producer being still forced to the former low rate. But when, in virtue of foreign bounties on exported sugar, the consumers of this nation were receiving among them a large annual bonus from theforeigner, the process was denounced as "unfair competition," and the last Government entered into the Sugar Convention in order to put a stop to it. How, then, will the protectionist party meet those traders who protest that unfair competition still goes on even under an import duty on the kind of goods they produce? If the foreigner competes unfairly when he undersells them now, will he not be competing just as unfairly if he leaps our tariff? And if he does not leap it, what becomes of the revenue he was to yield us?

Mr. Balfour's latest pronouncement is for a system of (1) small duties, on (2) a great many imported articles, (3) exempting raw materials, and (4) so adjusted that no extra burden shall be laid on the working classes. By this formula he is supposed to have "committed" himself definitely to tariff reform. It is difficult to see how practical men can hope to put such a scheme in operation. The four conditions are plainly incompatible; and Mr. Balfour is perfectly safe. If the mass of the people are not to be burdened by the extra prices they will have to pay for the newly taxed articles, the duties now levied on other articles must be lightened or removed; and in that case what becomes of the promised additional revenue? If the duties on tea, sugar, and tobacco, for instance, are proportionally reduced, or some of them abolished, the basis of taxation will in no intelligible sense be widened; and the argument for revenue goes by the board. Mr. Balfour's formula is once for all irreconcilable with the thesis that Protection means a source of greatly increased revenue.

There remains the plea once put by Mr. Chamberlain, that a really increased burden in the way of prices will be balanced by increased earnings. At an early stage of the discussion he asserted that a rise in the cost of food would be followed by a rise in wages. Later he explained that under his scheme there would be no rise in the total cost of food.[19] He had virtually promised, also, that the revenue from food taxes should go to providing Old Age Pensions. Now there is to be no such revenue. But wages, he predicts, will still rise, because under his policy there will be more employment.[20] That promise, we have already seen, cannot be fulfilled. Even if employment did somehow increase with raised prices all round, and without any such greatly increased output of raw material as has been possible in the United States and in Germany, their experience has abundantly shown that the rise in costs of living tends to distance the rise in wages. It has done so since Mr. Chamberlain spoke. To tax the worker, then, by new import duties on the promise of a rise in wages, would be sheer imposture.

What appears to be hoped by the majority of protectionists, in their confused way, is that if they can set up a tariff, prices will rise, to the advantage of the home producer, the consumer buying more than ever at higher rates, and that all the while foreign goods enough will come in to yield a considerable revenue. In that event the revenue would be got at the cost of an indefinitely greater amount paid by the home consumer in increased prices for British goods. From this dilemma there is no rational escape; and to state the case is to condemn, once for all, such a mode of raising revenue. It means a minimum return to the State, with a maximum burden on the average consumer – the negation of sound finance. Even the extra revenue available in the case put would in itself be wastefully won, for the system of small duties on many articles, as was long ago seen by most political financiers, means the maximum loss in cost of collection and prevention of smuggling. And all the while the revenue in question would be trifling in amount relatively to the alleged national needs.[21]

Our protectionists tell us alternately that we are of all nations the most heavily burdened by customs duties,[22] and that protectionist countries are to be envied because of the amount of revenue they receive from their customs.[23] This is but one more of the innumerable double delusions of their creed. Our high revenue from customs is relatively unburdensome, precisely because it is non-protective. It raises no prices save those of the articles actually imported. The import duties of the United States upon manufactures and raw material, and of France and Germany upon both foods and manufactures, raise the *home* prices of all the articles taxed, so that the amount received as customs revenue is but a fraction of the surplus payments made by the consumers. And if, on the other hand, as so many protectionists eagerly and suicidally claim, the revenue of those States from protective customs is really smaller than ours from non-protective, the more absurd is their proposal to make protective customs a large source of revenue for Britain. If, as seems to be implied in their ever-contradictory propaganda, we are to drop our present non-protective customs and substitute a protective set of duties, the result will be an absolute loss of revenue! And yet that loss would coexist with an increased burden upon the mass of the people.

The protectionist argument as to need for revenue is, in short (if it be possible), a worse argument than those we have already considered. So palpable is the central confusion that, as we have before noted, a number of protectionists disavow the demand for the "broadened basis of taxation," and claim that the essential object of their movement is increase of employment. The two theses are indeed ludicrously incompatible. But that does not prevent their being often used on the same platform by the same propagandist, to the edification of the same dupes.

NOTES

1 *Economic Notes*, p. 28.
2 *Economic Notes*, pp. 12–13.
3 *Id.* p. 14.
4 *Id.* p. 30.
5 *Economic Notes*, p. 30.
6 Cited by Prof. H. Dietzel, *Retaliatory Duties*, Eng. trans. 1906, pp. 29–30.
7 "France, Belgium, and Germany," he wrote to Croker in 1842, "are closing their doors against us." – *Croker's Correspondence*, 1884, ii. 383.
8 Work cited, p. 13.
9 Dietzel, ch. i.
10 Board of Trade *Reports on Tariff Wars between certain European States* (Cd 1938), 1904.
11 C.A. Vince, *Mr. Chamberlain's Proposals*, 1903, p. 62 [see also (Vol. III: 10)].
12 B. v. ch. iv. § 6, near end. People's ed. p. 515.
13 It will be observed that in the section cited Mill is reproducing parts of his early essay on International Commerce, and that in it he ostensibly contradicts another of his dicta. There he asserts that "a tax on imported commodities, when it really operates as a tax, and not as a prohibition either total or partial, almost always falls in part upon the foreigners who consume our goods." In the second section of the same chapter he affirms that "there are few cases in which" a tax on imports does not raise the value and price of a commodity by "more than" the amount of the tax. The passages are to be reconciled only by realising that in the one reprinted from his early essay he is driving at another point than that of the effect of an import duty on prices.
14 *A Short Handbook for Speakers*, etc., 4th ed. 1907, p. 157.
15 *Principles of Political Economy*, pp. 485–6.
16 J.S. Mill's argument that demand for commodities is not demand for labour is a confusion, now abandoned by nearly all economists.
17 *Economic Notes*, p. 21. The rest of Mr. Balfour's answer is beside the case, and indicates a failure to understand the issue.
18 *The Tariff Problem*, ch. iv.
19 Speeches, as cited, pp. 37, 39, 98.
20 *Id.* pp. 130, 138, 139.
21 On this see the speech by Mr. Alfred Mond, of March 31, 1908, published by the Free Trade Union.
22 *One Hundred Points on Tariff Reform*, reprinted from the *Globe*, p. 100.
23 *Id.* p. 29.

II

TARIFF REFORM: THE POLITICAL DEBATE

A

PAPERS, LETTERS, PAMPHLETS AND SPEECHES

14 PREFERENTIAL TREATMENT . . . *

E.W. Hamilton

The question of admitting colonial products into the United Kingdom on more favourable terms than foreign products is approached by Mr. Chamberlain, and naturally so, from a Colonial point of view, special weight being given to political and sentimental considerations; but it is bound to be approached by the Chancellor of the Exchequer from a financial point of view, special weight being given to economic and practical considerations. Preferential treatment differs only in one respect from what has been generally associated with the term Protection. Sixty years' ago the principal produce protected was the Agricultural produce of the United Kingdom. *Now*, it is proposed to include in the Preferential system Colonial produce as well as British produce.

From whatever point of view the question of according Preferential Treatment to our Colonies is approached, one thing is certain – it means a momentous and radical, change in our Fiscal system. It does not do to claim for that system immunity from imperfections and flaws, and it is certain that harm is done to the main principles that underlie it, and have underlain it for more than half a century, if a claim is put forward that those principles are the tenets of a sacred creed, and that to the system itself all our prosperity as well as commercial and industrial greatness are due.

What is our Fiscal system? At any rate, it is very simple and it is based on what even the most extreme protectionist must admit to be sound, if not the best, principles.

(1) It avoids taxing the prime necessities of life, which is most important for every country; and it avoids taxing raw materials for manufacture, which is most important for a manufacturing country.

(2) It limits taxes to the exigencies of the State; and thus it turns taxes to account for Revenue only.

(3) It raises Revenue in the most economical manner; that is, it puts into the Exchequer all that it takes out of people's pockets.

* E.W. Hamilton, "Preferential Treatment . . . ", Confidential Cabinet Paper (6 June 1903), British Museum Additional MSS, 49780.

It must be remembered that a change in our Fiscal system is a much more serious matter than ordinary changes initiated by the Legislature. It is not only a great "leap in the dark"; but the change involves the taxing of some things which are not taxed now, and of all things in taxation we ought to beware it is *change*, for I believe there is much truth in those who hold that there is nothing so unjust in taxation as change. Moreover, the very object of the change is to do what taxation ought not to do, that is, to interfere with trade, which it is very easy to dislocate and most difficult to organise.

What is the change to be? It is to be the taxing of imports from foreign countries which are now untaxed, allowing the same articles which are produced in our Colonies and in the United Kingdom to be free. Are all the commodities which come from foreign countries to be taxed without distinction? That is to say, raw materials for manufacture, articles of food, and manufactured articles? Or is it to be certain selected articles in one or other of the categories? It would probably be the most simple plan to impose an *ad valorem* tax on all foreign imports. Such a tax would lend itself best to the varying circumstances and conditions of the different Colonies, and it might be made to produce an large sum without being specially onerous, besides being applicable for retaliatory purposes in the case of foreign countries. But even those who advocate the imposition of taxing imports a great deal more than we now do, say we must draw the line at raw materials, in order that our manufactures may not be more heavily handicapped than they are now in the Industrial race in which the whole world competes. If raw materials are excluded, it is difficult not to exclude manufactured articles also; for many things that are entered in this category, though answering to the description of "manufactured articles" in one trade are practically the raw materials in another trade. It comes, then, to this – the foreign articles we must tax, in order to give the Colonies a "pull", are articles of food, and it must be an appreciable tax in order to raise a sum worth raising and in order to give the Colonies a preference worth having. Just think what a tax on food means! The nation as a whole may be lightly taxed; but we must remember that there is unfortunately always a by no means negligible quantity of the population who are in straits to keep body and soul together, and that anything which tends to enhance the cost of living – and it must do that – aggravates and extends those traits.

We are told that there will be a higher wage to compensate for the enhanced cost of living; but what is the use of holding out visions of a higher wage to those who have practically no wage, or at any rate no wage regularly?

Again, what consolation is it to a struggling artisan, who has to pay more for his bread and meat, to be told that the Agricultural Labourer is receiving better weekly wages? for, a tax on Agricultural produce can only place the

Farmer here in a better position to raise wages, and there is no certainty that he will, even if he can. So you are asking the working-man to incur a certain loss for a very uncertain gain. Can anything be more calculated to prejudice the ideas of Imperial unity in the eyes of the Working-classes than to tell that they will have to submit to increased taxation? Shall we not be told, and with great truth, that "charity begins at home", that it is paying too clearly for consolidation of the Empire, and that "the game is not worth the candle"?

But let us examine more closely the working of a Preferential system. That system involves, not only the raising of Revenue by new methods, but the raising of Revenue, and more of it, in a very wasteful and improvident manner. Let us, for the sake of example, suppose that by imposing a 5% tax on all foreign grain we raise 10 millions of money. But that won't represent the burthen on the consumer. The inevitable result of differentiation in taxation is to raise the price of the commodity wherever it is produced, that is, the price of grain grown in the United Kingdom and Colonies equally with that of the grain imported from foreign countries. The price of all grain will be raised, though it may not be to the full extent of the tax. Assuming that the foreign grain represents two-thirds of the total grain consumed here, the price to the consumer would be enhanced by 15 millions, or, allowing for the effect of competition, by say 14 millions, whereas 10 millions only would reach the Exchequer. Therefore, 4 or 5 millions more is taken out of the pockets of the consumers than goes to the credit of the Exchequer. Can anything be more wasteful or needlessly burthensome?

Let us follow up still further the working of the Preferential system. I assume that the whole of the 10 millions raised by the tax on grain are devoted to the payment of specific services, say old Age Pensions. We are at once landed in a dilemma. If, on the one hand, the Preference extended to the Colonies leads to the desired result, namely, that more Colonial grain and less foreign grain arrives here, then gradually the untaxed article takes the place of the taxed article, and the Revenue which is calculated upon for the payment of Pensions gradually dwindles, while the Pension charge gradually grows. It is easy to imagine the disappearance of 4 or 5 millions of Revenue, which would have to be made good in some other way, say by the addition of 2d. in the £. to the Income Tax, thus entirely upsetting the composition of the fund on which the Pension charge was originally placed and disturbing gravely the calculations of the Chancellor of the Exchequer. If, on the other hand, the Preference extended to the Colonies leads to no change in the grain trade, then the object aimed at will have failed, and we shall have changed our Fiscal system, and also have mulcted the consumer, to no purpose.

One would imagine from what one reads and hears that everybody's hand is against us – that every foreign nation has designed the tariff which will expressly impede and even shut out the arrival of British goods; but, as a matter of fact, not a single country has aimed its Protective tariff against us, and so far from succeeding in shutting our goods out we do an enormous business with them, and they do an enormous business with us. By adopting a system which favours our Colonies, we are, so far as that system succeeds, choking off our best and most numerous customers and trying to attract a much smaller set of less good customers in time, but they cannot possibly grow at the rate at which the rest of the world grows, and one cannot bear too constantly in mind that International trade is barter, and the more they send to us, the more they must take from us.

It is no doubt a most attractive idea that we should do more business with our own kith and kin. But, suppose that, in return for favouring their goods, the Colonies reduced their tariff in our favour and we succeed in introducing our manufactures into the Colonies in much greater quantities, what guarantee can we have that they will not be crying out about being made a "dumping-ground" for British goods, or complain of being hampered about raising Revenue? For, it must be remembered that the reason why Colonies have tariffs is not only to protect their own nascent industries, but because the tariffs afford the only means of raising Revenue in poor countries.

Having regard to these very grave considerations, can it be said that the uncertain political and sentimental advantages outweigh the certain economic and practical disadvantages? On the contrary, the Preferential system, grand though it may be in idea, seems to be fraught with danger to the Empire: – It may imperil its trade, hamper its finance, lead to strained relations with foreign countries, drag Colonial questions into Party politics, and increase the difficulty of the struggle for life with the poorest classes of the community, as well as hinder the prosperity of the mother-country as a whole.

[signed] EWH
[E.W. Hamilton]
6 June 1903

15 MOST-FAVOURED-NATION TREATIES v. RETALIATION*

Author Unknown

There is a wide-spread belief in the existence of a settled policy of active hostility on the part of foreign nations against British trade, which is held to call for reprisals on our part.

This belief is, however, quite at variance with the facts. There are, of course, many obstacles to the free exchange of commodities between various nations. Even we, who have made a special point of removing such barriers, have found it necessary, for the purposes of revenue, to maintain certain customs duties, which constitute a serious burden on particular branches of international trade. Other nations, taking a different view of the advantages of free exchange, aim at reserving a preference in their own markets for commodities which can be produced at home, and this they effect by the machinery of a "Tariff."

The fact that French brandy or American tobacco cannot freely enter the English market is, no doubt, prejudicial to the industries concerned in the production of those commodities. Further, when, as in the case of British manufactures entering France or the United States under a Tariff, there is also an untaxed home source of supply, the damage to the foreign trader is greater, since the artificial stimulus given to the home supply lessens the demand for the foreign product. But in neither case can the word "hostile" properly be applied to the attitude of the Governments in question. The protection of what they conceive to be the legitimate interests of their own subjects is clearly their first duty, and the incidental injury which the policy may inflict upon an outside person cannot correctly be described as an act of hostility.

"Hostility" may come in if unlike treatment is awarded in like cases. A country may open its markets fully to the products of all nations; it may close them absolutely; or, again, it may open them with such restrictions as it thinks proper: but, provided that the treatment is the same for all, none can be regarded as being actively attacked. The only real excuse for fiscal war is the infraction of this principle of equality of access, and "retaliation" may, in such cases, be applied by an aggrieved party against the products of the offender, and, as a consequence, in favour of those of other nations.

The loss of wealth to both parties which is occasioned by such conflicts is most serious, and in many cases the trades affected never recover. But, like other wars, they are occasionally unavoidable.

It is not, however, retaliation of this kind that we are asked to undertake. True, complaints have been made that certain foreign countries – notably, Portugal, the United States, and Russia – grant favours to imports from

---

* Author unknown, "Most-Favoured-Nation Treaties v. Retaliation", Confidential Cabinet Paper (29 August 1903), PRO, Cab. 37/66/56, pp 1–7.

other countries which are denied to those from the United Kingdom. If, and in so far as, such complaints have serious foundation, the adoption of fiscal reprisals might be justifiable. But the grievance ought to be a substantial one before such methods can be thought of, regard being had in general to the excessive damage invariably entailed by fiscal wars upon both parties, and in particular to the peculiar disadvantages – shortly to be explained – to which we should be subject in conducting warfare of this character, owing to the nature of our trade.

But, so far from the grievance being a substantial one, an examination of the facts shows that it is practically non-existent. Our own policy is the most liberal in the world and no Power has anything to gain from us by fighting. Under the "most-favoured-nation" Treaties we can send our goods into any market upon as favourable terms as any other foreign goods of the same description can be sent into that market.[1]

It is thus generally true that we obtain from all nations without bargaining all that other nations can hope to gain from each other by the most successful bargaining. The Tariff which is designed to obtain concessions from a neighbour is necessarily not put into force against us as we have already conceded everything that could be asked.

Hostile Tariffs in fact do exist; most nations have a "maximum" Tariff for fiscal foes and a "minimum" for fiscal friends. We belong to the latter category. A declaration of war will transfer us to the former.

So much for hostile Tariffs proper. There are, however, Tariffs in almost all countries – the Revenue and Protective Tariffs already referred to – which do in fact seriously hamper our trade, and which it would be to our interest to have removed. Can this be done by a process of bargaining? To answer this question we must look more closely at the nature of the Tariffs in question.

1. *Revenue Tariffs* are peculiarly susceptible to arrangements of this character. Taxes on articles not produced at home can be modified without seriously damaging any vested interest. We are at the present moment, without any change in our fiscal policy, in a position to offer concessions as regards wine to France, sugar to Germany, or tobacco to America, in return for any benefits which these countries might be disposed to confer on us in exchange. Further, it is a most significant fact that even when we had a general Tariff it was upon such articles and not upon the protective items that concessions were asked for. In this field there is an opening for negotiation and possibly in the last resort for retaliation.

2. *Protective Tariffs.* As regards duties intended to protect the home producer the case is entirely different. The protection of the home market is a settled policy with most foreign nations, and we shall not induce them to abandon it by duties on their products which will damage us more than they damage them. In other words the primary object of the duties we are asked to attack is to protect the home producer not to damage the foreign

producer or to obtain concessions from a foreign Government, and the home producer thus protected will not consent to forego his protection at home for the sake of advantages (most probably to another producer) in a foreign market.

The history of recent fiscal negotiations goes to show that a protective country is prepared, for a *quid pro quo*, to reduce any duty which it thinks it to be to its own interest to reduce. No doubt such reductions are postponed with a view to obtaining concessions in return, but where there is nothing to be asked in return they are not likely to be postponed.

The object for which we are asked to embark on a series of Tariff wars is very different. By denying or threatening to deny our free market to the goods of foreign countries we are to try to force those countries to free their protected market to our goods, or in other words to modify, if not to abandon, their protectionist policy.

For two nations to be in a position to make reciprocity arrangements each must have something up its sleeve and that something must be something which it is prepared to give away. At the present moment neither Great Britain nor her rivals, *vis-à-vis* with Great Britain, have anything substantial which answers to this description. We grant the foreigner complete equality in our markets; he grants us as favourable treatment, as he is prepared to grant to any one. Each might, of course, withdraw a portion of these favours and then make a solemn parade of regranting them as mutual concessions; or we might even at the end of the process get all we at present get by granting only a part of what we already grant. In the former alternative we should be left in the end precisely where we were in the beginning but permanently impaired by the struggle; in the latter we should have embodied certain elements of "Protection" on our fiscal system – a step which we are perfectly at liberty to take if we choose without the fuss of fighting.

Such would be the probable outcome of a policy of Tariff warfare. Most Tariff wars have in the past ended in almost exactly the *status quo ante bellum*. (*e.g.*, the Franco-Swiss Tariff War in the nineties), and a more successful issue to a contest which would appear to foreign nations as one to capture their markets and destroy their home industries, and therefore a question of national existence, is scarcely to be hoped for.

Nor are we in a favourable position for such a fight. To some countries foreign trade is of the nature of a luxury, to us it is a necessity, and our export trade is more vulnerable than that of any of our rivals.

Suppose we start operations against the United States. Here, if anywhere, we ought to be on strong ground as we have a trade of 127 millions on which to operate, while only 43 millions of our exports are liable to their direct attack.

But are we to impose a differential duty on raw cotton, food-stuffs or petroleum? The result would be either partially to exclude the American products from our market and to raise the price of the whole of our supplies by the amount of such duty, or to exclude the American products altogether. Even in the latter case a considerable rise in price must follow. We should thus be burdening our industries to provide bounties for Indian, Argentine, and Russian producers, while the Americans (though to some extent deprived of our market) would be able to pour their products into the vacuum caused in other markets through the natural supplies of those markets being artificially attracted to Great Britain. We should have diverted and disarranged the course of the trade – principally at our own expense.

Of the three, petroleum is perhaps the least unpromising, but here to differentiate against America is to give a bounty to Russia who is said to deserve of us very little, if any, better than the United States.

The truth is that food-stuffs and raw materials do not lend themselves to retaliation. The raw produce of any particular country has not as a rule any clearly recognisable peculiarity, and it is not limited to a particular market. The former characteristic makes it impossible to exclude it – you can only send it by a more round-about route at your own expense – while the latter makes the closing of a particular market less important, especially if such closing is accompanied by a shifting of the demand to other markets. About 107 out of the 127 millions of imports from the United States belong to this category, and are thus practically invulnerable.

The case of Russia is even more striking. Of our total imports from that country, in value about 26 millions, food-stuffs and raw materials amount to at least 23 millions, while of the remaining 3 millions (including more than $1\frac{1}{2}$ millions of flax) consist principally of articles in a comparatively elementary stage of manufacture.

If retaliation is to be practised we must turn our attention to manufactured articles – and indeed to finished manufactured articles, since to the partially manufactured the same arguments will apply as to raw materials – and the weakness of our position becomes immediately apparent. To the United States we send 20 millions of our own manufactures, exclusive of ships, as well as 20 millions of foreign and colonial goods in transit which could readily be diverted to another route by a hostile attack, while the British manufactured goods imported into Russia in 1902 exceeded 6 millions. Thus, even under present conditions, our assailable trade in these protected markets is greater in volume than their assailable trade in our markets. In other words, in fighting the two Powers which treat us worst, we stand to lose more from the destruction of the trade than they do.

Further, discrimination between various foreign countries, not because they discriminate between us and other foreign countries, but simply on the ground that they discriminate in favour of the home as against the foreign producer, would be regarded by the Power discriminated against as a wanton act of aggression, and as we should no longer be giving them most-favoured-nation treatment they would undoubtedly withdraw it from us forthwith.

Retaliation is a game at which two can play, and not only can the foreigner meet an attack by striking at our manufactured goods: he can in the last resort close his ports to, or levy differential duties upon, our shipping. As the great carrying Power of the world it is vital that we should be on friendly terms with our clients, and a fiscal rival could strike a more sure and deadly blow at our carrying industry than any we are in a position to inflict upon his commerce. The state of warfare which resulted would be more detrimental to our interests than his, and it is most unlikely that any breach would be effected in the protective Tariffs of our foreign rivals.

Retaliation without discrimination as between different Powers is not properly speaking retaliation at all – it is mere protection of home industries, and as such it is rather beyond the scope of the present Memorandum. Such protection might, of course, be adopted without our forfeiting most-favoured-nation treatment in other Protectionist countries. That adoption of this policy on our part would inflict injury on certain foreign industries is beyond question, but to expect that the hope of getting it reversed would induce foreign nations on their part to abandon a policy which we had just done them the compliment of copying would be unduly sanguine.

Protection of home manufactures may be a good thing or a bad thing in itself – to Great Britain it would be a fatal thing – but as a weapon for fighting hostile Tariffs abroad it is valueless. A protective duty may be put on for "diplomatic" purposes, but once imposed it creates a vested interest, and becomes practically irremovable, thus ceasing to be a diplomatic asset. Our commercial rivals know this much better than we do, and they are likely to estimate the value of our professions accordingly.

Note

1   There are indeed a few qualifications to this, but the Return prepared by the Board of Trade shows that the particulars in which we do not in fact actually obtain most-favoured-nation treatment are absolutely unimportant.

   Another complaint that is sometimes heard, viz., that most-favoured-nation treatment, while awarded in form, is denied in practice by giving concessions to other nations in respect of articles we do not export while maintaining high duties upon those we do export, is equally unsubstantial. Protectionist countries are naturally more willing to make concessions to raw materials than to manufactured goods. We fail to profit by these concessions because we are not large exporters of raw material. Instances have yet to be produced of favour shown to other foreign manufactures to the detriment of ours.

16 PREFERENTIAL TARIFFS*

Charles Thompson Ritchie

The Cabinet is placed in a position of extreme difficulty in being asked to come to a decision on the proposed fiscal changes without having before it a definite scheme. It is said that we are only asked at present to come to a decision on the principle of the proposed changes, and that, if an affirmative decision is given by the Cabinet and the country, the details of the scheme by which effect can be given to the principle will be a matter of discussion and settlement afterwards.

In a matter of such grave moment, however, before we are asked to decide on the principle, should it not have been explained to us what exactly is the plan, and how it is proposed to give effect to it? The necessity for this is amply shown by what has already occurred. Originally old age pensions were to form an important part of the proposal. I understand that has now been abandoned. A tax of 4*s.* or 5*s.* a quarter on corn and a corresponding duty on meat, &c., was suggested. This, I understand, has been considerably modified. It was also not denied that food would be raised in price by the scheme, but it was asserted that the people would be compensated by increased wages. We are now told that the cost of living, as a whole, will not be raised by the plan to be proposed.

I might refer to other changes which have been made since the discussion began, but I do not wish to insist upon the production of the plan in full detail merely because of the changes that have taken place in such particulars as have been already shadowed forth. We ought to know the plan, because it may turn out that however attractive the principle may seem to be in vague outline, it may prove impossible in practice to devise any scheme for carrying it out which would not involve us in insurmountable difficulties. I contend, therefore, that we ought to be made acquainted, not only with the scheme, but with its full details, before we are asked to take so vitally important a step as to assent to a principle, the effect of which would be to reverse the fiscal policy of the past sixty years, which has been so vastly beneficial to this country.

In the absence of a scheme, I shall assume that it involves (1) taxation of bread, meat, and dairy produce (but that it is claimed that the cost of living to the labouring classes will not thereby be increased), and that the new taxation is to be used for the purpose of giving preference to those Colonies who will accord a preference to our exports to them; and that (2) we are to be provided with some means by which we can bring pressure upon foreign countries to reduce their tariffs in our favour; further (3), that, in the event of any attempt on the part of foreign Governments, either to

* Charles Thompson Ritchie (Chancellor of the Exchequer), "Preferential Tariffs", Confidential Cabinet Paper (9 September 1903), PRO, Cab. 37/66/58, pp. 1–9.

penalize our Colonies for any preference they may give us, or to destroy any of our industries by what is called "dumping," we will adopt measures of commercial war against those Governments.

With regard to this last proposal (3), I think all the Cabinet will be, to a great extent, in agreement. We could not acquiesce in our Colonies being punished for their friendly attitude to the mother country. To do so would be a huge political mistake; but while they retain entire fiscal freedom, it is somewhat difficult to assume responsibility for their action, and the particular steps which we might find it advisable to take would greatly depend on the particular circumstances of each case. Tariff retaliation is not the only, and might not be the most effective, means of reprisal. So with regard to "dumping," if a deliberate attempt were made by any Power to destroy by means of that kind an important industry of ours, it would certainly justify reprisals; and if the attack promised to be successful, we might be compelled to take action. But it is worth remembering that this is a game at which foreign countries have burnt their fingers before now. In one very important case of bounty-fed competition – the case of merchant shipping – our unsubsidized trade has met the attack pretty fairly. Again, "dumping," while, of course, it benefits the whole body of consumers, is by no means altogether disadvantageous even to producers as such; it certainly often opens fields of remunerative employment which would otherwise be closed – e.g., cheap iron and steel have, beyond doubt, recently enabled us to compete advantageously in the trade for finished iron and steel goods, not merely in neutral markets, but, I believe, even in the German home market, to the loudly-expressed dissatisfaction of the German manufacturers themselves. Again, import duties in this country can do little to protect against "dumping" any trade that depends largely on exports, for it makes little difference to the exporter in this country whether the "dumping" takes place here or in the markets to which he exports. All I would insist upon in connection with colonial penalization and "dumping" is that each case should be dealt with as it arises, rather than that an attempt should be made to deal with the matter by general legislation, at least for the present.

With regard to (2) – the bringing pressure on foreign countries to reduce their tariffs – the matter is much more serious, and we ought to know how it is proposed to proceed. Is Parliament to be asked to place in the hands of the Government general powers to be exercised as they may think fit? I put this aside as quite impracticable.

Is it proposed to ask Parliament to impose a general import duty on all goods coming from foreign countries with a view of placing us in a position to remit the duty on goods coming from countries with which we are able by negotiation to secure a reduction in their Tariffs on our goods?

Or is it proposed to ask Parliament in each case to pass legislation imposing specific duties on particular goods coming from particular countries?

327

All of us who know the House of Commons must recognize the extreme difficulty of getting such tariff legislation through Parliament. The House is rightly jealous of its fiscal control; and the difficulties would be infinitely multiplied if the duties proposed were protective in character, *i.e.*, were calculated by a stroke of the pen to put considerable profits in the pockets of particular people.

From another point of view the question whether the duties are to be protective is of great importance. There is something to be said for doing what we can in the way of negotiation with our existing duties, and perhaps with similar *bonâ fide* revenue duties. But the moment a duty is imposed that is protective in effect – even if it is not protective in intention – we shall be entering on a path on which it is difficult to stop, and, I believe, almost impossible to go back. We have already seen how the almost infinitesimal preference to home milling under the recent corn duty created in a single year a vested interest of a formidable kind.

Again, is there any hope that the proposed negotiations can be conducted without breaking up the most-favoured-nation system, which (with whatever exceptions) has surely been very beneficial to us on the whole? Has sufficient consideration been given to the exasperating interference with business which must accompany any system of discriminating duties and certificates of origin? Is any such system likely to be effective in practice? Moreover, tariff changes must cause inextricable confusion in the long-period contracts for the supply of goods, which play so large a part in modern business. And must not all such interferences with trade fall with especial severity on our shipping and transhipment business? Surely also a war of navigation dues would be likely to follow, and would hurt us much more than any other country. And, after all, what should we be likely to gain in return for all this disturbance of trade – all this hostility that would be created? Is it conceivable that countries which have recently and deliberately adopted a given scale of protective duties would so reduce their barriers as to secure for our manufactures such favourable entrance to their markets as to enable us to compete successfully with their own manufacturers? The system of a definite minimum Tariff such as that recently adopted by France, and to some extent copied by other countries, seems to make negotiations especially difficult just now. If, therefore, there is not a reasonable probability that we should get what we want, would it not be in the highest degree unwise for us to enter upon such a thorny path – which, say what you like, would be a path leading ultimately to protection pure and simple.

Can any instance be given of substantial advantage resulting from retaliatory tariffs? I greatly doubt it. If not, are we likely to succeed where others have failed? Surely the fact that our imports consist to so large an extent of food and raw materials puts us at a disadvantage. Further, failure would mean much more to us than to any country already possessing a protective tariff, and, for my part, I should not see this country entering on such a course without the utmost misgiving.

I now proceed to consider the proposal to tax corn, meat, and dairy produce, in order to give preference to the Colonies, without increasing the cost of living to the labouring classes.

When this proposal was first shadowed forth, the ideal, as I understood it, was to place on these articles a considerable duty, 4s. a-quarter on corn and a corresponding duty on meat and dairy produce. I now gather that a duty of 1s. 6d. per quarter on corn and a corresponding duty on meat and dairy produce is contemplated. This modification is, no doubt, from the consumer's point of view a considerable amelioration, but from the colonial and farming point of view it will not be so acceptable. It is not sufficient to stimulate production substantially either at home or in the Colonies, while it is open to all the objections, on principle, to which the higher scale of duty would be liable, and it would certainly be regarded by the favoured parties as the "thin end of the wedge" merely. On the face of it there would appear to be considerable inconsistency in a proposal to reimpose one year a duty of a somewhat similar amount to that which we had abandoned the previous year. This abandonment no doubt was mainly owing to my action, but it has been defended by the Prime Minister on more than one occasion.

Putting aside, however, these considerations, let us see what the effect of such a duty is likely to be on the Exchequer and on the consumer.

I assume for my argument that the price of home-grown and Colonial produce will be raised by the amount of the duty. I do not argue this here. It would unduly prolong this paper. It is a matter on which I know there is a difference of opinion, and I will take another opportunity of discussing it.

I also assume that, in order to carry out the policy of not raising the cost of the working-man's Budget, the new taxes on food are to be met by a reduction of the duty on other articles of consumption.

I have made the best calculation I can of the probable burden which the proposed duties will impose on the consumer and the probable revenue they will yield to the Exchequer. For this purpose I have assumed a duty of 2s. a-cwt. on meat, and an all round rate of 5 per cent. on dairy products and other food-stuffs as being the equivalent of 1s. 6d. a-quarter on wheat. There are ample data for calculating the increase of cost to the consumer, so far as imported food is concerned; but only a very rough estimate can be made in the case of home-grown food, owing to the imperfection of our statistics. I have made use of such figures as are available, but there are no reliable computations of our domestic supplies of such important articles as butter, cheese, and eggs. Consequently, no allowance is made for any increase in the cost of the home supplies of these articles in my estimate of the additional burden on the consumer, which is, in round figures, as follows: –

		£
On food from foreign countries	..	5,500,000
On food from British possessions	..	1,000,000
On home-grown food	.. ..	4,500,000
Total	.. .. ..	11,000,000

It would appear, therefore, that the proposed duties, while yielding a revenue of 5,500,000*l*. to the Exchequer will increase the cost of living to the consumers by 11,000,000*l*. In other words, for every pound which the Exchequer receives the consumer will pay, on a low estimate, at least 2*l*. That will be the result while our supplies continue to be drawn from the present sources. But, of course, the object of preference is to reduce the proportion of the supplies from foreign countries, and the more that policy succeeds, the less will be the Exchequer share.

How then is the consumer to be recouped the 11,000,000*l*., so that the cost of living may not be enhanced? I understand that this is to be effected by repealing or reducing as far as necessary the existing duties on tea, sugar, coffee, cocoa, &c.

The present yield of these duties may be taken to be, roundly: –

		£
Tea	.. ..	6,000,000
Sugar	.. ..	6,000,000
Coffee, &c., and dried fruits	.. ..	1,000,000
Total	.. .. ..	13,000,000

If we may regard ourselves as free to deal with the whole of these duties for this purpose, their amount is sufficient to provide for the necessary relief, even when some allowance is made for the fact that the cost of the preferential duties is under-estimated at 11,000,000*l*. But it must be borne in mind that of the 13,000,000*l*. yielded by the duties on tea, sugar, &c., no less than 8,000,000*l*. is the result of war taxation. Whenever it becomes possible, and for my part I hope it may soon be found possible, to effect a substantial reduction in our expenditure, the taxpayers have an overwhelming claim to relief in respect of these taxes which were imposed for the emergencies of war. So long as the taxes are imposed on the present articles, there need be no difficulty about recognizing the claim. But when once the taxes on tea and sugar have been replaced by preferential duties, there will be no possibility of giving such relief. When it is realized in the country that the proposal involves giving up temporary taxes, of which the burden might soon be reduced, and substituting for them taxes which must permanently add to the cost of the necessaries of life, I doubt if the change will be looked upon as one which does not add to the cost of living.

I will not labour the point, which every one can appreciate for himself – that tea is after all a luxury, though nearly a universal luxury; and that many people would not regard an increased consumption of tea as an unmixed blessing.

Then, from the point of view of the Exchequer the proposal involves giving up revenue to the amount of 11,000,000*l.*, and receiving new revenue of only 5,500,000*l.* How is the deficiency of 5,500,000*l.* to be made good?

I believe there has been an idea in some quarters that the loss of revenue can be made good by imposing duties on articles of foreign manufacture. As, however, such duties must increase the cost to the purchasers of such articles in this country by at least the amount of the duties, it is clear that the loss to the Exchequer would only be made good by inflicting further loss on the consumer. Is the Exchequer account, then, to be balanced by adding to direct taxation? The circumstances of the present time are certainly not propitious for the launching of any scheme which would entail adding 5,500,000*l.* to the income tax or any other direct tax.

On the contrary, I think direct taxation as well as indirect ought to be further reduced as soon as possible.

I do not overlook the possibility that reduction of expenditure might enable an additional charge of 5,500,000*l.* to be borne without increasing the present revenue from taxes. But that would be no answer to my argument; the taxpayers, especially in view of the heavy burdens they have borne in recent years, are entitled to the full benefit of any relief which can be obtained by reduction of expenditure. To deny them such relief is to add to their burdens just as much as if new taxes were imposed.

The fact is that preferential taxes of the kind proposed must take far more out of the pockets of the taxpayers than they bring into the Exchequer, and consequently the problem of so arranging them as to provide the necessary revenue without increasing the burden on the taxpayer is in its very nature insoluble.

Lastly, from the Imperial point of view, a system of Preferential Tariffs, such as now suggested, would, in my opinion, so far from being a bond of union, have the opposite tendency. The people of the United Kingdom could not but feel that, while they already bear practically the whole burden of defence, and give the Colonies free access to the best market in the world, the new scheme would impose a further burden upon the industry of the country generally, and especially upon the poorest consumers, in the direct interest of a section of the producers of the Colonies.

It can hardly be denied that this feeling might, under circumstances which are by no means improbable, cause, to say the least, very serious friction, and might easily arouse an anti-Imperial feeling (now almost wholly absent) among large sections of our people. Again, as between

331

the several Colonies, it is quite impossible (at any rate while raw materials are untaxed) to treat them at all equally. Indeed, it would very probably result that Colonies which treat our produce comparatively well would be less favourably treated than others which maintain strict protective duties against us; and so that which is intended to bind the Empire together might have an altogether different effect. The case of India would present special difficulties.

Generally also, if preference to us is to be given, not by reduction of duties in our favour, but by increase of duties against foreign countries, it seems clear that, while the result to the mother country would be insignificant, the development of the Colonies might be much hampered, and I greatly doubt whether, in their own interest, it is wise to encourage them still further in the policy of closing the door against trade.

There is the further question whether preferential treatment of Canadian exports would not seriously interfere with the friendly relations between Canada and the United States, and between the United States and this country, which it is of the most vital importance to maintain and strengthen.

I have carefully studied the papers which have been distributed, but I find nothing in them which alters the view which I originally took. On the contrary, they confirm me in the opinion which I have expressed, that there is nothing in the state of the country which calls for such a momentous change in its fiscal policy as that which is proposed. Nor is there anything in the attitude of our Colonies, as a whole, which shows that they propose to press preferential treatment upon us, or to offer to us anything in return at all equivalent to the sacrifice we should make in taxing bread and meat, which I believe will meet with the most determined opposition in the country, but without which preferential treatment is impossible.

C.T. RITCHIE.

September 9, 1903.

17 LETTER FROM JOSEPH CHAMBERLAIN TO ARTHUR BALFOUR*

Joseph Chamberlain

'Highbury, Birmingham: September 9, 1903.

'My dear Balfour, – In anticipation of the important Cabinet which is to meet on Monday, I have most carefully considered the present situation as it affects the Government, and also the great question of fiscal reform. When you, in replying to the deputation on the coal tax, and I in addressing my constitutents at Birmingham, called attention to the changes that had taken place in our commercial position during the last fifty years, and suggested an inquiry into the subject, I do not think that either of us intended to provoke a purely party controversy.

'We raised, not for the first time, a question of the greatest national and Imperial importance in the hope that it would be discussed with a certain impartiality by both friends and opponents, and that the inquiry thus instituted might lead to conclusions accepted by a majority of the people of this country and represented accordingly in the results of the next general election.

'Whether our view was reasonable or not it was certainly not shared by the leaders of the Liberal party. From the first they scouted the idea that a system which was generally accepted in 1846 could possibly require any modification in 1903, and the whole resources of the party organisations were brought into play against any attempt to alter or even to inquire into the foundations of our existing fiscal policy.

'Meanwhile the advocates of reconsideration were at a great disadvantage owing to admitted differences of opinion in the Unionist party. The political organisations of the party were paralysed, and our opponents have had full possession of the field. They have placed in the forefront of their arguments their objections to the taxation of food, and even to any readjustment of the existing taxation with a view of securing the mutual advantage of ourselves and our colonies and the closer union of the different parts of the Empire.

'A somewhat unscrupulous use has been made of the old cry of the dear loaf, and in the absence of any full public discussion of the question, I recognise that serious prejudices have been created, and that while the people generally are alive to the danger of unrestricted competition on the part of those foreign countries that close their markets to us, while finding in our markets an outlet for their surplus production, they have not yet

---

* The Rt. Hon. Joseph Chamberlain, MP, 'Letter from the Rt. Hon. J. Chamberlain, MP to Arthur Balfour' (9 September 1903), in Arthur J. Balfour (ed.), *Fiscal Reform Speeches* . . . (London: Longmans, Green and Co., 1906), pp. 66–8.

appreciated the importance to our trade of colonial markets, nor the danger of losing them if we do not meet in some way their natural and patriotic desire for preferential trade. The result is that, for the present, at any rate, a preferential agreement with our colonies involving any new duty, however small, on articles of food hitherto untaxed, is, even if accompanied by a reduction of taxation on other articles of food of equally universal consumption, unacceptable to the majority in the constituencies.

'However much we may regret their decision, and however mistaken we may think it to be, no Government in a democratic country can ignore it.

'I feel, therefore, that as an immediate and practical policy the question of preference to the colonies cannot be pressed with any hope of success at the present time, though there is a very strong feeling in favour of the other branch of fiscal reform which would give a fuller discretion to the Government in negotiating with foreign countries for freer exchange of commodities, and would enable our representatives to retaliate if no concession were made to our just claims for greater reciprocity.

'If, as I believe, you share these views, it seems to me that you will be absolutely justified in adopting them as the policy of your Government, although it will necessarily involve some changes in its constitution.

'As Secretary of State for the Colonies during the last eight years I have been in a special sense the representative of the policy of closer union, which I firmly believe is equally necessary in the interests of the Colonies and of ourselves; and I believe that it is possible to-day, and may be impossible to-morrow, to make arrangements for such a union. I have had unexampled opportunities of watching the trend of events and of appreciating the feelings of our kinsmen beyond the seas. I stand, therefore, in a different position from any of my colleagues, and I think I should be justly blamed if I remained in office and thus formally accepted the exclusion from any political programme of so important a part of it.

'I think that with absolute loyalty to your Government and its general policy, and with no fear of embarrassing it in any way, I can best promote the cause I have at heart from outside, and I cannot but hope that in a perfectly independent position my arguments may be received with less prejudice than would attach to those of a party leader.

'Accordingly I suggest that you should limit the present policy of the Government to the assertion of our freedom in the case of all commercial relations with foreign countries, and that you should agree to my tendering my resignation of my present office to his Majesty and devoting myself to the work of explaining and popularising those principles of Imperial union which my experience has convinced me are essential to our future welfare and prosperity.

'Yours very sincerely,

'J. CHAMBERLAIN.'

18 LETTER TO JOSEPH CHAMBERLAIN*

Arthur J. Balfour

10 Downing Street, Whitehall, S.W.: Sept. 16, 1903.
My dear Chamberlain, – I did not answer your letter of the 9th, which I received shortly before my departure from Scotland for the Cabinet meeting, as I knew that we should within a few hours have an opportunity of talking over the important issues with which it deals. The reply, therefore, which I am now writing rather embodies the results of our conversations than adds to them anything which is new.

Agreeing as I do with you that the time has come when a change should be made in the fiscal canons by which we have bound ourselves in our commercial dealings with other Governments, it seems paradoxical indeed that you should leave the Cabinet at the same time that others of my colleagues are leaving it who disagree on this very point with us both. Yet I cannot but admit, however reluctantly, that there is some force in the arguments with which you support that course, based as they are upon your special and personal relation to that portion of the controversy which deals with colonial preference. You have done more than any man, living or dead, to bring home to the citizens of the Empire the consciousness of Imperial obligation, and the interdependence between the various fragments into which the Empire is geographically divided. I believe you to be right in holding that this interdependence should find expression in our commercial relations as well as in our political and military relations. I believe with you that closer fiscal union between the Mother Country and her colonies would be good for the trade of both, and that if such closer union could be established on fitting terms its advantages to both parties would increase as the years went on, and as the colonies grew in wealth and population.

If there ever has been any difference between us in connection with this matter it has only been with regard to the practicability of a proposal which would seem to require on the part of the colonies a limitation in the all-round development of a protective policy, and on the part of this country the establishment of a preference in favour of important colonial products. On the first of these requirements I say nothing; but if the second involves, as it almost certainly does, taxation, however light, upon foodstuffs, I am convinced with you that public opinion is not yet ripe for such an arrangement. The reasons may easily be found in past political battles and present political misrepresentations.

If, then, this branch of fiscal reform is not at present within the limits of

---

* Arthur J. Balfour, 'Letter to Joseph Chamberlain' (16 September 1903), in Arthur J. Balfour (ed.), *Fiscal Reform Speeches* . . . (London: Longmans, Green and Co., 1906), pp. 69–70.

practical politics, you are surely right in your advice not to treat it as indissolubly connected with that other branch of fiscal reform to which we both attach importance, and which we believe the country is prepared to consider without prejudice. I feel, however, deeply concerned that you should regard this conclusion, however well founded, as one which makes it difficult for you in your very special circumstances to remain a member of the Government. Yet I do not venture, in a matter so strictly personal, to raise any objection. If you think you can best serve the interests of Imperial unity, for which you have done so much, by pressing your views on colonial preference with the freedom which is possible in an independent position, but is hardly compatible with office, how can I criticise your determination? The loss to the Government is great indeed; but the gain to the cause you have at heart may be greater still. If so, what can I do but acquiesce? – Yours very sincerely,

ARTHUR JAMES BALFOUR.

P.S. – May I say with what gratification, both on personal and on public grounds, I learn that Mr. Austen Chamberlain is ready to remain a member of the Government? There could be no more conclusive evidence that in your judgment, as in mine, the exclusion of taxation on food from the party programme is, in existing circumstances, the course best fitted practically to further the cause of fiscal reform.

---

19 ECONOMIC NOTES ON INSULAR FREE TRADE*

Arthur J. Balfour

In the following Paper I propose to discuss some of the more fundamental economic questions which (as I think) require consideration on the part of those who desire to arrive at a sober and unprejudiced estimate of our fiscal policy. The present controversy has brought into existence, or at least into notice, masses of statistical information, official and unofficial; the documentary flood is rising, and for some time to come is not likely to diminish. But in order that the volume of facts thus provided should instruct and not merely overwhelm us, it is necessary to consider it in the light of theories and principles, always, of course, open to revision in the light of experience,

* Arthur J. Balfour, *Economic Notes on Insular Free Trade*, 5th impression (London: Longmans, Green and Co., 1903), pp. 3–32.

but without the provisional use of which experience itself can utter no intelligible oracles.

It may be as well to premise that I approach the subject from the free trade point of view: though the free trade is perhaps not always that which passes for orthodox in the House of Commons or on the platform. There is indeed a real danger of the controversy degenerating into an unprofitable battle of watch-words, behind which there is nothing deserving to be called independent reflection at all. Popular disputation insists on lables; and likes its labels old. It therefore divides the world, for purposes of fiscal controversy, into protectionists and free traders. Those who are protectionists are assumed to be protectionists after the manner of Lord George Bentinck. Those who are free traders are assumed to be free traders after the manner of Mr. Cobden. Does a man question the dogma that taxation must always be for revenue? Then evidently he hankers after the fiscal system of 1841 and a twenty-shilling duty on corn. Does he admire the tariff reforms of sixty years ago? Then evidently he regards the simple and unqualified doctrine of "free trade" as so fundamental in its character, so universal in its application, so capable of exact expression, that every conclusion to which it logically leads must be accepted without hesitation or reserve.

I am a "free trader," but not, it must be acknowledged precisely after this pattern.

I

1. That there may indeed be a collision between free trade and greater issues is easily seen if we reflect that an ideal world, from a narrowly economic point of view, would be one in which capital and labour would flow without hindrance to the places where profits were greatest and wages highest. Under the stress of economic forces they would immediately adjust themselves to a position of temporary equilibrium, as the ocean adjusts its level under the force of gravity. Such a system, were it possible, would certainly be one of "free trade" in the fullest sense of that much abused term, and under it the wealth-producing capacities of mankind would be all that free trade can make them.

2. But this perfect fluidity of capital and labour, however excellent its other consequences, would evidently be inconsistent with national life as we understand it. Nations could not be maintained, at least in their present shape, except through the accumulated effect of the various causes which in their sum total make up what may be called "economic friction," just as the continents on which they live are only prevented by cohesion and mechanical friction from merging in the ocean by which they are surrounded. It is because mankind are largely ruled by custom, are fond of home and country, cannot easily acquire new aptitudes and new languages,

cannot migrate without cost and risk, that labour is not "fluid." And though certain kinds of capital are really fluid, yet as a whole capital also is "viscous"; and partly because much of it is in a shape which cannot easily be moved or cannot be moved at all; partly because business channels are changed slowly and with difficulty; partly because, when the owner of the capital has to superintend its employment, he may, like other workers, be reluctant to change his home and his country, *it* also flows but gradually to the places where under a system of "free trade" as above described, it would find its most profitable employment.

3. Nations, as we know them, are therefore economically possible only because, for various reasons, mankind is both unable and unwilling to turn the natural resources of the world to the best economic account. It is the partial immobility of capital and labour to which this result is due, which makes it necessary for economists to distinguish between the theory of international, and the theory of internal trade. And though the "countries" which figure in economic treatises as the units between which international trade takes place, are not necessarily identical with the "countries" which are the subject of international law, the fact remains that these last, – the actual nations into which the world is parcelled out, – would never have come into being, and could never be maintained as they are, but at the cost of something which, from the point of view of pure free trade theory, must be regarded as economic waste. And inasmuch as they are thus a standing violation of cosmopolitan free trade (as above defined) it is not surprising that in their efforts at self-preservation they have not felt themselves bound to consider only arguments drawn from cosmopolitan economics. They have taken into account, not always wisely, something more than the present pecuniary interest of individual consumers and producers, they have recognised that the state is something more than the individuals composing it at any one time, and that not only is it irrational to suppose that what is good for the wealth-producing capacity of the world must necessarily be good for each particular state; but that quite certainly it is not.

4. This last proposition would have been accepted by Adam Smith; and so far as I know would be denied by no economist of repute. But there is nevertheless a widespread idea that what is economically "natural" as opposed to what is artificial or state contrived, is probably expedient, and that at least the burden of proof lies with those who take a different view. This theory, which belongs to a somewhat antiquated mode of thought, is I think incorrect. Each suggested example of state interference, in this or any other sphere of activity, has of course to make good its claim to acceptance. But it would be a most singular coincidence if (for example) every "natural" cause which promoted the easy flow of capital and labour from area to area, should also promote the interests of particular nations,

the number of whose population and the character of whose commerce are largely founded upon the partial immobility of these very partners in production.

5. There is no doubt a better argument against state intervention in matters of trade than any to be extracted from the *a priori* social theories so fashionable in the eighteenth century – an argument based on a deep-seated distrust of the competence of Legislatures. Adam Smith, for example, held much the same opinion of Kings and Parliaments as some persons do of doctors. He did not doubt that tonics might be found to invigorate national commerce, but he did most gravely doubt whether the authorised practitioners would find them. This however is hardly an assumption on which we can proceed in these days of Factory legislation, Housing legislation, compulsory Education, inspection of Mines, and Mercantile Marine Acts. Parliament can hardly assume its own incompetence as a fundamental axiom, however plausible this may appear as a working hypothesis. Having recognised the general truth that there is no pre-established harmony between economic world interests and national well-being, we seem required to abandon the "*laisser faire*" position as absolute dogma, and to accept provisionally the view that the character of our fiscal policy should vary with varying circumstances, and that we have no right whatever to regard any plan as perfect, merely because it is simple, unartificial, and, above all, familiar.

II

6. The plan we should adopt must evidently depend upon the end we wish to secure, upon the kind of state we desire to create or to maintain. Without considering the motives which have from time to time dominated the fiscal policy of other countries, it is only necessary here to say that so far as Great Britain is concerned, the contest which came to an end in 1846, was, in its inner reality, not a fight over an economic theory, but a struggle between two opposing ideals supported by two rival interests. Was the country to become more and more a manufacturing community? or was agriculture to be maintained, at whatever cost, in its ancient predominance, with all the social and economic consequences which were, or were thought to be, involved in such an attempt?

7. The country decided (in my opinion rightly) in favour of the first of these alternatives. Its benefits, to be sure, have not been unmixed; but it has this conclusive argument in its favour, – that a predominantly agricultural Britain could never have supported the men or furnished the money required for her imperial mission.

It must, however, be remembered that this "manufacturing ideal" can only be made tolerable, indeed can only be realised, if two conditions are satisfied: – (*a*) that inasmuch as conditions of climate render it obligatory to import many of our luxuries, and conditions of population and manufacture render it obligatory to import many of our necessaries, a large export trade is necessary in order that these things shall be paid for; (*b*) that sufficient capital shall always be forthcoming for *home investment* in order that this end may be attained, and employment provided for our growing urban population.

8. These corollaries which flow from the adoption of the manufacturing ideal in a country situated like Great Britain, suggested no anxious thought to fiscal reformers fifty or sixty years ago. They made, indeed, two mistakes, neither of which (as I shall show more in detail presently) would, perhaps, have greatly mattered without the other. They failed to foresee that the world would reject free trade, and they failed to take full account of the commercial possibilities of the British Empire. If they had been right on the first point, if free trade had indeed become a universal creed, no controversy about our commercial relations with any fiscally independent community could possibly have arisen. If, on the other hand, they had succeeded in giving us Imperial free trade, the protective tendencies of foreign nations would in the long run have been but of secondary importance. The double error has established insular free trade with its inevitable limitations, and left us bearing all the burden, but enjoying only half the advantages, which should attach to Empire.

9. It must, I think, be accounted a misfortune that the views of the great tariff reformers were thus restricted. The most momentous, perhaps the most permanent, victory for Free Trade was won when, rather on national than on economic grounds, inter-state tariffs were forbidden in the United States. I know not whether sixty years since a like victory might have been won for the same cause within the limits of the British Empire. In any case, the attempt was neither made nor dreamed of, and future efforts in that direction can, under altered conditions, be only gradual and tentative.

10. However this may be, we must now accept the fact that while our own free trade is rather insular than imperial, the most advanced of our commercial rivals are not only protectionist now, but in varying measure are going to remain so. Other nations have in the past accepted the principle of free trade; none have consistently adhered to it. Irrespective of race, of polity, and of material circumstances, every other fiscally independent community whose civilisation is of the western type has deliberately embraced, in theory, if not in practice, the protectionist system. Young countries and old countries, rich countries and poor countries, large countries and small countries, free countries and absolutist countries, all have been moved by the same arguments to adopt the same economic ideal. In circumstances so little foreseen we are driven to ask *whether a fiscal system*

suited to a free trade nation in a world of free traders, remains suited in every detail to a free trade nation in a world of protectionists.

III

11. As already stated, I approach this question as a free trader, *i.e.*, with the desire to promote free trade as far as contemporary circumstances permit. I throw no doubt on the free trade theory when expressed with due limitations. It tells us that international free trade promotes wealth, because it conduces to an international division of labour. Each country is enabled to turn its industrial capabilities to the best account; to purchase what it wants but cannot produce, or wants but cannot produce except at a relative disadvantage, by the export of those commodities for the production of which it is in a position of relative advantage. This system, therefore, tends to secure that each country does most what it does best, and buys what it needs at the least possible cost.

12. There can, I think, be no question that, speaking broadly, this is the best way of securing for the world the largest immediate results for international commerce and industry. It is by no means equally certain that it secures for each separate nation the maximum of well-being; nor even (under conceivable conditions respecting the flow of capital and labour) the maximum of wealth. Moreover, the majority of economists hold (I think rightly) that it may sometimes sacrifice the future to the present, and delay what might ultimately have proved to be the most productive distribution of capital and labour.

13. It is not, however, with these qualifications of the doctrine of universal free trade that we are now principally concerned. Our business is with the only free trade which we are ever likely to see; namely, free trade in some nations limited by protection in others. Of this partial free trade we may say in general, that its merits must be accepted with all the reserves already mentioned, and with this one in addition – that under conceivable circumstances free trade may not save a nation from suffering more by the adoption of a protective policy by its neighbours than do those neighbours themselves, nor even from being worse off than it would have been had it never pursued a free trade policy at all.

IV

14. In what way then can this take place, – what is the precise nature of the injury done to a free trade country by the adoption of protection by its neighbours? Presumably such a country bears its share in the general economic loss which the widespread adoption of a bad fiscal system inflicts on the world at large. Does it in addition suffer any special loss?

This is in other words to ask what is the special value to a free trade country of open markets. That our whole national policy implies their value is plain enough. We negotiate strenuously to maintain those that exist; there are some for which we should assuredly fight. It would be commonly admitted that the absorption by a protective nation of any rich non-protective area with which we had commercial dealings would produce not merely a temporary disturbance of our trade, but a sensible diminution of our permanent gains.

15. If this be true, it is of course because any check to our export trade is injurious. But why is it injurious? From the consumer's point of view, at least, it would seem that it is only what we import that matters. And in a sense that is so. But since the fortunes of the import trade are indissolubly united with those of the export, it may well happen that though the exporting manufacturer is the first to feel the pinch of hostile tariffs, it is the importing consumer who ultimately suffers.

16. Consider, for example, a simple case. Suppose that an island, which had shaped its industrial system on the Cobdenite model, found itself confronted by a world in which every other state adopted an extreme form of protection. What would be the consequence of such a situation to the island itself, and in a less degree to other countries? The answer to this question must, I conceive, vary according to the economic character-istics which we choose to attribute to our imaginary example.

17. Take for consideration three variations of the problem. Let us assume, in the first place, that the productive capacity of our imaginary island is small in amount, and restricted in range; and further, that it can neither grow nor manufacture anything which cannot, with the help of protection, be grown or manufactured at a profit in the protective coun-tries. In such circumstances I conceive that the fiscal policy of these countries would completely ruin it; and that they would suffer but little in the process. This case I may parenthetically observe is not unlike that of our own colony of St. Vincent where, according to the Commission of 1900, nothing could be produced but sugar, – sugar, which under the then prevailing system of bounties, could nowhere be sold except at a loss.

18. An economic area so situated is helpless. Having founded its indus-trial system on a free trade basis, having encouraged the growth of popula-tion and the investment of capital, in the belief that it could readily purchase what it needed by the sale of its exports, it discovers that, by no fault of its own, nor through any operation of nature, this sale is becoming more and more difficult; that only by the reduction of profits and wages can it be temporarily continued; and that finally it becomes impossible. Capital either flies to happier regions or is lost; labour either emigrates or sinks to savagery, and unless other help arrives our island

returns to the state of nature from which it had surely been better that it had never emerged.

19. This represents of course an extreme case of economic dependence. Let us now consider one of the opposite type. Assume that our imaginary island is of vast extent, enjoying consequently great varieties of climates, with a population small compared to its food-producing area, and with natural resources fitted to minister to all their needs. Such a country finding its exports gradually diminished by growing foreign tariffs, would, no doubt, suffer some economic loss. But it will be very differently situated from St. Vincent. Though it will have to manufacture at home much that it hitherto imported, though capital and labour would be diverted into channels which, at least for a time, would be less advantageous than those through which they had hitherto flowed, yet in the long run the condition of such a country would, I conceive, not be seriously worse than if it had been permitted by its neighbours to pursue its industrial development along free trade lines. Though the markets of the world might be closed to it by protection, its own would not be seriously insufficient. Domestic free trade would be enough.

V

20. But now take a third case. Let us assume our imaginary island to be rich in mineral resources, and adequately provided with capital and labour, but to possess no striking advantages over other areas, no natural monopoly in respect of the things it was best fitted to produce. Let us further suppose that owing to the law known to economists as that of "diminishing returns," it could not find food within its own limits for a growing population, except at rapidly increasing cost, and that therefore free trade and industrial expansion involved increasing dependence on external areas of food supply.

21. Now, what would happen to a country thus naturally endowed, and thus industrially organised, if it found itself confronted with a universal system of augmenting tariffs? As an economic example it stands between our first case and our second. Which does it most resemble?

It cannot be doubted, I think, that though it could never find itself in the position of St. Vincent, it would not only be incomparably worse off than the larger area of our second supposition, but worse off than it would have been had it never adopted the free trade policy, the advantage of which it has lost through the protective policy of its neighbour.

From the very nature of the case free trade requires open markets *somewhere*. If the free trade country is large enough and varied enough, the open markets within its own territory may, as we have just seen, be sufficient. They will not be sufficient if the character and capabilities of the

343

country are limited in such a way that, while large imports are a vital necessity, the exports required to pay for them are not of a kind which other nations – all, by hypothesis, protectionist – are obliged to take.

22. I imagine that in the conditions supposed, the free trade island would be compelled to change the character of its industries so as to find the weakest spot in the protective barrier. Each change would probably involve a double loss, – the loss of part of the capital and skill devoted to the abandoned industry, and the loss due to the fact that the new industry was presumably less remunerative than the old. Each change would also, by supposition, be sooner or later foiled by some corresponding augmentation of the hostile tariffs. When all was got out of this industrial re-arrangement which it was capable of giving, the free trade island would have no resource but to purchase its imports by lowering prices to the point at which it became possible to force its manufactures through the tariff obstacles by which its exports were impeded. If no diminution of profits or wages enabled such a point to be reached, the island would no longer be able to support its existing population; nor would any equilibrium be attained until, at the cost of much suffering, it was reduced to the position of being self-sufficient – producing that is to say, within its own area, all that it consumed – however little soil, climate, and mineral resources lent themselves to such a policy.

23. It may perhaps be objected that this imaginary case is not instructive even as a hypothesis, since the protective countries would never be so foolish as to injure their own export trade by impoverishing, and perhaps ruining, a good customer. They might do it in cases like St. Vincent where the amounts involved were small. But plain considerations of self-interest would seemingly forbid so suicidal a policy where the amounts involved were large.

But *are* the considerations of self-interest so plain? However sound be the economic doctrine on which they depend it is not one which easily appeals to protectionists. They would not be protectionists if it did. What they look to are the immediate and obvious consequences which are assumed to flow from high tariffs; and in the supposed case the obvious consequences are exactly what they desire. They would be so eminently satisfied with the successful "protection of Home Markets" and the weakening of a commercial competitor, that the more obscure causation of the counter-stroke which protection delivered against their own exporters would leave them unmoved. Here, indeed, if anywhere, the appeal to history should surely be conclusive. We have countless records of fiscal arrangements by which one nation has sought to benefit its commerce at the cost of another. Can a single example of the reverse process be produced? Has there ever been a nation which modified the commercial policy to which it was otherwise inclined, lest it should cripple the trade of a dangerous rival, who happened also to be an important customer? I trow not.[1]

VI

24. Among the three variations of our original supposition we are clearly most concerned with the last. The industrial characteristics with which in that case we credited our imaginary community, are precisely those actually possessed by Great Britain. Why then, it may be asked, does Great Britain not suffer all the ills with which our hypothetical island was threatened? That it does not is manifest. We imagined a free trade country completely environed by a wall of protection; a wall high enough to make export *first* difficult and *then* impossible. We inferred that it would find imports *first* costly, and *then* unattainable. In actual fact we see Britain hampered indeed by foreign tariffs, yet able, in spite of them, to carry on an export trade which, if it does not increase as we might wish, yet increases rather than diminishes, and an import trade of unexampled magnitude.

25. In what then resides the difference between the two cases? In three separate particulars.

(*a*) Foreign countries owe us a great deal of money, which they pay by means of imports into the United Kingdom.[2]

(*b*) Large areas still remain which are not protected at all.

(*c*) Existing protected areas are not completely protected.

It is these three causes, and these alone, which prevent this country undergoing the fate which, in the third example, befell the hypothetical island. Each, therefore, deserves careful consideration.

VII

26. As regards the national income from foreign investments, it has to be observed that while it must always be better for the inhabitants of any country to own capital than not to own it, it is better that the capital they own should be earning a profit at home, than that it should be earning the same profit abroad. If, indeed, there is no further room at home for the employment of capital, then, no doubt, it will be far better for all concerned that the overflow of wealth should be turned to account elsewhere than that it should run to waste. On the other hand, if capital which goes abroad might have increased the effective demand for British labour, its expatriation is *pro tanto* a loss to the labourer and the nation, if not to the capitalist himself.

27. Now it seems clear that in many cases this expatriation of capital can be, and is, encouraged by foreign protective tariffs. The imposition of a

protective duty upon any article of British manufacture has of course the double effect of discouraging its production here, and encouraging its production in the protectionist country – say Belgium. The popular free trade account of what happens in consequence is that, on the one hand, the English manufacturer and artisan are injured by the diversion of industry into some other, and presumably less profitable, branch of British industry; on the other, the Belgian consumer is mulcted in order to find a profit for the Belgian manufacturer. It is the latter, therefore, alone who profits by the transaction. All the rest are losers, though the British loss, so far as this particular industry is concerned, is confined to that part of it which supplied Belgium, and does not affect its success either in the home or in neutral markets.

28. But this is by no means what necessarily happens. It is assumed apparently that the British manufacturer adheres to his country and changes his business. But he may choose the other alternative. He may adhere to his business and (*quâ* manufacturer) change his country. He may transfer, that is to say, all that is transferable of his capital to Belgium; engage there, under the shield of protection, in the very industry from which foreign protection had driven him at home, and possibly compete not only in neutral but in British markets with his unprotected countrymen. It is, I think, manifest that if this should happen the fiscal arrangements of Belgium will have destroyed some invested British capital and some acquired British skill; will have directly injured the British workman and the Belgian consumer; will have directly benefited the British consumer; will have directly benefited the Belgian workmen and the English capitalist engaged in the Belgian industry; will have (if the capitalist continues to spend his profits at home) indirectly benefited England by increasing her foreign revenue; and will have indirectly injured her industries by giving them a subsidised rival. Without attempting to set out these various losses and gains in a national balance-sheet (which would, of course, show different results for each concrete case), it is, I think, plain that foreign investments of *this* description are by no means the unmixed benefit which some people appear to suppose.

29. We may, however, reasonably hope that the great bulk of our investments abroad are not of this character; but have been on the whole of advantage both to foreigners and to ourselves. It must not, however, be forgotten that the magnitude of these investments is due rather to the fact that we were first in the industrial field, than to the intrinsic merit of our fiscal system. Not every country which adopts free trade is destined to possess a large surplus of available capital, nor even to retain at home all the capital it requires for domestic use.

VIII

30. The second advantage which the actual Great Britain possesses over its hypothetical counterpart is to be found in the large portion of the earth's surface where protective tariffs are still, to all intents and purposes, unknown. These free trade areas consist either of countries which are protective in theory but not in practice, where the absence of manufactures makes importation an imperative though unwelcome need (*e.g.*, the States of South America and the small non-manufacturing States of Europe); or of countries whose tariff systems have, through historical circumstances, become more or less subject to international control (*e.g.*, Turkey and China); or of the Dependencies, Crown Colonies, and Protectorates of the British Empire.

31. Of the first it need only be said that so far they add to the neutral markets of the world not because they will, but because they must. They are not converts to the cult of free trade, though under the stress of necessity they obey its precepts. It rests not with us, but with circumstances depending upon the general movement of industry, and the character of their own internal resources, to determine how long they will thus remain fiscally "orthodox" against their wishes.

32. Our position in respect to the second and third class is very different. Here, it is neither the compulsion of economic need, nor the persuasive force of economic argument, which enables us to retain open markets for our manufactures. It is in the last resort on military power that our diplomatic rights in some of these regions, and our territorial rights in others, essentially depend. Without it they would ultimately lapse; and sooner or later these areas would become absorbed by one or other of the great protective powers, and their markets be lost to us for ever. When we reflect how necessary these are to the full success of insular free trade, and remember how in many cases they have been originally won, and how in all cases they are now maintained, I marvel that small armaments, small responsibilities, a small empire, and a large external trade should ever have been considered as harmonious elements in one political ideal.

33. If we look to the future of these various classes of non-protective areas there seems no probability of their increase; while industrial changes, political accidents, and international complications may at any time diminish them. The agricultural states who, if they had any manufactures to protect, would hasten to protect them, may in process of time become "industrialised." The expansion of the Empire has, broadly speaking, reached its limits. The countries whose markets are, by diplomatic arrangement, equally open to all the world, may, in whole or in part, fall under the control of some predominant protectionist Power. In many directions, therefore, there is a possibility of losing free trade territories. In none

does there seem any probability of gaining them; and it is therefore to the development of their wealth, not the increase of their size, that we must look for any improvement in the opportunities they offer to our enterprise.

IX

34. The third reason which prevents Britain from suffering the full penalty which might and would befall a free trade community in a completely protectionist world is that tariffs, even in the most protectionist countries, are not absolutely exclusive. In some of those countries, and for some of our main industries, indeed, no loophole is permitted. The barrier is impregnable. Bradford goods do not go to America, nor does bleach to Russia. Yet on the whole there is a large import into the protected area of the commercial world; protectionist nations and protectionist colonies are still our most important customers.

35. In order, however, to form an exact estimate of our industrial relation to those communities, we have to consider not merely what is, but what is to be. The tendency of trade, not its momentary position, is what chiefly concerns us. And this gives food for thought.

36. It is, I think, clear that our export trade, which should, other things remaining the same, have grown with our growth and with the yet more rapid growth of some of our customers, has, in fact, done neither one nor the other. Absolutely it may have increased, but its rate of increase has on the whole seriously diminished; in some important departments no increase is perceptible, in others there are symptoms of decay.

37. The cause of this is commonly set down to the "industrialisation" of the world. How, it is asked, can we expect to provide foreign nations with ever-increasing quantities of our manufactures, since they have learned, at our feet, so amply to provide for themselves? Britain had formerly an undisputed primacy in the industrial world; she has it no longer; she could not hope to have it. But, after all, the roots of this great change lie deep in the nature of things; why complain of the inevitable?

38. But this argument is wide of the mark. No complaint is made of the relative growth in wealth, population and prosperity of other nations. This ought, on the contrary, to be a matter of rejoicing. We might expect[3] on the free trade theory to gain, not to lose by it. It should increase, not diminish, the rate at which we get richer; and the tide of international commerce ought to flow, not merely without slackening, but in a volume proportionate to the growing numbers and wealth of the different populations to which it ministers.

If neither this nor anything like this is happening, it is not simply because "in the nature of things" and by the operation of some inevitable law it is impossible; but because it has been made impossible by the operation of hostile tariffs.[4] National industries have not been allowed to become mutually supplementary; they have been compelled to become mutually exclusive. Fiscal contrivances have forced them out of co-operative into competitive channels.[5]

39. That this is the true theory, on ordinary free trade principles, of what is now taking place, it seems to me impossible to deny. But there are two circumstances accompanying the diminishing rate of increase in our export trade by which some observers are greatly consoled.

They say, in the first place, that if we are losing our predominance in foreign markets, the home market is making corresponding gains. They say, in the second place, that if our staple industries are stationary or retrograde, this is more than made up for by the variety of goods we now manufacture for the foreign consumer. From neither circumstance can I derive much satisfaction. These are precisely the signs which would accompany the struggle of a free trade country so to modify its industries as to pierce the barrier of foreign tariffs. They are presumably, therefore, in part the consequences of protection. If so, the industrial changes in which they consist must surely involve an economic loss. It would be impossible to hold a version of the free trade theory so perverse as one which assumed that while any artificial diversion of industry due to home protection must necessarily be pernicious, the foreign protectionist accidentally confers upon us a benefit which we cannot confer upon ourselves!

X

40. A closer examination of the details of our export returns in no way allays the anxiety which theoretical considerations thus suggest. If we exclude coal from the sum of our exports, – still more if we also exclude machinery, – there are signs not only of a diminution relative to population, but of a diminution absolute.

Now what moral, if any, is to be drawn from this result?

I do not press the consideration that by exporting coal we are lessening our national assets – though this is both true and important. Nor yet do I think much illumination is thrown upon the subject by describing coal as "raw material." This is a phrase which easily lends itself to misconstruction; and if by raw material is meant material whose value is not due in any considerable measure to the expenditure of capital and labour, then coal is not raw material at all. Much labour and much capital has to be expended before what is stored in the seam becomes fit for the furnace.

41. It is not these considerations which make it desirable, in considering the condition of our export trade, to put coal, machinery, and ships in a class by themselves. The true ground of the distinction is to be found in the

fact that these commodities foster in an especial degree the competition of foreign protected manufactures. Though they may swell our exports now, they must therefore tend to diminish them hereafter; and we can hardly regard the very same phenomenon as at once an indication of prosperity and a cause of decline.

42. But why (it may be asked) is the export of coal and machinery more pernicious to the future of free trade than that of other British articles used abroad, either as instruments or materials in the production of tariff-protected goods?

43. In truth it is a matter of degree. And it may readily be admitted that in most cases foreign protection is but little assisted by these contributory exports. If we did not provide them others would, and almost as cheaply. They constitute, therefore, rather a symptom of the disease than an aggravation of it. Indeed, from one point of view the more we export the constituent elements of the protected manufacture, the less its protection injures us. If we imagine an extreme case in which *all* the constituent elements were exported, and nothing was left to the protectionist country but to fit them together, it is manifest that protection would be little more than a name.

When, however, our exports are of articles in the production of which we hold a privileged position, when they are necessary to the foreign protected manufacturer, and when their value is small compared with the total value of the final result to which they contribute, the case is different. Such exports do more than mark the development of protective tariffs; they add to their effect. And, therefore, it is that we may, or rather must, look otherwise upon coal and machinery than we do upon the manufactured and half-manufactured goods which constitute the rest of our outward-bound trade.

XI

44. If, then, an examination of the quantity and character of our exports to tariff-protected countries confirm the unsatisfactory conclusion which theory independently suggests, we have to ask ourselves whether there is reason to anticipate any improvement in the future. Are we to be permitted to take our fair share in the growing industrial labours of the world, and to reap our fair share of their reward; or is our position going to worsen relatively to that of other nations, or even to worsen absolutely?

45. I see no satisfactory symptoms. The highly developed industrial countries, like Germany, America, and France, give no sign of any wish to relax their protectionist system. The less developed protectionist communities, like Russia and some of our own self-governing colonies, are

busily occupied in building up protected interests within their borders – a process which is doubtless costly to them, but is not on that account the less injurious to us.

46. Nor has it, I think, been sufficiently noted that the injury in these cases is, or tends to become, a double one. The effect of any artificial stimulus to manufacturers in a country like the United States of America, or Russia, or Canada, is to ante-date the period when their food supplies will be required for internal consumption. Protection of manufactures diverts the supply of capital and labour from agriculture to manufactures. It diminishes the relative number of those who grow corn, and increases the relative number of those who eat it without growing it. To us, who not only wish to export manufactures but to import food or (if you prefer it) who have to export manufactures largely because we have to import food, this may become a serious matter; and in the interests of cheap bread, it is eminently desirable that the produce of the wheat-growing areas available for exportation should be kept at the highest possible level.

XII

47. So far I have only dealt with the injury inflicted on a free trade country by protectionist neighbours through the restriction of markets, the consequent loss of some of the capital and skill by which those markets were formerly supplied, and the diversion of industry into presumably less profitable channels. There is, however, another kind of injury which tariffs, working in alliance with modern methods of trade combination, may inflict upon national enterprise, on which something still requires to be said.

48. In the popular presentation of the free trade case, it is usually argued that howsoever differential tariffs may foster the protection of any articles intended for domestic consumption, the country imposing them cripples its power of competing, with that article, in outside markets. Clearly the manufacturer in the protectionist country (so runs the argument) can have no advantages apart from tariffs for the production for the home market of the protected article, otherwise protection would have been superfluous. His position, therefore, in the neutral markets would in any case be worse than that of the rival against whom he is protected. But it is still further worsened by the general operation of protection which raises the cost of living and therefore, it is urged, of production, in the protectionist country. From this it seemingly follows that the free trade manufacturer must always have a double advantage – one natural and one artificial – over his protected rival; so that his predominance is fully secured in neutral markets, and *a fortiori* in his own.

49. The argument is good as far as it goes, but it omits (among many other things) to notice the indirect effort of a contrivance which has only recently been adopted on any considerable scale.

Put shortly, the contrivance is this: In a trade where protective duties render outside interference in some industry (say steel) exceedingly difficult, the steel manufacturers combine to fix the home price at a level, which may vary from time to time, but is always well above the cost of production. So far the case does not differ from any other trade combination to raise prices, and protection only facilitates the operation by limiting to a single country the number of persons whose consent is necessary to make the combination effective.

Its further effects, those with which we are here alone concerned, show themselves only when the combination make the export of their protected manufactures play into their general scheme of profit-making.

50. Now there are three things which it is peculiarly difficult for a manufacturer or combination of manufacturers to do, and at the same time peculiarly desirable.

The first is to run their works evenly – that is to say, without undue pressure at one period, without dismissing workmen and leaving plant unused at another.

The second is to design their works on the scale which shall secure the greatest economy of production – which, in the language of political economy, shall take the utmost advantage of the "law of increasing returns."

The third is to secure a footing in foreign markets which are already occupied.

51. Now, in the attainment of all these objects, any manufacturer or combination of manufacturers who have, with the help of protection, obtained a command of their home market, are at an immense advantage compared with their rivals in a free trade country.

The unprotected manufacturer is compelled either to restrict his plant to a point well within what may sometimes be required of it, or, in ordinary times, to leave it partially idle. Even a small excess of supply may lower the price of his goods out of all proportion; and if it does, he not only loses heavily in respect to this small margin of over-production, but in respect of his whole output.

Now, there is no reason to expect that the plant erected to meet an average demand would reach the exact size most conducive to economy of manufacture. Should it prove to do so it could only be by accident. Neither is it practicable to arrange that the plant shall always be kept working full time. If it is, there must evidently be recurrent periods, during which over-production, with the consequent evils just described, must inevitably take place.

52. Such is the ordinary position of the manufacturer under free trade. Compare with it the position of his protected rival, who controls the home markets. *He* is not haunted by the fear of over-production. If the home demand slackens, compelling him, if he desires to maintain prices, to limit home supply, *he* is not driven, like his less-favoured brother, to attain this result by also limiting output. He is not obliged to close part of his works, or to dismiss some of his hands, or to run his machinery on half time. On the contrary, so long as other countries are good enough to offer him open markets, he can dispose of his surplus abroad, at prices no doubt lower, often very much lower, than the prices which his quasi-monopoly enables him to obtain at home, but at prices which nevertheless make the double transaction, domestic and foreign, remunerative as a whole.

53. Why, it may be asked, is no similar policy open to the manufacturer in a free trade country? Because free trade makes it difficult for him to obtain control of his home markets; and because, unless he has this control, it is difficult for him to fix two prices, a low foreign and a high domestic one. If he attempts it he will be undersold in the home market by his rivals, or even, if the divergence of price exceed the double cost of carriage, by himself! His own goods will be re-imported. He will become his own most dangerous competitor![6]

It is worthy of note that in theory it is not only possible that the foreign prices charged by the quasi-monopolist should be less than the home prices, but even that they should be less than the cost of production. And it has often been so in practice. German steel, for instance, has been sold in this country at a price for which no English manufacturer could produce it – or German manufacturer either, without the double aid of combination and protection.

54. But why (it may be asked) should any free trader object to such a proceeding? After all what it comes to is that the German consumer is amiable enough to make a handsome present to the British consumer and sometimes to the British manufacturer. Why should either the British consumer or the British manufacturer reject it? I was told the other day of a shipbuilder who was able to obtain contracts solely because he had secured a consignment of German steel at a price lower than it could possibly have cost either to a British or a German ironmaster. Why should we refuse to our shipping trade a bounty which the Germans are so generously anxious to confer?

55. The question is a pertinent one; yet I think the answer is conclusive. There is a utilitarian objection, as well as a sentimental one, to a form of competition which most persons would instinctively regard as unfair.

In the first place it disorganises industry. The manufacturing capitalist when investing his money in costly plant, has, in any case, many risks to run

– new discoveries, new inventions, new fashions. Add to these his loss, actual or anticipated, through the operation of foreign protection, and his burden becomes insensibly increased. But add yet again the further uncertainty and the further loss due to the system I have just been describing, and he is overweighted indeed. Will the hostile combination keep together long enough to ruin him? Can his credit stand the strain? Is it worth while holding on in the face of certain loss and possible ruin? These are questions which the leaders of the threatened industry cannot but ask. And surely the mere fact that they have to be asked must shatter that buoyant energy which is the very soul of successful enterprise.

56. This is serious; but this is not all. The "unprotected" manufacturer is not only attacked at home but abroad. He, perhaps, possesses what may be described as the "good will" of some neutral market. He has, in other words, a *clientèle* whom he has served well, and who, under ordinary conditions of trade, would never have deserted him. Suddenly, under the trust system, through no fault of his own, nor through any shortcoming of his staff or plant, he finds himself undersold. It is true that the power of underselling will last no longer than the ring whose monopoly has made it possible. It is also true that in some trades, though only in some, there is nothing so evanescent as these commercial conspiracies. Yet, however short-lived they may be, they have probably lasted long enough to destroy a valuable asset; and if his business survives at all, it will only be by slow and laborious stages that it can reconquer territory reft from it in a day by a tariff-protected combination.

XIII

57. I have now said enough to indicate the grounds of my difference with our commercial optimists. At first sight their case seems a good one. Judged by all available tests, both the total wealth and the diffused well-being of the country are greater than they have ever been. We are not only rich and prosperous in appearance, but also, I believe, in reality. I can find no evidence that we are "living on our capital," though in some respects we may be investing it badly. Why then, it is asked, do we trouble ourselves to disturb a system which has been so fruitful in happy results?

58. I will not take up the barren challenge contained in the last phrase, or add to the profitless and inconclusive dispute as to whether the growth in our prosperity is due to a good financial system, and the still greater growth in the recent prosperity of some other nation has been reached in spite of a bad one. The point to which I desire to direct attention is a different one. I ask the optimists to study tendencies – the dynamics not the statics of trade and manufactures. The ocean we are navigating is smooth enough, but where are we being driven by its tides? Does either theory or experience

provide any consolatory answer to this question? Consider some of the points on which I have commented in these notes: the injury which foreign protection is calculated to inflict on a free trade country; its need for open markets; the threatened contraction of existing free trade areas; the increasing severity of tariffs in protectionist areas; the building up of vested protected interests in new countries, which may be discouraged now, but not hereafter; the effect of this protection on our future corn supply; the uncertainty and loss which tariff-protected trusts are inflicting, and may hereafter inflict, upon British capital invested in Britain.

59. One and all of these evils, actual and prospective, are due to protection. The man who says that their cumulative effect is so small as to be negligible, can hardly describe himself as a "free trader" – at least he can attach but a very small value to free trade. The man who, admitting their reality, does not anticipate their increase has (it seems to me) not learned the lesson which theory and experience agree in teaching. The man who admits their present reality and the probability of their increase, and yet is too contentedly prosperous even to consider whether any mitigation is practicable, appears little short of reckless.

XIV

60. I cannot accept any of these positions. It seems to me clear that we are bound to seek for some mitigation; and that only in one direction can we hope to find it.

The source of all the difficulty being protective tariffs imposed by fiscally independent communities, it is plain that we can secure no concession in the direction of a freer exchange, except by negotiation, and that our negotiators can but appeal to self-interest or, in the case of our colonies, to self-interest and sentiment combined.

Now, on the free trade theory self-interest should have prevented these tariffs being originally imposed. But it did not; and if argument failed before powerful vested interests were created, it is hardly likely to be effective now.

The only alternative is to do to foreign nations what they always do to each other, and instead of appealing to economic theories in which they wholly disbelieve, to use fiscal inducements which they thoroughly understand. We, and we alone, among the nations are unable to employ this means of persuasion, not because in our hands it need be ineffectual, but because in obedience to "principle" we have deliberately thrown it away.

61. The "principle" to which we pay this strangely incongruous tribute is, of course, the principle of "free trade." But what a curious view of free trade it implies. The object which these fiscal inducements are intended to attain is increased free trade and nothing else; yet simply because the "fiscal

inducement" may, *if it fails of its effect but not otherwise*, involve duties not required for revenue purposes, or in certain cases even carry with it some element of protection to home industries, we are to turn away from it as from an accursed thing.

62. This seems to me, and has always seemed to me, extraordinarily foolish. It is certainly quite inconsistent with rational free trade. There is one, and only one, standard by which we can measure the free trade merits of any policy, and that is the degree to which it promotes free trade. This to be sure is as near a tautology as anything well can be, yet seemingly there are free traders to whom it presents itself as heresy, if not as paradox. They regard the maxim "thou shalt not tax except for revenue" not as the concise description of a fiscal ideal, but as a moral imperative of binding force. In their judgment it admits of no qualification or exception. It is, in school jargon, "universal" and "necessary," and could you prove to them that by risking the imposition of the most trifling protective tariff at home, it was possible to secure the greatest relaxation of protective tariffs abroad, they would only answer that we must not do evil that good may come of it!

63. This attitude of mind seems to me absurd. I hold myself to be in harmony with the true spirit of free trade when I plead for freedom to negotiate that freedom of exchange may be increased. This freedom to negotiate, like all other freedoms, may of course be abused. But are we therefore in a mood of irrational modesty to declare ourselves unfitted to enjoy it? I think myself that it ought not to be difficult to devise a method of turning it to most useful account. But were I proved to be wrong, my opinion on the fundamental question would remain unchanged. Where we fail others may succeed. It cannot be right for a country with free trade ideals to enter into competition with protectionist rivals, self-deprived of the only instrument by which their policy can conceivably be modified. The first and most essential object of our national efforts should be to get rid of the bonds in which we have gratuitously entangled ourselves. The precise manner in which we should use our regained liberty is an important, yet after all only a secondary issue. What is fundamental is that our liberty should be regained.

EXPORTS TO PROTECTED AND UNPROTECTED MARKETS OF ALL ARTICLES OF BRITISH PRODUCTION, EXCEPT COAL, MACHINERY, AND SHIPS.

I

Year.	All Countries.	Principal Protected Foreign Countries.	Principal Protected Colonies. (Victoria & Canada).	All other Countries and Colonies.	India.
VALUE.					
	Thousand £.	Thousand £.	Thousand £.	Thousand £.	Thousand £.
1880	205,423	87,124	11,498	106,801	29,278
1890	228,100	89,416	13,497	125,187	31,349
1900	224,364	80,906	12,879	130,579	27,784
1902	231,216	76,667	14,859	139,690	29,742
PERCENTAGE DISTRIBUTION.					
	Per Cent.	Per Cent.	Per Cent.	Per Cent.	Per Cent.
1880	100·0	42·4	5·6	52·0	14·3
1890	100·0	39·2	5·9	54·9	13·7
1900	100·0	36·1	5·7	58·2	12·4
1902	100·0	33·2	6·4	60·4	12·9

II

Year.	Value of	
	Exports of British Produce except Coal, Machinery, and Ships.	Ditto per head of Population.
	Thousand £.	£.
1881	215,277	6·2
1886	193,186	5·3
1891	213,270	5·6
1896	208,931	5·3
1901	222,726	5·4

NOTE. – The years selected are those for which the decennial census is in each case first available, and the years falling midway between them.

NOTES

1 It must be remembered that it need not be the protective policy of country B which *directly* and obviously makes it impossible for free trade country A to pay for B's exports. The direct cause might be protection in country C, through which A used to pay its debts to B, but can so pay no longer.

2 Under the first head I do not refer to freights or commissions. These it is more convenient to treat as payment, not for exported capital, but exported services. They should be classed with the payments for ordinary material exports, such as textiles or hardwares. At present we are concerned with the interest on foreign loans, and the profits on commercial undertakings abroad, paid to persons inhabiting this country.

3 Though not with absolute certainty.

4 The Board of Trade estimate the *ad valorem* equivalent of the duties levied on our principal exports to be – in the case of Russia, 130 per cent.; of the U.S.A., 72 per cent.; of Austria-Hungary, 32 per cent.; of France, 30 per cent.; of Italy, 27 per cent.; of Germany, 25 per cent.; of Canada, 16 per cent.; of Belgium, 13 per cent.; of New Zealand, 9 per cent.; of Australia, 7 per cent.; of the South African Customs Union, 6 per cent.

5 I do not, of course, mean that under a system of international free trade there would have been no competition between industrial nations; but only that there would have been much less competition and much more co-operation.

6 There are, indeed, exceptional cases, where, even in a free trade country, a monopoly can be established and where no re-importation is possible – certain shipping combinations provide a concrete illustration. Here no distinction can be drawn between free trade and protection.

---

20 MR. BALFOUR'S PAMPHLET: A REPLY*[1]

Harold Cox

Preface

The following pages had to be written at high pressure, and it is therefore possible that some words or phrases may have been used which appear unnecessarily harsh or even discourteous. If the reader should find any such, I hope he will accept my assurance that they are only due to the heat and to the hurry of the argument, and that no personal discourtesy has been intended either to Mr. Balfour or to any honest Protectionist.

H. C.

GRAY'S INN,
September, 1903.

It is alleged that on a famous occasion Mr. Gladstone banished political economy to the planet Saturn. Whether that allegation be true or false, it is

* Harold Cox, (Secretary of the Cobden Club), *Mr. Balfour's Pamphlet: A Reply*, 3rd impression (London: T. Fisher Unwin, 1903), pp. 2–16; 18–32.

certain that Mr. Balfour has derived his economic views from some equally distant planet. The pamphlet which he has issued to the world as a professed explanation of his opinions is founded entirely upon conjectures and suppositions, which have so little relation to the real facts of British life and British commerce, that it is hard to believe that the author is really an inhabitant of this planet and actually the Prime Minister of this country.

Indeed, it is charitable to suppose that Mr. Balfour in writing his pamphlet was compelled by pressure of other occupations to neglect altogether the ordinary sources of information with regard to terrestrial economics. For when, in the course of his argument, he ventures to depart from hypothetical cases and to appeal to facts, the statements he makes are, in at least five instances, untrue. That is a serious charge to make, but it will be proved up to the hilt in the following pages. No one of course believes that Mr. Balfour would deliberately state what he knows to be untrue, but the gulf between his statements and the facts is so wide that it is difficult on any theory to explain the discrepancy.

The following is a list of the more important misstatements made by Mr. Balfour. In order to understand the seriousness of this list it must be realised that the statements are made without reserve or exception, and are often rhetorically emphasised by repeated iteration. They are moreover the buttresses of supposed fact upon which the adjoining argument depends. They happen to be untrue – not merely inaccurate, but the direct reverse of truth.

> He clearly implies [p. 340] that at the time when England adopted Free Trade other nations were already Free Traders. *This is untrue.*
>
> He states [p. 340] that all Western nations, without exception, are Protectionists. *This is untrue.*
>
> He states [p. 342] that the commission of "1900" (*sic*) reported that the Island of St. Vincent could produce nothing but sugar. *This is untrue.*
>
> He states [p. 348] that no Bradford goods go to America. *This is untrue.*
>
> He states [p. 348] that no British bleach goes to Russia. *This is untrue.*

The above list does not include minor inaccuracies, nor does it include many statements which are fundamentally untrue, but which are made in somewhat vague language. The list is limited to definite and precise statements with which Mr. Balfour tries to support his abstract argument.

The apparent object of the pamphlet is to establish a proposition, and to present a demand. The proposition is that foreign protective tariffs injure Great Britain. The demand is that Great Britain should be endowed with the liberty of retaliating upon foreign protection. The first proposition is neither more nor less than a truism. No Free Trader has ever denied that foreign tariffs injure Great Britain. The injury is obvious and palpable. The whole of Mr. Balfour's laboured demonstration of this point is therefore waste of time and patience. Equally superfluous is his demand that Great

Britain should be endowed with liberty to retaliate. That liberty she already possesses. There is nothing whatever to prevent any Prime Minister from proposing a retaliatory tariff as soon as his own convictions are sufficiently settled to enable him to decide upon what country he wishes to retaliate and upon what articles his tariff is to fall. Indeed, Mr. Balfour's Government has already exercised this liberty of retaliation. The Sugar Bill of last Session was avowedly a retaliatory measure. It was directed not only against the money bounties which continental Governments pay, but also against the indirect bounties which continental producers are enabled to secure by forming a trust under the shadow of a protective tariff. This latter is the very evil of protection which Mr. Balfour specifies as his strongest argument for demanding the liberty to retaliate. Yet in the case of sugar he has already retaliated. Thus after thirty pages of print he arrives at a proposition which every man of common-sense, whether Free Trader or Protectionist, takes for granted, and formulates a demand for the creation of a liberty which already exists and which he has himself already exercised.

The Inner Purpose of the Pamphlet

Why, then, is it worth while to answer this pamphlet? For this reason, that Mr. Balfour, while professing only to lay down propositions which are innocuous because they are self evident, is in reality furnishing arguments to his Protectionist friends. The whole inner purpose of the pamphlet is to show that Free Trade, as practised in the United Kingdom, has been a failure, and the only practical conclusion which can be drawn from this argument is that we ought now to try Protection . . .

The Doctrine of *Laissez Faire*

The first point which calls for reply is in Clause 5 on page 6. Mr. Balfour here deals with the general doctrine of *laissez faire*, and he argues that because we have adopted factory legislation, compulsory education, and other interferences with individual liberty, therefore "we may accept provisionally the view that the character of our fiscal policy should vary with varying circumstances." It is a little surprising to find a man of Mr. Balfour's acute intelligence adopting as his own this familiar tag of the Protectionist rank and file. In order to make the argument logically valid it is necessary to prove that there is a direct connection between Factory Acts or Education Acts and Protective tariffs. A mere analogy is insufficient. The State forbids a man to take his bath in public, but even the author of the Birmingham leaflets would hardly argue that this establishes a *prima facie* case for an analogous law forbidding the public use of a pocket handkerchief. As a matter of fact, however, the examples which Mr. Balfour cites (with the single exception of Housing legislation) are not even analogous to the object at which he is aiming. Factory legislation, compulsory education, inspection of mines and mercantile marine Acts, all owe their existence to the principle that it is justifiable to limit the liberty of the individual for the advantage of the community. A Protective tariff, on the contrary, limits the liberty of the community for the benefit of a few favoured individuals. The only common feature of the two cases is the invocation of the power of the State. That is also an essential feature of the criminal law. Therefore Mr. Balfour's argument comes to this – that because the power of the State is daily invoked to prevent one man picking another man's pocket, it may also be invoked to assist one man to pick the pockets of many men and women, by giving him a legal right to extort a higher price for his goods than he otherwise would be able to obtain. This is the paradox to which Mr. Balfour's argument leads, and it is a fair specimen of his logical methods.

Early Free Traders and Foreign Tariffs

The second argument which Mr. Balfour employs has been culled like the first, and with equal carelessness, from the well-worn stock used by the commonplace Protectionist. For more than a generation Protectionists have been repeating one after the other, like parrots, the ridiculous tale that Free Trade was adopted in this country in the anticipation that all other countries would follow our example. Mr.Balfour adopts and expands this fiction. To quote his actual words [p. 340] the English Free Traders of fifty or sixty years ago "failed to foresee that the world would reject Free Trade." And again [p. 340–1]: "In circumstances so little foreseen we are driven to ask *whether a fiscal system suited to a Free Trade nation in a world of Free Traders remains suited in every detail to a Free Trade nation in a world of Protectionists*." (The italics are Mr. Balfour's.) If these passages mean anything at all they can only mean that at the time England adopted Free Trade, all the rest of the world was enjoying the same system. How this extraordinary delusion can have entered Mr. Balfour's head it is difficult to imagine. When England adopted Free Trade she was not surrounded by a world of Free Traders, but by a world of Protectionists. The Protection which France and Germany practise now is as nothing to the Protection which they maintained, not only at the time that we became Free Traders, but also for many years afterwards.

Cobden's Prophecy and Peel's Declaration

The important point, however, is that Great Britain adopted Free Trade, knowing that nearly all other countries were Protectionist, and having good reason to expect that they would remain so. It may be replied, But surely Cobden prophesised [*sic*] that other countries would become Free Traders. He did. He made that famous prophecy in January, 1846. But the final Free Trade victory had been won in December, 1845, when Peel decided to propose the abolition of the Corn Laws. Do modern Protectionists really believe that their great bogey man had such superhuman power, that he was able to bring about events by means of prophecies pronounced after the events had occurred? There is, as a matter of fact, not a tittle of evidence to show that the decision of England to adopt Free Trade was in the least influenced by the anticipation, or even by the hope, that other countries would follow her example. On the contrary, it can be proved conclusively that this decision was taken without regard to its effect on the policy of other countries. It is sufficient here to point to the great speech of Sir Robert Peel on January 27, 1846.[2] He then told the House of Commons that he had no guarantee to offer that other countries would follow our example. He went further. He admitted that our previous reforms had not produced any response from other countries. They continued to tax our goods although we had largely ceased to tax theirs. All this he admitted and emphasised, and then he proceeded to argue that it was our interest to open our ports regardless of the policy that other countries might pursue. Surely Mr. Balfour, who now stands in the place where Peel once stood, might have troubled to refer to Peel's own words before misrepresenting his work. That is enough to say about a myth that has already served as a substitute for argument to a whole generation of Protectionists.

An Imaginary Island

Two of Mr. Balfour's principal arguments have now been disposed of. We come next to an argument which has, at any rate, the merit of originality, and to which he devotes many pages. The argument begins with the statement that Free Trade will not "under conceivable circumstances" save a country "from being worse off than it would have been if it had never pursued a Free Trade policy at all" [p. 341].[3] This cryptic utterance is illustrated by an imaginary case of an island that "had founded its industrial system on a Free Trade basis," and "encouraged the growth of population and the investment of capital," only to discover that its industries were at the mercy of foreign Protectionists. From this imaginary island Mr. Balfour passes to the real island of Great Britain, and, after assuming that foreign countries are engaged in a deliberate conspiracy to destroy British industries, arrives at the conclusion that, if they succeed, "the island would no longer be able to support its existing population, nor would any equilibrium be attained until, at the cost of much suffering, it was reduced to the position of being self-sufficient" [p. 344].

This sounds very terrible, but what does it all mean? Let us deal with the real island first. If Mr. Balfour's pages [341] to [344] be examined carefully, it will be seen that he constantly confuses the real Free Trade system actually practised by Great Britain with the imaginary Free Trade system which he supposes the rest of the world at some unknown period to have

adopted. His assumption is that foreign Free Trade built up British industries. The assumption is absurd, for the simple reason that our principal
customers have never been at the best more than partial Free Traders, and
that only for a limited period. But even supposing that Mr. Balfour's fancy
were real, in what way would the position be improved by our adoption of
Protection? The terrible disaster pictured by Mr. Balfour is the reduction of
this island to the position of being self-sufficient through the action of
foreign Protectionists. But our adoption of Protection would only accel-
erate that end by doubling the barriers in the way of our foreign trade.
Indeed, most Protectionists advocate Protection because they want England to be self-sufficient. Mr. Balfour is able to see clearly that this
Protectionist ideal would be a national disaster, but while dreading the
goal he invites his country to follow the path that fatally leads to it.

The Legend of St. Vincent

Let us now turn to Mr. Balfour's imaginary island. This island is described
as being a small island unable to produce anything which the protective
countries do not produce for themselves with the aid of Protection. He
continues: –

> "In such circumstances I conceive that the fiscal policy of these
> countries would completely ruin it [the island]; and that they would
> suffer but little in the process. This case, I may parenthetically observe,
> is not unlike that of our own colony of St. Vincent, where, according to
> the Commission of 1900, nothing could be produced but sugar – sugar,
> which under the then prevailing system of bounties could nowhere be
> sold except at a loss."

The above statement illustrates, in a manner which the least intelligent
person will be able to understand, the extraordinary carelessness with
regard to facts which is one of the most unfortunate of Mr. Balfour's
characteristics. In the first place, the Commission to which he is obviously
referring, the West India Royal Commission, did not belong to the year
1900, but to the year 1897. But let that pass. The important point is that the
above-quoted statement with regard to the report of the Commission is
absolutely at variance with the real facts.

The Commission did not report that nothing could be produced but
sugar, nor is it true, as Mr. Balfour's statement implies, that the failure of the
St. Vincent sugar industry was due to the system of bounties. At the time
that the Commission reported, and for several years previously, the production of sugar was only one among several industries carried on in the
island of St. Vincent. In the appendix to their report the Commissioners
quote the following figures showing the exports from St. Vincent for the
year 1896: –

Collective Sugar Products £24,248
Subsidiary Products 33,188

Among these so-called subsidiary products arrowroot alone figures for £20,506, or nearly as much as all the sugar products put together. That is surely a sufficient answer to Mr. Balfour's statement that "according to the Commission nothing could be produced but sugar."

Equally misleading is his reference to the "then prevailing system of sugar bounties." It is true that the Commissioners reported that the sugar industry in St. Vincent was on the verge of extinction, but what was the reason they gave?

Here are their words: –

"§ 365. No improvements have been introduced in the manufacture of sugar, and the sugar canes have in recent years suffered very severely from disease, this disease being in all probability due, to some extent, to want of effective cultivation."

And again: –

"§ 372. We do not think that under the conditions that are likely to prevail in the future the production of sugar for export on a large scale could be permanently carried on in St. Vincent unless modern machinery were set up and the most approved processes of manufacture adopted."

These quotations are sufficient to show how completely Mr. Balfour has misrepresented the problem of the island of St. Vincent, as revealed by the report of the Royal Commission. The incident is of importance, not merely from the point of view of the influence his pamphlet may have on public opinion, but also as illustrating the kind of knowledge which guided his Government in framing the Sugar Bill of last Session. This Bill was avowedly intended for the relief of the West Indies. It was for the sake of the West Indies that British delegates were sent to the Brussels Conference; it was for the sake of the West Indies that the Government, in spite of the opposition of many of their supporters, forced the Bill through the House of Commons. Why did they thus press upon a reluctant Parliament a measure which can only benefit the West Indies by raising the price of sugar to the 41,000,000 inhabitants of the United Kingdom? They did it because they had been told, and apparently believed, that the West Indies would collapse altogether unless the owners of badly cultivated and ill-equipped sugar estates were endowed with additional profits at the expense of the people of Great Britain and Ireland. Their minds had been poisoned by the whispered mis-information of interested persons, and they refused to believe, or even probably to read, the report of their own Royal Commission. That is why the British nation now has to pay more than £7,000,000 a year for Mr. Balfour's first experiment in the policy of retaliation.

Hypothetical Ruin

We can now leave Mr. Balfour's imaginary island and this particular batch of imaginary facts. There are others to follow. After devoting three chapters to showing how "under conceivable circumstances" Great Britain might be reduced to a condition of self-sufficiency by a conspiracy of foreign nations to ruin her trade, he opens his sixth chapter [p. 345] by asking: –

"Why, then, is it that Great Britain does not suffer all the ills with which our hypothetical island was threatened? That it does not is manifest."

It is pleasant to find that Mr. Balfour is satisfied that Great Britain is not yet ruined. But having made this admission, it is clearly necessary for him to explain how the ruin which, according to his theory, ought to have befallen Great Britain, has somehow been avoided. His explanation is as follows: –

"(*a*) Foreign countries owe us a great deal of money, which they pay by means of imports into the United Kingdom.

"(*b*) Large areas still remain which are not protected at all.

"(*c*) Existing protected areas are not completely protected."

Those three points do not perhaps cover the whole ground quite so completely as Mr. Balfour seems to think, but it is not worth while here to enter into the close economic argument which a fuller consideration of the problem would involve. It is more important to see what Mr. Balfour makes of his three selected reasons.

He admits of course that it is an advantage to this country to possess investments abroad which bring in every year a handsome tribute of interest from those countries that are using our capital. He suggests, however, on page [345–6], that to some extent these investments may be due to the inducements which foreign Protection offers to British capital. There is undoubtedly some truth in this. British firms, finding their goods shut out by a foreign tariff, have established branch works within the ring fence of that tariff and continue to carry on a profitable business. Possibly Mr. Chamberlain could furnish Mr. Balfour with a practical example of this transference of British capital to foreign countries. That a transference of this character is injurious to British workmen nobody denies. But this evil of foreign Protection is in no way due to our practice of Free Trade, nor would it cease if we adopted Protection. Exactly the same process goes on, and upon a far larger scale, across the border between Canada and the United States, though both countries are Protectionist.

What Mr. Balfour fails to see is that while foreign Protection attracts some British capital, British Free Trade attracts other British capital and also capital from foreign countries. Why, for example, has the shipbuilding industry passed from the United States to the United Kingdom? No answer that meets all the facts can be given, except this, that in Great Britain all the materials employed in shipbuilding are free from taxation. Oh! but some Protectionist may reply, German shipbuilding is going ahead also, and Germany is a Protectionist country. Exactly! Germany is a Protectionist country, but as she wishes to develop a mercantile marine of her own she has had the good sense to abandon Protection absolutely so far as shipbuilding is concerned. Everything required by German shipbuilders is exempt from taxation. Even the cutlery and table linen that are placed on a transatlantic liner pay no duty. The German shipbuilding industry is, in fact, an admirable illustration of the way in which industries flourish under the influence of Free Trade . . .

An Extraordinary Blunder

Chapter IX. [p. 348] opens with the accurate statement that "tariffs, even in the most Protectionist countries are not absolutely exclusive." At this point Mr. Balfour seems to have reflected that perhaps he was admitting too much. He therefore pulls himself up, and proceeds to make the following qualification of what he had already written: –

"In some of those countries, and for some of our main industries indeed, no loophole is permitted. The barrier is impregnable. Bradford goods do not go to America, nor does bleach to Russia."

The average man, on reading this passage, would assume that of course the Prime Minister had taken pains to verify his facts, and that his assurance could be accepted without hesitation. The average man will therefore be surprised to learn that both the statements of fact contained in this sentence are absolutely untrue.

By Bradford goods Mr. Balfour evidently means woollen goods. If he had known anything of the woollen trade he would have known that America is one of the best markets for high-class woollens. Our woollen and worsted exports to America in 1902 were as follows: –

Yarns, woollen and worsted	£29,000
" alpaca, &c.	4,500
Tissues, woollen and worsted	1,481,000
	£1,514,500

So much for Mr. Balfour's "impregnable barrier" in the case of woollens. His statement with regard to bleach is equally remote from the truth. An examination of the last published "Annual Statement of Trade and Navigation" shows that Russia takes more British bleach than any other single country except the United States.[4]

After this unfortunate beginning, Mr. Balfour proceeds to consider what he calls the tendency of our export trade. He admits that our exports have

366

increased absolutely, but complains that they have not grown with our growth, nor with the yet more rapid growth of some of our customers. Assuming this complaint to be true, why does Mr. Balfour make it? The argument with which he sets out is, that exports are required to pay for imports [see p. 348]. He presses this point again and again, and insists on the danger to our imports if our export trade were destroyed. All this is perfectly legitimate as long as he confines himself to abstract argument. But when he comes to test his argument by facts, obviously the question he has to ask is not "Are our exports declining?" but, "Do our imports keep up?"

Mr. Balfour's Logic

Provided our imports do keep up, then the whole object for which exports exist is served, and there is no cause for further worry. Till recently the Protectionists would have replied by suggesting that we were living on our capital, and that British owners of American railway stock were generously parting with their scrip in order to buy foreign flour for our starving British poor. That ridiculous myth appears no longer to have currency even in Protectionist circles. Mr. Balfour emphatically dismisses it: "I can find no evidence that we are living on our capital" [p. 354]. If, then, we are not buying imports by selling capital, and if, nevertheless, imports continue to increase, clearly there is nothing left for Mr. Balfour to complain of. Why, then, does he complain? Because his whole economic argument has been twisted out of shape by the desire to say something that will give comfort to his Protectionist friends. It is this desire that leads him into logical as well as statistical absurdities.

Of his logical blunders an excellent illustration is to be found in the chapter we are now dealing with. After complaining that our exports have not grown with our growth, he goes on to examine the reply often made by Free Traders that other countries must inevitably, as time goes on, learn to manufacture for themselves. He answers as follows: –

"But this argument is wide of the mark. No complaint is made of the relative growth in wealth, population and prosperity of other nations. This ought on the contrary to be a matter of rejoicing. We might expect on the Free Trade theory to gain, not to lose by it. It should increase, not diminish, the rate at which we grow richer."

The "rate at which we grow richer"! ! ! Thus Mr. Balfour in his desire to be pleasant to Birmingham has actually adopted the vulgar Protectionist delusion that a nation grows rich by what it sends away. In defiance of all his previous argument "the rate at which we export" now becomes identical with "the rate at which we grow richer." Surely not in vain has Mr. Seddon lectured to His Majesty's ministers.

The same page contains the following curious footnote [note 5, p. 358] –

"I do not, of course, mean that under a system of international Free Trade there would have been no competition between industrial nations; but only that there would have been much less competition and much more co-operation."

What does this mean? International Free Trade could never be more complete than the Free Trade that exists between two countries of the United Kingdom or two States of the American Union. Does Mr. Balfour really imagine that competition only exists between manufacturers when they belong to different countries? Is he really unaware that the keenest competition, from which every manufacturer suffers, is the competition of the man in the same street?

On page [349] there is a phrase which it is important to notice. Mr. Balfour speaks of the struggles of a "Free Trade country" to pierce the barrier of foreign tariffs. In the same way on page [343] he says that "Free Trade requires open markets somewhere," and again on page [355] he speaks of the injury which foreign Protection is calculated "to inflict on a Free Trade country." These phrases must be slips of the pen, for it is extremely improbable that Mr. Balfour, in order to cast discredit upon Free Trade, would impute, to it alone, a weakness which equally belongs to Protection. Protectionist countries as well as Free Trade countries "require open markets somewhere," are injured by foreign Protection, and "try to pierce the barrier of foreign tariffs." Protectionist countries are, as a matter of fact, always negotiating with one another for the removal of the barriers which they respectively create, and the amusing feature of the situation is that whatever reciprocal concessions they may win from one another we as a Free Trade country at once enjoy by virtue of the most-favoured nation clause. But it is one of the curiosities of Mr. Balfour's pamphlet that he nowhere even mentions this important factor in our commercial relations with foreign countries.

Mr. Balfour's Statistics

In Chapter X. [p. 349] Mr. Balfour indulges himself in a dose of statistics. He cannot be congratulated on the result. Having adopted the Protectionist absurdity that the wealth of a country is measured by its exports, he wishes to justify by figures his contention that there is a tendency for our exports to decline. The figures of the Board of Trade do not quite bear out the case he wants to prove. He therefore deducts three of the most important items in our export trade – coal, machinery, and ships. His defence of these deductions is that: –

"The true ground of the distinction is to be found in the fact that these commodities foster in an especial degree the competition of foreign protected manufactures" [p. 349–50].

368

Let us leave the argument aside for a moment and look first at the facts. With regard to coal, the primary fact is that about half of all we export goes to feed the boilers of British ships.[5] This coal is sent to depôts at foreign ports, and British ships call to pick it up as they want it. In what way does this export "foster foreign manufactures"?

Next with regard to machinery! Mr. Balfour does not apparently know that machinery exports include agricultural steam engines and other agricultural machinery to the total value of £1,444,000. By the export of this machinery we are helping to develop the wheat-growing areas of the world – an object which on the very next page, in the course of another argument, Mr. Balfour declares to be "eminently desirable." Another large item in our machinery exports is locomotive engines – £2,299,000. These are probably employed to no small extent in dragging foreign or colonial wheat to the sea to be shipped to Great Britain. There is also a large item of £1,849,000 for "other steam engines," of which many would be for use in mines and at docks. Do these also "foster foreign maufactures"? Mining machinery proper accounts for £548,000, and there is an item of no less than £1,840,000 for sewing machines.

These items together account for more than a third of our total exports of machinery. So that even admitting Mr. Balfour's argument, he is only entitled to deduct two-thirds of our total export of machinery.

With regard to ships it is pertinent to compare his desire to limit the sale of ships to foreign purchasers, with the remarks which he makes in a footnote on [note 6, p. 358] as to the combinations formed by British shipowners. Surely one of the best ways of breaking down any ring of British shipowners is to permit foreigners to buy the best ships, namely British ships, and compete with the ring. The sea at any rate is open. However, the whole of his argument on this point is unsound. It is a mere repetition of the arguments that were used in the days when the export of British machinery was forbidden lest foreign manufacturers should benefit by the use of our inventions. Is Mr. Balfour prepared to revive this prohibition? If he really believes what he clearly states, that the export of coal, machinery, and ships is an injury to this country, it is his duty as Prime Minister to propose that the export of these commodities be entirely forbidden. Is that one of the proposals that is being prepared for the next Parliament?

Protection and Trusts

Of Chapter XI. nothing need be said except that Mr. Balfour appears to be ignorant of the fact that both in Germany and in the United States a powerful minority is in favour of Free Trade, and that even in France there is an appreciable Free Trade party.

Chapter XII. is devoted to describing in terms of envious admiration the system established by the trusts in the United States. According to Mr. Balfour, Protection has this glorious advantage, that it enables the protected manufacturers to form a ring for keeping up home prices and selling cheaply abroad. A delightful system that for the people who have to pay the home prices! But evidently it is the system that Mr. Balfour wants to establish here. He describes how this system enables the manufacturers "to run their works evenly – that is to say, without undue pressure at one period, and without dismissing workmen and leaving plant unused at another."

He apparently has never heard of the way in which American combines and trusts close down works and dismiss workmen by the thousand. He is so filled with admiration of the American system that he is blind to these little defects, and he appears to be seriously grieved because "no similar policy is open to manufacturers in a Free Trade country." The only disadvantage that Mr. Balfour can see in the Protectionist trust system is the fact that it enables and induces American and German manufacturers to assist British shipbuilders by giving them steel at less than the cost of production. He indignantly condemns this "as a form of competition which most persons would instinctively regard as unfair." He does not seem to know that such "unfair" competition has been part of commerce ever since the world began. If a man has goods on his hands and cannot find a purchaser for them at the price that they cost to produce, he will sell them for less, and wise men will seize the opportunity for making a bargain. The only new feature introduced by the Protectionist trust system is the regular practice of charging more to the home than to the foreign purchaser. This is the feature that appears to fascinate Mr. Balfour, but he is wrong in imagining that even this delightful system will guarantee the protected manufacturer against the vicissitudes of trade. The heavy fall in the value of the shares of the Steel Trust is an incident that might surely have arrested Mr. Balfour's attention when he was penning those pages.

A Certain Loss: A Problematic Gain

There remain only two chapters. These contain what, for want of a better word, we must call Mr. Balfour's "conclusions." He admits that "judged by all available tests, both the total wealth and the diffused well-being of the country are greater than they ever have been;" but he declares that there are dangers ahead against which we ought at once to guard. The remedy he advocates is the policy of retaliation. It is to this end that all his previous argument was intended to lead, and so far as any definite proposal can be extracted from his pamphlet at all, the proposal is that Great Britain should impose retaliatory tariffs upon foreign goods in order to force other countries to become Free Traders.

By way of commending this proposal to his Protectionist friends, some of whom would like something else, he elaborately mis-states the Free Trade case against it. He says, page [356]:–

"Could you prove to them that by risking the imposition of the most trifling Protective tariff at home it was possible to secure the greatest relaxation of Protective tariffs abroad, they would only answer, 'We must do no evil that good may come of it.'"

It is easy to score a dialectical victory by attributing to your opponents nonsense that they have never uttered. No Free Trader ever said that if you can "secure" a great Free Trade victory abroad by merely "risking" a small Free Trade loss at home, you ought not to do it. There is no man in the world who would not exchange the absolute certainty of a great gain for the mere risk of a small loss. But where is Mr. Balfour's certainty? Where is his "proof" that by risking Protection at home you can secure Free Trade abroad? From the very nature of the case no such proof is possible, and the real position of the Free Trader is that while the loss from retaliation is certain, the gain is at best problematic.

Of course, if we could frighten foreign countries by threats of retaliation which we did not intend to execute, well and good. But our foreign neighbours are not quite so foolish as to be taken in by that game. If retaliation is to be our policy, it must consist not merely of threats, but of executions. Parliament must authorise the imposition of some definite duty on some definite article, and then we must await events. The tax may or may not have the effect intended. Possibly, indeed, it may provoke fresh tariffs instead of diminishing those that already exist. At any rate, the gain is doubtful, while the loss is certain.

What, then, is that loss? In the first place, no tax can be imposed on any goods now entering this country without injuring the people who habitually buy those goods. Our countrymen will be deprived of the liberty to buy what they want at the price that suits them. Clearly that is a loss to them, and through them to the nation of which they form a part. It may be that the loss is merely a personal one, as when a lady is compelled to pay more for a French silk than she paid before. But it may also happen that the loss is industrial as well as personal, for the retaliatory tariff may fall – as in the case of the Sugar Bill –on the raw material of a British industry, and may thus diminish the power of that industry to compete in the markets of the world. In such a case as this even a trifling retaliatory tariff may work incalculable mischief.

The Creation of Vested Interests

These are not the only losses. Mr. Balfour talks as if it were a small matter to establish "an element of Protection to home industries." It is not a small matter; it is a very grave matter, for it involves the creation of vested interests which will afterwards be extremely difficult to remove. The "element of Protection to home industries" means that certain manufacturers are endowed by the State with the privilege of extracting from the British consumer a higher price for their goods than they could obtain if the market were open.

Having secured this valuable privilege at the expense of their fellow-citizens, they are not likely to be willing to lose it. People who imagine that the problem of retaliation is a simple one, may be advised to study the history of the British silk trade. The Protection given to that trade survived the great reforms of Sir Robert Peel, and continued down to the French Treaty of 1860. Here, then, were exactly the conditions that Mr. Balfour desires. We had something to bargain with. We had the revolver that Lord Lansdowne demands – wrapped in silk. The Treaty was negotiated, and France agreed to give us many valuable concessions in return for the abolition of our duties on silk. In the langauge of Protectionists, that was the price that we had to pay. In the language of accuracy, we, *i.e.*, the British nation, paid no price at all. We received all the profit. We got our silk cheaper and secured greater facilities for trade with France. The whole price was paid by the silk manufacturers, who lost a privilege which Parliament had previously conferred upon them. What has happened since? Have the British silk manufacturers patriotically welcomed their loss as a means of securing a greater good for their country? Not a bit of it! Men will lay down their lives for their country, but they will not forego their profits. The silk industry is the one British industry that has never ceased to clamour for Protection, and its spokesmen to-day even go so far as to attribute their ruin to one-sided Free Trade, whereas they are really the victims of reciprocity.

The Corruption of Parliament

There is still a third loss, and it is even more serious than the others. As already pointed out, Protection for home industries means the creation of a privilege for one or more favoured individuals. Most people like privileges and most people are willing to pay for them. Imagine an anxious minister eager to retaliate on somebody, and not quite certain where to begin. While he is still in doubt, information is conveyed to him by well-known channels that a little group of manufacturers is willing to make a handsome donation to the party funds if theirs is the trade selected for favour. No more need be said. The establishment of tariff privileges, whether under the name of Protection or under the name of Retaliation, means the death-knell to the purity of Parliament.

These, then, are the losses which the policy of retaliation must involve. They are certain. Now let us consider what are the possibilities of gain.

The assumption that foreign tariffs will fall down like the walls of Jericho before a blast of retaliation, is absolutely unwarranted either by the experience of the past, or by any reasonable estimate of the probabilities of the future. First, as to the experience of the past. Mr. Balfour appears to imagine that the idea of retaliation is entirely novel, and that the thing has never been tried before. Let him read again his Adam Smith. He will there find, in pages written one hundred and thirty years ago, a convenient summary of the more remarkable tariff wars for a hundred years preceding. Some of these tariff wars led to other wars with pike and musket. They certainly did not lead to Free Trade. Long after Adam Smith, the policy of retaliation continued to flourish in this country, as in others, but the tariff wall against British industries remained as high as ever, and no serious breach was made in that wall until England had abandoned the principle of retaliation and adopted the principle of free imports.

Contemporary experience is equally opposed to Mr. Balfour's theory. Other countries continue to maintain the policy of retaliation. Does it bring Free Trade to them? On the contrary, Mr. Balfour declares that their tariffs are growing higher and higher. Meanwhile, any incidental reduction of tariffs that may be brought about by their power of bargaining with one another, at once redounds to our advantage, for by virtue of our policy of free imports we are entitled to the lowest tariffs that foreign countries levy upon one another's goods.

Therefore there is nothing either in our own past experience or the present experience of our neighbours to give any support to Mr. Balfour's theory that Free Trade can be secured by means of retaliation.

Next let us look at the theory itself and ask whether there is any reasonable probability that it could be successfully applied. In the first place, it requires for its scientific application ministers who possess quasi-despotic powers, and who also possess a wide and an *impartial* knowledge of the requirements of British industry and the weaknesses of foreign competition. It is not easy to see how these two conditions could be satisfied under our system of Parliamentary Government. But suppose they were satisfied. Suppose we possessed the intelligent despot who knew how to prepare for battle as well as to provoke war. What could we do?

Why Our Hands are Tied

Few people seem to realise that it is generally impossible to retaliate directly. For example, Germany injures us by a duty on British iron and steel, but we cannot retaliate directly by a duty on German iron and steel, for the simple reason that our exports of these commodities to Germany are greater than our imports of similar commodities from Germany. Thus the German ironmaster has a greater interest in ousting us from his home market than in securing our market for himself. That is, indeed, the only reason why he wants a duty at all. Consequently, if we put a duty on German iron and steel, the German ironmaster would at once go to the Reichstag and ask for an increase of the duties already levied on British iron and steel. That would obviously be his interest, and it would be the interest of the German Reichstag to comply with his petition in order to prove to us that two can play at the game of retaliation. This consideration affects almost all our main industries. We cannot retaliate because we export so largely. Our hands are tied, not by Free Trade dogmas, but by the very magnitude of the export trade that we have built up since we took those dogmas as our guide.

All we can practically do if we wish to retaliate is to select some article which we import in large quantities, and which we export only in small quantities or not at all. Our importation of the penalised article must be large, or else the foreign country would not feel the penalty; our exportation must be small, or else we should lay ourselves open to a dangerous counter attack. Any one who will go through the list of our imports and exports will speedily discover that these two conditions exclude manufactured articles. In other words, the policy of retaliation which Mr. Balfour advocates involves either the taxation of raw materials, which he has explicitly condemned in the House of Commons, or the taxation of food, which he refuses even to mention in his pamphlet. Thus the very minister who advocates retaliation proves by his speeches, or by his silence, that he has not grasped the conditions under which retaliation would alone be possible. His own record achievement in the direction of retaliation is the Sugar Bill of last Session, which has not only imposed a heavy direct loss on the United Kingdom, but which has already provoked a serious counter-stroke from Russia.

Our Insular Free Trade

Yet he now asks for unlimited power to point a revolver at neighbouring nations – who like ourselves are not devoid of national pride – and who happen to be our best customers as well as our rivals. Such a proposal, so lightly made, after such a record, shows the utter unfitness of Parliamentary politicians to deal with commercial problems. This has always been the contention of Free Traders. They hold that men of commerce should be left free to deal with their own problems, without the attempted assistance of politicians who neither understand the difficulties nor have any real power to remove them. This has been the principle on which our country has proceeded now for sixty years. It is the basis of that Free Trade which Mr. Balfour would destroy. Our Insular Free Trade has secured to us the priceless boon of a Parliament that is free from pecuniary corruption; it has enabled us to maintain upon our little island, in ever-increasing prosperity, a population larger and already more prosperous than can be found on any equal area of the world's surface; it has added to the loyalty, and aided the expansion, of our world-embracing Empire; and it has helped to prolong for all mankind the blessing of peace.

NOTES

1 See (Vol. III: 19).
2 See (Vol. II: 5).
3 Mr. Balfour also says in this passage that Free Trade "may not save a nation from suffering more by the adoption of a protective policy by its neighbours than do those neighbours themselves." He offers no proof of this proposition, and indeed it is by its nature incapable of proof.
4 The exports of bleaching powder in 1902 were: – To Russia, 35,000 cwt.; Sweden, 19,700 cwt.; Norway, 9,800 cwt.; Denmark, 2,900 cwt.; Germany, 2,900 cwt.; Holland, 24,800 cwt.; Portugal, 11,600 cwt.; Spain, 9,200 cwt.; Italy, 34,200 cwt.; U.S.A., 649,700 cwt.; Brazil, 2,500 cwt.; other foreign countries, 38,200 cwt.; Cape of Good Hope, 4,300 cwt.; British East Indies, 31,200 cwt.; Canada, 14,900 cwt.; other British possessions, 5,700 cwt.
5 See paper by Mr. D.A. Thomas, MP, in the Journal of Royal Statistical Society.

---

21 SPEECH [ON TARIFF REFORM] DELIVERED AT SHEFFIELD . . .*

Arthur J. Balfour

My Lord Derby, Ladies and Gentlemen, – I mean to talk to you to-night upon one subject, and one subject alone, not because there are not many other topics of deep interest to this nation on which I should like to address you, but because I am well aware that you first want to hear what I have to say upon the subject of tariff reform – (hear, hear) – and that, if that subject is to be dealt with at all, it had better not be limited by the introduction of other and alien themes. Now, this is not a new subject. It is not a new subject in this hall; it is not a new subject to the National Union of Conservative Associations. On the contrary, all who will look back over the records of this great Association, drawn as it is from every part of

* Arthur J. Balfour, speech delivered at Sheffield . . . (1 October 1903) (reprinted, with revisions, by permission of the *Times* from the *Times* of 2 October 1903) in A.J. Balfour (ed.), *Fiscal Reform Speeches* . . . (London: Longmans, Green and Co., 1906), pp. 97–110.

England, may convince themselves that the subject of tariff reform has been never absent, or but rarely absent, from your deliberations, and that there have ever been a great variety of opinions held upon it within the limits of one united party. Well, what is it, ladies and gentlemen, which has suddenly brought this topic, so often before you on previous occasions, into that position of exceptional prominence which it now for the first time holds? There are those who would attribute this new importance to a great speech delivered by a great man – (loud cheers) – in the month, I think it was, of May last. But, after all, it was not in May last that Mr. Chamberlain – (cheers) – first uttered the sentiments which he expressed with such burning eloquence, and something more is required to account for a phenomenon unparalleled in the political experience of any man whom I am now addressing. What, then, is the reason why tariff reform has come so much to the front? I attribute it to more than one cause. In the first place, remember that the late war has brought us into closer and more conscious touch with the great Colonial Empire – (cheers) – of which this country is the centre. Remember, also, that the Prime Ministers and representatives of those colonies brought before this country and the Empire in the most categorical and explicit terms the question of tariff reform in connection with our Colonial Empire; and remember, lastly, that there has been for some time past – long, indeed, before the recent development of this tariff controversy – there has been among men of the most varied opinions a growing uneasiness as to the condition of British trade in its relation to the trade of the world. (Cheers.)

The Industrial Position of Great Britain

If you want to have evidence of this, do not look at the speeches that have been delivered since tariff reform came to the front; look at the speeches that were delivered before that· epoch. Then you will have an impartial guide to the opinions held on this subject before the perturbing effects of controversy made themselves felt. Call to mind the speeches, pamphlets, and articles written on the subject of technical education, and on the necessity of meeting foreign competition by increased educational efforts, a movement which I heartily sympathise with – (hear, hear)·– and which I have done my best to promote – (cheers) – I say, if you call to mind these utterances, delivered by men of all shades of opinion, you will see that I am not exaggerating when I allege that there has been for some years past a feeling of growing uneasiness as to the industrial position of Great Britain among the industrial nations of the world. (Hear, hear.) Therefore, when Mr. Chamberlain made his speech – a speech to which we naturally date back this particular movement – the speech itself would have had no effect comparable to that which it has actually produced had it not fallen on ground prepared for it by circumstances; had it not dealt with a problem about which men's minds were beginning to feel disquiet. Now that feeling was greatly intensified by what occurred in relation to Canada's Imperial effort to give preferential treatment to this country. You all have the particulars of that incident in your mind – how Canada gave preferential treatment to our manufacturers, and how thereupon Canada was threatened by at least one foreign Power with pains and penalties for what she had done. That brought home to many minds the consciousness of our helplessness under our existing fiscal system to deal with fiscal injuries. (Hear, hear.) You cannot go to war over tariff questions. Tariff attacks can only be met by tariff replies – (cheers) – and I think every Englishman felt, when he heard that there was some danger lest a British colony should be penalised for her efforts after closer Imperial union with Britain – every Englishman, I say, felt that if old weapons were insufficient to meet the peril, new weapons must be forged. (Hear, hear.)

Falsified Prophecies

And that feeling has not been diminished by a survey of the commercial history of the world during the last two generations. Sixty years have passed, or nearly sixty years, since the greatest, or at all events the most notorious, step was taken in the direction of tariff reform in the great epoch between 1841 and 1846. Those sixty years have been filled with refutation of the prophecies made by the great tariff reformers. (Hear, hear.) I am not going to say a word against their work; I believe it to have been necessary and appropriate to the times in which they lived. But those times are not as our times – (cheers) – and every year that has passed during the period of which we in this room have some personal recollections is a contradiction of all the hopes, all the aspirations, all the prophecies which then filled the mouths and the minds of men. (Hear, hear.) . . .

Mr. Cobden's Ideal

What was Mr. Cobden's ideal? No one will deny that he was a patriot. Yet few who have studied his life and writings will pretend that the sentiment of nationality had any large place in his philosophy of politics. He looked forward to a world in which national divisions might, indeed, remain, but with their emphasis largely diminished, if not wholly effaced; in which the divisions between nations would in no sense correspond with fiscal and commercial divisions; in which Free Trade would have swept away altogether all rivalry between men of different races, of different creeds, and of different political institutions; in which the world would commercially be one, in which production would follow natural lines, and in which international manufacture would take not a competitive, but a co-operative shape. (Cheers.) That was his ideal. He drew from it the conclusion that in a world thus industrially organised war would be a practical impossibility, that nation would be so linked to nation by industrial ties that it would be impossible either for national ambition or national vanity to break the great peace which was to brood over the face of the world. Who shall deny that that ideal had in it elements of great nobility? Not I for one; but, unfortunately, the world he thus pictured is not the world in which we live. (Hear, hear.) It is not merely that Protection has survived as a relic – a barbarous relic, as Mr. Cobden would have thought – of a past time; it is not merely that nation is still divided from nation by political and racial peculiarites. The actual facts are far stronger and more significant that any such statement would convey.

The Barrier of Protection and Nationality

What has happened is that the sentiment of nationality has received an accretion of strength of which no man then living could have dreamed; and that contemporaneously with this growing sentiment of nationality we have found Protection in foreign countries, not surviving as the creed of the obscurantist minority, but growing in strength day by day, and day by day more separating the nations commercially from one another. I regret it. I regret it deeply. But after all we have to take account of the facts of the world in which we live (hear, hear), and neither the individual nor the nation can venture with any prospect of felicity or success to act as if he lived in an ideal world, and not in the world which actually and in matter of fact surrounds him. (Cheers.) I am afraid that in these years we have too much been in the position of dreamers, confident in the consistency and the worth of our own ideal, refusing to see that it was not conformed to by our neighbours or the world with which we had to deal; and the result is that we have watched for fifty years – we have watched without saying a word or making a sign – we have watched a wall of hostile tariffs growing up, dividing nation from nation, and dividing us from the protective nations of the world. As we have seen our own colonies, our own flesh and blood, the very sinews of the Empire that is to be, building up one vested interest after another, by a system of protection which, when it reaches its logical conclusion, will make it hard for us, their Mother Country, pledged to defend them, bound to them by every tie of affection and regard – will make it hard for us to export the results of our industry, our enterprise, and our capital to them as we now find it to export those results to America or to other protective countries. I do not know whether there is anybody who, having faced these facts in their integrity, can look at them with indifference. In any case the fact remains that over the whole period of the lifetime of those whom I am now addressing we have done nothing whatever either in regard to foreign countries or our own colonies to remedy a state of things so absolutely inconsistent with Free Trade as Mr. Cobden understood it. (Hear, hear.)

The Commercial Treaty of 1860

I ought, however, to make one exception. I have said that no effort has been made. That I believe to be in strictness inaccurate. One great effort, and, in its measure, one successful effort, was made and it was made by Mr. Cobden himself. I allude to the famous commercial treaty with France, negotiated in 1859 and brought to a successful issue in 1860. When I consider the history of that treaty I ask myself whether Mr. Cobden was indeed a Cobdenite. (Laughter, and Hear, hear.) What was the essence of the treaty of 1860? We were then in process of completing a great series of tariff reforms, mainly due to Tory and Conservative statesmen, which did so much for English commerce and set so good an example to the world. In 1859 there were certain taxes still in existence which the then Chancellor of the Exchequer and other financial authorities thought might well be repealed, but for the repeal of which they desired to obtain from the Government of France – at that time perhaps the most Protectionist nation with which we had large dealings – some concessions in the direction of free exchange of goods. Now, I want to put to you the question. The duties the repeal of which was promised to the French Government as a consideration for some diminution of their protective tariffs were duties to which no value was attached, but the contrary, by the British Exchequer. When Mr. Cobden negotiated that treaty he and those who sent him must either have been resolved to keep on these duties if the treaty failed, or they must have been resolved in any case to give them up. If the latter, then the consideration they were offering to the French Government in exchange for fiscal concessions was purely illusory; and the most complimentary epithet that I can imagine for a diplomatic transaction of that kind is that it was extremely dexterous. (A laugh.) The epithets that I should be inclined to apply are all of a less complimentary description (laughter), but I do not think that those less complimentary epithets are deserved. I believe that Mr. Cobden, who was the emissary, and Mr. Gladstone, the then Chancellor of the Exchequer, when they were dealing with the French Government of the day, did not mean to indulge in those over-ingenious tactics. But what they did say to them, and meant to say to them, was: 'If you will give us increased facilities for our exports we will remit those taxes. If you will not give us increased facilities we will retain those taxes.' That is the only interpretation I can put, consistently with the honour of the persons concerned, upon that great commercial negotiation. But if so, then, in the opinion of Mr. Gladstone and Mr. Cobden, it was legitimate to keep on taxes which would have been from a purely Treasury and revenue point of view illegitimate in order to put pressure upon a foreign Government to relax its tariff. (Cheers.) There is no economical distinction whatever between the diplomacy which strives to attain its end by threatening to retain taxes which ought to be repealed, and one which threatens to impose taxes which, from a fiscal point of view, ought never to be put on. If Mr. Cobden approved the first, we must assume that he would not have boggled at the second. (Cheers.) I do not know whether that point has ever been dealt with by the Cobden Club. (Laughter.) If not, I respectfully commend it to their attention.

Well, that, so far as I know, is the one exception to our attitude of somewhat self-complacent indifference to the tariff policy of our great commercial friends and rivals and to the tariff policy of our own colonies.

Protection and Internal Free Trade

I do not think it is to our credit – (hear, hear) – and I confess that when I hear criticisms – criticisms with which I sympathise taken by themselves – upon the American and the German system, under which those great industrial nations have accompanied their marvellous commercial expansion with protective duties which must have thrown a most heavy burden upon the consumer, I feel that they have a retort to which I, ast least, have no reply. They may well say to us that, although their external policy has been thus Protectionist, at all events within the limits of their own country they have estabished permanent Free Trade – (hear, hear) – and that at this moment within the circuit of the German Empire and within the vast ambit of the American Commonwealth all duties, all restrictions which can hamper free exchange, have been abolished by their patriotism and their foresight. And they may well ask us whether we in the British Empire can point to a similar picture, and whether at this moment that Free Trade of which we talk so much, and of which we boast so loudly, is Free Trade extending beyond the narrow limits of the four seas, and whether it even includes those great self-governing colonies which we proudly boast are to be the great buttresses of our Empire. (Cheers.)

I take it, ladies and gentlemen, that it is quite impossible for any man to say – I know it is quite impossible for any Free Trader to say – that we have not suffered deeply and profoundly by foreign tariffs in this country. (Cheers.) Free Trade is indeed an empty name, a vain speculation, if the fact that foreign nations are setting themselves to work to divert our industries into channels into which they would never have naturally flowed, to exclude our manufactures from their appropriate markets, and to limit as far as they can the international play of supply and demand – I say that Free Trade is indeed a farce if those things do not produce an evil effect, not merely upon the country which imposes protective duties, but on the Free Trade country and there is still one – (laughter and cheers) – which has to endeavour to the best of its ability to meet them.

The Dangers of the Trust System

But real and great as these evils are, they are not the only ones inflicted on us by foreign protection. For there has been a development of which Mr. Cobden and Mr. Cobden's contemporaries never dreamed, the development of the trust system under the protection of these tariffs which inflicts an injury upon the capital and still more upon the workmen of these Islands. The phenomenon is so new that I dare scarce venture to prophesy what development it is likely to take, whether it is going to expand into a great national danger, or whether it is going to be limited to the evil which I fear it has already inflicted. But of this you may be absolutely sure, that in the alliance of trusts and tariffs there is a danger to the enterprise of this country which threatens not mainly the capitalist, for he is at liberty to establish his business in those countries where tariffs will benefit his industry, not injure it, but which will fall with the heaviest weight upon the artisan and labour classes of this country, who have no methods, or no methods known to me, by which they can protect their intersts against this particular danger. (Loud cheers.)

No Cure, but a Palliative

You will not get the great commercial nations of the world to abandon Protection; I fear you will not get our great self-governing colonies to retrace the steps which we have without remonstrance permitted them to take. I therefore say there is no cure for the evils that I have described, but I think there is a palliative, and it is that palliative which I am here to recommend to you today. (Cheers.) Remember what the situation is which I have endeavoured to describe to you. Mr. Cobden supposed that the world was going to be a Free Trade world in which commerce would follow its natural courses, unhampered by the devices of statesmen and politicians, untouched by the influence of international treaties. That is what he hoped, that is what he believed.

The Freedom of Negotiation

But what, in fact, we have got to deal with is a world in which international commerce is largely regulated by treaty, in which trade flows along channels engineered not by Nature but by diplomacy. Is it common sense that in such a world we, the greatest commercial nation of all, should come forward and say, 'We will endeavour to arrange treaties with you. We have nothing to give you – (laughter) – we have nothing to withhold from you, we throw ourselves upon your mercy, we appeal to your kindly consideration'? (Renewed laughter.) 'Remember, please remember, how good we are to your commerce' – (laughter) – 'how we throw no impediment in its way, how we freely open to it our markets; and treat it as if it were our own. And please don't forget us when you are making your next treaty.' (Renewed laughter and cheers.) I am incapable of believing that a nation which deliberately deprives itself of its power of bargaining is a nation which is likely to make very good bargains. I have been asked by friends of mine whether there really is any ground for supposing that we should make better bargains if we had the freedom of negotiation which I ask you to give us. (Loud cheers.) I confess that the very question seems to me to show that the questioner lives in a world of economic phantasma-goria – (laughter) – with no relation whatever to the realities in which, fortunately or unfortunately, our lot is cast. Are commercial bargains different from all other bargains? Are negotiations between nations which deal with duties upon manufactured goods different in essence and in character from other negotiations carried on for other purposes? (Cries of 'No'.) Did any man every hear of a country going into negotiations for these other purposes which came out of these negotiations with success unless it had in the course of these negotiations something to give, which, in case of necessity, it was at liberty to withhold? (Hear, hear.) My request therefore to you tonight – the fundamental and essential request to which everything I have to say in the remainder of my speech is subsidiary and accidental – is that the people of this country should give to the Govern-ment of this country, from whatever party that Government may be drawn, that freedom of negotiation of which we have been deprived, not by the force of circumstances, not by the action of overmastering forces, not by the pressure of foreign Powers, but by something which I can only describe as our own pedantry and our own self-conceit. (Hear, hear, and cheers; and a voice: 'How can we give you that power?') I have stated the fundamental proposition which I wish to affirm, but I agree with my friend opposite that it is necessary for me, though it may not be interesting to you, that I should answer some questions which will inevitably be asked as to the manner in which that freedom for which I ask is going to be used. I would, however, observe that this question is often put in a manner which I regard as highly unreasonable. I suppose there is not a man in this room who denies that we ought to have a fleet – (hear, hear); but am I, or is any other Minister, to tell you how that fleet is to be used in 1904, or 1905, or 1906 or 1907? That is a prophetic calculation which neither I nor any other man can make. (Hear, hear.) All you can say is this – that it is absolutely necessary for this country to have at its command in case of need a great navy – (cheers) – and it is necessary, though I admit less necessary – but it is necessary – in my judgement, that this country should also have at its command those instruments of negotiation for which in general terms I have already pleaded. How either of these instruments of national policy is to be employed must necessarily depend on the exigencies of the moment. (Hear, hear.) But though I think the question is thus put very often in a most unreasonable fashion, I am perfectly ready to answer it, so far as in my judgement it can be answered in general terms. Well, let it be noted that I brought before your attention two separate aspects of one great problem I have pointed out to you that we have allowed the industrial world to slide into a system of high protection duties against this country without effort and without remonstrance, and that the industrial world partly consists of our own colonies and partly consists of foreign nations. Now the problems raised by the protective policy of these two classes of autonomous communites are different, though they arise from the same difficulty and spring from the same root.

Fiscal Union the Prelude to Political Union

And as regards the first of those – namely, our colonies – let me say that I think we have in this country been strangely blind – (hear, hear) – to the anomalous situation in which the British Empire is placed in matters fiscal. You will find many cases in which fiscal union has been the prelude to that closer and more intimate union which is the basis of national strength. (Hear, hear.) I may mention, as a Scotsman (laughter), the case of England and Scotland. If any of you will consult your histories you will see that what reconciled the smaller kingdom to union with the greater kingdom was no love of being under a British Parliament, but the sense that it was absolutely necessary for national existence, or, at all events, for national prosperity, that England and Scotland should be fiscally one. (Cheers.) But that Union, originally based on mere material considerations, now depends on the yet stronger bond of sentiment; and it has welded the two peoples together into an inseparable whole, which it will not be possible for any hostile force to divide. And if I wished further to load my speech with historical illustrations I might, of course, point to the case of Germany. For Germany resembles Scotland in this respect, that fiscal union began before that political union which had been the greatest incident in modern history. We, on the other hand, have been content, apparently, as far as our Empire is concerned, to see fiscal divisions growing with our growth, and at the very moment when the population and wealth of our colonies are greatly increasing, and the sentiment of common interest, common blood, and common institutions is daily gaining strength, we see these fiscal divisions deepening and broadening, with results which no man can prophesy but which I venture to say no man of sober judgment or any knowledge of history can contemplate without disquiet. (Cheers.)

That is the first branch of the problem. I am disposed to say that in many respects it is the most important branch (hear, hear); and I have sorrowfully to admit that it is also the most difficult branch, and for this reason.

The Taxation of Food

The evil has been allowed to grow both by us and by our colonies to a point at which it is probably incapable of any complete remedy, and at which even an attempted remedy, so far as I am able to see, would involve the taxation of food in this country. Now, I do not think that public opinion is ripe for the taxation of food. (Hear, hear.) Of course, all must admit that the taxation of food, indeed every kind of taxation, is in itself an evil. (Hear, hear.) I think indeed that the evil of food taxation – provided that taxation is kept within narrow limits – has been exaggerated beyond what reason and logic justify. (Loud cheers.) But I think, nevertheless, that the feeling against it cannot be ignored. For it is due to historic causes, and is born of sentiments which have their root in far-off social conflicts. And the reason is not far to seek. Compare the case of France and England. In France at this moment it would be impossible for any legislator to attempt to make the smallest breach in that theoretical equality the passion for which has been burnt into them by the great struggle of the French Revolution. Every Frenchman, or most Frenchmen, believe it as an immutable creed. The Englishman, on the other hand, cares little for speculative equality. What he wants is liberty. (Hear, hear.) The Frenchman, however, is tolerant, to a degree incredible among us, of any taxation of food. Remember, that though France is a country governed under as democratic a Government as our own, taxation of food is part of its normal system. And Frenchmen submit not merely to taxation on food for what we should call national and Imperial purposes, but they pay what we pay out of rates very largely by such taxation. Now, take the case of England. In England we had no French Revolution. We have not suffered in our historic experience any of the ills which have given birth to the French sentiment on the subject of equality; but the memory of the misery endured by our working classes, and especially by the agricultural labourer – (hear, hear) – in the days when wheat was 70*s.*, 80*s.*, or 100*s.* a quarter has become associated, though I admit with very little historic propriety (hear, hear); but it has, as a matter of fact, become associated with the question of duty-free imports of corn. It has eaten into the historic imagination of our people. It cannot be eliminated by the best logic, the most conclusive reasoning, or the most eloquent speeches. I am, therefore, distinctly of opinion – I am speaking here as one who is bound to give advice to a great party on the policy which they should regard as their official policy – (hear, hear) – that a tax on food is not, with public opinion in the state in which we now find it, within the limits of practical politics. So much for the colonial branch of the question.

The Advantages of Freedom of Negotiation

Now you will ask me how I mean to carry out, or how I contemplate should be carried out, that liberty of negotiation for which I ask in respect of foreign countries. (Hear, hear.) Well, there are a great many people who seem to think that if we ask for liberty of negotiation in respect of tariffs with foreign countries we mean to enter into a general tariff war with the whole world. No such idea, no such expectation is entertained, at all events by myself. (Hear, hear.) I do not know whether most of you are acquainted with the practice of foreign countries in their tariff negotiations. What they commonly do is to have what they call a combative tariff, that is to say, a very high tariff placed upon all foreign goods, which they then proceed to reduce for the benefit of those nations which give them something in return. So that they start with a heavy duty on all manufactured imports, which they are prepared to reduce for consideration received. I contemplate no such procedure with regard to this country. I think it would involve too great a disturbance of our practice, and might risk the disorganisation of our trade. But I see no such objection to our proceeding, so to speak, from the other end, and if we thought we could do it without disadvantage to ourselves – which, after all, is the guiding consideration in these matters – (a laugh, and 'Hear, hear') – we might inform any foreign country which we thought was treating us with outrageous unfairness that unless they modified their policy to our advantage we should feel ourselves compelled to take this or that step in regard to their exports to our markets. (Cheers.) I do not for a moment suggest that foreign countries are animated by a desire to destroy our trade *simpliciter*. (Voices, 'They are.') What they want to do is to improve their trade at our expense – (laughter) – which is rather a different thing; but in any case are you not trying them too high by your present system? Are you not throwing an unnecessary temptation in their way? Supposing they want to do us justice – (a laugh) – is it fair to go to their negotiators and say, 'Well, we have nothing to give you, we have nothing to take from you; our principles are such that you may kick us round the room, and we will only say – "Please treat us as well as you can"'? (A laugh.) I do not think that is fair to the foreign negotiator, who has to consider public opinion in his own country. He will find it far easier to come to a fair 'give and take' arrangement if he knows that behind our request for justice there is a method of exacting it. (Cheers.) . . .

22 TWO SPEECHES*

Joseph Chamberlain

The Case for Tariff Reform
(St. Andrew's Hall, Glasgow, October 6, 1903)

I am in a great city, the second of the Empire; the city which by the enterprise and intelligence which it has always shown is entitled to claim something of a representative character in respect of British industry. I am in that city in which Free Trade took its birth, in that city in which Adam Smith taught so long, and where he was one of my most distinguished predecessors in the great office of Lord Rector of your University, which it will always be to me a great honour to have filled. Adam Smith was a great man. It was not given to him, it never has been given to mortals, to foresee all the changes that may occur in something like a century and a half; but with a broad and far-seeing intelligence which is not common among men, Adam Smith did at any rate anticipate many of our modern conditions; and when I read his books I see how even then he was aware of the importance of home markets as compared with foreign; how he advocated retaliation under certain conditions; how he supported the Navigation Laws; how he was the author of a sentence which we ought never to forget, that 'Defence is greater than opulence.' When I remember, also, how he, entirely before his time, pressed for reciprocal trade between our colonies and the mother country, I say he had a broader mind, a more Imperial conception of the duties of the citizens of a great Empire, than some of those who have taught also as professors and who claim to be his successors. Ladies and gentlemen, I am not afraid to come here to the home of Adam Smith and to combat free imports, and still less am I afraid to preach to you preference with our colonies – to you in this great city whose whole prosperity has been founded upon its colonial relations. But I must not think only of the city, I must think of the country. It is known to every man that Scotland has contributed out of all proportion to its population to build up the great Empire of which we are all so proud – an Empire which took genius and capacity and courage to create, and which requires now genius and capacity and courage to maintain.

I do not regard this as a party meeting. I am no longer a party leader. I am an outsider, and it is not my intention – I do not think it would be right – to raise any exclusively party issues. But after what has occurred in the last few days, after the meeting at Sheffield,[1] a word or two may be forgiven to me,

---

* Joseph Chamberlain, Two Speeches (6 and 7 October 1903), reprinted in Charles W. Boyd (ed.), *Mr. Chamberlain's Speeches*, vol. II (London: Constable and Company, Ltd., 1914), pp. 140–82.

who, although no longer a leader, am still a loyal servant of the party to which I belong.

I say to you, ladies and gentlemen, that that party whose continued existence, whose union, whose strength I still believe to be essential to the welfare of the country and to the welfare of the Empire, has found a leader whom every member may be proud to follow. Mr. Balfour in his position has responsibilities which he cannot share with us, but no one will contest his right – a right to which his high office, his ability, and his character alike entitle him – to declare the official policy of the party which he leads, to fix its limits, to settle the time at which application shall be given to the principles which he has put forward. For myself, I agree with the principles that he has stated. I approve of the policy to which he proposes to give effect, and I admire the courage and the resource with which he faces difficulties which, even in our varied political history, have hardly every been surpassed. It ought not to be necessary to say any more. But it seems as though in this country there have always been men who do not know what loyalty and friendship mean, and to them I say that nothing that they can do will have the slightest influence or will affect in the slightest degree the friendship and confidence which exist and have existed for so many years between the Prime Minister and myself. Let them do their worst. Understand that in no conceivable circumstances will I allow myself to be put in any sort of competition, direct or indirect, with my friend and leader, whom I mean to follow. What is my position? I have invited a discussion upon a question which comes peculiarly within my province, owing to the office which I have so recently held. I have invited discussion upon it. I have not pretended that a matter of this importance is to be settled off-hand. I have been well aware that the country has to be educated, as I myself have had to be educated before I saw, or could see, all the bearings of this great matter; and therefore I take up the position of a pioneer. I go in front of the army, and if the army is attacked, I go back to it.

Meanwhile, putting aside all these personal and party questions, I ask my countrymen, without regard to any political opinions which they may have hitherto held, to consider the greatest of all great questions that can be put before the country, to consider it impartially if possible, and to come to a decision; and it is possible – I am always an optimist – it is possible that the nation may be prepared to go a little further than the official programme. I have known them to do it before, and no harm has come to the party; no harm that I know has come to those who as scouts, or pioneers, or investigators, or discoverers have gone a little before it. Well, one of my objects in coming here is to find an answer to this question. Is the country prepared to go a little further?

What are our objects? They are two. In the first place, we all desire the maintenance and increase of the national strength and the prosperity of the

United Kingdom. That may be a selfish desire; but in my mind it carries with it something more than mere selfishness. You cannot expect foreigners to take the same views as we of our position and duty. To my mind Britain has played a great part in the past in the history of the world, and for that reason I wish Britain to continue. Then, in the second place, our object is, or should be, the realisation of the greatest ideal which has ever inspired statesmen in any country or in any age – the creation of an Empire such as the world has never seen. We have to cement the union of the states beyond the seas; we have to consolidate the British race; we have to meet the clash of competition, commercial now – sometimes in the past it has been otherwise – it may be again in the future. Whatever it be, whatever danger threatens, we have to meet it no longer as an isolated country; we have to meet it fortified and stengthened, and buttressed by all those of our kinsmen, all those powerful and continually rising states which speak our common tongue and glory in our common flag.

Those are two great objects, and, as I have said, we all should have them in view. How are we to attain them? In the first place, let me say one word as to the method in which this discussion is to be carried on. Surely it should be treated in a manner worthy of its magnitude, worthy of the dignity of the theme. For my part I disclaim any imputation of evil motive and unworthy motive on the part of those who may happen to disagree with me; and I claim equal consideration from them. I claim that this matter should be treated on its merits – without personal feeling, personal bitterness, and, if possible, without entering upon questions of purely party controversy, and I do that for the reason I have given; but also because, if you are to make a change in a system which has existed for nearly sixty years, which affects more or less every man, woman, and child in the kingdom, you can only make that change successfully if you have behind you not merely a party support – if you do not attempt to force it by a small majority on a large and unwilling minority, but if it becomes, as I believe it will become, a national policy in consonance with the feelings, the aspirations, and the interests of the overwhelming proportion of the country.

I was speaking just now of the characteristics of Glasgow as a great city; I am not certain whether I mentioned that I believe it is one of the most prosperous of cities, that it has had a great and continuous prosperity; and if that be so, here, more than anywhere else, I have to answer the question, Why cannot you let well alone? Well, I have been in Venice – the beautiful city of the Adriatic – which had at one time a commercial supremacy quite as great in proportion as anything we have ever enjoyed. Its glories have departed; but what I was going to say was that when I was there last I saw the great tower of the Campanile rising above the city which it had overshadowed for centuries, and looking as though it was as permanent as the city itself. And yet the other day, in a few minutes, the whole structure fell to the ground. Nothing was left of it but a mass of ruin and rubbish. I do not say to you, gentlemen, that I anticipate any catastrophe so great or so sudden for British trade; but I do say to you that I see signs of decay; that I see cracks and crevices in the walls of the great structure; that I know that the foundations upon which it has been raised are not broad enough or deep enough to sustain it. Now, do I do wrong, if I know this – if I even think I know it – do I do wrong to warn you? Is it not a most strange and inconsistent thing that while certain people are indicting the Government in language which, to say the least of it, is extravagant, for not having been prepared for the great war from which we have recently emerged with success – is it not strange that these same people should be denouncing me in language equally extravagant because I want to prepare you now, while there is time, for a struggle greater in its consequences than that to which I have referred – a struggle from which, if we emerge defeated, this country will lose its place, will no longer count among the great nations of the world – a struggle which we are asked to meet with antiquated weapons and with old-fashioned tactics?

I tell you that it is not well to-day with British industry. We have been going through a period of great expansion. The whole world has been prosperous. I see signs of a change, but let that pass. When the change comes, I think even the Free Fooders will be converted. But meanwhile, what are the facts? The year 1900 was the record year of British trade. The exports were the largest we had ever known. The year 1902 – last year – was nearly as good, and yet, if you will compare your trade in 1872, thirty years ago, with the trade of 1902 – the export trade – you will find that there has been a moderate increase of £22,000,000.[2] That, I think, is something like $7\frac{1}{2}$ per cent. Meanwhile, the population has increased 30 per cent. Can you go on supporting your population at that rate of increase, when even in the best of years you can only show so much smaller an increase in your foreign trade? The actual increase was £22,000,000 under our Free Trade. In the same time the increase in the United States of America was £110,000,000, and the increase in Germany was £56,000,000. In the United Kingdom our export trade has been practically stagnant for thirty years. It went down in the interval. It has now gone up in the most prosperous times. In the most prosperous times it is hardly better than it was thirty years ago.

Meanwhile the protected countries which you have been told, and which I myself at one time believed, were going rapidly to wreck and ruin, have progressed in a much greater proportion than ours. That is not all; not merely the amount of your trade remained stagnant, but the character of your trade has changed. When Mr. Cobden preached his doctrine, he believed, as he had at that time considerable reason to suppose, that while foreign countries would supply us with our food-stuffs and raw materials, we should remain the mart of the world, and should send them in exchange our manufactures. But that is exactly what we have not done. On the contrary, in the period to which I have referred, we are sending less and less of our manufactures to them, and they are sending more and more of their manufactures to us.

I know how difficult it is for a great meeting like this to follow figures. I shall give you as few as I can, but I must give you some to lay the basis of my argument. I have had a table constructed, and upon that table I would be willing to base the whole of my contention. I will take some figures from it. You have to analyse your trade. It is not merely a question of amount; you have to consider of what it is composed. Now what has been the case with regard to our manufactures? Our existence as a nation depends upon our manufacturing capacity and production. We are not essentially or mainly an agricultural country. That can never be the main source of our prosperity. We are a great manufacturing country. In 1872, we sent to the protected countries of Europe and to the United States of America, £116,000,000 of exported manufactures. In 1882, ten years later, it fell to £88,000,000. In 1892, ten years later, it fell to £75,000,000. In 1902, last year, although the general exports had increased, the exports of manufactures to these countries had decreased again to £73,500,000, and the total result of this is that, after thirty years, you are sending £42,500,000 of manufactures less to the great protected countries than you did thirty years ago. Then there are the neutral countries, that is, the countries which, although they may have tariffs, have no manufactures, and therefore the tariffs are not protective – such countries as Egypt and China, and South America, and similar places. Our exports of manufactures have not fallen in these markets to any considerable extent. They have practically remained the same, but on the whole they have fallen £3,500,000. Adding that to the loss in the protected countries, and you have lost altogether in your exports of manufactures £46,000,000.

How is it that that has not impressed the people before now? Because the change has been concealed by our statistics. I do not say they have not shown it, because you could have picked it out, but they are not put in a form which is understanded [*sic*] by the people. You have failed to observe that the maintenance of your trade is dependent entirely on British possessions. While to these foreign countries your export of manufactures has declined by £46,000,000, to your British possessions it has increased £40,000,000, and at the present time your trade with the colonies and British possessions is larger in amount, very much larger in amount, and very much more valuable in the categories I have named, than our trade with the whole of Europe and the United States of America. It is much larger than our trade to those neutral countries of which I have spoken, and it remains at the present day the most rapidly increasing, the most important, the most valuable of the whole of our trade. One more comparison. During this period of thirty years in which our exports of manufactures have fallen £46,000,000 to foreign countries, what has happened as regards their exports of manufactures to us? They have risen from £63,000,000 in 1872 to £149,000,000 in 1902. They have increased £86,000,000. That may be all right. I am not for the moment saying whether that is right or wrong, but when people say that we ought to hold exactly the same opinion about things that our ancestors did, my reply is that I dare say we should do so if circumstances had remained the same.

But now, if I have been able to make these figures clear, there is one thing which follows – that is, that our Imperial trade is absolutely essential to our prosperity at the present time. If that trade declines, or if it does not increase in proportion to our population and to the loss of trade with foreign countries, then we sink at once into a fifth-rate nation. Our fate will be the fate of the empires and kingdoms of the past. We shall have reached our highest point, and indeed I am not certain that there are not some of my opponents who regard that with absolute complacency. I do not. As I have said, I have the misfortune to be an optimist. I do not believe in the setting of the British star, but then, I do not believe in the folly of the British people. I trust them. I trust the working classes of this country, and I have confidence that they who are our masters, electorally speaking, will have the intelligence to see that they must wake up. They must modify their policy to suit new conditions. They must meet those conditions with altogether a new policy.

I have said that if our Imperial trade declines we decline. My second point is this. It will decline inevitably unless while there is still time we take the necessary steps to preserve it. Have you ever considered why it is that Canada takes so much more of the products of British manufacturers than the United States of America does per head? Why does Australia take about three times as much per head as Canada? And why does South Africa – the white population of South Africa – take more per head than Australasia? When you have got to the bottom of that – and it is not difficult – you will see the whole argument. These countries are all protective countries. I see that the Labour leaders, or some of them, in this country are saying that the interest of the working class is to maintain our present system of free imports. The moment those men go to the colonies they change. I will undertake to say that no one of them has ever been there for six months without singing a different tune. The vast majority of the working men in all the colonies are Protectionists, and I am not inclined to accept the easy explanation that they are all fools. I do not understand why an intelligent man – a man who is intelligent in this country – becomes an idiot when he goes to Australasia. But I will tell you what he does do. He gets rid of a good number of old-world prejudices and superstitions. I say they are Protectionist, all these countries. Now, what is the history of Protection? In the first place, a tariff is imposed. There are no industries, or practically none, but only a tariff; then gradually industries grow up behind the tariff wall. In the first place, they are primary industries, the industries for which the country has natural aptitude or for which it has some special advantage – mineral or other resources. Then when those are established the secondary industries spring up, first the necessaries, then the luxuries, until at last all the ground is covered. These countries of which I have been speaking to you are in different stages of the protective process. In America, the process has been completed. She produces everything; she excludes everything. There is no trade to be done with her beyond a paltry 6s. per head. Canada has been protective for a long time. The protective policy has produced its natural result. The principal industries are there, and you can never get rid of them. They will be there for ever, but up to the present time the secondary industries have not been created, and there is an immense deal of trade that is still open to you, that you may still retain, that you may increase. In Australasia the industrial position is still less advanced. The agricultural products of the country have been first of all developed. Accordingly, Australasia takes more from you per head than Canada. In South Africa there are, practically speaking, no industries at all. Now, I ask you to suppose that we intervene in any stage of the process. We can do it now. We might have done it with greater effect ten years ago. Whether we can do it with any effect or at all twenty years hence I am very doubtful. We can intervene now. We can say to our great colonies: 'We understand your views and conditions. We do not attempt to dictate to you. We do not think ourselves superior to you. We have taken the trouble to learn your objections, to appreciate and sympathise with your policy. We know that you are right in saying you will not always be content to be what the Americans call a one-horse country, with a single industry and no diversity of employment. We can see that you are right not to neglect what Providence has given you in the shape of mineral or other resources. We understand and we appreciate the wisdom of your statesmen when they say they will not allow their country to be solely dependent on foreign supplies for the necessities of life. We understand all that, and therefore we will not propose to you anything that is unreasonable or contrary to this policy, which we know is deep in your hearts; but we will say to you, "After all, there are many things which you do not now make, many things for which we have a great capacity of production – leave them to us as you have left them hitherto. Do not increase your tariff walls against us. Pull them down where they are unnecessary to the success of this policy to which you are committed. Do that because we are kinsmen – without injury to any important interest – because it is good for the Empire as a whole, and because we have taken the first step and have set you the example. We offer you a preference; we rely on your patriotism, your affection, that we shall not be losers thereby."'

Now, suppose that we had made an offer of that kind – I won't say to the colonies, but to Germany, to the United States of America – ten or twenty years ago. Do you suppose that we should not have been able to retain a great deal of what we have now lost and cannot recover?

I will give you an illustration. America is the strictest of protective nations. It is so immoderate, so unreasonable, so unnecessary, that, though America has profited enormously under it, yet I think it has been carried to excessive lengths, and I believe now that a great number of intelligent Americans would gladly negotiate with us for its reduction. But until very recent times even this immoderate tariff left to us a great trade. It left to us the tin-plate trade, and the American tin-plate trade amounted to millions per annum, and gave employment to thousands of British work-people. If we had gone to America ten or twenty years ago and had said, 'If you will leave the tin-plate trade as it is, put no duty on tin-plate – you have never had to complain either of our quality or our price – we in return will give you some advantage on some articles which you produce,' we might have kept the tin-plate trade. It would not have been worth America's while to put a duty on an article for which it had no particular or special aptitude or capacity. If we had gone to Germany in the same sense, there are hundreds of articles which are now made in Germany which are sent to this country, which are taking the place of goods employing British labour, which they might have left to us in return for our concessions to them.

We did not take that course. We were not prepared for it as a people. We allowed matters to drift. Are we going to let them drift now? Are we going to lose the colonial trade? This is the parting of the ways. You have to remember that if you do not take this opportunity it will not recur. If you do not take it I predict, and I predict with certainty, that Canada will fall to the level of the United States, that Australia will fall to the level of Canada, that South Africa will fall to the level of Australia, and that will only be the beginning of the general decline which will deprive you of your most important customers, of your most rapidly increasing trade. I think that I have some reason to speak with authority on this subject. The colonies are prepared to meet us. In return for a very moderate preference they will give us a substantial advantage. They will give us in the first place, I believe they will reserve to us, much at any rate of the trade which we already enjoy. They will not – and I would not urge them for a moment to do so – they will not injure those of their industries which have already been created. They will maintain them, they will not allow them to be destroyed or injured even by our competition, but outside that there is still a great margin, a margin which has given us this enormous increase of trade to which I have referred. That margin I believe we can permanently retain, and I ask you to think, if that is of so much importance to us now, when we have only eleven millions of white fellow-citizens in these distant colonies, what will it be when, in the course of a period which is a mere moment of time in the history of states, that population is forty millions or more? Is it not worth while to consider whether the actual trade which you may retain, whether the enormous potential trade which you and your descendants may enjoy, be not worth a sacrifice, if sacrifice be required? But they will do a great deal more for you. This is certain. Not only will they enable you to retain the trade which you have, but they are ready to give you preference on all the trade which is now done with them by foreign competitors. I never see any appreciation by the free importers of the magnitude of this trade. It will increase. It has increased greatly in thirty years, and if it goes on with equally rapid strides we shall be ousted by foreign competition, if not by protective tariffs, from our colonies. It amounts at the present time to £47,000,000. But it is said that a great part of that £47,000,000 is in goods which we cannot supply. That is true, and with regard to that portion of the trade we have no interest in any preferential tariff, but it has been calculated, and I believe it to be accurate, that £26,000,000 a year of that trade might come to this country which now goes to Germany and France and other foreign countries, if reasonable preference were given to British manufactures. What does that mean? The Board of Trade assumes that of manufactured goods one-half the value is expended in labour – I think it is a great deal more, but take the Board of Trade figures – £13,000,000 a year of new employment. What does that mean to the United Kingdom? It means the employment of 166,000 men at 30s. a week. It means the subsistence, if you include their families, of 830,000 persons; and now, if you will only add to that our present export to the British possessions of £96,000,000, you will find that that gives, on the same calculation, £48,000,000 for wages, or employment at 30s. a week to 615,000 work-people, and it finds subsistence for 3,075,000 persons. In other words, your colonial trade as it stands at present with the prospective advantage of a preference against the foreigner means employment and fair wages for three-quarters of a million of workmen, and subsistence for nearly four millions of our population.

Ladies and gentlemen, I feel deeply sensible that the argument I have addressed to you is one of those which will be described by the leader of the Opposition as a squalid argument. A squalid argument! I have appealed to your interests, I have come here as a man of business, I have appealed to the employers and the employed alike in this great city. I have endeavoured to point out to them that their trade, their wages, all depend on the maintenance of this colonial trade, of which some of my opponents speak with such contempt, and, above all, with such egregious ignorance. But now I abandon that line of argument for the moment, and appeal to something higher, which I believe is in your hearts as it is in mine. I appeal to you as fellow-citizens of the greatest Empire that the world has ever known; I appeal to you to recognise that the privileges of Empire bring with them great responsibilities. I want to ask you to think what this Empire means, what it is to you and your descendants. I will not speak, or, at least, I will not dwell, on its area, greater than that which has been under one dominion in the history of the world. I will not speak of its population, of the hundreds of millions of men for whom we have made ourselves responsible. But I will speak of its variety, and of the fact that here we have an Empire which with decent organisation and consolidation might be absolutely self-sustaining. Nothing of the kind has ever been known before. There is no article of your food, there is no raw material of your trade, there is no necessity of your lives, no luxury of your existence which cannot be produced somewhere or other in the British Empire, if the British Empire holds together, and if we who have inherited it are worthy of our opportunities.

There is another product of the British Empire, that is, men. You have not forgotten the advantage, the encouragement, which can be given by the existence of loyal men, inhabitants, indeed, of distant states, but still loyal to the common flag. It is not so long since these men, when the old country was in straits, rushed to her assistance. No persuasion was necessary; it was a voluntary movement. That was not a squalid assistance. They had no special interest. They were interested, indeed, as sons of the Empire. If they had been separate states they would have had no interest at all. They came to our assistance and proved themselves indeed men of the old stock; they proved themselves worthy of the best traditions of the British army, and gave us an assistance, a material assistance, which was invaluable. They gave us moral support which was even more grateful. That is the result of the Empire. I should be wrong if, in referring to our white fellow-subjects, I did not also say, that in addition to them, if any straits befell us, there are millions and hundreds of millions of men born in tropical climes, and of races very different from ours, who, although they were prevented by political considerations from taking part in our recent struggle, would be in any death-throe of the Empire equally eager to show their loyalty and their devotion. Now, is such a dominion, are such traditions, is such a glorious inheritance, is such a splendid sentiment – are they worth preserving? They have cost us much. They have cost much in blood and treasure; and in past times, as in recent, many of our best and noblest have given their lives, or risked their lives, for this great ideal. But it has also done much for us. It has ennobled our national life, it has discouraged that petty parochialism which is the defect of all small communities. I say to you that all that is best in our present life, best in this Britain of ours, all of which we have the right to be most proud, is due to the fact that we are not only sons of Britain, but we are sons of Empire. I do not think, I am not likely to do you the injustice to believe, that you would make this sacrifice fruitless, that you would make all this endeavour vain. But if you want to complete it, remember that each generation in turn has to do its part, and you are called to take your share in this great work. Others have founded the Empire; it is yours to build firmly and permanently the great edifice of which others have laid the foundation. And I believe we have got to change somewhat our rather insular habits. When I have been in the colonies I have told them that they are too provincial, but I think we are too provincial also. We think too much of ourselves, and we forget – and it is necessary we should remember – that we are only part of a larger whole. And when I speak of our colonies it is an expression; they are not ours – in the sense that we possess them. They are sister states, able to treat with us from an equal position, able to hold to us, willing to hold to us, but also able to break with us. I have had eight years' experience. I have been in communication with many of the men, statesmen, orators, writers, distinguished in our colonies. I have had intimate conversation with them. I have tried to understand them, and I think I do understand them, and I say that none of them desire separation. There are none of them who are not loyal to this idea of Empire which they say they wish us to accept more fully in the future, but I have found none who do not believe that our present colonial relations cannot be permanent. We must either draw closer together or we shall drift apart.

When I made that statement with all responsibility some time ago there were people, political opponents, who said: 'See, here is the result of having a Colonial Secretary. Eight years ago the colonies were devoted to the mother country. Everything was for the best. Preferences were not thought of. There were no squalid bonds. The colonies were ready to do everything for us. They were not such fools as to think we should do anything for them, but while things were in this happy state the Colonial Secretary came into office. Now it has all disappeared. We are told if we do not alter our policy we may lose our Empire.' It is a fancy picture, but I will not rest my case upon my own opinion. It is not I who have said this alone; others have said it before me. We have a statesman here in Scotland whose instincts are always right. What did he say many years before I came into office, in 1888? Lord Rosebery was speaking at Leeds, and he said this: 'The people in this country will in a not too distant time have to make up their minds what position they wish their colonies to occupy with respect to them, or whether they desire their colonies to leave them altogether. It is, as I believe, absolutely impossible for you to maintain in the long run your present loose and indefinable relations and preserve these colonies as parts of the Empire . . . I do not see that you can obtain the great boon of a peaceful Empire encircling the globe with a bond of commercial unity and peace without some sacrifice on your part.' Well, we have to consider, of course, what is the sacrifice we are called upon to make. I do not believe – no, let me first say if there be a sacrifice, if that can be shown, I will go confidently to my countrymen, I will tell them what it is, and I will ask them to make it. Nowadays a great deal too much attention is paid to what is called the sacrifice; no attention is given to what is the gain. But, although I would not hesitate to ask you for a sacrifice if a sacrifice were needed to keep together the Empire to which I attach so much importance, I do not believe that there would be any sacrifice at all. This is an arrangement between friends. This is a negotiation between kinsmen. Can you not conceive the possibility that both sides may gain and neither lose? Twelve years ago another great man – Mr. Cecil Rhodes – with one of those flashes of insight and genius which made him greater than ordinary men, took advantage of his position as Prime Minister of the Cape Colony to write letters, which have recently been published, to the Prime Minister of Canada and the Prime Minister of New South Wales, of that day. He said in one of these letters: 'The whole thing lies in the question – Can we invent some tie with our mother country that will prevent separation? It must be a practical one. The curse is that English politicians cannot see the future.'

Well, I ask the same question. Can we invent a tie which must be a practical one, which will prevent separation, and I make the same answer as Mr. Rhodes, who suggested reciprocal preference, and I say that it is only by commercial union, reciprocal preference, that you can lay the foundations of the confederation of the Empire to which we all look forward as a brilliant possibility. Now I have told you what you are to gain by preference. You will gain the retention and the increase of your customers. You will gain work for the enormous number of those who are now unemployed; you will pave the way for a firmer and more enduring union of the Empire. What will it cost you? What do the colonies ask? They ask a preference on their particular products. You cannot give them, at least it would be futile to offer them, a preference on manufactured goods, because at the present time the exported manufacture of the colonies is entirely insignificant. You cannot, in my opinion, give them a preference on raw material. It has been said that I should propose such a tax; but I repeat now, in the most explicit terms, that I do not propose a tax on raw materials which are a necessity of our manufacturing trade. What remains? Food.

Therefore, if you wish to have preference, if you desire to gain this increase, if you wish to prevent separation, you must put a tax on food. The murder is out. I said that in the House of Commons, but I said a good deal more, but that is the only thing of all that I said that my opponents have thought it particularly interesting to quote, and you see that on every wall, in the headlines of the leaflets of the Cobden Club, in the speeches of the devotees of free imports, in the arguments of those who dread the responsibilities of Empire, but do not seem to care much about the possibility of its dissolution – all these, then, put in the forefront that Mr. Chamberlain says, 'You must tax food.' I was going to say that this statement which they quote is true. But it is only half the truth, and they never give you the other half. You never see attached to this statement that you must tax food the other words that I have used in reference to this subject, that nothing that I propose would add one farthing to the cost of living to the working man, or to any family in this country. How is that to be achieved? I have been asked for a plan. I have hesitated, because, as you will readily see, no final plan can be proposed until a Government is authorised by the people to enter into negotiations upon these principles. Until that Government has had the

397

opportunity of negotiating with the colonies, with foreign countries, and with the heads and experts in all our great industries, any plan must be at the present time more or less of a sketch plan.

But at the same time I recognise that you have a right to call upon me for the broad outlines of my plan, and those I will give you if you will bear with me. You have heard it said that I propose to put a duty of 5s. or 10s. a quarter on wheat. That is untrue. I propose to put a low duty on foreign corn, no duty at all on the corn coming from our British possessions. But I propose to put a low duty on foreign corn not exceeding 2s. a quarter. I propose to put no tax whatever on maize, partly because maize is a food of some of the very poorest of the population, and partly also because it is a raw material for the farmers, who feed their stock with it. I propose that the corresponding tax which will have to be put on flour should give a substantial preference to the miller, and I do that in order to re-establish one of our most ancient industries in this country, believing that if that is done not only will more work be found in agricultural districts, with some tendency, perhaps, operating against the constant migration from the country into the towns, but also because by re-establishing the milling industry in this country, the offals, as they are called – the refuse of the wheat – will remain in the country and will give to the farmers or the agricultural population a food for their stock and their pigs at very much lower rates. That will benefit not merely the great farmer, but it will benefit the little man, the small owner of a plot or even the allotment owner who keeps a single pig. I am told by a high agricultural authority that if this were done so great an effect would be produced upon the price of the food of the animal that where an agricultural labourer keeps one pig now he might keep two in the future. I propose to put a small tax of about 5 per cent. on foreign meat and dairy produce. I propose to exclude bacon, because once more bacon is a popular food with some of the poorest of the population. And, lastly, I propose to give a substantial preference to our colonies upon colonial wines and perhaps upon colonial fruits. Well, those are the taxes, new taxes, or alterations of taxation which I propose as additions to your present burden.

But I propose also some great remissions. I propose to take off three-fourths of the duty on tea and half of the whole duty on sugar, with a corresponding reduction on cocoa and coffee. Now, what will be the result of these changes: in the first place upon the cost of living; in the second place upon the Treasury? As regards the cost of living, I have accepted, for the purpose of argument, the figures of the Board of Trade as to the consumption of an ordinary workman's family, both in the country districts and in the towns, and I find that if he pays the whole of the new duties that I propose to impose it would cost an agricultural labourer $16\frac{1}{2}$ farthings per week more than at present, and the artisan in the town $19\frac{1}{2}$ farthings per week. In other words, it would add about 4d. per week to the expenditure of the agricultural labourer and 5d. per week on the expenditure of the artisan. But, then, the reduction which I propose, again taking the consumption as it is declared by the Board of Trade, the reduction would be – in the case of the agricultural labourer 17 farthings a week; in the case of the artisan $19\frac{1}{2}$ farthings a week.

Now, gentlemen, you will see, if you have followed me, that upon the assumption that you pay the whole of the new taxes yourselves, the agricultural labourer would be half a farthing per week to the better, and the artisan would be exactly in the same position as at present. I have made this assumption, but I do not believe in it. I do not believe that these small taxes upon food would be paid to any large extent by the consumers in this country. I believe, on the contrary, they would be paid by the foreigner.

Now, that doctrine can be supported by authoritative evidence. In the first place, look at the economists – I am not speaking of the fourteen professors[3] – but take John Stuart Mill, take the late Professor Sidgwick, and I could quote others now living. They all agree that of any tax upon imports, especially if the tax be moderate, a portion, at any rate, is paid by the foreigner, and that is confirmed by experience. I have gone carefully during the last few weeks into the statistical tables not only of the United Kingdom, but of other countries, and I find that neither in Germany, nor in France, nor in Italy, nor in Sweden, nor in the United Kingdom, when there has been the imposition of a new duty or an increase of an old duty, has the whole cost over a fair average of years ever fallen upon the consumer. It has always been partly paid by the foreigner. Well, how much is paid by the foreigner? That, of course, must be a matter of speculation, and, there again, I have gone to one of the highest authorities of this country – one of the highest of the official experts whom the Government consult – and I have asked him for his opinion, and in his opinion the incidence of a tax depends upon the proportion between the free production and the taxed production. In this case the free production is the home production and the production of the British colonies. The taxed production is the production of the foreigner, and this gentleman is of opinion that if, for instance, the foreigner supplies, as he does in the case of meat, two-ninths of the consumption, the consumer only pays two-ninths of the tax. If he supplies, as he does in the case of corn, something like three-fourths of the consumption, then the consumer pays three-fourths of the tax. If, as in dairy produce, he supplies half of the consumption, then the consumer pays half of the tax. Well, as I say, that is a theory that will be contested, but I believe it to be accurate, and at all events, as a matter of curiosity, I have worked out this question of the cost of living upon that assumption, and I find that, if you take that proportion, then the cost of the new duties would be $9\frac{1}{2}$ farthings to the agricultural labourer and 10 farthings to the artisan, while the reduction would still be 17 farthings to the labourer and $19\frac{1}{2}$ farthings to the artisan. There, gentlemen, you see my point. If I give my opponents the utmost advantage, if I say to them what I do not believe, if I grant that the whole tax is paid by the consumer, even in that case my proposal would give as large a remission of taxation on the necessary articles of his life as it imposes. As a result of the advantage upon other necessary articles, the budget at the end of the week or the result at the end of the year will be practically the same even if he pays the whole duty. But if he does not pay the whole duty, then he will get all the advantages to which I have already referred. In the case of the agricultural labourer he will gain about 2d. a week, and in the case of the town artisan he will gain 2½d. a week.

I feel how difficult it is to make either interesting or intelligible to a great audience like this the complicated subject with which I have to deal. But this is my opening declaration, and I feel that I ought to leave nothing untold; at all events, to lay the whole of the outlines of my scheme before the country.

Now, the next point, the last point I have to bring before you, is that these advantages to the consumer will involve a loss to the Exchequer. And you will see why. The Exchequer when it reduces tea or sugar loses the amount of the tax on the whole consumption, but when it imposes a tax on corn or upon meat it only gains the duty on a part of the consumption, since it does not collect it either upon the colonial or upon the home production. Well, I have had that worked out for me, also by an expert, and I find, even making allowance for growth in the colonial and home production which would be likely to be the result of the stimulus which we give to them – and after making allowances for those articles which I do not propose to tax – the loss to the Exchequer will be £2,800,000 per annum. How is it to be made up? I propose to find it, and to find more, in the other branch of this policy of fiscal reform, in that part of it which is sometimes called 'retaliation' and sometimes 'reciprocity.' Now I cannot deal fully with that subject to-night. I shall have other opportunities, but this I will point out to you, that in attempting to secure reciprocity we cannot hope to be wholly successful. Nobody, I imagine, is sanguine enough to believe that America or Germany and France and Italy and all those countries are going to drop the whole of their protective scheme because we ask them to do so, or even because we threaten. What I do hope is that they will reduce their duties so that worse things may not happen to them. But I think we shall also have to raise ours. Now a moderate duty on all manufactured goods, not exceeding 10 per cent. on the average, but varying according to the amount of labour in these goods – that is to say, putting the higher rate on the finished manufactures upon which most labour would be employed – a duty, I say, averaging 10 per cent would give the Exchequer, at the very least, £9,000,000 a year, while it might be nearer £15,000,000 if we accept the Board of Trade estimates of £148,000,000 as the value of our imports of manufactured and partly manufactured goods. Nine milions a year – well, I have an idea that the present Chancellor of the Exchequer would know what to do with a full purse. For myself, if I were in that onerous position – which may Heaven forfend – I should use it in the first place to make up this deficit of £2,800,000 of which I have spoken; and, in the second place, I should use it for the further reduction both of taxes on food and also of some other taxes which press most hardly on different classes of the community. Remember this, a new tax cannot be lost if it comes to the Chancellor of the Exchequer. He cannot bury it in a stocking. He must do something with it, and the best thing he can do with it is to remit our taxation. The principle of all this policy is that whereas your present taxation, whether it be on food or anything else, brings you revenue and nothing but revenue, the taxation which I propose, which will not increase your burdens, will gain for you in trade, in employment, in all that we most want to maintain, the prosperity of our industries. The one is profitless taxation, the other scientific taxation.

I have stated, then, the broad outline of the plan which I propose. As I have said, this can only be filled up when a mandate has been given to the Government, when they have the opportunity which they desire to negotiate and discuss. It may be that when we have these taxes on manufactured goods, we might be willing to remit or reduce them if we could get corresponding advantages from the country whose products would thus be taxed. It cannot, therefore, be precisely stated now what they would bring in or what we should do, but this is clear that, whatever happened, we should get something. We should either get something in the shape of a reduction of other taxation or something in the shape of a reduction of those prohibitive tariffs which now hamper so immensely our native industries. There will be, according to this plan, as I have said, no addition to the cost of living, but only a transfer from one item to another.

It remains to ask, what will the colonies say? I hear it said sometimes by people who have never, I think, visited the colonies and do not know much about them, that they will receive this offer with contempt, that they will spurn it, or that if they accept it they will give nothing in return. Well, I differ from these critics. I do not do this injustice to the patriotism or the good sense of the colonies. When the prime ministers, representing all the several States of the Empire, were here, this was the matter of most interesting discussion. Then it was that they pressed upon the Government the consideration of this question. They did not press – it is wrong, it is wicked, to say that they pressed it in any spirit of selfishness, with any idea of exclusive benefit to themselves. No, they had Mr. Rhodes's ideal in their minds. They asked for it as a tie, a practical tie, which should prevent separation, and I do not believe that they will treat ungenerously any offer that we may now be able to make them. They had not waited for an offer. Already Canada has given you a preference of $33\frac{1}{3}$ per cent., South Africa has given you a preference of 25 per cent., New Zealand has offered a preference of 10 per cent. The premier of Australia has promised to bring before Parliament a similar proposal. They have done all this in confidence, in faith which I am certain will not be disappointed – in faith that you will not be ungrateful, that you will not be unmindful of the influences which have weighed with them, that you will share their loyalty and devotion to an Empire which is theirs as well as ours, and which they also have done something to maintain.

It is because I sympathise with their object, it is because I appreciate the wisdom, ay, the generosity of their offer, it is because I see that things are moving and that an opportunity now in your hands once lost will never recur; it is because I believe that this policy will consolidate the Empire – the Empire which I believe to be the security for peace and for the maintenance of our great British traditions – it is for all these things, and, believe me, for no personal ambition that I have given up the office which I was so proud to hold, and that now, when I might, I think, fairly claim a period of rest, I have taken up new burdens, and come before you as a missionary of Empire, to urge upon you again, as I did in the old times, when I protested against the disruption of the United Kingdom, once again to warn you, to urge you, to implore you to do nothing that will tend towards the disintegration of the Empire, and not to refuse to sacrifice a futile superstition, an inept prejudice, and thereby to lose the results of centuries of noble effort and patriotic endeavour.

Retaliation
(The Town Hall, Greenock, October 7, 1903)

I have dealt with the case of preferential arrangements with the colonies, and I proceed to speak a little more fully of the other branch of our policy, which is sometimes called 'retaliation' and which is sometimes called 'reciprocity.' Now, I begin with a confession of faith. I was brought up in the pure doctrine of Free Trade. I will not say that I believed it to be inspired, but I believed the statements of those who had preached it and who induced the country to adopt it. I accepted it as a settled fact; and nobody could have surprised me more than if, twenty, or still more, thirty years ago, he had told me that I should now be criticising the doctrine which I then accepted. But thirty years is a long time. Has nothing changed in thirty years? Everything has changed. Politics have changed, science has changed, and trade has changed. The conditions with which we have to deal are altogether different to the conditions with which we had to deal thirty years ago. Let no man say, because to-day you and I are in favour of retaliation, or what our opponents calls 'protection,' that that is at all inconsistent with our having been Free Traders under totally different conditions. When the temperature goes up to a hundred degrees, I put on my thinnest clothes; when it goes down below zero, there is nothing too warm for me to wear. When the prophecies of those who supported Free Trade appeared to be in the course of realisation, what reason was there why any of us should consider the subject or should express any doubt? And for something like five-and-twenty or thirty years after Free Trade was preached and adopted, there was no doubt whatever in my mind that it was a good policy for this country, and that our country prospered under it more than it would have done under any other system. That was for five-and-twenty years. What has happened during the last thirty years? In the last thirty years the whole conditions have changed; and it seems to me to be not the policy of a Liberal or the policy of a Radical, as I understood such a policy twenty or thirty years ago, but the policy of a rabid and a reactionary Tory to say that when all the conditions have changed you should not change your policy too.

Now, let us look at some of these changes. There was nothing upon which Mr. Cobden was more assured, more honestly convinced, than that Free Trade, as he understood it, was such a good thing that if we gave the example every other nation would follow. He said in the most positive terms that if we adopted the policy of Free Trade five years would not pass over before all the other nations adopted our views, and if they did not – he refused to conceive such a hypothesis – but his argument went to show that if they did not adopt our policy then they would be ruined, and we should gain by their distress. We are a great people, but, after all, I have never been able to believe that all the wisdom in the world was absolutely domiciled in this country. I have a great opinion of our American cousins. I have an idea that they are people with whom you ought to deal in the most friendly spirit, but you had better not shut your eyes. I have some considerable respect for the German people. I recognise that they have been and still are the most scientifically educated people on the face of the globe. I have a great regard for our neighbours the French. I think they have done immense service to knowledge and civilisation in our past history. I do not believe that all these people are fools; and when I find that they absolutely refuse to adopt the Cobdenite principle and to accept Free Trade as the model and example which it was represented to be, I say to myself, 'It is worth thinking over. I have perhaps been wrong to be as certain as I was of the wisdom of our policy,' – but that alone would not have moved me. If, in spite of my respect for the Americans, the French, and the Germans, I had found that the facts were against them, if I had found that they were being injured because they had adopted Protection, and that we were progressing enormously because we had adopted Free Trade, then I should be in favour of it in spite of the majority being against me.

What is the policy of these other nations? It has been, not a haphazard policy, but a policy deliberately adopted and deliberately pursued. It is a policy to use tariffs to increase home trade, and, if you like, to exclude foreign trade. All these nations to which I have referred, and every other civilised nation on the face of the earth, have adopted a tariff with the object of keeping the home market to the home population and not from any want of friendship to us. I do not believe they have been in the slightest degree actuated by ill-feeling to Great Britain; but because they thought it was necessary for their own security and prosperity, they have done everything in their power to shut out British goods. They have passed tariff after tariff. They began perhaps with a low tariff. They continued it as long as it was successful. If they found it ceased to do what it was wanted to do, they increased it; and what it was wanted to do was to exclude foreign manufactures, and above all to exclude the manufactures of this country, which at one time held the supremacy of trade in the world, and which was the greatest centre of industry in any part of it.

That was a deliberate policy; there is no doubt about that. Has it succeeded? It has, whether it was right or wrong. What these people intended to do they have done; and if you look back for any term of years you will find that the exports of British manufactures have fallen off to these countries, while their exports to us have risen. There may be something wrong in my constitution, but I never like being hit without striking back again. But there are some people who like to be trampled upon. I admire them, but I will not follow their example. I am an advocate of peace, no man more so. I wish to live quietly, comfortably, and in harmony with all my fellow-creatures, but I am not in favour of peace at any price. I am a Free Trader. I want to have free exchange with all the nations of the world, but if they will not exchange with me, then I am not a Free Trader at any price. And again I say it may be a defect in my constitution, but it seems to me that the men who do not care for the Empire, the men who will sooner suffer injustice than go to war, the men who would surrender rather than take up arms in their own defence, they are the men in favour of doing in trade exactly what they are willing to do in political relations. I do not care to what party they belong. I am not one of that party, and accordingly, when I find the effect of this policy on the part of other countries, I look about for a means of meeting it.

Last night I said, quoting from figures, that the exports of British manufactures to the principal protected countries had fallen over £42,000,000 in the course of thirty years. The *Glasgow Herald* this morning says incidentally that I ought not to have chosen that particular period. I assure the *Glasgow Herald* that I did not choose it with any sinister purpose. I thought thirty years was a good long time and a fair time to go back; but I invite them to choose any other period, I do not care what period. In this controversy which I am commencing here I use figures as illustrations. I do not pretend that they are proofs. The proof will be found in the argument, and not in the figures. But I use figures as illustrations to show what the argument is. The argument which I use, and which I defy the *Glasgow Herald* to contradict, is that since these tariffs were raised against us our exports to the countries which raised them have been continually decreasing. Yes; but that is not all. If their prosperity had been going down in equal proportion it would be no argument at all. While our exports to them have continually been decreasing, their exports to us have continually been increasing.

How do the Free Traders explain that? Their view is that these foolish Americans, these ridiculous Germans, these antiquated Frenchmen, have been ruining themselves all this time. They may have kept their home market; but they must have lost their foreign market. How can the good people whose cost of living has been raised – who have the little loaf and not the big loaf – who are hampered by tariff protection, though they may keep their own trade, how can they do a foreign trade? It may be very extraordinary, but they have done it. Their export trade has increased in very much greater proportion than our trade, the trade of the Free Trade country which has the big loaf, which has all this freedom and none of these disadvantages. I say that is a state of things which demands consideration. We are losing both ways. We are losing our foreign markets, because whenever we begin to do a trade the door is slammed in our faces with a whacking tariff. We go to another trade. We do it for a few months or for a few years, but again a tariff is imposed, and that is shut out. One industry after another suffers similarly; and in that way we lose our foreign trade, and, as if that was not enough, these same foreigners who shut us out, invade our markets and take the work out of the hands of our working people and leave us doubly injured.

Now, I say that is unfair and one-sided. In my opinion it threatens most seriously the position of every manufacturer, and, above all, of every working man in this kingdom. It threatens the position of the manufacturer. He may lose all his capital. His buildings may be empty; but he will perhaps have something left, and he can invest it in manufacture in some foreign country, where he will give employment to foreign workmen. Yes, the manufacturer may save himself. But it is not for him that I am chiefly concerned. It is for you – the workmen – I say to you that to you the loss of employment means more than the loss of capital to any manufacturer. You cannot live upon your investments in a foreign country. You live on the labour of your hands – and if that labour is taken from you, you have no recourse, except, perhaps, to learn French or German.

Now I go back for a minute to consider the importance of the question that I have asked. If there are Free Traders – I should rather say Free Importers, for in a sense we are all Free Traders – if there are Free Importers in Greenock you may have an opportunity of discussing this matter with them afterwards in a quiet and friendly way. Ask them this question: You say protection or retaliation will be very bad for this kingdom. How do you account for the fact that all these great nations, without exception, which have adopted the system which you say is bad, have prospered more than you have done? The Cobden Club says it is all right. But the Cobden Club has not answered that question; and I advise them to write to their foreign members and see whether they can tell them why Germany and France and the United States of America – and if you will remove all these from the calculation, then I take small countries, such a country as Sweden, for instance – why have all these countries prospered under a system which they declare would be ruinous to us? When that question is answered, I think that my occupation will be gone. I shall hide my diminished head, and make room for the foreign members. Now, I do not believe that these foreign countries are wrong. I believe they are better strategists than we have been. This policy, as announced by Mr. M'Kinley in America, and not by Mr. M'Kinley alone, but by the greatest Americans long before his time, by President Lincoln, by men like the original founders of the Constitution – this policy, announced in Germany by Prince Bismarck, who was in his time a rather considerable personage – this policy, announced in France by many of their most distinguished statesmen – here is no policy to take lightly.

Its main idea is to keep for a manufacturing country its home industry, to fortify the home industry, to make it impregnable; then, having left the fort behind, so protected that no enemy could attack it with possible success, to move forward and invade other countries, and attack especially one country, and that is our own, which we have left totally unguarded against all these assaults. We have left it unguarded because we think we are wiser than all the rest of the world; and the result has been, that although our fort has not been taken – well, it has received a very heavy battering. The time may come when we shall be unable any longer to defend it.

Now, these foreign countries have every advantage in their attack. They do not come like unarmed savages, even to attack such a defenceless village as Great Britain: they come with bounties of every kind. They have none of the disadvantages – I mean in an economic sense – from which we suffer. We, in a spirit of humanity of which I entirely approve, have passed legislation, to which I may say without boasting I have myself contributed, to raise the standard of living amongst our working people, to secure to them higher wages, to save them from the competition of men of a lower social scale. We have surrounded them with regulations which are intended to provide for their safety. We have secured them, or the majority of them, against the pecuniary loss which would follow upon accidents incurred in the course of their employment.

There is not one of those things which I have not supported. There is not one of them which I did not honestly believe to be for the advantage of the country. But they have all entailed expense. They have all raised the cost of production; and what can be more illogical than to raise the cost of production in this country in order to promote the welfare of the working classes, and then to allow the products of other countries – which are not

406

surrounded by any similar legislation, which are free from all similar cost and expenditure – freely to enter our country in competition with our goods, which are hampered in the struggle? I say to my fellow-countrymen, and especially to the great mass of the people who depend on their work for their wages and for the subsistence of their families – you are inconsistent, you are adopting a course that is suicidal. If you allow this state of things to go on, what will follow? If these foreign goods come in cheaper, one of two things must follow: either you will have to give up the conditions you have gained, either you will have to abolish and repeal the Fair Wages Clause and the Factory Acts and the Compensation to Workmen Acts, either you will have to take lower wages, or you will lose your work. You cannot keep your work at this higher standard of living and wages if at the same time you allow foreigners at a lower standard and lower rate of pay to send their goods freely in competition with yours.

The Cobden Club all this time rubs its hands in the most patriotic spirit and says: 'Ah, yes; but how cheaply you are buying!' Yes, but think how that affects different classes in the community. Take the capitalist – the man living upon his income. His interest is to buy in the cheapest market, because he does not produce. The cheaper he can get every article he consumes, the better for him. He need not buy a single article in this country; he need not make a single article. He can invest his money in foreign countries and live upon the interest; and then, in the returns of the prosperity of the country, it will be said that the country is growing richer because he is growing richer. But what about the working men? What about the class that depends upon having work in order to earn wages or subsistence at all? They cannot do without work; and yet the work will go if the article is not produced in this country. This is the state of things against which I am protesting.

Now, I call your attention to a matter of the greatest interest and importance which has just come to my knowledge. In a letter recently published in the *Times* a correspondent calls attention to an interview which was held in Philadelphia and published in the *Philadelphia Ledger*, a great newspaper of that city, between a director of the American Steel Trust and a reporter. The American Steel Trust is the greatest of all American Trusts. It produces at the present time about twenty million tons of steel and iron per annum, a very much greater quantity than is produced in this country. The director told the reporter that trade was falling off. There are many reasons for that. Financial difficulties in America seem likely to hasten the result. Orders are falling off; the demand for railways is less; and this director anticipated that before long the American demand would fall several millions of tons short of the American supply. 'What are you going to do?' said the reporter. 'Oh,' said he, 'we have made all our preparations. We are not going to reduce our output. We are not going to blow out a single furnace. No; if we did, that would be injurious to America. We

407

should have to turn out of our works into the streets hundreds of thousands of American workmen. And, therefore, what we are going to do, is to invade foreign markets.' And remember, it may not be easy for them to invade the German market, or the French market, or the Russian market, because in every case they will find a tariff which, if necessary, can be raised against them. They will go to the only free market, they will come to this country, and before you are two or three years older, and unless there is a change in the situation, I warn you you will have dumped down in your country perhaps as much as two million tons of American iron.

There is no iron manufacturer in this country who can regard such a proceeding as that without the greatest anxiety. You will see many iron-works closed, you may see others continued at a loss, struggling for better times; but what will become of the workmen employed? Hundreds of thousands of English workmen will be thrown out of employment in order to make room for hundreds of thousands of American workmen, who are kept in employment during bad times by this system. I sympathise with the American workman. I am glad that he, or any man, should be kept in employment; but, after all, I belong to this country. I admit that I am not cosmopolitan enough to wish to see the happiness, success, or prosperity of American workmen secured by the starvation and misery and suffering of British workmen.

I venture to say that no one has striven more continuously than I have done to advance the condition of the working people of this country; but of this I am certain – that what I and what others have done is a trifle in comparison with what may be done. It is as nothing in comparison with any policy or legislation which would ensure to every willing and industrious workman in this country continuous employment, full employment, at fair wages; and if your employment is filched from you, if you have to accept starvation wages, if you have to give up the advantages which you have obtained, then I tell you that your loaf may be as big as a mountain and as cheap as dirt, but you will be in the long run the greatest sufferers.

Let us look a little further into the matter; and, again, I will give you a figure or two as an illustration. Take other periods, if you like, this time, in deference to the *Glasgow Herald*. I will not go back to 1872 as a starting-point. I will take 1882 – that is twenty years ago. Since 1882 the total imports of foreign manufactures have increased £64,000,000, and, meanwhile, our exports of manufactures to these countries have increased £12,000,000, so that in the balance we have lost £52,000,000. I know perfectly well that it is very difficult to make people appreciate the meaning of a million. People who very seldom see many shillings or many pounds together find it very difficult to understand what ten hundred thousand pounds means, and still more what fifty-two times ten hundred thousand pounds means. Therefore I intend, as far as I can, throughout this discussion to translate money into work. What would this fifty-two millions of money have given to you if you had been able to get it? £52,000,000 a year of goods would cost £26,000,000 a year in wages alone, and £26,000,000 of wages would have provided constant employment at 30s. a week for 333,000 work-people, and it would have provided, of course, subsistence for their families, that is, for more than 1,500,000 altogether. I think we are all agreed that that would be worth having. If you gained this employment to-morrow, if any trade suddenly sprang up anywhere which employed 333,000 men and kept 12,500,000 people in comparative comfort, would you not say that the person who brought it to you was the greatest philanthropist you had ever known?

But what do the Free Traders say? No, I will not call them what they are not – Free Traders. What do Free Importers say? 'Yes, it is quite true that foreigners are doing the work of 333,000 British, and that they are earning the wages that would have supported 1,500,000 British people. That is true; but that does not matter in the least to the British workman or the British people, because they have found other employment. Having been turned out of their old employment, they have gone into something else, in which they are getting just as much. They are just as well off as they were before. They have not lost by the change, even if the foreigner has gained.' It is a very comforting doctrine for the armchair politician. But is it true?

I come to a subject which has a particular interest for a Greenock audience. It so happens that you have had in your midst a certain experience of a large trade which has been taken from you by the superior advantages of the foreigner. Has it injured you in the slightest degree or not? Do you care whether that trade went or not, or whether it should be re-established or not? Would you like to see your trade going, with one after another following it, always confident that your friends the Cobden Club would say, 'Oh, but you will find some other occupation?' I say you are an illustration. Of course, I refer to sugar. Greenock was one of the great centres of the sugar trade. You had many refineries; it was a profitable trade; it not only employed a great number of work-people itself, but it also gave employment in subsidiary industries to a great number of your countrymen.

Then came the foreign competition, aided by bounties, and your trade declines so seriously that only the very best, the very richest, the most enterprising, the most inventive, can possibly retain their hold upon it. If there had been no bounties and no unfair competition of this kind, what would have happened? In the last twenty or thirty years the consumption of sugar throughout the world has increased enormously. The consumption in this country has increased enormously; and you would have had your share. I do not hesitate to say that, if normal conditions and equal fairness had prevailed, at this moment in Greenock, quite independently of the other industries you may have found to occupy you, there would have been in sugar alone ten times as many men employed as there were in the most palmy days of the trade. But normal conditions have not obtained. You have been the sufferers; and a great number of your refineries have disappeared altogether. The capital invested in them has been lost, and the workmen who worked in them – what has become of them?

Free imports have destroyed this industry, at all events for the time, and it is not easy to recover an industry when it has once been lost. They have destroyed sugar-refining for a time as one of the great staple industries of the country, which it ought always to have remained. They have destroyed agriculture. Mr. Cobden – and again I am sure he spoke the truth as it appeared to him – was convinced that, if his views were carried out, not an acre of ground would go out of cultivation in this country, and no tenant farmer would be worse off. I am not here to speak to an agricultural audience; but if I were, what a difference could I show between that expectation and hope of Mr. Cobden's and the actual circumstances of the case! Agriculture, as the greatest of all trades and industries of this country, has been practically destroyed. Sugar has gone; silk has gone; iron is threatened; wool is threatened; cotton will go! How long are you going to stand it? At the present moment these industries, and the working men who depend upon them, are like sheep in a field. One by one they allow themselves to be led out to slaughter, and there is no combination, no apparent prevision of what is in store for the rest of them. Do you think, if you belong at the present time to a prosperous industry, that your prosperity will be allowed to continue? Do you think that the same causes which have destroyed some of our industries, and which are in the course of destroying others, will not be equally applicable to you when your turn comes? This is a case in which selfishness will not pay. This is a case in which you should take warning by the past, in which you can show some foresight as to the future.

What is the remedy? What is it that the Prime Minister proposed at Sheffield?[4] He said – I am not quoting his exact words – Let us get rid of the chains which we ourselves have forged, and which have fettered our action. Let us claim some protection like every other civilised nation. Let us say to these foreign countries: 'Gentlemen, we desire to be friends with you. We are Free Traders in the best sense of the word. We are ready to exchange freely; but, if you say that it is your settled policy that you will not buy from us, we will tax your exports to us. We will look further afield – no, not further afield, we will look nearer home. We will go to our own friends, who are perfectly ready to meet us on fair terms, who ask only for a reciprocal response.'

Then we are told that if we do this the foreigners will be angry with us! Has it come to that with Great Britain? It is a craven argument; it is worthy of the Little Englander; it is not possible for any man who believes in his own country. The argument is absurd. Who is to suffer? Are we so poor that we are at the mercy of every foreign State – that we cannot hold our own – that we are to fear their resentment if we imitate their own policy? Are we to receive their orders 'with bated breath and whispering humbleness'? No, if that were true, I should say that the star of England has already set; it would not be worth any one's while to care to speculate on her possible future. But it is not true. There is not a word of truth in it. We have nothing to fear from the foreigners. I do not believe in a war of tariffs, but if there were to be a war of tariffs, I know we should not come out second best. Why, at the present time ours is the greatest market in the whole world. We are the best customers of all those countries. There are many suitors for our markets. We may reject the addresses of some, but there is no fear that we shall not have other offers. It is absolutely absurd to suppose that all these countries, keenly competitive among themselves, would agree among themselves to fight with us when they might benefit at the expense of their neighbours. Why, at the present time we take from Germany about twice as much as she takes from us. We take from France about three times as much, and from the United States of America we take about six times as much as they take from us. After all that, do we stand to lose if there is to be a war of tariffs?

Ah! and there is something else. We have what none of these countries have. We have something, the importance of which I am trying to impress upon my country-men, which at present they have not sufficiently appreciated. We have a great reserve in the sons of Britain across the seas. There is nothing we want that they cannot supply; there is nothing we sell that they cannot buy. One great cause for the prosperity of the United States of America, admitted by every one to be a fact, is that they are a great empire of over 70,000,000 of people; that the numbers of these people alone, without any assistance from the rest of the world, would ensure a large amount of prosperity. Yes; but the British Empire is even greater than the United States of America. We have a population – it is true, not all a white population – but we have a white population of over 50,000,000 against the 70,000,000 – who are not all white, by the by – against the 70,000,000 of America. We have, in addition, 350,000,000 or more of people under our protectorate, under our civilisation, sympathising with our rule, grateful for the benefits that we accord to them, and all of them more or less prospective or actual customers of this country.

In times past we have in some inconceivable way ignored our colonies. We have not appreciated their greatness. We have not had imagination enough to see that, great as they are, there is no limit to what they may become. We have gone through a time (it is a most significant fact) when the men who advocated Free Trade in this country were at the same time absolutely indifferent to all idea of empire, and considered the colonies encumbrances which we should be glad to get rid of. That lasted for thirty years, and in the course of that time we tried the patience of our sons across the seas. We tried hardly their love of us and their devotion to the

411

mother country. They began to think that we had no sympathy with their aspirations; that we regarded them as troublesome children and wished to get them out of the house, and therefore that it would be their duty to break with the sentiment which would otherwise have held us together; that it would be their duty to fend for themselves, and to leave out of account everything which concerned the Empire of which they formed a part. That was not their fault; that was our fault, the result of our policy. Although we have done our best to correct that impression, although there is not a man living who thinks, or, if there is one who thinks, there is not one who dares to say, that he would wish to get rid of the colonies, that he does not desire their closer union with us, yet we have a good deal to make up, for we have to show that, whereas at one time we or our ancestors advocated separation, we are now prepared to do all that in reason can be asked of us in order to promote a greater and a closer union.

The colonies are no longer in their infancy. They are growing rapidly to a vigorous manhood. Now is the time – the last time – that you can bind them closer to you. If now you disregard their aspirations and wishes, if when they make you an offer not specially in their interests, but in the interests of the Empire of which we are all a portion, you reject this offer or treat it with scorn, you may do an injury which will be irreparable; and, whatever you yourselves may feel in after life, be sure that your descendants will scorn and denounce the cowardly and selfish decision which you will have adopted. We can if we will make the Empire mutually supporting. We can make it one for defence, one for common aid and assistance. We are face to face at this time with complications in which we may find ourselves alone. We have to face the envy of other people who have noted our wonderful success, although I do not think it has ever done them any harm. We have to face their envy, their jealousy, their desire, perhaps, to share the wealth which they think us to possess. I am not afraid. We shall be isolated. Yes; but our isolation will be a splendid one if we are fortified, if this country is buttressed, by the affection and love of its kinsmen, those sons of Britain throughout the world, and we shall rest secure if we continue to enjoy the affection of all our children.

When I was in South Africa nothing was more inspiring, nothing more encouraging, to a Briton than to find how the men who had either themselves come from our shores or were the descendants of those who had, still retained the old traditions, still remembered that their forefathers were buried in our churchyards, that they spoke a common language that they were under a common flag, still in their hearts desired to be remembered above all as British subjects, equally entitled with us to a part in the great Empire which they as well as we have contributed to make. The sentiment is there – powerful, vivifying, influential for good. I did not hesitate, however, to preach to them that it was not enough to shout for Empire, that it was not enough to bear this sentiment in their hearts, but that they and we alike must be content to make a common sacrifice, if that were necessary, in order to secure the common good.

To my appeal they rose. And I cannot believe that here in this country, in the mother country, their enthusiasm will not find an echo. They felt, as I felt, and as you feel, that all history is the history of States once powerful and then decaying. Is Britain to be numbered among the decaying States? Is all the glory of the past to be forgotten? Are we to prove ourselves unregenerate sons of the forefathers who left us so glorious an inheritance? Are the efforts of all our sons to be frittered away? Are all their sacrifices to be vain? Or are we to take up a new youth as members of a great Empire, which will continue for generation after generation, the strength, the power, and the glory of the British race?

That is the issue that I present to you. That is the great and paramount issue. It is also a question of your employment, of your wages, of your standard of living, of the prosperity of the trades in which you are engaged.

These are questions vital to the people of Great Britain. They are not to be decided by partisan outcries or personal abuse; they are not to be decided by a ridiculous appeal to the big loaf and the little loaf, to bogies which do not frighten sensible people, to bogies which are only addressed to the timid man, or to the man who is so prejudiced that he cannot open his mind.

Those are the issues that I present to you; and, gentlemen, the decision rests with you. Thank goodness, we enjoy a democratic constitution. Rightly or wrongly, and, as I think, rightly, the power lies with the people.[5] No dictatorship is possible; no policy can be forced upon you to give a preference to the colonies, or to put a duty upon foreign manufactures, or to protect your trade. If you choose to remain unprotected, if you do not care for your colonies, no statesman, however wise, can save those colonies as part of the Empire; for you cannot shift the responsibility upon us. We look to you; we appeal to you; we try to put the question fairly before you. The decision, as I have said, is yours.

I have been in political life for thirty years, and it has been a cardinal feature of my political creed that I have trusted the people. I believe in their judgment, in their good sense, their patriotism. I think sometimes their instincts are quicker, their judgment more generous and enlightened, than that even of classes who have greater education, who have perhaps greater belongings, who are more timid and cautious. One of the greatest of our statesmen said something to this effect – that the people were generally in the right, but that they sometimes mistook their physician. Gentlemen, do not mistake your physician. The other day, in the speech of a Scottish member, he referred to this subject. He said it was a matter for congratulations that in putting these views before my countrymen I was committing political suicide; my career would certainly be terminated. It was a kindly thought graciously expressed, worthy of the man who uttered it, but it does

413

not alarm me. I have in times past more than once taken my political life in my hand in order to teach that which I believe to be true. No man as a statesman is worth his salt who is not prepared to do likewise. I care nothing about the personal result. I beg you not to consider it for a moment; but I appeal to you to consider that in this matter the interests of your country, the interests of your children, the interests of the Empire are all at stake, and I ask you to consider impartially the arguments that I have put before you. I pray you may give a right decision.

NOTES

1 At which Mr. Balfour had declared himself in favour of the principle of Tariff Reform [see (vol. III: 21)].
2 The figures given in the then recent Board of Trade Blue Book are as follows: Total exports of British produce – 1872, £256,000,000; 1902, £278,000,000.
3 Who had published a joint remonstrance against any Tariff Reform.
4 See (vol. III: 21).
5 This was spoken in 1903, when such a boast was still apposite.

B

PARLIAMENTARY DEBATES

23 FISCAL POLICY*

John Morley

Mr. John Morley (Montrose Burghs) moved the Amendment of which he had given notice in regard to the fiscal policy of the country. He said: I am sorry to know, though this Amendment has been postponed for some days, that even now we shall not be able to have the advantage of the presence of the Prime Minister. I do not know whether he will be able to attend before the debate is concluded, but in any case, however that may be, I am sure I need not tell the House how much, both personally and on public grounds, I regret his absence. There is one other right hon. Gentleman, only less important, if indeed less important, than the Prime Minister, whose presence I understand we are not to look for during the course of this debate. I refer, of course, to my right hon. friend the Member for West Birmingham. I hope I shall not be trespassing beyond the proprieties of the occasion if I mention that I have known the right hon. Gentleman for half a life-time. During all those years I was in close and intimate relations with him, and I do not think I will allow any differences of opinion upon public questions – and between him and me they are, and have been, profound, and never more profound than they are to-day – to prevent me from saying, if the House will permit me, that he possesses in a most marked and peculiar degree the genius of friendship – sincere, kind, and staunch friendship. Mr. Powell Williams, who, a few hours ago passed away from our great world-theatre, found friends amongst us all. But to the Member for West Birmingham he was more than an ordinary friend. He was one who, in sunshine and in storm, was his close, faithful, and trusted adherent; and I for one, and I believe in all parts of the House hon. Gentlemen will agree with me, fully comprehend and entirely respect the feeling which has mastered the Member for West Birmingham.

It has been suggested to me that, as these two great protagonists of – I do not know whether I should call them rival policies or of identical policies – are unable to take part in this debate, we should postpone it. I cannot myself, for one moment, think that a well-founded view. I think we

* John Morley, *Parliamentary Debates*, 4th series (8 February 1904, House of Commons) (London: Wyman and Sons, Ltd.), cols 623–644.

are bound in this House to take the very first opportunity of bringing to the test of a discussion at close quarters the question that has agitated the mind of the country for the last four or five months, and we ought to know – it is our duty to know – where the House stands, where Ministers stand, and where the question stands. I think quite long enough, and too long, has it been the case that this House, of all places in the island, is the only place where this question has not been, and apparently is not to be, discussed. We think the House of Commons would be wanting in one of its first duties, perhaps its most fundamental duty, if it were not to take this opportunity of raising the question which arises on my Amendment. After all, its highest constitutional function is to examine the national charges, to survey national ways and means, to adjust the national burden. We are going this session to do so in remarkable – I think in unprecedented – circumstances. We have not only the well-known announcement of the Prime Minister, which I will not trouble at this stage to introduce, that he is for a deep and genuine change in our fiscal policy – that we are to annul and delete the traditions of two generations. We have also from the Chancellor of the Exchequer, the Minister who is specially responsible for the financial administration of the country, a strong declaration that "the time has come when we should make a breach with the traditions of the past" – I think he must have forgotten that he is on the Conservative side of the House – "and that we should allow ourselves to think for ourselves." That is very impressive, but does that Bench think for themselves? Then he says: – "We are making progress." Who are "we," and where is the progress to? The right hon. Gentleman will, no doubt, answer us those questions; but, be that as it may, it is indispensable that, if we are to discuss our financial situation, the supreme business of the House, with real efficacy, we must know whether we have got a protectionist or an anti-protectionist Government to guide us. It is not very easy to be quite sure of that. We are apt, in this House, to regard with suspicion, and perhaps with a trace of mockery, anybody who introduces a Motion, and begins by saying that it is not a Party Motion. I venture respectfully to submit to the House that I can make that claim to-day, because my Amendment will, unless I am greatly mistaken, be most powerfully reinforced, perhaps even more powerfully than we could argue it on this side, by Gentlemen, who are sitting among yourselves, by Gentlemen who a few months ago were amongst your most trusted and responsible and experienced leaders and Members. That is one thing which, I think, divests my Amendment of a Party aspect purely. And I would venture another, however insignificant, observation of a personal kind, that in economics and finance, so gravely do I, for my part, always regard these questions – much more gravely than purely political questions – that when the right hon. Gentleman the Member for Bristol was Chancellor of the Exchequer he will remember that I voted freely away from my friends who sit near me, and that I supported the Government on the coal tax and on the sugar tax. But the last straw – the corn duty – broke my back, and I could support him and the Government no more. I do not often regale myself by reading old speeches of my own, but when I went over again the observations which I had to address to the House in moving the rejection of the Report stage of the Corn Duty Clause of the Finance Bill, I really was astonished, not at my own moderation, but at my own foresight. Every observation that I made almost has been verified by the scenes of the last few months. I warned the then Chancellor of the Exchequer that he was entering upon a course which would inevitably lead him or his Party to colonial preference and to a tax upon food – to proposals for a tax upon food.

Well now, the Chancellor of the Exchequer on Tuesday last referred to some language I had used implying that the state of the industries of the country was not all that we could desire. I have always held for the last eight years the same language. I agree with the right hon. Gentleman the Member for West Birmingham on this point. I have said it again and again both inside this House and outside this House. There is a great deal in the state of the commerce and industry, and of the employment of our population which must give every serious and observant man plenty of food for reflection. I have always in the country wound up with the declaration of the late Lord Salisbury, which was that there is ground for anxiety, that no statesman can look around and see these new conditions without anxiety; but then Lord Salisbury went on to say –

"That is no reason why we should grasp at the first remedy that any man chooses to propose to us."

Sir, if the House will, for an instant, pardon an historical reference: during the last sixty years, which we are going to refer to so often in the course of this debate, the first step was Sir Robert Peel's liberation from the tariff of a certain number of articles in 1842. There then followed, in 1860, eighteen years afterwards, what Mr. Gladstone always used to call the cardinal and organic emancipatory free trade period. During that time, first by Sir Robert Peel and then Mr. Gladstone, an enormous number of articles were removed from the tariff which restricted trade, which interfered with the application of capital, and which prevented the free exercise of skill and industry. I am not sure that it was 1860; anyhow, by 1860 or 1866 that great emancipatory period was concluded. And these were all occasions of the most remarkable kind. And there was what the right hon. Member for Bristol will admit, a further important step taken, not in this House, nor by a statesman, but by the constituencies in the year 1874, when they by their rejection of the proposals then made to them for the abolition of the income-tax, settled finally that the income-tax was to be a permanent instrument of the national revenue. There are three or four stages of which I venture to remind the House. It may be; we do not know yet whether the

417

new movement that began on 15th May last year was a conflagration or whether it is to prove merely the flash of a meteor; I hope that this debate will perhaps clear the air a little on that issue; but anyhow there is this peculiarity in the situation in which we have now entered. In 1843 the state of the finances of the country, the state of the industry of the country, the dilapidation of the revenue, were so marked that it was the urgent duty of the Ministry of that day at once to set to work to remedy so deplorable a state of things. That was what Sir Robert Peel did in 1846. There was scarcity and famine which cried aloud for legislation; and in 1860 there were particular relations between this country and France. At that moment there was also an accidental state of things in the Exchequer which precipitated the occasion of which Mr. Gladstone took advantage. Upon all those occasions there was urgency; and even, if I may refer to 1886, when a very great and important step was taken by the Prime Minister of that day, which divided Parties, as Parties are divided now, there was urgency. If the Prime Minister had been here now I am sure he would have agreed with me that the solution which we then propounded to this House and to the country and which this House first and the country afterwards rejected – whether that solution of Home Rule was right or wrong – there was in the state of Ireland a condition of social order, and there was in this House a state of Parties which made it a question of urgency. But where is the urgency for the change that the Ministry now propose? What is the crisis, what is the emergency? I know that all controversies are liable to expand and to grow; and after the very effective treatment which my right hon. friend the Leader of the Opposition gave to the history of this crisis last Tuesday night, I am not going to repeat it to the House. But the change, everybody knows is expressed in a sentence. This new fiscal policy was sprung upon the country. I do not use the word "sprung" in an invidious sense; but it was launched from the colonial point of view. The colonial point of view pretty rapidly disappeared. [*Ministerial* cries of "No, no."] The hon. Member who says "No," if he takes part in the debate later, will perhaps tell us how he regards the position of the colonial policy. It disappeared, and a new case was presented. It was then that the industry and commerce of the country were languishing and declining, and demanded a prompt and immediate treatment (that was the new case), and that a remedy should be provided with the utmost despatch. It was rather odd, because it was not long before the Member for West Birmingham, who first launched the policy, had in tones of perfectly natural jubilation congratulated the country that it had been able to bear the enormous financial burden of the Boer war without turning a hair. But I see opposite to me the President of the Board of Trade. Very likely he will do me the honour to follow me in this debate. The President of the Board of Trade this time last year did not think that there was any crisis or any emergency. This is the language of the President of the Board of Trade to his constituents on 23rd January, 1903 –

> "He confessed that he did not see any signs of the decline and ruin of British industry which was the prominent topic with the British newspapers, and though the critics might have done good by drawing attention to the shortcoming, they could have too much even of a good thing, and he was bound to say that he thought the part of Cassandra had been somewhat overdone. He thought that in this matter they could do well with a little of the optimism which distinguished Mr. Chamberlain."

I respectfully ask the right hon. Gentleman to tell us when he rises whether in his view there was an emergency then. Surely not! Then what happened within three or four months? The President of the Board of Trade seems to have been led by the Member for West Birmingham into a completely new and reverse position, and we should be glad to know whether now he thinks, he having used the language which I have just read to the House, that agriculture is destroyed – [*Sir Howard Vincent*: Hear, hear!] – and all the rest of it. I should listen to him with the most respectful attention. Will he tell us why he has changed his mind, if he has changed his mind? Is there any indication or the smallest evidence of there being a crisis or an emergency except an artificial and invented crisis? The Prime Minister himself, I think at Bristol, said that he would have been very glad if circumstances – I do not know quite what the circumstances were – allowed him to leave this question, which was an urgent question, as an open question in his Cabinet. If it had been a critical or an urgent question, it would not have been an open question. There is no doubt about that. There is another point about that which I address to the President of the Board of Trade. The Government instituted what they called an inquiry – a proceeding which the Duke of Devonshire, although a party to it, describes publicly as having proved a deception. But the Member for West Birmingham speaks in the most contemptuous language of the inquiry instituted by the Board of Trade. He says that this Blue-book is the library of the free importers, meaning by that the whole contents of that Blue-book are a library of arguments for free importers. [Cries of "No."]

I will not detain the House long in arguing the second clause of my Amendment, namely, "that the removal of protective duties has for more than half a century actively conduced to the vast extension of the trade and commerce of the nation." You may dispute, if you please; I fully admit how many other elements there are that have entered into that most prosperous and satisfactory state of things which, until the other day, we were all agreed in recognising. Of course there were other elements which may have entered, but any hon. Member who endeavours to make an adjustment of the degree to which this prosperity is due to free trade, or to other elements, I warn him that he will enter upon a task of the most intricate and complex character. This I do venture to say, without fear of contradiction from hon. Gentlemen opposite or any where else, that the condition precedent to this country's being able to avail itself of the various other elements, such as railways and other things which have been good for the country, was free trade. If I may be allowed to indulge for a moment in a philosophical reflection, you may say, if you please, that the decision, by the repeal of the Corn Laws in 1846, to make the ideal of those islands a manufacturing community, instead of an agricultural community – you may say, if you like, that that was a wrong decision. But I am no great idolater of the factory system. I think it has produced, and I refer to them in my Amendment, a state of things which needs manifest and urgent remedies. I remember Mr. Mill, formerly a Member of this House and much more than a Member of this House. He used to tell us that if the alternative was between Socialism and the evil social condition then, as now, prevailing in many parts of these islands, though against Socialism, he would rather face Socialism with all its risks than acquiesce in the subsisting state of things. But it is not worth arguing now. If England is to be characteristically a manufacturing community, the man who denies that free imports actively conduce, and not only conduce but are indispensable, to our commerce and the welfare of our population – I say such a man, whoever he may be, shows himself so grossly ignorant of the social conditions of the country between the end of the great war and the time of Sir Robert Peel that I will not waste the time of the House in arguing against him. Then there is another position taken by some of the disputants in this controversy – I will not argue with them if they say it is matter of history and fact that protective duties were removed on the faith of anticipations and prophecies of imitation by other countries. To make that assertion is to be guilty of a ludicrous falsification of all you will read in speeches by Sir Robert Peel, Mr. Cobden, or anybody else; it is not worth argument. The effect of protective duties had been so examined by the country, had been so repudiated by the country, that the free trade policy, which was not only passed in this House in 1846, but was ratified by the general election in 1847, was held fast to all through the years from 1847 to 1852, when there was another general election, and the country still repudiated, having had bitter experience, anything like a return to protective duties. Mr. Disraeli himself, the Leader of your Party, said the country had decided, and therefore it would be a culpable waste of time to argue whether the country had good or bad reasons for its dislike of protective duties.

I am not going to take the House – and I am sure they will thank me for it – into all the controversy, or points of controversy even, in the discussions that have taken place during the last few months in the country; but I should like to call the attention of the House to what I call general fallacies – not fallacies of statistics, though they were fallacious enough – but general fallacies that seem to me to have pervaded these discussions. It is a very short list, though I do not believe there is a single fallacy that has not found illustration in speeches from hon. and right hon. Gentlemen on that Bench. This is the method. You take every case that is hypothetically possible, theoretically imaginable or conceivable, and immediately treat that as if it were an actual case and an urgent case. Then you begin with the economical argument, and when you find that the ground will not bear you you then change ground suddenly, and, dropping the economical argument, take refuge in sentimental, idealist, or political arguments. The third method, which has struck me very much, is that you show that circumstances might arise which might justify a tariff as the proper expedient, and then you proceed to infer that the argument is exactly as valid for existing circumstances, though these are entirely different from your hypothetical case. Then you state a fact, and if that fact is completely demolished in two or three days, you then say that it was an illustration, not an argument. I have read a number of speeches in which hon. Gentlemen opposite have been literally guilty of supposing that a protective duty is the same thing as a revenue duty, though, of course, a protective duty is the exact opposite of a revenue duty and thoroughly ill-adapted for all the purposes of a revenue duty. And then about the consumer and imports strange language has been used. The consumer has been spoken of as if he were a sort of habitual inebriate, and every import as if it were an affront to the British Empire. There is one argument I wish to deal with, the argument that times have changed and that conditions of industry have altered in our day. That is not at all an unnatural position to take, but I submit boldly to the House that not one of the changes that have taken place since 1846 – I think there is not one which does not make against protection and in favour of free trade. I maintain further that protection will aggravate every one of the mischiefs of which you complain. The first argument is, "Oh, since then – [*Sir Howard Vincent*, Hear, hear!] – there have sprung up great rivals." The hon. and gallant Member for Sheffield ironically cheers that. Does he suppose that any statesman deemed in 1846 that Great Britain was going to be the manufacturer to all eternity for the whole universe? [*Sir Howard Vincent*: Mr. Cobden said so.] I probably know a great deal more about Cobden than the hon. and gallant Gentleman, and I say that so far was he from saying that that he said exactly the opposite. I am prompted by the interruption of the hon. and gallant Member to read an extract of a few sentences from Mr. Cobden. When I regard the contemptuous language used about Mr. Cobden by men who are unworthy to loosen his shoe latchet, I venture to recall to the House language – very beautiful language, well worthy of his genius – used by Mr. Disraeli. Standing, I suppose, at this box, when Mr. Cobden died, Mr. Disraeli said –

"Thus our great men, when taken from us, are not altogether lost. Though not present, they are still Members of this House, independent of the caprice of constituencies, independent of dissolutions of Parliament, independent of the course of time. Their example will long be referred to and appealed to, and their words will often be quoted."

This was the language used by a Leader of your Party, a Leader who really led. Now, in reference to the hon. and gallant Member's statement that Mr. Cobden held out the expectation that this country would remain without manufacturing rivals, I will ask the House to listen to this extract –

"Looking at the natural endowments of the North American continent, at the boundless expanse of the most fertile soil in the world, at the inexhaustible mines of coal, iron, lead."

Looking at these, the writer reiterates the moral of his former work, declaring his conviction that it is from

"the silent, peaceful rivalry of American commerce, and the growth of American manufactures,"

and so on, that the

"grandeur of our commercial and national prosperity is most endangered."

Sir Howard Vincent: What is the date of this statement of Mr. Cobden's?
Mr. John Morley: I cannot say offhand, but I will satisfy the hon. and gallant Gentleman. It was the base of the whole policy, and it is, I hope, the base of the policy of us who sit on this side of the House, that it is exactly because you have this formidable competition to face that you should pursue a policy of peace, of reduced expenditure, and a policy of national education. That was the base of the whole of Mr. Cobden's national policy. But I must hurry on. The more formidable the competition is, the more reason is there why you should leave as much freedom as possible for the application of capital, for the exercise of skill and industry, and the general operations of trade. The second change is that you have all over the land enormous aggregates of population in manufacturing towns. Is that an argument for protection? Is it not an argument, the strongest you can use, for leaving all the channels by which food and raw materials find their way to our shores not narrow, not blocked? There is no argument for protection in that change. Then there have been, no doubt, enormous developments in steam locomotion and in telegraphic communication, having the effect of producing enormous mobility of capital and rapidity of transit of products from place to place. Granting all this, how can these great changes, these great material changes, be utilised to the uttermost unless you have open ports? Every change of this kind, if it means one

thing more clearly than any other, means that protection in any form would be the most ruinous step you could possibly take.

There is another change. The Colonies have accomplished great permanent power and prosperity. Yes, but I invite attention to this. Suppose that the policy of protection should tend to diminish the protective and accumulative power of this country, and should impoverish this country, what worse thing could happen to the Colonies than such an event as that? The Colonies have almost more to lose than we have by our impoverishment. Diminish our plentiful supply of capital, or our cheap and rapid means of locomotion, and all these boons which we are able to place at their disposal would be either stopped or limited; and I say that the demands of the Colonies are one of the strongest arguments for an anti-protection policy. There is another great change – the transfer of political power, since 1846, from the old £10 householders to the artisans of the towns and the labourers of the fields. I am not going to argue the effect of free trade upon political peace, but I would submit to the House that it cannot be quite an accident – it cannot be a fortuitous coincidence – that the great free trade country of Europe is the one great country of Western Europe which since 1846 has never known even a shadow of a civil convulsion. There is no great country in the West of Europe which equals us in the absence from class division, class envy, hatred, and strife which unfortunately prevails in some other countries. It cannot be that that circumstance is entirely unconnected with our fiscal policy. There is one other change of great importance, no doubt – the Suez Canal. That has made an enormous difference in many ways, and the effect upon the international trade of the world and the effect on our position as a great distributing centre has been of course enormous. But will the President of the Board of Trade tell me accurately, with chapter and verse, how a scientific tariff which is to affect the wool market or the tea market is to prevent that from having changed the position in London as I understand it has. This is the thing. You hear of the Suez Canal doing this or that in the redistribution of commodities, and then you say, "the thing is wrong, we will put it right," but a scientific tariff would not put it right. How could it? Many Members of the House who are well versed in these things will perhaps tell us. I will listen with absolute interest and candour to any demonstration they can offer that a tariff can affect this matter. A scientific tariff means really a tariff arrived at from a judicious computation of conflicting interests. I do not think that would do any good in this case.

Perhaps the House would now like me to turn to the question of the policy of the Government. We are opening a discussion which is no abstract economic discussion. In some ways it is only secondarily an economic discussion at all. We are face to face with a political situation, and it is of great importance that we should have that clearly examined. The Prime Minister, speaking at Bristol, said –

"Did anybody ever hear of a Cabinet which was not merely agreed upon a policy but was also agreed upon every principle upon which that policy was supposed to depend and upon every conclusion to which those principles might be pressed?"

I cannot find the Cabinet are agreed upon any policy which deserves to be so called in any better sense than tactics of Party managers and Party wire-pullers. They are the tactics of make-believe – make-believe that a Party which is divided is not divided. You cannot call these tactics a policy. You take great care that even as a make-believe you do your best to prevent anybody being taken in by it. The Prime Minister said it was –

"Most unreasonable to come forward and taunt us because my collea-gues who are agreed upon a policy do not pretend that they are agreed upon every conceivable development of that policy which that policy might under given circumstances take."

What is curious is that all the eloquence and all the energy is given to the "conceivable development." I would now ask the House to consider this agreement upon policy in the light of two or three utterances of important Gentlemen opposite, and I will begin, as indeed I ought, with the President of the Board of Trade. Speaking in October last, the President of the Board of Trade used this language –

"For the present, at all events, he did not consider it would be in the interest of the Party or of the policy they were recommending to include in the official programme (there were, it appears, two pro-grammes) of the Government, a preference carrying as it did with it taxation of food."

That is the President of the Board of Trade. But then there is the Parliamentary Secretary to the Board of Trade. He uses somewhat different language. He says he really believes that a trade preference to the Colonies is an essential part and would be an inevitable result of any change in our fiscal policy. He sympathised with Mr. Chamberlain's proposals. The President of the Board of Trade said one thing and his Parliamentary Secretary said quite the opposite. Then we come to the Postmaster-General, who said that with Mr. Chamberlain's scheme of preferential tariffs he could not agree. Then the noble Lord the Under-Secretary for Foreign Affairs made some very remarkable declarations indeed as a member of a Government which has quite agreed on its policy. He individually believed in Mr. Chamberlain's corn taxation proposals, and he said unhesitatingly that he believed it would be to the advantage of the country to adopt them. He frankly confessed that he did not think they would really benefit the agricultural industry at home. "For all his objects" – let the House notice this – let hon. Gentlemen opposite who are thinking how they will vote on this Amendment mark this – "for all his objects Mr. Chamberlain carries with him the hearty approval of his colleagues in the Government he has left."

Earl Percy: Objects, not methods.

Mr. John Morley: I invite the noble Lord in the course of this debate to draw a distinction between his sympathy with the objects of the Member for Birmingham and his disapproval of his methods. Then there is the President of the Local Government Board. I scanned his utterance very closely because he had taken the very striking step of going down to a constituency represented by a Conservative colleague and doing his best to turn that Conservative colleague out. He said it was not an inconsistent declaration for him also to say that while with his present information he was against the taxation of food – what is his present information? I wonder what information he does want? – while his present information is against the taxation of food, he could conceive the arrival of a time when Mr. Chamberlain's policy would be satisfactorily developed and the proper system discovered by which it could be applied.

The President of the Local Government Board (Mr. Walter Long, Bristol, S.): Is that not an extract from the speech of a Gentleman who had spoken before me and which I used as a quotation.

Mr. John Morley: I gave the right hon. Member my most studious attention, and I can assure the right hon. Gentleman I think not. Is a satisfactory development a development that ends in the taxation of the people? Then there is the Colonial Secretary, who went down to Leamington and recalled graceful reminiscences of Carlyle and Ruskin, and how they had overcome what he called the gloomy *doctrinaires* from Manchester. The gloomy *doctrinaires* of Manchester made short work of the sentimental idealist from Leamington. Does the right hon. Gentleman forget that if the Corn Laws and the whole policy of protection had two men more thoroughly opposed to them than Carlyle and Ruskin, I should be very much surprised? Carlyle's most saturnine, caustic, and picturesque descriptions are directed against the Corn Laws and against the Party of the kind of gentlemen who are now wanting to bring the Corn Laws back. The right hon. Gentleman shakes his head as if he did not want to bring the Corn Laws back. The right hon. Gentleman said he thought the ends of the right hon. Member for Birmingham were right and good ends, and he accepted as the expositor of those ends Mr. Charles Booth. Mr. Charles Booth is a protectionist. [No.] Is he not for a 5 per cent. duty? The right hon. Gentleman ought not to deny it.

The Secretary of State for the Colonies (Mr. Lyttelton Warwick and Leamington): Deny what?

Mr. John Morley: That you are a protectionist. To finish the extracts, I think they are most pithily summed up by the Secretary for the Local Government Board as follows –

"Some people said that Mr. Balfour and Mr. Chamberlain were in opposition. Others said that their policy was the same. He submitted that the true case was this – that Mr. Chamberlain was weaving a second string of the Government bow lest the negotiation string should snap before its work was done."

When these are the responsible governors of the country can you wonder that Consols are down to eighty-seven? I leave this part of the business with a quotation which expresses my view better than I can express it from the right hon. Member for Birmingham in a speech made in 1885 –

"I will say that Lord Salisbury does intend"

– and here I think he was unjust to Lord Salisbury –

"to put a duty upon corn, though he does not think it convenient at the present moment to say so, and although he allows some members of his Government to argue in favour of it in one place, he enjoins upon other members of his Government to repudiate it in another. Remember, this is not a question upon which the Government can be allowed to have two voices. If you are going to tax the bread of the people you will affect every household in the land; you will throw back the working classes of the country to the starvation wages and the destitution from which Mr. Gladstone and Sir Robert Peel have relieved them."

What is meant by retaliation? The word "retaliation" is used, I observe, by many gentlemen as a sort of formula by which they can escape the labour of a close examination of what the issue really is. Last summer, in this House the Prime Minister said –

"If other methods fail I do not shrink from retaliation, but I am not certain that there are not other methods."

I suppose he meant by "other methods" diplomatic negotiations of the ordinary sort. A case was brought to my notice the other day arising out of the reciprocity treaty between the United States and Cuba. Liverpool, Manchester, and, I think, the London Chambers of Commerce carried on a correspondence and had an interview with Lord Lansdowne, representing to him that the arrangements under that treaty would be extremely prejudicial and would in fact practically close the door to British manufacturers in Cuba. I wonder what "other methods" the Prime Minister would apply to a case of that kind? But now let us suppose a real case of outrageous unfairness perpetrated against us by a foreign Government. I am myself unable to find evidence of there having been any outrageous case of unfairness. [Cries of "Oh!"] I know some hon. Gentlemen regard a high tariff as an act of outrageous unfairness, but that is not what the Prime Minister means. If there be a case of outrageous unfairness the Minister of the day has only to satisfy this House of three conditions, and I am perfectly sure this House, whichever Party be in the majority, would support the Minister. What are the three conditions? The first is that the Minister would have to satisfy the House and make good the case on the facts, that outrageous unfairness had been or was being perpetrated; secondly, he would have to show that he had got a plan for reprisal that would effectually stop it; and, thirdly, he would have to persuade this House that his plan of reprisal not only was likely to effect the special object he had in view, but was not likely to do a great deal more harm in another way. If those conditions were satisfied, I do not think there would be any difficulty in carrying through this House whatever retaliatory powers were necessary. But do you mean power to impose a retaliatory duty independent of, outside of, and beyond Parliament? The Emperor of the French, in 1860, was able to carry the Cobden treaty with this country, though his two Chambers were both of them strongly and stoutly opposed to anything like free trade, because, happily for him and for us, there was a clause in the Imperial Constitution which allowed the Emperor to make a tariff binding if it was part of a treaty. Is that what you want? Do you want to be put in the position of the French Emperor? It is extravagant and absurd, the notion of any Minister having the power with his two Chambers both opposed to him, by decree to set up a tariff. I was much interested in another plan set out in a candid and well-argued book called "The Tariff Problem," by Professor Ashley of Birmingham University. What is his idea? He says –

"What seems dictated by the requirements of the case is a statutory authorisation of the Executive to impose the duties that may be required from time to time as circumstances arise. It will not be safe to wait until the need arises before appealing to Parliament, for the mischief is of a kind that can be accomplished in a very brief period."

Does the House really apprehend what is proposed by this excellent writer, who lives very near the centre of authority, very near to Mecca? To carry out the policy, in order to secure an economic revolution, it is proposed to make the most astounding political revolution in our history since the time of the Civil War. The writer supposes cases so urgent that you cannot wait from August or September, when Parliament rises, till January, when it reassembles. I cannot for my part realise any of those cases. What sort of powers of negotiation do you want? Let us suppose that the Steel Trust of the United States announced, projected, and carried out the landing of an enormous stock of their goods at a low price upon our shores. What are you going to do? I suppose Lord Lansdowne would invite the very distinguished man who represents the United States in this country to an interview with him at the Foreign Office. Lord Lansdowne would say to Mr. Choate, "Unless your Government put a stop to a certain set of traders sending us billets and blooms so cheaply we will impose a duty, or even prohibition as well, so as to close our markets to you."

Mr. Choate, however, has a very easy reply to Lord Lansdowne. He would say, "How can the American Government prevent a commercial company from selling so cheaply to British markets?"

Then supposing statutory authorisation were obtained, and suppose Mr. Secretary Hey said of Mr. Choate, "Are we to instruct him to come to you, who are so famous for selling cheap all over the world, and to say, 'if you do not give up selling cheap we will exclude you from the United States market.'" [*Ministerial* cries of "They would do it."] You have only to come to close quarters with the subject to see how absurd it is. There is tremendous suffering at this moment in Lancashire. It is not due to the Americans selling goods too cheap, but to the making of cotton too dear. What are hon. Gentlemen who suppose that by some formula you are going to remedy all the evils of the commercial system going to do about cotton? Are you to request the President of the United States to get Congress to pass an Act to prevent gambling in cotton? The idea is absurd. Then it is said that you want something to bargain with. This is the process I think that the Prime Minister has in his mind. But how do you start? Are you to set up a general or all-round tariff, to build up a general Customs wall with the view of frightening the foreigner into lowering the general level of his adverse tariff? The Prime Minister said in his Sheffield speech that he did not intend to set up a general tariff. What the Government is going to do is to set up a combative tariff, to start with a heavy duty on all manufactured imports. The Prime Minister is against that because he thinks it would be a disturbance of the existing practice, and would lead to the disorganisation of trade; therefore he abandons the general tariff. What does he say next? For a man so clear of speech, when he likes, this is the most nebulous declaration I remember to have seen from a man in a great station. He sees the objection to the combative tariff, but says –

> "I see no such objection to our proceeding, so to speak, from the other end; and if we thought we could do so without disadvantage to ourselves, we might inform any foreign country that we thought they were treating us with such outrageous unfairness that, unless they modified their policy to our advantage, we should feel ourselves compelled to take this or that step in regard to their exports."

I call that nebulous. I want to know what steps? When the Prime Minister announces a revolution in policy surely we have a right to expect that he should tell us what he intends to do, what "this or that step" is going to be. We have a right to ask also what is his "method" of settlement with a foreign negotiator. [Cries of "Speak up."] I suppose it would mean a threat to say to Russia to this effect, "Unless you reduce your general tariff we will impose an adverse discriminating duty on your wheat and hemp and other products," having free trade with the rest of the world. I do not know how that will work or what the effect would be on the corn market; but what is to prevent Russia from sending her grain through Holland and reaching us in that way? In the Napoleonic wars English goods got into the Continent despite all hindrances, and therefore we wish to know accurately what "step" it is that the right hon. Gentleman means.

There is another vital question I wish to put. Is this change to be a permanent or a temporary tariff? After all, that is the great issue. Do you want to put on duties to bargain with and after making your bargain and frightening the foreigner into lowering his tariff are you going to take them off again? Are you going to dismantle your fiscal batteries and to shut up your Customs house? I will not argue the point or dwell upon its prospect of success, but I think it will create a frightful dislocation of trade as well as embarrassing your Budget from year to year unless you know what all these extraordinary operations are to be. This is an urgently important point with regard to the political situation, because this policy of a temporary dealing with the tariff is absolutely inconsistent with the policy of the right hon. Member for West Birmingham. You do not believe in a permanent tariff; but he does. He wants a scientific protective tariff; but you do not tell us what it is you mean. The right hon. Gentleman appeals to the protective policy of the United States, of France, and of Germany, and he recites how they passed tariff after tariff. It was not a haphazard policy; it was a deliberate policy to use tariffs to increase home trade and, if you like, to exclude foreign trade. The right hon. Member for West Birmingham says these foreigners are not fools, and he winds up by asking about this foreign policy. "Has it succeeded? It has succeeded." Those who consider that they are not voting for a protective policy when supporting with cheers and enthusiasm the right hon. Gentleman the Member for West Birmingham cannot have read his utterances. Now what is your attitude towards these proposals? What, however, was the Government attitude? The Prime Minister's language is obscure and ambiguous; still he leaves room for some expectation that he is not committed to protection. But his language is one thing and his action is another. When a candidate stands for Norwich the Prime Minister sends down his blessing with the watchword "Union and fiscal reform." This gentleman at Norwich was a complete fiscal reformer in its extreme length; and that has been the attitude of the Prime Minister ever since the controversy arose. The great difficulty is to know whether you are men in masks or whether you are straightforwardly telling the country and the House what it is you want.

Now is the moment for hon. Gentlemen to make up their minds and for every individual Member to ask himself whether he is for protection or whether he is against it. It is in the highest degree distasteful to me to place any difficulties by the form in which I venture to put this question to the House in the way of hon. Gentlemen who, to their great honour and to the credit of English public life, have made the greatest sacrifice that any public men can possibly make. I think the case was worth the sacrifice. I do not believe there has ever been a more irresistible demand upon all of us for manliness, frankness, and moral courage; and I hope these hon. Gentlemen will not flinch from the views they have advocated with all the strength of their experience and responsibility. Let them ask themselves this question, "Am I going to vote for confidence in a protectionist Government or for confidence in an anti-protectionist Government." They will shirk the prime duty of political life at this moment if they are not satisfied on this point, and guided by the answer they give to themselves when they go into the Lobby. I, for my part, am not at all careful as to the numbers in the division when the division is taken. After all, what is important is this – What will be the result of that far greater division in the country when it takes place? I will not venture to predict, but I shall be very much surprised if the constituencies, when the time comes, express confidence in the Government at a time like this, when we have just barely emerged from the financial confusion and embarrassment caused by the late war, and when we are face to face with events threatening, or, I am afraid, I must say, events now happening, which, beyond almost any set of circumstances which have arisen in our recent history, impose the necessity on Great Britain, at all events, of keeping her powder dry, and of keeping her resources in steadfast charge. I say that if the country gives its confidence to any Government at a moment so grave as this, it will not be to a Government which, upon the plea of an emergency which does not really exist, and on behalf of a thing called fiscal reform which they cannot – I know they cannot – explain or define, are ready to plunge the country into confusion, and to pave the way to ultimate disaster.

Amendment proposed, at the end of the Question, to add the words –

"But it is our duty, however, humbly to represent to Your Majesty that our effective deliberation on the financial service of the year is impaired by conflicting declarations from Your Majesty's Ministers. We respectfully submit to Your Majesty the judgment of this House, that the removal of protective duties has for more than half a century actively conduced to the vast extension of the trade and commerce of the realm and to the welfare of its population; and this House believes that, while the needs of social improvement are still manifold and urgent, any return to protective duties, more particularly when imposed on the food of the people, would be deeply injurious to our national strength, contentmet [*sic*] and well being."

24 FISCAL POLICY*

Gerald Balfour

[*Mr. Winston Churchill*: I said the policy of the Prime Minister was not very important because it was not the issue before the country.]

Mr. Gerald Balfour: I beg leave to differ from the hon. Gentleman. It is the policy before the country. I think the real explanation of the language of my hon. friend is, that he, like others, can see nothing in fiscal reform except protection. Protection occupies the entire field of his vision, and my hon. friend is not alone in this because there seems to be something like an organised conspiracy to represent the issue before the country as an issue between free trade and protection. I absolutely deny that. I quite admit there is a natural temptation so to represent it. The old proverb, "Give a dog a bad name and hang him," has no doubt a good deal in it. If you can not only give your adversary a bad name, but retain a good one for yourself, double advantage is secured. But this way of presenting the issue is absolutely superficial and misleading. Let us look more closely at the various classes of opinion respecting this fiscal question existing in the country and this House at the present time. There are, at least, four such classes. First you have the free importers; next, those who approve the Government policy, who ask for a free hand to negotiate, and, if necessary, to retaliate; thirdly, there are those who follow the right hon. Gentleman the Member for West Birmingham, and who favour preferential arrangements with the Colonies; and, lastly, there are the protectionists. Anyone who is a protectionist will probably also be in favour of preference and of a free hand in negotiation: but the reverse by no means follows. There are many who are in favour of a free hand in negotiation who do not advocate preference, and others who advocate preference, but are by no means protectionists. The various distinctions have been so loosely appreciated in discussions on the platform that it is advisable to endeavour to define a little more precisely the essential characteristic of each class of opinion.

The free importers are free traders in intention, but not in reality. Free trade in its essence is bilateral. The characteristic mark of the free importer is not free trade. It is the refusal to adopt any other method than that of moral suasion in order to bring about free trade. They are the Quakers of finance. Their policy is a purely negative policy; they are the peace-at-any-price party in relation to industrial affairs. When Sir Robert Peel stated that in his view the best way of fighting tariffs was by free imports, he uttered a maxim which was no doubt a maxim of expediency at the time at which he spoke; but that maxim was subsequently converted into a fundamental

* Gerald Balfour, *Parliamentary Debates*, 4th series (8 February 1904, House of Commons) (London: Wyman and Sons, Ltd.), cols 656–664.

principle of English finance, that no taxation should be put on except for revenue purposes; and the principle itself became in turn something like a dogma, under no circumstances to be set aside or modified. You cannot hold that dogma and at the same time be in favour of freedom of negotiation; you cannot hold it to be final and unconditional and yet advocate preferential policy. *A fortiori* it is not possible to hold it and be a protectionist.

Let me pass to the fiscal reformers, and first of all to the protectionists. When I speak of protection I refer to the system existing at the present time in the United States of America, France, Germany, and other continental countries. What is protection? Protection is a system of artificial assistance deliberately accorded to particular industries by the State, generally by means of import duties, in order to give these industries advantages over and above what they would enjoy under conditions of natural competition. That is my definition of protection, and in order to illustrate it I should like to refer to what are called countervailing duties. Countervailing duties are duties imposed as a counterpoise to a bounty. They have to be most carefully discriminated from protective duties. They are really duties imposed in self defence. There is an ambiguity in the word "protection," and it would be greatly in the interests of clear discussion if, when we are speaking of protection to industry by a duty which is in the nature of a countervailing duty, we were to call it not protection but defence. There is a distinction between defensive duties and protection. Defensive duties are in my opinion perfectly legitimate even as part of the theory of free trade. Protective duties stand in a different category.

We have been challenged to-night to say whether the policy of the Government is protectionist or anti-protectionist. I have already stated, I hope in clear language, that the policy of the Government is not protectionist. If I am asked, not as a member of the Government but as an individual – the distinction is perfectly legitimate – what my own view of protection is, I am perfectly willing to state it. I do not think that protection is a wise policy for this country to adopt. I do not wish to make any absolute statement of faith with regard to protection in other countries. The effect of protection is, practically, to impose a tax on the consumer for the benefit of the producer. If the extra profits resulting from protection, or part of such profits, are employed, as may easily happen, to further the development of industrial enterprise, it is possible – I believe in some instances it is actually the case – that a policy of protection may really stimulate industrial development. I think protection has probably stimulated industrial development in Germany and also in the United States. Therefore I should be extremely reluctant to say that either Germany or the United States had adopted a policy which was wrong for these countries. On the contrary. I think very likely it was right for Germany and the United States. But for our country – which had such an immense start over all others, which was a highly developed manufacturing country at a time when such a description could not be applied to any other country – protection for such a country is, I believe, a bad policy, and I should be sorry to see a return to it now. I will even go so far as this – that if it was a choice between protection as we know it in Germany and America, and other countries and the existing system, I should be on the side of free imports. But, as a matter of fact, nothing of the kind is the case. It is possible to hold the views which I have just expressed and yet be a warm advocate of preferential arrangements with the Colonies. The object of preference is twofold. First, to draw closer the commercial relations between the mother country and the Colonies, and to make the exchange of commodities between them freer. That is the economic object. There is also a political object, namely, to draw closer the political tie between the mother country and the other parts of the Empire. What is there in these aims which has anything to do with the establishment of a protective system in this country? There is absolutely no necessary connection between the two things, unless indeed it be the circumstance that preference involves a small duty on certain food-stuffs, a duty which hon. Gentlemen opposite have repeatedly said in their speeches in the country would practically have no protective effect whatever. [*Opposition* cries of "Who said it?"] I have seen it stated over and over again. Lord Rosebery is among those who have stated it in very clear and very emphatic language. But then the right hon. Gentleman the Member for West Monmouthshire says, "What about the average 10 per cent. tax upon manufactured goods?" If I am to answer that question as a member of the Government and on behalf of the Government, I say that as preference is not in our programme, *a fortiori* any particular method of carrying out preference is not in our programme.

Sir William Harcourt (Monmouthshire, W.): It is quite independent of preference.

*Mr. Gerald Balfour. I am glad to hear that admission, because it is exactly the point which I am trying to drive home. If in my individual capacity I am asked to say what my view on the subject is, why, then, I say at once I should be very glad to see a state of public opinion in this country which would admit of the adoption of the policy of preferential arrangements with our Colonies. But in saying that I absolutely decline to pin myself to any particular method of carrying that policy out. I do not think my right hon. friend the Member for West Birmingham would say that this particular part of his plan is in his view absolutely essential to the policy preference. Why was this 10 per cent. adopted in the first instance by my right hon. friend as part of his scheme? It was because, in order to avoid the imposition of an additional burden on the working classes it was necessary to remit part of the duties on sugar and tea, and, therefore, to make good the deficiency resulting therefrom to the Exchequer. But that is purely a revenue question [Laughter.] Perhaps I have not made myself clear. It is

admitted that the policy of preference cannot be carried out without a tax upon certain food imports from foreign countries. The suggestion of my right hon. friend the Member for West Birmingham was that duties should be placed on corn and meat and dairy produce, and that they should be taken off tea, sugar, and coffee. As the result of that change in taxation would be to produce a deficit in the revenue, of course it would be necessary to make good this deficit it in some way or another; but the particular scheme by which my right hon. friend proposed to make good the deficit is not one which is essential to the policy of preference. For my part, speaking in my individual capacity, while I am in favour of the policy of preference, if the Colonies are able and willing satisfactorily to meet us, I am not equally bound to approve of the method of carrying it out which has been put forward and defended with such eloquence and ability by my right hon. friend the Member for West Birmingham. If protection is not necessarily implied in preference, still less is it implied in the policy of the Government. [Dissent.] Surely hon. Members have arrived at a more accurate conception of the policy of the Government than to suppose that it involves the taxation of food products.

Mr. Bryce (Aberdeen, S.): Do I understand the right hon. Gentleman to mean that his policy of retaliation will not take advantage of any duty on food in order to carry out retaliation?

*Mr. Gerald Balfour. I believe it has already been stated by the Prime Minister that his policy does not contemplate the taxation of food. [A *Unionist Member.* Of raw material?] Of course not; for the objections to taxing raw material are more serious than the objections to taxing food. I said a moment ago that the policy of the Government was not inconsistent with free trade principles. I think I may go even further than that, and say that those who advocate the policy of the free hand for negotiation may fairly declare that they are truer friends of free trade than hon. Gentlemen opposite, who, while they praise free trade, are not prepared to make any sacrifices on behalf of it. They have a platonic love for free trade. They will not do anything for it. They will not fight for it. But we are prepared to fight for free trade, and to that extent I think we may claim to be truer friends of free trade than hon. Members opposite. The line we have taken is this, that the policy of peace at any price with respect to commercial and industrial matters ought to come to an end. We are met by two arguments. We are told that we have the power to retaliate already. We are also told that if we did possess this power it would be of no use to us. As to the first argument, we are told that we have only got to come to Parliament and ask in each case for certain powers, and to act upon the powers to given. I do not think that that is an accurate statement of the position. No doubt Parliament is omnipotent. Parliament could to-morrow reintroduce the system of protection. Parliament could, so far as theory goes, restore absolute monarchy in this country. But would anybody suggest that any

Ministry would venture, in any single case, to impose for purposes of retaliation a duty which was incidentally of a protective character without having first got the general assent of the country to the change of policy which that involved? Hitherto we have observed the principle that taxation should not be put on except for revenue purposes, but if we are to have a free hand for negotiation we must abandon that principle, or regard it, at least, as a principle modifiable according to circumstances. Just imagine my noble friend the Secretary of State for Foreign Affairs, approaching a foreign Government under existing conditions, with a threat to impose this or that duty unless adequate concessions were made in favour of British interests. It would be out of question for any Minister of Foreign Affairs to do that unless he had the mandate of the country behind him, otherwise he would be making a threat which he would know perfectly well he would not have the power to carry out; and the negotiator, on the other side, would know it also, and would naturally say, "Your revolver is not loaded; you talk of putting on penal taxes, but we know that that is inconsistent with your general fiscal policy." Unless we have a mandate from the country behind us we never shall have the power to negotiate with real effect. Every Government in turn is constantly addressing appeals and warnings to foreign nations against some proposed action hostile to our interests. Those appeals are hardly ever effectual, and they never will be effectual unless the foreign country with whom we are remonstrating is aware that we have got the power of inflicting a penalty if our requests are not listened to. Then it is said, "It is all very well to talk about retaliation, but how are you going to retaliate against countries like Russia and the United States which send you raw material in a very much larger proportion than any other commodity?" Well, of course it would be more difficult for us to apply pressure to Russia and the United States than to some other countries which could be named. But really, the passion for uniformity of hon. Gentlemen opposite seems to me to amount almost to a mania. Because a preferential tariff might affect different colonies differently, therefore we are to have no preferential arrangements at all. And, similarly, because we are not in a position to apply as severe a pressure to the United States or Russia as we should be, say, to Germany and France, therefore we are not to attempt to apply pressure at all. Surely such an argument as that answers itself.

There is one other argument to which I would refer in this connection. It is perfectly true that we should find great difficulty – I fully appreciate it – in applying pressure to the United States; I believe that continental countries, which, as we all know, are equipped for retaliation, have not been successful in bringing pressure to bear on the United States. But they have successfully brought pressure to bear on other countries, though not on the United States. We have not merely to consider freedom of negotiation for the purpose of securing favourable commercial treaties, we have also got to defend our industries against illegitimate and unfair competition. One advantage secured by the Sugar Convention was that you had the representatives of all the principal commercial countries in Europe laying down the principle that high protective duties could under certain circumstances constitute a bounty. I believe that is absolutely true, and the whole system of modern dumping undoubtedly rests on the two factors – first, combination among the producers, and, secondly, the protection of a high tariff. Now, if we cannot induce the United States to lower their tariff, at least, it will be possible for us to provide against the kind of bounty which arises from the combination of producers operating from behind the shelter of a protection system. [An *Hon. Member*: How?] It is possible to put on duties if necessary.

Lord Hugh Cecil: On all goods of that class?

Mr. Gerald Balfour: I am not saying what we should do, but how it is possible – namely, by the imposition of a tax which would act as a countervailing duty, or even by the, in some way, more extreme measures of prohibition that we have taken in connection with the Sugar Convention.

Lord Hugh Cecil: Do you mean on all goods of one class as was done in the case of sugar.

Mr. Gerald Balfour: I am very sensible that it is impossible to cover so vast and complicated a subject as this is in a single speech. I have not entered elaborately into statistics on this occasion, for it is really only the policy of the Government with which I have to deal. That that policy is directed against a real and serious evil no one attempts to deny, and if I were to go through all the figures in the Blue-book bearing on this part of the subject I should only be proving in detail what is already admitted on all sides. ["No."] The hon. Gentleman must really be a very strange free trader if he does not admit that the closing of the markets of foreign nations to the exports of this country is a serious evil. Hon. Gentlemen opposite are of opinion that our remedy would be ineffectual, if not mischievous. Well, we do not agree, and we mean to ask the country to let us try the experiment. ["When?"] Of course it would be far easier to sit down and do nothing. For my own Department in particular Fiscal Reform means a vast addition of toil, trouble and anxiety. But we advocate the policy because we are convinced that it is required in the best interests of the commerce and industry of the country. I myself think that it would have an even wider influence and effect. I believe that the knowledge that the British market is always open to the exports of foreign countries, no matter what fiscal policy foreign countries may adopt towards us, has contributed very materially to encourage foreign nations in erecting those really ridiculous tariff barriers against each other and against us; and I regard it as not only possible, but probable, that if this fiscal reform, which hon. Gentlemen opposite deplore as retrograde, is adopted, it will contribute to the establishment, not, indeed of universal or complete free trade, but at least of a freer exchange of commodities than now between the nations of the entire civilised world.

---

25 FISCAL POLICY[*]

Lord Balfour of Burleigh

Lord Balfour of Burleigh: I can assure the House that it is from no desire or anxiety to speak that I am here. I am actuated solely by a desire to explain to the House and to the many personal friends I have in the House, the reasons which guided me in taking the step which I thought it my duty to take during the recess. I am told that it is customary that some such explanation should be made, that it is a duty to the House in which a resigning Minister sits, and perhaps it is in no small degree due to the Minister himself . . .

No man separates himself from colleagues with a light heart. No one willingly breaks those Party ties and Party friendships which form so large a part of the political life of this country. Certainly it is not to be done from any selfish or unworthy motive, nor is it to be done for personal convenience. If it is done at all, it must be done, in my opinion, from a sense of duty. If duty to oneself is so presented that such separation is demanded by it, and if at the same time one's conception of one's duty to the country also demands it, then I venture to say that your Lordships without exception will agree that no other consideration ought to be allowed to prevail for a moment.

What was the cause which in my opinion made it my duty to ask to be relieved of the office which I had held for some eight years? I am, of course, provided with the usual gracious permission to give any reasons that may be necessary, within the usual limits, to justify the position I took up, but I am glad to think that, at any rate on this occasion, I shall have no cause to avail myself of that permission, because I think, in fact I know, that I can find in the published speeches of the Prime Minister and of Mr. Chamberlain and in their letters sufficient in which they concur to justify the course which I thought it necessary to take. The Prime Minister in his second speech at Sheffield – his speech to the overflow meeting – used these words –

---

* Lord Balfour of Burleigh, *Parliamentary Debates*, 4th series (18 February 1904, House of Lords) (London: Wyman and Sons, Ltd.), cols 149–51; 153–62.

"I am one of those – I admit it – who when this topic was recently started and when it became a matter of common debate in the country would have been quite content to see it left an open question among members of the Government and among Members of the Party, but neither my colleagues in the Government nor the House of Commons nor the country would support that view."

The same statement was repeated in almost similar words at Bristol, with the addition that the Prime Minister thought that the old position should be maintained under which the fiscal question was regarded as an open question in the ranks of the Party. I quote these words not because I in any sense disagree with them as an accurate statement of the fact, but because I agree with them entirely, and because it seems to me that, in the very fact that it was thought possible for these great questions to be left open questions, one of the reasons which justify the course I took is to be found. The circumstances are not parallel. I know – I have known for years – that many of those with whom I have been acting had predilections in favour of another fiscal system. That was well enough so long as the system which prevailed in this country was accepted, but it seems to me to make all the difference when a prominent Minister proposed to reverse that system, and to bring it into discussion as a matter of practical policy. I venture to say to the House – I do not set up to be a great constitutional authority – but I do say that the established doctrine, the prevailing doctrine, the better doctrine, is that those who are responsible for a Government should speak with one voice on matters of that kind. But to understand how we really arrived at the position described by the Prime Minister, it is necessary to glance very shortly at some of the events of last summer . . .

There were then, as is perfectly well known, three main subjects of discussion. There was the question of preference to our Colonies, there was the question which is more particularly the subject of the noble Lord's Motion today – the subject of retaliation, or as, perhaps, it is more fairly and fitly termed, freedom of negotiation; and kindred to that, and alongside of it, there was the matter of "dumping" as it is called – I think the word has now been accepted into the English language – which certainly is a branch in close connection with the subject of retaliation. But at that time, neither in the Cabinet nor out of it, had we ever heard, I believe, of the average 10 per cent. duty on all imports into this country.

On the question of preference, of which the main advocate and proposer was the late Colonial Secretary, I wish to say a few words. I admit that it is not raised definitely in the Motion of the noble Earl, and I can only say what I want to say by the indulgence of the House, but my own explanation would not be complete, and I venture to think that the House itself could not fully understand the position of matters unless, by that indulgence, I am allowed to touch briefly upon some of the points involved in that question.

It always seemed to me that this suggestion of a colonial preference was no light demand to make upon this country. At any rate, there can be no question whatever that it is an abandonment – a complete abandonment – of the existing fiscal policy of the country. It may not be wise to pin oneself to any particularly abstract doctrine on the subject, but I venture to say that if there is one abstract doctrine which it is less unwise to pin oneself to than another, it is that taxation should not be levied except for revenue purposes. I say that on this ground – not on account of the great authorities by which it is supported, not on account of the length of time during which it has been the accepted policy of the country, but because, in my humble opinion, as a practical policy it is the best policy for this country, on this ground if upon no other – namely, that by that principle, and under that principle, you secure the end that the burden which you lay upon the consumer or upon whoever pays the tax (it does not matter to me for the moment who it is) will be, as a whole, transferred to the Exchequer. The point, then, that we had to ask ourselves in the summer was this: "Is there anything in our present circumstances which demands this great change? Is it in the interest of this country, looked at in its widest sense, that this great change should be made? Is it above all things necessary, as is suggested to us, for the maintenance of the Empire?" My Lords, I claim humbly to be as good a friend of the cause of the maintenance of the Empire as anyone else, but I venture to say that there has been no evidence whatever presented to us that this particular change is required, or even that it would promote the unity of the Empire. I know it is alleged upon great authority – upon the authority of Mr. Chamberlain, who, in my opinion, has rendered very great services – but I am not prepared, upon a matter of this kind, to accept or to advocate such a change, upon any authority, unless evidence in support of that authority can be adduced. I venture to add in proof of the fact that I desired to consider this with an open mind, that I asked certain questions, the object of which was to find out what amount of trade with the self-governing colonies it would be possible to acquire under a preferential system, and precisely what we were expected to do, or to bind ourselves to do, to get that trade. I was told that was not a wise way to approach the question. I was told that it would be an insult to the Colonies, that it would be improper, at any rate, to ask the Colonies to commit themselves until we had shown a readiness to meet them at least half-way. I was also told that we should be rejecting offers which had been made to us, unless we took the course that was proposed. I have never been satisfied that anything which could properly be described as an offer on the part of those who are authorised to make an offer, has really been transmitted to this country. I know there have been statements by individuals; I know there have been aspirations that it would be desirable to have a preferential system, and to bind the different parts of the Empire more closely together by that means, but I think it is stretching language and going beyond the actual facts of the case, to say that anything that could fairly be described as an offer in this matter has ever been made to this country. At any rate, I venture to say that if such exist, it would materially assist our deliberations if the actual text of those offers were communicated in a formal and deliberate manner to Parliament, in order that they might be considered upon their merits. I certainly would be glad, as I am sure many of your Lordships would also, to give such consideration to them. I venture to say, however, that it is a great deal more than doubtful whether this commercial union would be a better basis of union than the ties that already exist. I think the danger of differences would be very great. The case with us is not parallel with that of either the United States or Germany. We have no one authority which could settle the fiscal policy of the country. In the far future we may have such an authority, but it is perfectly certain that we have not got it at the present time; and until we have it, I venture to think that the danger of differences would be greater than with the complete freedom which we at present possess. I do not want to weary our Lordships with quotations, but on 20th August, a speech was made by Sir Wilfrid Laurier, Prime Minister of Canada – who, if there is a real Imperialist amongst our colonial statesmen, is that one – and in that speech he said –

> "Canada values too highly the system which made her what she is, to consent willingly to part with any portion of it for whatever consideration, or even for the maintenance of the British Empire. I think it would be a most evil thing if any of our colonies were to consent to part with any of their legislative independence, nor do I believe that in order to make such an arrangement of a commercial nature as I have spoken of some time ago, we should be called upon to make any sacrifices of dignity or independence."

We must make a sacrifice of freedom, and the Colonies must make a sacrifice of freedom, if they are to bind themselves by any arrangement whatever, of the nature which has been indicated.

There is one more point in connection with that matter to which I would allude. We are asked for a mandate, but it has never been authoritatively stated what is to be the extent or limit of the mandate which we are asked to give. It is suggested that the mandate should authorise, as I understand it, negotiations for a preference, with a duty of 2s., or something of that kind. But there is no security at all that that sum would be sufficient. What sort of a position would we be in, if in a year or two, after negotiations had been taking place, and after this mandate had been given, we found that a 2s. duty was not sufficient, and we had to make it 4s. or 5s.? What would be the position of this country? We should be asked "Are you really going to sacrifice the Empire for the mere difference between 3s. and 5s.? Is a difference of 3s. to make the difference between unity and separation?"

The only safe course to take is not to commit this country until you know the limit to which you are likely to be asked to go, not to depart from the principles which have regulated the policy of the country for so many years until the extent of the journey that you are asked to travel can be defined. We are now told that before a mandate can be asked for this proposal, there are to be two, or perhaps three, general elections. I do not know whether that is to be so or not, but if it is, is not that fact in itself a most complete and absolute justification of the line which those took who refused to allow the Government, and, so far as we could help it, the country and Parliament to be committed upon this question before any election at all had taken place? I pass from that; I will say no more about it; I am not going to discuss the question of which Minister was committed to this policy; it is certainly not my business to do that; it is sufficient for me that these things were before the Government, and that it was suggested that they were to be open questions. In my opinion, for those of us who are not able to accept the policy, it was impossible on that ground that we should continue to be members of the Government.

I pass to the question of retaliation or freedom of negotiation. It will not be difficult to show that the question is in a somewhat different position now from what it was in those days. I certainly have no doubt in my own mind that such arguments were used in support of it, and that such admissions were wanted about it, that if, so far as the arguments were concerned, we had admitted them, or if, so far as the admissions were wanted, we had made them, we should have been logically committed to a very large departure indeed from the principles of free trade. If I wanted a proof of that fact I could allude to the exact language used at Sheffield, where it was announced that the policy to be recommended to the country was to be a reversal of the existing policy, and subsequently at Bristol, where it was announced to be a great and serious change. On one point I do not agree with the noble Earl who spoke a few moments ago. I do not believe that it is fair to say that the Prime Minister is in any sense an advocate of protection. He has uniformly – publicly, and, I may say, privately – argued in favour of this policy, as a means of getting what he calls freer trade. I therefore feel bound to say that I do not think the remark which was made can fairly be applied to him.

The Earl of Crewe: I do not think I ever described the Prime Minister as being an advocate of protection. I said he was being drawn towards it.

Lord Balfour of Burleigh: Of course I accept the correction, but even in its modified form I do not think it is accurate. My recollection of what the Prime Minister has said in public and in private is to this effect, that if his policy involved a sort of flavour of protection, it was to be accounted as one of the disadvantages of the policy rather than as one of its advantages, and that he was not going for this policy because it was protective, but that he did not think its protective flavour was so great a disadvantage as to

441

deter him from endeavouring to get the benefits which he hoped to obtain. I hope I am stating it correctly, but I am only endeavouring to state it in order to say that I do not agree with the position thus taken up, because I think the protective flavour which is about some of the proposals that are made, is so disadvantageous that the disadvantages overbalance any advantages that might possibly obtain from them. I want to say this: I did not understand in August, and I do not understand now, if the policy of liberty of negotiation is to go no further than seems to be fashionable at this moment, why any mandate for it is required – if it is to be under the control of Parliament, as I understand is now admitted, although there seems to be some hesitation in accepting thecontrol of Parliament in every case. That is, as I understand, what happened in another place, but I am looking to this debate for light on that point. What I want to press on the House and upon the Government is that retaliation in itself is, as the noble Lord opposite has said, not really a final policy. It is an act of commercial war. I am not prepared to exclude war as a matter of policy either from wider politics, or from commercial concerns, but if it is really the case that those who are in favour of this policy are heart and soul intending to use it for the purposes of getting freer trade, then I would look at any rate with a tolerant eye upon it. But what made me doubtful in the autumn, and caused me to feel that I could not continue to advocate it, was not only the want of limitation, the want of actual definition of the objects and the methods which were set before the Government, but the fact, as I have said, that arguments in favour of it were used which seemed to me to lead to the direct reversal of the traditional policy of this country. It is a different thing to express a willingness to support those whom you trust on general grounds, even if you do not thoroughly understand at the moment everything they are proposing, than to remain a member of the Government undertaking to advocate a policy which you do not fully understand, and of which, as in this case, you have doubts as to the practical efficacy. This may be, as I have said, a free-trade policy for free-traders, but I have great doubts whether it is really a policy which, taken by itself, can effect the object in view. I hope before this debate closes the Government will tell us with absolute distinctness how they propose to carry this policy into effect. What do they intend to retaliate upon. We are told absolutely distinctly that their programme does not extend to the taxation of food or of raw materials. But are raw materials and food to be subject to retaliation? If they are, that is an extremely serious step, but if they are not, the revolver of which the noble Marquess spoke last summer will, in a great majority of cases, be an extremely harmless weapon, and he might as well load it with snipe shot and take it for the pursuit of big game in Central Africa.

But I have another difficulty. This policy may be a free-trade policy for free-traders, but I am speaking in the presence of some who do not regard it as a step towards freer trade, but as a step – perhaps a very short step, as some of them say, which is so insignificant as to be almost contemptible – leading to another and a very different policy. I hope His Majesty's Government will make it clear that they do not intend to be dragged along that path. Some of them I think, if I may say so in all friendliness, have gone rather too far along it at the present time. But I do not want to press matters too much, and I shall be only too glad to have an assurance that that is not to be the policy of His Majesty's Government. I recognise the difficulty of asking them for a concrete case in regard to the subject of retaliation, but there is this kindred subject of dumping. There are no international questions involved in that. Could not the Government mention some one of the trades which are especially affected, and which they desire to protect from dumping? Surely in regard to that we might have one or two concrete cases – cases put forward, not with the exaggeration of Party welfare, or, if I may say so without offence, with all the clap-trap of political oratory, but cases carefully selected, thoroughly investigated, and presented to Parliament in a form in which they can be discussed in a serious and anxious spirit. I admit that the difficulty and intricacy of the question is very great, but every trade which is distressed is not the victim of dumping, nor is every individual in every trade which is distressed the victim of dumping. These things require the most careful and anxious investigation. It is almost impossible without personal inquiry by some agent to get at all the facts in every case. I have no doubt that most of your Lordships have read the chapter in the fiscal Blue-book which deals with dumping. There was attached to it, when first circulated, an explanatory memorandum by somebody at the Board of Trade – I really do not know whom – but it was an exceedingly clever and good statement of the difficulties of getting at the truth in this matter. It was not intended that it should be circulated, because it was part of the canon of making up that book that nothing but facts – no individual opinion of any sort – was to be put forward. I think that was a wise rule under the circumstance; at any rate I myself was a party to it, and I make no complaint whatever about it. But this particular Paper to which I refer, although not circulated at the time, seemed to me so worthy of consideration that I would venture to ask His Majesty's Government whether they would consult the President of the Board of Trade with a view to publishing hereafter that Paper, upon the understanding that no member of the Government is committed to the opinions expressed. It seems to me that it would be so useful a guide that it would be for the advantage of Parliament and the country in considering this subject that that Paper should be in the hands of a much wider circle than at the present time.

But I come to what is to me a graver matter still, and that is the average 10 per cent. duty all-round. I know quite well that I shall be told that is not a part of the policy of His Majesty's Government at the present time. But can we be told distinctly by a representative of the Government from his place in Parliament what is the attitude of the Government towards it? I know it is not their policy but are their convictions settled in regard to it. How can we be sure that it never will be their policy? As I have said, I am afraid that some members of the Government have accepted it and have protectionist leanings. I make that no subject of reproach, for I recognise the right of everybody to have their own opinions upon that matter. I think, however, that, in a subject of such importance, Parliament and the country have a right to know what is the settled policy of the Government in regard to it. I venture to say that the country is thinking more about that at this moment than it is about the mere policy, the official policy, of the Government. I am afraid that too many of the supporters of the Government regard that as the most important part of tariff reform. Supposing the sympathy which is now expressed for this policy is translated into practical shape, and supposing we find at a subsequent time that a majority of those with whom we would like to act, find themselves in fact committed to that policy. I know quite well that it is unusual to give an illustration in this House, but there is a story going round at the present time which very well illustrates my position in this matter. I am told that a short time ago an American couple landed at Liverpool, and upon arrival at that port the husband received a message that his mother-in-law had died, within the last few days, while they were crossing the Atlantic, and he was asked to telegraph an answer to the message stating whether she should be buried, cremated, or embalmed. The husband went to the Post Office and telegraphed the following reply –

"Better try all three: take no risks."

That policy of protection is one, with which, so far as I am concerned, I am not prepared to take any risks, and what I am afraid of is that it will swallow up every other policy which is put before the country, and that it will be a sort of Aaron's Rod, which will devour every other question which comes into our public life so long as it remains there. The Government may not like it, and they may even shut their eyes to the fact, but I believe that it is that policy which is really before the country at the present time, and, that being so, I say, in my humble opinion, that the present position in which some of us are placed is not altogether a fair one. It is not fair to those of us who are loyal Unionists, and who remain free-traders to be left in the state of difficulty and uncertainty in which we are placed at the present time. I also venture to say that it is not altogether fair to Parliament itself. I am certain it is not fair to the constituencies who ought, in a matter of this kind, to have a clear and distinct lead from those who are the leaders of the people; and I am not quite sure that it is quite fair to the members of His Majesty's Government themselves. In spite of the precedent of the Home Rule Bill, which is sometimes put forward, I say that this state of uncertainty is, in my opinion, contrary to the best traditions of our public life.

One of the things that public men are distinguished for in this country is that we take a definite line, make it clear, and stand up and argue for it, and after declaring our opinions we take the consequences of them whatever they may be. Upon this question we must stand somewhere, and as far as I am concerned I am profoundly convinced that any departure from the policy of free trade or free imports, if you like to call it by that name, will be the first real blow to the prosperity of our British commerce; and that, so far from cementing the union of our Empire, it will render that union more difficult to maintain because it will be more complicated; and while holding these opinions I claim to be one who is as loyal a supporter of the unity of the Empire as any of His Majesty's Ministers themselves.

---

26 FISCAL POLICY*

The Duke of Devonshire

The Duke of Devonshire: My Lords, I have had considerable doubt whether it would be necessary for me to trouble your Lordships with anything in the nature of a personal explanation as to the reasons which caused me last autumn to resign the office in His Majesty's Government which I then had the honour to hold. But as two of my colleagues who resigned their offices about the same period have thought it due either to their constituents or to the House in which they sat or to themselves to enter upon some explanation of a personal character, and as, in addition, the Prime Minister thought it necessary – as he had not thought it necessary on the other occasions – to reply to my letter of resignation in a tone which perhaps was somewhat controversial, I hope that I may ask your Lordships to allow me in a few words to try to explain the reasons, not so much why I thought it necessary ultimately to resign my office, but why that resignation was for some considerable period delayed . . .

My colleagues, who have already made personal explanations, Mr. Ritchie and Lord George Hamilton, were perfectly justified in the statement they have made, that at the time when they resigned their offices they had every reason to believe from the communications which had passed between us that I intended to have taken the same course at the same time. I do not think it is necessary that I should enter at all fully into the reasons why I

* Duke of Devonshire, *Parliamentary Debates*, 4th series (19 February 1904, House of Lords) (London: Wyman and Sons, Ltd.), cols 348–50; 354–64.

formed that intention. Those reasons were, in the main, identical with those which have been fully stated by my colleagues. I perhaps could not have formulated so distinctly as they did the reasons for their action, because I had not at the time, and I have not even now, a very clear idea of what were the measures to which we were asked at that time to give our assent, or of what was the policy to which we were asked to commit ourselves. It may be enough for me to say that both the action and the language of the Prime Minister and of some of his colleagues since the first opening of this question had been to me a cause of great anxiety and doubt. I felt myself obliged to dissent from much that was contained in the pamphlet which has been published by the Prime Minister, and from some of the contents of the Memorandum which was circulated to his colleagues at the same time. I also had in my mind that two only of my colleagues had prepared for the Cabinet Memoranda dealing with the proposals which had been put forward by our colleague the late Colonial Secretary, and had made criticisms of those proposals with which I was on the whole in entire agreement.

At the Cabinet which met on 14th September it was clearly indicated that in the opinion of the Prime Minister the opinions of these members who had expressed themselves in these Memoranda were such as to make it impossible that they could give their assent to the policy which he was about to propose, and that it was not likely that it would be possible for them, with satisfaction to themselves, to remain members of his Government. Sharing as I did in the main the views which had been expressed by my colleagues, I did not see how, if in the opinion of the Prime Minister they could not with advantage remain in his Cabinet, the same considerations should not apply also to my own case. But there was, however, another reason, which was not referred to in the letters of resignation of my colleagues, but which had a great influence upon me, and I think must have had some influence also with them. I think we were, none of us, quite clear as to the nature of the declarations which the Prime Minister might think it necessary to make in his forthcoming speech at Sheffield; but what I felt, and what we all felt, was that, whatever might be the nature of these declarations, it would be impossible for us to continue to be members of a Cabinet in which the Colonial Secretary would be free to advocate principles which we knew he had adopted, which we also knew it was his intention, either in or out of the Cabinet, to advocate publicly throughout the country. Such a state of things would, I think, have been highly unsatisfactory to us, and contrary to the best interests of the public service. It would have been necessary in such circumstances for me either to remain silent – which would have been an intolerable position for myself – or to have taken an open part in combating a policy which my colleague was advocating, which, I think, would hardly have been a course that would have been decent to colleagues in the same Cabinet . . .

I desire to offer a few observations on the subjects which have been raised in the present debate. I think that my noble friend Lord Crewe has rendered no inconsiderable service to the House and to the country in raising a discussion upon one side of this question, which up to the present time, I think, has been inadequately discussed. A great deal has been said – not, in my opinion, at all too much – upon another side of the question, that of the attitude of the Government towards the policy which has been proposed, not by them, but by Mr. Chamberlain. But up to the present time very little, comparatively, has been said on the subject of the Government's own policy, or of the proposals which they intend to make either to Parliament or, before a general election, to the country. It is a somewhat curious and remarkable feature of the extraordinary position in which we find ourselves that ten times as much interest – I think I may say a hundred times as much interest – appears to be roused throughout the country in the policy which is advocated by Mr. Chamberlain, and in the attitude of the Government towards that policy, than is excited by the Government's own proposals.

The Government have asserted, and I believe still assert, that they have a policy. The Prime Minister at Sheffield declared that, this question having been raised, it was his intention to give a lead to his Party and to the country. I ask, Where are we to find this lead? It is unfortunate that the Prime Minister has been unable to further explain his views in the House of Commons; but surely he must have colleagues in the House of Commons who would have been fully capable of explaining those views if there had been anything further to explain. The Prime Minister has written a pamphlet and he has made three speeches; and in those, up to the present time, we must find the materials for forming an opinion on the policy of the Government and on the lead which he desires to give to his Party. In the pamphlet the most definite expression that I find is that he pleads for "freedom to negotiate in order that freedom of exchange may be increased." In the speech at Sheffield I find also the definite declaration that he intended to reverse the fiscal policy of the last two generations. That declaration would seem to imply that as the fiscal policy of the last two generations had been one of free trade the Prime Minister's intention was to revert to protection. But we have been assured that that is not the present intention of the Government, and therefore we have to fall back on the freedom to negotiate in order that freedom of exchange might be increased. That does not appear to me to be so much a declaration of policy as the expression of a sentiment; and until that sentiment is reduced to concrete proposals I maintain that we have not got – and the country has not got – the lead which we have the right to expect.

If the complexity and difficulty of this position could have been increased I think it would have been increased by the speech of my noble friend Lord Selborne last night. Lord Selborne told us that it was impossible to explain the details of a policy which was not yet born. I ask, how are we to accept as the policy of the Government or the lead which the Government have promised to give to the country a policy which, in the words of one of his colleagues, has not yet come into existence. Under these circumstances, it is perhaps not strange that we have not derived very much enlightenment from the debates which have taken place in the other House of Parliament. We have to-night one more chance of obtaining that enlightenment. My noble friend who leads the House holds a position only second in authority to that of the Prime Minister himself, and it may be – I hope it may be – that he will be in a position to throw some light upon this perplexed condition of things. He told us the other day, in words spoken with some deliberation, that the Government presented a solid front on that part of the policy which they had examined and to which as a Government they were committed. What we want to know is, What are the results of that examination which has been given? I trust that I do not put this question in a hostile spirit to the Government. As I have admitted, while I was a member of the Government I was perfectly ready to enter myself into an examination of certain proposals; but while I was a member of the Government certainly no examination of this policy had yet been undertaken, and if I had remained in the Government I should have expected that such an examination would be made before the meeting of Parliament, and that its results would be communicated to Parliament.

We have never got nearer to a definition of the policy of the Government than that which was given to us by the noble Marquess at the opening of the session. "The policy of the Government," he said, "might be summed up in the words negotiation and retaliation." It is perfectly possible that a policy which has been fully and adequately explained may be summed up in two words; but there never was a policy – and I do not think that there ever will be a policy – which, in the absence of such adequate explanation, could be summed up sufficiently for the consideration of Parliament or the country in a couple of words. Though we have often heard this summing-up of the policy of the Government we have never received any indications whatever as to the manner in which those principles are to be applied to our future fiscal policy. As to negotiation, the Government have always, in my opinion, been free to enter into negotiation.

The Prime Minister says that we deprived ourselves of the means of successfully conducting negotiations, and the other night, in the House of Commons, Mr. Wyndham attributed the failure of certain negotiations with France which took place in 1880 to the absence of any fiscal inducement which it was in our power to offer. I think Mr. Wyndham was not quite accurately informed with respect to that negotiation. It is not the fact that in that negotiation we had nothing to offer. Parliament had already been asked, and had assented, to a reduction of the duties on French wines in the event of the conclusion of a treaty. The obstacle which prevented the conclusion of that treaty was the pledge which was given to Parliament by the Government – rightly given, I think, at that time – that they would not assent to any treaty which should provide for the imposition of higher duties than those which had been agreed to by the French Government in 1860. The French Government, I believe, were perfectly willing to comply with that demand on the part of our Government; and the obstacle which prevented the conclusion of a fresh treaty with France was the unwillingness of the protectionist majority in the French Chambers to agree to the proposal to which their Government were quite ready to assent. That negotiation, therefore, did not fail in consequence of the absence of anything which we had to offer in the shape of inducement. It failed on account of the rigid protectionist principles professed by a majority in the French Chambers.

From negotiation we come to retaliation. I suppose my noble friend Lord Selborne was under the impression last night that he was defending the principles of retaliation. In my judgment almost the whole of his speech, although he every now and then used a phrase about retaliation, might have been just as well made in defence of a policy of protection, or the policy proposed by Mr. Chamberlain. My noble friend used all the arguments which are so familiar in the mouths of protectionist speakers. He asserted that our country had prospered under protection and also that other countries had in recent years prospered more under protectioin than we had under free trade.

The First Lord of the Admiralty (The Earl of Selborne): I made no comparison as to the respective degrees of prosperity. I simply said that foreign countries had prospered greatly under protection.

The Duke of Devonshire: I was under the impression that my noble friend used the words that other countries had prospered more in recent years under protection than we had prospered under free trade.

The Earl of Selborne: I said that their trade had progressed at a greater rate than ours.

The Duke of Devonshire: I accept my noble friend's correction; but if that is his opinion why does he not boldly advocate a return to a system of protection in this country? It may be that protection is a very good system, and that other countries may have prospered under a protective system; but I do not think that my noble friend can point to any instance where a country has prospered under a system of negotiation and retaliation, or to any country whose fiscal system is based on a formula so unmeaning. But we are not to-night discussing protection. The object of this debate I take to be to endeavour to find out, what, if it is not protection, is the policy of His Majesty's Government. If we were to discuss the question of protection I should find it necessary to challenge most, if not all, of the statements and arguments that were contained in my noble friend's speech; and especially should I think it my duty to call attention to the fact that he based an argument as to the stagnation of our trade upon the exports of our manufactured articles only, and that he altogether omitted to make the slightest reference in the course of his speech – an omission which was somewhat remarkable on the part of the First Lord of the Admiralty – to the enormous progress which has been made under free trade by our shipping industries, by our shipbuilding and our foreign shipping trade.

As to retaliation, it seems to me everything depends upon the meaning which we are to attach to the word and as to the spirit in which it is to be used. There was a somewhat ominous sentence in the Prime Minister's pamphlet, in which he said that the only alternative that was left was –

"To do to foreign nations what they always do to each other, and, instead of appealing to economic theories which they wholly disbelieve, to use fiscal inducement which they thoroughly understand."

If this means, as it seems to me, that we are to base our future fiscal policy on the model of foreign nations – upon what foreign nations do to each other – we can very easily form an opinion of what it comes to. If my noble friend Lord Lansdowne is to be free to present his big revolver at the head of every protectionist State which imposes protective duties against our exports, and to threaten, or to carry out a threat, of imposing similar duties upon their exports, we know very well what that would come to. We know that almost every nation of Europe and the United States of America attach far more importance to keeping control over their own markets than to opening our markets to themselves; and we know that all the fiscal inducements which they so thoroughly understand have never enabled them, if they have ever tried, to establish free trade between each other. If we are to model, as that sentence appears to indicate, our future fiscal policy upon what foreign nations do to each other, I cannot see what other result we can anticipate than the establishment of a system of protection all round.

The Government decline to discuss with us concrete cases. That is no reason why we should not put to them concrete cases of our own for the purpose of helping the country to see where this policy of retaliation may lead them. Lord Crewe referred last night to a suggestion which has been made that it might be possible in the case of Germany, for instance, by threatening to impose an additional tax upon her wines or upon the cheap toys that she exports, to obtain some concession on her part in our favour. It has also been suggested that in the case of France we might threaten to impose some duty upon her silks or fancy articles, and by that means obtain some concession from her. I admit that I am extremely doubtful whether the advantages which we could obtain from using such fiscal inducements as these would be very great. I can conceive that, if threats of this sort were made and carried out, it would certainly tend to dislocate a certain portion of our trade, and that it would infallibly diminish a certain portion of our exports which pay for those imports which would be thereby checked. But if, after full examination, His Majesty's Government had reason to suppose that by a threat or the imposition of duties of this kind there would be any probability of their obtaining larger and more important concessions in other directions, I should not have the slightest objection to seeing this experiment tried, to seeing it proposed to Parliament, and seeing on what grounds it could be defended. But let me instance another case of retaliation. I do not know that the proposal has ever been made in a more simple and naked form than it was made a short time ago in a newspaper which is a great supporter of His Majesty's Government and also of Mr. Chamberlain – *The Times* newspaper. *The Times* was discussing the question of our iron industry, and said –

> "By a hostile tariff America first shuts our iron out of her market and then invades our home markets and shuts up our manufactories. Would it really be no advantage to be able to retain our home market in spite of their tariff? We could do that by a retaliatory tax upon the iron of every country that taxes ours. Granting that we could obtain no power of negotiation that would open the American market to our own iron –
> "

It is not proposed that it should be done in order to secure greater freedom of exchange –

> "still to secure possession of our home market would immensely increase our power of competing with America in every foreign market open to both. All this is so elementary that no free-importer should spoil his case by directly contradicting it."

Well, this argument rather appeals to me. I happen to be considerably interested in the iron and steel industry as chairman of an iron and steel company, and I quite admit that it would be rather an attractive prospect to me to be relieved of American competition in our market and to be able thereby to charge higher prices to our customers at home. I have no doubt that if a tariff reformer were to go to Barrow-in-Furness and make the same suggestion to the workmen in our works they would see it in the same light as I do. But, in my opinion, Parliament has got to look a little further than the interests either of iron and steel companies, or even of the workmen engaged in this industry.

It is admitted that we cannot succeed in what we all desire to do – in opening the American market to our iron products; but, as a compensation, we are to be protected against competition in our own. Now the competition to which we are exposed is essentially of a temporary and fitful character; it is a competition of that kind which is now described as "dumping"; it is the occasional export by America or by Germany of a portion of their over-production which has been fostered by their

451

protective tariffs, and by their trusts which have grown up under protective tariffs. A portion of that over-production is priced below the cost of manufacture. But that competition must in its nature be of a temporary character. In order to relieve us from that temporary inconvenience we are to be compensated by a permanent protective duty. It is not easy to see that our power of competing in neutral markets would be increased by the adoption of that proposal. If America or Germany want to "dump" they will "dump" somewhere. If they cannot "dump" here, they will be driven to "dumping" in neutral markets in which we compete with them.

What this tariff would do would be permanently to raise the price of our products to our home customers. Who are our home customers? Nobody that I am aware of buys iron or steel to look at or to put in his pocket. The purchasers of iron and steel are a thousand different classes of manufacturers who convert iron and steel into hundreds of thousands of articles of general utility and advantage. Well, if the price of their material is raised to them, they also must be protected – the price of the article which they produce will also be raised, their consumption will be necessarily reduced, and the effect of this proposal would be that production would be diminished, and that a large number of workmen in these subsidiary industries – a far larger number than are employed in the ironmasters' works – would have their employment by so much reduced. I think it is a fair question to put to His Majesty's Government whether the proposal which I have just described comes under the head of protection, or whether it comes under the head of retaliation. If the answer is that such a policy as has been recommended by *The Times* comes under the head of retaliation, I think the country will be in a better position to judge than it is now of the consequences which may follow the adoption of the policy which was so simply described to us in a couple of words.

There is one point on which I desire to say a word, which seems to me more important even than the discovery of the proposals of the Government itself. It is the relation of the Government to the Unionist organisations which largely control the policy indicated by the tariff reformers. What are we all looking to? We know we are all looking to the future general election, to the preparations to be made for that general election, and the results of that election. The Government are using the whole of their influence to ensure that the results of that election should be a mandate for a change of some kind or another in our present fiscal policy. This is their irreducible minimum, and unless a candidate is prepared to proclaim himself a fiscal reformer of one kind or another he is no longer permitted to be a loyal supporter of the Government. Sometimes they profess a mild preference for their own proposals over the more extreme proposals of the Tariff Reform League. Some of them do not conceal, however, their sympathy with the more extended proposals than their own; but in no case, so far as I am aware, is the influence of the Government exerted, or will it be exerted, to impose any limit whatever on the extent to which their supporters may legitimately commit themselves. I submit that this attitude on the part of the Government is unfair to many of their supporters who desire to give them a loyal support.

I think we have a right to ask that there should be a superior limit as well as an irreducible minimum. Some of us here, and some of those who in the other House voted for the Amendment moved the other day, have endeavoured to induce the Government to fix some such superior limit; but hitherto our endeavours have been without success. I believe and I trust that the whole of His Majesty's Government are not committed to a policy of undisguised preference, protective taxation of food, or to the imposition of an all-round duty. But what is the use of the protests which some of them have made if they take no steps to secure that their protests shall be effective? And unless they take some steps to prevent the return to Parliament of candidates who are pledged to protection and preference, the responsibility of those members of the Government who are not prepared to go to these full lengths will not be, in my opinion, discharged if by their possible future resignations they decline a verdict on the part of the country which they have themselves been instrumental in obtaining and which by timely action on their part they might have averted.

There is only one hypothesis on which this attitude on their part can be justified. It is that in their judgment these questions are of minor importance as compared with the maintenance of the Unionist Party for other purposes – for purposes, I acknowledge, great and important, perhaps of resisting any revival of the Home Rule policy, of maintaining the principles of the Education Act, and, for all I know, there may be many others; but in comparison with these they hold that the most sweeping changes in our fiscal policy are matters of minor importance. I acknowledge that I am unable to hold this view, for I believe there is no subject which is the least likely to occupy the immediate or early attention of Parliament which compares in importance with that of the principles on which our fiscal policy is in the future to be based. In saying this I think I am taking a more consistent position than that which was taken by Lord Selborne last night. He reminded us that we were risking the existence of the great Unionist Party. But what are he and his friends doing? Are they doing nothing to risk the existence of the great Unionist Party? He has not even the excuse of thinking that these are great matters, for he told us that he considered that a wholly exaggerated importance was attached to the question both by the advocates and opponents of protection.

There are certain compensations for the absence of the Leader of the other House and for his place being occupied by Mr. Akers Douglas, who, speaking the other day, gave some novel definitions of the principles of Cabinet responsibility. He said –

"The noble Lord wants to know whether hon. Members supporting the Sheffield policy and hon. Members supporting a more advanced policy will receive the same support from the Conservative associations. I say certainly, as long as they receive the support of their local associations, and my hon. friend the Secretary of the Treasury has observed that he certainly will make no difference with regard to the candidates who are standing now; but the condition must be that they are supported by the local associations, and that they necessarily support the policy of the Government. How else would hon. members have it?"

I think that is a very frank expression of the opinions of an important member of the Government on this part of the question. We know now who are to control the decision of the future fiscal policy of the Government. It is to be left to individual opinion and the action of the local associations. If by any process of wirepulling a sufficient number of local associations can be got to support the policy of the Tariff Reform League, then it is the policy of the Tariff Reform League only and not their own policy which will be submitted to the country at the next general election. I confess I am not content to leave the decision of this question in the hands of the local associations. Local associations are a necessary and important part of our political organisations; but local associations do not always, and frequently do not represent the opinions of the constituencies which they profess to represent.

I have been reproached with disloyalty to the Unionist Party for having advised free-traders to vote against protectionist candidates. I have given that advice. I have never advised any one to vote against candidates who were pledged to the policy of negotiation and retaliation – partly because, as I have already said, I do not know what that policy means. But I do advise every man who professes free-trade opinions, and does desire that freedom of exchange should not be diminished but increased, to exact from every candidate who seeks to represent him in Parliament a pledge that he will oppose protection in whatever shape it may re-appear – to exact a pledge from the candidates that they will vote against protection, and that they will oppose protective taxes on food, that they will oppose the imposition of a protective duty upon foreign manufactured goods; and I will advise that, failing this pledge, he will refuse to support a candidate even if he professes to be a supporter of a Unionist Government.

27 COMMENTARY ON HANSARD'S PARLIAMENTARY DEBATES*

Author Unknown

Art. XII. – Free Trade and the Position of Parties

The free-trade cause wins all along the line!

Out of a vast mass of detail, and from amidst all the confusion of disputed facts and opposed statistics, certain broad features of Mr. Chamberlain's fiscal policy have most unfavourably impressed themselves on the imagination and intelligence of the people. In consolidating the Empire, and in recasting its constitutional framework, should this be found necessary, regard must of necessity be paid to the interests and welfare of the United Kingdom not less than to those of any other portion of the King's dominions. For a great and common purpose the people of Great Britain and the people of our great colonies are willing, doubtless, to make some sacrifice of local advantages. There must be some give and take all round. At the present time people at home feel, not unjustifiably, that though perhaps they talk less loudly about Empire than their fellow-subjects across the seas, they glory in it quite as much, and they bear a great deal more than their full share of supporting it. That very many Canadians, for example, are anxious to see a substantial tax placed upon American wheat sold in the English market is perfectly natural. But many Englishmen fail to perceive that an interest of this kind is more entitled to be called Imperial than the equally natural desire of people at home to purchase their foodstuffs as cheaply as they can. A home interest, or a colonial interest, may be in its nature rather local than Imperial. Every colonial interest is not necessarily Imperial, and a desire for the welfare of people at home is not necessarily mere insular selfishness. It will never be very easy to reconcile completely conflicting tariff interests throughout the widespread lands of the British Empire; and it may well be that for a long time to come a healthy Imperial sentiment in the Mother Country and colonies will best be preserved by abstaining from forcing on a fiscal unity for which the Empire is certainly not yet ripe.

Mr. Chamberlain's proposal to make a tax on imported foodstuffs the basis of a system of closer relationship between England and her colonies is singularly unfortunate. In the United Kingdom, alone of all the self-governing communities within the Empire, there is a large proportion of the population verging on absolute destitution. To tax the necessaries of life of

* Author unknown, 'Free Trade and the Position of Parties' (Commentary on *Hansard's Parliamentary Debates*), *Edinburgh Review*, 199 (408) (January–April 1904), pp. 547–55.

the very poor, in the supposed interest of regions where there are practically no poor, and where there is no poor rate, strikes the ordinary Englishman as neither wise nor just. Mr. Chamberlain has said that his projects will increase wages, and make employment more constant, and that therefore working-men will be benefited. But they do not think so themselves; and nothing deserving the name of argument has been produced throughout the debates in Parliament to show that farmers, railway companies, and employers generally would be willing or able to give better wages because the new system of taxation had increased the price of food and other commodities, or that under the new conditions there would always be abundance of work.

The corn-tax, fixed at 1s. a quarter two years ago, endured only twelve months. Mr. Chamberlain now advocates a 2s. duty; and his most zealous supporters are hopefully contemplating a much higher rate. The non-agricultural industries have no notion of tolerating protection for agriculture whilst their own productions are left exposed to foreign competition. Conversely, if the manufacturers are gratified by duties on foreign manufactures, the agricultural interests will undoubtedly press their equal or stronger claims to protection. Thus a corn-tax involves a tax on manufactures; and a tax on manufactures involves a corn-tax. It has always been found impossible to introduce just a little protection, and to stop there. It is due to the inherent necessities of the case, not to what protectionists describe as 'free-food claptrap,' that the broad issue of Free Trade *versus* Protection will have to be fought on the corn duty, which is in truth nothing more nor less than a bread-tax.

Free trade will be saved, in spite of Mr. Chamberlain. For that the country will owe small thanks to the Prime Minister and his colleagues. Mr. Balfour has written a pamphlet, and has made a speech at Sheffield, to which he constantly refers as embodying the fiscal policy of the Conservative party. He has made further speeches at Bristol, at Manchester, and in the House of Commons, without making at all more definite the hazy statements which fell from him at Sheffield. In Parliament, under pressure, individual Ministers have found themselves compelled to declare that the Government is *not* in favour of the corn duty, is *not* in favour of colonial preference, is *not* in favour of a general import duty on foreign manufactures. The natural conclusion would be that the Government is opposed to Mr. Chamberlain's policy, of which these are the three principal heads. They, however, refuse to allow the House of Commons to adopt a resolution affirming this position in plain English; and they give tariff reform candidates the full support of the Government wherever such a candidate has a chance of success.

In sober truth, Mr. Balfour at Sheffield propounded no policy at all. He merely suggested an expedient; and upon this expedient the life of the Ministry depends. The official view of the political situation is that Mr.

Chamberlain's policy is 'not before the country.' It will not be before the country, according to Mr. Balfour, at the earliest, till the general election after next. It is, therefore, quite unnecessary for any statesman, candidate, or elector to have any opinions upon it at present. His own policy of 'Fiscal Reform' is the only authorised policy of the Conservative party concerning which the electorate is to be consulted at the general election, and this policy only means that the British Government is to obtain 'freedom to negotiate' on tariff matters with foreign nations. It has, of course, been pointed out a hundred times that the British Government, subject to parliamentary approval, is absolutely free to negotiate at present with foreign nations – a freedom, however, which will be greatly limited if preferential arrangements are entered into with our colonies. All this make-believe, though it may serve a useful purpose for the moment in playing the party game in the House of Commons, entirely fails of effect upon the electorate. Since Mr. Chamberlain's campaign, the protectionists within the Conservative party have gained the predominance, they have captured the caucuses, and they have done their best in spite of occasional protests from the wiser heads among them to identify Conservatism with Mr. Chamberlain's policy. And as this process continues, the Conservative party steadily loses its hold on the constituencies.

Amongst Liberal-Unionists the free traders are, as might be expected, much more able to make a strong stand. There is something inherently absurd in Liberals of any kind adopting protection as one of their political principles. But here, as with Conservatives, 'the machine' works as it is directed to work. Between the Conservative machine and the Liberal-Unionist machine there is nowadays no difference of tendency whatever. Each is worked under practically the same direction for practically the same ends. But, nevertheless, in the central Liberal-Unionist associations and the local Liberal-Unionist associations there is keen and widespread dissatisfaction. Liberal-Unionists of mark, who in the past have done much to create these associations, are now leaving them altogether, or are holding aloof, whilst the rank and file of Liberal-Unionist electors are quietly all over the country in thousands rejoining the Liberal party.

We wonder how much longer it will be possible for people to blind themselves to facts. It may well be that Mr. Chamberlain did not wish to start a protectionist propaganda, and that his real aim was limited to the establishment of some kind of Imperial fiscal unity. A very slight acquaintance with recent elections is sufficient to show that the strength of his backing in the constituencies comes from those whose simple wish it is to use taxation for the purpose of enhancing the price of the commodities which they have to sell. In the House of Commons Mr. Bonar Law, on behalf of the Ministry, dwelt upon the great public advantage that would ensue from high prices in the iron and steel trade, which apparently only a system of protection could restore and maintain. Then and there, however, the Under-Secretary to the Board of Trade had his reply from no less a person than Sir James Kitson, as well qualified as any man in England to speak for those great industries, and these he maintained had grown and flourished to an extraordinary degree by reason of our free-trade system. It is beyond all doubt that many manufacturers have become bitten with the desire to exclude foreign competition in this country with their own finished products. In the interest of the manufacturer, producers like the British mine-owner and the British sheep-farmer are to be subject to the fiercest competition from foreign ore and foreign and colonial wool, whilst the manufactured article is to have the British market to itself and the foreign manufacturer is warned off! Where, however, in all this does the British public come in? Mr. Bonar Law will have to make many speeches before he can convince the mass of Englishmen that dear clothing and dear bread are objects proper to be aimed at by fiscal adjustments, though no doubt he will find many manufacturers and farmers to meet him in his 'fiscal reforms' half way.

The fiscal debate in the House of Commons on Mr. Morley's amendment to the Address was maintained at a very high level, and has done excellent service in bringing before the public the main features and the true turning points of the controversy, which the speeches made to party gatherings in the country had tended to obscure. Perhaps the most remarkable circumstance of the whole debate was that no one of any standing or mark gave his avowed support to the Chamberlain policy. Probably Mr. Bonar Law approached most nearly to Mr. Chamberlain; but even he had not a word to say in favour of the corn duty, which is the essential basis of the late Secretary of State's plan of colonial preference. No one attempted to show that protectionist countries get admission into markets from which our own free-trade country is excluded. No one attempted to show how, had we been a protectionist country, we should have prevented the more rapid proportionate growth of countries like the United States and Germany, which have developed new resources. No one showed that in protected countries periods of depression were less common, or less severe, than with ourselves. Whilst it was abundantly proved that, as regards the standard of living and rate of wages and amount of leisure, our working-men are infinitely better off than those of any European country. In the great controversy between free trade and protection in the House of Commons there was no one boldly to argue the case which Conservative caucuses and electors were supporting in the country. Ministers recognised this clearly enough. They were nervously anxious to give to the Chamberlain policy the go-by. 'It 'was not before the country. It was not the issue before the House of Commons.' The only question was whether the House and country were for or against 'fiscal reform,' for explanation of which inquirers were directed to the Sheffield speech. Mr. Balfour, unfortunately absent from the fiscal debate on the Address, could say no more than this when he took part in the renewed discussion of the subject at a later date. And so the matter stands.

Let us then take stock of the position. Let us face the facts. Upon the question of free trade *versus* protection the Ministry has broken up, and the Unionist party itself stands on the very verge of disruption. The Cabinet, constituted as it is at present, cannot possibly enjoy the same credit either with Parliament or with the country that Unionist administrations have heretofore possessed. No ministry could afford in the space of little more than three years to lose such men as Lord Salisbury, the Duke of Devonshire, Lord Goschen, Lord James of Hereford, and Lord Balfour of Burleigh, in the one House, and as Mr. Chamberlain, Mr. Ritchie, Sir Michael Hicks-Beach, and Lord George Hamilton, in the other, without being greatly weakened. It is no undue disparagement of their successors to hold that they are not the equals of the men who have gone. A prime minister can indeed always fill a place or places somehow; but political standing, personal weight in Parliament, some sort of reputation outside, have heretofore been generally considered desirable, if not absolutely necessary, qualifications for holding the highest political offices under the Crown. In any party the number of such men is limited. Mr. Balfour did the best he could in circumstances of much difficulty; but it was unfortunate for him that last year, whilst at one end of the scale the most experienced statesmen felt it impossible to continue in a Ministry clearly tending towards protection, at the other end of the scale the younger men in the House of Commons who had shown most brilliancy and political ability were almost without exception free traders, and were therefore equally unavailable for strengthening his administration under existing circumstances. The Government, which after the last general election reckoned its majority at 120, is now hardly able with the utmost pressure to get into the Lobby a majority of fifty in a full House! To all appearance the party is very much weaker in the country than in the House of Commons, where the dread of dissolution and the natural dislike of free-trade Unionists to vote against a Unionist Government tend to conceal the general distaste for Mr. Chamberlain's fiscal programme.

Free traders who are also Unionists have been very loth, and are still loth, to make a final breach with the Government of Mr. Balfour and with the party which he leads. It is in his power still to reassure them. The time has come when he must make his choice between supporting and opposing the fiscal policy of Mr. Chamberlain. Mr. Balfour's objections to that policy have appeared so far to be of a merely temporising character. The time has not yet come, he seems to say, for so large a change. Let us then take only a short step forward in the meantime. When the missionary efforts of Mr. Chamberlain have converted a majority of his countrymen, it will be time enough to sweep away the free-trade doctrine and system to which at present the British people are so strangely attached. It is very possible that, as public opinion makes itself felt, Mr. Chamberlain will do his best to minimise his demands, and that Mr. Balfour will talk less of 'fiscal revolution.' The question, however, about which free traders are anxious is not the length of the step to be taken in the first instance, but *the direction* in which it is intended to move. Free traders can no longer implicitly trust the Government. When Mr. Gerald Balfour in the House of Commons points out some objections to the Chamberlain policy, a supporter immediately behind him declares, without rebuke, that the speech of the President of the Board of Trade should be taken as an 'interim report,' and in no way represents the final views of the Government. When again Mr. Cripps, a faithful follower of the Ministry, makes it the basis of his speech that the policy of Mr. Balfour and that of Mr. Chamberlain are identically the same in spirit and intention, the Prime Minister listens to him without even a gesture of dissent. Free traders call to mind the good wishes for the success of his mission with which Mr. Balfour accepted Mr. Chamberlain's resignation, and the evident purpose with which his son was made Chancellor of the Exchequer. The least suspicious of men can hardly feel sure, having regard to still more recent events in the House of Commons, that the Prime Minister is able or willing to give effective opposition to pressure brought upon him by the devoted adherents of the Chamberlain programme.

It was made evident last autumn that there was no longer room in Mr. Balfour's Ministry for statesmen who believed in free trade and thought it worth a sacrifice. Has the time come when there is no longer room for free traders in the Unionist party? We hope not. But unless Mr. Balfour speaks out frankly, and speaks out soon, it will be with reference to free trade and protection that the two great political parties will be divided throughout the whole country. Free-trade Unionists are a very numerous and a very powerful body. Are they to be forced into opposition to the Government? That depends upon the policy of the Government. If Mr. Balfour chooses to identify his party or to allow it to be identified with the protectionism that is placed before the electorate by tariff reformers, and the adherents of Mr. Chamberlain, then rupture is inevitable. In that case free-trade Unionists must take all necessary measures to defeat a policy which they believe would bring irreparable mischief upon the State. They are, moreover, determined not to allow their Unionism to be made a pretext for furthering a policy of protection with which it has no connexion whatever. That the policy of maintaining the Union should be linked with a fiscal policy so essentially retrograde as the revival of protection is indeed lamentable. It is not free traders who are jeopardising the cause of the Union.

Those who have seen most of the difficulties which surround political and parliamentary leadership will best understand the magnitude of the troubles which Mr. Chamberlain's proceedings have brought upon the Prime Minister. It was Mr. Balfour's duty, if he could, to preserve the party. And so far he has succeeded, though he has lost many supporters, in averting complete rupture. But this has only been accomplished by the Government maintaining an attitude of studied ambiguity upon the fiscal question. Mr. Chamberlain, on the other hand, though he has not converted the country, has enlisted in his enthusiastic support the more Conservative elements of the Unionist party; and for the most part he now has at command the services of the Conservative organisations. He is recognised naturally as the leader of the protectionist party. Should that party prevail at the general election Mr. Chamberlain would necessarily be the statesman to whom the country would turn to carry into effect his fiscal projects. Mr. Chamberlain's programme is before us all. Little as we agree with him, we fully admit that his policy is intelligible and consistent, and that it deserves to be called a 'fiscal revolution,' for it involves a complete reversal of the principles and practice approved by all our statesmen for the last half-century. The position of free traders is also perfectly intelligible. If free trade was necessary and of advantage to this country in the days of Sir Robert Peel, it is in their opinion more than ever so to-day. To exclude, or obstruct, or hamper, commodities coming to the British market, because they are of foreign origin, is no true imperialism. If the United Kingdom is to maintain its commercial and industrial supremacy, it must continue to be the market of the whole world. A great gulf of principle divides protectionists from free traders.

That there was anything in the condition of this country to make it right and wise for Mr. Chamberlain to revive this very old controversy we do not believe. In our opinion this revival has been most unfortunate for the country and the Empire, as well as disastrous to the Unionist party. There is no use, however, in complaining of the situation in which the State finds itself. The Prime Minister and his Government have to face it and to make the best of it. The time for manoeuvring, for party management, is past. What the country has a right to know is the mind of the Government on the merits of the greatest question which for the last dozen years at least has occupied the thoughts of Englishmen.